Criminology

Criminology

Crime and Criminality

FOURTH EDITION

Lewis Yablonsky

California State University, Northridge

HARPER & ROW, PUBLISHERS, New York

Grand Rapids, Philadelphia, St. Louis, San Franciso,
London, Singapore, Sydney, Tokyo

1817

Sponsoring Editor: Alan McClare
Project Editor: Susan Goldfarb
Art Direction: Heather A. Ziegler
Cover Coordinator: Mary Archondes
Cover Design: Wanda Lubelska Design
Cover Photo: Courtesy Reginald Wickham
Production: Beth Maglione

Criminology: Crime and Criminality, Fourth Edition

Library of Congress Cataloging-in-Publication Data

Yablonsky, Lewis.
   Criminology : crime and criminality / Lewis Yablonsky. — 4th ed.
     p. cm.
   Rev. ed. of: Criminology / Martin R. Haskell. 3rd ed. © 1983.
   Includes bibliographical references.
   ISBN 0-06-047292-8
   1. Criminology. 2. Crime—United States. I. Haskell, Martin R.,
1912- Criminology. II. Title.
HV6025.H33   1990   89-36520
364—dc20   CIP

89 90 91 92 9 8 7 6 5 4 3 2 1

Contents

Preface

Criminology: Crime and Criminality, Fourth Edition, is a comprehensive survey of the discipline that focuses on the definitions and patterns of crime, the causes of crime, and society's responses to crime. Special attention is given to the social-psychological factors that contribute to crime and to the existence of criminal behavior at all levels of our society.

This new edition of *Criminology* is based on the many changes in the phenomenon of crime that have developed in the past decade. Crime exists in all societies. However, the pattern of crime changes over time, and there is often a corresponding shift in the attitudes of the general public. These changes prompted this extensive revision.

Part One, "Defining Crime," explores the latest trends in criminal law and the judicial process, analyzing the latest U.S. crime statistics in terms of modern trends.

Part Two, "Characteristics of Criminal Behavior," includes a new chapter on the victim's role in crime that considers the social-psychological forces that can make a person "victim-prone" and the degree some victims may participate in the crime. It explores the fact that most criminals were victimized during their early socialization and shows how child abuse is a significant factor in later criminal behavior, giving the reader a better understanding of the relationship between criminals and their victims.

Part Three, "Criminal Patterns," examines the links between substance abuse and criminality and the disastrous impact the drug problem has had on American society. Part Three also examines sex crimes and the enormous changes in both legal thinking and public attitudes towards sex offenses; it includes new information on acquaintance rape, the controversy over abortion, and the decriminalization of homosexuality.

Part Four, "Power-Status Crime," focuses on the increase in political crimes in recent years and on the relationship of political crime to ordinary white collar crime. The changing nature of organized crime is also considered, and organized crime, white collar crime, and political crime are compared and analyzed. Part Four ends with a study of how white collar criminals, political criminals, and organized crime offenders often interact and collaborate.

Part Five, "The Causal Context of Crime," analyzes the factors that lead people to crime. Classical sociological and psychological theories are considered, along with a new theory linking child abuse and later criminal behavior. This helps to explain how criminogenic families socialize children into criminal lifestyles.

Part Six, "The Treatment and Control of Crime," examines traditional and new methodologies used to prevent and control crime, both in prisons and in the community. Chapter 18 considers the therapeutic community as an effective alternative to incarceration.

I have an abundant faith and belief that the problem of crime can best be ameliorated through understanding and knowledge about the problem by people in all segments of our society. I am hopeful that this text—which presents relevant data and insights about patterns of crime, the factors that cause crime, and techniques and methods for effectively treating criminals—will contribute toward reducing the crime problem.

This new edition incorporates many of the viewpoints and clinical insights I have developed on the basis of my research and direct therapeutic work with criminals and delinquents over the past 40 years. I am grateful to the many social science researchers and writers who have granted me the permission to quote liberally from their work. Although he did not contribute directly to this edition, I want to acknowledge the contribution of my former coauthor, colleague, and friend, the late Martin Haskell, to the first two editions of *Criminology*. My editor at Harper & Row, Alan McClare, provided the valuable editorial guidance and support that was vital to the completion of the book.

Finally, I want to express my heartfelt thanks to my son Mitch, who has grown up from a loving child to become a trusted and valuable friend. He was very important to me in the process of working on this project.

LEWIS YABLONSKY

Criminology

DEFINING CRIME

Chapter
1

Crime and the Criminal Law

*C*rime encompasses a variety of behavioral acts. It can be the behavior of a drug addict holding up a store owner at gunpoint, a collusive bribery relationship between a Pentagon employee and a defense contractor, a member of Congress selling political favors, or a president of the United States illegally withholding evidence related to a criminal conspiracy. The behavior of an upper status criminal may be more complex and more difficult to prove in a court of law than a blatant armed robbery, yet all these acts are crimes according to our criminal justice system. Three basic elements are involved in defining crime: (1) the legal definition, (2) social perception, and (3) the self-concept of the offender.

1. *The Legal Definition* The *legal* definition of crime is fundamental, and it dominates our conception of criminality. This basically involves the arrest, prosecution, and conviction of an offender by due process. This category relates to the majority of offenders discussed in this book.

2. *Social Perception.* A second viewpoint of what constitutes crime is the *social perception* of an act by the general population. The social perception of a murder, a burglary, or an armed robbery is clear. However, there are offenses about which the public's view is not clear. For example, President Nixon was never convicted of a crime because his appointee, President Ford, pardoned him of all crimes he may have committed while he was in the White House. Despite this and Nixon's infamous "I am not a crook" speeches, there is taped and other evidence that he performed

criminal acts for which several members of his staff and his attorney general were convicted and served prison terms. In brief, despite the absence of a criminal conviction, Richard Nixon was socially perceived as a criminal by a large segment of the populace. In another case, the attorney general during President Reagan's years in office, Edwin Meese, was involved in a series of ethically questionable acts that were generally perceived by the public and the press as criminal behavior. In fact, the special prosecutor who investigated the alleged crimes concluded that there were several offenses for which Meese could be prosecuted. The social perception of the general population is a vital factor in defining criminality.

In contrast to Nixon, Meese, and others, Martin Luther King, Jr., was legally *convicted* on several occasions as a criminal, yet the general social perception of King was that he was not a criminal. Rather, he was perceived by the majority of society as a hero who advanced social justice.

3. *The Offender's Self-Concept.*   A third factor in "defining" crime and who is a criminal, one that goes beyond the criminal justice system, is the *self-concept* of the offender. Many blatant convicted criminals are self-righteous and, in their own minds, do not consider themselves criminals, despite the fact that they have been convicted of a crime and are locked up in prison. A side effect of this position is that such individuals are not easily rehabilitated because they do not define their behavior as wrong or criminal.

Many convicted offenders accuse the social system of being unfair and "criminal" in its effect, and in this way they avoid a criminal self-concept. Their self-exoneration, even though they are legally convicted felons, has its consequences. In terms of this rationale, many individuals perceive themselves as "freedom fighters" rather than criminals. An offender's self-concept is thus a significant factor in defining crime, and clearly it has an effect on the individual's readiness to be rehabilitated.

Despite the fact that we perceive three variables as affecting the criminal status of an individual, we have to rely most fundamentally on the criminal law and the machinery of the administration of justice to define the complex issue of who is a criminal.

THE LEGAL DEFINITION OF CRIME

The word *crime* has been used so frequently and heard so often that we take for granted that everyone who uses the term means the same thing. Yet definitions of crime differ. To the administrators of justice and to lawyers, a crime is an illegal act. Some social scientists tend to equate the term *crime* with all behavior that is injurious to society. Others view as crimes those acts that deviate greatly from the accepted norms of the society. Religious people regard crime within the same genre as sin. People whose personal codes emphasize truth as the ultimate value equate falsehood with crime. The most rational view is to apply the term *crime* to acts that deviate from rules of behavior valued highly by the majority of society, as written in laws.

The term *crime* is legally defined in the penal codes of all states in the United States. The following is a typical definition:

> A crime or public offense is an intentional act committed or omitted in violation of a law forbidding or commanding it, and to which is annexed either of the following punishments:

1. Death
2. Imprisonment
3. Fine
4. Removal from office; or,
5. Disqualification to hold and enjoy any office of honor, trust, or profit in this state.[1]

Most codes also provide that in every crime there must exist a union or joint operation of act and intent, or criminal negligence.

Some sociologists who object to the exclusive use of the legal definition of crime would broaden the definition to encompass other antisocial behavior. Two arguments in favor of this position are that some antisocial behavior more damaging to our social order than many of the traditional crimes is not made punishable by our criminal codes and that patterns of behavior closely resembling violations of the criminal law are not included in our criminal codes.

Reasons given for accepting the exclusive legal definition of crime incude the following:

1. Crime statistics are derived from violations of law known to the police, offenses cleared by arrest, court records, and data obtained from persons on probation, in prison, or on parole. Nonnormative and antisocial behavior that does not violate the law is not likely to become part of any public record.
2. There is no general agreement on what constitutes antisocial behavior.
3. There is no general agreement on norms whose violation would constitute nonnormative behavior of a criminal nature.
4. The U.S. Constitution and laws of the states have provided many safeguards to protect the individual from unjust stigmatization. It

---

[1] *West's California Codes* (St. Paul, Minn.: West, 1957), Penal Code, sec. 15, enacted in 1872.

would be a mistake to give these up to make the term *crime* more inclusive.[2]

Despite some inadequacies in the exclusively legal definition of crime, most sociologists and criminologists find the reasons for accepting it compelling. Immoral or unethical behavior, no matter how socially damaging or reprehensible it may be, cannot be meaningfully equated with criminal behavior because the status of criminal is not conferred on the perpetrator. This status, in our society, is conferred only upon those found guilty of a violation of a provision of the criminal law.

Several specific variables pertaining to the legal definition of crime deserve close attention. For an act to be a crime, all the following conditions must hold:

1. *There must be an act or omission.* That one intends to do something forbidden by law or plans to do a wrong in concert with others is not enough. There must be action. Even in the case of a conspiracy, intending and planning do not suffice. For example, if several people plan to rob a bank and have every intention of carrying out the plan, no crime is committed until there is an overt act in furtherance of the conspiracy. Stealing a getaway car, securing a weapon according to plan, or menacing a bank employee with a weapon would constitute an act in support of the plan. A member of the group who renounced the conspiracy before anything was done to carry the plan into execution, refusing to have anything to do with it, would not have committed a crime. The law takes cognizance of the fact that a person may wish someone dead, even plan to kill, and change his or her mind without committing a wrong.

   What constitutes an omission? There must be a duty or obligation to do something and a failure to perform that duty. In most states there is no obligation to interfere when one person sees another commit a crime. There are times, however, when the law requires one to take action. Most state statutes, for example, require a parent to furnish minor children with necessary clothing, food, shelter, and medical attention. Failure to do so constitutes an omission that is punishable as a misdemeanor.

2. *The act or omission must be in violation of a law forbidding or commanding it.* Somewhere in the statutory law or case law of the state, the act or omission in question must be formally defined as a crime.

3. *There must be criminal intent* (mens rea) *or criminal negligence.* The term *mens rea* is used to describe the nature of the intent. It

---

[2] Paul W. Tappan, *Crime, Justice and Correction* (New York: McGraw-Hill, 1960), pp. 3–22.

literally means "guilty mind," and it includes criminal negligence. The offense of larceny involves taking the property of another with *intent* to permanently deprive that person of the property. Taking something by mistake would not be a larceny because the requisite intent would be lacking.

Since people do not ordinarily publicize their intention to steal, direct evidence of intent is unusual. In most cases the court infers the intent from the circumstances surrounding the taking of the property. If the owner testifies, for example, that her automobile is missing and that she did not authorize anyone to take it, the apprehension of an accused driving the car might give rise to an inference that the accused took the automobile and that the taking was with the intent to steal it. The accused could overcome these inferences with other evidence, such as testimony of witnesses who saw the owner lend the vehicle to the accused.

Another complex facet of *mens rea* is that many sociopaths (persons who have no social conscience), including white collar and political criminals, do not see anything wrong in their criminal behavior. Consequently, they do not in fact have a "guilty mind." They often have a self-righteous, blameless self-concept.

Some crimes are defined by law in such a way as not to require criminal negligence or an intent to do wrong. Sexual relations with a person below the age of consent constitutes the offense of statutory rape even if consummated with the consent of or at the solicitation of the minor. Intent is not an element of the crime of statutory rape.

4. *There must be a union or joint operation of act and intent, or criminal negligence.* The act, to constitute a crime, *must be the act that the accused intended.* If an accused planned to shoot someone and en route to commit the murder accidentally struck the victim with his or her car, the killing would *not* constitute murder. There would not have been a joint operation of act and intent. The accused might have changed his or her mind about shooting the victim, and the murder might never have taken place.

Criminal negligence, as interpreted by the courts, involves the failure of an individual to exercise the degree of care required of a reasonable person under the circumstances. A man driving an automobile on the main street of a city at a speed of 100 miles an hour would be guilty of manslaughter if he killed someone. Under the circumstances indicated, a reasonable person should know that he was endangering the lives of others.

5. *Punishment must be provided by law.* Punishment was first introduced into criminal law to substitute collective vengeance for individual and family vengeance. Wrongs done to individuals

were redefined as wrongs done to the state. The state then acted to avenge.

In the eighteenth century, the idea of punishment as a deterrent to offenders was popularized by the Italian jurist Cesare Beccaria. It was assumed that if prospective offenders knew in advance the amount of punishment they were risking, they would not commit the crime. The assumption that *punishment deters* is still basic to our criminal law and influences the thinking of many of our legislators. When the incidence of a particular offense increases and this increase attracts public attention, there is generally a demand for more severe penalties for offenders.

The fact that the spirit of vengeance is still with us is evident when we read such statements as "We are coddling delinquents," "The courts are too easy," and "Criminals are getting away with murder." Unless the statute provides for *punishment* for the prohibited act or omission, the statute is not part of the criminal law and the act is not a crime.

An act or omission is a crime because the government, on some level, has promulgated a law making it a crime and providing for punishment of violators. The use of the criminal law is clearly one way in which our society attempts to get people to refrain from behavior considered undesirable. The political authority voted into power by the citizens reflects the majority opinion in most instances.

SOCIAL CONTROL AND THE CRIMINAL LAW

Every society exerts on its members pressures intended to procure a high degree of uniformity of attitude and behavior. Individuals living close to each other in a society and interacting with each other require some way of predicting in advance the response of others to their actions. The term *social control* has been applied to the system of measures, including suggestion, persuasion, restraint, and coercion, by which a society gets individual members to conform to approved patterns of behavior.

It is assumed in this context that the behavior of every member of a society may in some way affect other members. Each person depends on others with whom he or she has relationships to do what they are supposed to do as defined by the culture, the way of life of the people that make up the society. The "right ways" of doing things are defined for us by our society in rules of behavior that sociologists refer to as *norms*.

The principal norms are called *folkways*, *mores*, and *laws*. The individual who conforms to a norm is generally rewarded, and the one who deviates from it is in some way punished. Rewards are referred to as *positive sanctions* and punishments as *negative sanctions*. Rewards vary from words of approval and general acceptance to selection for positions of great prestige. Punishments—negative sanctions—vary from mild verbal disapproval to ostracism or death. They may be *informally* imposed by people who rebuke or snub the violator of the norm, or they may be formally imposed by an organized group or the society as a whole.

Norms may forbid certain actions. These have been called *proscriptive* norms. They warn that the violator will be punished if he or she does not obey. Those norms that tell us what we should do are called *prescriptive* norms. Compliance results in approval by others and by oneself. There is *consensus* that such acts as rape, murder, robbery, and violent assault are wrong, and the criminal law makes such violations of our norms punishable. There is not the same consensus with respect to such forms of behavior as gambling or possession of marijuana, which are also made punishable by law.[3]

Folkways and Mores

The concept of folkways, or the "ways of the folk," was introduced by William Graham Sumner.[4] The folkways and mores are inculcated early in life. Parents reward conformity and punish deviance in small children many times in an average day. As a result, conformity to these norms becomes almost automatic or habitual. They become invaluable guides to our behavior and help us to predict the behavior of others.

Violations of the folkways are punished by relatively mild sanctions. A violation of the folkways might be eating without using the appropriate utensils, wearing inappropriate clothing, or failing to show appropriate respect to another person. The violator would be punished mildly by being rebuked, by being criticized, and in some instances by being avoided.

Those folkways considered essential to the society are called *mores*. Incest, molestation of children by adults, murder, and rape are examples of behavior in violation of the mores of our society and, indeed, of all societies of which we have knowledge, though the definitions of the terms may vary in detail with time and place. The sanctions imposed on violators of the mores are usually more severe and often include some form of ostracism.

In small societies, informal sanctions are generally sufficient to ensure the maintenance of social control. People dare not risk being ostracized by their friends and neighbors. Since virtually everyone in

---

[3] Arnold Birenbaum and Edward Sagarin, *Norms and Human Behavior* (New York: Praeger, 1976), pp. 1–28.

[4] William Graham Sumner, *Folkways* (Boston: Ginn, 1906).

the small society knows everyone else, deviant behavior by a member comes to the attention of all the others and results in the widespread application of sanctions. In large groups and complex societies, more formal control is required. The deviant can escape informal sanctions simply by relocating to an area in which his or her deviant behavior is not known. The application of formal controls in the form of published rules with specific penalties contributes greatly to the maintenance of social control.

A group may enforce the mores by the imposition of informal or formal sanctions or by both when there is the *social perception* of crime. People who know that a man has committed incest may ostracize him even though no formal sanctions are applied by the state. In contrast, the excommunication of a priest who marries without special dispensation illustrates enforcement of the mores of a group by formal sanctions. The Roman Catholic church has a formal regulation forbidding the marriage of a priest. When it excommunicates a violator, the church employs its most severe sanction. In recent years, mores, once regarded as inflexible, have undergone great change. The Catholic church now grants permission for priests to marry without excommunication, though they must, if they marry, leave the priesthood. In recent years there has been considerable pressure exerted by large segments of the Catholic clerical and lay communities to do away with the celibate priesthood. Changing lifestyles in our society have made premarital sex, homosexual behavior, and out-of-wedlock childbirth—all once considered serious violations of our mores—acceptable to large segments of our population.

The Law

In complex societies many rules regulating behavior (including folkways and mores) are enacted into law. What distinguishes a law from a folkway, a mos (singular of mores), or a formal regulation of a group is that it is *promulgated* and *enforced* by *political authority*.

There are three types of law regulating behavior: *contract law*, *tort law*, and *criminal law*. *Contract law* provides standards for formal arriving at agreements and designates courts, the formal dispute-settling agencies of the state, to decide differences of interpretation in accordance with normative principles and to award damages for breaches of agreements. Every transaction involving the rental or sale or mortgaging of real property, the borrowing of money from a bank, or the purchase of insurance involves a written or oral contract and is obviously regulated by contract law. The pervasiveness of the influence of contract law on our lives becomes more apparent when we consider that the same applies to every situation in which one performs work, labor, and services in exchange for money or other services. Furthermore, virtually every purchase of food, clothing, furniture, or any other item of personal property is made pursuant to a contract—written, oral, or implied—with redress provided by contract law.

Tort law provides redress for one suffering an injury at the hands of another. The victim of a rape, an aggravated assault, or an automobile accident caused by the negligence of another may sue the wrongdoer for damages. Tort law specifies the circumstances under which such actions may be taken to court, designates appropriate courts, and outlines procedures to be followed. A person seeking redress in court for a breach of contract or a tort is awarded a sum of money as compensation for the loss or injury suffered. This disposition of a case is an example of *distributive justice.* The verdict of the court is intended to make the victim "whole," that is, to restore as nearly as possible the financial position that the victim occupied before the breach of contract or the tort occurred.

Criminal laws specifically forbid certain acts, command certain others, and provide punishment for violators. Police departments, prosecuting attorneys, courts, correctional institutions, probation departments, and parole agencies are assigned roles in the enforcement of the criminal law. Criminal laws differ from contract laws and tort laws in that they prohibit or command specified acts and provide for punishment of violators by the state and on behalf of the state. Violation of a criminal law therefore constitutes an offense against the state. A prosecuting attorney, an agent of the state, brings the case before a criminal court *in the name of the state* against one or more persons accused of violating one or more provisions of the criminal law.

Criminal law in the United States is derived from and contained in a great many documents, including the following:

1. The Constitution of the United States and the constitutions of all the 50 states.
2. Legislation of the Congress of the United States.
3. Legislative enactments made pursuant to provisions of the various state constitutions.
4. Court decisions interpreting the statutes and the constitutions.
5. Court precedents. English common law, upon which the U.S. criminal law is based, depended entirely on established practice of the courts. This body of precedent carried over to the colonies and continues to be applied by nearly all the state courts, unless superseded by statute.

The same act sometimes results in both a tort and a violation of the criminal law. Rape, for example, is a tort, a wrong done to a person. The victim may sue in a civil court to recover damages for injury. Rape is also a violation of the criminal law because the political authority has enacted a statute defining this act as a wrong to the state and providing for punishment of violators. In the United States the victim of rape, aggravated assault, or any other tort must resort to civil action to recover damages. Criminal courts can impose punishment only on behalf of the state and levy fines solely for the benefit of the state. A criminal court cannot award damages to a victim. Punishment provided by the sentence of a criminal court is an example of *retributive justice.*

The increased use of formal controls in our complex society does not eliminate the need for informal controls. Ideally, each type of control supplements the other. A form of behavior in violation of the folkways or mores is further deterred by the passage and enforcement of a law prohibiting it. For example, murder is forbidden by the mores. The law making it a crime provides an additional deterrent. By the same token, a law supported by the folkways or mores is easier to enforce than a law that does not have such support.

BASIC PATTERNS OF CRIME

We consider the four most significant patterns of crime to be *traditional crime, organized crime, white collar crime,* and *political crime.* In traditional crime we include such offenses as murder, felonious assaults, forcible rape, robbery, burglary, and larceny. Organized crime is a pattern of criminality engaged in by groups of criminals with formal organization and a hierarchical structure. Its activities include illegal gambling, prostitution, narcotics traffic, and coercive rackets in labor and industry. White collar crime includes offenses by "respectable" members of society who commit illegal acts in the course of their generally legitimate or professional business operations. Political crime includes such overt activities as assassination, sabotage, kidnapping, espionage, and terrorism clearly aimed at destroying the political authority structure as well as violent and nonviolent disruption undertaken to influence political or social changes. We shall here briefly define each of these basic criminal patterns. All of them are discussed more fully in later chapters.

Traditional Crime

The term *traditional crime* is used to describe behavior that has been defined as criminal for a very long time and that has been proscribed by laws in most societies throughout history. In the Judeo-Christian tradition, for example, acts forbidden in the Ten Commandments, the Law of Moses, have been established over the centuries as criminal, and their proscription is reflected in our laws against murder, forcible rape, robbery, burglary, and larceny. Violations of these laws have been traditionally regarded as crimes and are referred to as "serious crimes" in the *Uniform Crime Reports* of the Federal Bureau of Investigation. Seven categories of such crimes—murder and nonnegligent manslaughter, forcible rape, robbery, aggravated assault, burglary, larceny-theft, and auto theft—are used as a "crime index" by the FBI to determine the basic trend of crime in the United States. Known offenses are tabulated by local law enforcement agencies, and the statistics are relayed to the FBI for publication in its *Uniform Crime Reports*.

When people speak of a crime problem, it is to these seven crimes that they usually refer. The public tends to be particularly alarmed about traditional crimes of violence, such as murder, forcible rape, and aggravated assault, whereas such traditional crimes as burglary, larceny, and auto theft seem somewhat less threatening to the general public because they do not usually entail physical harm.

Most data available to criminologists concern the crimes in the FBI Crime Index and the people who commit them. These crimes represent the most common local crime problem and receive most of the attention of the police, courts, and criminologists.

Most traditional crimes are committed by people in a lower socioeconomic position in our society. The criminal categories discussed in the following sections are what I have termed power-status crimes. These crimes are committed by people with financial or political power or high social status in our society.

Organized Crime

Organized crime involves the operation of an illegitimate or illegal enterprise by a group with a hierarchical organization, or the control of a lawful business by such a group through use of unlawful force or the threat of force. The illegal enterprises of organized crime include gambling games, lotteries, commercialized prostitution, and narcotics distribution. Lawful businesses operated by organized crime include labor union locals taken over by racketeers, business protective associations run by racketeers, and various legitimate businesses operated by strong-arm men using duress to obtain business concessions.

Organized crime differs considerably from traditional crime. Any of the seven traditional crimes may occur in the course of the business of an organized crime syndicate, but when they do, they are incidental to the principal activity. It is reasonable to assume that relatively few of the crimes resulting from the business activities of organized crime are included in the FBI Crime Index.

White Collar Crime

The *Uniform Crime Reports* mention "white collar crime" as a type of crime not measured by the basic Crime Index. Edwin H. Sutherland, the first sociologist to study the problem of white collar crime extensively, presented considerable evidence to support his contention that white collar crime is widespread in American society. He defined a white collar crime as a crime committed by a person of respectability and high social status in the course of his or her occupation.[5] The types of law violations he included in this concept are restraint of trade; misrepresentation in advertising; infringement of patents, trademarks, and copyrights; "unfair labor practices" as defined by the National Labor Relations Act and other labor laws; financial fraud and violation of trust; and some miscellaneous offenses committed in the ordinary course of business.[6]

In an analysis of the business lives of 70 large corporations, he found that 980 court decisions, an average of 14 decisions per corporation, had been made against them. One hundred and fifty-eight of these decisions, 16 percent of the total, were made by criminal courts, and 60 percent of the 70 corporations had been convicted in criminal courts and had an average of approximately 4 convictions each.[7]

A similar study conducted in the 1990s would probably support the contention that white collar crime, as Sutherland defined it, had increased substantially, perhaps tenfold or more, since the 1940s, when white collar crime began to receive the extensive attention of sociological researchers.

Herbert Edelhertz, a former chief of the Fraud Section of the Criminal Division of the U.S. Department of Justice, broadened the concept still further in his study of white collar crime. He defined white collar crime as *an illegal or series of illegal acts committed by nonphysical means, and by concealment or guile, to obtain money or property, to avoid the payment or loss of money or property, or to obtain business or personal advantage.*[8]

Whether we accept the narrower or broader definition of the term, white collar crime differs from organized crime in that it does not necessarily involve the operation of an illegal business or include business conducted by means of unlawful force. The crimes that are considered white collar crime are not included in the Crime Index, and the seven index crimes traditionally regarded as serious do not usually occur in the course of the commission of white collar crime.

Political Crime

Every government, if it is to maintain its political authority, must insist on the acceptance of the decisions and actions of those who wield legal power. Authoritarian and totalitarian governments tend to suppress all

---

[5] Edwin H. Sutherland, *White Collar Crime* (New York: Holt, Rinehart and Winston, 1949), p. 9.

[6] Sutherland, *White Collar Crime*, p. 32.

[7] Sutherland, *White Collar Crime*, p. 29.

[8] Herbert Edelhertz, *The Nature, Impact, and Prosecution of White Collar Crimes* (Washington, D.C.: Government Printing Office, 1970).

opposition, seeking to equate the political authority structure with those who are in power at a particular time. The statement of King Louis XIV of France, "L'état c'est moi" ("I am the state"), typifies the attitude underlying such action. More democratically oriented governments limit suppression of individuals and organizations to those who engage in overt activities clearly aimed at destroying the political authority structure, as distinct from discrediting people in office or policies of the government. Such overt activities as assassination, sabotage, kidnapping, and espionage are clearly punishable by law. Persons or organizations engaged in such activities are punished for violating the appropriate statutes or prosecuted for participating in conspiracies to commit these acts. The justification for these laws and prosecutions is usually that the "conspiracies" and "acts" are intended to aid external enemies of the state.

We have broadened the definition of political crime to include the acts of people in political power and out of power to change the processes of government by illegal means. We would also include under the heading of political crime the illegal use of one's political status for personal gain. (These last three patterns of criminality are discussed more fully in later chapters on power-status crime.)

THE ORIGIN AND DEVELOPMENT OF THE CRIMINAL LAW

The criminal law is a body of rules promulgated by a political authority (some level of government) to regulate behavior and to provide punishment for violators of the rules. There is considerable disagreement as to how it originated. Four somewhat interrelated explanations have received the widest support:

1. The law originated out of attempts to formalize the folkways and mores. This explanation is based on the assumption that persons living in small groups had developed patterns of interaction that became habitual and customary. Customs were enforced informally through folkways and mores. As the groups grew larger, more formal control was required. The law, particularly the criminal law, originated in an effort to stabilize the existing mores of a period. The law was, in this context, a *conservative force* used by the leaders of a society as a means of deterring experimentation and resisting changes in established ways of doing things.
2. The law originated as a means of resolving problems within a society. Here the assumption is that a number of people living and working together had a need to regulate behavior and resolve their differences formally. Law, and criminal law in particular, developed as a rational and *reasonable* approach toward a solution of problems and the maintenance of intragroup peace.

3. The law originated in an attempt to supersede individual vengeance or family vendetta by a societal redress of wrongs. Here the assumption is that each person originally avenged wrongs through personal retaliation against the offender. Later on, families reacted to a wrong done to a member by retaliation against the offenders and/or their families. Private law, characteristic of the simpler social systems prevailing before the Middle Ages, provided redress in the form of compensation to the individual, the family, or the clan for wrongs committed by one person against another. Attacks, assaults, and thefts were considered to be offenses that concerned only the perpetrator, the victim, and the family of the victim. This system of law provided essentially *distributive justice,* righting of a wrong by compensating the victim. Where the perpetrator of the wrong could not or would not compensate the victim or the family, the action was avenged by the person wronged, the family, or the clan. *Retribution* was the way people obtained satisfaction for wrongs done them without subsequent compensation. The criminal law, then, originated in an attempt to supersede individual vengeance or family vendetta with a societal system of *retributive justice* through which a society punished the perpetrator of the wrong. Criminal law in this framework developed in an effort to redefine a wrong done to an individual (a tort) into a wrong done to the society (a crime).

4. The law originated in an attempt to manage conflicts of interest between groups within a society. Here the assumption is that several families living and working together in a society, no matter how small, had some interests that conflicted. One group or a coalition of groups became dominant in the society and imposed its will on the entire society. Criminal law thus developed as a means for one group to impose and exercise its control over all others, placing its interests over the interests of the other.[9]

Another formulation of an interest group theory was presented by Richard Quinney in the following terms:

1. *Law is the creation and interpretation of specialized rules in a politically organized society.* Law is not only a system of formal social control but also a body of specialized rules created and interpreted in a *politically organized society.* As a process, law is

---

[9] Georges Gurvitch, *Sociology of Law* (New York: Philosophical Library, 1942), pp. 1–67; Bronislaw Malinowski, *Crime and Custom in Savage Society* (New York: Harcourt Brace Jovanovich, 1926); Roscoe Pound, *An Introduction to the Philosophy of Law* (New Haven: Yale University Press, 1954); William Seagle, *The History of Law* (New York: Tudor, 1946), pp. 5–69; George B. Vold, *Theoretical Criminology* (New York University Press, 1950), pp. 203–219.

a dynamic force that is continually being *created* and interpreted. Furthermore, law in operation is an aspect of politics. As an act of politics, law does not represent the norms and values of all persons in the society. Legal decisions, rather, incorporate the interests of only some persons. Whenever a law is created or interpreted, the values of some are necessarily assured, and the values of others are either ignored or negated.

2. *Politically organized society is based on an interest structure.* Each *segment* of society has its own values, norms, and ideological orientations; when these concerns are considered as important for the existence and welfare of the respective positions, they may be defined as interests. Within these segments [Quinney lists six broad categories: political, economic, religious, kinship, educational, and public order], groups of persons may organize to promote their common interests. These groups may be simply called *interest groups.*

3. *The interest structure of politically organized society is characterized by unequal distribution of power and by conflict.* Interests are structured according to differences in power and are in conflict. Groups that have the power to gain access to the decision-making process are able to translate their interests into public policy.

4. *Law is formulated and administered within the interest structure of a politically organized society.* Law supports one point of view at the expense of others. Thus, the content of the law, including the substantive regulations and the procedural rules, represents the interests of segments of society that have the power to shape public policy. By formulating laws, some segments are able to control others to their own advantage. New and shifting demands require new laws. When the interests that underlie a law no longer are relevant to groups in power, the law will be reinterpreted or changed to incorporate the dominant interests.[10]

On the basis of his analysis of the criminal law, Quinney concluded that the prevailing criminological approaches were closely related to the maintenance of order as defined by the dominant or ruling class. Criminal laws were promulgated by the state, a political organization which maintains the interest of the ruling class over those ruled. He pointed out that our national commissions, the FBI, the Department of Justice, and other government agencies are run by people selected by the ruling class who do not question the established order. He proposed

---

[10] Richard Quinney, *Crime and Justice in Society* (Boston: Little, Brown, 1969) pp. 26–30. Used by permission of the author.

a socialist society whose goal would be a world free from the oppression produced by capitalism.[11]

THE CRIMINAL LAW AND DIFFERENTIAL CONSENSUS

Complex societies employ criminal law to provide punishment for behavior in violation of values considered essential to the general welfare, in much the same manner as simpler societies employed informal sanctions to support the mores. Statutes defining such crimes have traditionally been included in criminal and penal codes. In the course of the past several decades, however, our legislatures have added to the criminal codes sections regulating professional and business activities.

The federal government has enacted antitrust laws, patent and copyright laws, labor laws, pure food and drug acts, and other statutes intended to influence certain business activities. It has also set up administrative agencies to enforce the provisions of these statutes. Administrative codes have been enacted by our states to regulate transportation, taxation, health and safety, public utilities, financial establishments, insurance companies, and other enterprises in which there was deemed to be a public interest. Sections of administrative codes prohibit specific acts and provide punishment for violators. These sections are therefore part of the criminal laws of the states.

The criminal law has come to include criminal codes, portions of administrative codes, and constitutional provisions limiting the exercise of power by legislative bodies, courts, and enforcement agencies over the individual. The federal constitution and all state constitutions contain such provisions.

It is apparent from this review of laws that much of our criminal law is not related to values considered essential to the general welfare of all groups that make up our society. Thorsten Sellin pointed out the influence exerted by powerful minorities:

> The criminal law may be regarded as in part a body of rules, which prohibit specific forms of conduct and indicate punishments for violations. The character of these rules, the kind or type of conduct they prohibit, the nature of the sanction attached to their violation, etc., depend upon the character and interests of those groups in the population which influence legislation. In some states these groups may comprise the majority, in others a minority, but the social values which receive the protection of the criminal law are ultimately those which are treasured by dominant interest groups. In democratic states the essential character of the criminal law is not so easy to discern as in states with other forms of government, but even in democracies

---

[11] Richard Quinney, *Critique of Legal Order: Crime Control in a Capitalist Society* (Boston: Little, Brown, 1974).

the importance of strong minority interest groups can be seen shaping some part of the criminal law.[12]

The social values of dominant interest groups—religious, economic, and other—are usually protected by the criminal law, and these groups may or may not constitute a majority. The fact that a statute is enacted is usually evidence of two conditions: (1) the dominant interest groups wish a certain type of behavior to be discontinued or subject to punishment and (2) the undesired behavior is fairly widespread. A significant example is seen in the enactment of laws prohibiting sex between consenting adults and the heavy penalties attached thereto.

Behavior considered undesirable by the dominant interest groups may be defined as appropriate by some subgroups within the society. When this situation occurs, the enactment of a statute reflects a conflict between the culture of the dominant group and the cultures of one or more subgroups. In these instances the law formalizes culture conflict rather than consensus.

The conflict of interests of dominant groups and subgroups is evidenced not only in the enactment of statutes but also in differential enforcement of laws. The dominant interest groups generally control or influence law enforcement, and therefore laws considered important by these groups are more likely to be enforced than laws in which they have little interest. Violations of law by members of subgroups are more likely to be dealt with by law enforcement agencies than are violations by members of the dominant groups.

There is considerable consensus in support of most of our criminal laws; however, attitudes toward others vary from apathy to active opposition. The following analysis of the criminal law and differential consensus logically divides criminal law into five broad categories: (1) laws restating mores, (2) laws reinforcing mores and folkways, (3) laws formalizing folkways, (4) laws enacted to deter social change, and (5) laws enacted to promote "morality."

Laws Restating Mores (Category 1)

In one form or another, the criminal codes of most societies include statutes prohibiting murder, rape, robbery, larceny, burglary, and aggravated assault. There is almost complete consensus in support of these statutes. These offenses make up the Crime Index reported annually by the FBI in the *Uniform Crime Reports* and are considered *mala in se,* evil in themselves. In the Judeo-Christian tradition they have been considered illegal and immoral at least as far back as the announcement

---

[12] Thorsten Sellin, "A Sociological Approach to the Study of Crime Causation," in *The Sociology of Crime and Delinquency*, eds. M. E. Wolfgang, L. Savitz, and N. Johnston (New York: Wiley, 1962), pp. 4–5.

of the Ten Commandments on Mount Sinai. Not only do victims and persons sympathetic to them consider these laws just and necessary, but even perpetrators tend to agree that these laws are needed and that offenders should be punished.

Although the mores are slow to change, changes do occur over time. Laws restating the mores tend to stay on the books long after the support for them has diminished. The laws against adultery, for example, may be traced to the Ten Commandments. As recently as the nineteenth century, every state in the United States had such a statute in effect. By the middle of the twentieth century, these laws, although still in effect in most states, were not strictly enforced.

Columnist Stewart Alsop quotes the following from a book entitled *Acts and Laws of the Colony of Connecticut*, printed in New London, Connecticut, in 1715:

> If any Man have a Stubborn and Rebellious Son of sufficient understanding, viz. sixteen years of age, which will not Obey the Voice of his Father or the Voice of his Mother, and that when they have Chastised him he will not Harken unto them, then may his Father or Mother, being his Natural Parents, lay hold on him, and bring him to the Magistrates Assembled in Court, and Testify unto them that their Son is Stubborn and Rebellious . . . and such a Son shall be Put to Death.[13]

This was quoted as one of the 12 capital crimes, which included blasphemy, witchcraft, bestiality, and sodomy. Few would deny that our attitudes toward these laws have changed considerably.

Laws Reinforcing Mores and Folkways (Category 2)

Most states have statutes against indecent exposure, obscene exhibition, the reproduction or sale of obscene literature, prostitution, drug abuse, gambling, bribery, the falsifying of public documents, and corruption. These forms of behavior may not be considered evil unless prohibited by law. Each may be considered *malum prohibitum*—specifically forbidden by law, with the limitation on behavior specified in a statute. When these offenses are committed, formal controls are applied with the general support of members of the dominant group and most subgroups.

There is an important difference, however, in the imposition of informal controls regarding these crimes. Whereas people are likely to see themselves or those dear to them as victims or potential victims of the category 1 offenses, in the case of category 2 offenses they tend to see themselves as part of a *collectivity* that may be a victim or a potential victim.

The arrest, trial, and prosecution of violators of these statutes receive varying degrees of public support. Moreover, informal sanctions are not

---

[13] Stewart Alsop, "Quick Looks," in *Newsweek*, November 27, 1972, p. 112.

as likely to be applied when formal legal sanctions fail. Members of underprivileged subgroups tend to be apathetic toward violations of these statutes. Unless convicted of one of these offenses and given the status of criminal by a court, a violator is not likely to suffer any informal sanctions.

In New York, for example, there is a statute that makes the "forging, stealing, mutilating, and falsifying of judicial and public records and documents" a crime. John M., a 17-year-old boy with considerable skill in installing electrical equipment, was anxious to obtain employment as an electrician. The state law limited such employment to persons 18 years of age or over. John falsified the date of birth on his birth certificate to indicate that he was 18. He succeeded in obtaining work as an electrician's apprentice. After working at the job for two months, he was apprehended at work, and he acknowledged what he had done. Although he was held for trial, charges against him were dropped. There was no evidence that any of John's acquaintances or friends looked down on him for violating the statute in question.

There is general public support for laws barring children from dangerous occupations, and officials can count on mild public suport in prosecuting violators. However, when no formal sanctions are applied (charges are dropped), it is unlikely that informal sanctions will follow. Most people do not refuse to associate with accused persons, and some may even admire their courage and initiative. Consensus is not so complete as it is in the event of a violation of a category 1 statute.

A study of public attitudes conducted by the Wisconsin Survey Research Laboratory in a midsized industrial city in Wisconsin revealed that people were unconcerned about gambling, prostitution, and other mala prohibita crimes. Ninety-six percent agreed with the statement that "no matter what you do, people will always gamble." They also felt that a large proportion of their neighbors gambled and that some forms of gambling are not reprehensible. There was little awareness of the extent of corruption in the city. Although the people were strongly against dishonest public officials, they did not infer corruption from the simple presence of prostitution and gambling in the city.[14]

In instances such as these, there is mild public suport for the exercise of formal control. Where formal sanctions fail, informal sanctions are seldom applied. Category 2 offenses are less likely to come to the attention of the police, to result in prosecution, to lead to conviction by our courts, or to be sanctioned by imprisonment than are offenses in category 1. Essentially because most people do not consider themselves personally involved or harmed in any way, they do not assist in the enforcement of these laws.

---

[14] John A. Gardner, "Public Attitudes toward Gambling and Corruption," *Annals of the American Academy of Political and Social Science* 381 (January 1969):123–134.

Laws Formalizing Folkways (Category 3)

Violations of some sections of motor vehicle codes, labor codes, health and safety codes, and business and professional codes are punishable by the courts as felonies and misdemeanors. Motor vehicle codes, for example, provide for the punishment of speeders, reckless drivers, drunken drivers, and violators of all sorts of traffic regulations. In recent years, owing to such organizations as Mothers Against Drunk Drivers (MADD), public sentiment is increasingly for prosecuting drunk drivers and giving them severe sentences.

A large majority of our traffic accidents, estimated to be as high as 88 percent, result in part from a violation of some traffic law. Despite this fact there is a definite lack of social stigmatization. The traffic law violator may be just about anyone who owns a vehicle. The violator is rarely charged with criminal intent, but rather with having committed an act forbidden by statute. The tendency is not to treat the traffic law violator as a criminal. Standard schedules of fines are furnished, and attendance at court is waived if the fine is mailed in. In extreme cases, licenses may be revoked.[15]

Motor vehicle codes may be considered formalizations of folkways defining behavior appropriate for operators of motor vehicles. In many states there is so little support for the prosecution of violators that traffic laws are expressly excluded from consideration as crimes.

Category 3 offenses do not come to the attention of the police unless the police are engaged in the process of searching for violations of the law. Prosecutions tend to be routinized, and the penalty (usually a fine) is prescribed without trial. Imprisonment is rare. Informal sanctions are virtually nonexistent.

Laws Enacted to Deter Social Change (Category 4)

Most laws regulating business enterprises are designed to formalize folkways or to deter social change. Since violations of these laws are made misdemeanors by statute, and since punishment is provided by statute, such laws are part of our criminal law. For example, many of our states have placed in the criminal law statutes designed to protect businesses from the misrepresentations of unscrupulous suppliers, borrowers, and customers. The changeover from a cash-and-carry economy to one largely dependent on the expansion of credit places businesses in a vulnerable position. When the seller of personal property turns over custody of the property to the purchaser, the seller no longer receives a substantial payment. This is frequently true whether or not the purchaser is a good credit risk. To protect the businesses, statutes have been enacted making it a crime to sell mortgaged personal property, to move a

---

[15] Laurence H. Ross, "Traffic Law Violation: A Folk Crime," *Social Problems* 8 (Winter 1960–61):231–240.

motor vehicle outside the state without the consent of any finance company that has retained title to it, or to make false statements on credit applications. The federal patent laws were also designed to protect the businesses that had financed the research leading to inventions. Violations of these laws are defined as misdemeanors or felonies. Action to enforce them, however, is seldom taken unless initiated by an injured party. Persons not directly concerned are indifferent.

An example of a statute enacted to deter social change in family structure is one that makes it a crime for an adult son or daughter to fail to provide support for an indigent parent. A family is often unable or unwilling to assume obligations for the support of indigent relatives, even very close ones. In working class families in particular, the support of aged parents creates too great a burden for many married children to assume. The state, through its welfare agencies, has increasingly assumed this burden. When children neglect to support their parents, in violation of the law, a prosecutor seeking to enforce the law can expect little cooperation from the public and active opposition from those adversely affected. The fact that such laws remain virtually unenforced indicates the ineffectiveness of the law in maintaining the family status quo.

In view of the high rate of divorce and remarriage, it has become increasingly important for courts to ensure support for minor children and to impose sanctions on parents who fail to contribute. A study conducted in a metropolitan county of Wisconsin over a period of ten years indicated that compliance with court orders was less than complete. In 91 percent of a representative sample of families in which divorces were granted, fathers were obligated to provide child support for ten years. In each instance the court determined the obligation of the father and the amount of contribution he was required to make on the basis of his financial ability. Fathers who fail to pay may be held in contempt of court, be subject to civil action, or be prosecuted for a misdemeanor or felony. The study found 84 percent of the fathers in defiance of court orders during the ten-year interval. Only 36 percent of these were prosecuted. Following the second year of payment there was a steadily decreasing interest in securing compliance with the law.[16] In the late 1980s, there have been a number of law enforcement mass "sweeps" and arrests of errant fathers who have dropped out of paying child support.

To deter social change, statutes forbidding trespass have been employed to outlaw protest marches, demonstrations, and certain types of picketing. These forms of protest are considered essential to civil rights groups, student groups, antiwar protesters, other dissenting groups, and labor unions in their efforts to bring about social change.

---

[16] Kenneth W. Eckhardt, "Deviance, Visibility, and Legal Action: The Duty of Support," *Social Problems* 15 (Spring 1968):470–477.

When the political authority employs the criminal law or law enforcement personnel to prevent marches and demonstrations, the objective is to reinforce the power structure by reducing or minimizing all forms of resistance and maintaining the status quo. Although formal sanctions may be applied by agents of the society to those who violate these statutes, violators are likely to be considered heroes by their respective groups. Many who participated in the sit-ins, freedom rides, and civil rights marches of the 1960s considered their arrests as badges of honor. The same may be said for those who engaged in demonstrations and protests against racism in recent years.

Laws Enacted to Promote "Morality" (Category 5)

Smith and Pollack point out that hundreds of sections of our penal codes are concerned with acts that are criminal because we say they are. They include laws prohibiting "homosexuality between consenting adults, prostitution, gambling, adultery, marihuana use, possession of obscene and pornographic materials." They point out that only a small fraction of the time of police officers, judges, prosecutors, and correction officials is spent in handling what we have included as category 1 offenses: rape, murder, and aggravated assault. For every murderer processed through the system, there are dozens of gamblers, prostitutes, pushers, and alcoholics. They note that a common characteristic of violations of these "morals" laws (including drug laws) is that the resulting crimes have no victims. The prostitute's client has not been forcibly seduced; the person who makes a bet on the numbers has not been robbed; the drug user has directly harmed only herself. There are, in a very real sense, no complaining witnesses who can help the police in establishing the case against the accused offender. Because of the fact that there are no aggrieved victims ready and willing to testify for the state, the burden of producing evidence for the prosecution rests entirely on the police.[17] This situation places the police in direct conflict with a segment of the population defined by law as having committed crimes, without the active support of any significant portion of the population. That is the effect of giving police the task of enforcing a law which lacks consensus, because there are many differeing viewpoints on what constitutes morality.

In summary, the American legal system contains laws that are clearly agreed upon by the vast majority of the populace and laws which have limited consensus. What fosters equitable justice in America is the fact that written laws are tempered in the courts by a jury of peers and a judge in the process of the administration of justice.

---

[17] Alexander B. Smith and Harriet Pollack, *Some Sins Are Not Crimes* (New York: Franklin Watts, 1975), pp. 1–16.

Chapter
2

The Administration of Justice

A criminal justice system is the process that a government employs to enforce standards of conduct required by that government of people subject to its authority. We noted in Chapter 1 how a government formalizes standards of conduct through the enactment of criminal laws. The criminal justice system operates by apprehending, prosecuting, convicting, and sentencing those persons who violate the criminal law. Figure 2.1 presents a general diagram or flowchart of how the criminal justice system generally works in the United States.

THE CRIMINAL JUSTICE PROCESS

In our society a person convicted of a crime is given the status of criminal. Once given this status, he or she may be subjected to isolation, segregation, degradation, incarceration, and, in some instances, chemical, medical, or psychological treatment. A convicted person may be sent to prison for a long time, even for life, or executed. Under the most favorable conditions a criminal may remain in the community on probation. However, even on probation the criminal must conform to certain rules and restrict some activities and associations. Furthermore, the stigmatization that attaches to conviction for a serious crime may continue to affect the person for a lifetime. For these reasons it is important that every precaution be taken to protect the innocent from conviction of a crime.

In his book *The Innocents*, Edward Radin points out that "one of the most common American myths is the belief that innocent people are not

This chart presents a simple yet comprehensive view of the movement of cases through the criminal justice system. Procedures in individual jurisdictions may vary from the pattern shown here. The differing weights of line indicate the relative volumes of cases disposed of at various points in the system, but this is only suggestive since no nationwide data of this sort exist.

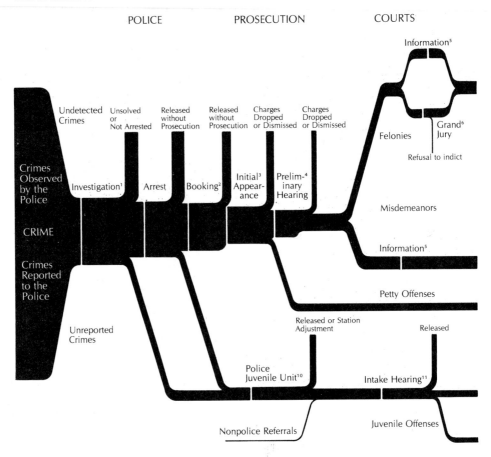

1. May continue until trial.
2. Administrative record of arrest. First step at which temporary release on bail may be available.
3. Before magistrate, commissioner, or justice of peace. Formal notice of charge, advice of rights. Bail set. Summary trials for petty offenses usually conducted here without further processing.

4. Preliminary testing of evidence against defendant. Charge may be reduced. No separate preliminary hearing for misdemeanors in some systems.
5. Charge filed by prosecutor on basis of information submitted by police or citizens. Alternative to grand jury indictment; often used in felonies, almost always in misdemeanors.

6. Reviews whether government evidence sufficient to justify trial. Some states have no grand jury system; others seldom use it.
7. Appearance for plea; defendant elects trial by judge or jury (if available); counsel for indigent usually appointed here in felonies. Often not at all in other cases.

Figure 2.1 A general view of the criminal justice system. [*Source:* President's Commission on Law Enforcement and Administration of Justice, *The Challenge of Crime in a Free Society* (Washington, D.C.: U.S. Government Printing Office, 1967), pp. 8–9.]

CORRECTIONS

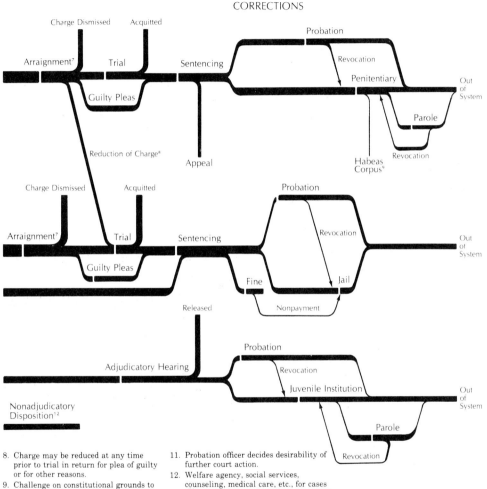

8. Charge may be reduced at any time prior to trial in return for plea of guilty or for other reasons.

9. Challenge on constitutional grounds to legality of detention. May be sought at any point in process.

10. Police often hold informal hearings, dismiss or adjust many cases without further processing.

11. Probation officer decides desirability of further court action.

12. Welfare agency, social services, counseling, medical care, etc., for cases where adjudicatory handling not needed.

convicted for crimes they have not committed." He presents documented instances in which people were convicted of crimes they did not commit, some for crimes that never even happened. According to Radin, it is generally believed that 95 percent of the persons convicted are guilty, but lawyers who have specialized in freeing illegally convicted prisoners believe that only about 80 percent of those convicted are guilty.[1] Radin's book shows how easy it is for an average, decent, hardworking American to be arrested for a crime he or she has not committed. It is easier for a person who is poor, or is also a member of a minority group, or has a criminal record to be convicted. When we consider these possibilities we are inclined to resist the pressures of "law and order" proponents to make convictions easier. It is no doubt true that current judicial procedures enable some guilty people to escape punishment. However, are we prepared to see more innocent people suffer so that more guilty people can be punished?

It is important, moreover, that the people—all the people, if possible—have confidence in the fairness of the system under which justice is administered. A political authority functions best when there is unquestioning acceptance of its decisions and actions. The more people lose faith in the system, the more they are likely to resist or even actively oppose it. The government can, of course, respond to resistance or active opposition with force. However, the more the government has to rely on power rather than authority, the weaker it becomes. In extreme cases a nation can become divided against itself.

The procedures required to determine criminal status have been in part established by the common law, in part set forth in statutes enacted pursuant to the provisions of our federal and state constitutions, and in part determined through judicial interpretation of constitutional provisions. The administration of justice preceding the determination of criminal status generally flows as outlined in the following sections.

The Arrest

Action against an individual charged with a crime usually begins with the individual's arrest. A private citizen may arrest another for any crime committed in his or her presence—but in doing so risks the possibility of a lawsuit for false arrest. A police officer may take a suspect into custody with or without a warrant of arrest. If the officer has reasonable cause to believe that a felony has been committed and that the suspect has committed it, the officer may make an arrest without a warrant. A police officer may arrest for a misdemeanor if the act was committed in the officer's presence.

A warrant may be issued by a judge when someone complains under

---

[1] Edward D. Radin, *The Innocents* (New York: Morrow, 1964).

oath that a crime has been committed and that there is probable cause to suspect the accused. Police and other peace officers usually take action on the complaint of a victim or some other person who has witnessed the commission of a crime. They are required to make an arrest when a warrant ordering it is issued by a judge.

Complaint or Accusations

Most arrests are made before any accusatory pleading has been filed. Once an arrest is made, the facts are presented to a prosecuting agency. This agency must either prepare a complaint or issue a dismissal. In the event of a dismissal, the accused can be rearrested when new facts or witnesses are obtained. This does not constitute double jeopardy.

In the event a complaint is filed and approved by the court, then the next step is the preliminary hearing.

Preliminary Hearing

The police are required to present the arrested party for a preliminary hearing before a magistrate of the court without unreasonable delay. In some states, 24 hours is considered reasonable. In others, a preliminary hearing is usually held within 10 days. The function of the preliminary hearing is to determine whether or not the accused should be brought to trial. This procedure requires law enforcement officials to publicly inform the accused of the nature of the charges against him or her and the type of evidence available to the prosecution. It also affords the accused an opportunity to contact family and friends, retain counsel, and obtain aid in the preparation of a defense. In most states the preliminary hearing takes place in an inferior court presided over by a magistrate. The magistrate may dispose of minor cases, but if she has reason to believe that there is enough evidence to convict a suspect of a serious offense, she must hold that person for a grand jury. The magistrate may fix bail and release the accused from custody if he or someone else posts bail on his behalf. The magistrate may also release the accused on his own recognizance. This means that the magistrate trusts the accused to appear at the trial. The magistrate may refuse release on bail to a person charged with murder or some other very serious offense.

Indictment or Information

In some states the accused may be brought to trial by an "information" prepared by the prosecutor, which is based upon an investigation conducted in the prosecutor's office. In other states indictment by a grand jury is required, and there is no provision for a preliminary hearing. In California and certain other states, an information can be filed only after a preliminary hearing is held.

Grand juries in the United States range in size from 5 to 23 members. The grand jury determines, on the basis of evidence submitted by the prosecutor, whether or not there is sufficient evidence to warrant a trial. A majority vote of the grand jury is sufficient to result in an indictment.

A finding of a grand jury is not the equivalent of a conviction because the grand jury does not weigh the evidence. It merely decides that the evidence presented by the prosecution, *if believed,* would warrant the conviction of the accused.

A grand jury holds both advantages and disadvantages for an accused. In certain respects it protects privacy, and if no indictment is returned the accused does not suffer public humiliation. On the other hand, it allows a prosecutor to gather evidence without the knowledge of the accused, and without the exculpatory evidence that an accused might offer.

The grand jury was introduced into England at the time of the Norman conquest in 1066. It was virtually abolished in England in 1933 for reasons of economy. In the United States the grand jury indictment procedure for prosecution of felonies in federal courts was established by the Fifth Amendment to the Constitution. Most states provide for grand jury indictment in their constitutions. Many, however, permit the prosecutor to proceed by indictment or information without a grand jury. Actually, grand juries have two completely different functions. The first is to determine, on the basis of evidence presented by the prosecutor, whether there is a prima facie case—that is, whether there is enough evidence to warrant trial. The second function performed by the grand jury, one that has resulted in considerable controversy, is to act as an investigating or inquisitorial body with broad powers to determine what crimes have been committed in its jurisdiction.[2] Using this power, grand juries have attempted to compel newspaper reporters, radio commentators, and journalists to reveal their information. In many cases, people refusing to reveal their sources have been placed in jail for indefinite periods.

The Trial

After an arraignment in which the charges against the accused are read in open court, an accused may plead guilty. If he or she does so, there is no trial, and the judge may impose sentence. If the accused pleads not guilty, the burden is upon the prosecution to prove guilt beyond a reasonable doubt. In a trial by jury, guilt must be determined by unanimous vote of 12 jurors in most states. The Sixth Amendment to the U.S. Constitution guarantees to those charged with crimes a trial by an

---

[2] Paul W. Tappan, *Crime, Justice and Corrections* (New York: McGraw-Hill, 1960), pp. 337–339.

impartial jury. The Fourteenth Amendment requires that the jury be drawn from a cross section of the community, avoiding the systematic and intentional exclusion of any qualified group of individuals. Discrimination resulting in the exclusion from jury service of members of minority groups has resulted in Supreme Court reversal of convictions by juries so selected. Before members of a jury are placed on the jury, there is a *voir dire* examination during which the prosecutor and defense may question them to determine their impartiality. Individual jurors may be challenged for cause if either counsel considers them biased or unqualified. The judge decides whether to excuse the juror or not. A number of peremptory challenges, challenges without any reason, are allowed each side. When a lawyer challenges peremptorily, the juror is immediately excused.

Objections to the jury system include the following:

1. The length of time required for impaneling a jury delays trials.
2. Persons selected to serve on juries are without legal or investigative training and are not qualified to analyze evidence or apply complicated judicial instructions.

Actually, a very small portion of criminal cases are tried by jury. Victimless crimes, which account for most of the congestion in criminal courts, may be greatly reduced by changes in criminal codes. Also, much of the court congestion may be attributed to the large number of automobile accident cases.

Those favoring retention of the jury system point out that it tends to reduce popular distrust of official justice. To many, the jury trial provides the best opportunity for the criminal justice system to display an unbiased and unhurried search for the truth.[3]

How does the criminal justice system operate? Here is one journalist's pertinent summary of its operation in Washington, D.C.:

> To begin with, you find that most criminals are never caught. For example, arrests are made in only 1 out of 4 reported robberies. So, only a small fraction of all crimes committed ever reach the criminal-justice system at all.
>
> Starting with those who are arrested, you find only 33 out of 100 will eventually be convicted of any crime. . . . Typically, for a variety of reasons, the prosecutor declines to prosecute 24 out of 100 cases that the police bring in. An additional 40 cases out of the original 100 will be dropped later by the prosecutor or dismissed by a judge. Only 10 cases will go to trial. About 26 defendants will plead guilty to some charge— sometimes a lesser charge than that on which they were originally arrested. Out of the original 100 arrested, only 3 will go free because of an acquittal at trial. The other 7 who will stand trial will be convicted.

---

[3] Paul Ligda, "Viva La Jury," *California State Bar Journal* (October 1974):453–457.

Of those who are convicted, about 4 in 10 will not be sentenced to jail or prison. Instead, they will be fined or placed on probation.[4]

This analysis is as appropriate now as it was in 1976.

The United States has an adversary system of justice. The prosecuting attorney, on behalf of the state, presents the evidence against the accused. The accused is entitled to choose an attorney to prepare a defense. If the defendant cannot afford an attorney, one is appointed by the court. Understandably, in the past, poor people have been inadequately represented. A court-appointed attorney may be unskilled or may be unwilling or unable to devote the time needed for adequate preparation of a case and may have been unknown to the defendant prior to the trial. In recent years, bar associations have made efforts to provide representation for persons tried in our criminal courts. In many jurisdictions public defenders are designated by the state to represent indigent people charged with crimes.

In the adversary system, the role of the judge is to determine the admissibility of evidence, rule on matters of procedure, and instruct the jury on matters of law. If the jury renders a verdict of guilty, the judge fixes and announces the sentence. At the trial the accused and the defense attorney may cross-examine witnesses presented by the prosecution, object to inadmissible evidence, present evidence on behalf of the accused, and avail the accused of all the protections guaranteed by the U.S. Constitution and the constitution of the state. The defense attorney is duty-bound to present the case of the accused in its most favorable light, *even if the attorney knows the person to be guilty.*

Mental Incompetence—Insanity

There are many variations on how the "insanity defense" operates in court. The following, however, is a general summary of the issues involved and how this plea is incorporated into the judicial system.

If, at the time of trial, it appears to the court that the accused is mentally incompetent and unable to participate in a defense, the judge may send him or her to a mental institution. The suspect then remains in the mental institution until deemed able to stand trial. The judge may, if in doubt as to the accused's ability to stand trial, order a psychiatric examination and postpone judgment until hearing testimony as to the person's mental competence. Again, if mental incompetence is established, the accused is sent to a mental institution until deemed competent by the psychiatric staff. Months or years may elapse before such a person is released from the hospital to stand trial. Some mental hospitals

---

[4] *U.S. News & World Report*, May 10, 1976, p. 37.

provide little treatment and operate largely as warehouses for these cases.

An accused who regains mental competence must then stand trial. In the event of conviction the accused gets credit for time already spent in custody.

In a unanimous decision in 1972, the Supreme Court ruled that under due process and equal protection clasues of the Constitution, a defendant who is found incompetent to stand trial is also subject to the procedural civil requirements:[5] The standards for involuntary civil commitment in a given state must be met before an accused can be subjected to prolonged commitment; an accused who no longer meets civil commitment standards must be released.

In most felony cases an evil intent, *mens rea*, is an essential element of the crime. If the accused is insane—is incapable of forming or harboring an intent to commit a crime—no crime has been committed. The plea is not guilty by reason of insanity, and the jury has to determine, on the basis of the evidence (including psychiatric testimony), whether or not the accused was insane at the time of the act.

Since 1843, courts in England have applied the *M'Naghten's Rule* in determining the nature and extent of unsoundness of mind which would excuse the commission of a felony. It was decided in this case that to establish the defense of insanity, "it must be clearly proved that, at the time of the committing of the act, the party accused was labouring under such a defect of reason, from disease of the mind, as not to know the nature and quality of the act he was doing; or, if he did know it, that he did not know he was doing what was wrong."[6]

Either by statute or by case decision, the M'Naghten's Rule is applied in most states. Some states combine it with an irresistible-impulse test, which may be applied where *the mind is powerless to control the will*. The individual knows what is right, desires to do right, but some uncontrollable impulse compels the person to commit the wrong.

In 1961, a federal court of appeals applied a new test in the case of U.S. v. Currens, 290 F. 751, 766. Since that time, other federal courts have adopted this so-called Model Penal Code test. The rule is stated as follows: "A person is not responsible for criminal conduct if at the time of such conduct as a result of mental disease or defect he lacks substantial capacity either to appreciate the criminality (wrongfulness) of his conduct or to conform his conduct to the requirements of law."[7]

Some objections to the M'Naghten's Rule are as follows:

---

[5] *Jackson v. Indiana*, June 7, 1972 (No. 70-5009).

[6] M'Naghten's Case, House of Lords (1843) 8 *Eng. Repr.* 718.

[7] American Law Institutes Model Penal Code, sec. 4.01, subd. (1).

1. It permits the punishment of people who are seriously psychotic.
2. A psychiatrist cannot reach any reliable conclusion on the accused's ability to distinguish between right and wrong.
3. A psychiatrist cannot determine whether or not an accused was insane at the time of an offense.
4. A psychiatrist is required to reply, in court, to hypothetical questions which do not relate to the diagnosis.
5. Since the adversary system results in each side presenting psychiatrists giving opinions in support of its contentions, psychiatry, which is an inexact "science," often appears debatable and confuses jurors.

The determination of mental competence or insanity is made by "expert witnesses" who are, in fact, often lacking in competence. In their book *Coping with Psychiatric and Psychological Testimony*, forensic psychologists Jan Ziskin and David Faust question the value of psychological testimony:

> Do mental health professionals—psychiatrists and clinical psychologists— aid courtroom justice or constitute a burden on the legal system? It has been estimated that psychiatrists and clinical psychologists participate in as many as 1 million cases a year. Their opinions as "experts" may play a role in determining whether a person is confined to a mental institution, obtains custody of a child, receives monetary damages for injuries, or is held not accountable for acts that otherwise would be considered crimes. Much of the related cost is borne by the taxpayers.
>
> Mental health professionals may provide helpful treatment for people with psychological problems. However, other than impressive-sounding credentials and a facade of scientific knowledge, there is little reason to believe these professionals possess the capabilities that the law normally requires to qualify for rendering expert opinions. The state of knowledge of scientific disciplines or professions is contained in their literature—books and journals. Overall, scientific literature fails to support a view of psychiatrists and psychologists as experts in assessing mental condition. They do not even have an adequate system for classifying disorders, although this is an essential prerequisite for developing a valid body of knowledge about such disorders. There is a substantial body of literature in psychiatry and clinical psychology that, at the minimum, creates serious doubts about whether psychiatrists and psychologists possess the kind of validated knowledge and methodology of assessment that would allow them to render opinions without, in effect, committing perjury.[8]

The laws of evidence require that expert opinions be admitted only if they can be stated with "reasonable certainty," or, in the case of mental health issues, with reasonable psychiatric or psychological certainty. But there is no validated body of knowledge or principles that

---

[8] Jan Ziskin and David Faust, *Coping with Psychiatric and Psychological Testimony* (Los Angeles, Calif.: Law and Psychology Press, 1988), p. 48.

provides a high probability of correctly determing whether, for example, an individual was able at some time in the past to distinguish right from wrong or whether someone is presently dangerous. The research shows the opinions are about twice as likely to be wrong as to be right in determining the dangerousness of a person. How, then, can an honest and informed psychiatrist or psychologist say under oath that such an opinion can be stated with reasonable certainty? And how can the trial process be aided by these opinions? An honest professional who is acquainted with the literature would have to acknowledge that any opinion is speculative, in which case the court would not allow it in evidence.

An accused who pleads not guilty by reason of insanity may be acquitted and may then be released to the community. This might happen either in the case of temporary insanity or where the insanity was of longer duration. If the judge considers the accused insane or in need of treatment, the judge can send the individual to a mental hospital.

Many people believe the community should have voice in this issue. In an article entitled "An Analysis of Public Attitudes Toward the Insanity Defense," sociologist Valerie P. Hans states this position:

> Results from a public opinion survey of knowledge, attitudes, and support for the insanity defense indicate that people dislike the insanity defense for both retributive and utilitarian reasons: they want insane lawbreakers punished, and they believe that insanity defense procedures fail to protect the public.[9]

The Sentence

In many states the indeterminate sentence is employed. The minimum and maximum terms are ordinarily determined by a provision of the law. Even where the definite sentence is employed, the possibility of parole makes it in effect an indefinite sentence in which upper and lower limits are set by law, a court, or an administrative agency. (In some states prison terms are fixed by an administrative agency rather than by a court.)

In those states in which the judge fixes the sentence, he or she usually has available the report of a presentencing investigation. This report contains a record of previous arrests and information regarding education, work history, family, and social relationships. In one representative study of sentencing by six judges for eight felonies, considerable disparity was found. Of 721 defendants, 46 percent were sentenced to imprisonment, 37 percent were given probation, 10 percent were fined, and 7 percent received suspended sentences. Courtroom deci-

---

[9] Valerie P. Hans, "An Analysis of Public Attitudes Toward the Insanity Defense," *Criminology* 24, no. 2 (1986):409.

sions often tend to reflect a judge's prejudices. Some judges see some offenses as more threatening to the community than others, and they sentence accordingly. Some have personal biases which they express in the form of severity of sentence. For example, black defendants have received more severe sentences than whites from some judges.[10]

The kind of sentence that a judge may impose on a person found guilty of crime is provided for in the statutes of the state. In general, a statute declaring that a specific violation of the criminal law is a crime also provides for punishment. At times a minimum punishment is specified, and invariably a maximum punishment is included. Judges may exercise discretion within these limits. In some cases they may fine the person found guilty. In most cases they will impose a prison sentence or place the person on probation. A person placed on probation serves this sentence in the community under the supervision of a probation officer. A probationer does not go to prison unless he or she is determined to have violated the conditions of probation. Prison sentences may be for a fixed term or for an indefinite period (one to three years, two to ten years, etc.). A person placed on probation may also be required to serve time in a local jail.

There is a continuing debate among criminologists and judicial administrators on the relative merits of short or long sentences in deterring crime. One study by Donald Lewis concludes that

> taken as a whole the studies reviewed constitute a substantial body of evidence which is largely consistent with the existence of a deterrent effect from longer sentences. This conclusion must still be considered tentative for several reasons. . . . There remains substantial room for improvement in the underlying theory, data sources and methods of statistical inference and design. In addition, the evidence concerning the magnitude of the deterrent effect of longer sentences for various crimes is far from uniform. Nevertheless, impartial analysis of the best available evidence suggests that criminals do respond to incentives and that longer sentences do deter crime.[11]

The Appeal

A person convicted of a crime may appeal the decision of the court to an appellate tribunal. Appeals are generally based on some alleged procedural error or some violation of the constitutional rights of the accused. Every state has at least one appellate court. When it is alleged that the rights of an accused under the U.S. Constitution have been violated, the individual may ultimately appeal to the U.S. Supreme

---

[10] Lenard Cargan and Mary Coates, "The Indeterminate Sentence and Judicial Bias," *Crime and Delinquency* (April 1974):144–156.

[11] Donald E. Lewis, "The General Deterrent Effect of Longer Sentences," *British Journal of Criminology* 26 N (January 1986):60.

Court. While the appeal is pending, the individual, although convicted by a court and sentenced, may be released on bail. In instances where a convicted person is out on bail, to all intents and purposes the status of criminal is deferred until appellate rights have been exhausted.

The procedures described above are those followed in criminal proceedings, as distinguished from the proceedings of civil courts and administrative tribunals. The emphasis in a criminal proceeding is on the protection of the accused. Thus, guilty people may not infrequently escape punishment, but these safeguards also protect innocent people from stigmatization and unmerited punishment.

In brief, the foregoing reveals the "rules of the game" under which a person accused of a crime is judged. Every person who has violated a section of the penal code, or a portion of an administrative code that is punishable as a felony or misdemeanor, may be given the status of criminal. Accused citizens cannot, however, be given legal criminal status until they have been found guilty of a crime by a court, even though anyone so accused is often perceived by the society as a criminal. It is also a fact that under the criminal justice system in the United States, people who have wealth, influence, and high social status can hire the best attorneys, and they consequently tend to have a better chance to elude conviction in the courts than poor people without power.

THE POLICE

The police perform their functions mainly on the street, where the going is roughest. Their job is quite hazardous. Because they are so visible, there is a tendency on the part of the public to blame the police for increases in crime, but the fact is that the police cannot resolve the social conditions responsible for the increases in crime. The police do exercise a considerable amount of discretionary power in the process of law enforcement. However, they do not enact the laws that they are required to enforce, nor do they determine the disposition of the criminals they arrest.

Functions of the Police

Most people tend to visualize police officers—on the basis of the television and movie images with which they are inundated—as spending most of their time investigating crimes, arresting criminals, engaging in daily gun battles, and pursuing suspects either in police cars or on foot. Actually, police officers can perform their duties for years without foot or car chases and without using their guns except for practice, and their felony arrests are not very frequent. Except for detectives (a small portion of an urban police force), few police officers spend much of their time in investigation. Most officers spend their time doing routine patrol. In some neighborhoods, they may have to intervene in fights between spouses, relatives, or friends, some of whom may be armed with guns, knives, or other weapons.

A great deal of the work done by patrol officers is service-oriented: taking an abandoned child to an agency providing shelter, calling an ambulance to the scene of an accident, rendering assistance to injured persons, and giving information to the public in general about legal and police issues. Many studies have reported that the primary role of the police is providing generalized social services to the public and that law enforcement tasks account for a relatively small portion of the patrol function. In one study it was found that service duties constituted 64 percent of total police duties. Only 36 percent of police work involved law enforcement tasks.

One of the most important functions of the criminal justice system is the *protective* function. By working to prevent crime and apprehend criminals, the police play a major part in *protecting society*. Total enforcement of the law, even if it were possible, is limited by generally applicable due-process restrictions on such police procedures as arrests, search, seizure, and interrogation. There is an area of *full enforcement* in which the police are not only authorized but expected to fully enforce the criminal law. Minimally, full enforcement, so far as the police are concerned, means:

1. The investigation of every disturbing event which is reported to or observed by police and which they have reason to suspect may be a violation of the criminal law.
2. Following a determination that some crime has been committed, an effort to discover its perpetrators.
3. The presentation of all information collected by police to the prosecutor.

Even if there were enough police, adequately equipped and trained, certain pressures could force the police to act selectively. Police officers themselves might decide not to take full enforcement action, and, in so deciding, would be administering justice on their own—without prosecutor, judge, or jury. For example, a police officer who decides to ignore a felonious assault because the victim will not sign a complaint has, in effect, disposed of the case. It is unlikely that the prosecutor or grand jury will ever take action to bring the case before a court. Trading enforcement against a narcotics suspect for information about other offenders, a common practice in police departments, involves police decisions not to invoke the criminal process fully.[12]

---

[12] Joseph Goldstein, "Police Discretion Not to Invoke the Criminal Process: Low-Visibility Decisions in the Administration of Justice," in *Criminal Justice, Law and Politics*, ed. George F. Cole, 2d ed. (North Scituate, Mass.: Duxberry Press, 1976), pp. 108–127.

Most police officers maintain that they enforce all laws; but Kenneth Kulp Davis, an administrative law expert who studied how police officers work, found that officers enforce many laws selectively or not at all. Davis interviewed 300 Chicago police officers about how they enforce laws. Among laws that he and his researchers found officers very rarely enforcing are those prohibiting social gambling, intercourse in automobiles or in parks, public marijuana smoking, curfew violations, juvenile drinking, adult drinking in parks, and attempts to bribe a police officer. Interviewed police officers said that when they investigated a crime such as armed robbery, assault with a deadly weapon, or shoplifting, *they would not arrest a criminal against whom the victim refused to make a complaint.*[13]

The Police Officer's "Working Personality"

Jerome Skolnick points out that doctors, janitors, lawyers, and industrial workers develop distinctive ways of perceiving and responding to their environment and that certain outstanding elements in the police experience also combine to generate distinctive responses which he calls a "working personality." Exposure to danger and the felt pressure to prove oneself efficient are the elements which in combination generate the police officer's working personality. The element of danger seems to make officers especially attentive to signs indicating a potential for violence and lawbreaking. As a result, police officers are generally suspicious people. The element of authority, combined with the element of danger, tends to isolate them. This is particularly true when they enforce unpopular laws related to puritanical morality. Furthermore, the element of danger makes it particularly difficult to use authority in a judicious manner.

Police officers are specifically trained to be suspicious. As a result of this training, and the fact that they share career and salary problems with each other, they tend to show an unusually high degree of occupational solidarity. Their best friends tend to be other police officers.[14] Every officer is aware of the Law Enforcement Code of Ethics, to which he or she is supposed to subscribe (see Figure 2.2). This code incorporates an ideal that is virtually impossible to attain. Considerable guilt may be involved when officers violate the code by permitting personal feelings, prejudices, animosities, or friendships to influence their decisions. When they violate this provision of the code, they tend to rationalize their behavior by exaggerating the "evil" activities of the persons who provoked them. They must exercise discretion in matters involving life

---

[13] Bryce Nelson, "Police Found to Enforce Law Selectively," *Los Angeles Times*, August 18, 1976.

[14] Jerome H. Skolnick, *Justice Without Trial*, 2d ed. (New York: Wiley, 1975), pp. 42–68.

Law Enforcement Code of Ethics

As a Law Enforcement Officer, my fundamental duty is to serve mankind; to safeguard lives and property; to protect the innocent against deception, the weak against oppression or intimidation, and the peaceful against violence or disorder; and to respect the Constitutional rights of all men to liberty, equality and justice.

I will keep my private life unsullied as an example to all; maintain courageous calm in the face of danger, scorn, or ridicule; develop self-restraint; and be constantly mindful of the welfare of others. Honest in thought and deed in both my personal and official life, I will be exemplary in obeying the laws of the land and the regulations of my department. Whatever I see or hear of a confidential nature or that is confided to me in my official capacity will be kept ever secret unless revelation is necessary in the performance of my duty.

I will never act officiously or permit personal feelings, prejudices, animosities or friendships to influence my decisions. With no compromise for crime and with relentless prosecution of criminals, I will enforce the law courteously and appropriately without fear or favor, malice or ill will, never employing unnecessary force or violence and never accepting gratuities.

I recognize the badge of my office as a symbol of public faith, and I accept it as a public trust to be held so long as I am true to the ethics of the police service. I will constantly strive to achieve these objectives and ideals, dedicating myself before God to my chosen profession . . . law enforcement.

Figure 2.2 Law enforcement code of ethics. [*Source:* FBI, *Uniform Crime Reports for the United States, 1987* (Washington, D.C.: U.S. Government Printing Office, 1988), p. 226.]

and death in an environment that they perceive as dangerous. Their actions may violate the rights of others.

Peter Manning points out that in modern society the police have an *impossible mandate*. To gain the public's confidence in their ability, the police have encouraged the image of themselves as an efficient, highly organized force in a dangerous and heroic enterprise: the prevention of crime and the apprehension of criminals.[15]

Police-Community Relations

Police have good to excellent relations with people in the suburbs and in urban middle-class neighborhoods. Except for occasional traffic tickets, or perhaps encounters when they are obnoxiously intoxicated, members of the middle and upper class experience largely positive contacts with the police. The car patrol may come to the house in response to a call when a house is burglarized or vandalized. These people will call the police if they are robbed, mugged, or assaulted. They may call the police in the event of a fire, and the police will protect their property. They may also have occasion to call the police department for any one of its many services. Generally speaking, the police respond to their calls, and they tend to view the police as necessary public servants. They support efforts to increase police power because they tend to see the police as protectors against the enemy: criminals who threaten life and property, minority group members who may invade their good neighborhoods, and other real or imaginary threats to their security.

Almost 30 percent of all persons arrested in the United States in 1987 were black. Since arrests of Puerto Ricans and Mexican-Americans are included with the white total, we have no way of knowing the number of members of these ethnic groups arrested.[16] However, if the percentages in our prisons are any indication, we can estimate that about 30 percent of the persons arrested in our cities are members of these two groups. In addition to the large number of minority group members arrested, a great many more have unfavorable contacts with the police. At least half the young men in our ghettos have been arrested one or more times, and half the remainder have been interrogated. Even middle-class black people have unfavorable attitudes toward the police. The results of a study comparing attitudes of unemployed blacks between 20 and 40 years of age with 200 middle-class household units indicated the following:

1. The more contacts with the police they have, the more negative are their attitudes toward law enforcement.

---

[15] Peter K. Manning, "The Police: Mandate, Strategies, and Appearances," in *Crime and Justice in American Society*, ed. Jack D. Douglas (Indianapolis: Bobbs-Merrill, 1971), pp. 156–167.

[16] FBI, *Uniform Crime Reports*, 1987, p. 182.

2. Street respondents (individuals who "hang out" on the street corner) expressed more negative ratings of police service in their neighborhoods.
3. Household respondents were dissatisfied with police service when they called for such service.
4. Persons of higher social status held even more unfavorable attitudes toward police than persons of lower status.[17] A possible explanation is that they expected the same services and treatment given by the police to white middle-class people.

According to Arthur Niederhoffer and Alexander Smith, the most common complaints about the police, based on a study in 1974 and still applicable, are these:

- Police act like an army of occupation.
- Police are brutal.
- Police are unconcerned and callous.
- Police are hostile.
- Police are corrupt.
- Police are not available when needed.
- Police do not respond promptly to emergency calls.
- Police ignore narcotics and gambling criminals.
- Police are racist.
- Police violate constitutional and civil rights with impunity.
- Police do not live in the community and have no personal stake in its improvement.
- Police discriminate against minority groups.
- There are no legitimate grievance mechanisms, when citizens desire to lodge a complaint against the police.
- Police humiliate the men in the community by field interrogation and "stop and frisk" procedures.
- Police are unresponsive to community demands.
- Police do not provide adequate protection against crime.
- Police are not representative of the community because they refuse to appoint black police officers.[18]

Table 2.1 shows the most common complaints in South Los Angeles after the 1965 riots. These attitudes are still current among many South Los Angeles citizens.

Whether or not these complaints can be substantiated is irrelevant. If a substantial number of people in the black community believe them to

---

[17] Sarah L. Boggs and John F. Galliher, "Evaluating the Police: A Comparison of Black Street and Household Respondents," *Social Problems* (February 1975):393–406.

[18] Arthur Niederhoffer and Alexander B. Smith, *New Directions in Police-Community Relations* (New York: Holt, Rinehart and Winston, 1974). Copyright 1974 by the Dryden Press, a division of Holt, Rinehart and Winston. Reprinted by permission of Holt, Rinehart and Winston.

Table 2.1 COMPLAINTS AGAINST POLICE

Complaint	Happened in area	Saw it happen	Happened to someone you know	Happened to you
Lack respect or use insulting language	85%	49%	52%	28%
Roust, frisk, or search people without good reason	85	52	48	25
Stop or search cars for no good reason	83	51	49	25
Search homes for no good reason	63	22	30	7
Use unnecessary force in making arrests	86	47	43	9
Beat up people in custody	85	27	46	5

Source: President's Commission on Law Enforcement and Administration of Justice, *Task Force Report: The Police* (Washington, D.C.: Government Printing Office, 1967), p. 147.

be true, then relationships with the police will be poor. Regardless of how police view themselves, there is no doubt that a substantial number of people in the black ghettos and Puerto Rican and Chicano barrios view the police as an occupying army. This view hampers any real cooperation between law-abiding citizens in these neighborhoods and the police. *If cooperating with the police means aiding the enemy, there can be very little of it.*

Niederhoffer and Smith list the following complaints voiced by police about the public:

- The community does not appreciate the work that the police do.
- The community makes no attempt to understand the problems of the police.
- The community does not cooperate with the police.
- The public, in many cases, actually obstructs the police, for instance, by helping prisoners to escape and refusing to come forward with information.
- The public complains about corruption, yet constantly attempts to bribe the police.
- The public wants police protection but complains when police take vigorous action on its behalf.
- The public does not realize how dangerous police work really is.
- The public registers false complaints against the police.
- The public is hostile toward the police.
- The public holds police in low esteem.[19]

---

[19] Niederhoffer and Smith, *New Directions in Police-Community Relations*, p. 38.

Many of these complaints are as true now as they were in 1974, but there is another side to police–minority community relations. This is related to increasing requests to the police from poor law-abiding citizens who want the police to clean up their neighborhoods, especially from the scourge of crack cocaine and PCP dealers. The following article reveals this demand, the police response, and the hazards of being a police officer.

THE NARCS: FRONT-LINE DUTY IN LA'S WAR ON DRUGS

Eleventh and Lake is like a lot of street corners in the city's ghettos.

Things have been getting out of hand. In a letter to Councilman Robert Farrell, police officials and newspapers, the Van Buren/Budlong Neighborhood Assn. near the Los Angeles Coliseum wrote:

"This is not the work of an overactive imagination. . . . It's real, when at any given time of day or night (we) find five to 15 men in our driveways and our yards selling drugs. . . . It's not our imagination when the lead starts to zoom past our children's head from rival drug pushers' guns claiming territorial rights in our neighborhoods. These are facts. We do find human feces along the sides and in the backs of our homes and apartment buildings. On hot days, our hedges reek of urine deposited there the night before and sometimes during the day."

The protesting residents fear being exposed as snitches. But they fear the growing menace of drug dealing more and want action.

"Please, we need your help. We are drowning in a sea of crime and drug traffic," they wrote.

When police raided one intersection known as a hot spot for the sale of codeine pills, four public telephones were ringing off the hook. Police said the callers, unaware the police were answering the phones, confidently sought to place orders for pills.

At 38th and Vermont, empty prescription bottles with the names of the patients torn off littered the area. Police said that was an indication of illicit drug sales.

The pleas of the neighborhood association were not exaggerated.

They call it Sherm Alley because it is a place where Sherman brand cigarettes dipped in PCP can be purchased for $30 each.

But Sherm Alley is more than a place. It is the passageway to a dark corner of human consciousness where the conjured devils of a troubled mind can be loosed with murderous ferocity.

Those under the influence of PCP have been known to drown because they could not distinguish up from down. They pulled out their teeth with pliers and have not felt a thing. Users have been known to set their chairs on fire and then burn to death because they had been immobilized by PCP.

PCP (phencyclidine), sometimes called "angel dust," has hallucinogenic properties and produces a total disorientation from reality, drastic personality changes, memory loss, severe depression, superhuman strength, and suicidal and homicidal tendencies.

In the world of the undercover narc, there is always a potential for something to go wrong, even during a nickel-and-dime marijuana bust. But PCP dealers are often under the influence of the drug themselves. They are unpredictable. An arrest is always potentially explosive.

And on this night, "B" platoon of the Metro Division and men from South Bureau Narcotics led by Detective Norman Eckles will raid a Sherm Alley apartment occupied by suspected PCP dealers believed to be armed and dangerous. The 22 men of "B" platoon, dressed in black military fatigues, crowd into a small office at Southwest Division station, trading jokes and friendly insults as they wait to be briefed before the raid gets under way. . . .

"There is some information they may be armed. If there is shooting, I don't want that house filled with holes. Only shoot when you see a threat."

"Any questions? OK. Mount up."

At a given signal, unmarked Metro cars move in on Sherman Alley. Others come to a halt on Santa Barbara Avenue where the apartment house is located. The "entry team" rushes up the stairs.

"Open up! Police! We have a search warrant!"

From inside, a woman is heard urging others to open the door. They tell her to shut up.

A few seconds pass and then . . .

Boom, boom, boom, boom. Crowbars and a battering ram assault the iron door. Officer Scott Reeves, slinging a sledge hammer, pounds a gaping hole in the stucco wall a few feet from the door to confuse the occupants and divert attention from the main entry team.

As he pierces the wall, Reeves spots a suspect with a handgun running out of sight into a rear bedroom. Reeves shouts a warning to the entry team. . . .

Within a minute, the entry team has forced the doors and four suspects are ordered to the floor. The apartment is secured. No shots are fired. There are no injuries. This time.

"You guys are going to jail for the rest of your life," Detective Norman Eckles shouts. Police find no PCP. They find a quantity of marijuana, and a shoe box containing $5,647 in cash.

Outside the apartment, a woman near tears is looking for her son. She had come to Sherm Alley to find him. He has been arrested on PCP charges before.

She prays he's not here again.

"There's nothing down here but death," she says.[20]

Police Officers and Stress

As the foregoing case illustrates, police work has an enormous impact on an officer's emotional state. There have been numerous reports of this factor in recent research. An article in *Newsweek* by Holly Morris and Emily Newhall delineates both the problem and the therapeutic work performed by a former Boston police officer named Ed Donovan:

---

[20] Larry Stammer, "The Narcs: Front-Line Duty in LA's War on Drugs," *Los Angeles Times,* March 15, 1982. Copyright 1982, Los Angeles Times. Reprinted by permission.

Stress is built into a cop's job. Part of each shift he does nothing but cruise. Then an emergency call comes and his adrenaline races along with the siren. There may not be time to unwind before a second alert, and even if there is, the cop could be headed for another rape or robbery or murder. He's frustrated by the courts and feels unappreciated by the public. His world view is in the gutter. He can trust no one outside his patrol car. Most cops manage in some fashion to hold this Wambaughian nightmare together. Others can't.

The point of Donovan's program is to get the cops who aren't coping to start talking. But first he has to get them in the door and it's not easy. Cops, like other people, don't want to be labeled weak. "The message is, 'Don't cry, don't feel, don't get carried away,'" says one Boston cop. "You're supposed to leave all your feelings behind with your uniform." Often, Donovan has to go looking for his targets. He follows tips from friends on the beat that lead to a parked cruiser or an after-hours bar where he can try to talk down an officer's guard. His message: you don't have to be alone.

The centerpiece of Donovan's work is his Wednesday-night ventilation session, when between ten and 40 cops gather for some Alcoholics Anonymous—style group therapy. "I've never gone anywhere that I've taken so much without taking a swing," says one. "But I keep coming back because I know it's good for me." Thirty-four-year-old Freddy came in out of the cold three years ago after his wife left him and his bottle. Freddy is sober now, but sometimes still tastes the bile of panic. "If I'm uptight I just call Eddie," he says.

Periodically Donovan takes his message on the road. This summer he flew to Atlanta to help run a five-day stress course with Jerry Brinegar, a former cop turned minister-therapist. At one session, Donovan asked the class, "Why are cops so suspicious? When I go into a restaurant I sit in a corner with my back to the wall. I feel safe that way. Too often we take the paranoia out of the job with us. Why?"

"Experience," said one cop. "When I'm in a restaurant, I always want to sit where I can see the cash register in case there is a holdup."

"Because you want to get the bastard and get your name in the paper?" asked Donovan. "But if a holdup went down and they went out the door and you didn't do anything, how would you feel?"

"Like hell," said another cop.

"Why?"

"Because it's your job."

"I don't think every doctor who drives along the highway thinks he should stop at every scene and perform an autopsy," said Donovan. "You need time away from your job to refresh your batteries, to get with positive people so that when you're back the next day you can handle it better."

From there he tried to lay down some rules of positive living, the two most important being: associate with some people who are not cops, even if they complain about their parking tickets, and don't treat your spouse and kids as though they were suspects. As the discussion continued, John Clendenen, a 35-year-old De Kalb County detective, looked transfixed. "This is the first time I've heard anybody say you don't have to be suspicious all the time, that you're not a police officer 24 hours a day," he said. A week later the relaxation effect still hadn't worn off. "A lot of pressure has been taken off me," Clendenen admitted. "I was getting to the point where I was thinking about having a rubber holster made so I could carry my gun in the shower with me."

It's just that fear of a gun in the hands of an overstressed cop that worries the public. Despite the potential menace, other police departments have not uniformly fallen into line behind Donovan. Many still prefer to rely on their chaplains. When breakdowns can't be ignored, they pull an officer's weapon and ship him off to a deskbound bow-and-arrow squad. Even Boston has pared back Donovan's budget, leaving him with just one paid associate. Such thinking is decidedly short range. A patrol car without brakes must be repaired; an overwrought patrolman deserves no less.[21]

COURT DECISIONS AND LAW ENFORCEMENT

The U.S. Supreme Court, in a series of decisions going back to 1914, has required that people dealt with by state law enforcement agencies be given the protection guaranteed by the Bill of Rights of our federal Constitution. In opposition, many law enforcement officials contend that as a result of the application of the federal rules, large numbers of guilty people escape punishment. Part of the reason for this reaction is that the success of law enforcement and prosecuting agencies is frequently measured by convictions; any policy that tends to reduce the percentage of convictions naturally wins their disfavor.

The Bill of Rights, however, was designed to protect the innocent and the helpless from abuse by powerful police and prosecuting agencies. Despite the claims of local law enforcement agencies, federal law enforcement officials have always been required to accept constitutional limitations on their activities, and their records of achievement do not appear to be inferior to those of state and local agencies.

Several specific activities of law enforcement agencies create areas of conflict between the police and the courts and affect legal decisions. These include (1) unlawful arrest, (2) unlawful detention and interrogation, (3) unlawful search and seizure, and (4) inadmissible confessions and admissions.

Unlawful Arrest

Police practices in many of our large cities are in violation of arrest regulations. Police officers often make arrests on suspicion when there is no specific charge and even when they cannot relate the arrest to a specific crime that has been committed. They tend also to make mass arrests of individuals with prior arrest records. While in custody, such

---

[21] *Newsweek*, September 14, 1981. Copyright 1981, by Newsweek, Inc. All Rights Reserved. Reprinted by Permission.

persons, after being interrogated, may confess to crimes. They may also provide clues to evidence that may involve them in violations of law not then being investigated.

The police may fingerprint people who are in custody. Under present New York law, in addition to the required fingerprints for persons arrested for felonies, misdemeanors, and loitering for homosexual purposes, the police may take fingerprints if the arresting officer

1. Is unable to ascertain such person's identity;
2. Reasonably suspects that the identification given by such person is not accurate; or
3. Reasonably suspects that such person is being sought by law enforcement officials for the commission of some other offense.

These provisions give the police almost unlimited power to fingerprint suspects. The use or misuse of such fingerprints and arrest records can do serious damage to an individual.

The claim that police harass people who support causes that the police do not like was examined by a professor at California State University, Los Angeles. He directed a study to determine whether or not there was any basis for the claim made by members of the Black Panther party that they were continuously harassed by law enforcement officers. The subjects for his study were 15 students: 5 black, 5 white, and 5 of Mexican descent, each group including 3 male and 2 female students. Each had to drive to and from school each day; the average distance was 10 miles, with some driving as much as 18 miles. All participants had excellent driving records with no moving traffic violations in the preceding 12 months. Each agreed to drive carefully and do nothing to attract the attention of law enforcement personnel. Cars driven had no defective equipment. All participants wore typical campus dress with the exception of one hippie and the militant blacks, who sometimes wore dashikis. Bumper stickers in orange and black, depicting a menacing panther with *Black Panther* in large letters, were attached to the rear bumper of each subject car.

The first student received a ticket for making an "incorrect lane change" on the freeway less than two hours after heading home in rush-hour traffic. Five other tickets were received by others on the second day for "following too closely," "failing to yield the right of way," "failing to make a proper signal before turning right at an intersection," and "failure to observe proper safety of pedestrians using a crosswalk." On the third day students were cited for "excessive speed," "making unsafe lane changes," and "driving erratically." And so it went every day. Altogether the participants received 33 citations in 17 days, and the violation fund of $500 was exhausted. Five of the cars were thoroughly gone over, and their drivers were shaken down. Students received citations equally, regardless of race, sex, ethnicity, or personal appearance. The researcher concluded that it was statistically unlikely that this number of previously "safe" drivers would amass such a collection of tickets without an assumption of real bias by the police against drivers with Black Panther party bumper stickers.[22]

In a San Francisco study of white, Mexican-American, and black gang youths over a two-year period, researchers found that a great many arrests resulted from disrespectful behavior rather than from crimes. Feeling themselves demeaned and challenged, the youths reacted with defiance and hostility. Police reacted by arresting the youths for vague or minor offenses such as suspicion of robbery, loitering, disturbing the peace, or violating curfew regulations. The San Francisco study concludes that "this is why criminal records of many gang boys are often heavily laced with such charges as 'suspicion of rape.'"[23] Similarly, a study of disorderly conduct arrests in the District of Columbia found that in almost a quarter of them the arrest had been made only for loud and boisterous talking or obscene remarks to the police.[24] In the wake of a number of "gang-related" murders in Los Angeles in 1989, police sweeps were initiated, which produced many irrelevant arrests.

A survey of police officers in one midwestern city indicated that many officers considered it justifiable to use force under many conditions that violate the rights of citizens. Police officers gave the following responses to the question "When do you think a policeman is justified in roughing a man up?" (Only one response was counted for each officer.)

Reason	Percentage
Disrespect for police	37
To obtain information	19
For the hardened criminal	7
When you know the man is guilty	3
For sex criminals	3
When impossible to avoid	23
To make an arrest	8

In their article "Deadly Force in Law Enforcement," Arnold Binder and Peter Scharf analyzed two highly publicized cases of police officers

---

[22] F. K. Heussenstamm, "Bumper Stickers and the Cops," *Trans-Action* 8 (February 1971):32–34.

[23] Carl Werthman and Irving Piliavin, "Gang Members and the Police," in *The Police*, ed. David Bordua (New York: Wiley, 1967), pp. 56–98.

[24] The President's Commission on Law Enforcement and the Administration of Justice, *Task Force Report: The Police* (Washington, D.C.: Government Printing Office, 1967), p. 180.

using deadly force.[25] In the Eulia Love case, police officers shot at Mrs. Love 12 times, hitting her 8 of the times, after she allegedly threw a knife at the officers. The second case involved a woman who was shot by officers in an automobile. In both cases, the women were black.

Binder and Scharf noted that "the legal right of police officers to use deadly force stems from specific statutes directed at enforcers of the law." Police, however, are subject to the usual penalties and criminal prosecution if they exceed the legal boundaries. Under English common law, a peace officer was permitted to use deadly force to stop a felony but not a misdemeaner. This law is still prominent in American common law.

In the case of Eulia Love, the statement issued by the Los Angeles Police Commission, and reported in the same article, exonerated the police:

> The Commission has reviewed the Department's policy on the use of firearms and finds that there are no inadequacies in that policy which contributed to the shooting of Eulia Love. On the contrary, if properly implemented, the policy provides sufficient safeguards against such a shooting. The Commission has concluded that further revision of the policy is not necessary at this time. No one has yet been able to come up with a precise directive to police officers on the use of deadly force, because each situation has its own dynamics. We believe that the only basis for the use of deadly force by a police officer is the criterion employed by the F.B.I. which states that deadly force can be employed when an officer's life is clearly threatened.

Unlawful Detention and Interrogation

Police rely heavily on admissions and confessions, and they engage in prolonged and persuasive interrogation of suspects in an effort to obtain evidence, admissions against the interest of the accused, and, if possible, confessions. This often involves holding suspects in custody for unreasonably long periods of time without benefit of counsel.

There is no legal basis for arresting persons simply to detain them while an investigation of their possible involvement in a crime is conducted. Yet this has been a common practice in a number of departments. The American Bar Foundation found that in cities with substantial crime problems, arrests are often made on suspicion—such as refusing to answer questions or giving an equivocal answer during a field interrogation.

---

[25] Arnold Binder and Peter Scharf, "Deadly Force in Law Enforcement," *Crime and Delinquency*, vol. 32 (January 1982), p. 18. Copyright 1982 by *Crime and Delinquency*. Reprinted by permission of Sage Publications, Inc.

In the case of *Miranda* v. *Arizona*, the Supreme Court ruled that once the police hold people in custody, and before interrogation, the accused must be advised that

1. They have the right to remain silent,
2. Anything they say may be used against them in a court of law,
3. They have the right to speak to an attorney and to have the attorney present during questioning, and
4. If they desire counsel and cannot provide their own, counsel will be provided without charge before questioning.[26]

Although some efforts have been made to change it, the *Miranda* decision is still in force in 1989. Police officials are very much opposed to the rules requiring them to advise each accused of his or her constitutional rights because they believe that this practice is a handicap to them.

A suspect who, after being advised of these rights, does not elect to remain silent and does not request counsel is regarded as having voluntarily consented to interrogation. Police skilled in interrogation have many techniques designed to trick a suspect into confessing. One officer interrogates the accused in privacy and tries to win the individual's confidence with friendliness. Another officer, the "bad guy," makes dire predictions about the accused's ultimate fate if he or she does not cooperate. This good guy–bad guy type of interrogation has been incorporated in police training programs for years, and it works fairly well. The rationale supporting the use of trickery is that the purpose of the interrogation is to get at the truth. Other tricks used by police are misinforming the accused regarding evidence in the hands of the police, lying about nonexistent testimony against the accused, or quoting from nonexistent confessions of others implicating the suspect. While physical duress is obviously illegal and is seldom used, many other forms of duress have been employed over the years.[27]

Wealthy people, when advised of their rights, immediately ask for counsel. Members of organized crime and professional criminals know their rights and demand counsel even before the police advise them. It is the poor and members of minority groups who can be and are tricked into confessions and admissions. In New York City in the six months between June 1966, when the police presumably began informing each accused in custody of his or her rights, and January 1967, only ten requests for counsel were made in the city's police stations. One of the ten requests came from a police officer suspected of a crime; two others, from suspects who spoke only French. We can conclude from this either

---

[26] Miranda v. Arizona, 86 S. Ct. 1602 (1966).

[27] Fred Inbau and John Reid, *Criminal Interrogations and Confessions* (Baltimore: Williams & Wilkins, 1967).

that poor people do not want to be represented by counsel and feel a need to confess to the police or that the police are not advising accused people of their rights until after they have obtained confessions. In court, the police testify that they advised each suspect before interrogation. However, a former prosecuting attorney, Richard H. Kuh, expressed some doubt when he said, "Police officers will tell these 'little white lies' in court to sustain a confession. Most judges and juries will tend to believe police testimony even over the denial of an accused, particularly if other evidence implicates him in a crime."[28]

The effects of the *Miranda* case were questioned by the action of the Supreme Court in the case of *Michigan* v. *Mosley*, decided in December 1975. In that case the Court ruled that the police had a right to resume an interrogation after the suspect had decided to remain silent. In the *Mosley* case the detectives read the suspect his rights, and he elected to remain silent. Two hours later a different detective resumed the interrogation. He read Mosley his rights and told him that an accomplice had named him as the gunman in the murder case. Mosley made several incriminating statements. Mr. Justice Brennan, in a minority opinion, said that the majority decision "encourages police . . . to continue the suspect's detention until the police station's coercive atmosphere does its work and the suspect collapses."[29]

The law still requires that persons who have become the target of a police investigation be advised of their constitutional rights. The Supreme Court has ruled that when a suspect is not so advised, a confession or admission obtained by the police is inadmissible in evidence.

Unlawful Search and Seizure

The following statements represent a bare outline of the rules for searches and seizures. As a result of recent rulings by the United States Supreme Court, many decisions vary from state to state and from the states to the federal courts. States reserve the right to lay down rules restricting the police if these decisions are based on the respective state court rulings.

The Fourth Amendment to the Constitution of the United States provides that "the right of the people to be secure in their persons, houses, papers, and effects, against unreasonable searches and seizures, shall not be violated, and no warrants shall issue, but upon probable

---

[28] Allen Harris, "Miranda Today—New York," *Bar Bulletin, New York County Lawyer's Association* 24, no. 4 (1966–67):168–173.

[29] Linda Matthews, "Court Again Narrows Miranda Guidelines," *Los Angeles Times,* December 10, 1975.

cause, supported by oath or affirmation, and particularly describing the place to be searched, and the persons or things to be seized."

Police officers may lawfully search a suspect in the course of an arrest. The officers may, if arresting someone they have reason to believe committed a robbery, search that person for weapons and stolen property. Officers may not, however, search people merely on the basis of suspicion, then arrest the one whom they find in possession of stolen property.

The police may, if arresting a person in a hotel room or automobile, search the room or car when they have reason to believe that they will find weapons used in a crime or property taken in the course of a crime. However, *lawful search and seizure not incident to an arrest requires a search warrant.* A judge may issue such a warrant when claim is made under oath that certain specified property is probably to be found in a specified place. The place to be searched and the things to be seized must be adequately described.

In 1914 the Supreme Court ruled that illegally secured evidence was inadmissible in federal court casts.[30] In a 1961 decision the Supreme Court held that evidence obtained in the course of an unlawful search was inadmissible in state courts as well.[31] As a result of these decisions, it is unlawful to search the home of an accused without a search warrant after the accused has been taken into custody.

A weapon or stolen property found in the course of an illegal search may not be used in evidence. Police believe that this ruling hampers them unnecessarily. When they arrest a thief, the police would like the right to search the suspect's home for stolen property.

The police are not permitted to obtain a warrant on suspicion alone, because the Fourth Amendment to the U.S. Consitution specifies that the person or things to be seized must be described. This provision protects people from unreasonable searches and from the planting of contraband in their homes.

Where police officers make a lawful arrest with an arrest warrant, a reasonable search of the person of an accused may be made, and items of personal property of an incriminating nature may be seized if found. Such reasonable search and seizure is permitted as incident to a lawful arrest. Also, where probable cause exists with regard to the commission of a felony by the accused, a search and seizure may be made incidental to an arrest. When a crime is committed in the presence of police officers, they may make what is called an "on view" arrest and undertake a "custody search." Contraband or arms found on the accused's person may be lawfully seized.

---

[30] Weeks v. United States, 232 U.S. 383 (1914).

[31] Mapp v. Ohio, 367 U.S. 643 (1961).

In July 1976 the Supreme Court ruled that defendants who claim that they have been convicted in state courts on the basis of illegally obtained evidence may no longer pursue their constitutional rights in federal court. The critical case came from Omaha, Nebraska, where Black Panther leader David Rice was convicted of murder, in part because explosives were found in his home by police in the course of a search.[32] The police admitted that their search warrant was faulty. The Nebraska courts upheld the conviction of Rice. A U.S. judge reversed the conviction by applying the *exclusionary rule*. Under the exclusionary rule, evidence obtained in the course of an illegal search must be excluded; that is, it cannot be admitted by a court. The Supreme Court reinstated the conviction, criticized the exclusionary rule, and upheld the state court decision. The rule remains in force.

Wiretapping Wiretapping is the act or practice of tapping telephone wires to get information secretly. At the time the Constitution was written and adopted, telephones did not exist. The Fourth Amendment forbidding unreasonable searches and seizures, while protecting us from invasion of privacy, did not specifically include wiretapping or electronic surveillance. In *Olmstead* v. *United States*, the Supreme Court ruled that a wiretap was not a search within the meaning of the Fourth Amendment.[33] To protect people from invasion of privacy by wiretapping, the Congress passed Section 605 of the Federal Communications Act, which provides that "no person not being authorized by the sender shall intercept any communication and divulge or publish the existence, contents, substance, purport, effect, or meaning of any such communication to any person." However, the Department of Justice and the FBI continued to conduct unauthorized wiretaps.

On October 9, 1975, former law enforcement officers and wiretap experts testified that illegal wiretapping was commonplace in the United States and that neither the Justice Department nor the FBI seemed interested in stopping it. Anthony V. Zavala, a former Houston police narcotics officer, testified that he took part in about 35 illegal wiretaps between 1968 and 1975. He estimated that the narcotics division in Houston, during the time he was there, conducted between 700 and 1,000 illegal wiretaps. All this, he said, took place with the help of the telephone company and federal employees. Since 1968, the law had forbidden wiretapping except by court order or for reasons of "national security." Nevertheless, Anthony J. Farris, former U.S. attorney for the southern district of Texas, testified that the FBI and Justice Department knew of the illegal wiretapping in Houston but did nothing about it. An

---

[32] Wolff v. Rice, 50 L.Ed. 2, 158.

[33] Olmstead v. United States, 277 U.S. 438 (1928).

expert in wiretap laws testified that illegal bugging had not substantially declined since enactment of the Federal Wiretap Act in 1968.[34]

No one knows how many illegal wiretaps are ordered by state and federal courts or how many are made by law enforcement personnel and others without any authorization. Estimates are that they run into the thousands each year.

Electronic Surveillance   In the case of *Berger* v. *New York*, the Supreme Court ruled that a person's right to conduct a conversation in private was protected by the Fourth Amendment and that using electronic equipment to spy on conversations was an unlawful search. To be lawful, the search had to be based on probable cause, and the crime, the place to be searched, and the conversations to be seized would have to be specified.[35] In *Katz* v. *United States*, a conviction based on evidence of acceptance of bets by public telephone was reversed because the telephone was bugged without a warrant having been obtained.[36]

In 1968 Congress passed the Omnibus Crime Control and Safe Streets Act, which provides ways of legally wiretapping telephones and using electronic surveillance. The regulations are similar to those that provide for lawful searches and seizures of property. The person and place to be searched (bugged) must be specified, the evidence used for a specified purpose, and authorization granted by a judge upon application.[37] Despite the fact that enforcement people can lawfully undertake electronic surveillance where a specific pattern of illegal behavior is under investigation, a great deal of illegal electronic surveillance continues. According to former attorney general Ramsey Clark:

> Developments in electronics beyond the telephone make it possible to totally destroy privacy. Privacy will exist tomorrow only if society insists on it. By placing a radio receiver-transmitter in a room, by directing a laser beam through a wall and focusing it on a resonant surface, by directing a parabolic scope toward two men in the middle of a field, every sound can be heard from afar. The speaker has no way of knowing who hears. . . .
>
> Invasions of privacy demean the individual. Can a society be better than the people composing it? When a government degrades its citizens, or permits them to degrade each other, however beneficent the specific purpose, it limits opportunities for individual fulfillment and national accomplishment. If America permits fear and its failure to make basic social

---

[34] "Illegal Wiretapping Called Commonplace," *Los Angeles Times*, October 10, 1975.

[35] Berger v. United States, 388 U.S. 41 (1967).

[36] Katz v. United States, 389 U.S. 347 (1967).

[37] Alexander B. Smith and Harriet Pollack, *Crime and Justice in a Mass Society* (Lexington, Mass.: Xerox, 1972), p. 190. Copyright 1973 by Rinehart Press, a Division of Holt, Rinehart and Winston.

reforms to excuse police use of secret electronic surveillance, the price will be dear indeed. The practice is incompatible with a free society.[38]

The government can, with a warrant, authorize wiretaps and electronic surveillance, and such evidence is admissible "with respect to conspiratorial activities, threatening the national security and organized crime." This power is provided by Title III of the Omnibus Crime Control and Safe Streets Act of 1968. Former attorney general John Mitchell claimed, under this provision, to have the right to use electronic surveillance in the case of the Chicago Seven, though no foreign interest was involved. His reasoning was also applied to the Students for a Democratic Society, the Black Panthers, and other organizations he considered dangerous.[39] This electronic surveillance may very well have been extended to millions of Americans with whom Mr. Mitchell or his successor strongly disagreed, people who were threatening not the United States but mainly the continuance in office of the incumbent administration. It is only a short step from this exercise of Mr. Mitchell's claim to the Watergate break-in, where employees of the Committee to Re-Elect the President (of which Mr. Mitchell was chairman) bugged Democratic party headquarters. The experience of Watergate has raised the following questions in the public mind:

1. How can privileged conversations be protected, conversations between husband and wife, lawyer and client, doctor and patient, and priest and communicant?
2. How can a defendant be protected against deliberate tampering with a tape?
3. How can we be sure that the tape recording introduced in evidence by police witnesses is intact?
4. Is a tap that is conducted over a period of time a single intrusion into the suspect's privacy, or a series of intrusions?
5. How can we protect the rights of innocent third persons who took part in conversations with a person under surveillance?

Electronic surveillance can be a dirty business regardless of who uses it, even under White House direction and reportedly in the interest of national security.

An article in the July 18, 1988, issue of *Newsweek*, "Fighting Crime by the Rules" by Tomar Jacoby, congently reviews a number of the legal issues discussed in the foregoing section and describes how they have affected and been integrated into law enforcement in recent years:

---

[38] Ramsey Clark, *Crime in America* (New York: Simon & Schuster, 1970), pp. 286–287. Copyright © 1970 by Ramsey Clark. Reprinted by permission of Simon & Schuster, a Division of Gulf + Western Corporation.

[39] "The F.B.I.: A Right to Eavesdrop?" *Newsweek*, June 23, 1969, p. 37.

Like many reforms of the 1960s, the changes in police procedure mandated by the Supreme Court in that tumultuous era have been under bitter attack ever since. From the start, critics predicted that the exclusionary rule (barring the use in court of evidence seized in illegal searches) and the *Miranda* warnings (informing suspects of their right to remain silent or have a lawyer present during interrogations) would cripple law enforcement. "In some unknown number of cases," Justice Byron White warned in his dissent from *Miranda*, "[the] rule will return a killer, a rapist or other criminal to the streets."

But today a new consensus among scholars and police chiefs suggests that these due-process reforms have done little to hinder the cops. Not only have officers learned to live with the rules, says Professor Yale Kamisar of the University of Michigan, but "most studies indicate that the prophecies of doom have not been fulfilled." Indeed, both rules are widely credited with improving professionalism among policemen—and as a result the reforms enjoy growing support among even the most hard-bitten cops.

Columbia University law professor H. Richard Uviller spent eight months in a New York City precinct, observing compliance with the rules. A former assistant prosecutor, Uviller had some experience in the gritty world of cops and criminals. And after 14 years in the Ivy League, he wondered how well the Constitution he was teaching in his classroom was being observed on the beat. His experience with criminals had left him with some reservations about both reforms. But out on the street he found that they have become "part of the legal landscape," as much as a part of police routine as using handcuffs, filling out forms and waiting around the station house for the next emergency call.

Uviller's new book, *Tempered Zeal*, reports some griping on the beat about both reforms. He also observed occasional violations, particularly when officers casually questioned suspects in the back of the squad car, saving the reading of their *Miranda* rights for the more formal setting of the station house. But on the whole, he found that the cops have "internalized" the rules and are sometimes even more scrupulous than the court requires in respecting suspects' rights. "To the extent that constitutional principles accord with what officers think is fair and decent," Uviller says, "they have no trouble applying the rules."

Others who have studied *Miranda* in a more systematic way say the warnings rarely stop people from confessing. Many suspects try to exonerate themselves in the eyes of the police and end up incriminating themselves instead; others simply don't grasp that they have a right to remain silent. "Besides," says former police lieutenant James Fyfe, now professor at American University, "hardly anybody walks": even when a suspect does not confess or his confession is thrown out in court because of a botched *Miranda* warning there is usually enough evidence and other testimony to make a case against him. Peter Nardulli of the University of Illinois finds that less than 1 percent of all cases in his large statistical surveys were thrown out because of illegal confessions. Says Houston Police Chief Lee Brown, "I don't see any detrimental impact [from *Miranda*]."

New Habits   Experts have reached similar conclusions about the exclusionary rule. One 1982 survey by the government's National Institute of

Justice warned that a large number of felonies were being thrown out of California courts because evidence was obtained in illegal searches. But later interpretations of the same data debunked this claim, proving that only a tiny percentage of cases were lost because of the rule. Says Fyfe, "There is not one study that shows it affects more than 1.5 percent of all cases." Even in narcotics cases, where the impact is greatest, Nardulli and others find that the rule has forced police to conduct searches more carefully. Says Uviller, "They have learned to stop and think before they search—exactly what the Fourth Amendment wants them to do."

By far the most striking findings suggest that cops are proud of the way the reforms have shaped up their departments. In 1987 law student Myron Orfield interviewed members of a Chicago narcotics squad and found that all opposed eliminating the exclusionary rule. "It makes the police department more professional," said one. Without it, said another, an investigating policeman "would be like a criminal released in the midst of society." Former Newark police director Hubert Williams reports a similar reaction to *Miranda*. "Officers want respect," he says. "We've gotten away from force and coercion. Nor do we want to be accused of that." And in his view, *Miranda* has made it much harder to level such charges.

Ideological Gap   Those who oppose the reforms are hardly convinced by these findings. Conservatives say history has more than borne out Justice White's grim predictions for *Miranda*. And the Reagan administration is still campaigning hard to overturn both measures. "The issue is not whether the police have learned to live with the rules," says Assistant Attorney General Stephen Markman, "but whether society has learned to live with unprecedentedly high crime rates." Markman argues that no one really knows how many offenders decide not to confess after hearing their *Miranda* warnings. His own suspicion is that many take that route and go free as a result.

In the end, the debate boils down to ideology: a quarrel between those who favor battling crime with all available weapons and those who worry as much about the rights of the accused. Neither station-house stories nor academic studies are likely to change minds on either side of that divide. But surely it is welcome news that most police, far from finding their hands tied, have learned to reconcile due process with the fight against crime.

SOME PROBLEMS IN THE ADMINISTRATION OF JUSTICE

Pretrial Confinement or Bail

We have already noted that at the preliminary hearing, a magistrate must decide whether to keep an accused in confinement awaiting trial or release the suspect with or without bail. Bail involves the posting of financial security by an accused or by someone acting on his or her behalf, guaranteeing that the accused will be present at the trial. The Eighth Amendment to the Constitution of the United States provides that *"excessive bail shall not be required, nor excessive fines imposed, nor cuel and unusual punishments inflicted."* That portion of the Eighth

Amendment relating to excessive bail was provided to prevent arbitrary imprisonment before trial. Since an accused is presumed innocent until guilt is established in court after a fair trial, it was deemed unjust to deprive a person of liberty for a long time while awaiting trial.

Rich people charged with crimes have no trouble posting bail; nor do members of organized crime. Poor people, on the other hand, must either spend long periods in jail awaiting trial or place their friends and relatives deeply in debt to raise the money to pay a fee for bail bond. If bail is set at $10,000, the fee, usually 10 percent, amounts to $1,000, an amount poor people cannot raise without great hardship. An accused who stays in jail may face loss of employment, long separation from the family, and the inability to locate witnesses or otherwise assist in preparing a defense. Ramsey Clark, commenting on the hardships resulting from inability to post bail, noted:

> Thousands jailed without bail were innocent. Hundreds of thousands were released after weeks or more in jail without trial. As to some, formal charges were never filed or were filed and later dismissed. Many prisoners served longer awaiting trial than the maximum sentence provided for the crime with which they were charged.
>
> Thousands were corrupted awaiting trial in jail . . . exposed to brutality, homosexual rape, drug addiction, insanity, senility, and hardened human beings capable of any crime.[40]

A publication of the New York County Lawyers' Association noted in its September, 1976, issue that a substantial number of the 4,000 inmates in New York City's detention facilities were deprived of their right to a speedy trial. It indicated that there was evidence that persons detained while their cases are pending are convicted more often and, once convicted, are sentenced to prison more frequently than those released prior to trial. As of May, 1976, approximately 300 inmates had been in jail for over six months awaiting trail in New York County, and 120 of these defendants had been detained for a year or more.[41]

An alternative to bail instituted in many jurisdictions provides for the issuance of citations in lieu of arrest. In 1976, California established this practice for persons found in possession of less than 1 ounce of marijuana. A modified bail system has been instituted in Illinois, which requires the defendant to deposit 10 percent of the amount of bail to the court as a condition for release. Ninety percent of this deposit is returned when the accused appears for trial. No fee is paid to a third party and the net cost to the defendant is 1 percent of the bail set.[42]

---

[40] Clark, *Crime in America*, p. 300. Copyright © 1970 by Ramsey Clark. Reprinted by permission of Simon & Schuster, a Division of Gulf + Western Corporation.

[41] "Vesey Street Letter," *New York County Lawyers' Association*, September 1976.

[42] Richard D. Hongisto and Carol Levine, "Alternatives to the Present Bail System," *California State Bar Journal* (November 1974):577–581.

It would appear that there is no real need for a bail system. Those not dangerous to the community could be released on recognizance or given citations. Those believed to be violent and dangerous should not be released at all until trial (30 days from date of incarceration). Speedy trials for incarcerated persons would protect people from long confinement without trial.

In 1970, at the request of the Nixon administration, a law was passed to allow "preventive detention" of suspects in Washington, D.C., who were considered dangerous. The reason given for support of this law was the sharp rise in violent crimes by suspects who were out on bail. There was much opposition to this bill on the ground that it would be a technique for harassing and detaining political opponents, minority group members, and poor people.

Persons accused of murder, rape, armed robbery, and other major crimes of violence are rarely released on their own recognizance pending trial. Money bail is not the answer for such persons. As for the others, who is to determine which are dangerous and should be kept in confinement before trial?

During the first ten months the law was in effect, it was invoked against only 20 of 6,000 defendants in felony cases involved in the Washington, D.C., criminal justice system. Of the 20 suspects held, 9 were subjected to hearings, 8 were ordered detained, and 2 were held in preventive detention by a judge without a detention hearing. Of the 10 preventive detention orders, 5 were reversed on review or reconsideration, and 1 was dismissed when a grand jury refused to indict.[43] There appeared to be no need for a preventive detention system.

Reducing Court Congestion

The court is the principal public arena in the system of criminal justice. Here we expect an impartial judge to decide controversies by objectively applying preestablished rules. Before any evidence is presented, the judge presides over the jury selection process. During the trial, the judge rules on the admissibility of evidence. After all evidence is presented, the attorneys for the defense and prosecution summarize the evidence, and the judge instructs the jury on how to interpret the evidence and arrive at a verdict. The jury makes a finding of guilty or not guilty. In most jurisdictions, the judge then fixes the sentence. That all this is done fairly and objectively is vital to the system of criminal justice.

The criminal court process is determined by the federal and state constitutions, federal and state statutes, and prior court decisions. While there is considerable variation because of differences in state statutes

---

[43] Nan C. Bases and William F. McDonald, *Preventive Detention in the District of Columbia: The First Ten Months* (New York: Vera Institute of Justice, 1972).

and procedures, the U.S. Supreme Court, in interpreting the constitutionality of state laws and state court procedures, sets the limits. However, important differences exist between the "ideal" and the "real" system. In terms of volume, most cases in the criminal courts are essentially violations of moral norms or instances of annoying behavior rather than dangerous crimes.

On this general issue of court congestion, former Los Angeles County deputy district attorney Aaron Stovitz stated:

> Most people think of the sensational criminal trial as an example of our criminal justice system. In the 80s there is a trend away from the typical. We must realize that in every large city, of every 100,000 persons arrested each year, 60,000 are for misdemeanors. The remaining 40,000 are treated as follows: 20,000 are released with no charges being filed, 10,000 are accused of felonies and 10,000 are accused of additional misdemeanors. We must also realize of this group that some are arrested several times a year, and for some it is their first arrest.
>
> Our criminal justice system must be fair and efficient for all these persons. Now that our courts guarantee a lawyer for every accused person who is in jeopardy of a jail sentence, the problem confronting our society is one of selective law enforcement.
>
> The following situation is illustrative of the problem. Suppose you have been given a $500 bad check by a stranger. You go to the police and wish to swear out a complaint. In some cities a crime report is not taken unless the suspect has been convicted of passing bad checks or has other bad checks outstanding. If a crime report is taken, a complaint for a misdemeanor is obtained. If and when the suspect is arrested, he is brought before a magistrate and then arraigned. At that time, he is given a court appointed lawyer if he is indigent. The lawyer marshals the facts and offers to plead nolo contendere if the judge does not impose a jail sentence. The victim is hardly ever consulted to see if this plea bargain is agreeable. If the defendant admits the charge, either by a plea of guilty or a plea of no contest, the court imposes a probationary sentence of thirty days in the county jail. This sentence is suspended on condition that the defendant make restitution and pay a $100 fine. Let us assume that the defendant is truly indigent, and that is the reason the check was not honored. He will then *not* be able to pay the restitution or the fine, and he will end up serving thirty days in jail.
>
> Look at the cost to society of this $500 check. A policeman's time, the court time, the court-appointed lawyer's fee, and finally the cost of incarceration. In addition to clogging the courts and jails, "crimes" of this kind, in total, cost the taxpayers millions of dollars each year.
>
> We are continually reading about congestion in the local jails and the need for more state prisons. One of the reasons for congestion in the local jails is that there are not enough public defenders and courts to take care of the growing caseload. Most defendants get unlimited continuances. They get credit toward their jail or prison time if they are convicted. They know that the longer a case takes to come to trial, the more chance of losing prosecution witnesses and evidence [that could convict them].[44]

---

[44] Personal communication from Mr. Stovitz.

On the same subject, Alexander Smith and Harriet Pollack reflect about the impact of court congestion:

> The criminal justice systems of our metropolitan areas are in such a precarious condition that only a degree of nonenforcement by police, nonprosecution by prosecutors, and nondefending by defense counsel saves these systems from a complete breakdown. If every violation witnessed by the police were to result in an arrest, if every accused person were presented to the courts for prosecution, if every defendant were to have a trial, the result, literally, would be anarchy within a few days.
>
> Americans are a law-minded people. If there is something wrong with the world their impulse is to pass a law against it. Our penal codes are, among other things, the heritage of two hundred years of reforming impulses; yet despite all our laws, at night we are afraid to walk the streets of our big cities. Something has gone wrong, and in our anguish our first impulse is to call for *more:* more police, more judges, more courts, more jails, more money to deal with the increasingly insistent problem of crime. But more is not the answer. What we need is *less:* less crime, fewer criminals, arrests, prosecutions, and prisoners. What we want more of is justice and order, which, paradoxically, we can hope to achieve only through decreasing rather than increasing the scope and sweep of our criminal justice system.[45]

---

[45] Alexander B. Smith and Harriet Pollack, *Some Sins Are Not Crimes* (New York: Franklin Watts, 1975) pp. 2–3.

Chapter
3

The Nature and Extent of Crime

Most people are concerned about becoming victims of basic street crimes—the possibility of being mugged or assaulted. In contemporary society we are also concerned with the possibility of the theft of our property, including burglary of our homes and theft from our cars. "Upper class crimes" committed by corporations, or even political crimes involving elected officials, are generally perceived as being of intellectual interest—but not as the type of crime that the average citizen feels most directly affected by.

The basic crimes which involve the theft of personal property or assault on a person are known as "traditional crimes." They are defined in the FBI annual report *Crime in the United States* as Part I offenses and are counted in the FBI Crime Index. These crimes are the basic concern of most Americans.[1]

Part I offenses (traditional crimes) are basically felonies, or more serious crimes. As listed by the FBI, they include criminal homicide, forcible rape, robbery, aggravated assault, burglary–breaking and entering, larceny-theft, motor vehicle theft, and arson.

It is apparent that the first four Part I offenses are the most horrendous forms of crime, because they involve a criminal assault on an innocent victim. A total of 13,508,700 Part I offenses, or felonies, were committed in 1987. This total breaks down as follows: 20,096 people were murdered; 91,111 women were forcibly raped; 517,704 people

---

[1] Unless some other source is specified, all the 1987 statistics cited in this chapter and the book are taken from *Crime in the United States: Federal Bureau of Investigation Uniform Crime Reports* (Washington, D.C.: Government Printing Office, 1988).

were robbed; 855,088 people were the victims of aggravated assault; 3,236,184 private structures (67 percent were private homes) were invaded for the purpose of burglary; and 7,499,851 acts of larceny and theft were committed.

Although property crimes rose 2.6 percent, violent crimes remained almost the same, comparing 1987 to 1986. However, from 1983 to 1987, violent crimes rose 18 percent. The "crime clock" sped up in 1987 to the point where there was one Crime Index offense every 2 seconds: one violent crime every 21 seconds, one murder every 26 minutes, one robbery every minute, one aggravated assault every 37 seconds, one property crime every 3 seconds, one burglary every 10 seconds, and one larceny-theft every 4 seconds.

THE CRIMINAL DRAMA

Statistics alone, as powerful as the figures are, do not communicate the drama of criminal events. All these Part I crimes inflict an enormous emotional impact on the victims and their friends and families. Moreover, the threat of being criminally victimized is a Sword of Damocles that hangs by a hair over each of us as we perform our normal daily activities. Violent crime is rampant not just in the ghettos of depressed cities, where it always has been a malignant force to contend with, but everywhere in urban areas, in suburbs, and in peaceful countrysides. More significant, the crimes are becoming more brutal, more irrational, more random—and therefore all the more frightening.

In an article in *Time* magazine, the impact of traditional crime on American citizens was graphically described through a sampling of criminal events. The following criminal incidents are prototypical felonies in the United States; they portray the criminal drama being enacted on a daily basis in both rural and urban areas throughout the United States.

Burglary in the Country   Vivian and Al Weber lived in Battle Creek, Mich., working 6:30 a.m.-to-3 p.m. shifts in two different factories—and hating city life. In 1976 they realized what Mrs. Weber calls "our dream, our lifelong dream," moving to a 50-acre site near the tiny village of Burlington and commuting 35 minutes to work. "Everything we had, we put into this home," she recalls. One afternoon the Webers came home to find "glass all over. They'd smashed the window into the kitchen. Everything was gone through—every drawer, every room."

Mrs. Weber felt that their house had been sullied. "I scrubbed the walls. I took the curtains down and washed them. I would open a drawer to put on clean clothes and think about my personal things, 'Oh, God, I've got to wash them.'" She and her husband took different shifts so one of them would always be home. They started locking their doors, even if one of them was merely going out to the garden.

Eventually they decided to work the same hours again. Al got home first one day and met Vivian outside the door. He was white as a sheet. "Honey," he said, "we've been ripped off again." This time the burglars took some of the items the Webers had bought as replacements—and keepsakes as well. "They've got us timed," thought Mrs. Weber. "They know when we go and when we come home." She quit work and would not even go shopping unless Al was home. He gave up his annual hunting trips. They put dead-bolt locks on all the outside doors, wired a back-room window with a siren, and even bought a third car to park as a decoy in the driveway if they could not avoid being gone at the same time.

The Webers placed their dream house up for sale, then reconsidered. "I have friends here who are more like family than friends," she explains. But their lives have changed. "I try to be normal, but I'm afraid. I have turned around and driven 15 miles back home because I had a funny feeling in my stomach. I feel watched constantly. I never feel safe."

Brutality in Phoenix   Suzanne Marie Rossetti, 26, a technician at a burn treatment center in Phoenix, had attended a performance of *Dancin'* at Arizona State University. On her way home, she drove into a grocery-store parking lot, and mistakenly locked her car with the keys inside. Two young white men helpfully unlocked the door, asked for a short lift—then forced her to drive to her apartment, where they beat and raped her for several hours.

According to Phoenix Police Detective Richard Fuqua, the men then drove 50 miles to an isolated desert area and hurled Suzanne off a cliff. They heard her moaning and climbed down to her side. She pleaded with them to leave her alone because, she said, "I'm dying anyway." The response was swift. "Damn right you are," one of the men said, and picked up a large rock and crushed her head to still her sounds.

Rape in Galveston   Marsha Walker, 30, asked a woman friend to stay with her while her husband, a doctor, was out of town. She heard her two dogs barking at 2:30 a.m. outside the Walkers' second-story garage apartment in a historic section of Galveston, Texas. She was not alarmed; there were three locks on the front door, there was no back door, and the apartment was 18 ft. above ground level. But as she went to check an open window, a bare-chested man wearing an Arab-style kaffiyeh over his head pressed a knife to her throat. He ransacked the apartment, put pillowcases over both women's heads, and raped the friend.

After that night of terror, Mrs. Walker, a magazine editor, began carrying a .45-cal. pistol. She and her husband put new locks on their windows and set up lights around the yard. When alone, she slept with all the lights in the apartment turned on. A few weeks after the attack, she returned from a brief vacation to find a makeshift ladder at one of their apartment windows and the screens ripped. But the prowler, whom Mrs. Walker assumes was the rapist bent on another attack, was heard by a friend of the Walkers and fled as police arrived.

"Victims don't stop being victims when the police leave," says Mrs. Walker. "Violence is disabling. It changes your life for years." The Walkers have moved from the apartment, and she says, "I will never set foot there again. The anger, the dread and the fear are receding. But the rapist is still in my head. I don't think he will ever go away."[2]

UNIFORM CRIME REPORTS

The most factual data on crime in the United States have been compiled since 1930 by the FBI. The overall data are based on information compiled by local, county, and state enforcement agencies regarding crimes committed in their jurisdictions. The data received are first compiled into biannual and then into annual reports, known as *Uniform Crime Reports*. Information relating to all the traditional crimes we have referred to may be found in these reports. Relatively few data regarding white collar crime, organized crime, or political crime are included. The reporting system set up by the FBI is voluntary. Each contributing agency remains wholly responsible for compiling its own crime reports for submission to the bureau. While local police departments may refuse to cooperate, their reliance on the bureau for assistance in information gathering and training induces them to cooperate. In 1987, law enforcement agencies representing 96 percent of the national population submitted reports.

City police, sheriffs, and state agencies report on a monthly basis the *total number* of criminal homicides, forcible rapes, robberies, assaults, burglaries, larceny-thefts, and auto thefts *that are known* to them. All *complaints* of these crimes, whether received from victims or from others, and all such crimes *discovered* by the police are included in the count, unless police investigation determines complaints to be without foundation. A compilation of these data is published annually by the FBI as a Crime Index. Table 3.1 (pp. 68–69) presents the Crime Index data for 1987, and Table 3.2 (pp. 70–71) provides the Crime Indexes for the decade 1978 to 1987.

CRIMES OF VIOLENCE

Murder, forcible rape, robbery, and aggravated assault are basic violent crimes; burglary, larceny, and auto theft are property offenses. People are most afraid of being victims of violent crime, yet Table 3.2 indicates that only slightly more than 10 percent of the total number of crimes reported are violent crimes. Furthermore, over a third of these are robberies in which the threat of violence is the only technique employed. The purpose of a robbery is to take property. Violence is often merely incidental to the principal objective of the crime.

---

[2] *Time*, March 23, 1981. Copyright 1981 Time Inc. All rights reserved, Reprinted by permission from TIME.

Criminal Homicide

This includes murder and nonnegligent manslaughter, the willful (non-negligent) killing of one human being by another. Deaths caused by negligence, attempts to kill, assaults to kill, suicides, accidental deaths, and justifiable homicides are excluded. Justifiable homicides are limited to the killing of a felon by a law enforcement officer in the line of duty and the killing of a felon by a private citizen. Manslaughter by negligence is the killing of another person through gross negligence. This category excludes traffic fatalities.

Murder is basically defined in the Uniform Crime Reporting Program (UCRP) as the willful killing of another. Classification as this offense, as for all other Crime Index offenses, is based solely on police investigation as opposed to the determination of a court, medical examiner, coroner, jury, or other judicial body. Following are the FBI summaries and analysis of murders in 1987:

- There were an estimated 20,096 murders in the United States during 1987. These offenses represented approximately 1.5 percent of the total number of violent crimes committed. The southern states, the most populous, accounted for 42 percent of the murders. The western states reported 21 percent, the north central states recorded 20 percent, and the northeastern states 17 percent. Murder offenses occurred more frequently during December than in any other month of 1987.

  Compared to 1986, the number of murders in 1987 dropped 3 percent nationally, with the only increase (4 percent) occurring in rural counties. This decrease in murder volume was reflected regionally by a decrease of 4 and 6 percent in the South and West, respectively. The Northeast and Midwest both showed relative

- The volume of murder offenses rose in the suburban areas to 5 per 100,000, and in cities with 250,000 or more inhabitants to 20 per 100,000. Rural areas experienced an upswing in the volume of murders to 6 per 100,000.
- Approximately 74 percent of the murder victims in 1987 were males. An average of 53 of every 100 victims were white, 45 were black, and 2 were persons of other races.
- Fifty-nine percent of the murders nationwide in 1987 were committed by use of firearms. Of all murders, 44 percent were by handguns, 6 percent by shotguns, and 4 percent by rifles.
- As has been noted, criminal homicide is primarily a societal problem over which law enforcement has little or no control. Supporting this statement is the fact that 57 percent of the murders committed in 1987 were perpetrated by relatives or persons acquainted with the victims.

Table 3.1 INDEX OF CRIME, UNITED STATES, 1987

Area	Population[a]	Crime Index total	Violent crime[b]	Property crime[b]	Murder and nonnegligent manslaughter	Forcible rape	Robbery	Aggravated assault	Burglary	Larceny-theft	Motor vehicle theft
United States total	243,400,000	13,508,708	1,483,999	12,024,709	20,096	91,111	517,704	855,088	3,236,184	7,499,851	1,288,674
Rate per 100,000 inhabitants		5,550.0	609.7	4,940.3	8.3	37.4	212.7	351.3	1,329.6	3,081.3	529.4
Metropolitan statistical area	186,637,562										
Area actually reporting[c]	98.1%	11,613,326	1,333,808	10,279,518	17,028	78,454	499,116	739,210	2,738,932	6,346,964	1,193,622
Estimated totals	100.0%	11,747,875	1,343,765	10,404,110	17,132	79,264	501,347	746,022	2,771,222	6,427,814	1,205,074
Rate per 100,000 inhabitants		6,294.5	720.0	5,574.5	9.2	42.5	268.6	399.7	1,484.8	3,444.0	645.7
Other cities	22,752,410										

Area actually reporting[c]	93.3%	1,039,689	74,045	965,644	960	5,161	10,499	57,425	220,550	702,052	43,042
Estimated totals	100.0%	1,114,517	79,814	1,034,703	1,032	5,541	11,357	61,884	237,082	751,440	46,181
Rate per 100,000 inhabitants		4,898.5	350.8	4,547.7	4.5	24.4	49.9	272.0	1,042.0	3,302.7	203.0
Rural counties 34,009,028											
Area actually reporting[c]	89.3%	592,456	54,930	537,526	1,720	5,846	4,572	42,792	208,390	294,997	34,139
Estimated totals	100.0%	646,316	60,420	585,896	1,932	6,306	5,000	47,182	227,880	320,597	37,419
Rate per 100,000 inhabitants		1,900.4	177.7	1,722.8	5.7	18.5	14.7	138.7	670.1	942.7	110.0

[a] Populations are Bureau of the Census provisional estimates as of July 1, 1987, and are subject to change.

[b] Violent crimes are offenses of murder, forcible rape, robbery, and aggravated assault. Property crimes are offenses of burglary, larceny-theft, and motor vehicle theft. Data are not included for the property crime of arson.

[c] The percentage representing areas actually reporting will not coincide with the ratio between reported and estimated crime totals, since these data represent the sum of the calculations for individual states which have varying populations, portions reporting, and crime rates.

Table 3.2 INDEX OF CRIME, UNITED STATES, 1978–1987

Population[a]	Crime Index total[b]	Violent crime[c]	Property crime[c]	Murder and nonnegligent manslaughter	Forcible rape	Robbery	Aggravated assault	Burglary	Larceny-theft	Motor vehicle theft
Number of offenses										
1978—218,059,000	11,209,000	1,085,550	10,123,400	19,560	67,610	426,930	571,460	3,128,300	5,991,000	1,004,100
1979—220,099,000	12,249,500	1,208,030	11,041,500	21,460	76,390	480,700	629,480	3,327,700	6,601,000	1,112,800
1980—225,349,264	13,408,300	1,344,520	12,063,700	23,040	82,990	565,840	672,650	3,795,200	7,136,900	1,131,700
1981—229,146,000	13,423,800	1,361,820	12,061,900	22,520	82,500	592,910	663,900	3,779,700	7,194,400	1,087,800
1982—231,534,000	12,974,400	1,322,390	11,652,000	21,010	78,770	553,130	669,480	3,447,100	7,142,500	1,062,400
1983—233,981,000	12,108,600	1,258,090	10,850,500	19,310	78,920	506,570	653,290	3,129,900	6,712,800	1,007,900
1984—236,158,000	11,881,800	1,273,280	10,608,500	18,690	84,230	485,010	685,350	2,984,400	6,591,900	1,032,200
1985—238,740,000	12,431,400	1,328,800	11,102,600	18,980	88,670	497,870	723,250	3,073,300	6,926,400	1,102,900
1986—241,077,000	13,211,900	1,489,170	11,722,700	20,610	91,460	542,780	334,320	3,241,400	7,257,200	1,224,100
1987—243,400,000	13,508,700	1,484,000	12,024,700	20,100	91,110	517,700	355,090	3,236,200	7,499,900	1,288,700
Percent change in number of offenses										
1987–1986	+2.2	−.3	+2.6	−2.5	−.4	−4.6	+2.5	−.2	+3.3	+5.3
1987–1983	+11.6	+18.0	+10.8	+4.1	+15.4	+2.2	+30.9	+3.4	+11.7	+27.9
1987–1978	+20.5	+36.7	+18.8	+2.8	+34.8	+21.3	+49.6	+3.4	−25.2	+28.3

Rate per 100,000 inhabitants

1978	5,140.3	497.8	4,642.5	9.0	31.0	195.8	262.1	1,434.6	2,747.4	460.5
1979	5,565.5	548.9	5,016.6	9.7	34.7	218.4	286.0	1,511.9	2,999.1	505.6
1980	5,950.0	596.6	5,353.3	10.2	36.8	251.1	298.5	1,684.1	3,167.0	502.2
1981	5,858.2	594.3	5,263.9	9.8	36.0	258.7	289.7	1,649.5	3,139.7	474.7
1982	5,603.6	571.1	5,032.5	9.1	34.0	238.9	289.2	1,488.8	3,084.8	458.8
1983	5,175.0	537.7	4,637.4	8.3	33.7	216.5	279.2	1,337.7	2,868.9	430.8
1984	5,031.3	539.2	4,492.1	7.9	35.7	205.4	290.2	1,263.7	2,791.3	437.1
1985	5,207.1	556.6	4,650.5	7.9	37.1	208.5	302.9	1,287.3	2,901.2	462.0
1986	5,480.4	617.7	4,862.6	8.6	37.9	225.1	346.1	1,344.6	3,010.3	507.8
1987	5,550.0	609.7	4,940.3	8.3	37.4	212.7	351.3	1,329.6	3,081.3	529.4

Percent change in rate per 100,000 inhabitants

1987–1986	+1.4	-1.3	+1.6	-3.5	-1.3	-5.5	+1.5	-1.1	+2.4	+4.3
1987–1983	+7.3	+13.4	+6.5	—	+11.0	-1.8	+25.8	-.6	+7.4	+22.9
1987–1978	+8.1	+22.5	+6.4	-7.8	+20.6	+8.6	+34.0	-7.3	+12.2	+15.0

[a] Populations are Bureau of the Census provisional estimates as of July 1, except April 1, 1980, preliminary census counts, and are subject to change.

[b] Because of rounding, the offenses may not add to totals.

[c] Violent crimes are offenses of murder, forcible rape, robbery, and aggravated assault. Property crimes are offenses of burglary, larceny-theft, and motor vehicle theft. Data are not included for the property crime of arson.

All rates were calculated on the offenses before rounding.

Source: FBI Uniform Crime Reports, 1987, p. 41.

- Seventeen percent of these killings were within family relation-ships, one-half of which involved spouse killing spouse.
- Arguments preceded 37 percent of all murders, while 20 percent occurred as a result of felonious activities such as robbery and arson. Another 1 percent were suspected to be the result of some felonious activity.
- Comparing 1986 to 1987, murder arrests for persons under 18 years of age increased by 6 percent, while adult arrests for this offense decreased 1 percent. In 1987, of all persons arrested for murder, 44 percent were under age 25, with 10 percent of the total being 17 or younger. The 18 to 24 age group showed the greatest involvement in this offense, accounting for 34 percent of the total 1987 murder arrests.

The clearance rate for murder in 1987 was higher than for any other Crime Index offense. Nationwide, law enforcement agencies were successful in clearing 70 percent of the murders occurring in their jurisdictions. This is largely due to the fact that a substantial number of murders are committed by people related in some way to the victim.

On this issue, former attorney general Ramsey Clark commented:

> Studies indicate that up to 85 percent of all murders occur within families or among acquaintances. Murder, usually a crime of passion, naturally occurs where emotions are strongest—husband and wife, father and son, a psy-chotic, a drunk, the angry neighbor, the lover's quarrel, beer-drinking buddies. The crime we fear most—murder by a stranger, the mad killer, the shadow in the night—accounts for fewer than one murder in five. If you are afraid of being murdered, there is more safety in deserting your family and having no friends than in additional police, who rarely have the opportunity to prevent friends and relatives from murdering one another.[3]

One study indicates that persons who commit murders were, prior to the murder, less likely to have a criminal history than others in prison. Basing a categorization of criminality level on three criteria, Gordon Waldo compared a group of 621 murderers with nonmurderers in a prison population. The criteria used were the extent of previous incar-cerations, the prevalence of infractions during previous incarcerations, and the number of escapes during previous incarcerations. He found that murderers were less likely to have been previously incarcerated than were nonmurderers; 62 percent of the murderers had not served a previous sentence, as against 38 percent of the nonmurderers. This was true when data were controlled for race, age, and intelligence. Fewer murderers who had served previous sentences had infractions or escapes than did nonmurderers. The researcher concluded that the murderer

---

[3] Ramsey Clark, *Crime in America* (New York: Simon & Schuster, 1970), pp. 51–52. Copyright © 1970 by Ramsey Clark. Reprinted by permission of Simon & Schuster, a Division of Gulf + Western Corporation.

would appear to have a lower "criminality level" than the nonmurderer, and the release of a murderer offers no more of a threat to society than that of other incarcerated offenders.[4]

Aggravated Assault

Aggravated assault is defined as an unlawful attack by one person upon another for the purpose of inflicting severe bodily injury, usually accompanied by the use of a weapon or other means likely to produce death or serious bodily harm. Attempts are included, since it is not necessary that an injury result when a gun, knife, or other weapon is used which could and probably would result in serious personal injury if the crime were successfully completed.

- The nearly 856,000 aggravated assaults in 1987 made up 6 percent of the total Crime Index and 58 percent of the crimes of violence. As has been the experience in previous years, aggravated assaults occurred more frequently in the summer months of 1987. Aggravated assaults increased 2 percent in volume between 1986 and 1987. Cities with 1 million or more population recorded an 8 percent upswing; suburban areas showed a 3 percent rise; and rural areas registered a 1 percent increase.
- In 1987, 21 percent of the aggravated assaults were committed by firearms; knives and other cutting instruments were used in 21 percent; 32 percent were committed with blunt objects or other dangerous weapons; and the remaining assaults were committed with personal weapons such as hands, fists, and feet. A comparison of 1986 and 1987 reveals that aggravated assaults committed with firearms increased 2 percent during the two-year period. Assaults with knives and other cutting instruments decreased 1 percent; assaults where blunt objects or other dangerous weapons were used increased 2 percent; and those aggravated assaults committed through the use of personal weapons climbed 7 percent. During 1987, the nation's law enforcement agencies cleared an average of 59 per 100 reported cases of aggravated assault. Again, this is because of the usual close relationship between the assailant and the victim.
- The number of persons arrested for aggravated assault in 1987 was nearly 353,000. The total was up 4 percent over the 1986 total and 22 percent over the 1983 figure. During the five-year period 1983 to 1987, arrests of persons 18 years of age and over for aggravated

---

[4] Gordon P. Waldo, "The 'Criminality Level' of Incarcerated Murderers and Non-Murderers," *Journal of Criminal Law, Criminology and Police Science* 61 (March 1970):60–70.

assault rose 23 percent, while the number of arrests of persons under age 18 increased 19 percent.
- Arrests of males for aggravated assault outnumbered those of females by seven to one.

In both aggravated assault and murder we find that the victim and assailant usually knew each other and were engaged in a serious quarrel in which a weapon was used. In some instances death resulted, and the crime was murder; in others the victim did not die, and the offense was aggravated assault. One might speculate that the distinguishing factor was the type of weapon used. The percentage of firearms used in murders was more than twice that used in aggravated assaults. This seems to support the view that if firearms were less available, we would have fewer murders.

Forcible Rape

Forcible rape, as defined by the FBI, is the carnal knowledge of a female through the use of force or the threat of force. Assaults to commit forcible rape are also included; however, statutory rape (without force) is not counted in this category.

- An estimated 91,111 forcible rapes came to the attention of law enforcement agencies in 1987. Duplicating the experience of past years, forcible rape accounted for 6 percent of the volume of violent crimes. The data reveal that more forcible rapes occurred in the summer months than during any other time of the year. The greatest number were recorded in August, after which the volume continuously dropped through the end of the year.
- Final 1987 national statistics revealed that reported forcible rape offenses decreased less than 1 percent from 1986 figures and increased 21 percent over the 1978 volume.
- By Uniform Crime Reporting Program definition, the victims of forcible rape are always females. In 1987, an estimated 73 of every 100,000 females in the country were reported rape victims, a 1 percent decrease from 1986. Since 1983, the forcible rape rate has risen 11 percent.
- Of all reported offenses in this category during 1987, 81 percent were rapes by force. Attempts or assaults to commit forcible rape made up the remainder. Even with the advent of rape crisis centers and an improved awareness by police dealing with rape victims, forcible rape, a violent crime against the person, is still recognized as one of the most underreported of all Index crimes. Victims' fear of their assailants and their embarrassment over the incidents are just two factors which can override their resolve to report these crimes.
- Fifty-three percent of known forcible rapes in the nation were

cleared by arrest in 1987. Total forcible rape arrests in 1987 decreased 2 percent from 1986 while a 9 percent increase was evident from 1983. Arrests of persons under 18 years of age for this offense increased 15 percent from 1983; adult arrests climbed 8 percent in the same time period. Forty-five percent of the forcible rape arrests in 1987 were of males under the age of 25 with 29 percent of the arrestees in the 18 to 24 age group.

Rape is one of the most damaging crimes. It is accompanied by violence; it humiliates the victim; and it may result in venereal disease, pregnancy, loss of employment, loss of the respect of family and neighbors, and emotional traumas. When the victim reports the rape, she may suffer again because of the methods of the criminal justice system. (The issues and problems that surround the crime of rape will be more fully discussed in Chapter 10.)

Robbery

Robbery is a violent crime against a victim for the purpose of acquiring the victim's property. Robbery makes up 4 percent of the total Crime Index and 35 percent of the crimes of violence. There were a total of 517,704 robberies reported during 1987. They occurred most frequently in the second half of the year, the highest volume being in December.

- The volume of robbery in 1987 decreased 5 percent from 1986 but increased 2 percent over 1983. For 1987, cities betwen 500,000 and 1 million in population reported decreases in robbery offenses of 8 percent, suburban areas decreases of 4 percent, rural areas decreases of 5 percent, from their 1986 volumes.
- In 1987, the robbery rate was 213 per 100,000 inhabitants, down 6 percent from the 1986 rate. Robbery is primarily a large-city crime. During 1987, the vast majority of robberies occurred in cities with populations of 100,000 or more. The robbery rate for these cities was 900 per 100,000 people.
- The value of property stolen during robberies in 1987 was an estimated $327 million, with an average property and dollar loss per incident of $637 and $292, respectively. However, the impact of this violent crime on its victims cannot be measured in terms of monetary loss alone. While the object of robbery is to obtain money or property, the crime always involves force or the threat of force, and many victims suffer serious physical and emotional injuries.
- Only some types of robbery increased in volume from 1983 to 1987. Bank robberies jumped 6 percent; convenience-store hold-ups were unchanged; street robberies climbed 3 percent; service-station holdups increased 2 percent; and robberies of other commercial or business establishments rose 16 percent. Residential robberies decreased 5 percent for the five-year period.

- Thirty-three percent of all robberies reported in 1987 were committed through the use of firearms; 44 percent by strong-arm tactics (hands, fists, feet, etc.); 13 percent through the use of knives or cutting instruments; and 10 percent through the use of other weapons.
- Data on arrests disclose that 61 percent of the persons arrested for robbery were under 25 years of age.
- An average of 8 out of every 100 persons arrested for robbery during 1987 were female. Arrests of women for this offense increased 6 percent compared to the 1983 figures.

Drug addiction accounts for a sizable amount of robbery. As drug prices rise and arrests for "dealing" drugs increase, street addicts often turn to robbery to support their expensive habits.

CRIMES AGAINST PROPERTY

In 1987, property offenses—burglary, larceny-theft, and auto theft—accounted for over 90 percent of all crime known to the police in the United States. Approximately 20 percent of these crimes were solved by the police. The perpetrators of 80 percent of these offenses remain unknown. With respect to this 80 percent, we have no way of knowing the age, race, sex, or anything else about the offender. We do know, however, that in the commission of these offenses no violence or threat of force was used on the victim. If force or threat of force were involved, the crime would have been classified as robbery. It is precisely for this reason that the percentage of solution is so low. Whereas in crimes of violence the victim is likely to know the accused or at least to have seen the perpetrator long enough to identify him or her later, in property offenses this is very seldom the case. Furthermore, the police are likely to be alerted immediately following a crime of violence. However, a burglary or larceny usually occurs in the absence of the victim, who may not be able to report it until hours or even days later. Thus, "hot pursuit," which is possible when a robbery is reported, rarely occurs when a property offense is reported.

Burglary

The FBI defines burglary as the unlawful entry of a structure to commit a felony or theft, even though no force was used to gain entry. Burglary is a crime that severely disturbs people. It involves invasion of a person's dwelling, a place that the average person feels is an extension of his or her self. Theft of personal property is annoying at the very least, and a disaster if the stolen goods are of great value or personal importance. The theft of an automobile, while inconvenient, is least disturbing because the vast majority of automobiles are insured against theft. Many others, however, are not insured. These simply become personal losses.

- An estimated 3.2 million burglaries occurred in the United States during 1987. These offenses made up 24 percent of the total Crime Index and 27 percent of reported property crime.
- Averages by month for 1987 show that burglary experience was lowest during the first half of the year and then rose during the third quarter. August was the month with the highest reported burglary volume, while April recorded the lowest count. Burglary offenses during 1987 dropped 7 percent from the 1978 volume and decreased 1 percent from the 1986 total.
- Residential property was targeted in two-thirds of the reported burglaries during 1987; nonresidential property accounted for the remaining one-third. Burglaries of residences remained the same in 1986 while nonresidential offenses were down 1 percent.
- Seventy percent of the burglaries in 1987 involved forcible entry, 21 percent were unlawful entries (without force), and the remainder were forcible-entry attempts.
- Daytime occurrences increased 12 percent for residential property and 16 percent for nonresidential property from 1983 to 1987. Nighttime burglaries dropped 2 percent for residential property and 9 percent for nonresidential structures.
- Burglary represents a substantial financial loss. In 1987, burglary victims suffered losses estimated at $3.2 billion. The average dollar loss per burglary was $975.
- Adults were involved in 81 percent of all burglary offenses cleared during 1987. Young people under 18 years of age were offenders in the remaining 19 percent.

In a number of cities police are experimenting with new approaches to curb burglaries. In one district in San Francisco, specialized units with portable crime-lab kits respond immediately to obtain physical evidence. Arrests increased substantially, and reported burglaries declined 25 percent over the year. Officers who specialize in intensive field interrogation carry lists of convicted burglars when they are on patrol. They are able legally to stop and search people on probation who, as a condition of the probation, have agreed to submit to search.

In some communities police have fed information on past burglaries into computers. They claim that the computer gives them information that helps them predict when and where burglaries are likely to occur. In one computer experiment, the rate of reported burglaries dropped 25 percent. In some areas, residents have established home security programs, known as neighborhood watches, on a block-by-block basis. These programs appear to have a positive effect in reducing burglaries. In 1989 Los Angeles County and Washington, D.C., introduced special police units to track down and closely follow repeat offenders.

Larceny-Theft

The most frequently committed crime against property is larceny. The FBI defines larceny-theft as the unlawful taking or stealing of property or articles of value without the use of force, violence, or fraud. It includes crimes such as shoplifting, pocket-picking, purse-snatching, thefts from autos, thefts of auto parts and accessories, and bicycle thefts.

- A high-volume property crime, larceny-theft totaled an estimated 7.5 million offenses in 1987. Fifty-six percent of the Crime Index total and 62 percent of the property crime total were attributable to the volume of larceny-theft.
- August was the month in which the number of recorded larceny-thefts was highest; February's count was the lowest. Compared to 1986 figures, the 1987 volume of larceny-thefts rose 3 percent in the nation, as well as in all cities collectively.
- In 1987, the average value of property stolen by larceny-theft was $407 per incident, up from $400 in 1986. When the average value is applied to the estimated number of larceny-thefts, the loss to victims nationally was $3 billion. While a portion of the goods stolen is recovered, the relatively low clearance percentage for larceny-thefts (20 percent) and the frequent absence of owner identification on recovered property indicate that the overall loss due to this criminal activity is not substantially reduced. In addition, other studies have indicated that many offenses in this category never come to police attention, particularly if the value of the stolen goods is small.
- The average value of goods and property reported stolen as a result of pocket-picking in 1987 was $286; by purse-snatching, $238; and by shoplifting, $96. Miscellaneous thefts from buildings and thefts from motor vehicles averaged $665 and $434, respectively; thefts of motor vehicle accessories resulted in average losses of $288 per offense.
- Thefts of motor vehicle parts, accessories, and contents accounted for 38 percent of the larceny-theft volume of 1987. Other major types of thefts which contributed to the large number of these crimes were those from buildings, 15 percent; shoplifting, 15 percent; and bicycles, 6 percent. The remainder was distributed among pocket-picking, purse-snatching, thefts from coin-operated machines, and miscellaneous types of larceny-thefts.

Motor Vehicle Theft

The third major crime against property is motor vehicle theft. The FBI defines motor vehicle theft as the unlawful taking or stealing of a motor vehicle, including attempts. This definition excludes taking for temporary use by those persons having lawful access to the vehicle.

There were 1,288,674 motor vehicle thefts in 1987. A rising trend in the volume of motor vehicle thefts began in the second quarter of 1987 and continued steadily through most of the third quarter. The greatest number of motor vehicle thefts occurred in August, and the lowest number in February. Of all motor vehicles reported stolen during the year, 77 percent were automobiles, 15 percent were trucks or buses, and the remainder were other types. The average value of the vehicles when stolen was $4,964, for an estimated total national loss of $6 billion.

As in prior years, motor vehicle theft arrests in 1987 primarily involved the younger segment of the nation's population; 58 percent of all persons arrested for motor vehicle theft were under 21 years of age, and those under 18 accounted for 40 percent of the total. Many of these "thefts" are really cases of youngsters engaged in joyriding. There are, however, highly organized adult auto theft rings that are engaged in theft for profit.

Arson

Arson is defined by the UCRP as any willful or malicious burning or attempt to burn, with or without intent to defraud, a dwelling house, a public building, a motor vehicle or an aircraft, the personal property of another, and so on. Only fires determined through investigation to have been willfully or maliciously set are classified as arsons. Fires of suspicious or unknown origins are excluded.

Arson was designated a Part I offense by congressional mandate in October 1978, and it was added to the FBI Crime Index in 1979. The data collection effort began after thorough study which enlisted the input of members of the law enforcement, fire service, and insurance communities regarding the types of information to be gathered and the design of the collection form.

Arson is sometimes referred to as a violent crime because it can result in injury or death. It can also qualify as white collar crime because fraud is often the motive, and the actual or attempted destruction of property is always involved.

During 1987, over 12,600 law enforcement agencies were able to provide at least partial arson statistics; in 1987, the participation grew to almost 13,000 contributors. The number of reported arsons also increased—from 77,147 in 1979 to 102,410 in 1987. That increase in volume must, however, be viewed as an increase in law enforcement participation in the data collection effort and not as a surge in the actual occurrence of arson incidents.

Representing 75 percent of the U.S. population, 8,507 participating agencies submitted all 12 monthly arson reports during 1987. From these submissions, a total of 102,410 arson offenses were reported for the year. Most of the agencies submitting arson counts were able to provide complete reports with detailed information, including type of structure and extent of damage.

The monetary value of property damaged due to reported arsons in 1987 was $907 million, and the average loss per incident was $10,755. Industrial and manufacturing structures registered the highest average loss, $37,187 per offense.

Of all persons arrested for arson, 40 percent were under 18 years of age, and 63 percent were under 25. Males made up 86 percent of all arson arrestees. Arson is often carried out by expert professional criminals hired by owners of failing businesses for the purpose of cashing in on insurance policies. The offense is also used on occasion in an attempt to disguise a murder. Some hotel fires, as for example the MGM Grand Hotel fire in Las Vegas in 1981, were major tragedies in terms of deaths. The convicted perpetrator was given a life sentence, which emphasizes the seriousness of arson as a crime. Even a small fire can result in deaths and thousands of dollars worth of property damage.

MISDEMEANORS

The discussion so far has dealt with the more serious crimes reported in FBI statistics. Crimes considered less serious are known as misdemeanors or, in FBI terminology, as Part II offenses. The following is a list of Part II offenses as defined by the FBI:

1. *Simple Assaults* Assaults and attempted assaults where no weapon was used and which did not result in serious or aggravated injury to the victim.
2. *Forgery and Counterfeiting* Making, altering, uttering, or possessing, with intent to defraud, anything false which is made to appear true. Attempts are included.
3. *Fraud* Fraudulent conversion and obtaining money or property by false pretenses. Included are larceny by bailee and bad checks, except forgeries and counterfeiting.
4. *Embezzlement* Misappropriation or misapplication of money or property entrusted to one's care, custody, or control.
5. *Stolen Property: Buying, Receiving, Possessing* Buying, receiving, and possessing stolen property, including attempts.
6. *Vandalism* Willful or malicious destruction, injury, disfigurement, or defacement of any public or private property, real or personal, without consent of the owner or person having custody or control.
7. *Weapons: Carrying, Possessing, etc.* All violations of regulations or statutes controlling the carrying, using, possessing, furnishing, and manufacturing of deadly weapons or silencers. Included are attempts.

8. *Prostitution and Commercialized Vice*   Sex offenses of a commercialized nature, such as prostitution, keeping a bawdy house, procuring, or transporting women for immoral purposes. Attempts are included.
9. *Sex Offenses*   Statutory rape and offenses against chastity, common decency, morals, and the like. Attempts are included. Does not include forcible rape, prostitution, and commercialized vice.
10. *Drug-Abuse Violations*   State and local offenses relating to narcotic drugs, such as unlawful possession, sale, use, growing, and manufacturing of narcotic drugs.
11. *Gambling*   Promoting, permitting, or engaging in illegal gambling.
12. *Offenses Against the Family and Children*   Nonsupport, neglect, desertion, or abuse of family and children.
13. *Driving Under the Influence*   Driving or operating any vehicle or common carrier while drunk or under the influence of liquor or narcotics.
14. *Liquor Laws*   State or local liquor law violations, except drunkenness and driving under the influence. Federal violations are excluded.
15. *Drunkenness*   Drunkenness or intoxication. Excluded is driving under the influence.
16. *Disorderly Conduct*   Breach of the peace.
17. *Vagrancy*   Vagabondage, begging, loitering, and so forth.
18. *All Other Offenses*   All violations of state or local laws, except the above offenses and traffic offenses.
19. *Suspicion*   No specific offense; suspect released without formal charges being placed.
20. *Curfew and Loitering Laws*   Offenses relating to the violation of local curfew or loitering ordinances, where such laws exist.
21. *Runaways*   Limited to juveniles taken into protective custody under provisions of local statutes.

Although many Part II offenses are minor crimes, some interlock with more major offenses. For example, fences and receivers of stolen property are part and parcel of the felony crimes of burglary and robbery. Drug abuses also are inextricably part of felonious behavior, as are simple assaults.

PEOPLE ARRESTED—AGE, SEX, AND RACE

The foregoing discussion deals with data concerning the extent of crime. We shall now shift our focus to the general characteristics of people who are arrested for crimes in the United States. We will analyze this issue on the basis of general crime data supplied by the FBI.

Criminality by Age

Most persons arrested are young. Since in most states persons under 18 years of age are referred to juvenile courts, the age group from 20 to 24 has the highest arrest rate.

- The arrest rate of young people for property offenses is particularly high. Almost three-fourths of those arrested for burglary, larceny, and auto theft are under 25 years of age.
- Nationally, 5 percent of all persons arrested were under 15, 16 percent were under 18, 30 percent were under 21, and 48 percent were under 25.
- A further examination of figures on youthful arrestees shows that persons under 25 years of age made up 59 percent of those arrested for Crime Index offenses, 47 percent of those arrested for violent crimes, and 62 percent of those arrested for property crimes.
- In the suburban areas, the volume of arrests of persons in the young age groups was greater than the national figures, with the age group under 15 representing 6 percent; under 18, 18 percent; under 21, 33 percent; under 25, 49 percent. The distributions of arrests in the rural areas were lower for the younger age groups, with the group under 15 being involved in only 2 percent; under 18, 10 percent; under 21, 24 percent; and under 25, 41 percent.
- For Crime Index offenses only (including arson), 11 percent of the arrestees in the nation were under the age of 15; 29 percent were under 18; and 44 percent were under 21.

The following explanations seem to account for the lower arrest rates of older people:

1. *Experience*   People who engage in crime to earn their livelihood learn from each mistake of their own and from the mistakes of those with whom they associate. When incarcerated they come into close contact with many people who have had varying degrees of success or failure in the commission of crimes. From these associates they acquire some basic skills that help them avoid detection and apprehension. By the time most boys graduate from a state reformatory, they have learned how to enter a building without breaking in, how to start a car without ignition keys, how to avoid leaving fingerprints, and how to carefully select potential victims.
2. *Maturation*   People who commit crimes in their youth often change their attitudes about crime as they grow older. Sociological research clearly indicates that most juvenile delinquents do not become adult criminals, although most adult criminals have a history of juvenile delinquency.
3. *Repression*   When a young man is sent to prison, he suffers a severe traumatic experience. He is taken from his friends and

family, deprived of the possibility of normal sexual relations, possibly subjected to homosexual aggressions, and otherwise demeaned. This treatment may result in his becoming embittered and violent. It may, however, deter him from taking future risks and encourage him to submit to the norms of the society to avoid a repetition of this horrible experience.

4. *Rehabilitation* Correctional institutions for juvenile delinquents and youthful offenders have vocational-training, educational, and therapy programs, Along with probation and parole, these programs help in the rehabilitation of some offenders. An individual who, upon leaving such an institution, is fortunate enough to obtain satisfying employment is likely to succeed on parole. The deterrence effect created by the repressive experience in the institution depends largely on the opportunities for success available to the person upon release.

5. *Length of Time in Prison* A person who is apprehended and convicted receives a more severe sentence each time. As criminals become older, they spend more time in prison and have less opportunity to engage in criminal behavior.

6. *Higher Death Rates* The death rate for persons convicted of crimes is higher than that of the general population. The criminal population is thus reduced to some extent by attrition.

Increases in arrests of young people have led to a prognosis of large increases in adult criminality for the future. While FBI data provide support for the conclusion that most persons treated as criminals (arrested and convicted) were first arrested as juveniles or in their early youth, *most juvenile delinquents do not become criminals*, although most adult criminals *were* juvenile delinquents.

The President's Commission on Law Enforcement noted the increasing size of the youth population and its restlessness. The commission attributed the rise in criminality of the young to the weakening of parental and especially paternal authority. In the late 1980s, a marked increase in fatherless families resulted in a further decline in the proper discipline of young people. As the commission concluded:

> Young people who have not received strong parental guidance, or whose experience leads them to believe that all of society is callous at best, or a racket at worst, tend to be unmotivated people and, therefore, people with whom the community is most unprepared to cope. Much more to the point, they are people who are unprepared to cope with the many ambiguities and lacks that they find in the community. Boredom corrodes ambition and cynicism corrupts those with ethical sensitivity.[5]

---

[5] President's Commission on Law Enforcement and Administration of Justice, *The Challenge of Crime in a Free Society* (Washington, D.C.: Government Printing Office, 1967), p. 6.

Because of these factors, an increasing number of young people are becoming committed to a criminal lifestyle.[6]

Sex Differences in Criminality: The Female Offender

Most persons arrested are males. Men are arrested over four times more often than women. The arrest rate for men is higher than for women for every offense except prostitution.

A comparison with 1986 figures shows that in 1987 arrests of males were up 2 percent and those of females rose 4 percent. Nationally, male arrests outnumbered female arrests by four to one, with males accounting for 82 percent of all arrests, 78 percent of those for Index crimes, 89 percent of the violent crime arrests, and 76 percent of those for property crimes.

As in previous years, female criminal involvement related mainly to larceny-theft, the crime which accounted for 20 percent of all female arrests and 80 percent of female arrests for Index offenses. The number of female larceny arrests increased by 6 percent from 1986 to 1987.

From 1983 to 1987, arrests of males under 18 years of age increased 5 percent; arrests of females in the same age group increased over 13 percent. Arrests for the eight Crime Index offenses during this period stayed the same for males under age 18 but increased almost 5 percent for females. Basic statistics on male and female criminality for 1978 to 1987 are given in Table 3.3 (pp. 86–87).

Some of the disparity between male and female arrest rates may be attributed to the underreporting of female crime, some to differences in social roles ascribed to women and men by most cultures. The role of wife, lover, or girlfriend is an important one to most women. Many female offenders engage in prostitution and property offenses to earn money to support the drug habits of husbands and lovers. When couples are involved in robberies, the woman is usually the girlfriend or wife of the male robber. To a very considerable extent, the criminal activity of women is influenced by the requirements of the men to whom they are emotionally attached.

Many young girls in urban ghettos become involved in delinquencies because of their associations with boys who are delinquent gang members. Female participants in gangs are referred to as "debs." They do not engage in gang fights of their own, but assist boyfriends by servicing them sexually, carrying weapons, spying on rival gangs, and sometimes serving as decoys. A girl's participation in a gang is in an auxiliary role.

The differences between roles ascribed to women and those ascribed to men account in part for the differences in types of crime in

---

[6] President's Commission, *The Challenge of Crime in a Free Society*, p. 6.

which they engage. Most activities requiring heavy physical labor, physical danger, or violence are performed by men rather than women. Because of this role differentiation, women are less likely to commit crimes of violence involving physical force, such as aggravated assaults and robberies. Differences in rates of property offenses may be due in part to the cultural requirement that the male assume the economic role of provider. As women move toward greater equality in economic roles, there is a tendency for their property offenses to increase. The female arrest rates for serious crimes have been increasing sharply. In the past decade, various movements directed at "women's liberation" have increased in strength, although militant preoccupation with feminist movements seemed slow in the 1980s. One result of such activity has been to greatly increase the number of women involved in social and economic roles that previously were largely monopolized by men. This increased exposure to opportunities, although not necessarily a reason for the upturn in female criminality, certainly has contributed to the likelihood of such an upturn.

The following reasons have been advanced for the lower female arrest rate and for the apparently lower female participation in crime:

1. *Female roles are more clearly defined.* The female child is likely to learn roles considered appropriate to a woman in her earliest years. She can observe her mother in the household and identify with her. The male child does not have the same opportunity to learn roles considered appropriate for the adult male. When parents are divorced or separated, the children generally remain with the mother. The male children do not have a father to observe or identify with. Even when father and mother live together, the father is likely to be absent from the home all day and be in the presence of his children only in the evening. At that time, when the children can observe him, he is not performing in an occupational role. In most homes, evening hours are spent watching television. While the young daughter watches mother at work in the home, the young son watches father at rest.

2. *Females are more closely supervised.* Young women and girls are more closely supervised than their brothers. Parents try to keep them at home more and show greater interest in their associations.

3. *Females receive greater protection.* Women—young women in particular—are protected to a greater extent than men. Parents are more likely to accept responsibility for their support, and other family members as well are more likely to assist them in times of adversity. There are also more social agencies in urban communities that provide support for the unattached female than for the unattached male.

Table 3.3 TOTAL ARREST TRENDS, SEX, 1983–1987

Offense charged	Males Total			Males Under 18			Females Total			Females Under 18		
	1983	1987	Percent change	1983	1987	Percent change	1983	1987	Percent change	1983	1987	Percent change
TOTAL	7,647,104	8,256,826	+8.0	1,227,278	1,288,914	+5.0	1,530,743	1,784,249	+16.6	330,327	373,446	+13.1
Murder and nonnegligent manslaughter	14,108	13,766	−2.4	1,102	1,365	+23.9	2,153	1,979	−8.1	121	130	+7.4
Forcible rape	26,616	28,913	+8.6	3,965	4,505	+13.6	265	334	+26.0	51	99	+94.1
Robbery	113,114	107,972	−4.5	30,666	24,700	−19.5	8,999	9,517	+5.8	2,160	1,820	−15.7
Aggravated assault	199,438	244,435	+22.6	25,462	30,494	+19.8	31,029	37,566	+21.1	4,890	5,512	+12.7
Burglary	347,221	321,920	−7.3	134,318	113,773	−15.3	25,764	28,3`5	+9.9	9,719	9,217	−5.2
Larceny-theft	740,899	809,686	+9.3	250,868	264,440	+5.4	312,471	366,089	+17.2	91,163	99,808	+9.5
Motor vehicle theft	86,461	124,988	+44.6	29,287	49,176	+67.9	8,555	13,309	+55.6	3,547	5,747	+62.0
Arson	12,858	12,019	−6.5	5,124	5,080	−.9	1,819	1,940	+6.7	549	582	+6.0
Violent crime[a]	353,276	395,086	+11.8	61,195	61,064	−.2	42,446	49,396	+16.4	7,222	7,561	+4.7
Property crime[b]	1,187,439	1,268,613	+6.8	419,597	432,469	+3.1	348,609	409,653	+17.5	104,978	115,354	+9.9
Crime Index total[c]	1,540,715	1,663,699	+8.0	480,792	493,533	+2.7	391,055	459,049	+17.4	112,200	122,915	+9.5
Other assaults	370,836	533,381	+43.8	56,783	70,995	+25.0	63,873	94,935	+48.6	15,667	20,943	+33.7
Forgery and coun-terfeiting	42,838	47,815	+11.6	4,047	4,332	+7.0	21,792	25,122	+15.3	1,948	2,163	+11.0
Fraud	140,116	147,853	+5.5	15,844	13,378	−15.6	93,386	113,275	+21.3	4,493	4,697	+4.5
Embezzlement	4,515	6,010	+33.1	288	439	+52.4	2,236	3,746	+67.5	117	272	+132.5

Stolen property: buying, receiving, possessing	86,327	98,435	+14.0	21,467	25,437	+18.5	11,023	12,890	+16.9	2,224	2,583	+16.1
Vandalism	172,019	190,428	+10.7	76,675	80,169	+4.6	18,323	22,627	+23.5	7,009	7,813	+11.5
Weapons: carrying, possessing, etc.	133,690	144,279	+7.9	19,449	22,658	+16.5	11,173	11,864	+6.2	1,295	1,751	+35.2
Prostitution and commercialized vice	33,872	34,565	+2.0	821	669	−18.5	79,724	63,171	−20.8	1,817	1,362	−25.0
Sex offenses (except forcible rape and prostitution)	64,591	74,183	+14.9	10,233	11,904	+16.3	5,286	6,503	+23.0	680	832	+22.4
Drug abuse violations	479,369	652,919	+36.2	55,959	62,740	+12.1	78,244	114,889	+46.8	10,788	9,409	−12.8
Gambling	30,933	18,977	−38.7	971	759	−21.8	3,857	2,947	−23.6	52	31	−40.4
Offenses against family and children	32,248	33,340	+3.4	676	1,448	+114.2	4,303	7,546	+75.4	380	902	+137.4
Driving under the influence	1,245,617	1,136,204	−8.8	18,874	15,506	−17.8	159,659	150,383	−5.8	2,828	2,461	−13.0
Liquor laws	315,433	381,676	+21.0	73,516	88,547	+20.4	61,503	82,199	+33.7	25,244	32,674	+29.4
Drunkenness	790,661	609,948	−22.9	21,397	16,277	−23.9	75,837	62,149	−18.0	4,022	3,124	−22.3
Disorderly conduct	506,872	453,373	−10.6	72,994	66,782	−8.5	96,542	105,515	+9.3	14,952	15,631	+4.5
Vagrancy	27,180	27,945	+2.8	2,046	1,874	−8.4	3,028	3,577	+18.1	359	395	+10.0
All other offenses (except traffic)	1,538,238	1,892,872	+23.1	203,412	202,543	−.4	277,157	351,659	+26.9	51,510	53,285	+3.4
Suspicion (not included in to- tals)	9,580	9,542	−.4	2,073	1,875	−9.6	1,652	1,601	−3.1	527	437	−17.1
Curfew and loitering law vio- lations	48,947	55,728	+13.9	48,947	55,728	+13.9	14,843	18,522	+24.8	14,843	18,522	+24.8
Runaways	42,087	53,196	+26.4	42,087	53,196	+26.4	57,899	71,681	+23.8	57,899	71,681	+23.8

[a] Violent crimes are offenses of murder, forcible rape, robbery, and aggravated assault.

[b] Property crimes are offenses of burglary, larceny-theft, motor vehicle theft, and arson.

[c] Includes arson.

8,692 agencies; 1987 estimated population 183,805,000.

Source: FBI Uniform Crime Reports, 1987, Table 30, p. 171.

4. *Females have the opportunity for household employment.* Unskilled women find it far easier to get work than unskilled men. There has been a shortage of household help in middle-class neighborhoods and suburbs for many years. An unskilled woman can obtain work doing house cleaning without much difficulty. Household work has been defined in our culture as appropriate for women and inappropriate for men. Unskilled men are not as likely to be offered this sort of employment and are more likely to consider it demeaning if offered. The result is that the unskilled male is more likely to be unemployed for long periods of time.

5. *Male roles are more active.*   When in the company of a woman, the male is likely to assume the more active role, one which involves greater risk. For example, about 12 times as many men as women are arrested for driving while intoxicated. In our culture when a man and woman are together in an automobile, the man generally drives. If both are drunk the man is more likely to be behind the wheel and is therefore more likely to be arrested for drunken driving. He is also the one more likely to be caught in possession of drugs, although both might be using them. Also, in a dispute with others involving physical encounter, the male is likely to strike the blows. Thus, although the female may verbally provoke the fight, the male is arrested for assault and battery.

6. *Men are likely to be chivalrous.*   When a man is in the company of a woman, he is expected to assume responsibility for any difficulty involving both of them. For example, if a couple is apprehended in flight from a robbery, the male is likely to testify that his female companion was "along for the ride" and played no part in the crime.

A study by Christy Visher supports the chivalry hypothesis. In her study, she concludes:

> Some chivalry appears to exist at the stage of arrest, but only for *selected* female offenders. Older white women who are calm and deferential toward the police are granted leniency, whereas young black or hostile women receive no such preferential treatment. Apparently, female suspects who deviate from a middle-class stereotype of the traditional female role (white, older and submissive) are not afforded any chivalrous treatment during arrest. But the hypothesis that police officers would be more lenient with female property offenders than with violent offenders was not supported. Females suspected of property offenses are arrested as often as violent offenders. Police officers respond to female suspects on the basis of the image they portray rather than the type of offense they may have committed.[7]

---

[7] Christy Visher, "Sex and Arrest: A Test of the Chivalry Hypothesis," presented at American Society of Criminology meetings, Washington, D.C., 1981.

7. *The public perceives men and women differently.* A woman is perceived to be less threatening than a man under identical circumstances. A woman using loud and abusive language in a public place is not as likely to be taken seriously. Persons at whom the abuse is directed may consider it annoying but are not likely to lodge a complaint with the police. This is particularly true if the abuse is directed at a man. In our culture it would be considered cowardly and unmanly for the man to call the police. A man using loud and abusive language is more likely to be charged with disorderly conduct.

8. *The police react differently to men and women.* Police are less likely to detain or arrest women than men under identical circumstances. A man walking alone at night in a strange neighborhood may be perceived by police as suspicious, dangerous, or involved in a criminal pursuit. A woman would be more likely to be viewed as someone in need of protection.

Male and female role expectations and behavior are stongly influenced by the larger cultural environment and by their subcultural identifications. Since men are expected to be aggressive, males are more likely to be delinquent than females, who are expected to adopt a more passive role. Despite this, the arrest rate of females is increasing. This may be a consequence of the narrowing of the difference between male and female cultural roles in recent years. The economic and social roles available to women in our society tend ever more closely to approximate those available to men. This is particularly true in the big cities. It is no longer unusual for a woman to work outside the home, to be a principal breadwinner, and to share equally with the male members of the household in the decision-making processes affecting all members.

In an analysis of the equal opportunity–equal crime concept, Figueira-McDonough and Selo conclude that the hypothesis is not that simple. They state in the conclusion of their analysis:

> The equal opportunity argument is that women's increasing access to positions long held by men exposes them to more opportunities to engage in criminal activities. Equality of legitimate opportunities will lead to similar behavior, legal and illegal. A simple interpretation of this argument is that, given similar conventional opportunities, males and females will behave in similar ways, both legitimately and illegitimately. However, we have shown in our inventory of opportunity-related delinquency explanations that other elements—namely, the access to illegitimate opportunities and the strength of attachments to conventional institutions and groups—are crucial links in the causal relationship between opportunity and delinquency.[8]

---

[8] J. Figueira-McDonough and E. Selo, "A Reformulation of the Equal Opportunity Explanation of Female Delinquency," *Crime and Delinquency* (July 1980). Copyright 1980 by *Crime and Delinquency*. Reprinted by permission of Sage Publications, Inc.

In an interview for *People* magazine in response to the question "How big a part does women's liberation play in female criminality?" criminologist Freda Adler replied:

> The dramatic rise cannot be directly attributed to one factor. The feminist connection is that women are taking on more of the behavior of men. This also means taking on the stress, strain and frustration that males have traditionally dealt with. Many of these women, unskilled and untrained, may turn in desperation to crime. There was a time when a female confined her criminal acts to prostitution and shoplifting. Now she is committing armed robbery, auto theft, and burglary, traditionally male crimes, so that we see a definite change in both the dimension and form of female criminality.[9]

In her larger work *Sisters in Crime*, Dr. Adler examined the extent and nature of the changing patterns of female criminality in America, describing the new female criminal and relating this phenomenon to social forces such as female assertiveness.[10] It is generally recognized that women are committing more crimes than before, and more violent ones—homicide, armed robbery, aggravated assault, and gang violence. In *Sisters in Crime*, Adler overcame a decade of resistance from traditional theorists, police chiefs, judges, and probation officers to take into account new social facts. She reassesed the scope, depth, and implications of female crime and showed that the exception has become the rule as thousands of women are stepping across the imaginary boundary which once separated crimes into "masculine" and "feminine" categories. Using original research conducted over several years, Adler explained how the rising tide of female assertiveness led women to break out of the traditional limits of prostitution and shoplifting into more serious and violent crimes. Adler noted the changing patterns in the female criminal and her relation to the larger social forces in our society, and she challenged a variety of stereotypes regarding women and crime, race and class, and wealth and power. Adler also examined and rejected the traditional myth of the genetic basis of the passive female.

Women now seem to be gravitating toward the center of the action in crime and delinquency. While this is not a positive outgrowth of the women's movement, it does nevertheless show that women's self-concept is approaching that of being men's equal more nearly than in the past. The general attitudes inherent in the women's liberation movement tend to filter down to adolescent girls—and no doubt are part of the causal backdrop to the current trend of increased female delinquent and criminal behavior.

---

[9] Freda Adler, in *People*, October 13, 1975, pp. 20, 22.

[10] Freda Adler, *Sisters in Crime—The Rise of the New Female Criminal* (New York: McGraw-Hill, 1975).

Darrell J. Steffensmeier assessed the impact of the women's movement on crime and delinquency as follows:

> It has become commonplace for analysts to point out that, although women defendants were treated more leniently in the past, if the current trend in relations between the sexes continues, this preferential treatment can be expected to change. The major reasons for this expectation of change have been: (1) Chivalrous attitudes of male judges toward protecting the "weaker sex" will probably decrease as women continue to demand equality, not protection. Increased participation of women in all aspects of life will diminish the view of them as frail and passive and result in respect for women as equals. (2) Equality of treatment may also be promoted by changes in the nature and extent of women's crime. In particular, the increased number of women before the criminal court may cause judges to see female crime as a real rather than a marginal problem. (3) An increase in women judges may lead to less preferential treatment. It is suggested that women judges have not been socialized to view themselves in a protective role vis-à-vis other women. Thus, their decisions affecting women offenders will be based more on the facts of the case and the circumstances of the crime than on a paternalistic view of the "weaker sex."[11]

In fact, women judges might instead feel that women criminals are reflections on them, and they might then give tougher sentences to women. This trend has persisted.

The Radical Feminist Viewpoint on Crime

Alongside the problems of women as offenders is their unfortunate escalating role as victims of crime. Although the role of female victims is not likely to be totally the problem of a "capitalistic system," the most vocal and articulate spokespeople on this subject are Marxist feminists. On this theme of females as victims, Nicole Rafter and Elena Natalizia make the following assertions:

> Although women in capitalist society are victimized by the same offenses as are men, some types of victimization are inherently or virtually the domain of women. These include rape, incest, wife abuse, sexual harassment on the job, and prostitution, all of which are rooted in the traditional patriarchal concept of women as sexual chattel. . . .
>
> From the perspective of Marxist criminology, the traditional "crime" of prostitution is instead another victimization of women, a matter of sexual slavery rather than sexual immorality. The prostitute may be seen, in fact, as the archetype of woman's traditional role of sex partner to man; however, because she performs this role outside the nuclear family model—and does it for profit—she is punished by bourgeois moral codes upholding a double standard of morality for men and women.

---

[11] Darrell J. Steffensmeier, "Assessing the Impact of the Women's Movement on Handling Female Offenders," *Crime and Delinquency* (July 1980). Copyright 1980 by *Crime and Delinquency*. Reprinted by permission of Sage Publications, Inc.

An increasing problem of juvenile delinquency is the escalation of teenage prostitution. The problem is increasingly more a function of economic necessity for young homeless girls than in the past when young female prostitutes were motivated to prostitution by emotional problems.

What would an alternative, egalitarian system look like in its handling of women as victims? Most important, it would undertake a massive commitment to the female victim, including the following:

1. Mandatory education in public schools on rape, incest, and employment rights. In addition, training of females in self-defense should be offered by the schools.
2. Employment of female staff in all parts of the criminal justice system dealing with female victims.
3. Training of all law enforcement personnel in the problems unique to female victims.
4. Establishment of rape crisis centers and shelters, and of other support systems to encourage bonding among female victims.
5. Encouragement of women who wish to prosecute men who have victimized them, and the provision of legal assistance for these women.

In addition, necessary legal reforms would include the following:

1. Removal of the husband exemption in rape statutes.
2. Making restraining orders against abusive husbands a more effective legal tool for battered women.
3. Recognition of self-defense as a legitimate legal defense for women who retaliate against men who repeatedly batter them.
4. Legalization of prostitution or, at the very least, sanctions directed equally at all parties involved.
5. Adoption of laws criminalizing sexual harassment on the job. Sexual harassment should be established as adequate grounds for leaving a job without forfeiting unemployment compensation.[12]

Many of the issues raised by Rafter and Natalizia have been effectively corrected through legal and social changes in the past decade. It is hoped that all of these inequities will be ameliorated by the twenty-first century.

Race and Criminality

The term *race*, as used by biologists and anthropologists, refers to a group of people characterized by certain hereditary concentrations of genes which determine their physical characteristics. Such characteristics as skin color and texture, texture and color of hair, thickness of lips, shape of nose, and type of eyelids have been used by anthropologists and biologists to group people into broad racial categories. The classifi-

---

[12] N. F. Rafter and E. M. Natalizia, "Marxist Feminism: Implications for Criminal Justice," *Crime and Delinquency* (January 1981):81–87. Used by permission of the authors.

cation most widely accepted recognizes three major racial groups: the Mongoloid, the Negroid, and the Caucasoid.

Anthropologists are agreed that all people have some mixed ancestry. It is generally recognized that the people referred to as blacks are a mixture of a great many ethnic and tribal groups originating in Africa and Europe. What is often overlooked is that the people we refer to as white are *also* a mixture of a great many ethnic and tribal groups originating in Africa and Europe. Estimates of the number of blacks who have "passed" into the white society run as high as 7 million. In addition to those millions who have introduced an African mixture into the "white" population of the United States in the relatively recent past, there must have been millions of Africans who were assimilated into the populations of Spain, Portugal, Italy, Greece, and other Mediterranean countries. Decendants of those people are now part of the "white" population of the United States. By way of preface, therefore, we state our belief that the concept of race is complex and a difficult issue to sort out. Given this caveat, we shall proceed to an examination of the data supplied by the FBI on arrest distributions by race. Table 3.4 provides the FBI breakdown of arrests by race in terms of whites, blacks, American Indians, and Asians.

Blacks and Criminality

Since more blacks are arrested than any other group except whites, black criminality requires some special analysis. About 30 percent of the persons arrested in 1987 were black. Because blacks make up about 14 percent of the population of the United States, the arrest rate is disproportionately high.

In general, the disparity in arrest rates for offenses of violence is much greater than that for property offenses. About half the people arrested for murder and nonnegligent manslaughter, robbery, and aggravated assaults were blacks. Basically, black people are not intrinsically more prone to commit crimes than white people; however, the socioeconomic forces that have oppressed black people since slavery have affected their crime rate. A major causal factor for black people is their relative lack of opportunity due to the continuance of discrimination and prejudice.

SOME PROBLEMS WITH CRIME STATISTICS

In general we have a limited idea of the percentage of crime that is committed by any category of individuals or groups in our society. The actual amount of crime in the United States today is, according to reliable surveys, several times that reported in the *Uniform Crime Reports*. We have no idea of the age, sex, or race of persons who

Table 3.4 CITY ARRESTS, DISTRIBUTION BY RACE, 1987

Offense charged	Total arrests					Percent distribution[a]				
	Total	White	Black	American Indian or Alaskan Native	Asian or Pacific Islander	Total	White	Black	American Indian or Alaskan Native	Asian or Pacific Islander
Total	8,362,736	5,462,663	2,740,348	93,914	65,811	100.0	65.3	32.8	1.1	.8
Murder and nonnegligent manslaughter	12,554	4,714	7,622	87	131	100.0	37.5	60.7	.7	1.0
Forcible rape	24,089	10,743	13,020	181	145	100.0	44.6	54.0	.8	.6
Robbery	108,342	36,323	70,831	501	687	100.0	33.5	65.4	.5	.6
Aggravated assault	232,123	125,208	103,205	2,073	1,637	100.0	53.9	44.5	.9	.7
Burglary	278,166	174,523	99,327	2,201	2,115	100.0	62.7	35.7	.8	.8
Larceny-theft	1,067,174	687,816	354,944	12,333	12,081	100.0	64.5	33.3	1.2	1.1
Motor vehicle theft	117,279	64,530	50,530	1,022	1,197	100.0	55.0	43.1	.9	1.0
Arson	11,353	7,861	3,293	107	92	100.0	69.2	29.0	.9	.8
Violent crime[b]	377,108	176,988	194,678	2,842	2,600	100.0	46.9	51.6	.8	.7
Property crime[c]	1,473,972	934,730	508,094	15,663	15,485	100.0	63.4	34.5	1.1	1.1
Crime Index total[d]	1,851,080	1,111,718	702,772	18,505	18,085	100.0	60.1	38.0	1.0	1.0

Offense									
Other assaults	539,168	313,906	214,936	6,202	4,124	100.0	58.2	39.9	1.2	.8
Forgery and counterfeiting	58,257	36,678	20,914	330	335	100.0	63.0	35.9	.6	.6
Fraud	154,733	96,252	56,958	549	974	100.0	62.2	36.8	.4	.6
Embezzlement	6,961	4,640	2,242	28	51	100.0	66.7	32.2	.4	.7
Stolen property: buying, receiving, possessing	94,913	52,868	41,053	473	519	100.0	55.7	43.3	.5	.5
Vandalism	186,373	135,232	47,715	1,898	1,528	100.0	72.6	25.6	1.0	.8
Weapons: carrying, possessing, etc.	134,714	76,558	56,333	751	1,072	100.0	56.8	41.8	.6	.8
Prostitution and commercialized vice	95,008	54,473	39,240	438	857	100.0	57.3	41.3	.5	.9
Sex offenses (except forcible rape and prostitution)	64,960	48,094	15,686	704	476	100.0	74.0	24.1	1.1	.7
Drug abuse violations	642,117	383,155	253,845	2,109	3,008	100.0	59.7	39.5	.3	.5
Gambling	19,915	7,308	11,440	8	1,159	100.0	36.7	57.4	—e	5.8
Offenses against family and children	24,346	15,108	8,385	377	476	100.0	62.1	34.4	1.5	2.0
Driving under the influence	867,646	754,507	97,167	9,542	6,430	100.0	87.0	11.2	1.1	.7
Liquor laws	397,610	342,916	42,270	10,112	2,312	100.0	86.2	10.6	2.5	.6
Drunkenness	587,334	453,074	118,153	14,704	1,403	100.0	77.1	20.1	2.5	.2

(continued)

Table 3.4 (Continued)

Offense charged	Total arrests					Percent distribution[a]				
	Total	White	Black	American Indian or Alaskan Native	Asian or Pacific Islander	Total	White	Black	American Indian or Alaskan Native	Asian or Pacific Islander
Disorderly conduct	540,310	331,643	199,800	6,400	2,467	100.0	61.4	37.0	1.2	.5
Vagrancy	30,139	17,680	11,569	822	68	100.0	58.7	38.4	2.7	.2
All other offenses (except traffic)	1,876,928	1,082,775	757,880	18,104	18,169	100.0	57.7	40.4	1.0	1.0
Suspicion	10,292	4,748	5,462	16	63	100.0	46.1	53.1	.2	.6
Curfew and loitering law violations	74,550	53,434	19,607	755	754	100.0	71.7	26.3	1.0	1.0
Runaways	105,382	85,896	16,921	1,087	1,478	100.0	81.5	16.1	1.0	1.4

[a] Because of rounding, the percentages may not add to total.

[b] Violent crimes are offenses of murder, forcible rape, robbery, and aggravated assault.

[c] Property crimes are offenses of burglary, larceny-theft, motor vehicle theft, and arson.

[d] Includes arson.

[e] Less than one-tenth of 1 percent. 7,187 agencies; 1987 estimated population 137,831,000.

Source: FBI Uniform Crime Reports, 1987, Table 44, p. 191.

committed crimes that were not reported to the police. Only about 20 percent of the crimes known to the police are cleared by arrest. We have no idea who committed the remaining 80 percent, and therefore we cannot attribute these crimes to any age, sex, or racial group. Moreover, people arrested by the police are not necessarily guilty. Many are released without being charged, and many more are acquitted. The statistics reveal that *almost half the people arrested were not found guilty of a crime.*

The general and complex statistical issue is that FBI statistics regarding the age, sex, and race of criminals are mainly based on data obtained from those arrested. These are the *suspects* and the *failures* in crime. We know little or nothing about people who successfully commit crimes and are not apprehended. Because these statistics are the ones we have used in discussing the age, sex, and race of "criminals," the discussion might more accurately be entitled "Characteristics of Persons Arrested" or "Characteristics of Failures in Crime." Figure 3.1 shows the percentage of crimes known to the police that were cleared by arrest in 1987, that is, cases that were solved.

As previously noted, all that we know about a crime before it is cleared by arrest is that someone reported the commission of that crime to the police. The number of such reports, for each of the seven crimes called "serious" by the FBI, is summarized in the *Uniform Crime Reports* Crime Index. Once a crime is cleared by arrest, we know something about the person arrested for the crime. The report of the local police to the FBI includes information regarding the sex, age, and race of the person arrested. This information is analyzed and reported in tabular form in the arrest section of the *Uniform Crime Reports.*

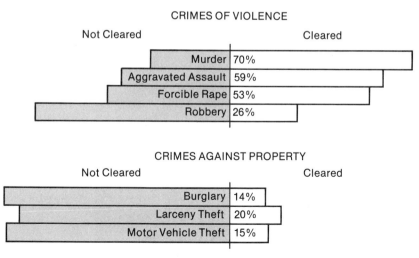

Figure 3.1 Crimes cleared by arrest, 1987. [*Source:* FBI, *Uniform Crime Reports, 1987* (Washington, D.C.: U.S. Government Printing Office, 1988), p. 154.]

As we have seen, crimes against the person are more likely to be reported to the police than crimes against property. Crimes against the person are also more likely to result in arrests than crimes against property. Three factors account in large measure for the relative success of the police in solving crimes against the person:

1. The offense occurs in the presence of a victim, and if the victim survives, he or she may be able to identify the assailant.
2. The victim and the assailant are likely to know each other. About one-fourth of willful killings occur within family units, and half result from altercations among acquaintances. About two-thirds of people killed are victims of assaults by persons with whom they had some relationship. Lovers' quarrels, quarrels over money, drinking situations, and revenge accounted for these killings. Similarly, about two-thirds of aggravated assaults involve persons within the same family unit or persons otherwise acquainted with each other.
3. The police place great emphasis on the solution of crimes against the person because the victim and persons close to the victim are sufficiently interested to exert pressures. The press also plays a part in influencing police activity by giving wide publicity to such offenses and by being sharply criticical of police failures.

Differential Reporting of Different Crimes

Another problem with the Crime Index developed by the FBI is that some crimes are more likely to be reported to the police than others. Homicide, for example, is the offense most likely to be accurately reported. This is due to several factors. The burial of a deceased requires that a death certificate be issued. A wrongful killing is likely to be discovered by the doctor issuing the certificate and brought to the attention of the authorities.

An aggravated assault is also likely to come to the attention of the police. The victim frequently requires hospitalization, and in most states the attending doctor is required to make a report. This is particularly true when the doctor attends someone who has been shot, stabbed, or otherwise injured by a dangerous weapon. Homicides and aggravated assaults in the Crime Index are most likely to reflect the accurate number of such crimes committed.

The statistics regarding crimes against property, however, do not provide so accurate an index. In this category auto thefts are most likely to be reported, since the recovery of the property is strongly desired by the owner. Moreover, the owner will no doubt notify the police as protection against liability for the vehicle while it is in the possession of unauthorized persons.

On the other hand, street robberies, which constitute more than 50 percent of all robbery offenses reported, are likely in many cases to go unreported. A victim unable in any way to identify the robber is often reluctant to accept the time loss and inconvenience necessary to notify the police. When the victim is robbed of money or other unidentifiable property, there is sometimes a reluctance to pursue the matter further. This reluctance also applies to the victims of burglaries and larcenies of unidentifiable property or money. We can therefore estimate that a substantial number of burglaries, larcenies, and robberies are not reported to the police and are not included in the *Uniform Crime Reports*.

Differential Enforcement Standards, Policies, and Practices

The Federal Bureau of Investigation, as we have noted, is not the original or primary source of the data it publishes. *The primary sources of the data contained in the* Uniform Crime Reports *are the local police and state agencies throughout the United States.* While the FBI may have been successful in achieving approximate uniformity in reporting procedures, there are considerable differences in law enforcement standards, policies, and practices.

Police policies and attitudes toward members of a particular age group or race often greatly influence the number and kind of arrests. Attitudes of members of an age group, class, or race toward the police may also influence the number of complaints reported to the police.

According to surveys evaluated by the President's Commission on Law Enforcement, the actual amount of crime in the United States is several times that reported in the *Uniform Crime Reports*. Reasons most frequently given by victims for not reporting to the police were: (1) the police could not do anything, (2) the victims did not want to harm the offenders, and (3) the victims feared reprisal.[13]

If these reasons are valid, we would be justified in assuming that with increased police effectiveness, statistical crime would *rise*. Increased police effectiveness would produce an improvement in the reputation of police. This increased confidence in police ability to solve problems would increase the number of crimes reported by victims.

The following series of events, which occurred in an apartment-house area in New York City, illustrates the way in which increased police effectiveness can result in a statistically higher crime rate. The events were reported by a New York City police official who was enrolled in a course I taught at the City University of New York.

The home of Mrs. J. was burglarized. The burglar or burglars had taken money, jewelry, and other personal effects. Mrs. J. immediately notified the police, and a detective went to her home to conduct an

---

[13] President's Commission, *Challenge of Crime in a Free Society*, pp. 21–22.

investigation. He searched the apartment for fingerprints and other clues, but found none. Mrs. J. told the detective that a few days prior to the burglary she had seen two men loitering in the vicinity of her apartment house. At the request of the detective, she spent an afternoon at police headquarters examining photographs of known criminals in an effort to identify the two persons she considered suspicious. She was unable to do so. A few days later, the apartment of Mrs. B., a neighbor of Mrs. J., was burglarized. She reported the burglary to the police, and her experiences were similar to those of Mrs. J. Shortly after that, the apartment of another neighbor, Mrs. C., was burglarized. By that time, everyone on the block was aware of the experiences of Mrs. J. and Mrs. B., and Mrs. C. did not bother to report to the police. During that month eight other burglaries were committed on the same block, but none was reported to the police.

The following month an alert police officer apprehended a man in the course of a burglary. A considerable amount of clothing, jewelry, and other articles were found in the course of a search of the burglar's apartment. When this became known, the nine victims who had not made reports to the police did so in the hope of recovering some of their property. The alert police officer with his fine arrest created a statistical crime wave.

Another example of police practice demonstrates how the crime rate can be affected. In a situation known to me, there were two police captains in a precinct over a two-year period. During the first year the first captain emphasized arresting, booking, and prosecuting any and all youth gang activity. As a result, delinquency arrests were high. During the following year the second police captain applied a fatherly approach to gang youths. Gang members were frequently brought into precinct headquarters, but they were seldom officially arrested. They received, instead, fatherly counseling. Statistics on juvenile delinquency decreased enormously in the second year, reflecting a difference in police practice rather than a decrease in actual illegal gang activity.

As another example, simply increasing police personnel may increase the number of arrests. This would raise crime statistics without necessarily affecting the actual amount of crime in the area.

Shifts in Laws

Theoretically, all crime can be eliminated tomorrow by eliminating all laws. Eliminating all drug abuse laws would substantially reduce crime statistics, even though the deviant behavior continued at the same rate. The point is that changes in laws, both nationally and locally, must be taken into account in considering shifts in crime statistics.

Treatment of Crime Statistics by the Media

Most people in the United States get their information about crime rates from the media rather than from any statistical source. Therefore, distortions in the media have a profound effect on the beliefs and fears of the people relative to crime and criminality. For example, there have been articles reporting that half the burglaries and larcenies in the United States were committed by persons under 18 years of age. Most people believe these figures to be true. Yet, as we have noted, there is no way of determining from the *Uniform Crime Reports* how many offenses are actually committed by any age or racial group. The FBI statistics relative to sex, age, and race deal only with persons arrested for particular crimes. Few people realize that only about 20 percent of the crimes known to the police are cleared by arrest. We have no way of knowing who committed the other 80 percent. Furthermore, about half the persons arrested are not convicted.

An illustration of distortion resulting from media interpretation is provided by two articles published in the same newspaper six days apart. Both articles were based on the same data. One article was by the United Press International and the other by the Associated Press—two of the most significant news sources in the world. The first was published in the August 20, 1972, edition of the *Los Angeles Times:*

LONDON SAFEST OF WORLD'S MAJOR CITIES

LONDON (UPI)—In an era of rising crime rates, London remains the safest of all great metropolises.

Most Londoners can't define it—perhaps it's the friendly, unarmed "bobbies," the placid British public, the reassuring red double-decked buses, the staid black beetle cabs—but for them there is a certain something that breeds a sense of security in a violent world.

The feeling is supported by statistics and, excluding strife-torn Northern Ireland, embraces the whole of the British Isles.

In many cases, especially crimes involving violence, the crime count actually is going down.

Muggings Rare
New York-type muggings with guns or knives were so rare in London last year they failed to rate a mention in the crime statistics. And in a metropolitan area with combined resident and transient population last year of about 16 million, there were only 6,000 purse-snatchings, pocket-pickings and other petty personal crimes.

That meant the odds against such a thing happening were about 2,500 to 1.

Police recorded only 77 cases of murder in London last year compared with at least 58 murders in a single week in New York in July of this year.

117 Murders in '71
There were 117 murders overall in England and Wales in 1971, or about three murders per million of the population. In West Germany, there were 700.[14]

---

[14] Reprinted by permission of United Press International, copyright 1972.

The second story appeared August 26, 1972, in the *Los Angeles Times:*

SERIOUS CRIME HITS NEW HIGH IN LONDON

LONDON (AP)—Serious crime in London reached a record high in the first six months of this year, with fraud and rape showing the biggest increases, Scotland Yard reported Friday. Rape was up 50%.

The categories listed in the report with the percentage increases over last year's six-month period were: violence up 10.3%, robbery up 18%, rape up 50%, shoplifting up 9.3%, fraud up 30.5%, and auto thefts up 11.4%.

The report said the June figure of 35,163 indictable offenses was the highest ever recorded in a month in the metropolitan area of London. The crime total for the January-to-June period was 181,899, up 7.8% from the same period of 1971.[15]

Support for both articles can be found in the data provided by the British government. Yet the interpretations of the two wire services leave entirely different impressions.

In summary, it must be mentioned that despite statistical problems, the FBI *Uniform Crime Reports* are the best collation of data on crime collected by any country in the world. The data do provide us with a reasonably good and useful profile of the nature and extent of traditional crime in the United States.

---

[15] Reprinted by permission of AP Newsfeatures.

PART Two

CHARACTERISTICS OF CRIMINAL BEHAVIOR

Chapter
4

The Victim Role and Crime

*T*he administration of justice involves three major societal components: (1) the criminal, (2) the general society, and (3) the victim. Each of these parties involved in the criminal situation deserves equity and protection under the law. The traditional focus of criminology has been almost exclusively on the criminal and society, and the role of the victim in crime has historically been shortchanged. As we approach the twenty-first century, greater emphasis is being placed on studying victims: their legal rights, the degree of emotional and physical harm perpetrated on them, their level of participation in the crime, and how to treat the short- and long-term harm they have experienced as victims.

This overall area of criminological analysis is often referred to as victimology. Victimology, simply defined, refers to the role of the victim in a crime, the degree of harm to the victim, therapeutic treatment of the victim, and ways of making restitution to victims of crimes.

In the following analysis I will focus on crime victims and will propose some general concepts related to how people become victims in their human relationships. My focus will be predominantly on crime victims; however, a better conceptualization and comprehension of how people become victims in life in general helps to understand the interaction that takes place between legally defined criminals and their victims.

A landmark contribution to understanding the interaction between criminals and victims is Hans von Hentig's provocative book *The Criminal and His Victim.*[1] In his book, in essence, von Hentig posits the

---

[1] Hans von Hentig, *The Criminal and His Victim* (New Haven: Yale University Press, 1948).

theory that crime has "a duet frame of reference," that on some level, more or less, victims are participants in their victimization. On the basis of my research into victimology, and building on von Hentig's viewpoint, victims can be perceived as participants in a crime on a scale of 0 to 10. For example, at the 0 level of participation, a victim is minding his or her own business in the normal course of life and is victimized by an unknown assailant. At a level of 9 or 10, the victim precipitates a violent interaction with another person by provoking or goading the other, who proceeds to inflict bodily harm on the provocateur. In this context the provocateur then becomes the victim. In effect, the provocateur has played a role in creating the situation in which he or she becomes a victim.

As a case in point, think of a driver who is cut off by another driver. The person who has been cut off has two main responses: to ignore the incident and continue on down the highway, or, as often actualized, to chase, pull over, and threaten the perpetrator. The perpetrator may then physically attack and cause bodily harm to the challenger. The victim had the option of continuing on down the highway and thus minimizing the situation, but instead has facilitated the crime.

In many criminal interactions, it is a toss-up as to who will, at the end of the scenario, become the victim and who will be the criminal. For example, in the much publicized case of Bernhard Goetz, four young men approached him on a subway and asked him for $5. They appeared to Goetz to be criminals about to mug him. When the target victim, Goetz, pulled out a gun and shot all four of the young men, he became the criminal and they became victims who had suffered bodily harm.

Many individuals start out as assailants and because they are "victim-prone," they become victims. Members of violent gangs are good examples of victim-prone people. Swaggering around in a macho-belligerent way in rival gang neighborhoods where they know they are unwelcome can often create a situation where they are victimized by an enemy gang. Many generally law-abiding citizens help in the process of their victimization by being careless with their property or through provoking an obviously hostile person to attack.

In the area of homicide and violence, criminologist Marvin Wolfgang, building on von Hentig's theories, carried out research that has contributed to our understanding of the victim role. On the basis of his research into over 588 consecutive homicides committed in Philadelphia from January, 1948, through December, 1952, Wolfgang concluded that 150 cases, or 26 percent, were what he terms "victim-precipitated homicide," which he explains as follows:

> In many crimes, especially in criminal homicide, the victim is often a major contributor to the criminal act. Except in cases in which the victim is an innocent bystander and is killed in lieu of an intended victim, or in cases in which a pure accident is involved, the victim may be one of the major precipitating causes of his own demise.

Various theories of social interaction, particularly in social psychology, have established the framework for the present discussion. In criminological literature, von Hentig, in *The Criminal and His Victim*, has provided the most useful theoretical basis for analysis of the victim-offender relationship. In Chapter XII, entitled "The Contribution of the Victim to the Genesis of Crime," the author discusses this "duet frame of crime."[2] In *Penal Philosophy*, [Gabriel] Tarde frequently attacks the "legislative mistake" of concentrating too much on premeditation and paying too little attention to motives, which indicate an important interrelationship between victim and offender.[3] And in one of his satirical essays, "On Murder Considered as One of the Fine Arts," Thomas De Quincey shows cognizance of the idea that sometimes the victim is a would-be murderer.[4] [Another criminologist, Raffaele] Garofalo, too, noted that the victim may provoke another individual into attack, and though the provocation be slight, if perceived [as an assault] by an egoistic attacker it may be sufficient to result in homicide.[5]

[Wolfgang provided many examples of the "victim-precipitator" patern of violence such as the two below.]

A drunken husband, beating his wife in their kitchen, gave her a butcher knife and dared her to use it on him. She claimed that if he should strike her once more, she would use the knife, whereupon he slapped her in the face and she fatally stabbed him.

The victim was the aggressor in a fight, having struck his enemy several times. Friends tried to interfere, but the victim persisted. Finally, the offender retaliated with blows, causing the victim to fall and hit his head on the sidewalk, as a result of which he died.[6]

Although victim-precipated homicide is obviously illegal and non-sanctioned, one can see some degree of rationality to it. Dr. George Bach, in a penetrating article based on his research into husband-wife murders, delineates the "rational" issues involved in spouse violence. Following is a summary statement of his research:

As an alternative to the sado-masochistic interpretation of violent spouse abuse, a quasi-romantic perspective sees abuse as a form of punishment of the partner who is experienced as the spoiler of the expectations, hopes and plans for a fulfilling long term, committed and attuned communion. He/she, who is perceived as the breaker of that intimate context, has to be penalized,

---

[2] von Hentig, *The Criminal and His Victim*, pp. 383–385.

[3] Gabriel Tarde, *Penal Philosophy* (Boston: Little, Brown, 1972), p. 466.

[4] Thomas De Quincey, "On Murder Considered as One of the Fine Arts," in *The Arts of Cheating, Swindling, and Murder* by Edward Bulwer-Lytton, Douglas Jerrold, and Thomas De Quincey (New York: Arnold, 1925), p. 153.

[5] Baron Raffaele Garofalo, *Criminology* (Boston: Little, Brown, 1914), p. 373.

[6] Marvin E. Wolfgang, "Victim-Precipitated Criminal Homicide," *Journal of Criminal Law, Criminology and Police Science* 48 (June 1957): 1. Reprinted by special permission of the *Journal of Criminal Law, Criminology and Police Science*. Copyright © 1957 by Northwestern University School of Law.

with the death-penalty being the extreme form of expression of outrage at the offense.

Both husbands who killed their wives, and wives who killed their husbands, in their interviews with the author displayed a deep commitment to their marriages. This explains why their leave-takings were so violent and their exits so final. By killing the spoiler they could bury and let go of their romantic dreams! Less lethal forms of spouse abuse-battering, enslavement, etc., often have the same element of punishment of the spoiler. . . .

[Dr. Bach asserts that] marital partners develop unrealistic expectations of their capacity for selfless caring, devotion and concern for each other's welfare. The painful suspicion that these high expectations will not be fulfilled arouses angry tensions. A common way of coping is to punish the spouse who is seen as having set up false expectations. The punishment for setting up false expectations may take the form of "spouse abuse," as well as the ultimate punishment of death.[7]

Dr. Bach delineates several factors that characterize abuse-prone man-woman bonds. The probability and intensity of violence increases with the number of factors or characteristics that are operative in a given couple's situation. Several of these factors reveal Bach's concept:

In our sample, the super-covert "nice people" tended to kill the relatively less covert more openly angry partners in a ratio of 3 to 1. . . . In our sample, 80% had severe power disparities, and we had more rebellious underdogs who killed their overbearing controllers than we had the bosses who delivered the "death penalty" to insubordinate followers.

Bach gives some examples that parallel Wolfgang's findings on victim-precipitated murder:

"I'll never let you go!" is a common enough warning—normally an attempt to block impulsive exits and prevent the love-object from falling into competitive hands. Usually the keeper will let the leaver go, especially if the leaver is unambiguous and straightforward about splitting. However, in our tragic cases, the supposedly-leaving partners tend to stick around intimidated. Sometimes a victim wants to get killed: "I feel so lousy, he might as well do away with me. It will get me out of my misery and he will get punished for it."

In the context of the research done by von Hentig, Wolfgang, and Bach, all of us are victims at some time in our lives. People tend to think of victimization in terms of an anonymous criminal offender. Most victimizers, however, are likely to be loved ones, friends, husbands, wives, employers, or parents who pollute others' lives by subjugating them in a victim role. In criminal interactions, over half of victims have some prior relationship with their offenders.

---

[7] George Bach, "Spouse Killing," *Journal of Contemporary Psychotherapy* 2, no. 2 (Fall/Winter 1980):91–105. Human Sciences Press, 72 Fifth Ave., New York, N.Y. 10011. Copyright © 1980.

THE PROCESS OF VICTIMIZATION

An analysis of the general process of victimization at the levels below violence or homicide provide insights into the general concept of victimization. *Webster's Dictionary* defines a victim as "one that is injured, destroyed, or sacrificed under any of various conditions." The degree of harm or hurt experienced by any victim is a unique subjective phenomenon that is difficult to measure, and people experiencing the same general kind of victimization tend to experience different levels of hurt and postvictimization response and damage.

The simplest human needs set a person up for victimization. The basic need for love can make a person vulnerable. The song "Looking for Love in All the Wrong Places" is a victim's lament—one of thousands of such songs. Desiring someone intensely sets a person up to ignore the other's obvious faults. Once a person becomes committed, it may be too late to pull out of a relationship and avoid the victim trap.

This trap is often the plight of the criminally assaulted battered spouse or family member. Some people are almost unerring in finding a person who at the outset of the relationship appears to be kind and loving but turns out to be a victimizer. As indicated, in over half of the various crimes of violence, the perpetrator is not a stranger but a spouse, family member, or "friend."

Victim Types

There are two basic types of offender-victim situations. One type involves a "crime" perpetrated by someone with whom the victim has an intimate or personal relationship. The offender can be a spouse or a loved one. This type includes battering husbands and wives, parents who abuse their children, and "lovers" who violate their partners. Intimate offenders are seldom prosecuted in the context of the law unless their crime is murder. The other type of offender-victim situation involves an anonymous offender, a stranger who commits an illegal crime against the victim.

Given these two types of offender-victim situations, there are generally three types of levels of identifiable victims: (1) nonparticipants, (2) victim-prone people, and (3) participating victims. On a scale of 0 to 10, nonparticipants are at 0, victim-prone people are at around 5, and participants often contribute to their victimization at a self-destructive level of 10.

1. *Nonparticipant Victims* These are people who are criminally harmed by an unknown assailant in the normal course of their lives. They are totally innocent and blameless. Children, for example, are usually nonparticipants in their victimization. Even though the offender is known to the victim, a child has limited

knowledge about the reality of the situation, and a child has little or no power to resist when placed in the victim role by a child-abusing adult.

Victims of anonymous criminals are not responsible for their unfortunate plight; however, they do have some control over their style of "combat" with their offender. For example, a woman "under siege" in a rape situation may use judiciousness in whether to fight back or not; and, in this regard, in some cases she may control the level of harm committed against her. In most cases with an anonymous offender, however, the victim has no responsibility for the criminal act.

2. *Victim-Prone People*   These are people who participate on some level in their own victimization by making themselves vulnerable to harm by another. They do not actively seek out a perpetrator, but they allow themselves to be victims because they have not taken realistic or obvious precautions to avoid becoming victimized. Some examples are people who are careless with their personal property; people who place themselves in "harm's way" in a violent bar or a hostile, strange neighborhood; and people who antagonize others who are obviously emotionally disturbed.

3. *Victim Precipitators and Participants*   These are people who consciously or unconsciously set themselves up as victims and therefore activate their own victimization. They are often people in search of a criminal victimizer. For example, some people frequently find themselves in unfulfilling relationships and have a proclivity for finding spouses who abuse them. These people are most likely to be very dependent. Their dependency needs make them vulnerable to victimization.

The main character in the book and film *Looking for Mr. Goodbar* was a woman who hooked up nightly in one-night stands, in some instances with sociopaths she picked up at bars. Such a person would be a good example of a victim precipitator.

Precipitators often initiate the interaction that results in their harm. For example, a victim-prone man might go to a bar, have a few drinks, and become belligerent and instigate a fight with a man twice his size. As a result of the fight he might be injured and end up in the hospital. There are many cases like this in which people precipitate their own victimization.

In another type of case that has similarities, a victim-prone participant in a therapy group I directed had, with great difficulty, exited from a relationship with an assaultive man. Three months after her separation she informed me she was in love with "a wonderful shy and gentle man." I saw her once a week on a regular basis. As if in a slow-motion film, she began to report in the group on how she and this formerly "wonderful" man were beginning to argue—and how their relationship was rather rapidly disintegrating into physical combat (a repeat of her former relationship). She, being the weaker of the two, was now being regularly abused by her "lover." This relationship was the fourth in a series over a three-year period. She had an uncanny ability for finding relationships with men who at the outset were "kind and gentle" but who rapidly began to victimize her. Her delusionary ability at entry was remarkable. She was able to incorrectly read the real person—who soon turned into her criminal victimizer.

FACTORS THAT CONTRIBUTE TO PLAYING THE VICTIM ROLE

My research into the criminal-victim interaction reveals several significant factors that seem to contribute to a person's enacting a victim-prone role. The factors include the following: (1) *A low self-concept or low self-esteem*—"I don't deserve any better." Many criminals have this problem, which often results from child abuse. A low self-concept often emanates from being devalued as a child. (2) *Delusions* about a relationship. This encourages victimization. The confidence artist, for example, about to criminally victimize a mark, is perceived by the incipient victim as really a legitimate investment broker. (3) *Familiarity with a victim's role.* The battered wife who states "That's the way my father treated my mother" reveals part of the reason that these individuals find and accept their victim roles. On some level they believe that they are fulfilling a "correct" role in their abusive relationships. In the following analysis, each of these victim factors will be discussed in greater detail.

Victim-Proneness and Self-concept

People who have a low self-concept or low self-esteem are more likely to be victim-prone than people who have a high regard for themselves. People with a low self-concept often feel they deserve what they get. People who were chastised during their early growth process and were habitually "put down" by their parents are likely to be victim-prone. They become accustomed to the role of "loser" and more accepting of this victim position in relationships.

Child abuse is usually a significant factor in this syndrome. The emotional, physical, and sexual abuse of children are problems that have existed for a long time. These issues have surfaced dramatically in recent years and have properly received considerable attention. Varied forms of child abuse—which basically involves treating children as objects of adult problems—have had an enormously deleterious impact on many children and their self-concepts. Children who are victims of these forms of abuse have great difficulty recovering from the abuse of their egos.

And, most regrettably, these same abused children will often act out the same problem on others later in life.

The dynamics of the replication of the problem operate as follows: People who are sexually, emotionally, or physically abused as children often develop a familiarity with the acts perpetrated on them and a rage about the powerless position in which they were placed. This may result in a motivation to assume the power role of abuser in their later life, in an effort to distance themselves as much as possible from the victim role. Also, in playing out the offender role later in life they ventilate their rage in the same type of situation in which they were formerly powerless.

I have observed hundreds of cases that substantiate this "transmission-belt" syndrome, in which the abused child later becomes the perpetrator of the same offense. There is considerable data that reveals this transmission belt of victimization rests on the foundations of a low self-concept.

The case of a boy I was attempting to treat in my work with delinquent adolescents reveals this pattern, in which the victim becomes the perpetrator. At the time I met Fred, he was 15. When he was 6, an older boy of 18 had criminally sodomized him several times against his will and threatened him with further violence if he "told." He finally reported the incidents to his father. His father, who beat him often "to discipline him," told him, "You probably brought it on yourself." Fred's father and mother did nothing about his reporting his abuse except to make him feel he was somehow responsible for his own victimization.

This led Fred to believe, on some level, that he was a person who "deserved what he got." Fred's low self-esteem was combined with a deep sense of injustice about the world. He was full of rage that was not understood by his parents, and he acted out the consequences of his own victimization on other victims. His acts spread the problem like a social virus.

When Fred was 15, out of hostility and a damaged self-concept, he began to criminally sexually abuse children. In several psychodramas I ran with him, it was revealed among other issues that he didn't feel sexually adequate and was unable to relate to girls his own age. He was afraid of them. He also was strongly motivated to overcome his lowly position in his victimization and become the transgressor. He was now the offender in the power position. Consequently, because of his rage about his own victimization, his low self-esteem, his familiarity with the behavior, and a strong motivation to be in the power position, Fred became a child molester himself.

Fred is one fairly typical example of the several hundred "victims" who became offenders with whom I have worked in psychodrama and group therapy. Most of these violently "acting-out" offenders have been victims of child abuse. And many of these children turn into hardened adult offenders. It is estimated, for example, that around 80 percent of all of the approximately 600,000 offenders doing time in American prisons were emotionally, physically, or sexually abused when they were children.

Many of these criminals were child-abuse victims of irresponsible "macho" fathers. A prototypical case is that of an 18-year-old youth I will call Mike. Mike was in a psychiatric hospital for the so-called criminally insane (where I worked) for, among other violent offenses, beating up another youth with a baseball bat. He was quite an intelligent youth who had been in therapy a long time. The following is his self-diagnosis of his plight:

> My father used to lock me in this room when I was a little kid around 5 or 6. And then when he came home from work, usually drunk, he used to beat the shit out of me. This went on for around seven years. When I became 13 I felt my power and I began to beat up on people. It felt good to get even with the world for what happened to me. I learned from my psychiatrist that part of why I do what I do as far as violence goes is connected to my feelings about myself. I don't care about myself. I don't care about me or what happens to me. I really hate my father. I have a lot of rage about what he did to me—and I take it out on the world.

A young woman named Alice, who was in the same group as Mike, began to cry when she heard his commentary. I asked her what was wrong. She talked about her own low self-concept that stemmed from a common cause for young women, sexual abuse:

> My father always put me down, too. And what happened to me is I became a victim of this motorcycle gang. I'm full of anger about how I let myself be fucked by all these creeps. I would get loaded and then they would pass me around.

I had Alice have a psychodramatic conversation with her former self. She became furious confronting this image of her own low self-esteem, and she began to scream at "herself" and how much she hated this "low-life victim." She was more angry at allowing herself to be a victim than at the offenders in her life. Given her insight into the problem, she vowed never to let it happen again.

People with a low self-concept or low self-esteem, like Mike or Alice, are more apt to play the victim role in a relationship because they do not feel they deserve any better. They can be easily coerced into accepting pain, humiliation, and the "short end" of a relationship. In contrast, people with high self-concepts are less susceptible to living out their lives in victim roles and becoming "born-to-lose" criminals.

The Delusion Factor in Victimization

Many victims I have studied have delusions about their victimizers and do not fully comprehend the reality of the situation in which the victimization takes place. The "delusion factor" involves an extravagant hope or delusion the victim has about the victimizer. For example, in the simplest, most absurd criminal confidence game, the victim deludes himself or herself into a belief that they can actually buy a money machine that converts $10 bills into $100 bills. In most cases of criminal spousal abuse that I have studied, victims stay in abusive relationships not necessarily because they are masochistic—but because they believe on some delusional level that their spouses will magically change into loving, affectionate people. There is often a tinge of reality to the situation since most abusers do act loving for brief periods of time. Participating victims almost *always* have a level of delusion that keeps them in their victim role.

The following summary statements by criminal victims I have treated or interviewed help to illuminate this point:

A *33-year-old housewife:* "Bill will stop drinking and being as-saultive with me and the children. There are weeks when he is a model husband and father. When he drinks he is wild and nasty—but he'll change. Yes, I know he's been abusing me for 12 years—but I have a dream that he'll change. I have to believe that, and that's why I stay with him."

A *70-year-old retired man:* "When I gave my life savings of $50,000 in payment for these worthless stocks to that vicious con man, I believed what he told me. He was a fast talker, but he had a nice office and he assured me the value would double in one year. I had this dream that with the $100,000 my wife and I could move to Hawaii and live in style for the rest of our lives. My optimistic hope made me a vulnerable victim."

A *15-year-old incest victim:* "My stepfather began to sexually abuse me from the time I was 10 till now. I kept it a secret because I hoped it would stop. He always told me before he did it to me that it would stop, and this would be the last time. Sometimes he would cry and beg me to keep it a secret because that would be the last time. I really didn't believe him, but I hoped and prayed that it would end someday. It went on for six horrible years."

A *25-year-old female office worker:* "Why do I keep going back to the singles bars and that sleazy scene where I always end up a loser? You're right, I have had some really rotten times. In the last year, I was almost raped twice, and, yes, I have picked up a disease or two. When something bad like that happens I quit going for a while. Then I began to think—who knows? You know, hope springs eternal. I guess I am a victim of the dream we all have that next Saturday night I'll meet Mr. Right."

A *40-year-old woman in prison for killing her husband:* "I was the high school cheerleader who married the football hero. At first life was good. After the first year of bliss, he began to drink and became constantly abusive. It escalated into weekly beatings—sometimes in front of the kids. I hung on for almost 15 years, then I couldn't take it anymore. I left because I began to feel it was hopeless. We reconciled about five times, so I guess my dream was revived a few times. . . . Finally, I warned him to stay away. I was really through with him. The night of the murder, he came to my apartment unannounced, broke the door open, and began to assault me. I went into the bedroom, got out the loaded gun I had bought for protection, and killed him. As I looked at him on the floor, I had a sense of relief. There would be no more fear, and I felt better knowing my stupid dream of an idealized romance was dead on the floor with the body of my husband."

All these examples have one thing in common: the victims were all vulnerable because they each had *delusionary* dreams about their victimizers. The ideas were delusionary because there was very little chance that they could become reality. Almost all participatory victimization begins with a false dream.

One of my basic hypotheses about victimization is that people are most vulnerable when they delude themselves about a relationship and situation they are in or entering. Moreover, people who maintain a delusion that things will change, or that the offender will stop the negative behavior, simply perpetuate their victim role in the relationship or the crime situation.

Hope seems to spring eternal in victims that their offenders will cease to harm them. This delusion of hope is often necessary for their survival during a difficult episode or period of life.

The Holocaust, a staggering and horrendous case of mass murder, was possibly perpetuated in part by the delusion on the part of the victims and the society that this level of murder and suffering was not humanly possible. It is impossible to summarily analyze a phenomenon of such epic social, historical, and psychological proportions—yet the delusion factor played a part in the catastrophe. Isaac Bashevis Singer, the brilliant Nobel Prize–winning writer, revealed in a television interview the role of the delusion factor in the Holocaust in his response to a question about his early years in a Polish ghetto that was tyrannized by the Nazis:

It was a civilized city: trolley cars, theaters, beautiful restaurants, museums. It was far from being the Middle Ages. I decided to leave in 1935 because Hitler was a neighbor and he promised to invade Poland any day. I just ran away for dear life. There were other Jews who also knew he was coming but stayed. We don't know why people act the way they do. Of course, poor Jews had no choice. They could not get a passport. Many rich people did leave. Many people didn't want to leave their apartments, their property; they thought, "Well, the enemy will come and after a while they would make peace."

This delusion, that the Nazi criminals would make peace, or that what happened was not humanly possible, cost the lives of millions of victims in the Holocaust, and it accounted in part for the murder of over 10 million people in one of the most homicidal events in recorded history.

Learning a Victim's Life Script

Children often tend to emulate the same-sex parent's role in their own adult lives. A boy who sees his father in a criminal role or a daughter who sees her mother in a victim role often emulates that role in later life. They do this, in part, because they see it as a familiar role and they identify with it. In this way the script for a future life as a victim is psychologically implanted in them.

A cogent TV documentary, "When Women Kill," about women who have murdered their abusing husbands or lovers, revealed the dynamics of learning a victim's script. One woman shown in the documentary had killed her husband after eight years of being violently assaulted by him. She described her life with him and the murder as follows:

> He beat me up at least twice a week—especially when he was drunk. He also fooled around a lot with other women, and then he would accuse me of having boyfriends. He used to slap and kick me. He broke my nose; he kicked me in the face with steel-toed shoes that he wore at work. He kept accusing me of having a boyfriend and I didn't. He wouldn't let up, so finally I said in anger, "If you think I'm cheating, I am." Then he said, "You old whore, I'll kill you." When I heard him firing shots in the bedroom in a drunken rage, I started to scream. He said, "I'm going to kill you." Then I saw the gun in his hand. Somehow I grabbed it from him, and I turned the gun on him. I jabbed it into his stomach and began pulling the trigger. They told me later I killed him with six shots.

One point about this violent episode is that it followed the pattern of victim-precipitated homicide described by Wolfgang: the final "victim" brought about his own demise from the primary victim after years of abuse. But a fundamental question is, why did this woman allow herself to take this abuse for eight years?

A partial answer is found in the "murderer's" own statement, in which she related how she learned her victim role in her family:

> My father physically abused my mother all during my childhood. When my husband began to assault me, I thought that's what husbands are supposed to do. To me, getting beat up seemed to be part of marriage. Only, he just went too far. I guess I accepted his beatings, that was familiar and acceptable, but I wasn't going to let him kill me.

A significant problem with these familiar abusive life scripts is that they are passed on from one generation to the next. Following is the commentary of the daughter of this same woman who killed her husband. It appears that she was acting out the same horrendous life script her mother had followed.

> My husband came home drunk one day. I had something on the stove. He threw it on the floor. Then he told me to clean it up. He told me to get down on my hands and knees and do it. I was pregnant with my second child, and there I was on the floor cleaning up this mess. While I was down on my hands and knees, he threw this glass pitcher at me. It shattered all over the floor. He then began kicking me while I was down on the floor, and he kept yelling to clean it up right, because if our kid or him cut their feet with glass, I was really going to get it.
>
> He would do these mean things and then say he was going to change and never do it again. Things would be okay for a few days and then he would do it again. One day he took a butcher knife after me. I'm lucky I'm still alive. To me, it just seemed like part of marriage. My grandfather beat my grandmother. My father beat my mother. The two husbands I had both beat me up. For me, in a way, getting beat up meant he loved me. That's what I saw in my family.

The basic point here is that the victim role and an accepting response was transmitted to these three generations of women. They all were familiar with and identified with this victim's script because they grew up with it. This three-generation case illustrates the victim problem of tens of thousands of people in American society, especially women.

How do we break this criminal cycle when the victim role is learned in families? A 15-year-old girl named Sally, who was in a psychodrama group I directed in a psychiatric hospital, was intent on breaking her family cycle of criminal victimization. After she had developed some insight into the problem, she told me about her goals in this regard:

> After being here in the hospital for over a year, I learned my mother had been an incest victim like me. Her stepfather abused her sexually. She had very low self-esteem, and she figured she didn't deserve much as a person. So she became involved with around four assholes—stepfathers who acted as if they were my father. They all abused me sexually—since I was 8. My mother must have known about it before I told her when I was 12. But she played dumb, and, anyway, she didn't see anything too wrong with it because, after all, it happened to her, too. She knew the territory.
>
> Now that I've been here all this time talking to psychiatrists and here in psychodrama, I've figured out how terrible those abuses have made me feel about myself. The way I was treated I felt like a piece of meat, or, really, a piece of shit.
>
> The thing I've learned in my therapy is that I have a lot of fear about doing this to my child—just like my mother. Because I feel shitty about myself, and I've seen the way my mother picked these low-life punks, I may do the same thing and wind up with husbands who will do this to my child.
>
> With the help of the therapists here, I'm beginning to learn I'm not a bad person, and maybe I'll feel I deserve more than my mother ever got from a

man. I've decided it will never happen to any child I have. I'm just not going to let it happen. I think enough of myself so I'll never marry a man who would do to my child what happened to me. I know from my psychiatrist that I have this kind of victim's life script, but I want to rewrite it.

In effect, Sally did escape from the criminal sexual abuse syndrome. Her therapy and insights worked—and at the age of 20, she became a peer counselor to other children who were sexually abused. She now has children, and, according to her, "a reasonable husband who is not abusive."

Before I discuss other methods and techniques for dealing with the victim problem, it is important to identify another aspect of victimology, the concept of the co-victim.

THE CONCEPT OF THE CO-VICTIM AND DOUBLE VICTIMIZATION

Almost everyone in American society has suffered at some time in their lives from the criminal victimizations of a friend or family member. When any person is victimized, it necessarily produces co-victims. These are people who are harmed along with the primary victim because they are an emotional part of the victim's social sphere. Some co-victims suffer more than the primary victim. In extreme cases, when a child is hurt or killed, the family often becomes lifelong victims.

For example, the survivors of a murdered child clearly become co-victims of the crime perpetrated on their child. Organizations like Parents of Murdered Children and MADD (Mothers Against Drunk Driving) reflect the increasing awareness by people of the concept of co-victims when a crime is perpetrated on a family member. My observation is that most of these organizations provide a form of group therapy for people who share the common pain of having had loved ones victimized. MADD may be an organization primarily devoted to getting criminal drunk drivers convicted in court; however, "revenge" in court against such criminals can also be a therapeutic catharsis for parent co-victims of the crime.

The revenge of a co-victim family member may simply be a judicial situation, in which justice is properly meted out by the courts. Too often, however, justice is not done and the co-victims are left with feelings of rage toward the criminal who has victimized their loved one.

In many cases, especially where a homicide has been perpetrated, our adversary system of justice inadvertently continues to punish the victim and the victim's family. Part of this problem is that in mounting a proper defense for the acknowledged murderer, the killer's defense attorney often places the dead victim on trial.

Obviously, the victim's role in his or her own demise is not presented; the person is dead and is not present in court to give the other side of the story. The admitted murderer can concoct any kind of bizarre excuse as a defense.

The Preppie Murder

A bizarre case that illustrates some of these issues is the so-called preppie murder. Here, the viewpoint of the self-admitted killer, Robert Chambers, was presented in court. The story that would have been told by the victim, Jennifer Levin, remains a mystery; and her parents, sitting at the trial as co-victims, were punished twice. An article in the April 4, 1988, issue of *Time* magazine describes the case:

> The basic facts were not in doubt. At 4:30 A.M., on August 26, 1986, Robert Chambers, 19, and Jennifer Levin, 18, left a popular hangout on New York City's Upper East Side and ventured into Central Park. There, just before dawn, the 6-ft. 4-in. college dropout killed Levin with his bare hands. Though Chambers confessed to this much, an eight-man, four-woman jury struggled last week, after nine days of deliberations, to determine exactly how and why he killed a girl with whom he had previously had a casual affair.
>
> For more than a year and a half, lurid details of the tragedy had splashed across the local tabloids: an apparent sex killing involving attractive, affluent young club-goers gave many New Yorkers both a voyeuristic tingle and an uncomfortable shudder of recognition. Throughout the eleven-week trial, arguments centered on the few seconds when Levin's life was extinguished. Did Chambers inadvertently kill her while blinded by pain during rough sex, as he maintained? Or did he strangle her purposely after becoming enraged by taunts of sexual inadequacy as the prosecution suggested?
>
> Chambers' attorney, Jack Litman, portrayed Levin as sexually aggressive and tipsy the night in question. Reportedly, she had approached Chambers at a trendy bar; Chambers, depressed by a friend's death and his own bouts with drugs, was reluctant. Still, they walked to nearby Central Park, where, the young man claimed, he rejected her advances.
>
> Chambers told the police that Levin became sexually playful, first tying his hands behind his neck with her panties, then straddling his body and fondling him. Chambers claimed that he remained uninterested and told her to let him go. Instead, said Chambers, she began squeezing his testicles. In the defense version of events, the frenzied young man freed his hand and hooked his arm around Levin's neck, flipping her over and accidentally crushing her throat. To support this scenario, the defense summoned Los Angeles County Chief Medical Examiner Dr. Ronald Kornblum, who testified that such a choke hold could have killed the victim in as little as five seconds.
>
> The prosecution had difficulty establishing a convincing motive for the crime, so Assistant District Attorney Linda Fairstein concentrated on the act of killing. "There was no sex, only death," Fairstein told the jurors, urging them to focus on how the vivacious brunette had died. Fairstein showed grisly photos of Levin's facial injuries to make the point that Chambers must

have beaten her during a prolonged struggle in which the girl had been fighting for her life.

For more than a week, the jury grappled with the question of Chambers' intentions. Did he purposely kill Levin (second-degree murder)? Did he mean to cause serious injury that resulted in her death (first-degree manslaughter)? Did he act recklessly (second-degree manslaughter)? Or did he choose to ignore the fact that his actions might lead to her death (criminally negligent homicide)?

In an unexpected turn late last week, as a possible mistrial loomed, the prosecution and defense struck a bargain. On Friday evening Chambers changed his plea to first-degree manslaughter. Asked by Judge Howard Bell whether he had intended to cause "serious injury" to Levin, the rock-jawed, glassy-eyed Chambers, who had shown no remorse during the proceedings, replied, "Looking back on everything, I have to say yes. But in my heart, I didn't mean it to happen." Chambers faces 5 to 15 years in prison, instead of the 25 years to life that he would have received for a second-degree-murder conviction.[8]

During the trial, the victim's parents became brutalized co-victims by having to endure the bizarre allegations made by the murderer of their daughter. They were not allowed a voice in the courtroom to respond to this judicial rape of their murdered daughter.

The Dominique Dunne Case

Another homicide that reveals the co-victim issue and placing the victim on trial was the horrendous homicide and murder trial of Dominique Dunne.

Ms. Dunne was an actress in her twenties who had a starring role in the original *Poltergeist* film. She had had a stormy romantic affair with a young man about her age, John Sweeney, who worked as a chef at a famous restaurant in Los Angeles. Because he had been physically and emotionally abusive, she broke off their relationship.

On the evening of October 30, 1982, around 9 P.M., Ms. Dunne was rehearsing a script with another young man when Sweeney appeared at the front door of her house unannounced. He rang the bell and through the door cajoled her into letting him ask for another chance to resume their relationship. She agreed to step out on the porch and talk to him for a few minutes. According to the actor who overheard the conversation, Ms. Dunne told Sweeney that there was no chance of reconciliation. When the argument grew louder the actor called the police, who responded within five minutes. By the time the police arrived Ms. Dunne was dead on the porch floor, a victim of strangulation. Sweeney admitted that he had strangled her but said, "I didn't think I choked her that hard. I just lost my temper and blew it again."

---

[8] Eugene Linden, "The Preppie Killer Cops a Plea," in *Time*, April 4, 1988, p. 22. Copyright 1988 Time Inc. Reprinted by permission.

Why would Ms. Dunne see this violent man one more time? Like many people in this type of "victimizer-victim" combat relationship, Ms. Dunne apparently wanted to make it a clean break. According to a friend of hers who was familiar with the situation, "Dominique definitely wanted out, but she was a nice person who wanted to end it clean. She told me she was going to make a final effort to have Sweeney understand and accept the break." She wanted to end the relationship rationally with a man who was clearly irrational. Like many victims, she was suffering under the delusion that she could bring it off. She paid for this delusion with her life.

Dominque's family were clearly co-victims in the murder. They were not only subjected to the loss of their daughter and sister, but they were victimized again by the court processes that dealt with her murderer, John Sweeney.

Dominick Dunne, her father and a professional writer, described how he and his family were victimized by the "administration of justice" in an article in the March, 1984, issue of *Vanity Fair*. His commentary may be more revealing than the words of most parents of victims, because of his literary talent. He incisively reveals a commonly felt set of emotions by many people who regrettably become co-victims of a crime.

> The night on the news we watched John Sweeney being arraigned for Dominque's murder, he was accompanied by the defense team of Michael Adelson and Joseph Shapiro. As we watched, we all began to feel guilty for not having spoken out our true feelings about Sweeney when there was still time to save Dominique from him. In the days that followed, her friends began to tell us how terrified she was of him during the last weeks of her life. I found out for the first time that five weeks previously he had assaulted her and choked her, and that she had escaped from him and broken off her relationship with him. Fred Leopold, a family friend and the former mayor of Beverly Hills, told us during a condolence call that he had heard from a secretary in his law office that John Sweeney had severely beaten another woman a year or so earlier. We passed on this information to Detective Harold Johnston, who stayed close to our family during those days. [Mr. Dunne reflects here on a commonly felt regret by co-victims that they might have prevented the tragedy that befell their loved one, if they had intervened.]
>
> On my first day back in New York after the funeral, I was mugged leaving the subway at twelve noon in Times Square. I thought I was the only person on the stairway. I was ascending to the street, but suddenly I was grabbed from behind and pulled off balance. I heard the sound of a switchblade opening, and a hand—which was all I ever saw of my assailant—reached around and held the knife in front of my face. From out of my mouth came a sound of rage that I did not know I was capable of making. It was more animal than human, and I was later told it had been heard a block away. Within seconds people came running from every direction. In his panic, my assailant superficially slashed my chin with the blade of his knife, but I had beaten him. I had both my wallet and my life, and I realized that uncourageous as I am about physical combat, I would have fought before

giving in. Whoever that nameless, faceless man was, to me he was John Sweeney. [This incident reveals the way in which the co-victim's life and behavior are significantly changed by the criminal event.]

If Dominique had been killed in an automobile accident, horrible as that would have been, at least it would have been over and mourning could have begun. A murder is an ongoing event until the day of the sentencing, and mourning has to be postponed. After several trips west for preliminary hearings, I returned to Los Angeles in July for the trial.

It is the fashion among the criminal fraternity to find God, and Sweeney, the killer, was no exception. He arrived daily in the courtroom clutching a Bible, dressed in black, looking like a sacristan. The Bible was a prop; Sweeney never read it, he just rested his folded hands on it. He also wept regularly. One day the court had to be recessed because he claimed the other prisoners had been harassing him before he entered, and he needed time to cry in private. I could not believe that jurors would buy such a performance.

A former girlfriend of Sweeney's, Lillian Pierce, in her testimony, revealed that Sweeney was a classic abuser of women. She said that on ten separate occasions during their two-year relationship he had beaten her. She had been hospitalized twice, once for six days, once for four. Sweeney had broken her nose, punctured her eardrum, collapsed her lung, thrown rocks at her when she tried to escape from him. She had seen him, she said, foam at the mouth when he lost control and smash furniture and pictures. As she spoke, the courtroom was absolutely silent. . . . [For some peculiar legal reason, the Judge ruled that Lillian Pierce's testimony was not admissible in the trial. This was a source of great chagrin to the Dunne family.]

The loss of the Lillian Pierce testimony was a severe blow to the D.A., Steven Barshop. Our hopes were buoyed by Barshop's opening argument in the case. He began with a description of the participants. Sweeney: 27, 6 ft. 1-in, 170 pounds. Dominique: 22, 5 ft. 1-in., 112 pounds. . . . He said that the coroner would testify that death by strangulation took between four and six minutes. Then he held up a watch with a second hand and said to the jury, "Ladies and Gentlemen, I am going to show you how long it took for Dominique Dunne to die." For four minutes the courtroom sat in hushed silence. It was horrifying. I had never allowed myself to think how long she had struggled in his hands, thrashing for her life. A gunshot or a knife stab is over in an instant; a strangulation is an eternity. The only sound during the four minutes came from John Sweeney and his lawyer, who whispered together the whole time.

Our daily presence in the courtroom annoyed Sweeney's lawer, Adelson, throughout the trial. Defense lawyers in general don't like jurors to see the victim's family. Friends of ours had advised us to leave town until the trial was over. The organization known as Parents of Murdered Children advised us to attend every session. "It's the last business of your daughter's life," a father of a young girl stabbed to death by a former boyfriend said to me on the telephone one night. We sat in the front row behind the bailiff's desk in full view of the jury; Lenny [Dominique's mother] in the aisle in her wheelchair, Alex, Griffin [Dominique's brothers] and I. We were within six feet of John Sweeney. As the weeks crept by, the boys became more and more silent. It seemed to me as if their youth were being stripped away from them.

In the row behind us sat representatives from Parents of Murdered Children; some had been through their trials, others were awaiting theirs. Many of Dominique's friends came on a daily basis; so did friends of ours and friends of the boys. There were also representatives from "Women Against Violence Against Women" and from "Victims for Victims," the group started by Theresa Saldana, an actress who was brutally stabbed a few years ago and survived.

"If any member of the Dunne family cries, cries out, rolls his eyes, exclaims in any way, he will be asked to leave the courtroom," we were told by the judge at the behest of Adelson.

From the beginning we had been warned that the defense would slander Dominique. It is part of the defense premise that the victim is responsible for the crime. As Dr. Willard Gaylin says in his book, *The Killing of Bonnie Garland*, Bonnie Garland's killer, Richard Herrin, murdered Bonnie all over again in the courtroom. It is always the murder victim who is placed on trial. John Sweeney, who claimed to love Dominique, and whose defense was that this was a crime of passion, slandered her in court as viciously and cruelly as he had strangled her. It was agonizing for us to listen to him, led on by Adelson, besmirch Dominique's name. His violent past remained sacrosanct and inviolate, but her name was allowed to be trampled upon and kicked, with unsubstantiated charges, by the man who killed her.[9]

The jury in this case concluded the offense was voluntary manslaughter, and that the earlier choking attack was a misdemeanor assault. The maximum sentence for the two charges was six and a half years, and with good time and work time, Sweeney could be paroled automatically, without having to go through a parole hearing, after he had served half his sentence. Since the time spent in jail between arrest and the sentencing counted as time served, Sweeney could be free after two and a half more years. The fact that justice was *not* done in this case intensified the harm and pain perpetrated on the Dunne family in their co-victim roles. This is too common a phenomenon in a criminal justice system that focuses almost entirely on the offender—with limited regard for the victim and co-victims.

The case also reveals the manner in which too many victims and co-victims are punished twice in the administration of justice: one time by the crime, the second time by the judicial process. This negative impact of double-victimization of victims and their families occurs in too many trials.

Sweeney was released from prison in 1987, and the Dunne family still agonizes over his short sentence for the murder of Dominique Dunne.

---

[9] Dominick Dunne, in *Vanity Fair*, March 1984.

SOCIETY AND THE VICTIM ROLE: THE GOETZ CASE

The average compassionate citizen is victimized daily by the horrendous crimes reported in the mass media. Feeling people respond to the atrocious crimes they witness on a daily basis in the press and on television. Some people become inured to this crime problem, but others are victimized daily through their emotional identification with crime victims.

A particular subway shooting received an avalanche of mass media coverage and catalyzed an outburst of divergent emotional reactions, polarizing American society. It is easy to describe what happened on the New York subway, though the bare facts do not tell the whole story.

Bernhard Goetz, while riding on a subway, according to his later testimony, was minding his own business when he was approached by four young black men who asked him for $5. Goetz had been robbed before, and from his viewpoint, he believed he was about to be robbed again. He pulled out a gun he had been carrying for protection and systematically shot each of his perceived assailants. Three of his assailants recovered from the gunshot wounds, and one was paralyzed by the gunshot wounds, probably for life. All of the alleged muggers had criminal records.

The citizenry of the United States projected a variety of interpretations onto this "Rorschach-like" criminal event. At one pole, some saw Goetz as a hero justifiably acting out a necessary collective societal revenge on criminals who victimize law-abiding citizens. At the other extreme, some saw him as a vicious racist vigilante who had unjustifiably attacked four young men who were members of a minority group. In a sense, the Goetz case became an interesting Rorschach test: society projected a variety of interpretations onto this criminal event.

A penetrating essay by Charles Krauthammer in the January 21, 1985, issue of *Time* magazine analyzed the range of societal projections onto the case:

> Rarely, apart from assassinations of the famous, has the act of a single anonymous person caused such a stir. Mild-mannered Bernhard Goetz gets on a New York City subway. Four young toughs surround him, asking first for a match, next a cigarette, then $5. He pulls a gun, shoots them all, two in the back. He runs away, then nine days later turns himself in. The town goes wild for him. Dubbed the subway vigilante, he is the talk, the toast, of every radio call-in show from Miami to San Diego. The outpouring of popular support becomes a story in itself. Mayors, governors and editorialists express dismay.
>
> How can good, decent citizens react this way?
>
> The short answer is rage, directed first at Goetz's harassers. It is hard for anyone to muster much sympathy for them or their Miranda rights. The loathing for these villians/victims is universal. Columnist Jimmy Breslin says it is because of race. The four youths are black, Goetz is white. There

may be some truth to that, but it does not begin to explain things. Millions of blacks and Hispanics ride the New York subways. Interviews with most show them to be as sympathetic to Goetz and as hostile to his attackers as whites.

Curtis Sliwa, leader of the Guardian Angels, gives a better clue. Interrupting a string of choice etymological epithets by which he characterizes the "muggers," he observes that they were not stealing for food. The $5 they wanted was to play video games.

This is violence of a special kind, not "brother, can you spare a dime" stuff but anarchic, pointless, *Clockwork Orange* violence. It is particularly reviled because it is perfectly senseless. We tend to call serial murders senseless, but we know that buried deep inside a Wayne Williams lies a horrible, though perhaps unfathomable, purpose. We suspect a reason, some powerful, twisted logic. Anomic violence, on the other hand, is truly senseless. Thus crimes of madness elicit from us revulsion; crimes of need (like Jean Valjean's) sympathy; but crimes for fun, for a video game, for no purpose, elicit rage.[10]

There was sufficient evidence for indicting and trying Goetz, the victim turned criminal. On June 16, 1987, he was acquitted of charges of assault and attempted murder but found guilty of illegal possession of a handgun. On March 5, 1989, the New York State Board of Parole ruled that he had to serve a one-year prison term minus time off for good behavior. Goetz began serving his sentence on January 13, 1989.

Many issues were raised in the Goetz case. Among them was the fact that Goetz transformed the situation when he began shooting, by becoming a criminal in the eyes of the law rather than a victim. The legal issue of probable cause is a debatable matter. Was Goetz a vigilante, or did he act in a way that any reasonable person might legally act in a similar situation? In his book *A Crime of Self Defense: Goetz and the Law*, law professor George Fletcher stated, "The case was a cliff-hanger legally and morally . . . the jury had doubts about whether Goetz had grounds for self-defense."[11] A clear effect of the case was that Goetz tapped into a large reservoir of rage and revenge felt by many people in American society who have in their lifetimes been victims or co-victims of crimes.

SOME IMPACTS OF VICTIMIZATION AND ITS TREATMENT

The Goetz case became a cause célèbre because many people identified with Goetz's "fighting-back" spirit. The fact is, however, that many

---

[10] Charles Krauthammer, "Toasting Mr. Goetz," in *Time*, January 21, 1985, p. 76. All rights reserved. Reprinted by permission from TIME.

[11] George Fletcher, *A Crime of Self Defense: Goetz and the Law* (New York: Free Press, 1988).

victims do not even report the crimes perpetrated on them. On this issue, Dean G. Kilpatrick summarized one study as follows:

> A sample of 391 adult females were interviewed about lifetime criminal victimization experiences, crime reporting, and psychological impact. In total, 75% of the sample (n = 295) had been victimized by crime, and 41.4% of all crimes were reported to the police. Reporting rates differed by crime type. Burglary had the highest reporting rate (82.4%); and sexual assault the lowest (7.1%). Of all crime victims, 27.8% subsequently developed post-traumatic stress disorder (PTSD). Major implications are the following: prevalence rates are extremely high and reporting rates are low.[12]

Secret Victims

In my research on victims, especially with basically normal people, I have been amazed at the large number of people who were victims yet never reported the crimes perpetrated on them to the police. These people were secret victims, as children, of sexual and physical abuse. These constitute a large number of unreported crimes. I have found this secret crime phenomenon in both normal college students and other segments of the general population I have studied. For example, in my criminology classes, when I lecture on victimology I often probe the students on their victim roles. I am often amazed at the number of individuals who reveal how they were secret victims.

Secret victims are people who carry the burden of their early victimizations into their later adult lives and, therefore, never have their problem treated or resolved. A large proportion of people in American society are secret victims.

The following interview reveals a regrettable situation that unfortunately is not an unusual one for many women who are secret victims of crime. The woman, Carol, is now 22 and asserts that she is disabled from having a relationship with a man because her father abused her when she was a child:

> When I was around 9 my dad would French-kiss me and stroke and fondle me and ask me who I belonged to—until I said, "I belong to you, Daddy." He wouldn't stop. I hated it. My father was very threatening and told me to never tell my mother about what we did. He said it was our secret and never, never tell anyone. There was no sexual penetration, but lots of fondling and touching.
>
> At the time I started school, I started eating uncontrollably because I was in charge of what I could eat, and maybe if I got real fat he wouldn't like me so much or find me attractive. I got horrendously fat, and the fooling around stopped. It worked! I saw closet monsters for years and still suffer

---

[12] Dean G. Kilpatrick, "Criminal Victimization: Lifetime Prevalence, Reporting to Police, and Psychological Impact," *Crime and Delinquency* 33, no. 4 (October 1987):479. Copyright 1987 by *Crime and Delinquency*. Reprinted by permission of Sage Publications, Inc.

from paranoia which I'm in therapy for. This whole incident came out in therapy under hypnosis *because* I had suppressed it and needed to deal with it. My parents divorced when I was 11, and I went to a foster home because neither one wanted to take care of the three of us. To this day, I call my foster parents Mom and Dad and feel as if their home is my home.

My real mother was so out of it, she acted as if she didn't know what was going on. And even if it had become public knowledge, she probably would've been noncommittal and denied it happened. She had no sensitivity. She died when I was 19 years old. I didn't even shed a tear. You can't cry for someone you never had.

I hardly saw my real father when I was growing up, and I felt that was a plus in my life. A few years ago he remarried and he invited me over for a visit. When I first walked in he complimented me and told me I looked very nice. Later, with his new wife next to him, he said, "Look, isn't she beautiful?" And just before I was getting ready to leave, he looked me up and down very slowly, licked his lips, and said, "You look delicious." When I got to my car, I threw up.

Sometimes when I'm driving down the freeway and I see a man in a car look at me, I have to pull off at the next exit because I'm scared. I feel like my body isn't mine, and I'm never going to be in control of it. And this is 13 years later! I am incapable of having a real relationship with a man because of what my father did to me.

Carol's case is somewhat extreme. It is, however, representative of the way many young girls are secretly victimized, and it does reveal some of the deleterious consequences of this type of child abuse. It reflects the impacts of a victimization phenomenon that happens to too many women on some level, from fondling to rape, in our society. The maintenance of this type of victimization as a secret, kept by both the man and the woman involved, compounds the original problem.

I have found many secret victims in the criminal population. The victimization issue surfaces in individual and group therapy—and in part explains their criminal behavior.

Psychological Impact

In regard to the psychological impact of crime, a study by Arthur J. Lurigio reported the following:

Samples of crime victims (burglary, robbery, felonious assault) and nonvictims were compared to examine the short-term differential and generalized effects of crime on psychological, behavioral, and attitudinal measure. Victims were more likely to report experiencing high levels of vulnerability, fear, and symptomology, and lower levels of self-efficacy. Also, victims were more likely to engage in protective behaviors. There were fewer differences, however, among the three groups of crime victims. Burglary victims were more likely to report feeling vulnerable and fearful, while assault victims were more likely to express more negative views of the police.

The existing literature on the psychological effects of criminal victimization is limited in several important respects. One notable gap in our knowledge about the effects of crime is an explicit documentation of its differential impact on victims of different categories of offenses, which lie between the extremes of obviously very serious (e.g., rape) and not-so-serious crimes (e.g., petty theft). Other limitations in our knowledge stem from the failure of prior investigations to include a control group of nonvictims for a baseline comparison of generalized effects, and to examine the impact of victimization across a variety of dependent variables. In the present study, we sought to overcome these shortcomings. Our efforts were aimed at exploring both the generalized effects of crime by comparing victims against a control group of nonvictims and the differential effects of crime by comparing separate groups of burglary, robbery, and nonsexual assault victims. We made these comparisons on a range of basic psychological, behavioral, and attitudinal measures.[13]

Lurigio's research revealed some of the effects of crime on victims. There are many factors that affect the impact of the crime on the victim and the recovery of people who become victims. My research and therapeutic work with victims reveals that the differences are related to the following three factors.

1. *The Horrendousness of the Offense*   Verbal abuse, bodily harm, and the level of physical assault and humiliation the crime victim has been subjected to are factors affecting the person's level of victimization harm. Someone who is severely physically or emotionally scarred may never fully recover from the experience. Some victims, like the Ancient Mariner, go through life repeatedly analyzing their plight in their dreams and meditations and will tell anyone who will listen about their suffering.

2. *Personality Prior to Victimization*   A person who has a solid level of mental health prior to being victimized is more likely to recover from a criminal act than is a person who already has emotional difficulties prior to victimization. For example, in a post-rape therapy group of ten women, one 21-year-old woman had been raped when she was 14. She was still a victim—seven years later—despite the fact that she had undergone therapy and had been involved with a number of groups for rape victims. She had had severe emotional problems when she was 14. The rape exacerbated her problems and gave her a "hook" on which to hang some of her pre-rape problems. The combination of her former problems, the crime, and her post-rape emotions made her life most difficult and blockaded her exit from the victim role.

   In the same group was a 21-year-old woman, a college graduate with a good job, who had been raped six months earlier. She was making excellent progress in becoming devictimized. In

---

[13] Authur J. Lurigio, "Are All Victims Alike? The Adverse, Generalized, and Differential Impact of Crime," *Crime and Delinquency* 33, no. 4 (October 1987):452–453. Copyright 1987 by *Crime and Delinquency*. Reprinted by permission of Sage Publications.

brief, various social factors in a victim's background prior to the experience is often a significant variable in successfully overcoming victimization.

3. *Resistance to Devictimization Because of Secondary Emotional Gain*   Even though remaining a victim is painful, there are some secondary gains from the role for some people who have been victimized. They therefore cling to their victim role in life because it has some unconscious emotional rewards. Some secondary gains for remaining a victim include the following:

   a. Other people may find the victim more interesting than he or she was prior to the victimization. They now have something interesting to talk about.

   b. The victim can activate a "poor me" role that facilitates and brings out a level of pity, sympathy, and compassion from others that was never in evidence prior to the crime.

   c. Some victims are not expected to do much. They are in a role which enables them to retire righteously from their usual work expectations and responsibilities.

   d. The newfound attention the victim role brings may alleviate an emptiness or loneliness in the person's life. The victim role may enable the person to avoid facing other problems.

For all these reasons, many victims cling to their victim role and resist devictimization. Many war veterans, for example, including some in Veterans Administration hospitals, cling to their victim roles and resist getting on with their lives. Once these issues are illuminated, a practicing victim can often overcome the problem and facilitate recovery.

The "Caring Circle" Factor   A very significant factor in a person's recovery from victimization is the size and quality of the "caring circle" of friends and family. A problem some victims encounter is related to the fact that their victimizers were once significant members of their caring circle, perhaps even people upon whom they depended. Consequently, after leaving the victimizing relationship, the victim has few friends. This often accounts for the victim's return to a relationship with the victimizer (the "best friend") in the delusional hope that he or she has changed. This problem is especially acute for a child, whose offender may be a parent. For this reason, children often cannot escape from the clutches of the offenders.

People who have a strong, caring circle of friends and family can more easily exit, and overcome, their victimization. They have people who can absorb and facilitate their treatment in the devictimization process.

In a sense, a person's caring circle can serve as a buffer to the criminal experience. (This is another aspect of the co-victim concept.) For example, victims of crime can cope better with their problems if there are relevant others to help them, to commiserate and sympathize with them. In contrast, people who are relatively alone in the world may become "stuck" with the pain of victimization. In brief, a caring circle may help a person to avoid being victimized, and it can also be enormously beneficial in helping a person disconnect from, and escape from, the deleterious effects of criminal victimization.

SUMMARY: ON THE VICTIM FACTOR IN CRIME

A number of issues that pertain to the victim factor in crimes deserve further research, analysis, and discussion.

1. The three major social-psychological elements that pertain to all crime are the criminal, the victim, and the general society. In criminology, our dominant emphasis has historically been on the criminal: the criminal's modus operandi, the causal background of crime, and treatment strategies for reaching the offender. A more intensive analysis of the role of the victim in the crime complex seems indicated. Moreover, greater attention should be focused on the crime problem as it affects the general population in the social system. More needs to be known about the effects of crime on citizens in general. To what degree are we all co-victims of crimes committed on people with whom we have no direct personal relationship? In brief, it is my view that attention needs to be focused more equitably on the criminal, the victim, and the impact of crime on society in general.

2. The von Hentig hypothesis of victim-precipitated crime also requires more research and theoretical analysis. In this regard, for example, rape represents a controversial type of violent crime. Around 20 years ago, most rape cases that were reported and brought to the courts involved a man raping a woman who was a complete stranger. In recent years, such offenses as acquaintance rape, date rape, and even husband-wife rape have been the subject of judicial review. In one sense, in this context, victims have been accorded more power and equity in the judicial system, even though many victims have had prior social relationships with their accused offenders. Does the fact that a victim had a personal relationship with an offender prior to the commission of a crime reduce the offender's culpability in both a moral and a legal sense? Or are all acts of rape equally heinous?

3. In studying the role of a victim in a crime, should the courts take into account the degree of involvement of the victim? As I have stated, there are three levels of victims: nonparticipants, people who are victim-prone, and precipitators of their own victimization. More research is required to delineate the victim's role in

crime and whether and to what degree it should diminish the responsibility of the criminal in the situation.

4. Another area for consideration is how and why some people are more crime-prone than others. My research indicates that the delusion factor, a family-induced victim's life script, and a low self-concept are personality factors which contribute to a person's susceptibility to victimization. In brief, the *delusion factor*, involving a distorted reality of the potential crime situation, makes a person more crime-prone; *life-scripting* involves a socialization process in which a person is more likely to be trained for a victim's role; and a *low self-concept* propels people into more situations where they might become victims, because they care less about what will happen to them.

5. Another significant issue in victimology is the degree to which people related to a crime victim become or do not become co-victims. This concept can affect the postcrime situation in at least two respects: (1) The co-victim is profoundly emotionally affected by the victimization of the loved one, and (2) the co-victim should be accorded some participatory role in the administration of justice of the crime. The trial of Dominique Dunne's murderer, so eloquently described by the victim's father, produced a situation in which the family was not permitted to play a role in the adjudication process. As a consequence, the family as co-victims were doubly victimized—first by the murder, and second by the fact that they had no voice in the judicial process.

    Victims and co-victims should in general be accorded more positive and therapeutic consideration in the administration of justice. In some jurisdictions, co-victims are allowed to testify and ventilate their feelings at the trial. The criminality of the offender should not be the only consideration in the judicial process.

6. The Goetz case was a lightning rod for the degree to which citizens in our society have pent-up feelings and react to crime as co-victims. The public's response was multifaceted and polarized. Many citizens perceived racism and took sides with the youths who were shot by Goetz. Many people saw Goetz as a heroic person fighting back against vicious criminal behavior. And many people were unsure whether or not Goetz had acted appropriately or properly for a citizen in a crime situation.

    In brief, the Goetz case revealed the fact that most people are enormously emotionally concerned about crime and are somewhat unsure about what the average citizen's role should be in counteracting crime. The issue turns on the question of whether Goetz's behavior made him an offender or a valiant victim who fought back against great odds.

7. Since all crimes produce victims and co-victims, more attention

needs to be paid to the postcrime treatment of victims and co-victims. Our society's concerns have been concentrated more on the treatment of the criminal than the victim. There are at least four factors that affect the treatment process for victims: (1) the horrendousness of the crime, (2) the precrime personality of the victim, (3) the victim's "caring circle" of friends and family, and (4) treatment procedures for ameliorating the negative impact of the crime.

In general, in the study and treatment of the crime problem, the criminal has been the central focus. Criminologists need to pay more attention to research about the victims of crime, the impact of crime on the general society, and the proper balancing of each of these three components in the proper administration of justice.

Chapter
5

The Criminal Personality

*T*here is a continuing controversy about whether criminal behavior is a manifestation of mental illness, the result of negative social factors such as poverty or depressed socioeconomic factors, a reflection of deviant socialization, or a combination of all these factors. My own first-hand observation and analysis of relevant research in these areas reveals that all these forces create a personality that acts out criminal behavior; however, certain factors may be more dominant in a particular case.

In an article entitled "Addressing Inmate Mental Health Problems," Kenneth Adams describes some of the complexity of analyzing mental health issues and crime:

> In the early nineteenth century, as scientific approaches to the study of crime were starting to appear, psychiatric theories vigorously stressed the notion that mental illness is the major cause of crime. These theories outlined a "medical model" of crime causation which viewed crime as a "disease of the mind" that needed to be "cured." From about the middle of the ninteenth century to about the middle of the twentieth century, psychiatric theories of criminality were widely accepted. Once the proposition that mental illness is the cause of crime was accepted, it followed logically that in order for therapeutic services to be rehabilitative in the penological sense, they must be designed to address mental health problems. From this point of view, there was little to be gained from distinguishing between correctional rehabilitation services and mental health service.[1]

---

[1] Kenneth Adams, "Addressing Inmate Mental Health Problems," *Federal Probation #49* (December 1985), p. 27.

From the social-psychological perspective, it is apparent that various sociocultural factors enter into personality formation and criminal behavior. It is important to research and analyze these sociological factors; in addition, we foster a better understanding of the general arena of criminality by examining the emotional factors that produce criminal personality types. It is of great value to comprehend not only the sociological value systems that cause criminality but also the psychological emotional disorders that relate to criminal behavior. In this regard, before discussing the basic criminal personalities we will analyze three aspects of the relationship between emotional disorders and crime:

1. Most psychotherapy in the field of criminology is based on the assumption that criminal behavior is an overt symptom of some underlying emotional disturbance or disorder. There is no doubt that many criminal acts are committed by people who are emotionally disturbed and that some "normal" people commit criminal acts when under great emotional strain. In brief, some criminal behavior is a symptomatic acting out of underlying emotional pathology.
2. Behavior considered symptomatic of emotional disturbance is likely to receive more attention when exhibited by someone charged with or convicted of a criminal act. One conclusion, therefore, is that a certain amount of criminal behavior is a result of underlying emotional problems; however, because there tends to be a greater focus on the emotional background of a criminal than on that of the average person, more emotional problems may be attributed to criminals than to law-abiding people.

    Criminal behavior may emanate from an emotional disorder, but in some cases there may not be any causal connection between the two. In other words, a criminal may be emotionally disturbed but the emotional disorder may not be related to the criminal behavior.
3. Criminal behavior may cause emotional disorders. What is suggested here is that criminals may develop an induced emotional disturbance as a result of their nerve-racking lives: committing criminal acts, being arrested, spending a long time in prison, and dealing with the variety of abnormal social forces involved in the administration of justice. In some cases "normal" criminals are incarcerated in facilities where the emotional stress produces personality problems unrelated to their former criminal behavior. Being a criminal is often an exceedingly nerve-racking occupation or status that can cause emotional problems for the individual who becomes involved in this lifestyle. Rather than a causal factor, the emotional disorder may be more of an occupational disease that results from a criminal lifestyle.

On the basis of my firsthand research in a variety of settings and a review of the relevant research literature, I group criminals into four types in terms of the manner in which their personalities affect their criminal behavior.

1. *Socialized Criminals*   These are people who are no more emotionally disturbed than the average person. They become criminals as a result of the social context within which they learn deviant values. They are more likely to become property violators than violent offenders.

2. *Neurotic Criminals*   These are people who become criminals as a result of personality distortions and distortions in their perceptions of the world around them. They may have a need to commit deviant, perhaps violent acts to prove to themselves that they are not insecure, or they may become deviant because of some anxiety or neurotic compulsion. For example, people who become kleptomaniacs, shoplifters, and pyromaniacs often have neurotic compulsions that can result in criminal behavior.

3. *Psychotic Criminals*   These are people with severe personality disorders, who have a significantly distorted perception of the society and world around them. Unlike socialized offenders, psychotics do not plan their crimes; however, their distorted view of reality and their delusional thoughts may compel them to commit acts which violate the law. Psychotic offenders are prone to commit acts of violence, including murder. These criminals are the ones who tend to commit the most bizarre and senseless acts of violence.

4. *Sociopathic Criminals*   These offenders are characterized by an egocentric personality. They have limited compassion for others, or none at all. Because of this character disorder, they can easily victimize others with a minimum of anxiety or guilt. The sociopathic element is present in most criminals, although not all criminals are clear sociopaths.

Many power-status offenders fit this fourth category. They have a marked blindness and inability to comprehend unethical behavior. Amazingly, some of these individuals become involved in law enforcement roles.

These four categories account for most of our criminal population. It should further be noted, by way of preface to our more intense analysis of these categories, that there are few pure cases. Many socialized criminals have sociopathic tendencies, and many murderers manifest a combination of socialized and sociopathic characteristics. Most white collar and political criminals have sociopathic personality characteristics.

THE SOCIALIZED CRIMINAL

This type of offender is socialized into crime. Edwin Sutherland explains that because of "differential association," the socialized criminal learns "a preponderance of values, attitudes, and techniques that make law violation a more desirable way of life than becoming a law-abiding citizen."

The community in which the offender grows up is apt to significantly affect his or her values, ethics, and choices in life. There are high-crime neighborhoods where becoming a criminal is an attractive choice for a person growing up with criminal role models. When the neighborhood stars are "successful" criminals or racketeers, many youths may seek to emulate their "heroes'" patterns. For many children growing up in this social content, becoming a criminal is therefore, paradoxically, more a matter of conformity than deviance.

In this context, we should consider the existence of organized crime in a neighborhood. Donald Cressey makes the point that the Mafia, or organized crime, is a most attractive potential field of endeavor for poor youths growing up in urban ghettos.[2] Cressey asserts that the Mafia feeds on the urban poor. Of the thousands of people involved in organized crime, the "street men" or street-level commission agents are visible manifestations of a seductive criminal lifestyle, and they exert a primary influence on training future criminals. The agents of organized crime have high status in their neighborhoods and are the idols of young ghetto residents; they are the men who have "made it." In the eyes of many urban youths, the image of success is that of a hustler who promotes his interests by using others.

Cressey takes the position that organized crime influences the general crime and delinquency rate in the inner city in three ways. First, it demonstrates to young people that crime does pay. Second, according to Cressey, the presence of organized crime exhibits the corruption evident in law enforcement and political organizations. This makes it more difficult for parents to teach their children to achieve in the world by "hard honest labor in service to their family, country, and God." Third, organized crime, through the numbers rackets, prostitution, gambling, and drug dealing, appreciably affects and lowers the economic status of the people in the community; thus, the people have less to lose if convicted of crime. Delinquency therefore becomes attractive to lower-class youth as a stepping stone to bigger and better crime. Cressey separates his observations into three dimensions: attraction, corruption, and contamination.

1. *Attraction*   Because of varied forces, according to Cressey, slum boys grow up in an economic and social environment that makes some participation in organized crime attractive, natural, and relatively painless. Cressey cites Irving Spergel, who, in his studies of juvenile delinquents in three different neighborhoods

---

[2] Donald R. Cressey, "Organized Crime and Inner City Youth," *Crime and Delinquency* (April 1970):129–138.

in Chicago, concluded that developing specific social skills is less necessary than learning the point of view or attitudes conducive to the development of organized crime.

In response to Spergel's question to delinquents, "What is the job of the adult in your neighborhood whom you would want to be like?," eight out of ten responded by naming some aspect of organized crime. Spergel's "Racketville" delinquents believed that connections are the most important quality in getting ahead. Seven out of ten chose education as the least important factor in getting ahead. A youth who can make $1,000 a day dealing drugs is not likely to aspire to a fast-food job.

An illustration of this continuing influence and "attraction" to youngsters in a high-crime neighborhood was revealed by the death and burial of a well-known pimp and drug dealer in Oakland, California, in the summer of 1986. The criminal was gunned down in a prototypical drug war slaying. In a paradelike atmosphere, over 50,000 people witnessed his elaborate hearse rolling down main street on the way to the cemetery. The funeral reputedly cost over $40,000. Journalists interviewed a number of teenagers who responded with variations on a theme of hero worship: "He was an important man in the neighborhood. He was well liked and I hope I'll be as successful as he was"; "Money's the name of the game. I worked for him, and I'll get my share when I get older."

2. *Corruption* Organized crime, in its alliances with politicians and law enforcement officials, helps, as Cressey sees it, "to break down the respect for law and order. How can a boy learn to respect authority when that authority figure is known to be on the payroll of criminals?" The "sleaze factor" in the Reagan administration, in which over ten of his government staff were convicted of crimes, is not lost on youthful offenders in the 1980s.

3. *Contamination* Cressey asserts that because the areas of low socioeconomic status are the areas of high delinquency and crime in American cities, it must be concluded that in some areas lawlessness has become traditional. He reasons that in poverty areas, the values, social pressures, and norms favorable to crime are strong and constant. The persons responsible for enforcing these moral systems and concepts are organized criminals. Cressey quotes Dr. Martin Luther King, Jr., who once stated, "Organized crime flourishes in the ghetto as 'permissive crime' because no one cares particularly about ghetto crime."

Cressey concludes his observations by stating:

Keeping vice out of affluent areas while allowing it to flourish in the ghettos, together with corruption that supports the practice, [contributes to] the traditions of delinquency and crime characterizing our inner city areas. In these areas opposition to crime and delinquency is weak because the city is poor, mobile and heterogeneous and people can't act effectively to solve their problems.[3]

In his paraphrasing of Sutherland's theory of differential association, Cressey asserts that most people living in low-income or poverty areas are either delinquent or criminals because they are isolated from law-abiding behavior patterns and are in close, continuing contact with criminal influences "that affect forces favorable to delinquency." Cressey believes that the "incidence of inner-city delinquency may be reduced by eliminating the behavior patterns spread by organized criminals or by expanding those anticriminal patterns that keep inner-city youth out of trouble."

The contemporary version of these dynamics is related to drug dealing. Many urban "socialized delinquents" are making enormous amounts of money, especially in ghetto areas, by dealing drugs—particularly "crack," a highly marketable form of cocaine.

John and Jim: Two Socialized Delinquents

John   John grew up and was essentially socialized by the criminal forces in the inner city of New York described by Cressey. I became closely acquainted with John in the course of my early research in New York City, and I met him at a later date when he was in his twenties and in the Syranon program in California attempting to overcome his heroin addiction problem. The following analysis is based on five in-depth taped interviews with John.

John grew up in a delinquent subculture on the West Side of Manhattan. His neighborhood "naturally" socialized him into a de-linquent–drug addict style of life. The process involved the development of a delinquent mask or "tough-guy" image that was necessary for survival on the streets.

John was first institutionalized in a "juvenile jail" at the age of 10 by his parents, for being incorrigible. From then on, he felt extreme hatred for his parents, especially his father. In the institution, he "always felt a need to protect the underdog in a fight." He had several fights each day and found that the "home" or juvenile detention facility he was periodically in was a "house of horror." He was later sent to a long-term facility for two years and learned all about crime from the older boys.

When he left the institution at about the age of 13, he began running with various youth gangs in New York on the Upper West Side of Manhattan. They were involved in petty theft and destructive acts. He remembered learning to hate his father more and more. "I always stayed

---

[3] Cressey, ibid.

out late, and when he would get me at home, he would beat me up pretty badly. Then he would actually sentence me, like a judge. For example, he would give me 'sixty days in the bedroom.' I began my jail time early." John, like many children in his situation, seldom went to school.

During most of his early life, John worshipped older gangsters and criminals. He wanted to be like them. In his neighborhood there were many to imitate. A criminal he especially admired was one who, according to John, "killed a few wrong guys and died in the hot seat at Sing Sing without a whimper."

When John was 14, he took his first fix of heroin. In the course of his delinquency apprenticeship, he says, he "used to run dope and deliver packages of heroin to older addicts. One day, out of curiousity I asked this guy for a little. He fixed me, and that was it. I began using from then on. It's hard to describe my first feelings about heroin. The best way I can describe it is that it's like being under the covers where it's nice and warm on a cold day."

John continued to run the streets, used drugs whenever he could, and received more training for a life of crime. "In my neighborhood, when I was around 13, I was considered a 'cute kid.' The whores liked me, and once in a while, for a gag, they would turn a trick with me. I admired the stand-up guy gangsters. They were my idols. My main hero at that time was the local head of the Mafia family."

John, in his teenage years, was a thin, baby-faced young fellow. His pale, ascetic face had an almost religious quality. In his neighborhood on the Upper West Side of Manhattan, he became known to some of his peers as "Whitey the Priest."

He received this nickname from an addict who was kicking a habit. As John relates it:

> Once, when I was in jail in the Tombs, some Spanish guy who was kicking a bad habit came to for a minute. He saw me and began to scream hysterically in Spanish that I was a priest. Later on, it was picked up by other people who knew me around the city. Some of the whores on Columbus Avenue would even "confess" to me as Whitey the Priest. First I made sure they gave me a good fix of heroin, or money for a fix, and then I would actually listen to their "confession"! They weren't kidding; they were dead serious. After the "confession" took place, usually in some hallway or in a bar, after they poured out their tragic story, I would lay a concept on them. Something like "into each life some rain must fall." I'd bless them and cut out.
>
> I took my first big fall at 14. I was sent to the reformatory at Otisville. I hated everyone there and wanted to kill the director and some of the guards. I was always fighting and spent a lot of time in the hole [solitary confinement]. This gave me a chance to think and plot different ways to kill the guards and the man who ran the joint.

At age 16, John was transferred from Otisville to another reformatory for older boys. From then on he spent time in various institutions. These included trips to Rikers Island Penitentiary, to Lexington Hospital for a "winder" ("you wind in and out"), to Riverside Hospital for addicts, and to various New York City jails.

John always considered himself to be a "stand-up guy" (a criminal with ethics); and he had set his personal goal as becoming a professional criminal. At one point he tried to learn from an old-timer how to be a safecracker. "Somehow I wasn't very good. I did go on a few jobs, but it wasn't right for me. Whenever I was out of jail, which wasn't too often, I would just use drugs and steal. I became a baby-faced stall for some cannons [pickpockets]. The stall sets up the mark, and the cannon picks his pocket. I made a fair living in this business. I used to like to pick pockets in museums. In fact, I don't know why, but I spent a lot of time walking around museums." (Certain works of art tend to mesmerize the pickpocket's victims and render them oblivious to having their pockets picked.)

In my lengthy discussions with John, I never determined that the young man had any significant neurotic, psychotic, or sociopathic personality traits. It appeared that his delinquent lifestyle resulted from the "straight-line" learning of delinquent behavior in a neighborhood social milieu that presented delinquency as a correct and logical way of life.

Socialized delinquents growing up in a delinquent subculture acquire skills useful in crime, along with values and attitudes that make a later criminal career attractive. They learn the skills needed to commit burglaries, thefts, and other property offenses, and they engage in these acts to earn a livelihood. They desire a career that involves professional crime. In later life, young delinquents like John usually develop into what Edwin H. Sutherland has defined as "the professional criminal."

Sutherland's conception of the professional criminal parallels the sociological model of socialized delinquents. Sutherland's classic theory of differential association, grossly oversimplified, states that delinquents learn to become delinquent from association with other offenders. They are trained into delinquent patterns at an early age. Sutherland's "professional thief" is the role that the socialized delinquent will achieve after becoming a specialist in a particular criminal activity. Sutherland and Cressey describe the professional thief as follows:

> Professional thieves make a regular business of theft. They use techniques which have been developed over a period of centuries and transmitted to them through traditions and personal association. They have codes of behavior, esprit de corps, and consensus. They have a high status among other thieves and in the political and criminal underworld in general. They have differential association in the sense that they associate with each other and not, on the same basis, with outsiders, and also in the sense that they select their colleagues.
>
> Because of this differential association they develop a common language or argot that is relatively unknown to those not in the profession, and they have organization. A thief is a professional when he has these six characteristics: regular work at theft, technical skill, consensus, status, differential association, and organization.

Professional thieves have their group ways of behavior for the principal situations that confront them in their criminal activities. Consequently professional theft is a behavior system and a sociological entity.[4]

This model image characterizes the professional criminal as resourceful, well trained, and effective, a member of a profession (albeit illegal) with certain ethics and values that dictate conduct. In criminal jargon, the professional thief has "class." A thief would not "rat" on fellow thieves, and even certain victims were proscribed. Assault and violence were used as means to an end, not as ends in themselves.

Jim Jim, like John, is a socialized delinquent. Following is Jim's story as he told it to me:

> When I was 16 or 17 I used to hang around a pool hall in our neighborhood a lot. I could shoot pool pretty good and once in a while I would make a couple of bucks. But there were older guys there who were really doing good. They had good reputations in the neighborhood and they always had money, cars, and broads. Me and some kids my age were doing a lot of petty stealing at this time, cars and things from cars, but we didn't know how to make any real money. What we wanted to do was get in with the older guys we admired so we could learn something and make some real money.
>
> One day, I remember, I had just got out of juvenile hall for some petty beef and one of the older thieves, a guy that was supposed to be one of the slickest safe men around, came over to me and talked to me for awhile. This made me feel pretty good. Later one of his friends asked me if I wanted to help him carry a safe out of some office. We worked half a night on that safe and never did get it out of the place. But from then on I was in with this older bunch. Every once in a while one of them would get me to do some little job for him, like "standing point" [lookout] or driving a car or something like that; and once in a while when they had snatched a safe, I would get to help open it. I was learning pretty fast.
>
> By the time I was 18, me and a couple of my buddies had real solid names [reputations] with the older thieves. We were beating a lot of places on our own and we handled ourselves pretty well. But we were still willing to learn more. We used to sit around some coffee shop half the night or ride around in a car listening to a couple of the old hoodlums cut up different scores [crimes]. We would talk about different scores other guys had pulled or scores we had pulled, and we would also talk about how you were supposed to act in certain situations; how to spend your money, how to act when you got arrested. We discussed different trials we knew about, we even talked about San Quentin and Folsom and prisons in other states, because usually the older thieves had done time before in these other places. We talked about the laws, how much time each beef carried, how much time the parole board would give you for each crime. I guess we talked

---

[4] Edwin H. Sutherland and Donald R. Cressey, "Developmental Explanation of Criminal Behavior," in *Criminology*, 10th ed. (Philadelphia: Lippincott, 1978), pp. 80–82. © Copyright 1978 by J. B. Lippincott Company. Reprinted by permission of the Estate of Donald R. Cressey.

about everything that had anything to do with stealing. Of course we didn't talk about it all the time. Lost of the time we just shot the bull like anyone else. But by the time I was 18 I had a pretty good education in crime.

John and Jim *learned* their criminal behavior in a relatively normal fashion. It was my opinion that neither of them had any special personality problems. They became criminals as a result of the deviant value system they were exposed to as youths growing up in a neighborhood where becoming a criminal was a "legitimate" and desirable way of life. They were thus socialized into a criminal lifestyle and can be clearly categorized as socialized delinquents.

THE NEUROTIC CRIMINAL

The general heading of emotional disorders includes neurotic and psychotic behavior. Neurosis is a less severe form of emotional disorder than psychosis. Neurotic compulsions can cause certain types of delinquent behavior. People suffering from one or another type of neurosis are typically capable of functioning in everyday life. Unlike the psychotic, the neurotic generally does not perceive the world in a distorted way. Moreover, neurotics typically are aware that there is something wrong with their thinking and behavior.

The principal symptom of neurosis is evidence of anxiety. Anxiety involves a visceral sense of fear and personal distress not brought about by any clear stimulus in the social or physical environment. In mild cases of neurosis, anxiety may be expressed directly. In some severe cases, a neurotic person may appear to be in a state of panic. According to psychiatrists, anxiety may also be expressed indirectly—showing up as a variety of other problems, such as blindness; deafness; exhaustion; inexplicable fear of objects or particular situations; and compulsive activity, including offenses such as kleptomania, pyromania, and shoplifting.

Some burglars manifest neurotic tendencies in their modus operandi. Eric, a 16-year-old offender with whom I worked in a juvenile jail, presented a clear pattern of neurotic compulsion. He was a compulsive house burglar. When he was finally arrested, the police cleared more than 60 burglaries he had committed over a three-month period during one summer.

Eric's neurosis was reflected in his repeated modus operandi. His burglary pattern always took the following unalterable form. He would locate and break into a house whose residents were on vacation. Once inside the house, he would make himself at home. He would cook himself a meal, read a paper, and then take a nap. Upon awakening he would loot the house of all valuables. Prior to leaving, almost as an afterthought, he would return to the bedroom and feel a compulsion to defecate on the bed.

I had many lengthy counseling sessions with this neurotic delinquent. We concluded that this last act of defiance and hostility was related to his hostility toward his own parents. He felt that they never had provided him with an adequate home situation, and his delinquency revolved around his unconscious hostility toward people who had "nice homes." Eric's neurotic burglaries and defiant acts of defecation were a form of revenge directed at "good homes." He talked further about how he would sometimes walk around for days with an inner feeling of fear and hostility—manifestations of his anxiety. He explained how, when he would act out his compulsions in his form of burglary, it would relieve his anxiety and he would feel better for a period of time.

Freud and others have hypothesized that neurotic anxiety is reduced by various *ego defense mechanisms*. Following are several of these basic ego defense mechanisms and a discussion of them as they relate to the neurotic criminal.

1. *Denial of Reality* Protecting the self from unpleasant truths by refusal to perceive or face reality, often by escapist activities such as using drugs or acting out criminal behavior.
2. *Fantasy* Gratifying frustrated desires in imaginary achievements. The violent gang in many ways has a pseudoreality component, where criminals picture themselves as heroic embattled individuals fighting a courageous war for their "turf."
3. *Projection* Placing blame for difficulties upon others or attributing one's own unethical desires to others. Violent criminals project onto others their own violent motivations, often in a paranoid way, and then attack an innocent victim.
4. *Reaction Formation* Preventing insecure feelings from being expressed by exaggerating opposed attitudes and types of behavior and using them as "barriers." The neurotic male criminal is often a person who is insecure about his power and masculinity. He tends to act out in violent behavior to prove that he is a "powerful man."
5. *Displacement* Discharging pent-up feelings, usually by hostility, on objects less dangerous than those which initially aroused the emotions. Displacement is a common defense mechanism for neurotic offenders, and it accounts for their violent behavior. For example, many rapists act out their unconcious hostility toward women in an act of rape.

In several psychodramas I directed with a 15-year-old violent youth who was in a psychiatric hospital, the process of neurotic displacement was revealed. The young man had enormous feelings of hostility toward his stepfather, which were displaced onto the world at large in a series of muggings. As indicated in the ego defense explanation, he found strangers less dangerous objects for his hostility and displaced his rage onto these innocent victims.

PSYCHOTIC CRIMINAL TYPES

Psychosis is a more severe type of mental aberration than neurosis. Individuals diagnosed as psychotic have their own unique versions of reality and thus are often unable to perform the roles expected of them in everyday life. Consequently, treatment of psychoses commonly involves voluntary or involuntary confinement.

Psychotics may suffer from hallucinations, hearing voices, deep changes in mood, or an inability to think, speak, or remember. While psychiatrists have found that some psychoses are *organic*—that is, a result of actual physical damage to the brain, of hereditary malfunctions, or of chemical imbalances in a person's system— they claim that most types of psychosis are *functional*. In other words, in most psychoses there is no known physical reason for the symptoms of illness that are displayed; the causes of the psychoses are to be found in defective socialization backgrounds.

One of the more common psychoses is called *schizophrenia*. This term is applied to people who are extremely withdrawn from their surroundings or who act as if they were living in another world. Schizophrenics' thoughts may appear disorganized and bizarre, their emotions inappropriate for the situation, and their behavior unusual. Various types of schizophrenia have been identified and categorized. Persons who exhibit delusions of being persecuted by others are called *paranoid* schizophrenics. *Catatonic* schizophrenics act in an excessively excited manner or, alternatively, exist in a mute vegetative state.

When psychotics are in their "excited" state, they can explode into murderous acts of epic proportions. Cases of this sort in recent years include the Texas rampage of Charles Whitman, the Hillside Strangler murders in Los Angeles, the murderous spree of Herbert Mullin, Mark David Chapman's slaying of John Lennon, and the "Son of Sam" murders by David Berkowitz that terrorized New York City. These horrendous murders were committed by offenders with psychotic criminal personalities. We shall discuss each of them in turn to reveal some of the psychodynamics that resulted in these crimes.

The Madman in the Tower

In the forenoon of a blazing August day, a blond, husky young man strolled into a hardware store in Austin, Texas, and asked for several boxes of rifle ammunition. As he calmly wrote a check in payment, the clerk inquired with friendly curiosity what all the ammunition was for. "To shoot some pigs," he replied. At the time, the answer seemed innocent enough, for wild pigs still abound not far from the capital. The horror of its intent became obvious a few hours later, when the customer, Charles Joseph Whitman, 25, a student of architectural engineering at the University of Texas, became the perpetrator of one of the worst mass murders in recent U.S. history.

That morning, Charles Whitman entered two more stores to buy guns before ascending, with a veritable arsenal, to the observation deck of the limestone tower that soars 307 feet above the University of Texas campus. There, from Austin's tallest edifice, the visitor commands an extraordinary view of the 232-acre campus, with its green mall and red tile roofs; of the capital, ringed by lush farmlands; and, off to the west, of the mist-mantled hills whose purple hue prompted storyteller O. Henry to christen Austin the "City of a Violet Crown." Whitman had visited the tower ten days before in the company of a brother and had taken it all in. Today, though, he had no time for the view; he was too intent upon his deadly work.

Methodically, he began shooting everyone in sight. Ranging round the tower's walk at will, he sent his bullets rasping through the flesh and bone of those on the campus below, then of those who walked or stood or rode as far as three blocks away. Somewhat like the travelers in Thornton Wilder's *The Bridge of San Luis Rey,* who were drawn by inexorable fate to their crucial place in time and space, his victims fell as they went about their various tasks and pleasures. By lingering perhaps a moment too long in a classroom or leaving a moment too soon for lunch, they had unwittingly placed themselves within Whitman's lethal reach. Before he was himself killed by police bullets, Charles Whitman killed 13 people and wounded 31—for a staggering total of 44 casualties. As a prelude to his senseless rampage, it was later discovered, he had also slain his wife and mother, bringing the total dead to 15.

It was later determined that Whitman had emotional problems and had sought psychiatric help. He had several counseling sessions, but apparently the depths of his emotional disorder had not been revealed.

Kenneth Bianchi: The Hillside Strangler

Many recent psychotic murderers have not confined their homicidal tendencies to one outburst, like Whitman. There appears to be an increasing number of serial psychotic murders in the United States. One such notable case involved the so-called Hillside Strangler in Los Angeles, Kenneth Bianchi.[5]

Kenneth Bianchi, along with his partner in crime, Angelo Buono, was allegedly responsible for the murders of at least 13 and possibly over 20 young women during a period from September, 1977, to February, 1978. Almost all the victims were found nude, all were strangled, all were sexually assaulted, all had been handcuffed or bound prior to death, almost all the cases involved sexual intercourse, and all the bodies were later found on hillsides.

After Bianchi's arrest, Dr. John G. Watkins, professor of psychology

---

[5] This summary of the case of Kenneth Bianchi is based on my collation of numerous articles on the subject and various court transcripts.

at the University of Montana, interviewed him and later put him under hypnosis. During the time Bianchi was under hypnosis, Dr. Watkins found him to have multiple personalities.

Under hypnosis the personality of "Steve" came to life. Unlike Bianchi, who was polite and courteous most of the time in his sessions with Dr. Watkins, Steve appeared to be rude and hostile. Dr. Watkins identified the killer personality as Steve.

In the context of one interview, under hypnosis, Steve told Dr. Watkins that he hated Ken because Ken was always nice to people. Steve also said he made Ken lie and said he liked to hurt anyone who was nice to Ken. Steve also said that one night Ken went to his cousin Angelo Buono's house. Angelo had a girl over, and Ken walked in while Angelo was killing the girl. Steve said that he and Angelo talked a lot about killing women. Steve asked Angelo what it was like to kill someone and how many others he had killed. About a week later, Steve and Angelo went out together and picked up a girl. They both had sex with her and then killed her. This was, according to Bianchi, the first of a series of killings that he and Buono would commit together.

Steve explained that whenever the murders took place, he was in control of Ken's body, and Ken would have no recollection of what had happened. Bianchi had complained to Dr. Watkins of frequent losses of memory even before he was put under hypnosis. Steve told Dr. Watkins that he could become sexually aroused only when he knew he was going to kill a woman. Ken, on the other hand, apparently had a normal sex life with a girlfriend.

Dr. Ralph Allison, a theorist in the field of abnormal psychology, also put Ken into a state of hypnosis. Dr. Allison asked Ken to tell him when he started to have problems at home. Ken responded by going back to when he was 9 years old. Apparently, the Bianchis were having financial problems at this time, and Mrs. Bianchi was constantly upset. Bianchi said she was always yelling at him or hitting him. Ken felt he needed his mother's approval; when she became upset with him, he would run and hide from her. It was at this time that Steve appeared. Steve was at first Ken's imaginary friend. This is a normal occurrence for some children, but most of these imaginary people disappear in time. In Bianchi's case, however, Steve became the "bad" Ken Bianchi. This enabled Bianchi to defend his "self"—so he did not have to accept personal responsibility for his horrendous homicidal behavior. He could displace this negative side of himself onto Steve.

When he was on trial, Bianchi was examined for several months by a number of psychiatrists and psychologists. He was diagnosed by several as psychotic with multiple personality problems. Several psychiatrists disputed the Steve personality that appeared under hypnosis. They alleged that Bianchi was faking the Steve personality in order to mount an insanity plea. If he was successful with the insanity plea, he could escape the death penalty. If Steve was real, we can speculate that

Bianchi's multiple personality was a complex defensive psychotic syndrome emanating from an early life that involved severe problems with his mother.

One psychiatrist's analysis of Bianchi's psychosis related to the fact that his mother was a prostitute. In one interview, Bianchi revealed his hostility toward his mother as he lay awake in the next room hearing her having sex with many men. Whether Steve was a reality to Bianchi or faked, his repressed hostility toward his mother when he was a child was later displaced onto women he perceived as being like her. Part of his psychotic compulsion was to kill women who were or appeared to be prostitutes.

Another aspect of Bianchi's repressed hostility toward his mother was revealed in psychiatric observations made when he was a child. Clinical reports stated that she beat him physically, often without any justifiable reason. In 1984 he was interviewed and hypnotized by a number of psychiatrists who videotaped the sessions; the sessions supplemented the data found in the reports made when he was a child.

In his commentary, under hypnosis, Bianchi focused on the violent assaults perpetrated on him by his mother. His mother, according to Bianchi, "would hit me almost every day. Most of the time she hit me for no reason. I was mad at her all the time—but I would never hit her back. I was fully controlled by her and under her thumb." The psychiatric videotapes revealed that Bianchi repressed all of his enormous hostility toward his mother and avoided any encounters with her. It was during these childhood years that he developed Steve to help him deal with his anger and his furious feelings toward his mother.

Bianchi's torment and anger were expressed later in life in his ritualistic, torturous, and brutal murders of women. His homicides can be partially explained as the expression of the rage he felt as a child toward his mother, which was later displaced through the torture and murder perpetrated on his female victims.

In a sense he practiced a kind of role reversal. When he was a child, his mother had all the power. She was the offender and he was the victim. As an adult, in his ritualistic vengeance against his mother, he had all the power and the women he killed (who were often tied up) became the helpless victims of his rage. In this bizarre way he seemed to achieve a kind of revenge against his mother.

Many homicidal psychotic criminals like Bianchi manifest another personality that is held responsible for their heinous acts. In my work I have encountered several violent criminals who attribute their darker side to a manufactured other person in their body. This other personality, they allege, takes over and commits the horrendous act. This enables psychotic criminals, in a convoluted way, to rationalize away their violence, to escape responsibility for their deviance, and to maintain a self-concept of being a good person. In Kenneth Bianchi's case, Steve was the villain and Ken remained a "good guy." It was, however, the total Kenneth Bianchi who became the vicious Hillside Strangler.

The "Astrological" Mass Murderer

Dr. Donald T. Lunde and Jefferson Morgan detailed the life of Herbert William Mullin, a convicted mass murderer, in a book entitled *The Die Song*.[6] Mullin killed 13 people over a four-month period (October 13, 1972, to February 13, 1973). Mullin had been in and out of mental institutions prior to the killings; he had entered the hospitals on his own for treatment of instability. Mullin was evaluated by numerous psychiatrists while in a state mental facility and was diagnosed as a paranoid schizophrenic. During his trial, however, it was curiously determined that he was sane during the time he committed the murders. Mullin was sentenced by a jury to prison, and not to a mental hospital for treatment of his problem. This often happens in cases where a judge and jury ignore a killer's emotional disorder, because the public clearly wants to put the murderer away for life in prison. The goal is to incapacitate the offender for as long a time as possible.

Despite the judicial decision, there is strong evidence that Mullin was psychotic. He was obsessed with earthquakes and how to avoid them, with hearing voices (voices which he claimed were from his father), and with numbers, especially the number 13.

The number 13 came up too often to be overlooked. Mullin chose the number because of his belief in numerology. He started killing on October 13, and stopped killing on February 13, after 13 people were dead. He believed that the number 13 was a necessary sacrificial number. The two examples he cited were Jesus and the 12 disciples and Jonah when he threw himself into the sea to save 12 men. He believed that the number 13 was not a coincidence in the cases of Jesus and Jonah but was a message—a message to sacrifice (kill) others to avoid disaster. Mullin saw himself in his paranoia as a person who carried out the sacrifice of others to save humanity.

The disasters Mullin sought to avoid were earthquakes. He believed, in his clearly delusionary psychotic mind, that people in the past and present sacrificed themselves to avoid earthquakes. He believed that there was a significant correlation between death rates and earthquakes—the more deaths, the fewer quakes. To prove this theory, he wrote to the United Nations for documentation of death rates around the world and of earthquake activity during the same period.

Mullin claimed that 13 people were ready to die to avoid the earthquakes and that they knew he was the one to sacrifice them. He

---

[6] This case analysis is summarized from *The Die Song*, a book about Herbert Mullin, by Donald T. Lunde and Jefferson Morgan (New York: Norton, 1980).

believed they were ready to die through some form of mental telepathy known to him, the victims, and his father, who "told him to kill."

Prior to the murders Mullin was self-admitted three times to mental facilities and was an outpatient in various group therapy clinics. But when the state budget for mental health facilities was cut, Mullin was discharged, despite the fact that he was diagnosed as a dangerous paranoid schizophrenic personality by all the psychiatrists who knew him. Without question, Mullin's underlying emotional disorder produced his horrendous criminal behavior.

Mark David Chapman

Many psychotic killers like Mullin have, in their convoluted inner minds, a self-concept of being "humanitarian." This type of murderer often manifests a self-righteous—at times extremist—system of religious beliefs. Several of the Manson gang, who participated in ritual murders of a brutal nature, later on in prison became born-again Christians. "Tex" Watson, who killed one man over a period of several days under instructions from Manson, became a prison minister. Susan Atkins, another Manson disciple who stabbed pregnant Sharon Tate in her stomach, also manifested deep religious beliefs in her later prison years. Even Charles Manson has wrapped himself in the cloak of a humanitarian out to save the planet earth from destruction.

An obviously psychotic killer who manifested characteristics of self-righteousness and humanitarianism in the genre of Mullin and Manson was Mark David Chapman, now serving 20 years to life in prison for the senseless, atrocious murder of John Lennon. Chapman actually worked with children, played in his high school band, and claimed to idolize John Lennon and The Beatles. He strangely attemped to emulate and identify with Lennon. Like Lennon, he had a Japanese wife, had an avid interest in modern music, and had an interest in "humanity." After obtaining Lennon's autograph in front of the latter's home in New York, he shot Lennon to death with a gun that contained four hollow .38-caliber bullets. He was arrested moments later carrying J. D. Salinger's compassionate book on adolesence, *The Catcher in the Rye.*

In June, 1981, Chapman, a born-again Christian, told the court that God had told him to plead guilty and take his punishment. At his sentencing in September, 1981, he announced a vow of silence and stated as "my final spoken words" a fundamental passage in *The Catcher in the Rye:* "I keep picturing all these little kids playing some game in this big field of rye and all. Thousands of little kids, and nobody's around, nobody big, I mean, except me. And, I'm standing on the edge of some crazy cliff. What I have to do, I have to catch everybody if they start to go over the cliff . . . I'd just be the catcher in the rye."

Chapman had a peculiar and ambivalent attitude toward children. In an article in the February 23, 1987, issue of *People* magazine, reporter James R. Gaines wrote:

> In fact, Chapman's feelings about children, which were deeply involved in his eventual identification with *The Catcher in the Rye*, were complicated . . . . in an interview with the defense team's Milton Kline, he said he feared he might have gotten too close to his young charges. "I have always loved children," he said. "I think maybe I loved them so much, identified with them so much, that it became a confused kind of thing."
>
> His confusion, he remembered now, had once led to a peculiar act of half-intentional violence. "I never told anybody this. I was driving down the road in my car, and there was a small boy on the curb. I remember thinking he shouldn't be so close to the road, and then . . . . I looked in the rear-view mirror and I had knocked him down."
>
> At that point Chapman began to cry, in long, heaving sobs. When he could speak again he was nearly beside himself. "I don't want to cry," he gasped. "I haven't cried before. I can't take this. . . . I don't want to be crazy."[7]

Son of Sam

Another murderer whose deeds emanated from a psychotic personality was David Berkowitz. He terrorized the entire city of New York for a year with his grisly, senseless homicides. He was known as the .44-caliber killer to the police and public, and he called himself Son of Sam. His motivation and crimes were detailed in a *Time* magazine article after his capture. Basically, Son of Sam's personality could be characterized as psychotic, reflecting a paranoid delusionary system.

> "Kill! Kill!" chanted the vengeful crowd outside Brooklyn's Central Court Building, even though the object of their hatred was nowhere in sight. . . .
>
> The fury was directed at David Berkowitz, 24, a U.S. mail sorter, who was captured by police and identified as the lone gunman who had terrified much of New York in a yearlong series of eight nighttime attacks in quiet residential neighborhoods. But as the city's most massive manhunt ended, the killer of six young people (seven others survived their wounds) did not fulfill public expectations of the type of man who would automatically arouse suspicion, fear and hate.
>
> To be sure, the thin half-smile he wore as flashbulbs assailed him was infuriating. But the paunch, the round and smooth face, the short, curly hair and calm manner all seemed far from menacing. Rather than sinister, Berkowitz looked innocuous, an unexceptional figure unlikely to attract attention anywhere. As the facts of his life began to emerge, the much-sought gunman turned out to be the loner the psychologists had predicted. He had apparently abandoned the few friends acquired in his earlier years, lived alone in a sparsely furnished apartment in suburban Yonkers, got along comfortably with fellow postal workers but rarely initiated a conversation, and kept his personal feelings to himself.

---

[7] Copyright 1987 by *People* magazine. Reprinted by permission.

Even as police finally grilled the man who had caused them so many hours of frustration and drudgery, he was neither sullen nor hostile. He talked readily of his crimes, showing amazing recall of each attack, correcting police on details that only he could know, never refusing to answer their impatient questions.

But then that twisted side of the mild-mannered killer's mentality exposed itself. Why, why had he murdered? "It was a command," he said in a soft, nonaggressive voice. "I had a sign and followed it. Sam told me what to do and I did it." Again: "Sam told me to do it. Sam sent me on an assignment. I had to do what I had to do. I had my orders. Sam sent me." Who is Sam? Berkowitz said Sam is at the moment a neighbor of his named Sam Carr, but "really is a man who lived 6,000 years ago. I got the messages through his dog. He told me to kill. Sam is the Devil."

Clearly Berkowitz is crazy or, much less likely, feigning insanity. At his arraignment in the Brooklyn court, the judge ordered psychiatric examinations to determine whether he is sane enough to be prosecuted. Chances are he will spend the rest of his life in a mental institution.

The question of how the once unremarkable Berkowitz acquired his demonic delusions will, of course, be the object of intense psychiatric study. Born Richard David Falco, but given up for adoption by his mother at birth, the killer was raised by Nathan Berkowitz, a respected owner of a small hardware store in the Bronx. His first wife pampered David, but one family friend recalls that the boy sometimes would "curse her because he knew he was adopted." Nevertheless, when she died of cancer in 1967, her teenage son sobbed openly at the funeral; nobody could remember his crying since then. The youth apparently was never close to Berkowitz's second wife, a congenial woman, active in charity work. After his father retired two years ago with his wife to Boynton Beach, Fla. David occasionally visited the couple. . . .

If Berkowitz had no continuing attachment to a mother, he also seemed to have little affinity for women of his own age. According to Columnist Jimmy Breslin, a detective asked Berkowitz: "Do you go with girls?"

"No," he replied.

"Did you ever go with girls?"

"Yeah."

"How long back was that?"

"Couple of years."

"And you don't get invited a second time?"

"That's right."

Said the same detective: "He killed people, and I asked him about it. But he has no remorse. To him it was the same as eating an ice cream cone. He doesn't know the difference." . . .

Nothing seems to have been unusual about his education. He attended Christopher Columbus High School in the Bronx, where he rarely dated and was teased for being fat, and he stuck to Bronx Community College for only one year. He spent some of his free time with the New York City police auxiliary service. This did not involve training in the use of firearms or crime detection. He was taught how to direct traffic, administer first aid and perform other rescue-related duties. Fellow trainees considered him introverted but not particularly reclusive.

Berkowitz's rather withdrawn personality seems to have developed its more ominous oddities after he joined the Army in 1971. He flunked his first rifle-shooting test but eventually qualified as an infantry sharpshooter (the middle ranking between marksman and expert) with the M-16 rifle. Early in his Army service, for unknown reasons, he left Judaism to become a fundamentalist Baptist after attending hand-clapping revival meetings. . . .

Berkowitz's apartment was a mess, furnished with little more than a low mattress. The windows were covered by sheets to keep neighbors from seeing in. Pornographic magazines were strewn near the bed. One large hole had been knocked in a wall, with an arrow pointing to it and a puzzling hand-printed message: "Hi. My name is Mr. Williams, and I live in this hole." Also on the wall was another irrational declaration: "I have several children who I'm turning into killers. Wait til they grow up."

More often, Berkowitz couched his strange ideas in vivid verbiage. Said part of a note found in his car. "And huge drops of lead/Poured down upon her head/Until she was dead. Yet the cats still come out at night to mate; and the sparrows still sing in the morning."

From a letter sent to Columnist Breslin: "I am a spirit roaming the night. Thirsty, hungry, seldom stopping to rest, anxious to please Sam. I love my work."

The torments within Berkowitz, a man who sometimes greeted people in his apartment building with a friendly smile and even gave a newspaper delivery boy a $30 tip one Christmas, also surfaced in anonymous crank letters to neighbors—notes that helped lead to his capture. Two were to Sam Carr, the fatherly figure Berkowitz was to fancy as a source of the commands to kill. Carr, 64, a frail, grizzled man who operates a telephone answering service from his home and maintains an astonishing arsenal of guns (he said he has a .22 automatic, .32 revolver, .38 revolver, .30-06 rifle, .410 shotgun and .357 magnum), suspected that Berkowitz sent the anonymous threatening letters that complained about the howling of Carr's black Labrador retriever Harvey.

The first letter declared that "our lives have been torn apart because of this dog." The second said that "my life is destroyed now. I have nothing to lose anymore. I can see that there shall be no peace in my life or my family's life until I end yours. You wicked, evil man—child of the devil—I curse you and your family forever." Carr claimed that Berkowitz later shot Harvey in the leg with a .44-cal. gun.

The other recipient of hate mail was Craig Glassman, 29, a male nurse and part-time corporal in the Westchester County sheriff's emergency force. He lived directly under Berkowitz's apartment and got four letters. They accused Glassman of being a "demon" and a "wicked person," who (like "Sam") was forcing the writer to kill. Said one letter: "My master Craig, You will be punished. Craig, how dare you force me into the night to do your bidding. I promise you, Craig, the world shall spit on you and your mother . . . Sure, I am the killer, but Craig, the killings are at your command." On the same day that he received two of the letters (Aug. 6), Glassman was startled to find a fire burning outside his apartment door. When firemen put it out, they found .22-cal. shells in the ashes. . . .

Incredibly, Berkowitz, who had so cleverly eluded police for so long, had used his own properly registered 1970 Ford Galaxie sedan as his getaway car for each attack, not bothering even to acquire stolen license plates. When New York police checked parking tickets for the murder night in the Gravesend neighborhood, they found one issued to Berkowitz; it led to his Yonkers address. They wondered: What was a Yonkers resident doing 25 miles away in Brooklyn at 2:30 a.m.?

With that, New York detectives went to Berkowitz's apartment house, and they found his car parked handily in front. Peering inside, they spied a rifle butt protruding from an Army duffel bag in the back seat and a note on the front seat. It bore the highly distinctive hand printing of the .44-cal. killer's letters to police and Breslin. A dozen officers staked out the car and the building, while a search warrant was sought.

At 10:30 p.m. Berkowitz walked calmly out of the building, got into his car and started the engine. A couple of officers ran out of the darkness, their guns drawn. They ordered Berkowitz to turn off the ignition, get out of the car and place his hands on top of it. Having followed the mountains of clippings about Son of Sam closely—a scrapbook of them was found in his apartment—Berkowitz recognized the arresting officers' leader, Deputy Inspector Timothy Dowd. "Inspector, you finally got me," he said quietly to Dowd. "I guess this is the end of the trail."

When he was seized, Berkowitz was carrying a manila envelope; in it was the .44-cal. pistol that had been used in all of the Son of Sam murders. He also had a semiautomatic rifle, simulated to look like a submachine gun, in the car.

Telling his story later to police, Berkowitz destroyed some misconceptions that had been spread, sometimes by authorities, more often by frenzied New York tabloids. No, he did not always fire his jolting .44 Bulldog revolver with two hands from a crouch. "The first three times I shot with one hand." No, he was not a skilled marksman. "I was lousy." No, he did not always keep one of the five bullets in his revolver in reserve in case he faced capture. He twice emptied the gun in his attacks. No, he did not look only for dark-haired girls, haunt discothèques for victims or carefully case a site before striking. His hunt was random. "When I got a calling," he said, "I went looking for a spot."

He often crusied various neighborhoods in his car after such a "calling," looking for some "sign" that the timing was right. Even such a chance event as the appearance of a convenient parking space was such a sign to Berkowitz. He did choose victims whom he considered "pretty," claiming he favored the Queens borough for a time because "Queens girls are prettier." He did not walk casually away from the murder sites and slip into the dark. "I ran like hell." He revisited at least two of the scenes of his crimes and tried to find the grave of his first victim, Donna Lauria, 18, whom he had not known but for whom he seemed to develop a posthumous affection. . . .

The work of criminal psychologists in providing police with personality profiles of the likely killer was more accurate and perhaps did help narrow the search. Such a profile issued by police last May described the killer as "neurotic, schizophrenic and paranoid, with religious aspects to his thinking process, as well as hints of demonic possession and compulsion. He is probably shy and odd, a loner inept at establishing personal relationships, especially with women." Psychologists say Berkowitz is a psychopath, and all evidence points to his lonely nature and inability to relate normally to women.[8]

Raw Violence and the Psychotic Criminal Personality

All these crimes were committed by psychotic people. Most violence has a cloak of rationality and sanction in the social conditions, issues, and situations that surround its expression. The concept of *raw violence* refers to violent action that does not flow from any readily comprehensible social conditions or issues. It is a direct expression of an individual's psychological disorder at a given time, when that person commits a bizarre criminal act of violence.

Legal, sanctioned, rational violence, such as war or police violence, constitutes acts motivated by a fundamental desire to maintain the norms and equilibrium of the social structure. War is generally seen by its proponents as an effort to defend or restore the social structure, and violence in law enforcement is justified as an effort to maintain the legal structure. The violence that flows from these circumstances is comprehensible even if there is disagreement about its use. The defense of one's honor or the unauthorized illegal use of force to defend certain values is also understandable within the framework of societal norms.

Violence that emanates from or is a part of the socialized criminal's behavior is also more easily understood than raw violence. The use of violence by organized crime or the shooting of a robbery victim who does not cooperate has a great degree of rationality in the criminal context. Here we would have to search for the causes of the violence in the causal context of the crime.

The causal background of crime per se thus accounts for most violence. Raw direct violence, however, must be studied and explained within its own context. It is not a secondary act flowing from criminal behavior. It is a primary, not a secondary, criminal act.

Psychiatrists attribute most acts of raw violence to a psychotic condition. They describe this condition as a type of emotional breakdown that causes an individual to have hallucinations or to fantasize that people are out to get him, and he assaults or kills them before they can harm him.

A considerable proportion of incidents of raw violence may be accounted for by a psychotic or sociopathic personality; individuals with limited social conscience have no real compassion for others.

An aspect of the psychotic criminal personality's breakthrough into violence may be termed "existential validation." When a person feels constantly alienated from other human beings, he begins to lose the

---

[8] "Sam Told Me to Do It . . . Sam Is the Devil," in *Time*, August 22, 1977. Copyright 1977 Time Inc. Reprinted by permission.

sense of his own humanity and requires increasingly heavier dosages of bizarre and extreme behavior to validate the fact that he really exists. This extreme behavior gives him a glimmer of feeling when nothing else does. As one gang killer commented to one of the authors, "When I stabbed him once, I did it again and again, because it really made me feel alive for the first time in my life."

There are, then, two dominant patterns of criminal violence. One involves, in a sense, a criminal sheath. Violence is a secondary act that is instrumental to or a by-product of other criminal activity (e.g., organized crime or robbery). The other pattern is primary, raw, senseless violence that emanates from an individual's psychodynamic condition. Whitman, Bianchi, Mullin, and Berkowitz are cases in point. Part of the dynamics of the psychotic criminal personality is explained in Norman Cameron's concept of "the paranoid pseudocommunity." His penetrating analysis tends to explain in some measure the psychotic criminal personalities of these murderers.

According to Cameron, a group makes certain demands upon the individual, and in the normative pattern of life the individual makes a personal contribution to group demands. This the normal individual finds satisfying. On the daily level of group interaction, relevant "others" validate the individual's group participation at a minimal level of social expectation. However, "Under certain circumstances individuals with socially inadequate development fail progressively to maintain such a level, with the result that they become socially disarticulated and very often have to be set aside from the rest of their community to live under artificially simplified conditions."[9]

The person who requires this forced or voluntary dissociation from the general community has psychotic characteristics. A psychotic person's essential limitation is an inability to take the role of another, except for egocentric purposes. The individual lacks a social conscience. To oversimplify, this type of individual tends to become paranoid and to have interchangeable delusions of persecution and excessive grandeur. These emotions result from an essentially correct assessment of existing personal and social disability—a disability developed in a vacuum lacking effective socializing agents and processes. The paranoid's reactions of delusion and persecution are useful in enabling the person to fool himself or herself into feeling powerful and at the same time to blame his or her social disability on any unfair societal persecution. Both paranoid devices (grandeur and persecution) tend temporarily to relieve an already battered, ineffectual self of blame for any problems.

The delusional process is at first internal and on the level of personal

---

[9] Norman Cameron, "The Paranoid Pseudo-Community," *American Journal of Sociology* 49 (July 1943):32–38.

thought; however, in time it tends to become projected onto and involved with the surrounding community. According to Cameron:

> The paranoid person, because of poorly developed role-taking ability, which may have been derived from defective social learning in earlier life, faces his real or fancied slights and discriminations without adequate give-and-take in his communication with others and without competence in the social interpretation of motives and intentions.[10]

This type of person, whose role-taking skills are impaired, lacks the ability adequately to assess the "other" in interaction. The paranoid psychotic begins to take everything the wrong way and, because of an inability to think as others do, becomes increasingly alienated and dissociated from the real world. Delusional fantasies become hardened, and the person begins to see and experience things not consensually validated or similarly felt by others. As Cameron specifies, the psychotic "becomes prejudiced with regard to his social environment." His responses tend first to select reactions from his surroundings that fit into his personal interpretation and then to reshape in retrospect things that seemed innocent enough when they occurred, until they support the trend of his suspicions. Because of this already incipient disturbance, and particularly if the individual is evolving in a defective socializing community, the person is unable to get relevant responses from others to counteract a developing reaction formation that finally hardens into what Cameron has termed a *paranoid pseudocommunity*.

As he begins attributing to others the attitudes he has toward himself, he unintentionally organizes these others into a functional community, a group unified in its supposed reactions, attitudes, and plans with respect to him. In this way he organizes individuals, some of whom are actual persons and some only inferred or imagined, into a whole that satisfies for the time being his immediate need for explanation but which brings no reassurance with it and usually serves to increase his tensions. The community he forms not only fails to correspond to any organization shared by others but actually contradicts the consensus. More than this, these others do not actually perform the actions or maintain the attitudes he ascribes to them; they are united in no common undertaking against him. What he takes to be a functional community is only a pseudocommunity created by his own unskilled attempts at interpretation, anticipation, and validation of social behavior.

This pseudocommunity of attitude and intent that the individual succeeds in thus setting up organizes his own responses still further in the direction they have been taking; and these responses in turn lead to greater and greater systematization of the surroundings. The pseudocommunity grows until it seems to constitute so grave a threat to the individual's integrity or life that, often after clumsy attempts to get at the

---

[10] Cameron, "The Paranoid Pseudo-Community," p. 33.

root of things indirectly, the person bursts into directly defensive or vengeful activity. This brings out into the open a whole system of organized responses to a supposed functional community of detractors or persecutors which the individual has been rehearsing in private. The real community, which cannot share in these attitudes and reactions, counters the person's actions with forcible restraint or retaliation.[11]

The real community's response and retaliation only serve to strengthen the individual's suspicions and distorted interpretations: these actions are seen as further evidence of unfair discrimination. The pseudocommunity calcifies, becomes more articulate and real to him. He begins after a while to live in his delusional realm almost to the exclusion of other social alternatives. He may break out of this shell through bizarre acts of violence against his imagined enemies in the real world.

There are in our society many criminal psychotic personality types, like Whitman, Bianchi, Mullin, and Berkowitz, who live in the paranoid pseudocommunity described by Cameron. We need to develop effective techniques for identifying and then treating them if we are to avoid the conflagrations of raw violence that they produce.

THE SOCIOPATHIC CRIMINAL

For many years the catchall label *psychopathic* was applied by psychiatrists to all persons whose behavior deviated markedly from the normal yet who could not be clearly categorized as severely neurotic or psychotic. In the last decade, the term *sociopath* has been used interchangeably with the term *psychopath* to describe individuals who, because of a severe character defect involving a lack of compassion, act out self-destructive and other destructive behavior. In the following analysis I will use the term *sociopath* to describe this personality disorder.

A dominant theme of the sociopathic offender is what has varyingly been called "moral imbecility" or "character disorder." This type of offender may know right from wrong but still lacks any coherent, appropriate discretionary ability in the realm of compassionate or moral behavior.

A number of sociologists and psychologists have attempted to define this personality syndrome. Paul Tappan describes the sociopath as follows: "He has a condition of psychological abnormality in which there is neither the overt appearance of psychosis or neurosis, but there is a chronic abnormal response to the environment."[12]

---

[11] Cameron, "The Paranoid Pseudo-Community," p. 35.

[12] Paul W. Tappan, *Crime, Justice and Corrections* (New York: McGraw-Hill, 1960), p. 137.

According to Harrison Gough, the sociopath is "the kind of person who seems insensitive to social demands, who refuses to or cannot cooperate, who is untrustworthy, impulsive, and improvident, who shows poor judgement and shallow emotionality, and who seems unable to appreciate the reactions of others to his behavior."[13]

In brief, from my viewpoint, the prototypical sociopathic criminal has a persistent pattern of deviant behavior characterized by an almost total disregard for the rights and feelings of others. A summary listing of the sociopath's overt personality and behavior traits would include most, if not all, of the following factors: (1) a limited social conscience; (2) evidence of egocentrism dominating most interaction, instrumental manipulation of others for self-advantage (rather than affective relating); (3) the inability to forgo immediate pleasure for future goals; and (4) a habit of pathological lying to achieve personal advantage.

The Mask of Sanity

Dr. Hervey Cleckley, a psychiatrist who has contributed much to the clarification of the psychiatric terminology on the sociopath, defines the sociopath as follows:

> This term refers to chronically antisocial individuals who are always in trouble, profiting neither from experience nor punishment, and maintaining no real loyalties to any person, group, or code. They are frequently callous and hedonistic, showing marked emotional immaturity, with lack of responsibility, lack of judgement, and an ability to rationalize their behavior so that it appears warranted, reasonable, and justified.[14]

In a book (aptly titled *The Mask of Sanity*, since sociopaths usually appear normal), Cleckley developed comprehensive criteria for viewing this criminal personality. Cleckley noted that most sociopaths manifest the following personality characteristics:

1. Superficial charm and good "intelligence." The typical sociopath, when first encountered, seems friendly and well-adjusted, appears to have many interests, and is also likely to possess superior intelligence.
2. Absence of delusions and other signs of irrational thinking. The sociopath can recognize the physical realities of the environment, does not hear voices, and reasons logically.
3. Absence of "nervousness" or psychoneurotic manifestations. The sociopath is usually free from the minor reactions popularly

---

[13] Harrison G. Gough, "A Sociological Theory of Psychopathy," *American Journal of Sociology* 53 (March 1948):365.

[14] Hervey M. Cleckley, "Psychopathic States," in *American Handbook of Psychiatry*, ed. Silvano Arieti (New York: Basic Books, 1959), p. 568.

called "neurotic" and is typically immune to anxiety and worry that might be considered normal in disturbing situations.

4. Unreliability. The sociopath, after making substantial gains personally and often financially, will for no predictable reason abruptly throw these gains away in an irresponsible manner. A sociopath cannot be counted on in any way.

5. Untruthfulness and insincerity. The sociopath's disregard for truth is remarkable. Such a person seems confident and comfortable when making a solemn promise that will never be kept. Sociopaths will lie recklessly, but with great conviction, to extricate themselves from any accusations.

6. Lack of remorse or shame. The sociopath cannot accept blame for any misfortunes, no matter who caused them. Although he or she may insincerely claim some responsibility for troubles, this is probably done to elicit confidence and trust from others. Also, the sociopath displays virtually no sense of shame, even though such a person's life is filled with immoral exploits.

7. Inadequately motivated antisocial behavior. The sociopath generally follows a course of behavior that is antisocial—cheating, lying, and fighting even when such actions do not serve any personal goal.

8. Poor judgment and failure to learn by experience. Although more than capable of rationality, the sociopath displays terrible judgment about how to achieve a goal. There is no evidence that such a person ever learns from continuing negative experiences. The sociopath compulsively repeats failures, even to the point of repeating antisocial behaviors that lead to second or third incarcerations.

9. Pathologic egocentricity and incapacity for love. Though the sociopath often manifests the overt signs of affection and love, there is no indication that he or she actually experiences these emotions in any real sense. This is a person who cannot and does not form enduring relationships. Despite surface indications of love and compassion, the sociopath is usually callous and destructive to others.

10. General poverty in major affective reactions. The sociopath may display peevishness, spite, and false affection, but such a person is incapable of experiencing, deeply and truly, such emotions as pride, anger, grief, and joy.

11. Specific loss of insight. The sociopath has limited insight, is apparently not introspective, and is unable to understand others' viewpoints. The sociopath who has committed a crime assumes that "the legal penalties . . . do not, or should not apply to him."

12. Unresponsiveness in general interpersonal relations. Although perhaps superficially courteous in minor matters, the sociopath is incapable of sacrifice or true generosity and does not demonstrate appreciation when others perform acts of trust or kindness.

13. Fantastic and uninviting behavior with drink and sometimes without. The sociopath typically uses alcohol and drugs to excess. Unlike most alcoholics, the sociopath under the influence of even a modest amount of alcohol may become extremely irrational and destructive. This bizarre behavior can continue even when the person is not drinking.

14. Suicide rarely carried out. The sociopath often threatens suicide but rarely carries it out. The lack of real guilt or shame about personal behavior does not produce a true motivation for suicide. The threat is used egocentrically for immediate personal advantage.

15. Sex life impersonal, trivial, and poorly integrated. The sex lives of both male and female sociopaths are generally promiscuous and, for the most part, emotionally unfulfilling. The sex partner is viewed as an object rather than as a person with feelings. The sociopath often seems to choose sexual exploits solely to put "himself, as well as others, in positions of sharp indignity and distastefulness."

16. Failure to follow any life plan. The sociopath makes no steady effort toward reaching any long-range personal goals. One of the remarkable features of the sociopath is a consistent pattern of self-defeat. It is one of the few predictable behavioral characteristics of these people.[15]

By applying Cleckley's criteria, we can distinguish the sociopath from the psychotic—a person whose reasoning is disturbed by delusions and hallucinations—and from the neurotic—a person who suffers from an excess of anxiety and guilt. We can also distinguish the sociopathic personality from the "normal" personalities of career and professional criminals, who are motivated by monetary gain rather than emotional problems. The diagnostic criteria employed by Cleckley clearly illuminates the sociopath as a criminal personality type.

Two other social scientists, William and Joan McCord, helped define the sociopathy syndrome. The McCords' profile of the psychopath (or sociopath) parallels Ceckley's categories and may be summarized as follows in further defining the sociopathic criminal:

1. The sociopath is asocial. No rule, however important, can stop this person. The professional criminal, the gang criminal, and others may be asocial or antisocial, but they do not share the character structure of the true sociopathic personality. Any adequate study of the sociopath must look beyond asociality.

2. The sociopath is driven by uncontrolled desires. Much of the

---

[15] Summarized from Hervey Cleckley, *The Mask of Sanity* (St. Louis: Mosby, 1976). Used by permission.

sociopath's asociality can be traced to this quest for immediate pleasure. The sociopath often seems to know no greater pleasure than constant change and does not seem to receive satisfaction from productive work.

3. The sociopath is highly impulsive. Unlike the normal person, or even the average criminal, the sociopath's adventures often seem purposeless. Even the person's crimes are rarely planned: there seem to be no stable goals.

4. The sociopath is aggressive. The individual characteristically reacts to frustration with fury because the uninhibited search for pleasure often clashes with society's restrictions. The conflict frequently results in aggressive action.

5. The sociopath feels little guilt. In the usual sense, the sociopath has no conscience. The sociopath can commit any act with hardly a twinge of remorse, showing very little anxiety or inner conflicts.

6. The sociopath has a warped capacity for love. This type of person has been characterized as a "lone wolf." The individual seems cold and compassionless and treats people like objects—as means for egotistical pleasure. The sociopath wards off close attachments, either lacking the capability to form them or because experience has not provided a model of how to form them.[16]

The pattern of the socialized criminal, who is a relatively well-trained type of offender, differs considerably from that of the sociopathic offender. The following commentary, made by a sociopathic youth who was involved in a brutal gang homicide, reveals the compulsive abnormal behavior of the sociopath:

> Momentarily, I started thinking about it inside; I have my mind made up I'm not going to be in no gang. Then I go on inside. Something comes up, then here all my friends coming to me. Like I said before, I'm intelligent and so forth. They be coming to—then they talk to me about what they gonna do, like kill this guy! Like, "Man, I just gotta go with you." Myself, I don't want to go, but when they start talkin' about what they gonna do, I say, "So, he isn't gonna take over my rep, I ain't gonna let him be known more than me." And I go ahead, just for selfishness.[17]

The senseless "other-directed" violence of such sociopathic offenders is perpetrated for ego status—for "kicks" or "thrills." The kicks involve a type of emotional euphoria that the sociopathic criminal maintains "makes me feel good." The motive is "selfishness." The goals of the offender are self-oriented in a primary fashion, with material gain

---

[16] Summarized from William McCord and Joan McCord, *The Psychopath* (New York: Van Nostrand, 1964).

[17] Lewis Yablonsky, *The Violent Gang* (New York: Macmillan, 1962; reprint, Irvington Press, 1988).

as a secondary consideration. Socialized criminals do not place themselves in jeopardy for this type of senseless gang-violence offense. Socialized offenders use violence as an instrument for material gain, not for an emotional charge which serves to validate their existence.

Violence is often used in a "rational" way as an instrument in the activities of the socialized criminal. The violence of a sociopathic offender, on the other hand, is characterized by the following:

1. There is no evidence of prior contact or interaction between the assailant and the victim.
2. The violent act often occurs in an unpremeditated, generally spontaneous and impulsive manner.
3. In some cases (particularly, for example, in gang assault), there is a degree of prior buildup to the act; however, the final consequence (often homicide) is not really anticipated.
4. The offender's expressed reaction to the violent behavior is usually lacking in regret and inappropriate to the act that has been committed.

Causal Factors in the Development of the Sociopathic Criminal Personality

An adequate social self develops from a consistent pattern of interaction with rational adults in a normative socialization process. The parent or adequate adult role model is someone who helps a child learn social feelings of love, compassion, and sympathy. The proper adult role models necessary for adequate socialization are absent from the social environment of many children growing up in depressed disorganized slum areas.

The basic ingredient missing in the sociopathic delinquent's socialization is a loving parent or adult. On the basis of their extensive analysis of the literature, the McCords state: "Because the rejected child does not love his parents and they do not love him, no identification takes place. Nor does the rejected child feel the loss of love—a love which he never had—when he violates moral restriction. Without love, from an adult socializing agent, the psychopath remains asocial."

Dr. Marshall Cherkas, an eminent psychiatrist with over 20 years of experience as a court psychiatrist, interviewed several hundred delinquent sociopaths. He has come to similar conclusions about the etiology of the sociopathic criminal's personality. In the following statement he presents his viewpoint on the causal context of the sociopath's early life experience:

> Children are extremely dependent upon nurturing parents for life's sustenance as well as satisfaction and avoidance of pain. In the earliest phase of life, in their first year, infants maintain a highly narcissistic position in the world. Their sense of security, comfort, reality, and orientation is focused on

their own primitive needs with little awareness and reality testing of the external world. As the normal infant develops, its security and comfort is reasonably assured. There occurs a natural attachment, awareness, and interest in "the Other." As the child matures, the dependency upon "the Other," its parents, diminishes, but the strength of the self is enhanced, and the child develops an awareness that its narcissistic needs are met through a cooperative, adaptive, and mutually supportive relationship to its parents and others. In other words, the child recognizes that even though its selfish (narcissistic) needs are extremely important, they can best be served by appropriately relating to other people, especially its parents.

This cooperative process is repeated many times in the development of the individual, and there are stages of recapitulation where dependence and narcissistic interest are heightened. There are other stages where the child's sense of social recognition and cooperativeness are greatly increased, with less emphasis upon its own narcissistic needs.

Infants whose needs are not adequately met because of the parents' own exaggerated narcissistic needs develop feelings of mistrust, insecurity, and wariness about the capacities of their provider. In order to protect itself, the child may perform many tasks to gain attention, support, and interest from the parent. The child also begins to feel that it cannot trust others, and that its needs can only be met through self-interest. The child who cannot count on its own parents begins to become egocentric and therefore sociopathic in its behavior.[18]

Edwin Megaree and Roy Golden carried out research into this element of causation related to the sociopath. They based their research on the reasoning that sociopathic offenders have a significantly poorer relation with their parents than do either noncriminals or the normal, socialized criminals. The purpose of the study was to partially test these formulations by comparing the attitudes toward their parents held by sociopathic and socialized criminal offenders and a noncriminal group of comparable socioeconomic status.

Megaree and Golden advanced the following hypothesis:

1. Sociopathic criminals' attitudes toward their parents are likely to be significantly more negative than those of noncriminals.
2. Sociopathic criminals' attitudes toward their parents are likely to be significantly more negative than those of socialized criminals.
3. There is probably no noteworthy difference between socialized criminals' and noncriminals' attitudes toward their parents.[19]

Using various psychological inventories, Megaree and Golden cross-compared a sample of identified sociopaths from a federal correctional institution and a matched control group of students attending a technical

---

[18] Adapted from an unpublished paper, "The Sociopathic Delinquent Personality," by permission of the author, Dr. Marshall Cherkas.

[19] Based on Edwin I. Megaree and Roy E. Golden, "Parental Attitudes of Psychopathic and Subcultural Delinquents," *Criminology*, vol. 10, no. 4 (February 1973), pp. 427–439.

trade school. Both institutions were located in Tallahassee, Florida. The correctional institution's final sample of 31 was divided into two groups of "subcultural delinquents" and "psychopathic delinquents." (The subcultural delinquents would parallel our socialized delinquents.)

The delinquent groups (both subcultural and psychopathic) were contrasted with the nondelinquents with regard to parental relationships. On the basis of their research, Megaree and Golden came to the following conclusion:

> The nondelinquents expressed the most favorable attitudes toward both their parents, and the psychopathic delinquents the most negative. For these two groups there was little difference between the ratings for the mother and the father. The subcultural [socialized] delinquents displayed a different pattern, however; their attitude toward mother was as favorable as that of the nondelinquent group, but their attitude toward father was as negative as that of the psychopathic sample. . . .
>
> The data . . . highlighted the important role played by the mother. While the attitude toward the father was the crucial variable separating the delinquents from the nondelinquents, it was the attitude toward the mother than differentiated the subcultural from the psychopathic delinquents. One might speculate that it is this positive relationship with the mother that permits the subcultural delinquent to appear well adjusted and capable of loyalty to his group and adherence to a code of values, albeit a socially deviant code.[20]

The notion of adequate self-emergence through constructive social interaction with others, especially parents, is grounded in the theoretical works of Charles Horton Cooley and was later developed by J. L. Moreno and George H. Mead. Mead developed the theme as follows:

> The self arises in conduct when the individual becomes a social object in experience to himself. This takes place when the individual assumes the attitude or uses the gestures which another individual would use and responds to it himself. Through socialization, the child gradually becomes a social being. The self thus has its origin in communication and in taking the role of the other.[21]

Harry Stack Sullivan saw the self as being made up of "reflected appraisals":

> The child lacks equipment and experience necessary for a careful and unclouded evaluation of himself. The only guides he has are those of the significant adults or others who take care of him and treat him with compassion. The child thus experiences and appraises himself in accordance with the reactions of parents and others close to him. By facial expressions, gestures, words, and deeds, they convey to him the attitudes

---

[20] Megaree and Golden, "Parental Attitudes of Psychopathic and Subcultural Delinquents," pp. 433–437.

[21] George H. Mead, *Mind, Self and Society* (University of Chicago Press, 1934), p. 236.

they hold toward him, their regard for him or lack of it. A set of positive sympathetic responses, necessary for adequate self-growth, is generally absent in the development of the youth who becomes a sociopath.[22]

In summary, therefore, the sociopathic criminal is produced by a socialization process that does not include loving role models. Because of this lack of loving role models in the social sphere in early life, the sociopathic criminal tends to be self-involved, exploitative, and disposed toward violent outburts. This sociopathic individual lacks social ability, the ability to adequately assess the role expectations of others. Lacking the ability to identify or empathize with others, such a person is characteristically unable to experience the pain of the violence he or she may inflict on another. The sociopath is thus capable of committing spontaneous acts of senseless violence without feeling concern or guilt.

The sociopath is highly impulsive and explosive. For this person, the moment is a segment of time detached from all others; actions are unplanned, guided by whims. The sociopath is an aggressive individual who has learned few socialized ways of coping with frustration. The sociopath feels little if any guilt and can commit the most appalling acts, yet view them without remorse. The sociopath has a warped and limited capacity to love and be compassionate. Emotional relationships, when they exist, are shallow, fleeting, and designed to satisfy only egocentric desires.

A Classic Sociopath: The Case of Jose

The emergence of the sociopathic criminal personality is an enigma that has not been fully clarified. Yet there are patterns that recur consistently enough to enable us to identify them as probable causes of the development of the sociopathic personality. As noted earlier, one is the lack of a proper parental role model of love or compassion, which would demonstrate the ability to involve oneself with another human being without egocentric designs. Most sociopaths have grown up in a predatory, exploitative, and manipulative social situation. Love and compassion are generally foreign to their lives.

The evolution of a sociopath may be seen in the case of a boy we shall call Jose Perez, who was known to me for several years during my five-year study of sociopathic gang youths in New York City.[23] Jose had brutally participated in the stabbing and killing of another youth and was convicted of homicide. I had the opportunity to observe his behavior on the streets prior to the murder and to interview him several times in the state reformatory where he was incarcerated after the murder.

---

[22] Harry Stack Sullivan, *Conceptions of Modern Psychiatry* (Washington, D.C.: William Alanson White Psychiatric Foundation, 1947).

[23] See Yablonsky, *The Violent Gang.*

Jose migrated from Puerto Rico to New York City with his family when he was 8 years old. Jose's first remembered reaction to New York City was to the cold and dirt. "It's always summer in Puerto Rico," he explained. Although in San Juan he had lived in a run-down slum called La Perla, it was heaven to him compared to the slum where he now lived on Manhattan's Upper West Side. On the island, Jose could step out of his shack to find sunlight and ocean breezes and the friendly greetings of his neighbors. In New York City, he would leave his tenement to enter a cold world of hostile and indifferent strangers.

On the island Jose was somebody. He had an identity. Although the family was poor, the Perez name meant something, and Jose sought to live up to it. His family and friends identified him as an individual; he had a position in the community, even though he was still a child. Everyone knew everyone else in the huddle of poor shacks where he lived; they all had some concern for one another.

In New York he was shocked to discover that he was considered "different." The first time he was cursed at school as a "dirty spick" he became severely upset and angry. His response became aggressive. He retaliated; finally he began to attack other children without provocation in anticipation of their insults.

"Outsiders"—whites and some blacks—were not his only antagonists. He was often picked on by other Puerto Ricans who had lived longer in New York City. To them he was a foreigner, a "tiger." (The *Marine Tiger* was one of the ships that carried many Puerto Ricans to New York City early in the Puerto Rican migration. The name was shortened and applied to all newly arrived "greenhorns.") He embarrassed them because he was a Puerto Rican greenhorn and reflected negatively on earlier arrivals who had become assimilated. Other Puerto Ricans, suffering from self-hatred as a result of their lowered status, took out their resentment on someone they needed to feel was even more inferior than they.

Jose had a good school record in Puerto Rico, but in New York he hated school and became a habitual truant. His despised identity as a "spick" was accentuated by his inability to speak English. The teacher tried to help, but, overwhelmed by a large number of students with various problems, she was unable to do much. Her students' personal problems, combined with their language difficulties, made teaching specific subject matter almost impossible.

The one available school guidance counselor (for some thousand students) tried to talk to Jose, but by this time Jose was considered a serious behavior problem. His hatred for school became more intense each time he played hookey. Going back to school seemed increasingly difficult, if not impossible. He spent his days at the movies, when he could raise the price of a ticket by petty thievery, or simply sat and daydreamed. He felt weak, inferior, and alone. His favorite cartoon hero was Mighty Mouse: "You know he's a mouse—he's dressed up like

Superman. He's got little pants—they're red. The shirt is yellow. You know, and then he helps out the mouse. Every time the cats try to get the mouse, Mighty Mouse comes and helps the mouse, just like Superman. He's stronger than he acts. Nothing can hurt him."

Jose alternated between fantasy and direct acts of violence—increasingly delivered to undeserving and often unsuspecting victims. Lectures and threats to have him sent to a reformatory meant little to Jose. He already knew from a friend that the state reformatory was "all filled up, and they ain't going to send you there for just playing hookey." Roaming the streets produced other delinquent activities: petty thievery and vandalism. These, plus a developed pattern of purse-snatching, with greater emphasis on violence than on financial gain, helped provide the necessary background for his sentence to the reformatory.

Yet it was not so much what happened to Jose that caused his unfeeling, asocial behavior to grow; it was what did *not* happen. In his world there was a dearth of law-abiding young people and adults from whom he could learn any social feeling toward another person. To Jose, people became things you manipulated to get what you wanted. He discovered that "being nice" was often useful, but only if it helped get what you wanted. When caught stealing, he learned that "sometimes if you hang your head down right and looked pitiful, you could avoid punishment."

There were few people in Jose's world who ever considered another person's feelings or welfare unless they expected to get something in return. Everything Jose saw was a con game. The two most successful types of behavior were manipulation and violence. When one didn't work, the other would. Jose found violence and the threat of violence most effective. As his "rep" for sudden, unexpected violence grew, others responded by complying with his egocentric needs.

Jose "naturally" learned to manipulate others and to use violence "properly." He learned to feel no affection for anyone, not even the other members of his family. No one taught him to express positive emotions or set an example by displaying human feelings. In the hostile and asocial world that surrounded him, he learned the most effective adaptation, and his sociopathic personality became more developed with each day's experience.

Jose's family was of little help to him in New York. His family's rules, language, and appearance were considered old-fashioned and inappropriate. Also, his parents and older brothers were busy battling their own enemies in the cold city. His family was generally not available to fill his needs for human contact and compassion. He sometimes dreamed with fondness about pleasant evenings of the past, in Puerto Rico with his family. They used to go to a park near their home in the evenings. Mostly the children would play, and the adults would sit around and discuss the day's events. At these times children and adults talked easily with each other. In these old days, now gone, Jose had the opportunity to discuss his personal troubles with his parents and older brothers. It was even pleasant to be criticized, since it gave Jose a secure feeling to know someone was concerned. In the park not only his own parents, but relatives and other adults also took an interest in children. One man took the boys swimming; a group of older men from a social club formed a baseball league for the younger boys. Jose belonged to a community.

All this changed in New York. His father, an unskilled laborer, found it hard to get a job that paid a living wage. Jose's father earned a modest amount when he worked. He was often unemployed. During these periods, quarrels and conflict developed between his parents, and his father became less and less the man of the house—the role he had clearly occupied in Puerto Rico. Beset with their own overwhelming problems, Jose's parents sometimes unfairly attacked their children, who increasingly became a burden to them.

There was no one for Jose to talk to about his feelings. His father began to drink excessively to escape from immediate realities and a sense of inadequacy he could not face. The more he drank, the more violent he became. In his seemingly senseless rages, he beat Jose's mother and often attacked Jose for no apparent reason. Violence surrounded Jose, and he became indifferent to his family. About his father Jose said, "I'll ask him to take me boat riding, fishing, or someplace like that, ball game. He'll say no. He don't go no place. The only place where he goes, he goes to the bar. And from the bar, he goes home. Sleep, that's about all he do. I don't talk to my parents a lot of times. I don't hardly talk to them—there's nothing to talk about. There's nothing to discuss about. They can't help me."

Family trouble was compounded by the need for Jose's mother to take a menial job to help support the family. This removed her further from the home. Rents were exorbitant. The family was barred from moving into certain neighborhoods where Puerto Ricans were not welcome. In any case, their erratic income was insufficient for a steady monthly rental in a more stable neighborhood. The family of six continued to live in a rat- and roach-infested two-room hotel apartment, though they had originally moved in on a temporary basis. They shared kitchen facilities and an outside toilet with eight other families and paid a rental of over $150 a week. Close quarters intensified the family conflict. Jose increasingly resolved his problems outside the home.

At one time Jose became friendly with Juan, an older youth from the neighborhood who took an interest in him and attempted to help him. Juan was a leader in a social gang called the Braves. This group was well organized; the members participated in sports, ran dances, and belonged to the local community center. The Braves were tough, but they did not go in for gang wars or other violent activity. Although most members of the Braves engaged in occasional fights and petty thievery, they stayed clear of mass fighting and participated in more socially accepted activities. Juan tried to get Jose into the Braves, but Jose was voted down. He lacked the social ability to be a member.

Then Jose met a violent gang leader called Loco. As his name implies, Loco was thought to be a little crazy, and this did not displease him. His reputation for sudden violence with a knife or a homemade gun made him greatly feared. As part of his usual gang-leader activity, Loco was organizing a West Side Dragons division. Jose was accepted without question and was appointed a war counselor after Loco saw him stab a younger boy on a dare.

Jose and other Dragons enjoyed the exciting stories Loco told about Dragon gang divisions throughout Manhattan. Jose learned, and he began to make brother-gang pacts of his own. Also, as a war counselor for the West Side Dragons, he had what seemed like a good excuse to commit acts of violence every night. His sudden temper and quick use of a blade increased his rep. With Loco he organized a brother-gang pact with another gang on the Upper West Side called the Egyptian Kings. Membership did not really give Jose a feeling of belonging or provide a comfortable way of life. Instead, the violent gang affected his anxieties and troubles in the same way alcohol "resolves" problems for the alcoholic and drugs "help" the drug addict: it served to destroy him further.

The Kings provided a vehicle for expressing much of the hatred, disillusionment, and aggression that existed in Jose. The group also was compatible with the acompassionate, unfeeling, and manipulative socio-pathic personality he had developed. Violence was expressed at the right opportunity, or opportunities were created. Also, the gang helped minimize feelings of guilt and anxiety about violence at the increasingly rare times such feelings existed in Jose. Any limited concern he had with feelings of worthlessness were diminished by the recognition that there were others like himself. All the Kings were "down cats." "Everyone puts you down" and "Get your kicks now—make it today" were his slogans. "Sounding on people" and "putting them down" were central King activities, and Jose became an expert in all the gang activities.

The violent gang gave Jose a feeling of power. He was a core member and accepted the mutually supported gang fantasy that he was now "a leader." In the position of war counselor, he enjoyed the gang's violence. He found it gratifying and exciting to strike out at others for whom he had no feeling. Violence was a useful instrument for him, and he was well trained for this activity. Quick, senseless violence gave him a "rep." Success, prestige, and fame were achievable through the quick, unexpected stroke of a knife.

On the night Jose went to Highbridge Park in the Bronx, the trip was just another gang fight. It had all the usual elements of gang activity— mostly talk about violence, about "what we're going to do," "getting even," "being a big shot." Afterward, Jose's comments that "they called me a dirty spick" and "we fought for territory" were rationales. All of

Jose's negative social background converged the night he plunged a bread knife into another boy's back.

ATTEMPTS TO TREAT THE SOCIOPATHIC PERSONALITY

Despite the large number of sociopaths in our correctional institutions, little progress has been made in providing treatment for such persons. This is partly due to the fact that most experts in the field consider the sociopath untreatable. Hervey Cleckley notes that, in spite of the fact that psychoanalysts have reported a few successes in the treatment of patients regarded as sociopaths, a review of analytic treatment of the sociopathic personality leads to the conclusion that the treatment has proved a failure. He notes further that "all other methods available today have been similarly disappointing in well-defined adult cases of this disorder with which I am directly acquainted."[24] He suggests setting up facilities specifically designed to deal with problems of the sociopath, pointing out that our large state and federal psychiatric institutions are organized for psychotic patients and are not well adapted to handling the sociopath. Cleckley states further, "Even if no really curative treatment should be discovered, despite organized efforts over the years in institutions specifically adapted to the problems of the psychopath, a great deal might be accomplished through careful supervision and control of destructive activities that today seem to run virtually unchecked."[25]

The National Training School for Boys attempted to evaluate the effect of an action program specifically designed for sociopathic youths in residence. The separation of sociopaths from the general population for treatment purposes was prompted by the same considerations applicable to all correctional institutions: not only do the sociopaths fail to benefit from institutional treatment programs, but their unruly behavior disrupts treatment for the rest of the population. The treatment program for sociopaths was designed with an emphasis on recreational activities providing novelty and excitement. The only therapeutic activity scheduled for the group under study was psychodrama.

Using established Quay Personality Classification instruments, it was possible to identify sociopaths within two weeks of admission to the institution. Sociopaths had a higher rate of commitment, a longer term of stay in the security unit, a higher rate of being absent without permission, and a higher rate of transfer to more secure institutions. The project group consisted of the 20 most recently admitted sociopaths. A "contem-

---

[24] Hervey M. Cleckley, "Psychopathic States," in *American Handbook of Psychiatry*, ed. Silvano Arieti (New York: Basic Books, 1959), pp. 585–586.

[25] Cleckley, "Psychopathic States," p. 586.

porary control group" of 21 consisted of 3 recently admitted sociopaths plus all sociopaths admitted after the project began. Two other control groups were made up of sociopaths already in the institution. The subjects in the project group and the control groups were matched on the Quay Personality Classification and in race, scores on intelligence tests, and type of commitment. All the statistical comparisons of the youths in the project group with the control groups indicated far better adjustment of those in the project group. They averaged fewer days in segregation, committed fewer assaultive offenses, provided fewer security problems, and adjusted better to institutional life.[26]

In an attempt to study the effect of the milieu therapy provided at Wiltwyck, a school for emotionally disturbed delinquent boys, the McCords administered a number of personality tests and questionnaires and obtained behavioral ratings of children admitted to the school. The children were tested and then retested a year later, providing before and after measures of change. The McCords found that milieu therapy had a decidedly positive effect on the sample of sociopathic boys at Wiltwyck:

> Wiltwyck milieu therapy provided an instrument for the treatment of psychopathy. The warm supportive environment could serve to satisfy the childrens' dependency needs, which had been frustrated by their families. The consistency, nonpunitiveness, and social controls of the Wiltwyck staff could provide the prerequisites for the establishment of a conscience.[27]

Dr. Raymond J. Corsini reported on the successful use of psycho-drama with sociopaths in prison. He also described in detail a psycho-drama session with Don, a young inmate of a state school for boys, who had been diagnosed by a psychiatrist as a "primary psychopath, with no apparent conception of right or wrong." Corsini explained why psycho-drama was successful in changing this boy's behavior patterns and personality:

> In summary, it can be said that some people are impervious to certain kinds of symbols. There are, for example, nonreaders who just cannot comprehend written language. Some of these can be taught to read by motor procedure rather than by the ordinary visual procedures. It may well be that much the same is true with that class of people who appear deaf to reason and logic, who are labelled "psychopaths." In the treatment of such cases, actional procedures such as psychodrama do appear effective.[28]

In my book *Psychodrama* I describe the case of Ralph, a young man I successfully treated in several psychodrama sessions. The patient had

---

[26] Gilbert Ingram, Roy Grant, Herbert Quay, and Robert Levinson, "An Experimental Program for the Psychopathic Delinquent: Looking in the Correctional Wastebasket," *Journal of Research in Crime and Delinquency* 7 (January 1970):24–30.

[27] McCord and McCord, *The Psychopath*, pp. 138–165.

[28] Raymond Corsini, "Psychodrama with a Psychopath," *Group Psychotherapy* 11 (March 1958):33–39.

been diagnosed by the psychiatric staff at Atascadero State Hospital in California as a "psychopath."

Ralph, at eighteen, was in custody for blacking out of control and attempting to kill his father. He almost succeeded. The verbal interactions he had with various therapists in the hospital about his "past behavior" (which we learned through psychodrama was constantly on his mind) had admittedly been of limited help in reaching him. His immediate therapist had participated in several psychodrama sessions and requested that I direct a session with Ralph to help him explore some of Ralph's psychodynamics in action. Ralph's therapist was present at all of the sessions and very productively followed the leads we produced in our psychodramas into his private therapeutic verbal sessions with Ralph. In this case, psychodrama became a valuable adjunct to Ralph's individual therapy.

In addition to Ralph's potential for violence, another symptom that he manifested was a body tic. When it was active, his body would writhe in an epileptic fashion. The tic usually seemed to appear whenever he felt anger or was under pressure. According to a medical report by a doctor who had examined Ralph, there appeared to be no physiological basis for the tic. In the first psychodrama session I ran with Ralph as the protagonist, I noted that the tic was enacted and accentuated whenever there was reference to his father, or sometime even when the word *father* was used.

In one session, Ralph led us back to a basic and traumatic scene in his life with his father. He acted out a horrendous situation that occurred when he was eight: his father punished him by tying him up by his hands to a ceiling beam in their cellar—like meat on a hook—and then beat him with a belt.

We determined from several later sessions with Ralph, and my consultations with his therapist, that the traumatic experience of the whipping and other parental atrocities produced his tic, because the tic appeared after this particular beating and, as indicated, there did not seem to be any physiological basis for it. The tic seemed to be a way he controlled striking back at his basic antagonist, his father. In brief, Ralph had two extreme postures that emerged from his father's abuse: one was the tic that incapacitated him from the other extreme—uncontrolled violence. Other sessions revealed that his rage toward his father was often displaced onto others, especially other children at school.

The father, who had Ralph hospitalized, was obviously the arch object of Ralph's hatred. Ralph could seldom talk to his father in life. He would either manifest the incapacitating tic, run away, or, as he finally did, attempt to kill him. . . .

We had progressed to a point where he accepted a male nurse as an auxiliary ego in the role of his father. In the psychodrama scene, Ralph would alternately produce the tic or attempt to attack his "father." There was hardly any verbalization of Ralph's rage—he required an action form [such as psychodrama] to express his emotions—and the time factor was in the psychodramatic "here and now" that included varied time frames.

After Ralph had physically acted out much of his rage, I finally improvised a psychodramatic vehicle that facilitated a conversation between Ralph and his auxiliary ego "father." I put a table between him and his "father." At the same time he talked to his father, I gave him the option and the freedom to punch a pillow that he accepted symbolically as his father. This combination of psychodrama devices enabled Ralph to structure in thought and put into words his deep venom for his father. He blurted out much of his long-repressed hatred in a lengthy diatribe. Finally, we removed the props, and after his rage was spent, he fell into his "father's" arms and began to sob, "Why couldn't you love me? I was really a good kid, Dad. Why couldn't you love me?" . . .

In a later session, we had him play the role of his father, and he for the first time began to empathize with the early experiences in his father's life that brutalized him. Ralph's grandfather—who beat his son—was the original culprit and Ralph was indirectly receiving the fallout of his father's anger toward his father, or Ralph's grandfather. When Ralph reversed roles and returned to himself, it diminished his hostility toward his father and he, at least psychodramatically, that day forgave him.

All of the material acted out in the psychodrama sessions was more closely examined in his private sessions with his therapist. Also, I had a number of productive discussions with both Ralph and his therapist on an individual basis. This combination of therapeutic activity seemed to be most effective in helping Ralph reduce his homicidal sociopathic behavior.

In my follow-up of Ralph's case, I learned that he had made a reasonable adjustment after leaving the hospital. He stayed clear of his father because he couldn't fully handle that relationship. The positive results were that he went to work, married at 20, and, according to the reports I received, for the most part adjusted to a law-abiding life.[29]

A central point in explicating Ralph's extreme psychodrama experience is to reveal that the "learning in action" on his part, combined with his private sessions, was effective. Ralph could not just talk about his anger. He required a vehicle such as psychodrama, which gave him the opportunity to physically and psychologically reenact the scenarios of the early parental crimes against him in their bizarre details. The total treatment he received at Atascadero, including psychodrama, may have helped prevent Ralph from committing the kinds of murderous acts carried out by criminally sociopathic personalities such as Manson and Bianchi. Ralph was provided with some insights into his violent sociopathic nature and was able to overcome his problem sufficiently to function in a law-abiding way in our society.

---

[29] Lewis Yablonsky, *Psychodrama* (New York: Basic Books, 1976, and Gardner, 1981). Used by permission.

Chapter
6

Situational Criminals and Career Criminals

*C*areer criminals are people who spend most of their lives committing acts of theft and violence for an elusive profit—and they also spend a lot of time in courts, jails, and correctional institutions. As a study by sociologist John Irwin points out, most of the over 600,000 offenders in American prisons are unskilled criminals who profess a desire to lead a law-abiding life; however, because they lack opportunity and because of the criminal socialization process that exists in their environment, they fall into a life of crime. In an article titled "Who Goes to Prison," John Irwin says of the convicted career criminals in his study:

> Most of them expressed a sincere desire to live a conventional life. Moreover, their conception of a desirable conventional life was very modest:
>
> "I want to go to school and get a trade. Then when I get out I want to have my kids with me, have a good job so I can support them. I want to get the drugs out of my life." [28-year-old black drug addict convicted of armed robbery and episodically involved in crime]
>
> "I think I will pass up getting involved in the gangs in prison. I'm going to go to school and get me a trade. I want a nice job, paying pretty good. Something to keep me busy instead of running the streets." [21-year-old black ex–gang member episodically involved in crime and convicted of armed robbery][1]

This projects a picture quite different from the popular imagery. Instead of a large, menacing horde of dangerous committed criminals,

---

[1] John Irwin and James Austin, "Who Goes to Prison" (San Francisco: National Council of Crime and Delinquency, 1989), p. 32.

apparently our cities contain a growing number of young men, mostly members of racial minority groups, who become involved in crime because there are no avenues to a viable, satisfying life.

Most career criminals fit this model. They are losers who do not find a legitimate role in the social system, and consequently, despite the positive aspirations described by Irwin, they fall into a life cycle of committing crimes, getting arrested, and going to jail and prison. In terms of criminal personality, most of them are socialized offenders; however, some career criminals have neurotic, psychotic, and sociopathic personalities.

In this same category of career criminals are a small percentage of professional career criminals. These are offenders who have developed some special criminal skills. The more highly trained professional career criminals include safecrackers, computer criminals, counterfeiters, pickpockets, major drug dealers, professional arsonists, and effective confidence artists. Most of these offenders, like average career criminals, spend a large part of their lives in the courts and in jail and prison.

A second major category of criminal is the situational criminal. This category is composed of normally law-abiding people who upon finding themselves in an emotional or a financial position where they can make an illegal profit take advantage of the situation. Most situational criminals are not recidivists, and they do not spend as much time in courts, jails, or prisons as do career criminals. The general public does not perceive these offenders to be as criminal as the person who devotes a lifetime to a criminal career. Some situational criminals are emotionally disturbed, but most situational criminals would fit the personality curve of most people in the larger society. However, many situational criminals who commit white collar or political crimes are sociopaths.

In the following analyses, I will further delineate the different characteristics of these two main categories of criminals, the *situational criminal* and the *career criminal*.

SITUATIONAL CRIMINALS

Many normally law-abiding citizens become criminals because they cannot say no when confronted with the possibility of garnering large sums of money in a corrupt situation. The unfolding Pentagon defense contract scandal is a cogent example of situational crime. When this enormous national crime scandal was exposed in 1988, it revealed the criminal greed of respected people who held power and status. Avarice had led them to this form of situational crime.

Another aspect of situational crimes is that they often take place in emotionally destabilizing circumstances in which relatively normal people perform criminal acts that are unlike their usual behavior. In general, so-called crimes of passion fit this situational category. A close examination of the approximately 25,000 murders committed each year reveals that about half of these are emotional situational crimes involving family, friends, or loved ones. This violence is often perpetrated in the heat of an emotional situation by people who would ordinarily not commit criminal acts.

Situational crimes often become the subjects of news stories and headlines. They are committed by people who have not been socialized in a criminal or delinquent subculture and do not accept a criminal value system. As a result of despair, terror, hate, or thoughtlessness, any person could commit an act that might lead to his or her being given the status of criminal. A quarrel between husband and wife could lead to an aggravated assault; a fight between friends, even brothers, could lead to a homicide; a sudden desperate need for money could lead to robbery, burglary, embezzlement, or some other form of theft.

Situational crimes cannot be understood except as they relate to the social context in which they happen. The general characteristics of the situational criminal are:

1. The individual was confronted with a problem that required action.
2. The individual took action that was in violation of criminal law.
3. The person was apprehended, convicted, and given the status of criminal.
4. Until the time of the offense, the criminal was committed to the normative system of our society.

This last characteristic means that the situational criminal basically accepted as appropriate the goals defined by our culture, along with the means for achieving them institutionalized by our society, and that the individual was not committed to a criminal value system or to criminal associations, as in the case of the career criminal.

There are two broad categories of situational criminals: those who fall prey to some emotional situation, and those who cannot resist their greedy impulses when they find themselves in a situation in which they can garner some illegal financial gain.

An Emotional Situational Crime

A case of an emotional situational crime was the act of Billy Don Jackson, a football star at the University of California at Los Angeles. He stabbed a drug dealer to death in 1980, in an altercation that revolved around the purchase of a small amount of marijuana, and he was sentenced to one year in the county jail. In comments leading up to the sentencing of Jackson, Judge Woodmansee said, "To reduce a killing from murder to manslaughter, it has to be shown it was the result of a sudden quarrel and that the slayer was acting under the influence of that quarrel and in the heat of passion. . . . This was not a deliberate and premeditated murder and the police and prosecution agree with the propriety of the [voluntary manslaughter] plea."

Woodmansee gave Jackson the jail sentence as a condition of placing him on five years' probation. Jackson's defense attorney, Charles English, in asking for probation instead of prison, said Jackson "is totally remorseful for what he did and concedes he went berserk."

Jackson admitted that he used a knife to kill Mark Bernolak in an altercation over a marijuana deal in the victim's West Los Angeles apartment in October, 1980. During testimony at a preliminary hearing on the case, Los Angeles police detective Steve Osti said Jackson and a friend went to Bernolak's residence to buy drugs. The friend was identified by police as a person who was dealing drugs. According to Osti, the fatal stabbing occurred when Bernolak tried to back out of a narcotics deal because he did not know the potential customers. Jackson initially tried to break up a knife fight between Bernolak and his friend. But when he himself was slashed, Jackson seized the knife and killed Bernolak.

Billy Jackson fits the pattern of the emotional situational criminal. Although he apparently used marijuana, he did not use hard drugs. He had no prior criminal record, and it was reasonable to expect that he would not commit any further crimes after his jail sentence.

Situational criminals are often individuals who have committed an act of violence in the family. Many murders are committed within the family in the United States, and half of these involve the killing of a spouse. Most aggravated assaults also occur within the family unit or among neighbors and acquaintances. Many of the offenders, despite the seriousness of some of their offenses, can be classified as situational criminals.

The individual who has led a normal life but then, under sudden and immediate financial pressure, embezzles money or even commits a burglary or robbery also fits into the category of situational criminal, provided that previous to the crime this person was *not* committed to a criminal value system.

Financial Situational Criminals

White collar workers, politicians, and corporate executives who commit crimes while engaging mainly in lawful occupations sometimes become situational criminals. Included are people who misappropriate money entrusted to them or commit acts of embezzlement or fraud, which all constitute financial situational crimes.

The misappropriation of money in business or financial situations is a major form of situational crime. Many enterprises of this type begin with the best of intentions; however, the person who controls the funds may get a sense of power over other people's money and may begin to utilize the money for personal gain. Such a situation encourages the formerly ethical person to cross over the legal line into a situational crime.

In the United States, it is a common practice for people to turn over their money to bankers, stockbrokers, commodity brokers, and others to keep or to invest for them. At times such persons may appropriate some or all of the money for their own use. Such action is punishable as a crime and is generally referred to as embezzlement. In virtually every business, some people occupy positions of trust. Some keep the books, others handle deposits, still others handle sums of money as part of their duties. Many, for various reasons, divert some of their employers' money to their own use. The amounts misappropriated vary from a few dollars a day to millions. A bus driver becomes a "partner" in the company by keeping fare money. The amounts embezzled are small, but the penalty is severe if the bus driver is caught. The treasurer of a corporation may misappropriate far larger sums with far less severe punishment.

Donald R. Cressey, on the basis of his study of trust violators, concluded that trusted persons become trust violators when they conceive of themselves as having a financial problem they cannot share, are aware that this problem can be secretly resolved by violating the position of financial trust, and are able to apply to their conduct in this situation verbalizations that enable them to adjust their conceptions of themselves as trusted persons to their conceptions of themselves as users of the entrusted funds or property. When asked why they had not violated other positions of trust, or why they had not violated their present positions at an earlier time, those who had an opinion expressed it in ways equivalent to one of the following: (1) "There was no need for it like there was this time." (2) "The idea never entered my head." (3) "I thought it was dishonest then, but this time it didn't seem dishonest at first."[2]

When persons incur debts, they frequently feel they must keep them secret; meeting the debt therefore becomes a nonshareable financial problem. In all cases encountered by Cressey, a nonshareable problem preceded the criminal violation of financial trust. Many different situations are considered by individual trust violators to have produced problems that are structured as nonshareable. All these problems are related to the status-seeking or status-maintaining behavior of the violators. Many of the persons who have studied embezzlement have attempted to show that immorality, emergencies, increased needs, business reversals, or a relatively high scale of living are "causes" of embezzlement. However, Cressey's analysis indicates that these conditions are significant to criminal trust violation if they produce nonshareable problems for the trusted person, who is in a situation in which it is

---

[2] Donald R. Cressey, *Other People's Money* (New York: Free Press, 1953), pp. 159–166. Reprinted by permission of the Estate of Donald R. Cressey.

possible to misappropriate funds. The structuring of a problem as nonshareable has the effect of creating in the trusted person a desire for specific results, all of which are related to the solution of the problem and all of which can be brought about by criminally violating the financial trust.

Big business executives who commit white collar crimes do not appear to have the same or even similar motives for their criminal activities as do trust violators. Their actions are not precipitated by personal financial problems. Their crimes occur in the normal course of their jobs, where they have a situation that is compatible with the commission of the illegal acts.

Many executives have maintained that their actions, while technically criminal, served a worthwhile purpose—for example, "stabilizing prices." Some acknowledged that their actions were illegal but did not consider them criminal. For the most part, they justified their actions as conforming to corporate pressure from their bosses. An executive joining a company may find that illegal price fixing is going on and that he or she is expected to perform the illegal duties. The crime is part of the executive job; the executive is simply conforming to the norms of the company. These people do not consider themselves criminals because they believe on the basis of their experience that corporations engage in illegal price fixing in the ordinary course of their business. Executives singled out for prosecution believe that they have simply been unlucky.

The following account of a corporate executive convicted of a situational financial crime illustrates how a person who does not have a criminal self-concept can end up in a situation that causes him or her to become a criminal. The man described was involved in a corporate conspiracy case.

> The highest-paid executive to be given a jail sentence was a General Electric vice-president. . . . The details of his career and his participation in the conspiracy provide additional insight into the operations of white collar crime and the white collar criminal.
>
> The General Electric vice-president was one of the disproportionate number of Southerners involved in the antitrust violations. He had been born in Atlanta and was forty-six years old at the time he was sentenced to jail. He had graduated with a degree in electrical engineering from Georgia Tech and received an honorary doctorate degree from Siena College in 1958; he was married and the father of three children. He had served in the Navy during World War II, rising to the rank of lieutenant commander; he was a director of the Schenectady Boy's Club, on the board of trustees of Miss Hall's School, and, not without some irony, he was a member of Governor Rockefeller's Temporary State Committee on Economic Expansion.
>
> Almost immediately after his sentencing, he issued a statement to the press, noting that he was to serve a jail term "for conduct which has been interpreted as being in conflict with the complex antitrust laws." He commented that "General Electric, Schenectady, and its people have undergone many ordeals together and we have not only survived them, but

have come out stronger, more vigorous, more alive than ever. We shall again." Then he voiced his appreciation for the "letters and calls from people all over the country, the community, the shops, and the offices . . . expressing confidence and support." . . .

Previously, he had been mentioned as a possible president of General Electric, described by the then president as "an exceptionally eager and promising individual." Employed by the company shortly after graduation from college, he had risen dramatically through the managerial ranks, and [had] passed that point, described by a higher executive, "where the man, if his work has been sufficiently promising, has an opportunity to step across the barrier out of his function into the field of general management." . . .

The witness was interrogated closely about his moral feelings regarding criminal behavior. He fumbled most of the questions, avoiding answering them directly, but ultimately coming to the point of saying that the consequences visited upon him represented the major reason for the re-evaluation of his actions. He would not behave in the same manner again because of what "I have been through and what I have done to my family." He was also vexed with the treatment he had received from the newspapers: "They have never laid off a second. They have used some terms which I don't think are necessary—they don't use the term 'price fixing.' It is always 'price rigging' or trying to make it as sensational as possible." . . .

All things said, the former General Electric vice-president viewed his situation philosophically. Regarding his resignation from the company, it was "the way the ball has bounced." He hoped that he would have "the opportunity to continue in American industry and do a job," and he wished some of the other men who had been dismissed a lot of good luck. "I want to leave the company with no bitterness and go out and see if I can't start a new venture along the right lines." Eight days later, he accepted a job as assistant to the president in charge of product research in a large corporation located outside of Philadelphia. Slightly more than a month after that, he was named president of the company, at a salary reported to be somewhat less than the $74,000 yearly received by his predecessor.[3]

The rationalization that illegal price-fixing is useful to the society because it contributes to price stability may be compared to that advanced by the thief who claims to contribute to increased retail business by personally effecting a redistribution of wealth. Financial situational criminals often present outrageous rationalizations for their crimes.

Political Situational Criminals

Recent history has provided a rash of this type of political and white collar crime that fits the situational crime category. These criminal cases, referred to as the "sleaze factor" in government, were a notable part of the eight-year term of former president Ronald Reagan.

[3] Reprinted from Albert Geis, *The White Collar Criminal* (Atherton, 1968).

The Reagan administration was characterized in many reports by staff intimates as a laissez-faire, hands-off approach to the presidency. Possibly, as a consequence of Reagan's approach, along with the influence of an ethically bankrupt attorney general, political white collar crime flourished during the Reagan years.

The criminal record of Reagan appointees, who used the status and power of their situation to commit crimes, was extensive. A partial list of criminal activities that have plagued the courts connected to the Reagan administration includes the illegal diversion of funds known as the Iran-Contra scandal; the gross collusion of the Pentagon in criminal "sweetheart" contracts with defense contractors, which have cost the taxpayers billions of dollars; and the use of former White House connections by Reagan appointees for personal illegal profit.

Almost all these cases fit the situational crime model. None of the convicted criminals involved had a criminal history; however, when confronted with a situation that would enhance their personal power, financial situation, or political ends, they violated the law.

Many of the offenders in the Reagan administration clearly violated the law and were convicted of specific crimes. Former attorney general Edwin Meese III was, however, in the context of my three perspectives on crime, a socially perceived criminal who had a noncriminal self-concept. He was involved in a large number of activities which were perceived as criminal behavior—but he was never indicted or convicted of any of these acts. In an 830-page report in late July, 1988, Special Counsel James C. McKay asserted that Meese had probably committed four crimes for which he could be prosecuted, but there was inconclusive evidence. When Meese resigned as attorney general on July 5, 1988, he declared that the 830-page report by a special prosecutor (which Meese had not yet read) "completely vindicated" him. Meese's behavioral record presents a prototypical case of a socially perceived criminal who had no criminal or even unethical self-concept; however, when confronted with situations from which he could personally profit, he used the quasi-illegal situations for his own ends. (This assertion, and a more general analysis of political and white collar situational crime, will be more fully developed in Part Four, "Power-Status Crime.")

CAREER CRIMINALS

In contrast to the types of criminals just described, the career criminal is seldom a situational criminal. Career criminals have usually been trained and socialized into a life of crime in a crime-compatible social environment. Most of these people have been socialized or trained into systems of values and role definitions different from those of the majority, by subcultures favoring criminal behavior over law-abiding behavior. They tend to take the initiative in committing crimes, even in situations where they are very vulnerable to being arrested and prosecuted.

An extreme example of this pattern of being socialized from an early age into a criminal lifestyle may be seen in the criminal tribes that were of national concern to the government of India in the 1920s and 1930s. These tribes socialized their children into criminal activities. At early ages they were trained to commit acts of burglary and to operate confidence games. The girls were encouraged to be prostitutes. The training or socialization was methodically carried out by parents and tribal elders. The tradition of crime as a means of earning a living was passed on from generation to generation. No moral stigma was associated with a life of crime, and children growing up in this subculture had no guilt or conflict about committing crimes. This was what they were supposed to do. The deviants in the criminal tribes of India were paradoxically the few youths who did not adhere to the values and behavior of the dominant criminal ethos.

Young men growing up in urban slums in Western societies are often confronted with a similar type of criminal socialization. Although the pull toward criminality is not so overwhelmingly clear-cut or persuasive as in the Indian criminal tribes, it is seductive. When one's peers hold delinquent norms, when the neighborhood hero is a "successful" criminal or racketeer, a child may seek to emulate these patterns. A criminal career for many children growing up in this social context is therefore more a matter of conformity than of deviance.[4]

One concept of the "career criminal" was developed by Professor Walter Reckless. According to Reckless, some of the essential characteristics of the career criminal are as follows:

1. Crime is his way of earning a living. Although he may occasionally work at conventional jobs, when he does so it is usually as a result of extreme pressures from members of his family, probation officers, or parole officers. He considers crime his main occupation. Since crime is his way of earning a living, he commits property offenses: burglaries, larcenies, and robberies. He is not likely to become involved in a crime of violence.

2. The career criminal develops technical skills and techniques useful to the commission of property offenses. He learns how to break into a house, climb through a transom, start a car without an ignition key, and other tricks of the trade.

3. He develops attitudes favorable to crime and unfavorable to the police and the larger society. He tends to see the police, judges, politicians, and business people as dishonest.

---

[4] For an excellent case-history description of the career criminal, see Clifford Shaw, *Brothers in Crime* (University of Chicago Press, 1938).

4. He starts as a delinquent child. Not all delinquent children become criminals, but most career criminals have had records of juvenile delinquency. They are recruited from the sandlots of crime. Most of them are of lower-class origin.

5. He expects to do some time in prison and considers this a normal hazard of his occupation. He makes the best use of his time in prison by learning new methods of criminality. For him prison is a crime school.

6. He is usually psychologically "normal." There are no special psychological characteristics that distinguish him from the noncriminal. The career criminal has chosen crime as his occupation, develops skills to enable him to pursue this occupation effectively, and develops attitudes supporting his behavior. For the career criminal, the choice of crime as an occupation is for the most part a "rational" choice.[5]

A basic concept that seems applicable to career criminals is that they see their work as a "legitimate" occupation. Given this theme, sociologists Francis Cullen and Bruce Link suggest that it would be useful conceptually for crime to be studied as an occupation:

> The "normal concept" of occupation may [also] be employed to analyze . . . criminality. Once this conceptual leap is taken, it becomes possible to achieve new visions of the criminal world by investigating criminal work in the same ways in which conventional work has been examined. Thus, we have seen that just as conventional occupations are socially stereotyped and stratified by prestige, criminal occupations are characterized by these same social phenomena. We have explored the possibility that stereotypes may regulate the occupational choices and options of individuals not only in the legitimate workforce but also in the illegitimate workforce.[6]

A factor that lends weight to crime as an occupation is that career criminals are chronic criminals. Career criminals are intractable recidivists who commit the same type of crime over and over again—and who, because of their usually well established modus operandi, become known to the local police. Many law enforcement agencies have developed special programs for dealing with the repeater career criminal. A typical program is one that was developed by the city attorney's office in Los Angeles. The Los Angeles program was described in an article by Sandy Banks in the *Los Angeles Times:*

---

[5] The characteristics of the career criminal and professional criminal as here presented are modifications of those delineated by Professor Reckless over the years. For his description, see Walter C. Reckless, *The Crime Problem* (New York: Random House, 1961), pp. 153–177. Used by permission of McGraw-Hill Book Publishers.

[6] Francis T. Cullen and Bruce G. Link, "Crime as Occupation," *Criminology* 18 (November 1980).

CITY MOVING AGAINST CHRONIC CRIMINALS

The Los Angeles city attorney's office is stepping up its efforts to win long jail terms for chronic lawbreakers who have been falling through the cracks of the criminal justice system, City Atty. Ira Reiner said Monday.

Habitual criminals—particularly those convicted of serious misdemeanors such as theft, assault, drug violations and sex crimes—will be singled out for special prosecution that will begin with an extensive background check for probation violations, prior convictions under aliases and previous jail sentences, and end with a plea for the judge to impose maximum jail time, Reiner said.

This new effort involves expansion of the Chronic Offender Prosecution Emphasis (COPE) program. . . . The crux of the program is pretrial preparation that includes extensive investigation of a habitual criminal's background for grounds to justify the imposition of maximum jail time.

"We don't just look at arrests and convictions, but we dig for probation violations, whether [the defendant] has been convicted under any aliases, what each case involved," explained Deputy City Atty. Sue Frauns. . . .

Misdemeanors are punishable by a maximum one-year county jail term on each charge. But by conducting a fingerprint check to determine if a defendant has been convicted previously under an alias or by searching probation records to find out if he has fulfilled all court orders, such as payment of restitution, prosecutors have been able to come up with grounds for longer, consecutive jail terms, according to Frauns. . . .

"What we're looking for are people who have been through the system, been given the opportunity of probation repeatedly, been jailed repeatedly and nothing has worked," Reiner said.

"At that point, deterrence is pointless. Rehabilitation is pointless. Our objective is to get them off the street for as long as possible."[7]

Case History of a Career Criminal

The case history of Bill, an inmate of Riker's Island Penitentiary in New York City, is similar to many I have encountered. Bill was a member of a role-training group I directed as part of an experiment. The information contained in the following case history was excerpted from Bill's prison file and revealed in role-training sessions.

Description   Male, white, 28 years of age at the time of the interviews, single. Apparently in excellent health. Weight, approximately 170 pounds. Height, 5 feet, 10 inches. No visible physical defects. Normal medical history. Considered handsome by women. Soft-spoken and pleasant in demeanor. Normal intelligence. Completed ninth grade in school. Wide Range Reading Test placed him at sixth-grade level in reading ability. Vocabulary used in role communication creates impres-

---

[7] Sandy Banks, "City Moving Against Chronic Criminals," *Los Angeles Times*, March 16, 1982. Copyright, 1982, Los Angeles Times. Reprinted by permission.

sion of higher education. While in correctional institutions, he received training in printing and passed a high school equivalence test.

Family History Bill was born in rural Ohio. He had a sister two years older than he who had been married for several years to a truck driver. He also had a younger brother ten years his junior. At the time of the interviews, the brother was in a state training school. Bill moved to Brooklyn, New York, with his father, mother, and older sister. His father deserted the family and never rejoined it. The mother became ill, and the family encountered serious economic difficulties shortly after the father's desertion. The mother had been supported by the Department of Welfare. Bill still considered her home as his own, although he had lived elsewhere most of his adult life. He expressed great fondness for his mother, sister, and brother and hatred for his brother-in-law.

History of Juvenile Arrests and Confinement Bill stated that he had engaged in shoplifting in downtown Brooklyn department stores for about two years prior to his first appearance in juvenile court. He had been apprehended on five occasions, and each time he was released by the store detective or manager with a warning.

He was finally brought before the juvenile court. The petition alleged truancy and stealing an overcoat. The method used for stealing the coat displayed some ingenuity. He and another boy, neatly dressed but not wearing coats, entered the clothing department of a department store. They struck up a conversation with a woman, apparently the mother of a boy shopping for an overcoat. As the woman's son tried on several coats, Bill and his friend did also. When a salesclerk observed them, he assumed they were with the woman customer. Bill and his friend selected an opportune moment and left the store wearing the stolen coats. They were apprehended on this occasion. However, Bill stated that prior to this arrest he had successfully stolen seven coats in the same manner. He said that he had sold the coats. Apparently even before he was 13 years old, Bill had acquired a knack for stealing. This arrest led to probation. He was continued on probation after a subsequent arrest for allegedly attempting to break into a candy store. Bill denied that he and his friends were attempting to break in. He described their activity as "horsing around." According to him, the plate glass door was broken accidentally, attracting a police car and an arrest.

Bill was later arrested with two other boys, both a few years older, for burglary. They broke into a candy store and stole about $300 worth of cigarettes and cigars. After a two-month stay in detention, Bill was brought before the juvenile court and referred to a residential treatment center for boys.

About two months after his release from the residential treatment center, he was rearrested for burglary. He and two older boys had broken into a store and removed 12 cases of liquor. They succeeded in gaining entry without triggering the burglar alarm system. The two older youths were tried in a criminal court. Bill was sent by the juvenile court to the New York State Training School for Boys.

After his release, Bill was arrested with two other persons, a man and a woman. He was allegedly waiting in a getaway car while the two were holding up a liquor store. After spending two months in detention, Bill was released on court probation to await trial. By the time he was 17, Bill had spent three years in correctional facilities. While on probation, Bill left the jurisdiction of the court without permission and went to Ohio to live with an aunt. The state of New York made no effort to extradite him, and he remained in Ohio about three years. Bill stated that he did not get into any trouble in Ohio. He helped out on his aunt's farm and did odd jobs in a neighboring town during the winters. He then returned to New York City.

Arrest and Confinement Record as Adult Back in New York, Bill was arrested with two other men and charged with armed robbery. Bill was apprehended sitting in the driver's seat of a stolen car some 20 feet away from a liquor store that was being held up. He denied any knowledge of the holdup, although it was established that the two robbers were acquaintances of his. He pleaded guilty to a misdemeanor, joyriding in the car, and was placed on probation. The robbery charge was withdrawn. Bill persisted in maintaining that he was not involved in the robbery attempt.

Two months later he was arrested with another man for burglary. The two had broken into a clothing store on a Sunday morning and were moving racks of clothing into a rented truck. People passed by without suspecting that a burglary was in progress; they apparently assumed that the loading was part of a delivery or a move. The operation was so well executed that Bill and his accomplice might have succeeded except for the fact that one of the store owners happened to pass the store in his car, saw what was going on, and called the police. Bill stated that twice during his criminal career such burglaries had been successfully completed. Bill was tried and convicted for this offense and was given an indefinite sentence to Riker's Island Penitentiary. After his release he was rearrested many times and sentenced to serve various prison terms. He showed little or no guilt about the commission of his offenses. His essential regret was not that he was a criminal but rather that he had failed too many times in his chosen occupation.

A Career Criminal's Story

The following is the statement of black career criminal Louis J. Bean:

> I was thirteen years old when I first encountered the protectors of society and when I first learned what it really meant to be poor in a society that

measures a man more or less by his wealth. I had run away from home and left town with a carnival that had completed its week's stand in Dayton, Ohio. I began by working at odd jobs, such as putting up and tearing down tents and concession stands. I liked the excitement and hustle of the carnival, and soon I had graduated to being a ticket seller at one of the several burlesque shows. I soon became wise to the fact that I could make ten to fifteen dollars extra every night if I would cooperate with the ticket taker, who would give me a handful of tickets that could be resold and we would split the profits.

I worked on this job for a couple of months, until the manager saw the ticket taker shove me a fistful of tickets which had just been deposited in the ticket-taker's box. First the manager threatened to knock my head off, then he decided to call the sheriff. While he went to the office trailer to call the cops, I took what money I had in the money box and went to the highway and hitched a ride into town. I was arrested just outside the city limits by a deputy sheriff. He promptly clamped the long arms of the law on my wrists and carted me off to the city's juvenile center. I was there eleven days before they released me to my mother, who immediately went into her act and spanked and screamed at me until I promised that I would never do anything again. The officials kept my money, even the money that was really mine.

I was released to my mother and was back in Dayton that evening. I was reenrolled in the parochial school and was doing all right until about a year later when a buddy of mine decided that he wanted to join the navy and forged his birth certificate. I did the same, and we wound up in the Great Lakes Naval Training Center in the state of Illinois.

We soon tired of the rough training program and we decided to go over the back fence and enjoy a little freedom. We enjoyed our freedom and were in jail in Hot Springs, Arkansas, exactly ten days later. We had been arrested for speeding in a car that we had stolen in Chicago the previous day. The FBI charged my buddy and me with taking a stolen vehicle across the state line, and I received a three-year sentence in the federal reformatory and an undesirable discharge from the navy.

After my release from the federal pen, I roamed around my hometown for a few months and finally took a job in a war plant that made, of all things, machine guns. For some reason the steady work bugged me, so after about three months I quit the job and started driving stolen cars from one town to another for a friend of mine who I had met while in the federal pen. I made good money for the chances I took; I received $250 for each car I delivered no matter what the distance.

This went on for about seven months, until I was stopped one day in a roadblock that had been set up because a bank had been robbed in the area. The cops at the roadblock asked for my driver's license and auto registration, which I, of course, didn't have. So I was arrested on some kind of charge that slips my mind at the present time. The car was checked out, and me also. I was taken to jail and in due time I was sentenced to five years.

I did every day of the five years because I could not stay out of trouble. If you're seventeen you get into a lot of fights in prison. I was put in the hole several times for fighting, making booze, and gambling.

When I was finally released from the federal prison again, I had made up my mind that I would get a job and settle down and try the so-called good life, but I soon found out that it takes money for the good life as well as for the bad life. About nine months later I ran into an old buddy that I had done time with and he had some very good ideas, at least they seemed so at the time. We started pulling stickups. One night after a drugstore holdup, my buddy gave me my first shot of narcotics. I started taking cocaine whenever we had a job to pull because I felt that I could carry my part of the job better and faster. But one day I was shot in the leg while robbing a supermarket and was caught hobbling down an alley a couple of blocks away. I was taken back to the store and identified by the clerks. I was sentenced to ten years for this job, but I appealed the sentence and was granted bond. While out on bond I was stopped by a state trooper for speeding. I knew that if I was taken to jail I would forfeit my bond.

I have almost always carried a pistol of some sort. So I pulled it and told the state trooper to turn his back to me and raise his hands. I jumped into my car and drove about three miles down the road and right smack into a roadblock that the trooper had called in for.

For that I received another ten years. So I'm now doing two ten-flat sentences which means that I will have to do six years and eight months for each sentence.[8]

PROFESSIONAL CAREER CRIMINALS

Most career criminals, as indicated, are relatively unskilled offenders like Bill and Louis Bean. Some, however, have some "professional" training in crime. These professional career criminals include criminals with special skills: safecrackers, skilled pickpockets, confidence artists, pimps, professional arsonists (who are skilled at burning down buildings for a price), "hit men" and "soldiers" for organized crime, and counterfeiters.

The essential characteristics of the professional career criminal are the following:

1. Crime is his way of earning a living. In this respect he does not differ from the ordinary career criminal. The objective of his criminal activities is basically financial gain, and he is not as likely to become involved in crimes of violence unless violence is his specialty.
2. He is a specialist. It is this characteristic that most distinguishes him from the ordinary career criminal. Because he is highly specialized, he is able to plan his activities, choose his victims, and carry out his crimes in such a way as to avoid detection in many instances.

---

[8] Ethridge Knight, *Black Voices From Prison* (New York: Pathfinder, 1970), pp. 33–35. Reprinted by permission of Pathfinder Press, Inc. Copyright © 1970 by Pathfinder Press, Inc.

3. He is highly skilled, frequently as a result of intensive training in his specialty. His teachers are usually older professional criminals.

4. He is more likely to be recruited from the skilled technical ranks and professional occupations than from juvenile delinquent or career criminal types. Many safecrackers, for example, were formerly employees of safe companies, and counterfeiters often worked for engraving companies.

5. He is usually "normal" psychologically. In this respect, he does not differ emotionally significantly from the general population. He is generally prepared for arrest and trial. He is likely to know and be known by an attorney. Thus, if he is apprehended, he has someone to call upon for legal assistance. He also has money put aside for bail, his attorney's fees, and other expenses of his trial. Some con artists even have a confederate ready to offer to make restitution of money stolen on condition that the victim withdraw the charges against him.

6. He plans his crime far more extensively than does the ordinary career criminal. This is true of the con artist, who, if he is to attract investors in a venture, must establish an identity over a period of weeks and often months. The professional thief who works a jewelry switch at one jewelry store has to study the quality and size of diamonds offered at several other jewelry stores before starting the venture.

A great deal has been written about the activities of professional criminals. Art forgery; professional theft, including picking pockets, shoplifting, and jewelry switching; and confidence games of every sort have been described in the literature of professional crime. It should be emphasized, however, that our categorization is based on *patterns of behavior and lifestyle of the criminal,* and not only on the specific crime.

Some embezzlers could be included in the category of professional career criminals, but they tend more often to be situational criminals. Donald Cressey lists three essential kinds of psychological processes involved in embezzlement: "the feeling that a personal financial problem is unshareable; the knowledge of how to solve the problem in secret, by violating a position of financial trust; the ability to find a formula which describes the act of embezzling in words which do not conflict with the image of oneself as a trusted person."[9] I would view the person who embezzles for the first time as a situational criminal. The person who makes a living at embezzling as a criminal activity would be considered a professional career criminal.

Through careful planning and specialized skills, the professional career criminal is more likely than the other types to be successful in

---

[9] Donald R. Cressey, "The Respectable Criminal," *Trans-Action* 2 (March/April 1965):13.

avoiding detection, arrest, and conviction. Thus, he does not usually spend as much time in detention or prison as the ordinary career criminal. He often lives like a successful person in American society and conceives of himself as being successful. Since he often earns far more at his chosen occupation than he would if he obtained employment, he resists all efforts to change his career. He generally believes that he is simply another member of the community with a highly specialized trade. He doesn't think he is any more crooked than most politicians and business people. The professional career criminal does not have a guilty self-concept.

David Dressler described a type of professional criminal of lower status, one who was often "on the road" plying his trade:

Maxie the Goniff is a professional. Practically all cannons [pickpockets] are. . . . His body is slight and springy; his fingers are long, tapering, and nervous. His face resembles a parrot's, the beak long and hooked downward. His eyes are furtive. He decided over fifty years ago that picking "pokes" was a fine way of making a living. He apprenticed himself to a master, studied hard, graduated with honors, and went on his own. He wouldn't tell me how old he was at the time we spoke, but my guess is that he was at least sixty-five. . . .

Like most of his kind, Maxie has a long criminal record. He has been arrested seventy-one times in twenty-two states.

"Doesn't speak so well for you, Maxie," I goaded him. . . .

He flushed angrily. "Every one of them pinches came after a whole season's work. In fifty years I done six years' time. I'm living good—well, pretty good—for forty-four years and it cost me six years! You should have it so good!" . . .

For a time he was a petty thief, then a shoplifter, and finally, while still a kid, he met a man who took him on as an apprentice dip and taught him the business.

Picking pockets *is* a business, Maxie insists. "You've got to figure a certain amount of risk in any business. Suppose I open a saloon. I'm taking a chance, no? I might go broke, I might have to pay too much protection—it's all business."

Like all commercial enterprises, Maxie's has its seasons. "Summers we work the resorts, like Coney Island and the buses and subways going to and from. Beaches are good too. Certain holidays is season for us. Before Easter and Christmas. There's lots of shopping. That's when I hit department stores. In the elevators or even on the floor."

When he has had a run of bad luck he will depart from his more accustomed beat and cover a church wedding. "You don't often find much dough on the guys, but brother! are they easy to take! They don't expect a thief in a church." . . .

Maxie takes pride in his technique. He has little use for the lone operator, although he admits there are some good ones. He considers they take too many risks. . . .

He likes to work in a mob of two or four people. "Say you're on a subway or elevator. You pick your mark and try to figure where he keeps his wallet.

It ain't hard to find out. You just jostle the sucker and move off. Right away he puts his hand where he's got the wallet to see if it's there. He tips you off.

"Of course, if he don't fall for that, you've got to *fan* him. You feel around, very easy, until you locate the poke.

"Then comes pratting. You prat the guy around. That means you push him around, edge him around, not hard, gentle, just enough to distract his attention. Also to get him into position—the position you want him in for the score." . . .

Maxie is proudest of the fact that he is a specialist among specialists, "a left-breech hook." That's a man who can draw a score out of a left pants pocket. "There ain't many can do that. It's hard. Try it!" . . .

Maxie insists there is honor among thieves in his game. "Sure, a guy rats now and then. That don't prove nothin'. You'll always find a few rats. But most of us stick together. We help each other. We put up fall dough for a guy in trouble."

"Did you ever rat, Maxie?"

"Like I said, we stick together. We put up fall dough." . . .

"Maxie," I asked, "if you had it to do over again, what would you be instead of a pickpocket?"

"What's wrong," he snapped, "with this racket?"[10]

The Pimp

To become a professional career criminal requires considerable training. Youths brought up in disorganized slums do not usually have experts to teach them the required skills; nor do they have the necessary role models. Furthermore, advances in police technology have made it more difficult for the professional to succeed. A high degree of specialization on the part of the professional makes it easier for the police, with the aid of computerized modus operandi files, to apprehend him. One type of professional criminal that has been successful in the black ghetto is the pimp or "player." The pimp is an aristocrat among hustlers in the black ghetto. He is admired as a culture hero who makes a lot of money, has an expensive lifestyle, and has a high income. The Milners summarize the mechanisms of the pimp's control over women:

> In summary, the mechanisms of male control over women among the players are mental, physical and social structural. All mechanisms function to reverse the American man-woman game so that the female is put in the position of petitioner for the male's sexual favors. Male solidarity helps the pimp keep his game together. If the mental games fail, violence is an effective and ever-present threat in the fabric of this ideally male dominated culture, although it is seen as a last resort.
>
> There are seven principal spheres of male control: the training and

---

[10] David Dressler, "Maxie the Goniff," in *Readings in Criminology and Penology*, ed. David Dressler (New York: Columbia University Press, 1964), pp. 43–46; originally published in David Dressler, *Parole Chief* (New York: Viking, 1951). Used by permission.

guidance which a pimp provides for his woman as she becomes increasingly proficient at her trade, including setting her minimum acceptable earning per night; the maintenance of her proper role as a submissive woman by insisting on money in return for sex and affection, by insisting that she be an attentive handmaiden to his every demand, and by requiring that she show conspicuous respect for him and his friends in social situations and that she never divulge private information or behave in any way which might embarrass or show disloyalty to him; the ability to keep peace in a stable of two or more women; the complete control of how the money is spent, what the woman's allowance is, how much will be saved and for what purpose or future goal; the decisions regarding where they will live and with whom (adults and children), and decisions about where and when his women might occasionally be sent to work outside The City (Las Vegas, Seattle, Denver, etc.); the decisions surrounding an arrest, such as which lawyer to use, which bail bondsman, how much money will be spent on the case, and whether to leave the ho sitting in jail or not; and finally, the decision whether to hire or fire a ho.[11]

The Hustler

A group of sociologists headed by Leroy Gould researched professional crime under the auspices of the President's Commission on Law Enforcement and the Administration of Justice. They defined professional criminals as "individuals whose major source of income is from criminal pursuits and who spend a majority of their working time in illegal enterprises (excluding) regular members of crime syndicates or . . . people who engage in illegal activities as part of an otherwise legal profession."[12] When researchers asked professional criminals what they did, so as to determine their criminal specialty, a great many replied, "I hustle." "To 'hustle' is to be persistently on the lookout for an opportunity to make an illegal buck. A criminal 'on the hustle' will do whatever is required; he will consider whatever comes up."

The term *hustling* encompasses a wide range of activities. Hustling does not necessarily mean simply looking for someone to rob. It means moving around bars and making connections, contacting other professionals to see "what's up," reading the papers to see if there are any opportunities, contacting fences to see if any special orders have been placed, and so on. To hustle is to use every bit of knowledge about crime, criminals, the "straight" world, and "straight" people to make money, with no holds barred.

If the idea of hustling is accepted as fundamental to a life of professional crime, it should be obvious that a hustler requires versatil-

---

[11] From *Black Players: The Secret World of Black Pimps* by Richard and Christina Milner. Copyright © 1972 by Richard B. Milner and Christina Andrea Milner. By permission of Little, Brown and Company.

[12] Leroy Gould, Egon Bittner, Sheldon Messinger, et al., "Crime as a Profession" (Washington, D.C.: Department of Justice, 1966), p. 10.

ity. The hustler must be able to commit a burglary, pass forged checks, work confidence games, and "boost" from a department store—possibly all on the same day. In Gould's view, the professional criminal is in business to cash in on opportunities, and "if one specializes too narrowly, he is likely to miss too many opportunities."[13]

The more successful a criminal is, the more he can afford to specialize. All other things being equal, the professional engages in a specialty, a preferred activity. The most successful, however, accepts jobs outside his specialty. According to Gould, "Present day relationships between professional criminals . . . are not structured by strong ongoing group relationships. There are two classes of people with whom the professional does maintain stable relationships, the fence and the loan shark. He needs the fence to dispose of stolen articles and the loan shark to pay for lawyers, bail and court costs when he is apprehended.[14]

In a study of the interrelationship between drug use and hustling, researchers found that higher levels of drug use apparently led to more hustling, which included the following activities:

> [Drug] distribution-related activities such as street dealing, touting [steering purchasers to supplies], "juggling" [i.e., purchasing a quantity of drugs and selling it in smaller quantities so as to finance one's own habit], or renting out one's "works," and so on. Burglaries accounted for the next highest proportion followed by muggings. Addicted respondents relied much more heavily on illegal activities than nonaddicted subjects.[15]

According to Ianni, hustling in penitentiaries is as old as the penitentiary system itself. Authorities allow a certain amount of inmate hustling; they place informers in many key jobs in the contraband networks engaged in hustling and thus maintain control. Ianni describes a wine-making hustle in a prison as follows:

> There are always batches of hooch fermenting in any of dozens of hiding places throughout the prison. Watkins' brands are known as potent (though still more wine than liquor) and potable. In about four weeks, the rather sweet, raw-tasting beverage will be divided up into six or eight one-quart jars, distributed and consumed.
>
> On the day when this vintage hits the market, Angel Parilla receives one quart as his fee for providing the yeast. Ben Hicks receives one jar plus a percentage of the profits in cigarettes for his versatile and mobile efforts. An unforeseen hassle in getting the goods out of the laundry costs another jar to an inmate on one of the internal gates. Hicks receives a work order from a guard as he is transporting the finished product and must deposit the wine with the man on the gate, for a fee of one jar. The remaining jars are sold for

---

[13] Gould, Bittner, Messinger, et al., "Crime as a Profession," p. 27.

[14] Ibid., p. 29.

[15] R. B. Smith and Richard C. Stephen, "Drug Use and 'Hustling', A Study of Their Interrelationships," *Criminology* (August 1976):155–175.

cigarettes, mostly to men on or near Watkin's cell gallery. The concentration of booze in one cellblock produces a rather boisterous night, including a keeplock on one partying inmate who decided to challenge a guard.

In terms of social organization, the most interesting aspect of this winemaking hustle is the complete interdependence among several parties required for the successful completion of the project. Although George Watkins' entrepreneurial and manufacturing abilities and Ben Hicks' mobility were perhaps the key elements in the hustle, other men were just as important at various stages of the operation. Angel Parilla, Daniel McChesney, Luis Santiago, Watkins' friend on the front gate and the man on the internal gate were all indispensable to the hustle.[16]

The Racketeer as a Career Criminal

The racketeer engages in an activity that exploits the victim's fear of violence. The successful racketeer does not often have to resort to violence. His reputation for violence is usually sufficient to ensure compliance with his demands.

Racketeers are active agents in lawful as well as illegal activities of organized crime. In fact, it is frequently easier to apply the threat of force to legitimate business people, who are usually of the middle class and likely to be intimidated by threats of harm, than to persons who are engaged in illegal activities.

Most rackets are not owned or controlled by large organized crime syndicates. Many smaller operations exist in both large and small cities. Independent racketeers have succeeded in forming "protective associations" and "encouraging" (by threats of violence) business people to join. Many witnesses appeared before the Kefauver and McClellan committees of the U.S. Senate to present testimony about these patterns of racketeering exploitation.[17]

Newspaper accounts generally refer to those racketeers who are not known to be associated with organized crime as "small-time racketeers" or "petty racketeers." Their activities may be as small as the extortion of a few dollars monthly for useless burglar-alarm services or as large as the collection of tribute from all companies trucking food products into a city. It is the nature and not the extent of the activity that classifies these people as racketeers.

Before discussing the independent racketeer further, we shall consider the personnel employed by organized crime. Organized crime, like any big business, employs people with all sorts of specialized skills for work in its varied enterprises. Recruitment is from the ranks of ordinary

---

[16] Francis A. J. Ianni, *Black Mafia* (New York: Simon & Schuster, 1974), pp. 12–13. Copyright © 1974 by Francis A. J. Ianni. Reprinted by permission of Simon & Schuster, a division of Gulf + Western Corporation.

[17] Estes Kefauver, *Crime in America* (Garden City, N.Y.: Doubleday, 1951). See also Robert F. Kennedy, *The Enemy Within* (New York: Harper & Row, 1960).

career criminals, professional criminals, and legitimate business people and professionals, depending on the nature of the tasks involved. However, because in many of its activities organized crime utilizes force or the threat of force, there are also people who may be regarded as specialists in this type of criminal activity.

The essential characteristics of the racketeer working for organized crime are the following:

1. He uses force or the threat of force to coerce and intimidate others. This is the service he renders, and it is for this service that he is paid.
2. He does not usually commit property offenses.
3. He is involved in planning crimes of violence but does not usually commit these crimes himself. The violent acts are performed by specialists in violence.
4. He usually has an alibi. When a crime is being committed by persons acting in his behalf, he makes it a point to be either away from the city or in a conspicuous public place within the city. There are usually reputable witnesses to support his alibi.
5. He is skilled at building an organization or giving the appearance of having an organization. He exercises pressure and force not as an individual, but on behalf of an organization. It is always clear to the person being intimidated that reporting the racketeer to the police will result in violent action against him by "associates" of the racketeer.
6. The racketeer is likely to be recruited from the ranks of gang members and aggressive career criminals. With few exceptions, those who came to the attention of the Kefauver committee or the McClellan committee had records of conviction for traditional crimes.

In most respects independent racketeers do not differ much from members of a crime syndicate. The independent racketeer is, however, less able to protect himself than the syndicate racketeer. Because he does not have a large organization, he may become personally involved in violent crimes. Even if he has subordinates who actually perform the violent acts, they know him personally and can lead the police to him if they are caught. Furthermore, the independent racketeer is less likely to be able to secure immunity from arrest and prosecution than the one working for organized crime.

Organized crime contributes to political campaign funds, furnishes volunteer workers in campaigns, and helps in other activities on behalf of politicians. This aid is extensive and valuable. The independent does not have equivalent resources. He also has less support of reputable people as alibi witnesses and business associates. He is usually associated with from one to ten others—hardly enough to intimidate a city government.

Racketeers commit offenses we have referred to as traditional crimes. If they kill someone or conspire to have someone killed, they can be and are prosecuted for murder. Beating up an uncooperative person constitutes aggravated assault. Thus the racketeer is vulnerable to prosecution, and the syndicate racketeer is more vulnerable than other members of organized crime. Federal criminal statues may also be employed to prosecute racketeers who are active in labor unions or interfere with interstate commerce.

The gangster, or gunman, does not often control a racket. He is a paid worker who carries out an assignment for a price. Few racketeers have gunmen as part of their organization. They simply hire them when they need them, usually to protect their business from rival racketeers or to persuade stubborn people who refuse to cooperate with them.

A classic racketeer killer was Abe Reles, one of the gunmen for the infamous killer organization Murder, Inc., a group headed by the legendary organized crime kingpin Meyer Lansky in the 1920s. Reles agreed to turn state's evidence and testify against his partners in crime. Harry Barnes and Negley Teeters present a cogent description of Reles and his criminal activity within the framework of the rackets that is as relevant today about paid killers as it was in the 1920s:

> This sadistic gangster, a product of the Brooklyn slums, confessed to at least eighteen murders during his relatively brief career. He told Mr. O'Dwyer [William O'Dwyer, then district attorney of Kings County] that the Combination operated like banks and was spread all over the country. He compared it to a "tree with all its branches branched out" and to "an airplane trust." He added that there are hundreds of thousands in the nation-wide monopoly, and in the five boroughs of New York, several thousands. He stated, with relish, that "the old rule was, I'll do you and you'll do me . . . I looked to kill you and you looked to kill me. . . . There was no sense in that. So the leaders of the mob said, why not stop this crazy competition and go out and make money instead? So the leaders got together and said, 'Boys, what's the use of fighting each other? Let's put our heads together, all of us, so that there can't be a meeting without one another.' That's how they all got together, to make no fighting." Killing is an impersonal business proposition in this giant illegal combine.[18]

The career criminal, the professional, and the racketeer share a common characteristic: they have a commitment to crime based on socialization orientation that convinces them that they are engaged in a valid (albeit criminal) lifestyle.

Racketeers and Organized Crime

A contemporary example of a racketeer in organized crime is personified by John Gotti, alleged head of the New York rackets. A clip from an

---

[18] Harry E. Barnes and Negley K. Teeters, *New Horizons in Criminology*, 3d ed. © 1959. By permission of Prentice-Hall, Inc., Englewood Cliffs, N.J.

article about him by Andrea Chambers in *People* magazine (March 27, 1989) reveals part of his daily activity and his status in his community:

> For lunch he prefers Teresa Mimmo's in Manhattan's Little Italy. A plate of pasta. A small salad. A glass of wine. And then he walks it off on Mulberry Street. He moves in the eye of a small hurricane of flesh. In front there is Angelo Ruggiero, his boyhood friend, his gumbah and deputy, along with Bartolmeo Borriello, a trusted crony. Walking behind are Anthony Mascuzzio and Mike Napolitano, the bodyguards, who watch for the inevitable assassins. From doorways of the shops come the greetings, "How are you, John?" "Nice day, John." "You look good, John." Like a Florentine prince passing in procession, John Gotti, 48, waves and nods graciously the salutes of respect demanded by his position. John Gotti is the *capo di tutti capi*—the Godfather.

In the same article Ronald Goldstock, head of the New York State Organized Crime Task Force, who for years has been listening to government wiretaps and bugs planted around Gotti and his gang, depicts Gotti's position as a boss racketeer this way:

> "To a lot of people, John Gotti is a hero. All the other mob chiefs were sent to jail after the Pizza connection trials and the Mob Commission trial [federal prosecutions aimed at crippling the underworld leadership]. The organization is in shambles. The government is ahead. Or so it appears. Only Gotti looks like a winner. You know what he's like? He's like the last piton on the mountain. All the little mob guys are hanging on to him for dear life."
>
> If the future of the Mafia is riding on his back, Gotti shows little sign of the strain. He is the last of an old-style breed—that included Lucky Luciano, Vito Genovese, Al Capone, and Frank Costello—a swaggering crime chief running a multimillion-dollar-a-year illicit empire built on violence, prostitution, extortion, gambling, theft, and drugs. Gotti conducts his public life flamboyantly like his forerunners, and like them, he has an air of invincibility about him when it comes to immunity from the law. Despite this seeming invincibility, Gotti was arrested in 1989, and charged with a number of crimes, including conspiracy to murder, that could put him in prison for life. If the social system of racketeering and organized crime in the United States persists, inevitably a new Capone or Gotti career criminal is now moving up the status ladder of organized crime to assume their predecessor's godfather role. Despite the increasingly intense efforts of law enforcement, career criminal racketeers seem to be an ingrained facet of the American way of crime.[19]

Chapter 13, on organized crime, will explore this phenomenon in greater detail.

---

[19] Andrea Chambers, "Cold-Blooded King of a Hill Under Siege," *People* (March 27, 1989), pp. 70–72.

LIFESTYLES OF CAREER CRIMINALS

Most of the full-time crime careers I have discussed in this chapter have the following characteristics in common:

1. They involve offenses for material gain.
2. They are motivated by the desire for material gain.
3. The perpetrators all have rationalizations to justify their actions.
4. The perpetrators are usually psychologically "normal," or at least their criminal activities can be explained by other than psychological abnormality.
5. Violence, if used, is employed for the purpose of the commission of a crime for financial gain. Violence is not used gratuitously or as an emotional outlet.

There are great differences in the lifestyles of practitioners of the varied categories, and even greater differences in the reactions of society to the offenses and the offenders. The lifestyles of the economically deprived career criminals include a life "on the lam" to avoid apprehension, associations limited largely to poor people and other deprived career criminals, and long periods of time spent in prison. Bill, Louis J. Bean, and the thousands like them that we find in our prisons have had little or no opportunity to succeed in earning a decent livelihood in an affluent society, using the means lawfully available to them. To them, crime was one way to obtain some of the material goods that everyone is encouraged to acquire by our materialistic society.

The "jewel switcher," Maxie the Goniff, Reggie, and other professional career criminals also live on the fringes of society. They are more successful and more affluent than the usual career criminal, but they, too, must constantly look over their shoulders in fear of the law. They, too, associate most frequently with other criminals. They, too, must seek to avoid apprehension on a daily basis and prepare in advance for bail, lawyers, and trials. They spend far less time in prison, but they are not immune from prosecution and, when sentenced, usually receive stiff penalties. The same may be said for racketeers like Al Capone and John Gotti. Even men like this, who are at the top of their criminal profession, are convicted and go to prison because of increasingly vigorous law enforcement.

PART Three

CRIMINAL PATTERNS

Chapter

7

Patterns of Violence

Albert Camus, in *The Rebel*, his philosophical essay on the meanings of rebellion and revolution, had this to say about the contemporary violence that engulfs all citizens:

> The poets themselves, confronted with the murder of their fellow men, proudly declare that their hands are clean. The whole world absent-mindedly turns its back on these crimes; the victims have reached the extremity of their disgrace: they are a bore. In ancient times the blood of murder at least produced a religious horror and in this way sanctified the value of life. The real condemnation of the period we live in is, on the contrary, that it leads us to think that it is not bloodthirsty enough. Blood is no longer visible; it does not bespatter the faces of our pharisees visibly enough. This is the extreme of nihilism; blind and savage murder becomes an oasis, and the imbecile criminal seems positively refreshing in comparison with our highly intelligent executioners.[1]

There are still types of "senseless" violence and homicide that produce emotional reactions in the mass mind. These phenomena are almost unreal since they are mainly experienced secondhand on television, in the newspapers, or on the movie screen. This blurring of reality is quite evident with relation to television. For many people, the violence shown in a real war report on TV, as, for example, a pile of real bodies massacred on some battlefield, may not seem too different from the fictionalized war of a dramatic program.

---

[1] Albert Camus, *The Rebel*, trans. Anthony Bower (New York: Knopf, 1954), pp. 279–280. © 1954, Alfred A. Knopf, Inc. Reprinted by permission.

THE SOCIOCULTURAL CLIMATE OF VIOLENCE IN CONTEMPORARY SOCIETY

It would be logical to speculate that a child growing up in a nonviolent social system would be less inclined to be violent than a child growing up in a climate of violence. War, parental aggression (overt and covert), institutionalized violence by political leaders, mass media presentations of violence—all are factors that produce a violent environment.

More specifically, the violence-proneness of adults in a society affects the degree of violence committed by young people in the same society. Obviously, in a nonviolent social system most people would not ordinarily commit acts of aggression. The opposite would also hold true. Within the climate of Nazi Germany, for example, it would be expected that children growing up would be more amenable to violent behavior. A general hypothesis that would be affirmed by most people is that a person (young or old) in Nazi Germany would be more likely to follow orders and commit aggressive acts than the average individual in American society. Here we are essentially concerned not with the acting out of violence but with the predisposition of Americans to commit acts of aggression. Information on this theme provides some clues to the violence of young people that often stems from the "violent characteristics" of their adult role models in American society.

One set of experiments that fits into this category was the research of psychologist Stanley Milgram at Yale University in the early 1960s.[2] These experiments appeared to point up a continuing pattern. In his studies Milgram was concerned with the conditions under which people would be obedient or disobedient to authority. In his overall project, which extended over a period of several years, almost a thousand individuals were subjects of his research. He investigated a variety of experimental settings and modifications of variables. The results, however, were frighteningly uniform. On the basis of this research, Milgram concluded that a majority of "good people," who in their everyday lives were responsible and decent, could be made to perform "callous and severe" acts on other people when they were placed in situations that had the "trappings of authority."

The "harsh acts" included giving electric shocks to another individual who might have just died of a heart attack. The following detailed description of one of Milgram's projects more clearly illustrates the general research approach that was used.

The subjects in this prototype example of the Milgram experiments on obedience were a random sample of New Haven adult males who came to Milgram's Yale Research Center in response to a newspaper advertisement. They were paid by the hour and individually brought to a

---

[2] Stanley Milgram, "Some Conditions of Obedience and Disobedience to Authority," *Human Relations* 18 (1965):57–76.

laboratory and introduced to their "partners," who were, in reality, members of the research team. Each subject was told that he was going to participate in a learning experiment with his partner. One of them was to be the "teacher" and the other the "learner." It was contrived that the subject always wound up as the teacher and the research assistant always became the learner. The subject was then told, incorrectly, that the research was being conducted to determine the effects of punishment on learning.

The subject, now the teacher, witnessed the standard procedure by which the learner (in reality a member of the research staff) was strapped into a chair that apparently had electrical connections. The subject was then taken into another room and told to ask the learner certain questions from a questionnaire he was given. The teacher was told to administer electric shocks every time the learner gave a wrong answer. (In some cases, before the learner was strapped into his "electric chair," he would comment, "Take it easy on me, I have a heart condition.")

In the room with the teacher was another member of the research team who served as an authority figure and as a provocateur. He was present to make sure that the subject administered the proper shocks for incorrect answers.

The subject was told by the authority figure to give progressively stronger shocks to the learner when the latter's answers were incorrect. In front of the subject was an elaborate electric board that, as far as the subject knew, controlled shock levels from 15 to 450 volts in 15-volt gradations. The last two switches were ominously labeled XXX.

The researcher in the room would admonish the subject to increase the shock for each incorrect answer. In a short time the subject was repeatedly, as far as he knew, giving shocks of up to 450 volts to the person in the next room. The "victim" would often dramatically pound the wall and shout, "Stop it, you're killing me!" Some subjects balked at continuing but proceeded on the orders of the authority figure, who would simply say, "Continue the experiment."

At a certain point, the "victim," after pounding on the wall, would "play dead," or act as if he passed out and make no sound. The researcher in the room would instruct the subject to count "no response" as an incorrect answer. He would then order the subject to continue to shock an apparently inert or dead body with heavy electric shocks.

In several cases, the subject refused to act out his robopathic behavior of continuing to shock the victim ("Christ, I don't hear him anymore, maybe I killed him! You know he said he had a bad heart," said one.) The researcher would say, "Go on with the experiment." The authoritative voice of the Yale researcher caused more than half the subjects to continue to shock what might very well have been a dead body!

In a part of the experiment, some subjects refused to go on. The researcher would tell the subject to continue and say, "Go ahead, I'll be responsible for what happens to the 'learner'. " When this was done, the subject would usually say, "O.K., I'll continue. Remember, you're responsible, not me!"

One of Milgram's experiments, conducted with 40 subjects, was typical of the overall series of experiments carried out with almost 1,000 men. All 40 subjects complied by shocking their "victims" with up to 300 volts. Fourteen stopped at that point or at slightly higher levels. But the majority—26 subjects—continued to administer increasingly severe shocks until they reached 450 volts. This was beyond the switch marked *Danger: Severe Shock.* Thus 65 percent of this representative sample of "good people," paid a few dollars an hour, conformed to the dictates of an experimental authority to the point that they supposedly inflicted severe pain or possible death on another human being.

The research essentially validated the assumption that people would conform to dictates of people in authority even when they knew they were inflicting severe harm on another person, up to and beyond homicide. Authority, in a legitimate social context, thus produced obedience and conformity to inhuman goals—even in America.

It would be difficult to measure the proportion of violent components in an individual and perhaps even more difficult to estimate the number of such individuals in a society. (A wild speculation, in accordance with the Milgram experiments, would be: more than half the population.) Perhaps even more difficult is the measurement of the number of what Jules Feiffer calls "little murders," which people "just doing their job" inflict on others in everyday life.

Several issues are blatantly clear. The majority of people tend to support illegal and immoral wars and their concomitant killings. Common people do sanction many little murders and big murders, especially if the perpetrators are legitimately acting within the proper formal societal contexts. This climate of violence surrounds the socialization of young people—and helps to account for the acceleration of "senseless violence" within the population.

Another reason for the developing climate of violence that effects violence in people is the growing alienation of people in a machinelike social system. One observer of the scene, Lynne B. Iglitzin, comments:

> By far the most potent source of violence is the ubiquity of feelings of alienation and anomie which plague so many human beings in modern society. Feelings of normlessness and meaninglessness, of estrangement from one's self and from others are generally accepted characteristics of alienation. The alienated person is out of touch with himself and with other persons; he is at the mercy of his technological creations, a "thing" dependent on unknown powerful forces.[3]

---

[3] Lynne B. Iglitzin, *Violent Conflict in American Society* (San Francisco: Chandler, 1972), p. 97.

R. D. Laing, the British psychoanalyst, defines alienation in his poignant description of the human condition, particularly of the white European and North American, as a sense of "being at an end: of being only half alive in the fibrillating heartland of a senescent civilization."[4] This pervasive condition of estrangement from ourselves and from the human community provides a setting in which people have perpetrated incredible acts of violence upon each other and have been able to rationalize such behavior as "normality." According to psychiatrists such as Laing and Erich Fromm, it has become "normal" to be alienated, and the more one thus behaves like everyone else—that is, treating others as commodities rather than as human beings—the more one is taken to be sane. It is Laing's belief that those who are considered sick in an alienated world might be the healthiest of all. Laing conceptualizes that "the condition of alienation, of being asleep, of being unconscious, of being out of one's mind, is the condition of the normal man."[5] As support for this premise, he notes that "normal men have killed perhaps 100,000,000 of their fellow normal men in the last fifty years."[6]

In brief, the described "climate of violence" in society is a vital ingredient to violent behavior on the part of many criminals. Murderers are not dropped into our society from outer space. These individuals grow up under conditions that can effect the most prone members of society to commit acts of violence.

The Family as a Cradle of Violence

In an article aptly titled "The Family as a Cradle of Violence," Suzanne K. Steinmetz and Murray A. Straus state:

> It would be hard to find a group or institution in American society in which violence is more of an everyday occurrence than it is within the family. Family members physically abuse each other far more often than do nonrelated individuals. Starting with slaps and going on to torture and murder, the family provides a prime setting for every degree of physical violence. So universal is the phenomenon that it is probable that some form of violence will occur in almost every family . . .
>
> A survey conducted for the National Commission on the Cause and Prevention of Violence deals with what violence people would approve. These data show that one out of four men and one out of six women approve of slapping a wife under certain conditions. As for a wife slapping a husband, 26 percent of the men and 19 percent of the women approve. . . .
>
> Richard Gelles of the University of New Hampshire, who has done a series of in-depth case studies of a sample of 80 families, found that about 56 percent of the couples have used physical force on each other at some time.

---

[4] R. D. Laing, *The Politics of Experience* (New York: Pantheon, 1967), p. xiii.

[5] Ibid., p. 12.

[6] Ibid.

In a second study, freshman college students responded to a series of questions about conflicts which occurred in their senior year in high school, and to further questions about how these conflicts were handled. Included in the conflict resolution section were questions on whether or not the parties to the disputes had ever hit, pushed, shoved, thrown things or kicked each other in the course of a quarrel.

The results show that during that one year 62 percent of the high school seniors had used physical force on a brother or sister and 16 percent of their parents had used physical force on each other. Since these figures are for a single year, the percentage who had *ever* used violence is probably much greater.[7]

In most juvenile institutions it is usually apparent that delinquent, emotionally disturbed, or schizophrenic teenagers have been subjected to abusive treatment and family pathology from the time of birth. Many admissions to institutions are occasioned by bizarre retaliatory acts teenagers perpetrate against themselves or family members. Even when instances of gross abuse come to "public" attention, there is no guarantee of appropriate intervention. Most adults who become violent offenders were abused children.

In a basic book on the subject of family violence, *The Violent Home* by Richard Gelles, the phenomenon of family violence was explored in detail.[8] Gelles asserted that the family is the major source of the most violent acts. He defined these acts as homicides, aggravated assaults, and child abuse. Familial homicides constituted approximately one out of four murders, and half of these were between husbands and wives. Husbands and wives accounted for 11 percent of aggravated assaults. Gelles estimated that between 200,000 and 500,000 children are abused each year. It is likely that the more extreme forms of violence—those just mentioned—will be reported, but that violence in more moderate forms (slapping, pushing, hitting, battery) tends to go undetected.

Gelles researched 80 families concerning family violence. Because of the sensitivity of the subject matter, he used informal interview techniques. The questions asked of the family were in the form of problems and solutions that the interviewee would feel free to discuss. Half of the population of 80 was drawn from families where known violence had occurred, half from families with no known violence. The violent families were found through a social agency and were police blotter cases in a New Hampshire city (that is, homes where police

---

[7] Abridged and adapted from "General Introduction: Social Myth and Social System in the Study of Intra-Family Violence," Suzanne K. Steinmetz and Murray A. Straus in *Violence in the Family*, edited by Suzanne K. Steinmetz and Murray A. Straus. Copyright © 1974 by Harper & Row, Publishers, Inc. Reprinted by permission of the publisher.

[8] The following discussion is derived from an analysis of Richard Gelles, *The Violent Home: A Study of Physical Aggression Between Husbands and Wives.* Paper, Sage Publications. Sage Library of Social Research, Vol. 13 (1980).

intervention was called for). The families without known histories of violence were neighbors of the violent families. This research design allowed Gelles to compare violent families with nonviolent families.

More than half the families interviewed recalled one or more incidents of violence. This included the families with no *known* history of violence and supports the idea that much violence goes undetected. Half the families recalling at least one recorded incident of violence reported violence on a regular basis.

Husbands were the most violent. Forty-seven percent had hit their wives at least once, and 25 percent hit them regularly. Wives, as expected, were more passive. In the families that exhibited the most violence, however, wives hit their husbands as frequently as husbands hit them. Because of physical inequalities, wives reported using more extreme tools of violence—knives and hard objects—to initiate attacks or to retaliate for attacks.

In the interviews, Gelles noted many accounts of violence rationalizations. These rationalizations categorize some violent incidents into what Gelles termed "normal" violence. This violence is thought of as necessary in the normal routine of family life. It is the "spare the rod and spoil the child" type of violence. Such violent acts are, to some extent, even acknowledged as normative by the victim. Gelles also presented many cases of wives who approved of violent acts against themselves when the occasions were "appropriate." These victim-precipitated violent acts were often accompanied by the "I deserved it" attitude. The husbands justified the physical brutality as "knocking some sense" into their wives.

Acts of physical violence against children were construed as acts of communication. The parents were conveying a message, teaching something to the child. Force was seen as unavoidable. There were countless incidents of disciplinary actions that included hitting, with the "this is gonna hurt me more than it hurts you" attitude. Parents and spouses thus tended to neutralize acts of violence by attaching "rational" meanings to those acts.

Gelles discussed another type of violence, which he called "volcanic" violence. This act apparently has no goals in its execution or any rationalizations attached to it. It is an act that erupts from accumulated frustrations, and the family victim just happens to be in the wrong place at the wrong time.

There was a high association between violence and alcohol, especially on the part of the husband. The victim and the offender took the attitude that the alcohol caused the release of impulses toward aggression and violence. The cause of violence was the alcohol and not the offender. When sober, it was claimed, the offender was not an abuser.

Another typology of violence and abuse to women is that in which the fearful wife will not retaliate in a defense against the abusive husband. This is what Gelles called "one-way violence." The female victim feels either that her femininity will not permit retaliation or that any defensive action would bring harsher violence against herself. Gelles's data revealed that those wives who did not fight back were the ones most subject to repeated beatings. Numerous reports of violent attacks centered around sex-related incidents. Gelles contended that these violent outbursts, mainly about extramarital affairs, are learned in the socialization process and are given a high degree of social sanction. They are typically equally distributed between male and female offenders; females showed as much aggressiveness as males. The victim usually displayed the "I deserved it" attitude and did not retaliate.

Gelles presented the typology of family violence in three dimensions. The first dimension ranges from expressive violence, where the use of physical force is a means in itself (volcanic violence is an example of this), to instrumental violence, which is violence used to restrain or induce a particular behavior pattern on the part of the victim (such as disciplinary action taken on a child). The second dimension ranges from legitimate or socially sanctioned violent acts to illegitimate acts—for example, from beating an adulterous spouse (socially sanctioned) to simply beating a spouse (not socially sanctioned). The third dimension of violent acts is that which is victim-precipitated. Here the victim plays a major role in victimization by provoking the offender.

Gelles concluded that in general, violence in a family results from the numerous stresses that the members experience in everyday life. He stated several propositions to support his structural theory of family violence: (1) Violence is a response to a particular structure and situation. It is not usually an irrational phenomenon. (2) Stress is differentially distributed in the social structure. Families of lower economic and occupational status are more likely to encounter stressful situations. The ability to cope with this stress is also unequally distributed, and these same families live with a higher degree of isolation and less chance of getting qualified psychological services. (3) A child learns through exposures and experiences that violence is the normative approach to stress. When there is a model of approved violence, the chances are greater that violence will be used.

The family is too often a subculture of violence in our society. Its set of norms and values, through law, is informally sanctioned by society. Expressions like "a man's home is his castle," where he is lord and master, support this prevailing attitude. Violence is often used in the family by the husband, to enforce *his* norms and values.

A famous case that illustrates this pathological condition in a family is the web of violence in the Joel Steinberg household that resulted in the death of Steinberg's illegally adopted 6-year-old daughter, Lisa. In an article in the *Los Angeles Times* titled "Maximum Sentence in Girl's Death," John Goldman cogently summarizes the case:

> Declaring the defendant never showed any remorse, a judge Friday angrily sentenced disbarred lawyer Joel Steinberg to the maximum of 8½ to 25 years

in prison for killing his illegally adopted daughter in a case that focused national attention on the growing problem of child abuse linked to drugs.

Acting New York State Supreme Court Justice Harold Rothwax brushed aside Steinberg's plea that he should be pitied as a "victim" and accused him of "extraordinary narcissism and self-involvement." Rothwax also fined him $5,000.

"The defendant . . . has never accepted any responsibility. I have come to believe he is incapable of accepting responsibility," Rothwax said. "He has never offered any explanation except those that have been shown to be demonstrably false.

"His extreme need to control everyone in his ambit led him to become the instrument of Lisa's death," the judge added. "There is nothing in the record to mitigate the extreme callousness and harshness of his conduct, and he is deserving of the maximum sentence provided by law. . . . The court strongly recommends against the release of this defendant on parole."

Lisa Steinberg, 6, died in St. Vincent's Hospital in Manhattan on November 5, 1987, after being beaten and left on the bathroom floor of the Greenwich Village apartment Steinberg shared with his then lover, Hedda Nussbaum. During [the] trial, in which Nussbaum was a principal prosecution witness, there was testimony that Steinberg went out to dinner with a client, then returned home and took cocaine for several hours before summoning help for the child 12 hours after the beating.

When police entered the apartment, they found another illegally adopted child, Mitchell, 16 months old, drinking spoiled milk.

A jury convicted Steinberg, 47, of first-degree manslaughter January 30 [1989]. He did not take the stand in his own defense during the trial, but in an extraordinary scene televised on two New York local stations . . . , Steinberg spoke for the first time in court and sought leniency.

Steinberg attacked the credibility of his probation report and medical testimony about the children during the trial.

"At no point did I ever strike them in any form," Steinberg told the court. "I did not hit, strike or use any form of forceful discipline to those children. Those children were not locked in a house of horrors."

Referring to Lisa, he added: "I had a consistently joyous, happy relationship with her."

Steinberg claimed that when he left the apartment, he did not sense there was anything wrong with his daughter.

"The thing I feel the most difficulty about," he said, his voice breaking, "is not making the judgment to seek medical attention the moment I came home. . . . I did not make the judgment it was necessary. . . . If there was anything wrong with Lisa I would not have left.

"I made an error of judgment. On reflection, after hearing the testimony, I should have sought medical attention. I did not make that judgment. . . .

"I feel that pain every day. That is my loss. It is not like a defendant who stands before you and perpetrates a crime on an outside victim. I'm the loss, the victim." [This type of lying, egocentrism, and self-pity is characteristic of sociopaths like Steinberg.]

But prosecutors, in asking for the maximum sentence, painted a grimmer picture.

As the child "lay dying, he went to dinner with a drug-dealing friend of his and came back and free-based cocaine," Assistant District Attorney John McClusker charged.

McClusker told the court that Steinberg exhibited a "total lack of concern for anyone else but Joel Steinberg."

The prosecutor said that during their relationship, Steinberg "single-handedly reduced [his companion Hedda] Nussbaum to a horrible battered shell of a human being."

"It is clear Mr. Steinberg has no qualms about destroying human life," McClusker charged, adding that the defendant enjoyed "a life of violence and self-gratification."

". . . He has never shown any sorrow or remorse [that] a young child's life was taken and he was responsible. He has never shown any responsibility for his actions." [These attributes are also typical of sociopaths.]

Nussbaum, 46, also had been charged in the girl's death, but the counts were dropped on the grounds that 12 years of battering by Steinberg made her incapable of either violence or coming to Lisa's aid.

Nussbaum watched the sentencing on television at the Manhattan office of her attorney, Betty Levinson, who quoted her as saying, "How can he stand there and lie with such a straight face?"[9]

The Mass Media and Violence

Another general societal context of violence is the mass media. Virtually every family in the United States owns at least one television set, and, according to data available from broadcast rating services, these sets are turned on an average of about six hours each day. Children are the heaviest viewers. We know that a great deal of violence is exhibited in television programs.

If TV has a negative impact as a framework for violence, many films are even more negative. Violence has been a major attraction in films for some years; however, there has been a change in the way violence is presented. In films prior to 1960, the violent characters met with a bad end. The scene was characteristic of most gangster pictures; even in the westerns the violent "bad guys" were punished. Movie heroes were violent, but usually in self-defense. In the 1970s, violence was presented as the best solution and often the only solution for dealing with those with whom the characters had differences. As one writer put it, who-dunits have been replaced by everyonedunits. We have arrived at a point in movie violence where anything goes, from dismemberment murders to grotesque graphic shootings.

In these films, violence is presented as an effective way of handling problems, not only for ordinary people but also for "heroes" and for representatives of the state—police officers and people in authority. If we accept the available data on the relationship between viewing

---

[9] John J. Goldman, "Maximum Sentence in Girl's Death." *Los Angeles Times*, March 25, 1989.

violence on television and increased aggressive behavior, we must conclude that watching violent films is likely to increase violent crime. People—particularly very young people—watching stars perform the violent "hero" role are likely to consider violence as an approved way of asserting themselves and of solving their problems. I do not, of course, recommend or support censorship, but parents of young children should be alert to the possible dangers of allowing their children to watch such violent films.

There is increased evidence that some young people become more and more inured to violence because of the constant bombardment of the mass media. A case in point is the response of one relatively normal young man who witnessed an actual homicide. His father, a social psychologist, related the story of his son's response to the murder and his own reaction to his son's response as follows:

> The movies I saw during my childhood years contained simple human stories and had very little violence. Today the movies are full of mutilations, grisly murders and outrageous horror scenarios.
>
> My son is an afficionado of these modern horror films, and I detest them. He thinks they are fun and exciting, and I think they are the crass product of the typical banal, narrow Hollywood mind out to make a fast buck without a sliver of social conscience. He sees them all, and I see only a few purely for research interest in understanding modern tastes.
>
> In this context, my son recently had what would have been a horrendous emotional experience for me. The experience and his reaction to it reveal something about the conflict of perceptions on violence and the generation gap. During the summer he became friends with a young man—I will call him Jim—a twenty-five-year-old who seemed more like sixteen, my son's age at the time. The "man" was quite immature and had the basic personality of the standard Hollywood hustler who had no special talent yet was trying to break into the film and music business. He would do anything but *work* for his glorified and exorbitant goals. He did not have to work because he had a wealthy father who regularly sent him a sizeable allowance. My son would tell me about his friend's escapades with dope and prostitutes.
>
> Jim's story is rather complex, but the bottom line is that one day he got into an altercation (in my son's presence) with a man who lived near his apartment across their back alley. Apparently Jim owed him money (probably for drugs) and refused to pay up. The man physically assaulted Jim. Jim went into his apartment, got a gun he had bought that day and shot his adversary in the head, killing him.
>
> My son was an eyewitness to this horrible event. He was interrogated by the police for several hours. Knowing something about the psychological impact of such bizarre emotional events, when I saw my son after the police interrogations, I pressed him to open up and freely discuss his deeper emotional feelings about his dreadful experience. He ran through it one time, and in response to my continuing concern about how it affected him personally, he finally said in an exasperated voice: "Dad, I know what you're getting at. But you have to understand. When you were a kid, if something

like this happened to you, I know you would have been really upset. But it really doesn't bother me that much. I've seen plenty of killings on the tube and in the movies. It really is okay. You don't have to worry about me." Based on the emotional tone of his response, I accepted what he told me as valid.[10]

Guns as Part of the Violent Framework

An editorial in the August 22, 1988, issue of the *New York Times* reveals some of the social dimensions of guns:

> The first shots erupted at 12:23 A.M. when a group of six men surrounded two others, killing one and wounding the second. An hour later, a few blocks away, gunfire from a passing car raked a group of 25 listening to rap music on a streetcorner, wounding seven. Police recovered cartridges from military assault rifles. "Every day this is a war zone," a neighbor said. "The [drug] dealers have bigger guns than the police." . . .
>
> The story about yet another gang skirmish in a Brooklyn housing project illustrates an alarming national trend—the drug problem is becoming a gun problem. Yet unlike the drug problem, much could be done to reduce the gun problem with simple legislation.
>
> Sophisticated military assault weapons are now standard issue for the adolescent drug thugs who terrorize urban communities—homemade zip-guns went out with "West Side Story." Though Federal law bans fully automatic machine guns, semiautomatics, requiring a trigger pull for each shot, are subject only to local law. The distinction is all but meaningless, since many semiautomatics are easily converted to machine guns.
>
> One remedy would be a flat ban on civilian possession of semiautomatic military assault rifles. Designed for killing humans at close quarters, such guns are easily distinguishable from hunting rifles designed to kill animals at a distance. But Congress need not even go that far. It could also require a uniform national waiting period between purchase and delivery of a gun to allow for a check of the purchaser's background.
>
> The lack of such a law now creates a powerful incentive for gun-running from states like Ohio and Florida, where weapons are easily purchased with few questions asked, to New York City, where laws are strict. The dealer willing to go out of state may pay as little as $70 for a gun he can sell on New York streets for more than $200. The drug gangs, with cash to burn, willingly pay the markup. A uniform waiting period would take the profit out of interstate trafficking.
>
> The National Rifle Association fiercely opposes a waiting period, telling gun fanciers that "you will be forced to ask a government bureaucrat's permission" to make a purchase. The complaint is nonsense: the state has every right to inquire about fitness to own a gun, just as it asks about fitness to drive a car.[11]

---

[10] Lewis Yablonsky, *Fathers and Sons* (New York: Simon & Schuster, 1982), pp. 109–110. Copyright © 1982 by Lewis Yablonsky. Reprinted by permission of Simon & Schuster, Inc.

[11] "War on Drugs, War on Guns." Copyright © 1988 by The New York Times Company. Reprinted by permission.

In 1987, 59 percent of all homicides known to the police were committed through the use of firearms. The ready availability of handguns is blamed by many criminologists and law enforcement authorities for the increase in such violent crime as murder and robbery. Around 20,000 Americans are killed with guns each year, including homicides, suicides, and accidents. The homicide rate per capita in the United States is reported to be 35 times higher than the rate in Germany or in England, yet a substantial portion of the American population appears to support the view that everyone should be entitled to own a gun. A law in California requires prison sentences for criminals who use firearms in committing serious crimes, ranging from robbery to attempted murder. A small community in Illinois passed a gun control law in 1982 and spurred consideration of similar action by many other communities. In another American community, a radical gun advocate was attempting to pass a law making it mandatory for every family to have a gun. In 1988, Florida liberalized its gun control laws, and murders with guns have increased sharply in that state.

The British do not subscribe to the view held by many in the United States that because one is a citizen one is entitled to own a gun. They control the use of guns in the following ways:

> Under Britain's firearms control laws, no one may own a firearm without a police certificate, except for antique weapons and certain types of airguns.
>
> To get a certificate, the applicant must have a "good reason" which in the vast majority of cases is the desire to have a weapon for hunting or sport shooting. Membership in a gun or hunting club is usually the way to get the certificate.
>
> "The gun clubs," Russell said, "are mindful of the danger of a person joining for the purpose of getting a certificate that might otherwise be withheld."
>
> "We have worried about that," he said. "That's why virtually all clubs have a six-month probationary period for new members which enables the club's officers to find out if the new member is really interested in sport shooting."
>
> The certificates are issued for periods of up to three years. Police are not required to state a reason for rejecting an application, unless the applicant challenges the rejection in court. Aside from the "good reason" requirement, the applicant must show, usually through completion of a safety course, that he knows how to handle a firearm properly. . . .
>
> There are especially heavy penalties for possession of a firearm, whether used or not in the commission of a crime, and the intended use of a fake gun in the commission of a crime carries a maximum penalty of 14 years in prison. This is only one of 80 different offenses linked to the illegal possession of firearms. . . .
>
> As a result, firearms play a relatively small role in British crime.[12]

---

[12] Harry Trimborn, "Britain Dismayed by U.S. 'Myth'—Right to Own Guns," *Los Angeles Times*, September 25, 1975. Copyright, 1975, *Los Angeles Times*. Reprinted by permission.

Why is there so much opposition to gun control in the United States? For one thing, the manufacture and sale of firearms is a very big business, with gun owners spending an estimated $3 billion a year on guns. Gun and ammunition manufacturers, retail gun dealers, gun magazine publishers, and hunting resort owners make a great deal of money from the sale and distribution of weapons. They also spend a good deal of money in the form of contributions to the political campaigns of congressional and state legislative candidates. The National Rifle Association, probably the most effective lobby in Washington, carries on a continuous campaign against gun control legislation. Its officials have boasted that they can get their million members to send at least half a million letters to Congress on 72-hour notice. Very few politicians want to present an image that they are soft on guns or crime. Consequently, the NRA wins its fights against gun control legislation, and the death toll from guns will no doubt continue to rise in the United States into the twenty-first century.

In an article in *Psychology Today*, psychologist Leonard Berkowitz directs our attention to a phenomenon he calls "the weapons effect." He says past and present research reveals that weapons have an aggressive effect on our behavior. In his studies and those of others, he notes that the sight of a weapon increases any aggressiveness that one is already experiencing. In a study done in Sweden, it was found that the weapons effect occurred even without previous frustration being introduced. Still other studies have shown that children, when given toy guns to play with, will act more aggressively than when they play with other toys. A group of field studies revealed that when weapons were present the subjects behaved more aggressively than when no weapons were present.

Berkowitz offers two theories as to why the weapons effect occurs:

1. Weapons function as a conditioned stimulus eliciting associated responses.
2. Guns might remind people of earlier occasions when they have seen aggression rewarded (as on TV and in movies).

Berkowitz thinks it is this increase of aggression when a gun is present that leads to the "trigger pulling the finger."[13]

As a criminologist, I have an extreme zero tolerance to *all* types of guns in the hands of *any* citizen. The only people who should have gun firepower are the police and the military. A citizen's right to bear arms as specified in the Constitution is a totally outdated concept and should be eliminated. Citizens no longer need arms to protect themselves from the government of the United States. As for hunters, our wildlife is being sufficiently decimated by pollution without their assaults on animals and

---

[13] Leonard Berkowitz, "How Guns Control Us," *Psychology Today* (June 1981):11–12.

birds. In my view, citizens who love guns as hunters or collectors should forego their attachment in the interest of significantly reducing this country's murder rate in the coming century.

One piece of evidence, among many recent studies, that supports my assertions is found in the following study reported in the *New York Times* (November 9, 1988). The study revealed that restricting access to guns can reduce a community's homicide rate. The study, as yet unpublished, by Dr. John Henry Sloan, a research associate at Seattle's Harborview Injury Prevention and Research Center, reported that death by firearms is almost five times as high in Seattle as in Vancouver, British Columbia, a city with stricter gun laws. The two cities are very comparable in terms of population and a variety of other significant social factors. Consequently, the fact that the number of gun-related deaths in Seattle was 139, as opposed to 25 for Vancouver, provides significant support to the theory that stronger gun control could reduce homicide.

BASIC PATTERNS OF VIOLENCE

What factors delineate "logical" from "senseless" violence? My context for analysis is the viewpoint on violence of the dominant segment of the society. Four categories encompass almost all patterns of violence:

1. *Legal, Sanctioned, Rational Violence*   Many violent acts are supported in law. The soldier is rewarded as a hero for the intensity of his violent behavior in the line of duty. He is accordingly well trained for violent action. In fact, a nonviolent soldier may, under certain conditions, be court-martialed and executed. Police officers enact another role that is supported by legal violence. Other legally justified violence is found in certain aggressive sports (football, boxing) and in certain acts of self-defense, as for example, in the Goetz case.

2. *Illegal, Sanctioned, Rational Violence*   A significant factor in any analysis of violence is its degree of social sanction or support. No one would argue that an assault committed by a deceived husband on an adulterer is legal, but many would sanction this violence. Even when homicide is the result, the "unwritten law" has wide support. Other examples of violence that are illegal yet sanctioned and considered rational would include violent responses to insults or an attack upon one's honor. Another case of this type would be a woman's violent defense against an attack by a battering husband. In a number of court cases, wives who killed their assaultive husbands were exonerated.

   Violence, even when it is illegal, thus has varying degrees of acceptance within different segments of American society. Dr. S. J. Ball-Rokeach cogently comments on the issue of what he terms "social violence" as follows:

   [If] we define violence as primarily goal-oriented and therefore rational human behavior, then it permits exploration of "normal" social processes and "functioning" personal and social systems as possible causes of violence. The issue becomes not whether violence is prescribed or proscribed, but how violence is incorporated into everyday systems of social action. Violence caused by "normal" social and personal processes may be called *social* violence to distinguish it from "asocial" violence caused by "abnormal" or deficit states. Asocial violence thus becomes a residual category of acts that are caused by such abnormal or deficit states as psychopathology, biochemical disorder (e.g., certain drugs or blood sugar levels), neurological, hormonal or genetic malfunction, or acute breakdown of reasoning faculties (e.g., drunken rage or panic). Acts of violence would certainly vary in the extent to which they are or are not perceived by their perpetrators to fit the present definition of social violence.[14]

3. *Illegal, Nonsanctioned, Rational Violence* Some violent acts that are neither legal nor sanctioned are still considered rational in a criminal context. Our most prevalent form of serious crime, violence for financial gain, would generally fit into this category. Robbery and assault upon the person, or the commission of homicide within the framework of organized crime, would be rational behavior within the criminal context.

4. *Illegal, Nonsanctioned, Irrational Violence* This category, popularly referred to as senseless violence, or what I have termed raw violence, includes such crimes as the methodical murder of 8 student nurses in sequence, the shooting to death of 15 people (and the wounding of 31) from a university tower, the "kill-for-kicks" assault by three youths on an elderly man who was whistling a tune they didn't like, the stabbing and bludgeoning to death of a 15-year-old polio victim by a gang, or the Hillside Strangler murders. This kind of violence outrageously defies the law, social sanction, and rationality, yet under a sociological microscope certain facets of this deadly social virus can be isolated, analyzed, and understood.

See Figure 7.1 for a schematic representation of these four patterns of violence.

Violence generally has the effect of social disorganization. Figure 7.1, however, shows that categories 1 and 2 tend to have the impact and intent of affirming the social order and its norms, whereas categories 3 and 4 have the impact of producing social disorganization. This element of social disorganization is especially true of category 4, senseless violence. We shall now examine these four categories in order, providing case material that helps to illuminate each of them.

LEGAL, SANCTIONED, RATIONAL VIOLENCE

War is the ultimate violent activity undertaken by a society. Under some circumstances it is considered justified by virtually all segments of the

---

[14] S. J. Ball-Rokeach, "Normative and Deviant Violence from a Conflict Perspective," *Social Problems* (October 1980).

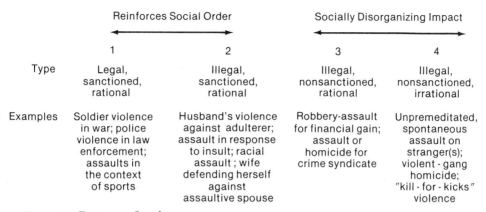

Figure 7.1 Patterns of violence.

society, as when the country is the victim of what is defined as an unprovoked attack. In general, wars are considered justified by the dominant groups in the society when the nation is committed to them in an effort to defend the status quo of its social structure. War obviously produces enormous casualties. For example the Iran-Iraq conflict, a relatively minor war, had resulted in 1 million casualties as of 1988.

When law enforcement officials engage in violent activities, they justify their actions as necessary for the maintenance of "law and order," which they tend to equate with the maintenance of the status quo of the social and political structure. In many situations, violent actions by the nation (war) and by law enforcement officials are forces mitigating against social change. Violent efforts to maintain present (or idealized versions of former) standards of morality, national boundaries, or spheres of influence and to resist ethical or moral shifts are regarded as legal, sanctioned, and rational by large segments of our society, including the dominant ones.

The field of anthropology reveals many examples of legally sanctioned and rational violence in smaller social systems. Among certain Eskimo tribes, homicide was a perfectly legal and rational way of freeing the tribe of the burden of the aged when food was difficult to find.[15]

Peter Freuchen describes other patterns of violence among Eskimos, and specifically how one man could "legitimately" take over another man's family by homicide.

> Sekrusuna had been a great one to tease poor Quanguaq (who was a young widower). He would taunt him by suggesting, when they were hunting together, that they go home to their "wife" now. . . . Sekrusuna also tantalized the poor man by promising him he might sleep with his wife when they returned, but whenever Quanguaq attempted to take advantage of this favor, he found the woman's lawful husband at her side. The husband thought this a great joke. . . . Besides all this, Sekrusuna beat his wife in

---

[15] E. M. Weyer, *The Eskimos* (New Haven: Yale University Press, 1932).

order to demonstrate to Quanguaq the many advantages of being happily married. He beat her only when the widower was present.

One day in the spring . . . Quanguaq drove his harpoon straight through the body of his friend Sekrusuna. . . . Quanguaq came home with both sledges and teams. He drove straight to the dead man's wife and told her that he was going to stay with her. . . . The widow meekly accepted her altered status.[16]

Other examples include authorized infanticide and the treatment of delinquency by killing the offender. Here is a complicated case:

The boy's debut in terrorism had taken place at Cape York, where he collected a load of rotten birds' eggs and hid them high up on a hillside. Then one day he became loudly hysterical and shouted: "A ship! A ship! A big ship is coming!" Magic words, of course, to natives who were seldom visited by outsiders.

They all hurried up on the hillside to get a look at the boat. Meanwhile the boy crouched behind a rock, and when his friends were close enough he jumped out and pelted them with his peculiarly offensive cache. This naturally reflected upon Kullabak's house, and she had tried to apologize, but being a lone woman, without a husband, there was not much she could say to reestablish herself.

So she asked Mayark to help her get rid of the boy, and Mayark took him up onto the glacier and pushed him down in a crevasse. That, by all rights, should have been the end of him. Kullabak went into traditional mourning, but her mourning was pretty effectively interrupted when the boy came walking into the house. By some miracle he had escaped death in the fall, and had followed the crevasse to its portal near the sea.

After that no one dared touch him, and the boy played all manner of tricks to revenge himself. He was a big, strapping youngster, but he had no hunting gear of his own and had to borrow what he wanted from the hunters while they slept. One day, while Mayark was away on a hunting trip, he went to Mayark's house and told his wife that he had followed Mayark some distance and that when they had parted, Mayark had told him that he might stay in his house and take all a husband's privileges. Mayark's wife was an obedient, loving wife, and not until her husband returned home did she realize that she had been tricked. All the villagers had the laugh on Mayark.

The boy also helped himself from various caches and never took the trouble to close them. His mother was at her wits' end, and finally decided that if she wanted to save the honor of her house she must do something desperate. One night while he was asleep with his head protruding beyond the end of the ledge, she made a sealskin-line noose, slipped it over his head and pulled it tight.

Thus ended the criminal pranks of one young man, and his mother was highly honored for her good deed. Now she was remarried, and her great, booming voice was always an asset at parties.[17]

---

[16] Peter Freuchen, *Arctic Adventure: My Life in the Frozen North* (New York: Holt, Rinehart and Winston, 1935). Copyright © 1935 by Peter Freuchen, copyright renewed 1963. Reprinted by permission of the Harold Matson Co., Inc.

[17] Ibid., pp. 123–124.

Legal, sanctioned, rational violence may provide the rationalization for illegal violence, some of which may be sanctioned by sizable segments of our society. Euthanasia is one debatable form of "homicide." In the 1980s it became a legal, rational, and sanctioned action in many countries, most notably in the Netherlands. Another sanctioned form of violence is illustrated by the activities of the armed forces and police. Such violence has further effects on the soldiers and police officers involved and on others who know about these activities.

Violence by the Military

Killing the enemy is a military duty. Effectiveness in this pursuit may be rewarded by promotion, which includes both higher pay and higher status within the military. Other rewards include medals, decorations, favorable press reports, favorable comments by friends and relatives, and high status in the civilian community, which accompanies high rank in the military. Bomber pilots boast of their achievements. No one ever comments on how many civilians they may have killed or injured or how many schools full of children or hospitals full of patients they may have destroyed. The emphasis is always on destruction of the enemy and enemy installations. The same is true of artillery units who do long-range shelling and infantry units who fight their way into a town and through it. The combat soldier becomes so oblivious to destruction that he is almost unaware of it. He really knows that when he takes part in saturation firing in inhabited areas, whether the firing is from the air or on land, he may be killing women and children and old people. He just doesn't think about it. When he sees the results of such military action he rationalizes it as unavoidable: "The enemy was hiding there," "We couldn't tell them from the enemy," "A nine-year-old child can throw a hand grenade," and so on. Killing has become routine, a duty. That may be why so many veterans were sympathetic to Lieutenant William Calley, a young officer convicted of killing over a hundred helpless civilians in My Lai, Vietnam.

Civilians back in the United States had heard so many reports of killing in Vietnam from the news media that killing Vietnamese appeared normal. Evidence in this case indicated that women, children, and old people were lined up in front of large pits and executed and their bodies were piled into the pits, but these facts passed almost unnoticed.

Lieutenant Calley did not deny that he personally produced the effects he was accused of and that he intended to do so. His defense rested on the assumption that actions ordered by legitimate authorities must be carried out. The prosecution maintained that either Calley acted without orders or that if he did receive orders to massacre civilians, those orders were clearly illegal. A sample of 989 persons representing a cross section of the American population was interviewed by the Roper organization on attitudes toward the trial and the actions of Calley at My Lai. The following are some of the findings:

1. Sixty-seven percent disapproved of Lieutenant Calley being brought to trial.
2. Eighty-three percent of those disapproving of trial agreed with the statement, *"It is unfair to send a man to fight in Vietnam and then put him on trial for doing his duty."*
3. Eighty-two percent of those disapproving of the trial replied *"Follow orders and shoot"* to the question, "What would most people do if ordered to shoot all inhabitants of a Vietnamese village suspected of aiding the enemy, including old men, women and children?"[18]

The researchers concluded that a large segment of the population regarded Calley's actions as normal. Most people, therefore, approve of extreme forms of violence when it is condoned by legitimate authority.

Violence by the Police

William A. Westley traces the development of extreme forms of violence through a three-stage process of escalation from initial support by the public for mild violence by a special group, through support for extreme forms of violence by this special group, to the actual practice of the extreme forms of violence by a small number of people who enjoy it.[19] He points out that among the police, violence is committed by only a small portion of the officers but is usually sanctioned by the entire department (despite official disapproval of the chief and penalties imposed by the courts). The sadistic officers within a police department are tolerated and, by implication, supported. The ideological support of the use of violence by the police and the extreme emphasis on secrecy make it difficult to organize support against them.

The social foundations of police ideology supporting the use of violence are rooted in their occupational culture. Violent acts on the part of a police officer are believed to protect the officer against violence. In using these tactics, the ordinary officer comes to accept violence as a good and necessary part of police work. There is good reason to believe that the police officer is mistaken in this definition of the situation, that is, in the belief that the use of violence reduces the likelihood of counterviolence. It is very possible that, instead, it elicits counterviolence: that by using violence the police officer defines the relationship to a suspect as a violent one. This may lead the suspect to violent resistance. It is likely that the criminal who knows that the approaching

---

[18] Herbert C. Kelman and Lee H. Lawrence, "Assignment of Responsibility in the Case of Lt. Calley," *Journal of Social Issues* 28 (1972):177–212.

[19] William Westley, "The Escalation of Violence Through Legitimization," *Annals of the American Association of Political and Social Science* 364 (March 1966):120–126.

police officer is likely to shoot will shoot first in self-protection. Under the circumstances, one wonders whether the police may not be mistaken in their continued support of capital punishment as a protective device. It may have quite the opposite effect, for the murderer with nothing to lose may decide to prevent capture at any cost, even by shooting a police officer.

ILLEGAL, SANCTIONED, RATIONAL VIOLENCE

Classic cases of illegal, sanctioned, rational violence are to be found among people devoted to maintaining what is from their viewpoint a high level of morality. An Italian patriarch in Sicily is thoroughly justified in killing the sexual violator of his daughter, even though his homicidal act is illegal. A 1988 report indicated that in Argentina, men who kill their adulterous wives are usually pardoned by the courts.

Several cases of murder by women involved in love affairs have also been clearly illegal, yet have received the sanction of a segment of the populace and to some appear to be *rational* murders. An example was the notorious case of Jean Harris, 57, accused of murdering Dr. Herman Tarnower, 69, the "Scarsdale diet" doctor. During the three-month trial, Harris admitted driving five hours from her home in Virginia to Tarnower's home in Westchester County, New York, with a gun in her purse. She did not dispute the fact that, late that night, she pulled the trigger five times, wounding the doctor four times. However, she maintained that she wanted to kill herself, not Tarnower, and that Tarnower was mortally wounded trying to save her from committing suicide.

Prosecutor George Bolen insisted that Harris, who had been Tarnower's lover for 14 years, was jealous over Tarnower's affair with his lab assistant, Lynne Tryforos, 38. Bolen argued that "there was dual intent, to take her own life, but also an intent to do something else . . . to punish Herman Tarnower . . . to kill him and keep him from Lynne Tryforos."

Perhaps the most dramatic piece of evidence was a ten-page letter that Harris had sent to Tarnower on the morning of the shooting. She wrote, "I have to do something besides shriek with pain." She called Tryforos "a vicious, adulterous psychotic" and "a thieving slut." Harris said she felt "like discarded trash."

The lovers' triangle, the renowned victim, the evidence presented in court, and the social standing of the participants—all made for a spectacular and melodramatic trial. After deliberating for eight days, during which they reviewed every piece of trial evidence, the jury of eight women and four men found Jean Harris guilty of second-degree murder.

In another highly publicized case, there seemed to be an effort by some—especially writer Norman Mailer—to provide a murderer with a *sanctioned* "poetic license to kill." The case of murderer Jack Abbott is worth exploring in detail because it reveals positions that reflect a softened and mitigated response on the part of society to violence—when the violence has some special characteristics.

In his book *In the Belly of the Beast*, written in prison, Jack Abbott says:

> You are both alone in his cell. You've slipped out a knife (eight to ten-inch blade, double-edged). You're holding it beside your leg so he can't see it. The enemy is smiling and chattering away about something. He thinks you're his fool; he trusts you. You see the spot. It's a target between the second and third button on his shirt. As you calmly talk and smile, you move your left foot to the side to step across his right-side body length. A light pivot toward him with your right shoulder and the world turns upside down: you have sunk the knife to its hilt into the middle of his chest.[20]

Jack Abbott had practiced on a fellow inmate while doing time in a Utah state prison, and he had killed the inmate. He described the act of murder in one of some 1,000 letters that he wrote to author Norman Mailer between 1977 and 1980, providing a cool but furious description of life behind bars. It was an existence filled with violence—the violence that Abbott, long a prison incorrigible, did to others.

Abbott began his correspondence with Mailer after reading that Mailer was at work on a book about Gary Gilmore, a Utah inmate who was executed for murder in 1977. Abbott had spent all but nine and a half months of his adult life in prison. He offered to give Mailer a sense of "the atmospheric pressure" endured by long-term convicts like Gilmore. Mailer accepted the offer and was impressed by the hard-edged eloquence of the self-educated Abbott. Mailer helped Abbott publish *In the Belly of the Beast*, which was based on his letters. Mailer and others then attested to the convict's talent and promised him a job in New York. This helped persuade the Federal Parole Board to release him in June, 1981.

After his release, Abbott stayed at a Salvation Army halfway house in lower Manhattan until his parole became official on August 25. He was required to check in seven times a day, but otherwise he was free to tour the city. Around 5:30 A.M. on Saturday morning, July 18, 1981, in the company of two attractive, well-educated young women he had met at a party, he stopped at a restaurant near the halfway house. Behind the counter was Richard Adan, 22, an aspiring actor. Abbott asked Adan the direction to the men's room and was told it was for the help only. Abbott calmly asked if he could use it anyway. Adan told him it was against health rules. Abbott calmly asked Adan to step outside to "talk this over." The young man agreed. Around the dark street corner, a knife appeared. Adan was stabbed in the chest, in almost exactly the way that

---

[20] Jack Abbott, *In the Belly of the Beast* (New York: Random House, 1981).

Abbott had described in his book. Abbott fled the scene but was later arrested and convicted of the crime.

After Abbott was convicted of the killing, a number of articles appeared that attempted, in a bizarre way, to rationalize the murder on the basis that Abbott was an artist. Among Abbott's apologists was Norman Mailer, who had helped engineer Abbott's release from prison. Mailer implied that an artist had special prerogatives and should not be punished as severely as the average killer because it could stifle his creativity. This absurdist reasoning is prevalent among certain intellectuals who believe that individuals with special talents are above the laws that apply to ordinary people. This theme was the subject of what I consider to be the best analytic book on criminology ever written— Fyodor Dostoyevski's *Crime and Punishment*. I do not share this "criminal elitist" viewpoint and affirm the position that all offenders, regardless of their status or talent, should receive equal justice.

ILLEGAL, NONSANCTIONED, RATIONAL VIOLENCE

Illegal, nonsanctioned, rational violence is the dominant pattern of the career criminal using violence in a robbery, the racketeer, or the organized crime syndicate. Violence is often used as an instrument in the commission of a crime that is itself nonviolent. For example, when setting out to commit a robbery, a gang may take along someone who has an established reputation for forcibly handling people who might interfere with the crime.

Another pattern in this context is the use of violence, including homicide when necessary, within the framework of the rackets or organized crime. The pattern of violence used in organized crime is notably businesslike.

> Persons involved vocationally in organized crime—in activities such as gambling, prostitution, and traffic in narcotics—have traditionally used violence for the achievement of their goals to a much greater extent than persons in the surrounding culture. The regular outbreaks in the larger society of war—a term also prominent in the catalogue of behavior of organized criminals—indicate that the society itself is not altogether unaware of the expedient value of force. It is partly in the designation of legitimate targets that the wars of gangsters and those of patriots differ, though civil wars, with opponents drawn from the segmented ranks of what had previously been viewed as an amalgamated group, are in this regard not unlike the conflicts of organized criminals.
>
> It is also the directness and the ease with which death is dealt in organized crime that seem to differentiate it from violence in the larger society. The violence of organized crime is neither so fiery nor so inarticulately vicious as much explosive murder in families, nor is it hidden behind inflammatory and rationalizing slogans like much international murder. Rather, *the violence of organized crime is usually inexorable, spare, and*

businesslike, an enterprise deriving its rationale from the exigencies of the immediate situation.[21]

Another rational pattern of violence includes Hans von Hentig's theme of interactions between criminals and victims and Marvin E. Wolfgang's viewpoint on victim-precipitated homicide, which were delineated in Chapter 4. In many cases, a victim's response to the threat of assault is a debatable act of violence. Some responses, however, fit this category of being illegal and nonsanctioned but having a degree of rationality.

ILLEGAL, NONSANCTIONED, IRRATIONAL VIOLENCE

The most disturbing pattern of violence in most societies is popularly termed senseless violence. The crimes are unprovoked, and there is no logical motivation. Many murderers of this type are "drifters" who suffer from alienation and loneliness. The 1976 film *Taxi Driver* dramatized the contemporary conditions and factors that produce senseless violence. In it, the taxi driver is a lonely man, untouched by ordinary life because of his own secret world of fantasy and his inability to communicate with his fellow humans. Paul Schrader, the writer, made his protagonist a Manhattan cabbie because he thinks the cab driver is a prime example of a man who moves, works, walks, and talks and yet somehow is invisible to the eyes of other people. He is not really a human being in the minds of his customers; he is part of the mechanics of the automobile, an inanimate thing like the steering wheel or the ashtrays or the headlights. Dark confidences are freely discussed by his passengers within his hearing; obscenities are performed in the back of his cab within the scope of his rear-view mirror. He is acknowledged briefly when the passenger enters the taxi and is then consigned to limbo, to nonexistence, until, at the end of the film, he goes on a brutal "senseless" murder spree.

This brand of dehumanized violence found in film is clearly linked to reality. The rambling aimlessness of the taxi driver was absorbed into the life of John Warnoch Hinkley, Jr., another drifter, who patterned his violent fantasies into an attempted assassination of President Ronald Reagan. The literary image of the taxi driver (the film featured Jodie Foster) had its impact on Hinckley, but it is by no means a cause-and-effect phenomenon. Many violent sociopaths seek out literary and historical materials that synthesize the violent fantasies they already harbor in their minds. The murder of musician-poet John Lennon by Mark Chapman resembles the Hinckley assault in that Chapman, too, had both his distorted fantasies and an easily available weapon.

---

[21] Gilbert Geis, "Violence and Organized Crime," *Annals of the American Academy of Political and Social Science* 364 (March 1966):87. Italics added.

In most cases of senseless violence of the type perpetrated by Hinckley, we hear nothing about motivations directly from the perpetrator of the crime. Hinckley, however, wrote to *Newsweek*, offering to respond to "a typewritten list of 20 questions, none dealing directly with my case." *Newsweek* submitted the typed questions to Hinckley by mail; he responded in a letter, answering the questions on lined yellow legal paper in his own handwriting. The following are *Newsweek*'s questions and Hinckley's answers:

NEWSWEEK: You seem to have liked the movie "Taxi Driver" very much. What was your favorite scene?

HINCKLEY: I liked the scene where Travis and Jodie are seated at a table having breakfast. Jodie looks so perfect in that scene because she isn't wearing that awful hooker costume. Their conversation is relevant to me because Travis keeps telling Jodie that he wants to help her escape all of these sordid characters that are ruining her, but she doesn't understand what he is talking about and resists him. I know exactly how Travis felt.

Q: What is it about Jodie Foster that makes her so attractive?

A: I try to think about the real Jodie Foster, not the characters she portrays in her films. The sweetness and innocence she displays in the movie "Echoes of a Summer" is what attracts me. It carries over into her real life. Unfortunately, Jodie is now at Yale where sweetness and innocence are not allowed.

I just like the way she looks, the things she says and the life she leads. I like her hair and smile and lucky face. Her youth and personality are just as attractive to me. Jodie is a bright girl and this overflowing brilliance used to intimidate me. But now I think we are equal and rather compatible. Don't you agree? [Perhaps Hinckley believes this because he is now a celebrity in his own right.]

Q: Do you think that seeing movies and reading books influence the way people behave in real life?

A: Yes, Yes, Yes. The line dividing Life and Art can be invisible. After seeing enough hypnotizing movies and reading enough magical books, a fantasy life develops, which can either be harmless or quite dangerous.

Q: Do you think that watching television is a good way to pass time and learn what's going on in the world?

A: Watching too much television can cause numerous social disorders. The damn TV is on all day and night in most homes, and is probably more harmful than movies and books. It is not a good way to pass time because, once again, a fantasy world tends to develop the longer a person stays in front of the tube.

Q: Your older sister was a great success in high school, at the same time that you were a student two years behind her, and your brother is a great success in business. Do you think that younger children suffer if their older siblings are that successful?

A: Probably. Young children suffer greatly when they are constantly compared to their perfect siblings. The pressure to become just as perfect causes most younger children to retreat when they realize they can't be the most popular student, the best football player or happiest all-around person.

Q: Your father is a successful businessman and a very religious man. Is this kind of model especially hard for a son to live up to?

A: It is difficult for a son to follow in his father's footsteps when the two of them have different goals, aspirations and outlooks on life. Let's leave it at that.

Q: You wrote a paper while you were in college on Adolph Hitler's "Mein Kampf." What do you think of Hitler's political and social ideas?

A: I think his political and social ideas are atrocious. "Mein Kampf" is a very difficult book to read and almost impossible to understand. Most college kids read "The Catcher in the Rye"; I read "Mein Kampf." It's another example of a book having the potential of being very dangerous.

Q: What do you think of the role of the American Nazi party in American life today?

A: The role of the party in American life is zilch. They are completely irrelevant, but sometimes they manage to draw attention to themselves, thanks to the media.

Q: Do you think that there ought to be stricter laws controlling the sale of handguns in the United States, and why did you buy so many handguns?

A: I believe in gun control. They cannot be banned or eliminated, but some stricter laws could be applied when buying a handgun. In most states, guns are as easy to buy as candy bars. A person's background and criminal record should be checked in all states before a gun can be purchased. Saturday-night specials should be banned altogether.

I bought so many handguns because Travis bought so many handguns. Ask him, not me. [Travis is the killer of *Taxi Driver*.]

Q: Do you think that a person accused of shooting a political leader in the United States can receive a fair trial?

A: Because public sentiment plays such a great role when a person shoots a political leader, the assassin has a very difficult time getting a fair trial. The pretrial publicity itself almost guarantees that the jury and public cannot be impartial.

Q: During your confinement, how well have you been treated by the authorities?

A: I have no complaints about my treatment by authorities, whether they be the Butner prison guards or U.S. marshals. They have all been fair with me and the measures they go to in order to protect me are simply staggering. I feel like the President myself, with my own retinue of bodyguards. We both wear bulletproof vests now.

Q: Do you think that there is any pattern in the personalities of people who attack or kill political figures, such as Lee Harvey Oswald with President Kennedy, Sirhan Sirhan with Robert Kennedy, Arthur Bremer with George Wallace?

A: Most assassins are disillusioned with everything, most of all politics. The ideology of the target doesn't matter. Politics has nothing to do with political assassinations in America.

Q: Ronald Reagan is making important changes in U.S. Government—for example, in cutting taxes and building up the military. Which Americans are being helped most by Reagan and which are being hurt most?

A: I believe all Americans will eventually be helped by Mr. Reagan's changes. He is the best President we've had this century. Let's give the man a chance.

Q: What political leaders do you most admire, and why?

A: I don't admire any political leaders, except perhaps, Mr. Reagan. The only person I ever idolized throughout my life was John Lennon, and look what happened to him.

Q: Do you think it matters who is President of the United States, or do you think the government goes on about the same whoever is President?

A: A President can make small changes if he is strong and effective or be nothing more than a figurehead if he is ordinary. It makes little difference whether the person is a Republican or Democrat. No one votes anymore because the government grinds on and on in bureaucratic splendor no matter who is the leader.

Q: Do you think that the protection of the President by the Secret Service is as good as it could be, or how could it be improved?

A: The Secret Service could improve its protection of the President. I can think of a half-dozen measures that could be taken by the Secret Service that could greatly reduce the risk to the President. I'd be happy to chat with them someday and give them my ideas concerning security. It might do the Secret Service well to listen to me very carefully.

Q: Do you think it is possible to protect the President completely from someone who wants to attack him and is not worried about getting caught?

A: No.

Q: As far as you can tell, has the press reported the story of the attempted assassination of President Reagan fairly and accurately?

A: I would say 85 percent of the reporting has been accurate and fair. The other 15 percent could be called yellow journalism. Too many journalists have played the role of amateur psychiatrists in this case.

Q: Much has been written about you and your background in the press. Do you think the coverage has been fair and accurate?

A: Considering that I came out of nowhere and my life story was pieced together within a week, I think the journalists did a pretty good job.

Q: Why did you choose to go to Nashville, Tenn., last October on a day when President Carter was to speak there, and why did you have three guns with you on the trip?

A: Be patient. You'll get the answer someday.[22]

After his final response to *Newsweek*'s questions, Hinckley added a personal note to Foster: "In closing, I would like to say hello to Ms. Foster and ask her one small question: Will you marry me, Jodie?" Hinckley signed his correspondence "The End, John Hinckley Jr." Hinckley's responses reveal something of his pathology and his obsession with Jodie Foster and his hero Travis, the "taxi driver." His adoration of President Reagan is curious, given the fact that he almost killed him. On June 21, 1982—15 months after Hinckley shot President Reagan and three other men—a federal grand jury in Washington, D.C., pronounced him not guilty by reason of insanity. He was committed to St. Elizabeth's Hospital in Washington for an indefinite period. In 1989,

---

[22] From *Newsweek*, October 12, 1981. © 1981, by Newsweek, Inc. All rights reserved. Reprinted by permission.

he was still a prisoner in the hospital, and still obsessed with a bizarre attraction to Jodie Foster.

The Buddy Killer Syndrome

Hinckley and Chapman were loners, and they reflected a certain pattern of the violent offender. A bizarre characteristic of a considerable amount of recent senseless violence is the fact thay many grisly killings have been committed by two or more killers in concert. This pattern of violence can be called *buddy killing*. In the past, murder had some level of sense or rationality when it was committed by two or more individuals. The killers would serve as checks on each other's extreme and horrendous acts. But in recent years, it appears that anything goes when it comes to murder. It was found, when the cases were solved, that two individuals were involved in the so-called Hillside Strangler murders in Los Angeles, and several men were involved in the so-called Los Angeles freeway murders. These cases are prime examples of the buddy killer syndrome.

The Hillside Strangler murders, perpetrated by Kenneth Bianchi and his cousin Angelo Buono, were described in Chapter 5. The Los Angeles freeway murders provide another prototypical case of senseless buddy killing. Although several other individuals were involved, the two principals were Vernon Butts and William Bonin. Their 21 teenage victims, most alleged to be homosexuals, were typically sodomized, tortured (several with icepicks through their ears), and then killed; one victim was castrated. Each of the young victims was picked up while hitchhiking, and the bodies were found near freeways throughout most of Southern California. Bonin was convicted of a number of the murders in 1982 and sentenced to death.

Bonin was a convicted sex offender; it was said that he, Butts, and others engaged weekly in "some sort of occult activity." The prosecutor at Buono's trial remarked that when he and his cousin were together, personality traits in the two combined to create a "chemical reaction" that resulted in the murders of these young women.

There has been no intensive research to date on buddy murderers. Some of the questions raised are: Do the two killers set each other off psychologically? What do they talk about during and after their buddy murders? How does one dominate the other(s)? Isn't there any kind of superego or moral quotient that surfaces between the two to stop their horrendous spree? Are buddy murderers individuals whose pathological backgrounds have similarities?

Solving Senseless Murders

Most murderers stumble at some point in their lives and are revealed and caught. It appears that increasingly, perhaps because of the bizarre nature of recent violence, there are many unsolved murders. Senseless crimes of violence are more difficult to solve than crimes involving situations where the killer and victim are known to each other. According to FBI statistics, more and more murders are unsolved because of the senselessness of the violence. As Ted Gest and Douglas Lyons reported in 1981:

> Murder is fast losing its reputation as one of the easiest crimes to solve. In 1970, only 14 percent of the homicides in the U.S. went unsolved, according to the Federal Bureau of Investigation. By 1979, the rate stood at 27 percent. . . .
>
> The majority of homicides still occur among friends or relatives, and police usually are able to identify suspects quickly. But killings by someone who has no connection to the victims tend to go unsolved—and such murders are becoming more and more common.
>
> In these so-called stranger-to-stranger crimes, authorities are often left with few clues. [As] Public Safety Director Lee. P. Brown says: "The three traditional reasons for *closing* homicides are missing. We have no eyewitnesses, no motive and no hard physical evidence."[23]

In 1987, over 30 percent of murders were not cleared. It appears that as murders became more "senseless," fewer can be solved. The increase in unsolved murders may very well be a function of the fact that killer pathologies are increasingly more senseless. It is increasingly difficult to ascertain the killers' motives.

Serial Killers and Mass Murderers

Buddy killers and serial killers increasingly account for America's illegal, nonsanctioned, and irrational homicides. An analysis of these increasing crimes provides some insights into this murderous trend.

Serial Killers   Buddy killers often kill a number of people; however, serial killers usually commit a large number of homicides over a long period of time before they are apprehended.

One of the most notorious serial killers was never clearly caught, although some police officers believed they knew who he was. He was identified by London police as "Jack-the-Ripper." He brutally murdered at least six prostitutes in London over a hundred years ago. Notable among contemporary serial killers are John Wayne Gacy, David R. Berkowitz, and Theodore Bundy. Gacy, 45, was convicted of murdering over 30 men and young boys in Chicago and burying their bodies under his house. Berkowitz, 33, New York's "Son of Sam" murderer, killed six

---

[23] Reprinted from *U.S. News & World Report*, March 16, 1981. Copyright 1981, U.S. News & World Report, Inc.

people in 1977 and is now serving a life sentence. Bundy, 40, was executed in Florida for killing two women and a 12-year-old girl and was suspected of murdering over 40 other women around the United States.

In 1988, Robert Ressler of the FBI's National Center for the Analysis of Violent Crime interviewed 35 serial killers, including Gacy, Berkowitz, and Bundy.

Profiles drawn from the interviews show that in outward appearances the killers seemed ordinary: they were usually white middle-class men with no physical handicaps, of average or above average intelligence, and of normal heights and weights.

But their youths were problem-ridden. Some things they had in common were the following:

- Parents with criminal records and histories of drug or alcohol abuse. The father often deserted the family when the killer was a child.
- Homicidal sexual fantasies in preteens, including a fetish for things such as underwear.
- Nightmares, compulsive masturbation, chronic lying, bed-wetting, setting fires, and cruelty to other children.
- An experience or experiences of being physically or sexually abused.

According to Ressler's research, homosexual killer Gacy, a construction contractor, said he was sexually abused by a construction worker as a child. Some of Gacy's victims were young construction workers he lured to his house.

Criminologist Edward Hickey surveyed the records of over 100 serial killers who had slain as many as 1,647 victims. He concluded that 28 percent had accomplices; the killers averaged 9 to 12 victims; up to 51 percent of victims were strangers to their killers; and sex, money, or both were alleged motives in at least 86 percent of killings. Hickey also distinguished three types of serial killers. Forty-seven were transients who went from state to state seeking victims. (Theodore Bundy was suspected in several states.) Fifty-eight operated in a single area. (David Berkowitz roamed the New York City area for victims.) Thirty-eight killed at a specific site. (John Wayne Gacy committed his crimes at home.)

Mass Murderers Mass murder differs from serial murder in that the homicides occur in one event. Sociologists Jack Levin and James Fox identify four common characteristics of mass murderers:

1. They had led a life of frustration and failure;
2. They felt threatened by a breakup in their family or were spurned in a relationship, and there was a precipitatory event that involved rejection;

3. They were loners living in a state of isolation; and

4. They were familiar with and had access to firearms.[24]

A mass murderer who fit these four criteria was R. Gene Simmons, Sr., a 47-year-old former Air Force sergeant who allegedly killed fourteen family members and two others over the Christmas holidays in 1987 and then reportedly said, "I've gotten everybody who wanted to hurt me."

At least three other incidents in 1987 drew national attention. In April, a gunman, 60-year-old William B. Cruse, randomly killed six people and wounded ten in Palm Bay, Florida. In July, 36-year-old Daniel Patrick Lynam shot his parents, his parents-in-law, his wife, his two children, and then himself in the Tacoma, Washington, area. In September, seven family members, including four children, were killed in Elkland, Missouri. Police arrested John Schnick in the case after Schnick tried to blame a 14-year-old nephew for the deaths. In 1989, five children were murdered and twenty-nine were wounded in a Stockton, California, school playground by a deranged killer, Patrick Purdy, who used a semi-automatic assault gun in the murders.

According to FBI statistics, there have been about 20,000 murders each year in the United States over the past decade. However, the patterns of murder appear to be more bizarre—including serial and mass murder. A marked characteristic of murder is its increasingly senseless nature.

Homicide: In the Future?

An unusual case that highlights these bizarre and senseless homicidal crimes took place in Milpitas, California, in 1981. In part, this case reveals the increasing influence of substance abuse on murder in the United States. A film, *The River's Edge*, was made of this crime in 1987. A reporter, Elizabeth Kay, incisively delineated some of the forces at work in this irrational murder that may regrettably be an example of the violence of the future.

> At moments in history, events occur that mirror society in so fundamental a way that they become metaphorical and reveal us to ourselves with the indisputable clarity of a traffic signal. An event such as this gave rise to the notoriety of Milpitas, a Northern California town.
>
> November 3, 1981, was a Tuesday, and on that day a sixteen year old named Jacques Broussard cut school with a fourteen year old named Marcy Conrad. This, in itself, was unexceptional. Jacques and Marcy were stoners. Stoners smoke a lot of pot and cut school often. They are also given, as are many children nowadays, to the utterly unchildish apprehension that life is

---

[24] James Fox and Jack Levin, *Mass Murders: America's Growing Menace* (New York: Plenum, 1985).

not necessarily getting better, for they are part of the first generation of Americans raised by parents who no longer have reason to believe the sustaining tenet of the American dream: that the reward for hard work and sacrifice is the privilege of making one's children's lives far better than one's own. As members of that generation, they view the world through the tarnished prism of their parent's disappointment and conclude that they may as well live for today since being young may very well be the best thing that will ever happen to them.

So it may have been in the name of living for today that Jacques and Marcy cut school and eventually went to his house, a one-story, dark green house six blocks from hers, with a BEWARE OF THE DOG sign on the door, in the sort of neighborhood where houses are neatly centered between tiny front and back yards and where the color television is, as a rule, the focal point of the living room. Homes such as these were once a mere rung on the American ladder of acquisition and success, but in this era of diminished prospects they simultaneously constitute the end of the line and the apogee of a certain level of middle-class attainment.

Jacques's family had lived in this house for many years, and it was here that his mother had died. His mother's death was one of two things that set Jacques apart from everyone. The other was that he was black, while all his friends were white. Of these two things, his mother's death was the more significant by far.

Gloria Broussard died when her son was eight years old. Jacques was the one who found her body, so the impact of her death transcended grief and became one of abject horror. On what was an otherwise ordinary day Jacques came home from school, and the harbinger that something was dreadfully wrong was the living room rug, which was sodden with water. When he heard the shower running he treaded his way to the bathroom door, opened it, made his way through the water-soaked room, and drew back the shower curtain. He saw his mother's naked body. She had died of natural causes a few hours earlier.

Jacques never quite recovered from that day, and all his friends knew it, which is why it was understood among them that they never breathed a word to Jacques about his mother. But Marcy Conrad dispensed with this crucial amenity, it seems, and said something about her, something truly mean. Or so Jacques told his friends. He also told them that is why he killed her.

Marcy became a corpse on Jacques's living room couch. The corpse was half naked, and this was because before Marcy died Jacques either made love to her or raped her. Were stoners at all interested in irony or observation, Jacques might have been taken by the fact that the corpse was clad in nothing but a tank top with the words SPOILED ROTTEN on it and a necklace decorated with a gold marijuana leaf–shape charm.

Once Marcy was dead Jacques was confronted with a succession of practical considerations, to which he apparently responded quite methodically. First he went ouside, backed his pickup truck into the garage, and set about gathering up Marcy's purse, jeans, and schoolbooks. He then lifted her body from the couch and began the formidable task of getting it out of the house. Jacques weighed 280 pounds and stood six foot four, and Marcy was just a little girl, but she was dead weight now. Jacques would later tell his friends that he had one hell of a time moving her. But finally he got the body into the back of his truck. The white truck was an unlikely hearse, with its KOME and KSJO stickers that appear on the cars of most stoners, letters that also appear as patches on their jeans and as decals on their schoolbooks. They are the call letters of two rock stations. The only thing the average stoner likes as well as weed is fine rock music. . . .

Jacques drove on to Old Marsh Road, and then the scenery abruptly changed, and the trees and grass beside the road became as sensuously moist as those in the center of a rain-soaked forest. This spot is a gathering place for many young people in Milpitas, and the pungent blanket of fallen leaves and bright green clover that covers the earth shares its space with empty, crushed beer cans and shards of broken wine bottles.

It is here that Jacques scattered Marcy's purse, jeans, shoes, and schoolbooks. Then he drove on, a half mile or so, to where Old Marsh Road merges again with the sun, and where the land to the south of the road slants down sharply to a barbwire fence. . . .

This place was selected by Jacques Broussard as his final destination. He stopped the truck and took the half-naked corpse from it. He carried it down the incline and pushed it beneath the barbwire fence. The body rolled and was stopped by the thick trunk of the oak tree. There it remained for the next two days, in the sun and the wind and the cold and the dark, face down.

In the days that followed, the murder of Marcy Conrad assumed its allegorical significance and ultimately became that rare event of equal interest to newspaper reporters and to poets. It is at this stage in the narrative that the focus shifts and both the murderer and victim become oddly peripheral to its telling. Events center instead on nine young people, all of whom are self-described stoners.

In retrospect, it seemed inevitable that others be drawn into it. It was not all that likely that a sixteen year old could indefinitely keep to himself the amazing fact that he has just become a killer. So it was, on the day following the murder, that three teenage boys were told of it by Jacques Broussard himself. They did not believe him, so he took them up the hill and showed them what all the horror movies and all the televised violence they had ever seen could not have conceivably prepared them for, just as they had hardened them to it.

There was no requiem at the oak tree. There was only gazing. And there was this thought in the mind of one of the boys: "Jacques is in real trouble now."

The hours that followed were extraordinary only for their ordinariness, only for the way the three boys managed to proceed as if nothing had occurred that was in the least unusual. One fell asleep in his room listening to the radio and did not wake up for dinner. Another would later say he thought the body was a mannequin and didn't think anymore about it. The third was met at his door by his mother, who told him not to come in. She had discovered he had stolen her marijuana. This was something that had happened before; he had been warned that he would not be welcome in the house if it happened again.

The boy's name is John Hanson. He went out into the night and later met up with a friend named Robby Engle. He told Engle about the corpse, and when Engle wanted to see it, Hanson said he would show it to him the next day since it was now too dark to see anything. Instead they walked to

Engle's house, went to his room to smoke some dope, and fell asleep. The night air was cool. In the hills where Marcy Conrad's body lay it was even cooler. Both boys slept dreamlessly.

All the next morning at Milpitas High, the huge bulk of Jacques Broussard traversed the grassy campus, telling students that he had killed Marcy and conveying that information with the reckless resolve of a man committing suicide because he is afraid of dying. Among the students, many of whom knew Marcy, though she had been enrolled at another school, the consensus was that Jacques couldn't have killed her, that he was simply "bragging" about it. Students at Milpitas High do not place too high a premium on the subtleties of words, which may be why the thought that bragging about a murder is kind of a contradiction in terms did not seem to occur to any of them.

Later in the day, Jacques, perhaps resenting that the most significant thing he had ever done had proven too significant to seem feasible, took a young girl and two boys up the hill so they might make witness to his claim, and having done so they, too, joined the circle of silence, increasing its number to six.

And now the passive silence was augmented by an action, when one of the boys aided Broussard in covering the corpse with a plastic bag and a scattering of leaves. Eventually he would be charged as an accessory after the fact, sentenced to three years at a county ranch for delinquent boys, and his existence would become a study in the curious way an entire life can be irrevocably altered in a single moment.

After lunch hour at the high school, John Hanson made a second sojourn to Old Marsh Road. He took Engle and two other friends, Mike Irvin and Dave Leffler, with him. Hanson was low on dope that day, so he bet Irvin a joint that the human form at the foot of the giant tree was an actual corpse. All right, he was told, but if it isn't, you give me your shoes and socks and walk home barefoot. It was on this note that they began to drive up the hill. They parked the car just as the oak tree became discernible. They scrambled down the incline. They stopped when they saw what they came to see.

The four young men stared down at Marcy Conrad's earthly remains. Moments passed; nothing was said. The only sound was the insistent yammering of a few distant birds. Then Hanson wanted to collect on his bet. Leffler said, "This is no time to smoke," but they climbed up the incline and smoked anyway.

On the way down the hill Mike Irvin said he was going to the police. Hanson and Engle wanted to go back to class. "As far as we're concerned," Engle said, "the body doesn't exist." All Hanson could think of was that he had seen the corpse the day before and not reported it and that if he got involved at this point he might be arrested as an accessory. And he thought of how he had hated the time he once spent in juvenile hall after committing a burglary. And he thought of one of the terms of his parole, which was that he not associate with Mike Irvin, his alleged partner in that crime, the same young man who wanted to go to the police at this moment.

So Hanson and Engle went back to class, and Irvin and Leffler drove to the Milpitas police station. Leffler waited in the car. It was left to Irvin to walk alone up the sidewalk and to open the thick glass door and, once inside, tell of the incredible thing he had seen in the hills, so that 48 hours after the murder of Marcy Conrad, the silence of the young people who knew she had died would be forever broken.

While Mike Irvin was in the office of the Milpitas police, Sergeant Garry Meeker was driving on Interstate 680. Meeker is the homicide and assaults investigator for Santa Clara County. . . . He takes a cop's pride in being tough and when he is summoned to view a corpse tries to regard it not as a body but as a piece of evidence. He often apologizes for the coldness of that attitude but has never doubted that if he's going to do his job, that's the way to do it.

It was two-thirty in the afternoon when he got the radio dispatch about the body up on Old Marsh Road. Meeker knew the area well. For one thing, it was something of a dump ground for corpses. . . .

When Meeker got to the oak tree, five of his colleagues were already there, men who were also paid to think of Marcy Conrad as a juvenile female, deceased. Before they left, two or three cars came up the hill and turned around when they drew near the police. Meeker did not give it much thought at the time; an hour or so would pass before he would learn of Broussard's boasts and the young people who had not reported the murder, and then he figured that the cars must have been those of young kids coming to see for themselves whether or not Broussard was lying.

The Milpitas police picked up Jacques Broussard later that evening. Shortly afterward Meeker questioned the young people who had gone up the hill to see Marcy's body. It had been an unsettling experience, though it was not the murder that was troubling. Meeker had seen a lot of murder victims, and murder itself was old as dirt. There was really nothing else you could say about it. But this case was different, and what made it so was the silence of the youngsters. "They were supposedly normal people," Meeker said. "But people who see dead bodies get shook. It bothers them. It still bothers me if you want to know the truth. But these kids . . . it didn't seem to bother them."

The silence of the children was the issue. The silence was the metaphor. And the only question of pertinence was, metaphor for what? "There's a moral breakdown somewhere," Meeker concluded. "That's what this thing represents. And it's not the kids' fault. The kids are a product of what we made them."[25]

The murder was shocking in and of itself, but not nearly as unsettling as the circle of young people who knew what happened and maintained their silence for 48 hours. It wasn't "reefer madness" that produced their response. Smoking marijuana does not usually produce the extreme indifference noted in this case. It may be, however, that a steady day-to-day diet of smoking dope, dropping pills, watching horrendous acts of violence on the tube and in the movies, and the continuing nonuse of one's intellectual capacities lead to a cool boredom that produces this indifference to human life.

This murder was a harbinger of a considerable number of drug-

---

[25] Elizabeth Kaye, "Growing Up Stoned," *California*, April 1982. Excerpted with permission from the April 1982 issue of CALIFORNIA. Copyright 1982 by CALIFORNIA.

related homicides, some including satanism, that characterized the late 1980s. Increasingly, drug wars and substance abuse lower the value that people place on human life; this has created an increase in strange violent behavior.

The gloomy prediction of Albert Camus on violence—"the whole world turns its back on these crimes; the victims have reached the extremity of their disgrace: they have become a bore"—may have become a social reality that will characterize the violence of the twenty-first century.

Chapter
8

Crime in a Substance-Abusing Society

*T*he substance abuse problem has reached awesome proportions in the United States and on an international level. The problem not only affects the self-destructive abuser and his or her family but has also insidiously intruded into the political relationships between nations. In the countries that supply the drugs (which have their own share of addicts) and in the nations that illegally import the various drug poisons, the problem is increasingly part of everyone's life. In recent years, the United States has launched major interdiction efforts to control the flow of drugs into the country, including the use of the armed forces. In these massive efforts to prevent the flow of drugs into our society, the political authorities have too often lost sight of the simple fact that if there were no consumers there would be no problem.

Some relevant statistics collated by the National Institute on Drug Abuse reveal that in the United States, there are about 5 million regular cocaine users; there are 20 to 24 million people who have tried cocaine; there were over 1,000 cocaine-related deaths in 1988; 30 percent of all college seniors have tried a form of cocaine; 42 percent of all college students have tried marijuana; and there are over 500,000 hard-core heroin users. In brief, a large segment of the population has become involved in the criminal politics of substance abuse. A collation of studies reveals that about 80 percent of our criminal population have been substance abusers.

Despite the variety of efforts to combat the problem on all levels, there has been an increase in the number of substance abusers in the United States. Not only has the number of addicts increased; the problem has become more "democratic" and widespread. Formerly, severe addiction was primarily restricted to the lower socioeconomic segments of society. Today, the problem is found among people in all groups. People of all ages—students in high schools and universities, sports figures, people involved in publishing and entertainment, corporations and industry—have become addicted to drugs and alcohol. The current problem has infected people of both high and low status in these varied walks of life. Consequently, the crippling effects of substance abuse have had a profound impact upon millions of people and upon the major social institutions in America.

Another factor in the United States is the proliferation of the *variety* of drugs in the illicit marketplace. The former staples of substance abuse, such as alcohol, marijuana, and heroin, have been joined by PCP, "ecstasy," "designer" drugs, cocaine in various forms, including "crack," and an increasingly larger selection of addictive pills.

Along the way, certain drugs which were formerly perceived as "fun and games" by many people have turned out to have long-term and even lethal consequences on the user's personality and life. Notable in this context are marijuana and cocaine.

Individuals who began smoking marijuana in the past decade for "fun" discovered too late that they have become amotivational, "vegged out," and strongly psychologically dependent on the drug. Cocaine, formerly a rich person's party drug, in the more marketable form known as crack has penetrated all segments of society—and has destructively affected many users' lives.

Another cataclysmic problem related to substance abuse is the complex relationship that exists between intravenous use of certain drugs, promiscuity, and acquired immune deficiency syndrome (AIDS). In a 1988 research report from New York City, over 50 percent of intravenous drug users tested were found to carry antibodies against the human immunodeficiency virus (HIV), which causes AIDS. Many substance abusers of both genders, especially those involved in prostitution, are vulnerable. The complex of intravenous substance abuse and AIDS is a national plague that has especially affected the criminal population in the United States.

DEFINING THE SUBSTANCE ABUSER

The use of illegal drugs has ensnared many normally law-abiding citizens in criminal activities. The mélange of more widespread drug abuse and the variety and combinations of drug abuse in all segments of the society have somewhat clouded the important question: When does a user become a substance abuser?

This cutoff point is, of course, a significant variable in determining the validity of any trends or statistics on addiction. The issue of when a person is truly addicted and what form of help is needed is very complex. In most cases, when a user's family and friends perceive the person as addicted to a drug or alcohol, the "addict" denies there is a problem. Because of their self-deception and denial, addicts usually refuse to take the basic first step in their treatment: admitting they are substance abusers.

In my research and observation of substance abusers over the past 35 years, on the street and in therapeutic settings, I have found the following four elements are basic in answering the complex question of who is a substance abuser:

1. *Overwhelming Need* Substance abusers have an intense conscious desire for their drug of choice—or for a variety of drugs. They have a mental set in which acquiring and using drugs becomes the paramount fixation or concern in their lives. In the clutches of their overwhelming need, users are more likely to commit criminal acts to support their drug habits.

   The Alcoholics Anonymous program recognizes the issue of overwhelming need. The first step requires the alcoholic to admit that the need has taken power over the person and that life has become unmanageable.

2. *Self-deception and Denial* When confronted about their addiction, almost all substance abusers practice self-deception and denial. This takes the form of lying to others and themselves about the amount of drugs they use, lying about the degree to which they are dominated by their drug habit, lying about the fact that the drug has become an integral part of their day-to-day behavior, and lying about the fact that their use of drugs has negatively affected their personal relationships. In regard to denial about the amount of drugs used, I use what I term the Yablonsky principle, which I developed in my work with addicts. This principle basically asserts that whatever amount the substance abuser gives when first asked the question, "How much and what kinds of drugs or alcohol do you use, and how often?", the true answer should be at least double that amount. In groups I have directed, in which I have interviewed several thousand substance abusers, the interviewee always admits, on further probing, to *at least twice* the amount given in the initial response.

   The substance abuser's favorite defensive denial, in one form or another, is "You're crazy. I can quit any time I want to." Somehow, they do not decide to quit unless some strong outside pressure is brought to bear on them or they become involved in some type of resocialization or therapeutic process.

3. *Periodic Abstinence* Most addicts occasionally become drug-free for a period of time when their habits become too onerous. They often stop using drugs for a brief period to prove to themselves that they really could quit if they wanted. The period

of abstinence is usually very short compared to the length of time of the overall abuse. The cunning, self-defeating substance abuser often uses the "periodic abstinence" ploy to mask or deny a serious problem.

4. *Self-image and Primary Group Relationships*   After a period of time as a user, the addict's substance abuse becomes a central focus of her behavior—and in many cases represents her identity. The addict no longer denies being an addict after she has tried to quit a number of times and failed. The true addict now begins to feel most at ease with peers, "friends" and cohorts who have the same drug problem she has, and these people gradually take over her primary group relationships. The addict increasingly becomes alienated from friends and family who are not drug abusers. She becomes identified by others as a pillhead, an alcoholic, a junkie, or a cokehead, even if she does not accept the label herself.

The perceptions and the responses of others tend to become a self-fulfilling prophecy; their effect begins to sink into the addict's self-concept. This perception by other people reinforces the addict's self-image and identity as a drug abuser. The substance abuser has now developed a firm self-concept of being part of a substance-abusing criminal subculture, and this perpetuates her problem with addiction.

HISTORICAL TRENDS IN SUBSTANCE ABUSE

A central issue of substance abuse is the fact that the use of an illegal substance involves a person in a criminal activity with criminal cohorts. Many people who become addicted were formerly law-abiding citizens; however, their drug involvement ensnares them into the criminal subculture. A notable example was the case of John Zaccaro, son of vice presidential nominee Geraldine Ferraro. He was convicted in 1988 on charges of cocaine dealing.

Most substance abusers are more enmeshed in the criminal underworld than John Zaccaro. The issue of which came first, the substance abuse or other criminal activity, is often difficult to sort out. Most criminals use drugs, and many substance abusers commit crimes to support their habits. The only fact that is clear is that drugs and crime have been related to each other for centuries.

In the past 50 years, most Western societies have had serious problems with the abuse of alcohol, morphine, opium, heroin, cocaine, and marijuana.

The first half of the twentieth century was marked by a more accepting attitude toward drugs, especially marijuana and cocaine. For example, in his early work in the field of psychotherapy, Sigmund Freud discovered and praised the use of cocaine as a possible treatment for certain psychological problems, especially depression. Until he became addicted himself and confronted the downside of cocaine use, he was an advocate.

The 1960s were a peak period in the use of psychoactive drugs by people around the world, and especially in the United States. Early in the decade, the "Harvard Group" (led by psychology professors Timothy Leary and Richard Alpert, who experimented with hallucinogenic drugs) ushered in such drugs as marijuana, LSD, and methamphetamine or "speed." Leary admonished America's youth to "turn on" (use hallucinogenic substances), "tune in" (explore the inner emotional world through "consciousness-raising" drugs), and "drop out" (quit playing along with society's rules). The so-called pop culture saw a major explosion in abuse of hallucinogens and other substances by young people around the country. The "hippies" of that era, many of whom are the parents of today's substance-abusing generation, set an ethos of embracing drugs as a way of exploring one's inner world and raising a person's level of consciousness. This attitude was carried over and was prevalent in the 1980s; it still affects our contemporary drug problem.[1]

The opiate drugs, especially heroin, have traditionally been used to block out an onerous social environment, to attempt to resolve personal problems, and to escape into a state of pleasant reverie. Especially among lower socioeconomic groups, heroin has been a persistent drug abuse problem since the 1930s in American society. Although heroin has been used to some extent by young people in the middle and upper segments of society, it has been and remains a predominantly lower-class phenomenon.

In recent years cocaine has become one of the most widely abused drugs, in an inexpensive form known as "rock cocaine" or "crack." The drug is usually smoked, rather than snorted as was the case when it was expensive and in powder form.

An analysis of substance abuse in the United States over the past 50 years reveals the following evolutionary phases:

1. In the 1940s, very few people used illegal substances. Marijuana and especially heroin were part of the criminal drug scene in the ghettos of large cities. Cocaine was restricted to the wealthy and some jazz musicians.

2. In the 1950s, along with the advent of rock and roll music concerts, marijuana, amphetamines, and alcohol became more widely used. Heroin and marijuana increasingly became a problem among minority groups growing up in depressed socioeconomic conditions.

---

[1] See Lewis Yablonsky, *The Hippie Trip* (Baltimore: Penguin, 1969).

3. In the 1960s, with the hippie "greening" of America on a philosophical pretext of raising consciousness, a variety of psychedelic substances were advocated and used by a large number of people of all ages and classes. Many people, especially young adult "dropouts," used hallucinogens (LSD, mescaline, psilocybin, etc.). In the context of a new sociocultural awakening, users sought to free themselves from the "heavy trips" of the larger society. In the hippie orbit marijuana was the "black bread" staple drug, used on a daily basis by millions of people to maintain their plateau of being and staying high. They referred to this process as "maintaining." LSD and other psychedelics became part of this social exploration scene. Toward the late 1960s, many users began to "crash" and run into serious emotional problems because of substance abuse. Also, methamphetamine ("crystal" or speed) began to intrude on this fading social movement.

    In the depressed socioeconomic areas of the city, marijuana and heroin continued as the drugs of choice to achieve euphoric highs that would block out a sense of hopelessness and the awareness of a lack of opportunities in the overall society.

4. In the 1970s, many people who had been part of the "psychedelic revolution" now moved back into the mainstream of society. Their more accepting attitude toward marijuana made it an easily accessible drug. Marijuana was tacitly condoned by many parents who had been into the hippie scene in the 1960s. Some of these parents used drugs with their children, partly to rationalize their own substance abuse as acceptable behavior.

5. In the 1980s, and especially since 1986, cocaine has strongly affected our society. In the form of crack, cocaine is readily available to consumers who pay $10 to $50 in a "rock house," on the streets, or in the business sections of large cities during the noon lunch break. Drug use and abuse has reached grotesque proportions, and the federal government has declared "war" on this severe national problem that has pervaded all segments of society. Young people growing up under these conditions have become heavily involved in substance abuse. Although crack came into vogue, all the other substances continued to be used. Substance abuse in the 1980s has had a profound impact on the crime problem. More than 80 percent of all criminals have used illegal substances, and most of this group has had a serious substance abuse problem. In contemporary society, therefore, substance abuse has become an integral and significant part of the overall crime problem in the United States.

Since 1965, the drug problem has stimulated a variety of legislation directed at controlling the problem. Following is a summary of this legislation:

1965 Congress passed the Drug Abuse Control Amendments providing for special controls over the manufacture, distribution, inspection, and record-keeping requirements for depressant and stimulant drugs.

1966 The Narcotic Addict Rehabilitation Act was passed by Congress. It provided for civil commitment and treatment of narcotic addicts charged with federal law violations.

1967 The United States ratified the Single Convention on Narcotic Drugs of 1961. It replaced previous multilateral international treaties controlling narcotic drug traffic.

1968 The Bureau of Narcotics and Dangerous Drugs was created through the merger of the Federal Bureau of Narcotics (Department of the Treasury) and the Bureau of Drug Abuse Control (Department of Health, Education, and Welfare).

1970 The Comprehensive Drug Abuse Prevention and Control Act was passed by Congress. Title II is more familiarly known as the Controlled Substance Act. There are four fundamental parts: (1) mechanisms for reducing the availability of controlled substances, (2) procedures for bringing a substance under control, (3) criteria for determining control requirements, and (4) obligations incurred by international treaty arrangements.

1971 President Nixon signed the Foreign Assistance Act, which included a program to encourage international narcotics control and reduce drug dependence among individuals in other countries.

1973 The Drug Enforcement Administration (DEA) was created.

1974 Passage of the Narcotics Treatment Act provided for the registration of professional practitioners who use narcotic drugs in the treatment of addicts.

1976 The Crime Control Act of 1976 required the Institute of Criminal Justice to consult with the National Institute on Drug Abuse to provide research priority in determining the relationship between drug abuse and crime.

1980 The United States signed the Convention on Psychotropic Substances, providing international control on depressants, hallucinogenic substances, and stimulants.

1981 The Attorney General's Task Force on Violent Crime released its report emphasizing the seriousness of illegal drug trafficking. In December, President Reagan signed legislation containing a provision that authorized the armed services to cooperate with various civilian authorities that enforce drug laws.

1982 In January, the attorney general agreed to give the FBI concurrent jurisdiction with the DEA to investigate federal drug law violations. In March, Vice President Bush was given direction of a special task force to combat illicit drug traffic in South Florida. In October, President Reagan created 12 regional multiagency task forces under the Organized Drug Enforcement Program to investigate and prosecute drug trafficking offenses.

1983 The National Narcotics Border Interdiction System was created to coordinate federal interdiction efforts.

1984 The Comprehensive Crime Control Act was signed into law, with a number of provisions aimed at illicit narcotics and dangerous drug traffic.

1986 In April, President Reagan signed a directive noting that international drug traffic was becoming a threat to national security. In July, U.S. Army transport helicopters and 160 support troops were sent to Bolivia to help raid cocaine-processing facilities along with local police. In August, President Reagan announced a new effort to test for drug use among federal employees who have jobs related to national security, safety, or health. In September, Attorney General Meese announced Operation Alliance, utilizing an additional 600 federal agents to combat drug trafficking along the border.

1988 Congress resisted committing financial aid to various countries that were considered not to be adequately enforcing drug laws. In Panama and Honduras, where government officials were engaged in drug trafficking, aid was withheld and certain individuals were indicted. In this context, drugs became a major issue in the political relationships between the United States and some countries in Central and South America.[2]

THE SOCIOCULTURAL CONTEXT OF SUBSTANCE ABUSE

A major component in the burgeoning criminal drug problem in the United States is the sociocultural attitude toward adult substance abuse, especially in regard to parents as negative role models. Consider the old story about the father admonishing his teenagers about the evils of drug abuse—with a tinkling alcoholic drink in his shaking hand.

The parent-child drug abuse syndrome was a particular problem in the late 1960s and early 1970s. The attitudes and behavior toward drugs

---

[2] "Evolution of Current Drug Legislation," from the *Congressional Digest*, Omnibus Drug Legislation, July 1988.

during that time set the stage for an explosion of substance abuse in the 1980s, which will hopefully peak and then decline in the 1990s. An increasing amount of research data supports the theory that the children of substance-abusing parents, especially alcoholics, are most likely to become substance abusers themselves, both in adolescence and later on. Several factors link parental substance abuse and its impact on children: (1) Parents may influence a child to become an abuser through role-modeling. (2) Parents who do not use drugs but are severe disciplinarians may cause their children to rebel, and the rebellion may include substance abuse. (3) Substance-abusing parents may genetically or physiologically transmit the problem to their children. In this regard, there is clear evidence that the children of addicted mothers are often born addicted to the same drug their mother was abusing, and that the offspring of such mothers are born emotionally or physically handicapped. (4) In some cases parents clearly and directly influence their children's drug abuse by using drugs with them.

Many parent-child links on the subject are debatable; however, the most clear-cut connection is revealed in situations where parents and children use drugs together. This connection was cogently described in an article titled "The Parent as Drug Supplier" by Mike Granberry:

Bob is 41. His daughter, Melissa, is 16. They first "did drugs together" when she was 11. Their basic high? Marijuana.

"I never considered marijuana a drug," he said. "I thought of it as a sacrament—a religious experience. I actually quit drinking before I quit using marijuana."

Melissa says that her mother, Doris, 39, also used drugs. By the time she was 15, Melissa was smoking marijuana, drinking, "doing crystal and coke, LSD, mushrooms. . . . The way I got into drugs was totally through the family," she said. "They were so [messed] up, I had to start using, just to fit in."

Once, in front of friends at a birthday party, Melissa was given a "giant joint" [marijuana] tied with a bow and ribbon—Mom's gift to her. "I thought it was so cool," Melissa said, "I think back on it now and realize how bizarre it really was."

Today, Bob and family appear to be normal middle-class Americans, living in the San Diego suburb of Chula Vista. They agreed to be interviewed as long as their real names were not used. They are recovering drug addicts and alcoholics, under the care of a program for the children of alcoholics in San Diego. They chose to share their story, hoping it might give some insights to parents giving drugs to children. At the end of the interview Bob remarked, "I can't smoke one joint, and I can't drink one beer. If I do, I lose my entire sobriety. My chief symptom was denial—even to giving drugs to my kid. Denial is what keeps you going. It can keep you going for a very long time."

He glanced at the floor, then at his daughter's face. "Wow," he said. "I could have killed her."

In another case of this type, Debbie, the 16-year-old daughter of parents who continue to abuse drugs, has heard talk about the horrible influence of peers, school and MTV (the rock video channel on cable television) on the teenage drug problem. She disputes this by stating: "MTV wasn't my problem. My dad was my problem. He's the one who first . . . gave me drugs."[3]

In my own work I have encountered many situations of the type described in the foregoing article. In one case, a 14-year-old girl in a drug treatment group I directed revealed that she had been given drugs by her grandfather. Many children who become serious substance abusers first use a substance such as alcohol or marijuana, which they get from their parents' bar or stash in their own homes.

A Society of Quasi-Legal Substance Abusers

In the sociocultural context of substance abuse in the United States, mind-altering pill popping has had an enormous impact. People are inundated by advertisements on TV and elsewhere for nonprescription headache and sleeping pills. These set the tone for the belief that emotional pain is easily cured by ingesting pills. In a complex way, the model influences people to try to cure their personal emotional problems with mind-altering drugs.

Pill popping has produced a paradoxical situation with regard to the drug-crime problem. If you are affluent and your "dealer" is a medical doctor, you are a crime-free addict. In contrast, if your connection is dealing in the black market in a crack house or on a street corner, you are a criminal. A review of the problem of quasi-legal drugs reveals some of the elements of this issue, and how a large segment of the law-abiding population has become hooked on psychoactive drugs.

In 1988, over 500 million prescriptions were written by physicians for psychoactive drugs such as amphetamines and barbiturates. These drugs were essentially used by "right-thinking," generally conservative middle- and upper-class people who had no reason to have a criminal self-concept. This use, however, indirectly facilitates juvenile use because it demonstrates to children that drug use is an acceptable way to cope with the stresses and strains of living. The paradox is that an adolescent who turns to drugs to solve personal problems may be labeled a "juvenile delinquent."

In a penetrating article, Drs. Henry Lennard, Leon Epstein, Arnold Bernstein, and Donald Ransom made a devastating comment on this pattern of drug abuse. They alleged that pharmaceutical companies are engaged in promoting drug use: "In order to extend the potential market for its product, the pharmaceutical industry, in its communications to

---

[3] Mike Granberry, "The Parent as Drug Supplier," *Los Angeles Times*, March 17, 1987. Reprinted with permission.

physicians, all too often practices mystification in relabeling an increasing number of human and personal problems as medical problems."[4]

They continued by elucidating their meaning of *mystification:*

It is apparent that the pharmaceutical industry is redefining and relabeling as medical problems calling for drug intervention a wide range of human behaviors which, in the past, have been viewed as falling within the bounds of the normal trials and tribulations of human existence. Much evidence for this position is to be found in the advertisements of drug companies, both in medical journals and in direct mailings to physicians.

A series of examples will be sufficient to illustrate this point. The first involves the potential personal conflict a young woman may experience when first going off to college.

On the inside front cover of one journal [*Journal of the American College Health Association*] an advertisement states: "A Whole New World . . . of Anxiety" . . . "to help free her of excessive anxiety . . . adjunctive Librium." Accompanying the bold print is a full-page picture of an attractive, worried-looking young woman, standing with an armful of books. In captions surrounding her, the potential problems of a new college student are foretold: "Exposure to new friends and other influences may force her to reevaluate herself and her goals." . . . "Her newly stimulated intellectual curiosity may make her more sensitive to and apprehensive about unstable national and world conditions." The text suggests that Librium (chlordiazepoxide HCI), together with counseling and reassurance "can help the anxious student to handle the primary problem and to 'get her back on her feet.'" Thus, the normal problems and conflicts associated with the status change and personal growth that accompany the college experience are relabeled medical-psychiatric problems, and as such are subject to amelioration through Librium.

Another journal has an advertisement that advises a physician on how he can help deal with such everyday anxieties of childhood as school and dental visits. This advertisement, in the *American Journal of Diseases of Children*, portrays a tearful little girl, and in large type appears the worlds: "School, the dark, separation, dental visits, 'monsters.'" On the subsequent page the physician is told in bold print that "the everyday anxieties of childhood sometimes get out of hand." In small print below he reads that "a child can usually deal with his anxieties, but sometimes the anxieties overpower the child. Then, he needs your help.

"Your help may include Vistaril (Hydroxyzine pamoate)."

The advertisement, in effect, presents an oversimplified conception of behavior and behavior change. Potential anxiety engendered by new and different situations is defined as undesirable, as constituting a medical and psychiatric problem which requires the intervention of a physician and, most particularly, intervention through the prescription of a psychoactive drug.

Physicians and parents with low tolerance for anxiety, or those with

---

[4] Henry L. Lennard, Leon J. Epstein, Arnold Bernstein, and Donald C. Ransom, "Hazards Implicit in Prescribing Psychoactive Drugs," *Science* 169 (July 31, 1970):438. Copyright 1970 by the American Association for the Advancement of Science.

limited ability to meet the demands of even a temporarily troubled child, are more prone to believe that the child is disturbed and in need of drug treatment.

There is, however, no substantial evidence for the proposition that the prescribed drug does indeed facilitate children's participation in school situations. *What is especially disturbing about advertisements such as this is that they tend to enlist the help of physicians to introduce children to a pattern of psychoactive drug use. Paradoxically, such drug use, at a later date, without a physician's prescription, is deplored both by the medical profession and the community at large.*[5]

Psychoactive drugs, according to Lennard and his colleagues, play an important role in many parent-child relationships. The authors described an ad on a box of physicians' samples of Tofranil (imipramine hydrochloride), a psychic energizer used to combat depression:

> On the box is a picture of an adolescent girl. Above the picture in bold print is the legend, "Missing, Kathy Miller." Below the picture we read, "$500 reward for information concerning her whereabouts." Alongside in white print we read the plea, "Kathy, please come home!" Inside the box is a letter entitled, "Kathy, We love you. . . . Please come home." We quote: "Dear Doctor: For parents, inability to communicate with their children is a significant loss. The 'What did I do wrong?' lament of the parent may be accompanied by feelings of incapacity, inferiority, guilt and unworthiness. Many may, in fact, be suffering from symptoms of pathological depression. What can Tofranil, imipramine hydrochloride, do for your depressed patient?"[6]

The advertisement then went on to describe how Tofranil can relieve these symptoms.

The drug manufacturer thus suggested a fascinating method of handling a delinquent runaway: first remove the delinquency problem from the realm of family dynamics, then convert it into a medical problem that can be "cured" by drugs. The parents, rather than dealing with the behavioral situation, are encouraged to allay their fears and anxieties with a drug. In this way, the authors pointed out, drug use is set up as a model for the false resolution of an intrafamily problem:

> Thus, when a physician prescribes a drug for the control or solution (or both) of personal problems of living, he does more than merely relieve the discomfort caused by the problem. He simultaneously communicates a model for an acceptable and useful way of dealing with personal and interpersonal problems. The implications attached to this model and its long-term effects are what concern us.[7]

---

[5] Lennard et al., "Hazards Implicit in Prescribing Psychoactive Drugs," pp. 438–439. Italics added.

[6] Ibid., p. 438.

[7] Ibid., p. 439.

A gross error in reasoning is also emphasized by these advertisements of the pharmaceutical establishment. Promotion pieces describe specific psychotropic drugs as altering specific emotional states and affecting specific psychological processes—this even though it has been clearly established that any agent produces multiple effects. In other words, the manufacturer singles out the desired components of a drug's impact and labels them "main effects"; all other changes are labeled "side effects," regardless of whether they are positive or negative, merely uncomfortable or highly dangerous. Using this philosophy, an advertisement for heroin could read: "Here is the solution to all your problems. Relief is just a fix away. Warning: may be addictive." Essentially this statement is true. But it is totally misleading because it fails to mention that the addictive "side effects" are so horrendous that they negate any positive benefits of the drug.

"Mystification" in legal drug use is a complex matter that undoubtedly influences the way people perceive their personal and interpersonal problems. Lennard and his colleagues concluded:

> Drug giving and drug taking represent all too brittle and undiscriminating responses, and ultimately, in our view, they will breed only more frustration and more alienation. Changing the human environment is a monumental undertaking. While seeking to change cognitive shapes through chemical means is more convenient and economical, the drug solution has already become another technological Trojan horse.
>
> The ultimate task is to alter the shapes of human relatedness and social arrangements that determine the context and the substance of our existence. To maintain, as do significant groups within the pharmaceutical industry, the medical profession, and the youth culture, that this can be accomplished merely through chemical means is indeed to have fallen victim to mystification.[8]

There is little doubt that this adult concept of the power of psychoactive drugs affects the patterns of drug use of youth. The concept of drug use to alter and resolve human problems was a central theme of the 1960s. The tremendous growth of drug use among young people stems in part from the tremendous affirmation of its use by adults in legal form.

The problems created by the production and use of quasi-legal pills may be summarized as follows:

1. There are valid reasons for a person to use some form of physician-prescribed tranquilizer: to get through a life crisis, or for some other therapeutic purpose.
2. Despite these legitimate uses, the widespread abuse of psychoactive substances tends to relabel human problems as medical problems. It sets up an ethos where drugs are used in an attempt

---

[8] Lennard et al., "Hazards Implicit in Prescribing Psychoactive Drugs," p. 441.

to solve human problems—which might be better solved by introspection or therapeutic counseling.

3. An ironic situation is created: it is legitimate for a doctor to prescribe drugs, but a person who self-administers a drug is violating the law and may be judged a criminal.

4. The supplying of psychoactive drugs may be more beneficial for the parents, caretakers, and doctors who give the drugs than for the patient. A person under the influence of a psychoactive drug is sedated and is not usually belligerent or argumentative. As in Aldous Huxley's *Brave New World*, in which the Soma pill tranquilized people, the users become more malleable in their sedated state.

5. When proponents advocate the extensive use of some pills, such as tranquilizers, they tend to emphasize only the immediate positive effects and not the longer-term negative side effects. For example, a good case can be made for the powerful energy one achieves by using cocaine or amphetamines; however, the downside longer-term consequences can be addiction and then depression when the user stops using the drug.

6. Finally, the use of psychoactive substances which tranquilize people and oversimplify their human problems may sidetrack them from getting the effective long-term psychotherapy or counseling which can be more beneficial to their emotional health and life situation.

WOMEN WHO ABUSE DRUGS: A SPECIAL PROBLEM

In American society, women and men have achieved equality as substance abusers. There are, however, some special issues and hazards related to women's substance abuse: (1) A substance-abusing pregnant woman can deleteriously affect her fetus. (2) In American society mothers are most likely to be the primary socializing agents for their children. As a consequence, they have a special responsibility to their children.

How do most women become substance abusers? There is considerable research evidence that suggests many young women are first "turned on" to drugs by male companions. Early research by Lee Bowker suggested that girls' use of alcohol and marijuana is influenced more by their boyfriends than by their girlfriends. For boys, he noted, peer influences appear to be "homosocial" (that is, boy influencing boy), whereas for girls, peer influences appear to be "heterosocial" (boy influencing girl). It appears that drug use spreads more from males to females than from females to other females. There is a good deal of evidence that males provide illicit drugs and receive sexual favors in return. Bowker has summarized the situation as follows:

> The combination of biological and social pressure may lead to ambivalence about sex among females. For males the pressures are all toward engaging in sexual behavior. As a result, males try to get their girlfriends to agree to participate in sexual intercourse. Females are socialized to please males (on dates and everywhere else), yet expected to avoid pleasing them so much that they ruin their reputations. A reasonable solution to this double bind is for females to join their boyfriends in recreational drug use and use [drugs] as an excuse for participation in initial and subsequent drug seduction ("I'm not that kind of girl, but I was just so drunk. . .").[9]

In recent years adolescents have referred to this phenomenon as the "coke whore syndrome." This relates to the sexual favors which are accorded men who supply a woman with cocaine. It is a form of what I would term "soft prostitution." A special issue of substance abuse and women is that many women support their habits through the "coke whore syndrome" or in more clear-cut, direct forms of prostitution.

Paula Paula was a New York prostitute and drug addict for many years. Her story provides a prototypical case history of the path traveled by many women who become substance-abusing prostitutes.

> Before I was 9 or 10, I was a problem child. I was put into a problem child's institution at a very early age. I think I was a year or a year and a half old when I was placed. I progressed from there to different institutions until I was 16. The last reformatory I was in was a so-called treatment center. Here I got my final street education.
>
> Most of the kids there, including myself, were considered incorrigible. Most of the guys had criminal records. Some of the girls had been runaways and whores from the age of 12.
>
> The guys were violent and some were accomplished thieves and con men. I absorbed all of their teachings readily. I enjoyed it.
>
> I think I always knew I was going to use drugs. I used my first form of drugs when I was 12. There were two guys who lived in the same apartment house with my family. I admired and looked up to them. They were about 17 or 18 at the time. I was allowed home visits once or twice a year for a weekend (when my behavior, in the institution I was in at the time, was good enough).
>
> Whenever I did manage a home visit, I looked forward to hanging out at night in front of the house with these guys. They seemed to know I was hurting inside and tolerated me. One summer night I saw them going to the roof of the house, and I followed them. They were smoking marijuana. It smelled good to me, and I asked for a drag. I turned on. I remember that I felt it was the most beautiful thing that ever happened to me. I was very

---

[9] Lee H. Bowker, *Women, Crime and the Criminal Justice System* (Lexington, Mass.: Heath, 1978), p. 90. Copyright 1978, D. C. Heath & Company.

happy and started to imitate all the singers I like. The guys gave me lots of approval for my singing. From then on, I was one of them and got all the pot I could use.

After that year, I was introduced to cocaine by the same two guys, and I snorted it whenever the opportunity arose. For 14 years I enjoyed all the drugs I ever used. Heroin crept up on me. I normally weighed 125 pounds. There was a period when I was badly strung out [addicted] on heroin and weighed 90 pounds. I thought my clothes had stretched!

I had a six-year period of using every form of narcotic and everything that went with it. Maybe if I describe the average life of an addict in New York City, you will get an idea of what my life was like. . . .

My hours were from six to six. That is, six in the evening to six in the morning. . . . I'd get up as late as possible, because the sun hurt my eyes. I didn't want people to look at me.

You know something's terribly wrong. You're different. Squares are scurrying around, bumping up against each other. They look insane to you. Addicts talk a lot about how crazy squares are.

You get dressed, and if you happen to have some drugs you take your morning fix. From there on in, you begin to scramble for bread [money] and drugs, and anything goes. I would buy and sell drugs. Most pushers are addicts. They're not the big-time people you read about with beautiful apartments. The heavier pushers [those with large quantities of drugs] are usually addicts too. That's the reason they're pushing. It's a simple matter of economics. You buy a quantity. You cut the drugs yourself. You sell a little bit. You make a little money to buy more dope.

Most of the time you're broke, so you use your wiles. You'll use anything you've learned. You con, and being female you have a few tools that guys don't have. I did a few nasty things in my time. I turned out as a whore. I participated in many degrading acts. If you check Krafft-Ebing, you will find a pretty good catalog of what I had to do to make my money.

If you get drugs that are pretty strong, you can go along on them for a few hours. But usually drugs are so weak and cut down, you have to fix [inject the drugs] six or eight times a day to feel normal. When you have a real habit going, you don't really get loaded like you see acted out in the movies or read about. You need the drug to feel normal.

After the first few months of addiction, the stuff takes over. The demand builds higher and higher and the supply is never enough. You need more and more drugs and money. I spent as much for myself as I did for my old man. (You would call him a pimp—I didn't think he was.) If I made $200 a day, it would be spent on drugs.

Maria Paula could have been the mother of Maria, a 13-year-old crack addict and prostitute. Maria lived with her prostitute-addict mother, turned tricks, and used drugs with her in San Francisco.

Maria was torn between two worlds when she cleaned up her habit in a drug rehabilitation therapeutic community. Her mother often called, begging her to return to their life on the streets. According to Maria, "The most important lesson I've learned in the program is that I'm worth something." Maria at 13 looks twice her age. A small "12" tattooed on her hand betrays her past. It was tattooed there one night after she did 12 lines of cocaine. Now, it reminds her of the 12 stages of her drug abuse recovery program.

Maria's family background is prototypical. When she was 5, her drug addict parents left her to be raised near Oakland by her grandmother. She was 7 when she began experimenting with marijuana and PCP. At 11, she went to live with her mother and joined her world of sex and drugs. She turned to prostitution when her habit reached $200 a day. She returned to her grandmother the following year, but soon she ran away. She was raped twice and arrested for heroin use, and even when she moved back to her grandmother's house, she continued using crack. One night she returned home intoxicated and high on PCP. "I walked into the house, then I fell on the floor and started kicking and screaming, telling my grandmother to kill me." Instead, her grandmother enrolled her in a drug treatment program. "It was the first time I was strong enough to say, 'That's it.'"

The beginning was difficult. She was hard to reach—cold and distant. "I don't always trust others with my feelings." Soon, however, she was talking openly in groups which emphasized and discussed family problems along with detoxification. The program taught Maria that she will probably never be free of the urge to use drugs to help her face the pressures of the world outside. Despite her problems, Maria was learning to live one positive, drug-free day at a time in the therapeutic community. Maria is typical of many young women who have been resocialized in recent years in a therapeutic community. (This type of program is more fully discussed in the section on treatment programs in Chapter 18.)

Andrea   Paula's and Maria's substance abuse problems emanated from their position in the lower socioeconomic class. But substance abuse in adolescent females appears at all levels of society.

> Andrea had it all. She was a cheerleader in suburban Atlanta, a member of the homecoming queen's court and an honor student who thought that taking drugs was dumb. But Andrea did an abrupt about-face when she was suspended from the cheerleader squad for putting on lipstick during class. She bleached her hair white and cut it in a Mohawk. As her mother, Jan, remembers, "She went from preppy to punk in seven months."
>
> No longer in the teenage social elite, Andrea sought acceptance in the school's drug culture. "I just wanted to be 'in' again, and I was, with another group," she says. Soon her grades dropped to F's, she couldn't wake up in the morning, and she had screaming fights with her divorced mother. "I was strung out on coke, acid—everything I could put into my body," Andrea recalls. Jan suspected drugs, but when she broached the subject, Andrea ran away. Friends found her a sanctuary in a run-down Atlanta neighborhood called Cabbagetown and introduced her to free-based crack cocaine. Andrea called an old school friend, giving her a phone number "in case anything happens to me." The call probably saved her life.

The friend finally betrayed Andrea's secret to Andrea's frantic parents. Two juvenile officers plucked her from a seedy apartment about 4 A.M., and later that day she was committed to . . . a drug-rehabilitation center. "She was screaming and carrying on," Jan says. But shortly after admission, Andrea grew determined to come clean. "I wanted help," she said. "I was about dead."

Andrea's most vivid memory of treatment was being able to see colors again. In the depths of her addiction, she saw everything in shades of black and gray. She stayed in the locked inpatient program for seven months, then attended public school part-time for five months. In January she was released to the third phase of the program—called aftercare—and still attends Narcotics Anonymous meetings every night. She changed schools to avoid her old drug-based friendships and has to fight temptation constantly. "Most everyone in high school uses in some way or other—even if it's just drinking on the weekends," she says. But Andrea is determined to stay off drugs. "Look at what staying clean has done for me. I'm going to go for it." She is earning straight A's. She hopes to attend college after graduation and is living in a far happier household with a new stepfather who has taken an active role in her recovery. "Now, I tell my mother I love her—more than once a day," Andrea says. "It's been a miracle."[10]

Addicted Mothers

A special and significant problem for women is that they can transmit substance abuse problems to their children before birth. There is considerable research evidence that substance abuse has a physical impact on the fetus.

Mary Mary was a 12-year-old girl on her way to becoming a delinquent when a teenage boyfriend shot her up with heroin for the first time. "I liked the way it felt, and I wasn't thinking then about babies." But when she first became pregnant three years later and tried, cold turkey, to kick what had become an addiction to heroin and cocaine, the consequences were devastating. Her severe physiological withdrawal killed the fetus.

After that, Mary gave birth to two children during a period when she used "speed" (methamphetamine) and cocaine. She was using a considerable amount of cocaine while she carried her first child, a son. The boy was born premature, brain-damaged, and he exhibited the irritability, jitteriness, and slow development that are characteristic of children who are born addicted to cocaine.

During her second pregnancy, Mary went into premature labor after injecting herself with her drug of choice at the time, speed. Her daughter nearly died at birth. The infant spent three weeks in intensive care and was then placed by social workers in a foster home.

Mary's case raises a number of questions. When and how should

---

[10] From *Newsweek*, March 17, 1986. © 1986, Newsweek, Inc. All rights reserved. Reprinted by permission.

society intervene to protect a substance-exposed baby from its addicted parent? Should a mother be held legally accountable for not following sound medical advice during pregnancy?

In New York City, 8 out of every 1,000 infants are born as "drug addicts," according to a 1988 City Health Department estimate. This figure is up from 1.5 per 1,000 in the mid-1960s. This horrendous statistic is further complicated by a growing rate of HIV infection among children of intravenous substance–abusing HIV-positive mothers. These mothers and their children are a significant factor in the growing AIDS plague in America.

Heroin was at one time the drug that most affected births. In hospitals around the country, cocaine is now the drug that most negatively affects newborn infants.

A recent study found that stillbirths and fetal deaths occur twice as often among cocaine-exposed babies as among infants exposed to other drugs. Often, physicians say, the placenta tears away from the mother's uterus prematurely, leaving the fetus without a life-support system.

Alcohol abuse also remains a major danger. Research reveals that about 6,000 children annually are born with fetal alcohol syndrome. This malady is characterized by distinctive facial and body malformations, mental retardation, and inhibited growth. Another 36,000 infants are born each year with more subtle forms of alcohol-related damage.

The response to maternal substance abuse is in disarray in most communities. There is a lack of money for prevention, intervention, and rehabilitation programs—from detoxification, counseling, and social work for pregnant drug users to special nursery care and developmental follow-up for drug-affected newborns. The increasing numbers of addicted teenage mothers exacerbate the problem.

The behavior of criminal substance abusers is sure to have a major influence on the next generation. We have seen that the following sociocultural factors profoundly affect the substance abuse of juveniles:

1. The social-psychological influence of drug-using parents.
2. Negative role models presented by adults who implicitly instruct children to "do as I say, not as I do."
3. A pill-popping philosophy that erroneously states human problems can be resolved with psychoactive drugs.
4. Substance-abusing mothers who directly transmit addictive problems to their children.
5. HIV-positive substance abusers who spread AIDS, not only to their children and to other substance abusers but to the general population.

All these factors converge in the criminal behavior of substance abusers in contemporary society. People will take these negative attitudes into the twenty-first century unless some major treatment and policy changes are made.

Chapter
9

Types of Substance Abuse and Crime

*T*he abuse of mind-altering substances affects the crime problem in several specific ways. The use of certain substances such as heroin, cocaine, and marijuana is illegal, and consequently the user is committing a criminal act in many jurisdictions in the United States. The United States Department of Justice released some pertinent data about the relationship between substance abuse and crime in a 1988 report. According to the Department of Justice analysis, well over half the men arrested for serious crimes in a dozen U.S. cities tested positive for illegal drug use.

The testing program, sponsored by the National Institute of Justice, found that 79 percent of those arrested in New York from June through November, 1987, tested positive for drug use. In Washington, the rate was 77 percent, and in San Diego, it was 75 percent. Drug use was least frequent in Phoenix, where 53 percent of those arrested tested positive. In other cities, the proportions of arrestees testing positive were: Chicago, 73 percent; New Orleans, 72 percent; Portland, Oregon, 70 percent; Los Angeles, 69 percent; Detroit, 66 percent; Fort Lauderdale, Florida, 65 percent; Houston, 62 percent; and Indianapolis, 60 percent.

The figures were based on a sample of more than 2,000 men placed under arrest who underwent urine tests voluntarily. Most of those tested were charged with street crimes such as burglary, grand larceny, and assault, officials said. The sample contained few men charged with drug sales, drunk driving, or disorderly conduct.

A psychoactive substance creates in the user a state of mind which often facilitates deviant behavior. Many criminals "get high" prior to a crime, and some offenders become more deranged and violent than usual under the influence of a drug. In particular, alcohol creates the condition for an outrageous number of "manslaughter" deaths on our highways; and the combination of a mind-altering substance, conflict within the family or between lovers, and the presence of a gun is too often lethal. In addition, conflicts and territorial disputes between drug dealers account for an increasing percentage of murders in the United States.

In order to support a drug habit, most users have to resort to an auxiliary life of crime. For example, heroin and cocaine addicts seldom earn enough money from a legal job. Consequently, their drug habits force the addicts to commit such acts as burglary, theft, prostitution, and often armed robbery to pay for their illegal drugs.

The commerce in illegal drugs is a very significant part of the criminal substance abuse problem. At the top of the drug-dealing hierarchy, drug importers are running a billion-dollar criminal empire that has a deleterious effect on our economy and also facilitates criminal corruption in our federal government.

For example, during the Reagan years (1981 through 1988), our foreign policy was corrupted through our government's relationships with "friendly" heads of government who were heavily involved in the flow of drugs into the United States. There is evidence that Marine Colonel Oliver North, operating out of the Reagan White House, knew that planes illegally delivering arms to the Nicaraguan Contras were returning to the United States with large caches of illegal drugs and that President Bush, once head of the CIA, knew many drug-dealing dictators.

Moving down to the street level of drug commerce, here again we find that many violent acts, including homicide, are perpetrated by dealers in the maintenance of territorial rights. Many members of violent gangs have become part of the drug-dealing process, and their "business" disputes have accounted for hundreds of homicides.

The federal government's programs to control drug abuse fail because they emphasize a futile crackdown on suppliers while neglecting the more important task of weaning the American public from its habits.

The administration's crackdown on drug suppliers is by far the most costly ever conducted. The budget for enforcement of drug laws surged to over $1 billion in fiscal year 1989, more than tripling the funds available for interdiction, investigation, prosecution, intelligence, and international activities. This represents the largest increase in funding for enforcement of drug laws in the nation's history.

SPECIFIC DRUGS: THEIR EFFECTS ON USERS AND ON CRIME

In the following analysis I will examine in detail the substances commonly abused in the United States. I will focus on the emotional effects of the substances, the context in which the drugs are used, and how each type of substance abuse is related to the overall crime problem.[1]

ALCOHOLISM AND CRIME

Alcoholism may be defined as a chronic behavior disorder manifested by repeated drinking of alcoholic beverages in excess of the dietary and social uses of the community, and drinking to the extent that it interferes with the drinker's health or social or economic functioning. According to the National Institute on Alcohol Abuse and Alcoholism, in 1988 there were 15 to 20 million alcoholics in the United States. Alcoholism is considered the nation's fourth greatest health problem, and since it results in serious economic consequences to alcoholics and their families, its prevalence contributes substantially to crime and delinquency. Another major consequence of the use of alcohol is that it contributes to hundreds of thousands of injuries and approximately 25,000 deaths each year on our highways.

There is increasing evidence that the problem of alcoholism affects an increasingly younger population. The National Institute of Alcohol Abuse and Alcoholism reports that the proportion of high school students who drink more than doubled from 1969 to 1988 and that in the same period the age of the youngest alcoholic dropped from 14 to 12.

The Research Triangle Institute carried out a nationwide study for the National Institute on Drug Abuse in 1988, which pointed out some interesting facts about teenage alcoholism. The study found that most American teenagers drink alcoholic beverages and one-third of the nation's high school students are "problem drinkers." Drinking among girls is increasing. The study showed that despite laws against minors purchasing alcohol, seven out of ten high school students said they could "usually" or "always" obtain what they wanted in an alcoholic beverage.

Probably because drinking alcoholic beverages is a positive experience for about half the population, the person addicted to alcohol is not rejected by society to the same extent as the person who abuses illegal drugs. Despite this, there is an increasing tendency to regard alcoholism as a disease that requires hospitalization and treatment. Evidence to support this position is based on physiological and psychological data. Medical experts maintain that excessive use of alcohol results in such physical complications as malnutrition, cirrhosis of the liver, polyneuritis, and gastrointestinal bleeding. Psychologists and psychiatrists note the compulsive nature and self-destructive characteristics of the alcoholic's drinking patterns.

---

[1] For a fuller description of the physiological effects of various substances, see Carl E. Pearl and Rochelle J. Haskell, *Understanding Cocaine Use, Understanding Alcohol Abuse,* and *Understanding Marijuana Use* (Role Training Associates, Long Beach, Calif., 1988).

Alcohol is a drug that seemed to be back in vogue with the young in the late 1980s, after having been "put down" to some degree during the 1960s. Despite the fact that alcohol remains illegal in most jurisdictions for young people under 18, drinking alcoholic beverages appears to be a growing pattern of accepted behavior in juvenile peer groups. Most youths appear to drink because of the immediate positive effects it has on the personality. Drinking tends to mask feelings of inadequacy, gives some people a sense of power, and provides euphoric feelings. In some instances alcohol is used to overcome inhibitions—as, for example, to have sex.

A number of sociologists see adolescent drinking as a form of rebellion. In an early study on this issue, Robert F. Bales reasoned that abstinence norms may actually encourage the use of alcohol as a symbol of aggression against authority:

> The breaking of the taboo becomes an ideal way of expressing dissent and aggression, especially where the original solidarity of the group is weak and aggression is strong. This total prohibition sometimes overshoots the mark and encourages the very thing it is designed to prevent. This situation is frequently found among individual alcoholics whose parents were firm teetotalers and absolutely forbade their sons to drink.[2]

Further support for the Bales rebellion thesis, especially in regard to relationships between fathers and sons, is reported by psychiatrists Henri Begleiter, Bernice Joyesc, Bernard Bithari, and Benjamin Kissin. On the basis of their research, they assert:

> Genetic factors may be involved in the development of alcoholism. Sons of alcoholic fathers represent a special group at high risk for developing alcoholism even when they are separated from their biological parents soon after birth. Studies of male adoptees indicate that the biological rather than the adoptive parent is predictive of later drinking problems. Further evidence for a genetic predisposition comes from twin studies indicating that the concordance rate for alcohol abuse among identical twins is almost double the rate for fraternal twins; patterns of alcohol consumption are also highly concordant among identical twins. This evidence suggests that a genetic factor may be involved in the presence of natal pathophysiology associated with alcohol abuse.[3]

G. Lawson, J. Peterson, and A. Lawson identified four parental types associated with the development of alcoholism in children. According to these researchers, one or both parents of an alcoholic typically fit into the following categories:

---

[2] Robert F. Bales, "Cultural Differences in Rates of Alcoholism," in *Drinking and Intoxication*, ed. Raymond G. McCarthy (New York: Free Press, 1959), pp. 263–267.

[3] Henri Begleiter, Bernice Joyesc, Bernard Bithari, and Benjamin Kissin, "Event-Related Brain Potentials in Boys at Risk for Alcoholism," *Science* 225 (September 1984).

1. *The Alcoholic Parent*   While alcoholic parents encourage development of alcoholism in their offspring in many ways, the most important way is through role modeling. Thus, if the child's parent deals with problems by drinking, so too will the child.
2. *The Teetotaler Parent*   In general, teetotaler parents provide their children with rigid rules and expectations which are unrealistic and inconsistent with basic human needs. In response, the child of a teetotaler parent may display his or her contempt for such unreasonable expectations by abusing alcohol, typically during adolescence or early adulthood.
3. *The Overdemanding Parent*   The high expectations of overdemanding parents make it impossible for the child to develop a positive self-image. In response, such children may turn to alcohol or drug abuse or may become mentally ill or commit suicide.
4. *The Overly Protective Parent*   As a result of being overly protected, children of these parents have been deprived of opportunities to develop self-confidence or feelings of self-worth or to learn how to deal with life's problems. Thus, such children, as adults, may respond to problems by drinking.[4]

Another significant correlation between alcohol abuse and crime and delinquency is that alcohol is often a "stepping-stone" to the use and abuse of other, illegal substances. John Welte and Grace Barnes summarized their findings on this subject as follows:

> The "stepping-stone" theory of progression into drug use was examined, based on the alcohol and other drug use of over 27,000 seventh- through eighth-grade students in New York State. The data show that students do not use illicit drugs unless they also use alcohol. White, black and Hispanic students all tend to initiate the use of drugs in the following order—alcohol, marijuana, pills, and "hard" drugs.[5]

Considerable evidence supports my own conclusion that alcoholism deleteriously affects families. Family violence that never gets recorded in police and FBI statistics includes covert sexual, physical, and emotional abuse of their children by alcoholic parents. These forms of violence by alcoholic parents cause some children to become teenage runaways, to engage in prostitution or rebellious and assaultive behavior, and to become substance abusers who grow up to inflict the negative effects of alcoholism on their own children. This spiral of self-destruction and other undesirable behavior is revealed in a fact cited

---

[4] G. Lawson, J. Peterson, and A. Lawson, *Alcoholism and the Family* (Aspen, Colo.: Aspen Publications, 1983).

[5] John W. Welte and Grace M. Barnes, "Alcohol: The Gateway to Other Drug Use Among Secondary-School Students," *Youth and Adolescence* 14, no. 6 (1986).

earlier, that most of the approximately 600,000 incarcerated offenders in American prisons were victims of abusive alcoholic parents.

MARIJUANA

According to the National Institute on Drug Abuse, there were 25 million marijuana smokers in the United States in 1988. Marijuana is an intoxicant used daily by many people. "Grass" is plentiful, and usually the only questions raised about its use relate to concern about its strength. It is generally used without guilt and with little self-examination, especially in our highest-crime neighborhoods.

Although marijuana remains an illegal drug, its use is increasingly accepted and the laws against it are seldom enforced. This situation is reflected in a somewhat absurd but factual statistic reported by the California Youth Authority in a "Criminal Justice Data Profile" in 1985: there were fewer juvenile arrests for marijuana use in California in 1985 than in 1975. There is ample evidence that if anything, marijuana use significantly escalated between 1975 and 1985; however, because the attitude of the general public on marijuana use has softened, the police now seldom arrest users. They usually let them go completely or issue a citation that carries a small fine. This portends the possibility that marijuana use may be further decriminalized and might even become legalized in the 1990s.

There are mixed opinions on the deleterious effects of marijuana on users; however, it is increasingly perceived as a harmful drug. Constandinos J. Miras studied chronic users in Greece, where the marijuana is more potent. He defines a chronic user as one who has smoked at least two marijuana cigarettes a day for two years. Dr. Miras alleges that chronic users have "slowed speech, lethargy, and lowered inhibitions." Some become "suddenly violent without any apparent provocation." Dr. Miras' most serious charge is that prolonged marijuana use produces brain damage. His studies with THC (tetrahydrocannabinol, the psychoactive component found in all parts of the marijuana plant) have shown that the substance passes through the brain very quickly. In a lecture at the University of California at Los Angeles, Dr. Miras stated that chronic users are prone to anemia, eye inflammations, and respiratory infections, and there is also good evidence of abnormal brain wave readings.

It is important to note that Dr. Miras' research is concerned with marijuana usage in Greece. There is evidence that the marijuana used in Greece is somewhat different in nature and strength from the type used in the United States and northern Europe, although research carried out in 1988 revealed that marijuana used in the United States has steadily increased in THC content.

In an interesting discussion of the pharmacological effects of marijuana, noted pharmacologist Frederick H. Meyer concluded:

> The effects of marijuana, both operationally and in its mechanism of action, correspond exactly to those of other sedatives and anesthetics, especially alcohol. The apparent distinctiveness of marijuana is due mostly to the use of a route of administration that permits the rapid development of an effect and to properties of the active components that lead to rapid decrease in the effects. One is driven to the conclusion that the differences between the dominant attitudes and consequent laws toward marijuana and alcohol are unrelated to the pharmacologic effects of the drugs but are due to a conflict between the mores of the dominant and one or more of the subcultures in this country.[6]

Dr. Norman Zinberg carried out an extensive survey of several major areas of concern about marijuana: its emotional syndrome, possible psychosis, brain damage, chromosome damage, marijuana as a stepping-stone to heroin, sex impairment, and general health hazards. On the basis of all the evidence on both sides of the subject, Zinberg summarized his conclusions as follows:

> Obviously there are areas of concern. Drawing any hot substance into the lungs cannot be good for anyone, but we should remember that no marijuana smoker in this country uses as many cigarettes a day as tobacco smokers do. Also, marijuana is an intoxicant; and despite the research showing that someone high on marijuana does better on a driving simulator than someone high on alcohol, driving under the influence of any intoxicant must be considered a real danger. Finally, it is my absolute conviction that adolescents below the age of 18 should not use intoxicants of any kind, whether nicotine, alcohol, or marijuana. The 14- 15-, or 16-year-old struggling to develop in this complex society needs as clear a head as possible. One argument made some years ago for the legalization of illicit substances was based on the possibility that parents and other authorities could more readily control aboveground use of licit substances than they could control the underground use of illicit substances. . . .
>
> In the end, after all this work and all these words, I still find myself echoing the remark made by Dr. Daniel S. Freedman of the University of Chicago, after a Drug Abuse Council conference on marijuana. "Nobody can tell you it's harmless."[7]

Dr. Robert DuPont, former director of the National Institute on Drug Abuse, stated in 1979, "In all of history, no young people have ever before used marijuana regularly on a large scale. Therefore our youngsters are, in effect, making themselves guinea pigs in a tragic national

---

[6] Frederick H. Meyer, "Pharmacologic Effects of Marijuana," in *The New Social Drug*, ed. David E. Smith (Englewood Cliffs, N.J.: Prentice-Hall, 1972), p. 39.

[7] Norman E. Zinberg, "The War Over Marijuana," *Psychology Today* (December 1976).

experiment. Thus far, our research clearly suggests that we will see horrendous results."

There is increasing evidence that Dr. DuPont's predictions are being scientifically confirmed. A study in 1981 by Dr. Robert Heath of the Tulane University School of Medicine reported that regular marijuana smoking may, in the long run, widen the gaps (synapses) between nerve endings in vital parts of the brain. Dr. Heath administered marijuana smoke and its active ingredient, THC, to rhesus monkeys over a period of six to eight months. At doses that are comparable to those inhaled in moderate to heavy smoking, THC caused structural changes, widening synapses by 35 percent. The most marked effects occurred in the septal region (which is associated with emotions), the hippocampus (which is concerned with memory formation), and the amygdala (which is responsible for certain behavioral functions).[8]

A study that also tends to confirm Dr. DuPont's dire prediction was carried out by the Institute of Medicine of the National Academy of Science in 1980. The research committee produced data indicating that persistent marijuana usage can produce severe health problems. Their research report revealed that over 25 million Americans spent some $24 billion in 1980 for the illegal privilege of regularly smoking marijuana. Another 25 million have tried the drug at least once, making it the most widely used illegal substance in the country.

The institute determined that the principal active element in marijuana, THC, like alcohol, impairs motor coordination, the ability to follow a moving object, and the ability to detect a flash of light. Since these functions are necessary for safe driving, among other activities, impairment "may suggest a substantial risk." The effects of THC may last four to eight hours after the time the user feels a "high," whereas alcohol is more quickly metabolized. Marijuana hampers short-term memory, slows learning, and produces distortions of judgment, including reactions of panic and confusion.

There is special concern about marijuana use since much of the heavy use of marijuana takes place within the school setting. Charles O'Brien, a professor of psychiatry at the University of Pennsylvania School of Medicine and a member of the committee, stated in the report, *"There's no way a student's brain can function normally when he uses marijuana daily."* [Italics added.]

A Perspective on Marijuana

In recent years, due in part to the increased potency of the marijuana used and the accumulation of research evidence that marijuana has a variety of negative effects on users, the pendulum of societal opinion

---

[8] Robert Heath, *Science Digest* (October 1981).

is swinging toward a perception of marijuana as a clearly destructive drug.

In the 1960s and 1970s most of the marijuana smoked in the United States came from northern Mexico. Its potency was relatively low. A crackdown on drug smuggling from northern Mexico was effective, but more potent marijuana from southern Mexico, Colombia, and Thailand began to flow into the country. A further war on drug smuggling caused an increase in homegrown marijuana production, especially in California. Domestic marijuana growers and some of the foreign suppliers have developed the "art" of growing more potent marijuana.

One longtime researcher in the field, Sidney Cohen of the University of California at Los Angeles (UCLA), recently estimated that THC now makes up about 7 to 14 percent of the content of marijuana. In contrast, ten years ago THC was 0.5 to 2 percent of the content. Researchers who have tested the potency of the marijuana smoked in the United States estimate that it is now about *ten times* stronger than it was a few short years ago. Dr. Cohen says that the marijuana currently in use is almost a different drug. Dr. Cohen and other researchers assert that the new, stronger marijuana has the following deleterious effects:

- THC causes changes in the reproductive systems of test animals.
- Marijuana smoking by pregnant women can adversely affect fetal development.
- Marijuana has been documented to cause extensive lung damage in chronic smokers.
- THC impairs the immune system in test animals and decreases resistance to infections.
- The already critical problem of drunk driving is exacerbated by marijuana smoking.

Some research has been conducted using marijuana with extremely high THC content, and drug clinics are beginning to see the same effects. Darryl Inaba, director of the Haight-Ashbury Drug Clinic in San Francisco, noted in 1986 that since the potent California marijuana became available in the early 1980s, he has begun treating patients suffering from "acute anxiety reactions." At first those at the clinic assumed the marijuana was laced with PCP, but it was actually just high-grade pot.

> The patients who smoke too much strong marijuana too fast require talk-down treatment, just like we treat a bad LSD trip. Ten years ago people would have laughed at the idea that marijuana could cause such an adverse reaction or that users would have a difficult time giving up smoking pot. But now several patients a month check into the detoxification clinic because they cannot quit smoking this potent pot.

Doctors recently have been reporting a new phenomenon among pregnant women who smoke marijuana. Some are now giving birth to children who have symptoms similar to the fetal alcohol syndrome reported in Chapter 8. The syndrome, previously only associated with pregnancy in alcoholic women, causes a number of abnormalities, such as an unusual facial appearance, deficient fetal growth, reduced central nervous functioning, mental deficiency, and an increased frequency of major physical abnormalities. Studies on these issues have also revealed that marijuana use is associated with lower weight and shorter length at birth and with a higher incidence of premature births. In a study in 1986 at Brigham Young University and Women's Hospital in Boston, the children of mothers who smoked marijuana had five types of malformations, including congenital heart disease and spinal problems, at a rate twice as high as a control group. Although the overall rate of all malformations was only slightly higher in the Boston study—which surveyed about 12,000 women, 1,200 of whom smoked marijuana—the association between marijuana usage and major malformations is "suggestive" and "merits further investigation," the study concluded.

Recent drug testing for marijuana has revealed that THC stays in a person's system from three to five weeks. Many researchers and medical experts maintain it is significant that marijuana smokers retain the drug in the system for so long. Cocaine and heroin are water-soluble; they are quickly metabolized and usually cannot be detected by urine tests after 48 hours. But marijuana is fat-soluble, so it lodges in the body's fat deposits and can be detected in chronic smokers up to 40 days after use. Dr. Forest Tenant, director of a hospital project, commented in a lecture: "It's scary to think that any drug is floating around in your system that long. The question is, what is it doing? We can only conjecture that the health implications are not good."

Many doctors are concerned about the effects of more potent marijuana on people's reproductive systems. Recent research in primates has revealed that THC causes decreases in the female sex hormones, estrogen and progesterone, interfering with ovulation and other hormone-related functions. Marijuana use is also associated with a reduction in the male sex hormone, testosterone. In one study, the administration of THC to male mice for as little as five days caused a reduction of sperm production and an increase in abnormal sperm forms.

Although some of these changes are reversible when marijuana use is halted, many questions remain about long-term use. The findings have serious implications for adolescents, who are still maturing.

Dr. Sidney Cohen said in a lecture at UCLA that "animal studies have indicated that THC interferes with the immune system. In tests with guinea pigs, the drug was shown to decrease resistance to herpes simplex virus. And other studies have shown that THC appears to inhibit the production of lymphocytes, which are important in the synthesis of antibodies."

On the issue of marijuana's effect on the lungs, Dr. Donald Tashkin, a professor at UCLA Medical School who has been studying the effects of marijuana smoking since 1972, concluded in 1987 that chronic marijuana smokers face a greater risk of developing lung cancer than cigarette smokers. In one of his studies of 74 subjects, Tashkin found that "even smoking one joint a day for at least two years causes abnormality of air passages and increases the effort necessary to breathe by 25 percent. One marijuana cigarette is as deleterious as 20 tobacco cigarettes."

Tashkin recently completed another study of about 275 marijuana smokers who smoked at least two marijuana cigarettes a day for several years. About half of the group also smoked tobacco. He conducted bronchoscope studies, which allowed him to view and biopsy samples of lung tissue. Tashkin concluded that "the marijuana smokers who didn't smoke cigarettes had extensive lung changes—things you wouldn't expect to see in young individuals. They were the kinds of changes you see only in older, long-term cigarette smokers. Some of the changes could be considered precursors of lung cancer. . . . Every marijuana smoker had some kind of abnormality."

Because marijuana is smoked in a different fashion than cigarettes—marijuana is inhaled deeply and held in the lungs longer—those in the test group had damaged different parts of the throat and lungs. As a result, according to Tashkin, they could run a greater risk of lung cancer and cancer of the larynx than tobacco smokers, even though they smoke much less. Tobacco smoking further exacerbates the problem. Tashkin stated, "Marijuana smoking now is where cigarette smoking was in the 1940s. With something like smoking, you've got a precancerous [condition] smoldering, and it takes decades for the cancer to develop."

On the issue of marijuana and death on the highway, a study undertaken in 1987 by the Insurance Institute for Highway Safety conducted autopsies on 440 Southern California males who had died in traffic accidents. Thirty-seven percent had recently smoked marijuana and many of them had also consumed alcohol. The men were between the ages of 15 and 34—an age group responsible for more than half of all fatal accidents.

The recent research reports on the negative consequences of marijuana use are not restricted to the United States. Parallel findings were presented at a conference I attended in Amsterdam in April, 1986:

> During recent years an increasing number of young male patients with a heavy abuse of cannabis have been referred to one of the Drug Dependence Units in Stockholm and to the Detoxification Unit at St. Lars Hospital in Lund. . . . A few of the patients are "pure" cannabis users; they abandon all other psychotropic drugs including alcohol and stick to a very strong hashish. When they come for treatment they seem to have in common a general bluntness of feelings and intellectual functions.[9]

---

[9] K. Tunving, J. Risberg, O. Thulin, and S. Warkentin, "Long-Term Effects of Cannabis Use," paper presented at the Fifteenth International Institute on the Prevention and Treatment of Drug Dependence, Amsterdam, April 1986.

All of this research that reveals the negative physical and emotional impact of marijuana use argues against those who want to legalize the drug. My own research, discussed in the following sections, provides more evidence against decriminalizing this destructive drug.

The Socialization Process, Marijuana Use, and Delinquency

All these recent studies point to the highly harmful social, physiological, and psychological consequences of smoking marijuana. I am convinced of the dire negative effects of marijuana revealed by the recent research. There are, however, other negative consequences. On the basis of my own research into marijuana as it affects young users, I find additional problems that relate to the defective socialization of children, adolescents, and young adults. I perceive harm to two significant aspects of the social development process: (1) The user loses the chance to learn basic social and educational skills during a significant developmental period of life, and (2) The user may develop an amotivational syndrome. These two factors are interrelated.

Social and Educational Deficits in Marijuana Users

The following observations are based on my study of over 500 adolescent marijuana users. All these young men and women smoked marijuana almost daily for a period of from 18 months to 5 years. Although many also used other drugs, such as alcohol, cocaine, and LSD, the *primary* drug of choice was marijuana.

About 90 percent of these marijuana users had educational problems, which took the forms of excessive truancy and a failure to learn in school. These young people missed out on learning educational processing techniques and subject matter acquired by most adolescents. This deficit is cumulative and results in an increasingly alienated posture toward school and working.

About 90 percent of the sample studied presented a flat, listless personality in social relationships. They were alone a lot or in the presence of peers who shared their retreatist posture. Basic human interaction in their lives not only was blocked by their "stoned" condition but was made almost impossible by a continuing intrusive diet of television or loud music. Their speech patterns were curt and minimal. They showed limited or no signs of any intellectual curiosity or concern.

Almost all these individuals had family problems. It was difficult to ascertain whether family problems caused the marijuana abuse syndrome or the drugged behavior created a problem between the abusers and their parents. In some cases it appeared that abusive or neglectful parents caused the use of marijuana in their adolescents. The adolescents used the drug to cope with or block out the emotional pain that resulted from their pathological and emotionally painful family situations. In some families, the drug abuser was the "identified patient," who smoked marijuana as a self-administered therapeutic sedative. In other family configurations, it appeared that the family was reasonably healthy and the use of marijuana by the child created rational concern and disruptions.

Whatever the specific cause, it was my observation in nearly all cases that the long-term (one to five years), almost daily use of marijuana prevented these adolescents from acquiring social skills needed for effective participation in society. Marijuana abuse interfered with their passage through the normal developmental phases in socialization.

The Amotivational Syndrome in Marijuana Users   The complex of social-psychological problems caused by marijuana use may be termed an amotivational syndrome. In this regard I am not describing the listlessness and withdrawal that are immediate effects of marijuana intoxication. The amotivational syndrome refers to the long-term personality consequences of the abuse of marijuana.

The amotivational syndrome creates a person who (1) has limited ability to concentrate on any subject for any length of time; (2) does not learn any new data brought to his or her attention, in spite of having intelligence enough for the task; (3) has difficulty relating to others and carrying on a normal social conversation; (4) has difficulty acquiring employment because of deficits in attention span and occupation-related achievement; (5) has a high level of apathy and boredom in relationship to subjects that go beyond the immediate life situation (a form of sociopathic egocentrism); and (6) in general, has difficulty in relating on a meaningful and intimate level to other people.

The amotivational syndrome that results from marijuana use refers in more common parlance to an alienated, bored, "vegged out," self-centered adolescent. Apart from the fact that adolescent marijuana abusers are already delinquent due to their buying and using an illegal substance, long-term abuse renders them susceptible to other kinds of self-destructive deviance.

Abusers are more prone to lie, cheat, or commit acts of theft to get their parents "off their backs" and to support their habit. They often deal with an illegal underworld in the process of acquiring their drug. Both males and females are more prone to participate in irresponsible sexual acts with partners they would not select if not under the influence of the drug. They are also less likely to take precautions to avoid unwanted pregnancies. In the context of the contemporary proliferation of sexually transmitted diseases, unsafe, irresponsible sex can be enormously self-destructive and can even lead to death from AIDS.

It should be noted that there are some marijuana users who get good grades in school, relate well to their families, have healthy personalities, are sociable, and enter adult life with no special social deficits. These few "invulnerables" are exceptional. Most marijuana users—as indicated, about 90 percent—have family, school, and personal problems and are victims of self-destructive behavior and the emotionally crippling amotivational syndrome.

HALLUCINOGENS

The use of hallucinogens such as LSD, peyote, and various "magic mushrooms" did not begin with the psychedelic revolution, but it was accelerated by the counterculture of the 1960s. Among the various hallucinogens, the use of LSD is widespread, and it remained a drug of choice and popularity for adolescents in the 1980s. I will concentrate on the use and abuse of LSD, or "acid," in the following discussion because its effects and the social context of its use are similar to those of other hallucinogenic drugs.

LSD

LSD (lysergic acid diethylamide) is often abused. The mental distortions produced by the chemical have an emotional impact that often meshes with the user's search for emotional liberation or consciousness-raising. Despite its misuse for fun and "highs," the LSD trip sometimes, under proper circumstances, appears to be a deep and meaningful spiritual experience.

Compared with the opium derivatives, LSD is a very recent discovery.[10] The ergot alkaloids are a group of drugs obtained from the fungus ergot, which grows on rye and gives rise to a great number of medically useful compounds, such as ergonovine and ergotamine. These latter compounds are used to contract the uterus after childbirth and to treat migraine headaches. LSD was first synthesized in 1938 as an intermediate stage leading to the synthesis of ergonovine. Its profound psychological effects were completely unknown at that time.

Dr. Albert Hoffman was one of the people involved in the original synthesis of LSD. In 1943, he was trying to synthesize a stimulant, using lysergic acid (the base of all the ergot alkaloids) in combination with a chemical similar in structure to nikethamide, a central nervous system stimulant. One day when he was working with these drugs, Dr. Hoffman began to experience some peculiar psychological effects, which he later described as follows:

> On the afternoon of April 16, 1943, when I was working on this problem, I was seized by a peculiar sensation of vertigo and restlessness. Objects, as well as the shape of my associates in the laboratory, appeared to undergo optical changes. I was unable to concentrate on my work. In a dreamlike

---

[10] With the permission of David E. Smith and the *Journal*, the following commentary is derived from his excellent article, "Lysergic Acid Diethylamide: An Historical Perspective," *Journal of Psychedelic Drugs* 1 (Summer 1967):2–7.

state I left for home, where an irresistible urge to lie down overcame me. I drew the curtains and immediately fell into a peculiar state similar to drunkenness, characterized by an exaggerated imagination. With my eyes closed, fantastic pictures of extraordinary plasticity and intensive color seemed to surge toward me. After two hours this state gradually wore off.

When a person ingests an average dose of LSD (150 to 250 micrograms), nothing happens for the first 30 to 45 minutes. The first thing the individual usually notices is a change in perception. The walls and other objects may become a bit wavy or seem to move. Colors may look much brighter than usual. As time goes on, colors can seem exquisitely more intense and beautiful than ever before. It is also common to see a halo or rainbow around white lights.

Hallucinations, or false sensory perceptions without any basis in external reality, are rather rare with LSD. More common are what may be called pseudohallucinations. The individual may see something out of the ordinary, but at the same time he usually knows this perception has no basis in external reality; if he sees dancing geometric forms or brilliantly colored pulsating shapes, he realizes that they don't really exist out there.

There is another kind of rather remarkable perceptual change referred to as synesthesia—a translation of one type of sensory experience into another. If the LSD user is listening to music, for example, she can sometimes feel the vibrations of the music surging through her body; or she may see the actual notes moving or colors beating in rhythm with the music.

A third kind of change is in the area of cognitive functioning, or ordinary thinking. When someone is under the influence of LSD there is no loss of awareness. The tripper is fully conscious and usually remembers most of the experience. Thoughts move much more rapidly than usual. One doesn't necessarily think in a logical way or on the basis of causal relationships. Things that are ordinarily thought of as opposites can now exist together in harmony, and in fact become indistinguishable; black and white or good and bad are equal. A person can feel heavy and light at the same time. There is a kind of breakdown of logical thinking; but if the tripper is asked to perform some ordinary task—write his name or take a psychological test—he can usually do it, although he will resent the interruption of his drug-induced experience.

The time sense is frequently affected. Past, present, and future get mixed up. Strange bodily sensations may occur. A tripper's body may seem to lose its solidity and distinctness and to blend into the universe. Sometimes the hands seem to flicker and become disconnected from the body. The LSD user may feel his neck elongate and experience other Alice-in-Wonderland phenomena.

The effects of LSD are largely psychological and can be divided into acute immediate effects and chronic aftereffects. When a person takes LSD, she may feel that she has lost control of herself—as indeed she may have done. Under this circumstance, some people panic. In their desperation to escape from this powerless state, they sometimes literally run away in blind terror. If they do not run away, they may become excessively fearful and suspicious of the people who are with them. Convinced that their companions are trying to harm them, they lash out first.

In other ways, too, people under the influence of LSD often show very poor judgment. More than one person on a trip has jumped out a window under the impression that he could fly. There have been reports that LSD users have actually walked out of windows or have committed suicide by strolling into the ocean, feeling they were "simply part of the universe." Many people have experienced feelings of invincibility and omnipotence, have stepped confidently into the paths of cars and trains, and have never stepped anywhere again.

Further adverse effects sometimes occur ofter the acute effects of the drug have apparently worn off. Some people have had prolonged psychotic reactions to their drugged experience. These psychotic consequences do not appear to be totally irreversible, but in some cases the emotional disorders have lasted for many months, and in a few cases they have involved long-term hospitalization.

Another adverse side effect, the flashback, involves a recurrence of the acute effects of the drug many days, or sometimes weeks or months, after the individual has taken it. This recurrence of symptoms can have a frightening impact. The person may feel he is losing his mind. The flashback phenomenon is relatively rare but seems to occur more frequently in individuals who take the drug regularly.

A self-destruct condition that has emerged for many young users of psychedelic drugs, the "crash," is a personality pattern that defies description. It is hard to know in many cases whether the hallucinogenic drug-induced personality is a traditional psychosis or a flashback phenomenon caused by an extended period of drug abuse.

The LSD-induced hallucinogenic experience seems to produce personality reactions that shatter older modes of definition. Some individuals who take LSD seeking a religious experience or conciousness-raising may end up in a psychotic state in a psychiatric hospital. One case involved a 16-year-old boy who claimed to have been on a "religious trip." He had taken LSD around 40 times and "smoked pot as a daily religious sacrament." His parents took him to a psychiatric hospital, where I worked, because he claimed he had talked to God and on occasion still could. Shortly after he was admitted, we had the following conversation:

LY: How old are you?

BOY: You obviously want to know my chronological age. In your terms I am 16. However, in *my reality* I have lived for 4,000 years. [Long dialogue about reincarnation and the cosmic view of life.]

LY: Tell me about your family.

BOY: You are obviously referring to my mother, father, and two sisters. However, my real family is in a commune in Northern California. That's where my spiritual heart is. [Long dialogue about the "family of man and nature."]

LY: Do you believe in God?

BOY: I am God. God is in me. When I have had some acid [LSD] I am tuned into the universe. I can now tune into God and communicate with him without drugs. I can meditate and reproduce the acid experience. Acid helped get me to this point, but I can achieve this state without drugs now.

Is this young man deeply religious or spiritual? Or is he a psychotic having a flashback experience? These are questions for which there is no simple answer. All these roles, emotions, and states of being tend to be parallel and overlap.

One of the primary characteristics of most psychoses is a belief in a fantasy world that supersedes the consensual reality felt by the majority of people. Many hallucinogenic drug-induced psychotic states enable a person to balance several worlds adequately. These people are not usually blocked from communicating with anyone in terms of the real world, and yet many appear to be on their own cosmic trip. The fact that people in this condition can communicate in terms of simple everyday reality tends to diminish the possibility that they are clinically psychotic.

The effects of psychedelic drugs confuse the usual psychological categories and cause many problems for practitioners of standard psychotherapy. New clients often view the "headshrinker" forced upon them by their parents with mingled feelings of spiritual superiority, condescension, and even pity. They have no self-concept of having a problem or any pathology.

The use of LSD and other hallucinogens was an integral part of the hippie consciousness-raising movement in the 1960s. The powerful drug was still found in the 1980s, but in a context of recreational use.

Other hallucinogens include a variety of so-called designer drugs. Many were developed in laboratories to thwart the intent of specific listings by the United States Drug Enforcement Administration. Some have dire consequences. One of these substances, MDMA or "ecstacy," was placed on the DEA's dangerous drug list in 1986. These hallucinogens are not used by many people.

PCP: Angel Dust

A drug that is a serious problem in some urban areas around the nation is PCP (phencyclidine), or "angel dust."[11] PCP is a potent hallucinogenic

---

[11] The following discussion of PCP is derived in part from George Gay, Richard Rappolt, and R. David Farris, "PCP Intoxication," *Clinical Toxicology* 14, no. 4 (1981):509–529. Reprinted by courtesy of Marcel Dekker, Inc. 1981. Updated in 1986.

anesthetic agent. Exhibiting high potency with almost no respiratory depressant effect, it seemed to fulfill the promise of the long-sought "perfect" anesthetic. It is dealt on the streets with names like angel dust, crystal, hog, K.J., the pits, and rocket fuel. Often, because of its extreme potency, it may be misrepresented as a "consciousness-altering" drug, such as cocaine, LSD, mescaline, or psilocybin. It is easy to make in a kitchen lab, and it is therefore relatively cheap.

The favored route among chronic abusers of PCP is smoking, usually rolling the drug into a joint of marijuana or tobacco leaves. This and snorting permit the user to titrate to some degree the level of intoxication. The onset is rapid, and profoundly incapacitating symptoms occur at relatively light levels of anesthesia. Oral ingestion of PCP is now rare for the sophisticated drug user, although this method may be employed in a suicide attempt.

Even the mildly intoxicated PCP user presents a bizarre clinical picture. One description of a PCP user by an observer in an emergency ward is typical:

> The PCP patient is sometimes "zombielike" but quite often "combative and hostile." . . . An orderly said that a lot of patients come in after they punched out a window or something and that they liked to make animal sounds . . . barking, growling, and gorilla-like snorting. . . . They seem to gain enormous strength, crazy strength. It takes a lot of people to hold them down. . . . You can hit them in the face, break their noses, and that would stop anyone. On PCP it might just agitate them.

Disorientation, hallucination, extreme agitation, loss of motor control, drooling, and vomiting create a frightening emergency room experience for the uninitiated health professional. The mildly intoxicated patient who is still upright will exhibit a slow, awkward, stiff-legged, lurching gait.

Drs. Rappolt, Gay, and Farris depicted the symptoms of PCP in the following case history:

> Dr. Gay called to see a young person who had smoked a "duster" at a Led Zeppelin rock concert (one of 13 people so seen that day). The patient was a 13-year-old Chicana from the South San Francisco Bay area. She was of slight habitus, and reportedly had just inhaled "only a few tokes." History available indicated that she was not new to this form of recreational drug use.
>
> The patient arrived by stretcher to a medical field tent. She was comatose, and her posture was a board-stiff extensor rigidity. Her extremities showed a tonic-clonic spasticity, accentuated by stimulus (movement of the stretcher, loud noises). Her eyes were open and staring, nonblinking.
>
> She was moved to a quiet area, and counselors proceeded to gently talk to her and to massage the muscles of her legs, upper back, and arms. At 15 min. her muscle spasms appeared much improved, but she was still unresponsive to voice. . . .
>
> At 30 min. she appeared visibly more relaxed, and responded to voice.

Within an additional 15 min. she was sitting up, appeared weak but with voluntary muscular control, and was sipping water and conversing.

One hour after admission she was released to the care of her friends, and walked out unassisted. Several hours later she was seen in the crowd, animated and enjoying the music.

At this time PCP is a less attractive drug to inner-urban ghetto dwellers than crack cocaine; however, it remains a problem for many youths.

HEROIN AND CRIME

Since the early 1940s, heroin has been a drug primarily used in the urban ghettos of American cities. The drug has essentially been used to escape from the oppressive conditions of poverty and racial discrimination. For many people living in depressed socioeconomic conditions, heroin provides a way to blank out a dim future of limited opportunity and little hope. A dramatic portrait of the meaning of heroin to a ghetto person is almost poetically provided by Piri Thomas, a former criminal-addict himself, in his perceptive book on Spanish Harlem:

> Heroin does a lot for one—and it's all bad. It becomes your whole life once you allow it to sink its white teeth in your bloodstream. . . . Yet there is something about dogie—heroin—it's a super-duper tranquilizer. All your troubles become a bunch of bleary blurred memories when you're in a nod of your own special dimension. And it was only when my messed-up system became a screaming want for the next fix did I really know just how short an escape from reality it really brought. The shivering, nose-running, crawling damp, ice-cold skin it produced were just the next worst step of—like my guts were gonna blow up and muscles in my body [were] becoming so tight I could almost hear them snapping.[12]

Heroin abuse is cyclical, but it appears to have held steady in the 1970s and 1980s, alongside a rising use of crack cocaine. Between 1969 and 1971, a virtual epidemic of heroin abuse hit the United States. Whether through the intervention of drug treatment centers or more effective law enforcement (including the disruption of the famous French-Corsican connection), figures on heroin use declined sharply in major U.S. cities in 1972 and 1973. What appeared to be a decisive victory, however, was apparently no more than an extended time-out.

Heroin use is still a major problem, judging from the heroin-positive urine samples collected from arrestees and people entering addiction programs. According to the U.S. Public Health Service, the continuing use of heroin and the rise in heroin overdose deaths coincide with a

---

[12] Piri Thomas, *Down These Mean Streets* (New York: Knopf, 1967), pp. 200–201. © 1967 by Alfred A. Knopf, Inc.

trend toward increased purity of street heroin. Many middle-class youngsters who were introduced to drugs in the psychedelic scene of the 1960s stayed on to become adult heroin addicts. About these trends in heroin use, Dr. George Gay and Anne Gay stated:

> It is no longer buried in Black and Puerto Rican ghettos; no longer confined to the "ignorant" poor. Heroin is in the suburbs, and white parents are beginning to know the impotent range of fear and despair that black parents have lived with for decades; the call from school, from the police, from some hospital somewhere. The call that rips you from complacency and tells you the cold, mean, street-corner truth: your kid has been arrested; your kid is a junkie.
>
> Your daughter, the lovely, clear-eyed child who was going to marry a nice attractive, sensible, hard-working young man, who was going to give you grandchildren and comfort your old age—well . . . she ran off with a greasy slob on a motorcycle. When he got tired of fucking her, he split, so now she is turning tricks on the street, hustling for enough bread to cop a balloon [a bag of heroin actually sold in a rubber balloon].[13]

Recent research indicates that heroin is increasingly more widely used by members of the middle class as an arch tranquilizer for their problems. Although it remains a drug of choice among poor people in the depressed socioeconomic areas of large cities, more and more affluent people are using the drug. The more widespread heroin addiction problem is delineated in the following article:

> To exploit the boom, dealers use what one drug-treatment specialist calls "sophisticated marketing techniques, like the ones used to sell soap." To help buyers find the potency they can tolerate, for example, dealers are labeling their packages with colored tape (red for a "dynamite high"). Another ploy: starting new users on high-purity heroin at bargain prices, which builds up need quickly; then diluting the dose once the customer is hooked, so that he must buy more to meet his needs—at higher prices.
>
> One of the early signs that heroin trade was no longer off limits to middle-class shoppers came in September 1979, when David Kennedy, a son of the late Sen. Robert Kennedy, reported that he had been beaten and robbed in a Harlem hotel that police said was a notorious heroin "shooting gallery." Since then, some dealers have relocated to less dangerous "transitional" neighborhoods. And a few are even providing their own security patrols to ensure safe conduct for their clientele.
>
> When the Asian heroin first appeared, a generation of potential users was seemingly waiting for it, prepared by decades of casual pill-popping and, more recently, cocaine chic. "If you're into recreational drug use," says Frank McGurk, director of Manhattan's Greenwich House treatment center, "whatever good and new comes along gets tried out." Dr. Robert Millman,

[13] Anne C. Gay and George R. Gay, "Evolution of a Drug Culture in a Decade of Mendacity," in *"It's So Good, Don't Even Try It Once"—Heroin in Perspective*, eds. David E. Smith and George R. Gay. © 1972. Reprinted by permission of Prentice-Hall, Inc., Englewood Cliffs, N.J.

an addiction specialist at New York's Payne-Whitney Clinic, agrees that cocaine opened the doors to the harder drug. "The same people who would have run out of the room at the mention of heroin a few years ago are buying it intermittently and using it."[14]

The actual variability in the quality of heroin currently being sold on the streets is rather problematic. Most informed sources say that, *in general,* the purity ranged from 2 to 5 percent throughout the late 1970s and early 1980s. This range is considered poor by heroin users, and many older addicts fondly recall the 1950s and early 1960s when the heroin was allegedly much more potent. One addict stated in an interview: "Years ago we used to get a bag and on that bag seven of us used to get straight. On that $5 bag. Now you have to shoot three, four, five bags to feel as high. It's a lot of money that you have to get and it may not be worth it. Sometimes it's garbage, and it's hard. . . . People don't appreciate that."

Most street addicts "trust" their dealers. They usually don't experiment with other dealers. But if word gets out that a particular dealer has "dynamite stuff," they may pursue the lead. One woman addict described her copping procedure as follows:

> I don't know how the word gets around which is the best, but the word gets out. If you're going up to the bar on 116th and Eighth it's "get the red and black tape." Or "today it's the yellow" or whatever, and that's how you get off. When I used to go uptown, I'd usually talk to the people outside the bar, who's got what and what is it. I don't know how the word gets out that morning, but it does.

Heroin is a lethal drug. In 1985, a form of potent heroin known as "black tar" was imported from Mexico; it resulted in over 224 overdose deaths in Los Angeles County alone. But despite the fact that heroin remains widely used by people of all ages in all socioeconomic strata, this problem has been dwarfed by the enormous increase in cocaine abuse.

COCAINE AND CRIME

Cocaine was formerly considered to be the Rolls-Royce of drugs. It was used only by a select number of affluent people and musicians. Recently it has become a drug abused by people of all ages, in all strata of society. The drug has been snorted in powder form, smoked and inhaled in a "freebase" form, "slammed" (injected intravenously), and smoked in a pipe in the form of "crack" or "rock."

---

[14] "Middle-Class Junkies," *Newsweek,* August 10, 1981. Copyright 1981, by Newsweek, Inc. All Rights Reserved. Reprinted by Permission.

The Inca people believed that the coca leaf was a gift to them from Manco Capac, son of the sun god; it was bestowed as a token of esteem and sympathy for their suffering labor. Coca served as stimulating tonic to those working in the thin mountain air of the Andes. Further, anthropological documentation indicates that the highly sophisticated surgical procedure of trephination was repeatedly successful in this era, as the operating surgeon allowed coca-drenched saliva to drip onto the surgical wound, thus providing adequate (and very real) anesthesia. This permitted the operation to proceed efficiently in relative quiet.

The coca boom began in Europe when, in 1884, a cocaine "kit" was delivered to Dr. Sigmund Freud in Vienna. Ever the visionary experimenter, Freud was shortly using coca in the treatment of various medical and psychological disorders. Between 1884 and 1887, he wrote five papers extolling coca as a wonder drug. His "coca euphoria" subsided abruptly, however, when he began to experience the devastating side effects of addiction, and he subsequently deleted these laudatory writings from the collected papers of his autobiography.

When "coke" entered the drug-using consciousness of middle America, the earlier historical pattern of injection was largely supplanted (in a needle-fearing society) by the inhalation route in which a "line" of coke was "horned" or snorted. Self-styled elite users often used high-denomination Federal Reserve notes (to denote affluence), or a red, white, and blue sipping straw. Some users bought various expensive instruments sold in boutiques.

A side effect of this nasal method of cocaine ingestion is septal perforation, due to intense and repeated vasoconstriction. Snorters are also prone to infections of the nasal mucosa and upper respiratory tract, due to chronic local irritation. Smoking crack cocaine, or freebasing, has introduced a much less expensive habit, and a method whereby a much greater quantity of substance is introduced per unit time (being almost equivalent to the rate of intravenous use) with a concomitant increase in euphoria, but leading to dysphoria, toxicity, and in some cases death.

Prolonged or chronic use of cocaine may lead to an irrational affect not unlike paranoid schizophrenia. Plagued with the dark shadows of increasing nervousness, an inability to concentrate, and disturbed sleep patterns, the chronic user is increasingly prone to violence. Owing to these paranoia-producing qualities, coupled with the very real heavy legal sanctions involved in the possession of cocaine, the user will seldom be seen in the offices or emergency rooms of traditional medical facilities.

A case pointing up the ravages of cocaine use is that of John Phillips, the musician, and his daughter, actress Mackenzie Phillips: They admitted in the national media that they had both become addicted to cocaine and it had almost killed them.

Richard Pryor, the comedian, admitted that he almost died of burns from an explosion and fire while freebasing the drug. This method of cocaine use, adopted by many users, is exceedingly dangerous. The purified cocaine base is smoked in a "base pipe" or sprinkled on a tobacco or marijuana cigarette for a sudden and intense high. The substance reaches the brain within a few seconds. However, the euphoria quickly subsides into a feeling of restlessness, irritability, and depression. The freebase post-high is so uncomfortable that, to maintain the original high and to avoid crashing (coming down), users often continue smoking until they become exhausted, pass out, or run out of cocaine.

Smoking cocaine is much more dangerous than snorting the drug. An enormous craving results from the rapid high-low shifts, and the smoker tends to become compulsive, less able to control the amounts of the drug used. Consequently, dosage and frequency of use tend to increase rapidly, so that cocaine smokers are likely to develop extreme dependency.

Crime and Crack Cocaine

From a historical perspective, the cocaine problem in the United States has increased enormously. The most significant aspect of the problem may be related to the degree to which crack cocaine has pervaded the lives of people in all strata of society. It is a deadly form of cocaine.

Crack is named for the popping sounds made by cocaine crystals when heated. It is different from the cocaine we have always heard about. Generally, cocaine is inhaled or snorted, a practice which causes some constriction of the nasal capillaries and thus some limits to its absorption. Also, most of the cocaine available for drug use is diluted, making it less potent. But crack is 99 percent pure cocaine. It is prepared by adding ammonia to a solution of cocaine. The resultant precipitate is smoked. The immediate euphoria is usually followed by a sudden depression that demands more and more of the drug until the person is addicted. It happens fast.

Although the element of danger is always present for anyone using unprescribed drugs, crack is life-threatening. The drug may bring about seizures and deadly changes in heart rhythm. A user who escapes death may develop a frank psychosis or paranoia or may experience a loss of consciousness. An article by Peter Kerr in the August 2, 1988, issue of the *New York Times* delineates some of the impacts of crack. Although the article is about New York, a similar problem existed in almost every city in the United States in the late 1980s.

> A life inside the drug trade is often solitary, brutal and short.
>
> But to many poor or working-class New Yorkers—victims of a decline of the blue-collar industries that once offered high-paying jobs to people without college degrees—the rewards of the drug business now seem so great, and the risks of punishment so slight, that entering the trade is a powerful lure.

The multibillion-dollar drug business, in fact, is one of the city's largest employers. And those who engage in the traffic explain their decision as a choice between the long struggles of legitimate life and a chance to earn quick and sometimes staggering amounts of cash. What follows are the accounts of three young crack dealers, how they entered the drug trade and how they ran their businesses.

In some ways they are exceptional accounts. All three were ambitious and well organized when they started selling drugs. And even after they became crack addicts, they retained enough insight to realize that they had to escape the drug world to survive . . .

The Young Entrepreneur

His was a crack business with a well-to-do clientele. Until he left the trade this year, at the age of 21, he counted among his customers four doctors, a psychotherapist, a diamond merchant and two very dependable police officers.

All told, there were 40 people who knew the number of his telephone beeper. Business was conducted a few hours a day, from 6 P.M. to 9 P.M., when he drove around in a blue sports car, watching telephone numbers appear on the beeper, stopping at pay telephones and meeting his clients on street corners or at their apartments to sell them white rocks of cocaine. "I am selling a higher quality product, a much purer form of cocaine," he recalled telling his customers. "When you deal with me, there are no worries, because you are dealing with the best."

Although crack use is most widespread among the poor, experts said they believed that there was also an uncounted but significant number of middle-class users.

As he described his clients, the dealer's face broke into the sort of salesman's smile that in another place, with another product, might be considered quintessentially American. His dark eyes turned boyish. His voice, usually weighted with the diction of an old-time mobster, turned crisp . . . as a junior executive's.

Each night, he was buying a quarter of an ounce of cocaine for $300. He cooked it into crack in the basement of his mother's house, using her lasagna pan, and sold it for $600. He could have earned more than $300 a night, he says, but he found no reason to be "a greedy monster."

One evening, he recalled, he was called to the apartment of a customer, a Hasidic Jew, who had smoked all the cocaine he had bought with cash. Overwhelmed by his craving, the customer offered an antique gold menorah, a family heirloom.

"No, I won't take that," the dealer recalled saying, despite having taken gold chains, jewelry and videocassette recorders as payment in the past. "When the holidays come, you are going to look youself in the mirror. And then what are you going to do, buy a plastic menorah at K-Mart?"

Like many drug dealers, he entered the business in a calculated way, first weighing the risks and the gains. And, like others, he decided drug dealing was too lucrative and too safe to resist.

He had been raised in Florida and Brooklyn by a Puerto Rican mother, who admonished him to pursue an honest career, and an Italian-American father, who had worked in low-level jobs for one of the five organized-crime families of New York. The young man had always received good grades in school and imagined himself someday as a legitimate businessman with a college degree.

"I always expected to be a suit-and-tie kind of guy," he said. "But you have to go to college and you have to wait before you make real money. I wanted to put away a nest egg first."

At 17, he recalled, he and three other young men organized a marijuana-distribution location on a Brooklyn street corner. His part of the operation sold $8,500 worth marijuana a week. He paid each of three salesmen $1,000. Later, he said, he paid $1,000 a week to a major Mafia figure for protection.

After a police crackdown on the corner, the dealers began a marijuana-delivery service, distributing a calling card printed with a beeper number and a marijuana cigarette as a trademark. Customers would dial the beeper and then their own phone numbers. The dealers would call back to arrange meeting places. By late 1985, cocaine replaced marijuana as their main product.

Meanwhile, he kept a daytime job with a construction business; lived with his mother, who knew nothing of his second career; and kept a list of his clients on his home computer. He also kept four guns locked in a safe, he said. But by last year, the competition was becoming stiff, and violence between crack dealers commonplace. He hired a bodyguard to accompany him on his deliveries. One night, he said, as he stood in front of a nightclub on a Brooklyn street corner, he heard a voice scream, "Watch out!"

As he turned his head, he saw another dealer, a competitor, lunge at him, swinging a baseball bat riddled with nails. He dove between two parked cars, but the nails tore into the back of one leg. The competitor drove off. Just before dawn, he said, his bodyguard found the assailant and shot him in the knees.

Several months later, the dealer's partner was shot to death, and the dealer realized that he was a crack addict himself, working just to support his habit. Several months ago, he left the business and entered treatment.

The Young Mother
Last January, she stood shivering outside a dilapidated Chinese restaurant, a crack dealer peddling $20 vials with a .38-caliber revolver tucked under her coat.

The crack business, once a free-for-all, where anyone with a frying pan and a source of cocaine powder could double money overnight, was being taken over by gangs with machine guns. But she still worked alone, a small woman, terrified, and with a brutal craving for cocaine to satisfy. She knew, she said, that unless she quit soon, she would probably be dead.

Just four years earlier, when a friend first offered her a job in the drug trade, her decision seemed perfectly logical. The business was the sole industry that would offer a high-paying job to a black mother on welfare. The threat of arrest seemed slight. And an alternative, a legitimate career that might help lift her family out of poverty, just did not seem to exist.

"You can make more money than you have ever imagined," she recalled a friend as having told her, "just sitting in a bar selling packets of cocaine."

She was a 20-year-old mother with a 2-year-old child living in a public housing project. Each day, she said, she strained to make a weekly budget of

$200, from welfare and her husband's tiny salary, cover rent, food, diapers and baby formula. At night, she would peer down on her sleeping daughter or stare out the window at the rows of boarded-up storefronts, roofs and subway tracks that stretched to the horizon.

But her friend belonged to one of the successful families of the ghetto. His father was one of a generation of black entrepreneurs who had made a fortune in the numbers industry and invested the profits from illegal gambling in real estate all around the borough. To people in her neighborhood, she said, there are really two thriving industries from which real money can be made, numbers and drugs.

Her friend, a young man with an eye to the future, was beginning to invest some of his father's capital in the cocaine business. He had made contact with a ring of Cuban cocaine traffickers and was selling the drug in an unlicensed club the family owned in the neighborhood. He needed a pleasant salesperson. The pay was $300 to $400 a night.

In the club, a darkened disco with ear-splitting music, she sat at a bar stool. When customers approached, she said, she would take them to a restroom or alcove. Customers bought $20 packets of cocaine wrapped in aluminum foil.

The club flourished, and soon she was a junior partner, employing nine dealers who sold cocaine in the club and outside on surrounding blocks. As she walked from her housing project to work each night, dozens of people would approach her, asking to buy drugs.

Now four gold rings adorned each hand. Her income was sometimes $1,000 a night, and she dressed well, she recalled. But most of the money disappeared in the free drugs she gave to friends and into her own growing cocaine habit.

One night in late 1985, she was standing outside the club when she saw nine plainclothes police officers jump out of cars and scramble through the front door. In the raid, her partner and six underlings were arrested. Although she was not caught, she only had a few dollars left in savings.

But crack was replacing the powdered form of the drug in New York, and she knew that for people who sold crack, making money was even more magical. Together with three friends, she purchased an eighth of an ounce of cocaine for $250, cooked it with baking soda in a frying pan, and sold it as 50 capsules for $500.

The next day the four bought more cocaine, cooked it into crack and sold $1,000 worth of crack on the street. In five days, they had turned $250 into $7,000.

"At that time, anybody who had crack could sell it," she said. "But then it got to a point where one guy who invested all his money and never got high would say, 'This is my corner.'"

The rules of the street suddenly changed. Death became the penalty for any transgression. And by this year, she said, more than 25 people she knew in the neighborhood had been shot to death in drug-related violence.

One day last winter, another dealer beat her severely with brass knuckles and slashed her face with a three-inch knife blade. She now rarely had time to see her daughter, whom her mother cared for. Six months ago, with her dreams of a new life lost long ago, she decided to enter a treatment program, far from the battleground she knew as home.

The Jamaican Mafia

It is not hard to make a fortune running two locations to sell crack, the 26-year-old dealer said, speaking with a light Carribean lilt. Just follow a few simple rules, and, when necessary, do not hesitate to use your gun.

He had joined a subculture of Jamaican immigrants who established themselves in the marijuana business in New York in the mid-70's and, in the last two years, have become some of the most successful and violent street distributors of the smokable form of cocaine.

To neighbors in his middle-class neighborhood in Brooklyn, he recalls, he appeared to be a stable businessman with a pleasant family. He commuted to work in Manhattan each morning, maintained a tidy home and appeared to love playing with his children in the evenings. His legitimate job, in fact, was real. But on his way home from work at night, he said, he stopped at two Brooklyn apartments in buildings where the superintendents had been generously paid off. At each apartment, the knobs had been ripped out of the front door, and customers stood in line in the hallways to pass cash through the holes in exchange for vials of crack.

He would drop off a new shipment of the drug, and the two employees in each apartment would hand him the day's earnings.

"My nice neighbors just thought of me as a regular Jamaican guy, looking good, dressing good," he said. "See, I am careful not to put myself in a position to get busted. I've never been busted yet."

The dealer had learned the ways of the drug trade from his older brother, another immigrant from Kingston, who avoided taking drugs himself, owns nine apartment buildings, he said, and has a tax-free income of more than $300,000 a year.

His father had been a successful engineer who urged his son to find legitimate work. But his older brother was involved with the highly organized and well-financed marijuana-smuggling organizations, which he called the Jamaican Mafia. At 17, he told his brother that he, too, wanted to join the business.

"I was saying, 'The cars they have, the clothes they have, why not me?'" he recalled. "'I want some of the things they've got. I want in.'"

After proving that he could peddle packets of marijuana on the street, he recalled, his brother showed him how superintendents of buildings could be bought for $300 every two weeks and how marijuana, double-wrapped in plastic and smuggled in luggage through customs on flights from Kingston, could be purchased at $500 a pound and sold in $10, $45 and $60 packets for $4,000.

The income from his brother's two marijuana locations brought him $1,200 a week in income, which he supplemented with $300 from his regular job. He invested some money to buy a house and lavish cars, jewelry and clothing. But he reported to the Government solely the income from his legitimate job.

Like many drug dealers, he said, the brothers found the profits and quick turnover of the crack trade irresistible.

One night, he said, as he waited to enter a sales apartment, two armed men jumped him and hurled him through the half-open door. His employees, however, were quick to react. They opened fire first, wounding an intruder.

Later, they dumped his blood-soaked body on a nearby street. The second intruder fled.

For Jamaicans in the street crack trade, he said, shootouts quickly became an expected part of the business.[15]

TREATMENT ISSUES IN RESOCIALIZING SUBSTANCE ABUSERS

Many efforts have been made at various law enforcement levels to cut into and smash the illegal sale of drugs. In my view, the major effort of money and treatment should be directed not at the supply side but at the consumers of drugs. Following is my analysis of the significant issues involved in reducing the substance abuser's need and demand for illegal drugs.

It is difficult in treating the addict to counterattack the euphoria of the drugs for users, especially adolescents, with admonitions that continued drug use is ultimately self-destructive. At the time they are using, the hedonistic "fun and games" pleasure of the drug far outweighs the pain and problems they will inevitably have to face when they hit bottom. In my group treatment work with adolescent abusers, I include recovering veterans who were once in the teenagers' position. They can often convey to the adolescents that drug abuse involves deficit emotional spending and that eventually they will pay a high price in future pain for their current euphoric lifestyle.

In Chapters 16 and 18, I will describe and discuss a variety of specific treatment approaches, including various anonymous treatment groups and the "therapeutic community" concept. It is relevant here, however, to delineate a number of issues that need to be assessed and resolved if substance abusers are to recover. These issues, which often came up in my experience in research and treatment, reveal some of the problems inherent in changing the addicts self-destructive behavior and treating the substance-abusing consumer.

1. *Addict-Alcoholic Self-Concept* *"I am an addict or an alcoholic."* Even after an addict is entered in treatment and has evidence he is an addict or an alcoholic, he continually attempts to deceive himself about this fact of his life. An encounter-group process is vital in order to constantly remind the addicts about their problem. The abuser's self-delusion in this area needs constant emphasis.

2. *The "Co-Addict" or "Enabler" Issue* A considerable amount of research has established the fact that a family's sociometry and

---

[15] Peter Kerr, "Crack at Retail: Experiences of Three Former Dealers," *New York Times*, August 2, 1988. Copyright © 1988 by The New York Times Company. Reprinted by permission.

psychodynamics can reinforce addiction. A mother's admonition to her addicted child—"It's OK for you to drink at home, but don't smoke marijuana or use cocaine"—is an example of the way family members sometimes facilitate the addict-alcoholic's return to the poison. In treatment, extreme language and harshness are often required to communicate to addicts the way in which their families might reinforce their habit at that time or at some time in the future. The substance abuser needs to understand how family or friends may subtly push her toward drugs. She needs to be eternally vigilant so she can assess when a loved one or friend is unconsciously facilitating the slide back to drug abuse. In many cases, substance abuse is reinforced or facilitated because the addict's parents are substance abusers.

3. *Friends or Peers*   A teenager in an encounter group I directed remarked, "My best friend offered me some crack yesterday when I was at school, and he knows I'm trying to quit drugs." It takes an enormous amount of energy and discussion in the group to prove to a recovering substance abuser that no one who uses drugs or offers them drugs is a friend:

ADDICT: But I've known him for ten years.
 GROUP: He is not a friend, if you want to stop using drugs.

Peer pressure is a most significant factor in substance abuse. It is enormously difficult to extricate a person from a substance-abusing peer group and involve him or her in an antidrug support group.

4. *Projected Despair: A Life Without Drugs or Alcohol*   One of the most difficult issues substance abusers must confront is the fact that they can never "use" again. For most addicts or alcoholics, this issue produces feelings of gloom and despair: "You mean, later on I can't have one drink or smoke one joint without falling back into my habit? That's really depressing." Most addict-alcoholics who want to stop using continue to harbor a covert idea that some day, after they're drug-free for a certain period of time, they can successfully "use" again or "party" on a recreational basis. The treatment group has to hammer away at this self-deceptive, self-destructive notion over and over again. The Alcoholics Anonymous concept of staying drug-free "one day at a time" is often a helpful slogan for the recovering person to keep in mind.

5. *Are Drugs Fun or Destructive?*   Drug use is quite pleasurable in the short run; repeated group discussion and attack are needed in order to point to the long-term negative effects of substance abuse. Many recovering alcoholics and addicts believe on a deep emotional level that giving up drugs will take away their main or *only* source of fun, recreation, and enjoyment. Recovering sub-

stance abusers fight the issue in a variety of ways. They tend to remember the pleasurable aspects of drug abuse rather than the long-term deficit and the negative and self-degrading effects the habit has had on their lives. The recovering substance abuser needs to be constantly reminded of the real long-term impacts and consequences of drug use.

6. *Slippage and Regression*   Substance abusers often (normally) slip at some point in their recovery process. *Verbal punishment deters this*, when properly administered in an encounter-group process. People who have regressed or slipped should know that if they use drugs, they can expect to be *verbally* brutalized by the indignant group of holier-than-thou addicts who make up their support group (Alcoholics Anonymous, Cocaine Anonymous, etc.). It can prove most humiliating when the group pours out its righteous indignation at the "offender." The fear of this flood of wrath from the support group often serves as a valid deterrent when temptation appears. I recall a recovering addict commenting to his fellow group members, "When I weighed it up against what you guys would do to me when I copped out in this group—something I would have to do—it wasn't worth it."

7. *Painkiller and/or Social Lubricant*   "Why do I use drugs?" is a topic that is repeatedly discussed by recovering addicts. Two of the most common responses to this question (beyond deeper psychodynamic reasons) include variations on "It helps kill the pain of my personal problems" and "It's the only way I feel a sense of belonging in a group." Of course, what is pointed out to the drug abuser is "It's difficult, but the only way you'll resolve your problems is to encounter them head on, without submerging or complicating them with drugs."

In considering substance abuse as a psychological painkiller, it is valuable to have some awareness of the issues that affect the addict's pain. In the short term, drugs do provide a sense of belonging and do assuage feelings of alienation: the group's answer is that it is necessary for the abuser to learn how to relate and communicate with people when drug-free. It is difficult for the recovering addict to learn how to confront day-to-day situations without using the drug as an arch painkiller (for depression) or as a social lubricant. In their former situations, the addict and the alcoholic had friends and social scenes (the corner, the bar, the party, etc.) where their addicted identity was validated and rewarded. They are often resistant to giving up this past identity because of a fear of having to relate to a new set of friends in a drug-free social setting.

8. *The Life-and-Death Factor in Drug Abuse*   An allegation that is often hurled at an addict in a drug treatment encounter group is

"You are committing suicide with drugs." This forces the user to assess what Albert Camus has referred to "not as a philosophical question but the *only* question: life or death." This is a critical and often dismal subject for a substance abuser to discuss in a group because many group members are forced to confront the fact that on some level their drug use *is* a slow form of suicidal behavior.

In an adolescent group I directed, a 15-year-old girl revealed how she immediately went back to drugs and prostitution to support her habit when she left the group. She talked about her despair of ever stopping: "I have no self-control." Because of her openness and vulnerability, the group was very supportive. One group member, trying to pull her out of her abject state of depression, asked her to "tell us about some of your positive fantasies." She responded, "I do have one positive fantasy." The group members eagerly awaited her response, hoping that her comment about something positive would cheer her up. They asked, "What's that?" She replied, "My positive fantasy is being dead, and free from my depression and pain."

It is obviously difficult for an addict to confront the fact that drug use may be an expression of an unconscious suicidal tendency. Yet this is a bottom-line issue that must be encountered by all substance abusers. The life-death issue in substance abuse leads to a basic premise about the abuser, which is that on some level such behavior is related to a self-destructive pattern which in its extreme form is short- or long-term suicidal behavior.

Given the nature of substance abuse and its effects on the personality, it is no wonder that alcohol and drugs are inextricably related to the crime problem. We must keep in mind the following points about substance abuse: (1) It usually involves illegal behavior. (2) Drugs have a mind-altering effect (in some cases, for life) and consequently affect users' judgment. Drug abuse makes people more vulnerable to deviance and more likely to commit illegal acts. (3) The process of acquiring an illegal substance to support a habit usually involves a variety of subsidiary criminal acts. (4) There is a relationship between drugs and criminal violence. (5) The vast profits of the criminal drug empire in the United States involve millions of people, and the influence of this fact extends to our government's often corrupt political relationship with other countries.

Chapter
10

Sex Crimes

Sex offenders given the status of criminal in our society may be considered in two broad categories: those who harm others, and those who deviate from the sex norms prevalent in our society but do not directly harm others. Those in the first category use force or the threat of force on an unwilling victim in a sexual attack. Included would be rapists and others guilty of sexual aggressions on others, and those who molest children. Those in the second category are guilty of such crimes as pornography and prostitution. Many of these "secondary crimes," traditionally viewed as illegal, are increasingly being viewed as nondeleterious, and the laws proscribing them are being changed or eliminated. Recently, however, a new form of sexual violence has emerged which baffles our legal system. This involves *knowingly* transmitting the AIDS virus to a sex partner. The AIDS carrier who has sex with another person is not easily or clearly convictable under current law, and this raises a controversial problem for the administration of justice related to sexual offenses in the 1990s.

SERIOUS SEX OFFENSES: THOSE HARMFUL TO OTHERS

Sex offenses deemed to be serious are classified as felonies. These criminal acts include rape, incest, and child molestation. Statutory rape, or sex relations with a person below the age of consent set by statute, also constitutes a felony. Men are sometimes guilty of this offense without being aware that they have violated any law. If a person engages in a sex act with a cooperating person who is below the age of consent, the fact that the perpetrator is unaware of the minor's actual age does not provide him or her with a legal defense.

Rape

The most serious sex offense is forcible rape, which is included by the FBI as one of the serious crimes tabulated in the Crime Index. Forcible rape has long been regarded as a serious crime. The act of rape involves a person imposing a sexual act upon another person by force or threat of force. It is the clear or inherently violent nature of forcible rape that makes the crime reprehensible. And a considerable amount of research evidence reveals that rape has a devastating physical and emotional impact on the victim.

In a landmark study, Susan Brownmiller carried out a historic social analysis of rape. On the basis of her analysis, she makes the controversial assertion that rape is only the tip of the arrow of men's domination over women. She perceives men exploiting women in many areas of life and concludes that rape is the final act that is unconsciously approved of by most men.

According to Brownmiller, "Rape is an act of physical damage to another person, and like robbery it is also an act of acquiring property: the intent is to "have" the female body in the acquisitory meaning of the term. A woman is perceived by the rapist both as hated person and desired property."[1] She further asserts that when men rape in groups, it is an act of males against females. These men are showing their hatred for all females. Such gang rapes, according to Brownmiller, are also latently homosexual in nature; to get together and watch male friends have sex is, at least covertly, a homosexual act.

Brownmiller correctly attacks the myth that women somehow instigate rape. Even in recent years, some judges and other men have asserted that women cause the crime themselves. She quotes one prominent man who remarked, "Many women break the most elementary rules of caution every day. The particularly flagrant violators, those who go to barrooms alone, or accept pickups from strangers or wear unusually tight sweaters and skirts, and make a habit of teasing, become rape bait by their actions alone. When it happens they have nobody to blame but themselves."[2]

Brownmiller asserts that rape is an act of humiliation, aggression, trespassing, and possession. There are many reasons behind the act of rape, but the desperate need for sex is not high on the list of reasons. The

---

[1] Susan Brownmiller, *Against Our Will: Men, Women, and Rape* (New York: Simon & Schuster, 1975).

[2] Ibid., p. 88.

current viewpoint is that rape is a violent act committed as an expression against either a woman personally or women in general.

In one study of rape, Peggy Reeves Sandy asserted that rape is not an inherent tendency of male nature. She began with the assumption that human sexual behavior, though based in a biological need, is an expression of cultural forces. She analyzed the incidence, meaning, and function of rape in a cross-cultural sample of tribal societies. Two general hypotheses guided her research: first, that the incidence of rape varies cross-culturally, and second, that a high incidence of rape is embedded in a distinguishably different cultural configuration than a low incidence of rape. Her data validate the assumption that rape is part of a cultural configuration which includes interpersonal violence and male dominance.[3]

Acquaintance Rape

In the 1980s, in general, there was an increasing awareness of many forms of rape. The society has come to recognize that rape is not restricted to the sexual attack of a stranger on a female victim and that, in fact, many husbands rape their wives clearly against their will. This is especially true of husbands who batter their wives and then rape them. Reliable statistics on this pattern of rape are difficult to acquire because most of the victims are trapped in violent marriages and are fearful of revealing their problems because they will be subject to further criminal violence.

Another form of rape, aquaintance rape, was increasingly exposed in the later 1980s. Prior to this time most women thought that if they were raped on a date by a man they knew or with whom they had even had prior sexual relations, the police and the courts would not consider the act as a criminal rape. Increasingly, however, judicial agencies have come to recognize any forcible sexual act against a woman who does not want the act perpetrated on her as rape.

A prototypical case of date rape was reported to me by a 22-year-old student. She told me about this traumatic event in her life in private, after I had given a lecture on the general subject of rape in a criminology class.

> This was my third date with this guy and I liked him. We had not yet had any sexual intercourse, although there was a lot of kissing and embracing. We had a good time that night, but I was not prepared for what happened. I invited him into my apartment for a nightcap.
>
> After we kissed for a while, without warning, he began to take off his clothes like I was supposed to go to bed with him. I told him I wasn't ready

---

[3] Peggy Reeves Sandy, "Rape in Its Cultural Context," *Journal of Social Issues* 37, no. 4 (1981).

and didn't know him that well. I was really concerned about sexual diseases, especially AIDS.

He began to call me a c-teaser, and told me he was going to get what he wanted. He grabbed me by my hair and pushed me into the bedroom. I resisted and he slapped me. I had a feeling of stark terror—when I looked at his face I realized he was going to get what he wanted by doing whatever it took. He slapped me again, pushed me onto the bed, raped me, and then left without a word.

The next day I was emotionally destroyed and couldn't go to work or school. I never reported him because I felt I didn't have a case. I had been out with him three times. He called again, and I threatened him with the police. He never called back.

This happened a year ago and this is the first time I've talked about this to anyone. I think about this horrible experience almost every day, and I hardly go out on dates anymore. I used to worry about strangers who might rape me. Now I worry about all men.

Date rape happens most frequently to women between the ages of 15 and 24, and most frequently on the first, second, or third date, according to one report. The impact on victims is that they often lose the ability to make decisions in their lives. Many victims also find it very difficult to form intimate relationships with men after they have been raped. College women are especially vulnerable to acquaintance rape, according to a 1988 report by the Association of American Colleges, because they are away from home, often for the first time, and are unsure of how to protect themselves in new situations.

A three-year *Ms.* magazine study covering 35 campuses found in 1985 that 90 percent of the women surveyed did not report date rape experiences to the police. This reluctance to report the crime is due to the fact that the victim blames herself because she chose to date the offender, to attend a particular party, or to accept a ride from the male "friend" who raped her. One victim stated, "I began to doubt my own judgment and found it difficult to trust men."

There is some evidence that in many cases, acquaintance rape is more psychologically damaging than other sexual assaults because the victim believed one of the myths about rape, that the rapist is usually a stranger and not someone she knows as a friend. The victim may think that she has no control over what a stranger does; however, when a "friend" rapes her she becomes distrustful of all men and may have difficulty in the future forming a close relationship with any man.

Andrea Parrot, a professor of psychology and human sexuality at Cornell University, gave a lecture at a conference on coercive sexuality in which she said that although women often admit to being forced to have sex with men against their will, they often do not call it rape:

They will say, "he pushed me further than I wanted to go; he made me do something I didn't want to do"—but they don't say, "I was raped." Women often refuse to view themselves as being raped because they see themselves as contributing to some extent to the outcome of the evening; perhaps because they invited their date up to their apartment or wore a "sexy" dress.

Part of the problem in American society is that most boys are socialized to be sexually aggressive and most girls are raised to be passive. Girls are told to say "no" in certain sexual situations where they may mean "maybe." Consequently, in many sexual encounters there may be doubts about the definition of the situation. The current viewpoint about date rape, however, is that when a woman says "no," her definition of the situation must be acknowledged by the man. If he goes against the woman's definition of the situation, the courts will probably rule that he has committed a criminal act of rape.

Although there are no clear-cut descriptions of the types of personalities a woman should steer clear of in dating, several aggressive personality types have been identified. In the September, 1985, issue of *Human Sexuality*, characteristics of three types of potential sexual aggressors were defined: (1) *sexually coercive men* who use extreme verbal pressure to induce a woman to have intercourse; (2) *sexually abusive men* who use threats of force; and (3) *sexually assaultive men* who use physical means to force a woman to engage in oral, anal, or vaginal intercourse. In the sample of 1,846 male college students who were studied, 15.9 percent were classified as coercive, 4.9 percent as abusive, and 4.3 percent as assaultive.

According to Gail Abarbanel and Aileen Adams, who are director and legal counsel of the Santa Monica Rape Treatment Center in California, they began noticing a significant increase in the number of cases involving campus rape, many of which were acquaintance rape situations. The women were from small colleges and large universities all over the country—Texas, Boston, Chicago, New York, and California. Those from out-of-town schools were either home for the summer or had dropped out, often because of the rape. There were instances of fraternity party gang rape, dormitory rape, date rape, and stranger rape.

On the basis of their experiences, Abarbanel and Adams wrote a booklet titled "Sexual Assault on Campus." Drawing on several recent national surveys, the booklet cites a 1987 survey that found that out of 6,000 students polled in 32 colleges across the country, 1 out of every 6 female students reported being a victim of rape or attempted rape during the preceding year. The majority of the cases reported were acquaintance rapes. In addition, 1 out of every 15 male students in the survey reported committing rape or attempting to commit rape during that same period. Another national survey cited in the booklet found that more than 90 percent of the rapes among college women went unreported. The Rape Treatment Center booklet recommends these steps by colleges:

- Issue a clear, written policy statement defining rape, condemning it and outlining criminal penalties and disciplinary steps that can be taken against assailants. Chancellor Ira Michael Heyman of the University of California, Berkeley, issued such a statement after two campus rapes, and his action added to the understanding of the issue on that campus.

- Set up a process for an immediate hearing to determine whether the victim or the alleged assailant should be moved if they live in the same dormitory.
- Establish a program providing medical treatment and counseling for victims.
- Encourage victims to report attacks and provide statistics concerning attacks on campus. Many colleges are reluctant to acknowledge assaults, but everyone is safer if accurate information—not rumor—guides behavior.
- Increase security to prevent attacks. Colleges should avoid scheduling classes in otherwise deserted campus areas, install telephones linked to security stations in potentially dangerous areas, improve dormitory locks, and offer escort services. Students and administrators can help reduce the incidence of rape by making it clear that rape is a crime—one that especially creates barriers to the trust that is so essential on a college campus.

On the basis of the various cases and research reviewed here, it appears that either campus rape and acquaintance rape are significantly on the rise, or in the past decade a criminal phenomenon that has been kept secret for many years has surfaced and is receiving more attention. In any case, most victims are still reluctant to prosecute rapists because of anxiety and fear about going to court.

Legal Aspects of Rape

In the past, many women would not report rapes for fear that they would become victims twice. The first victimization was the rape experience itself. The second would be in court, where the accused rapist's defense attorney would invariably attempt to bring out the victim's past sex life and, too often, place the victim on trial. As the following article from *Time* magazine points out:

> Since rape trials often hinge on the victim's word against the defendant's, a standard defense tactic has long been to make the woman appear to have been seeking sex. Courts allowed this, generally following the admonitory dictum on rape laid down in the 17th century by the English jurist Sir Matthew Hale: "An accusation easily to be made and hard to be proved, and harder to be defended by the party accused, tho never so innocent." Over the years, rape became encrusted with rules to protect men from vengeful women: almost anything about the victim's sex life was relevant, and the prosecution had to prove that she had tried to resist the attack. As a result, conviction rates had been much lower for rape than for other violent crimes.
>
> But now the laws are changing. Since the mid '70s Congress and half the

states have adopted "rape shield laws" that protect rape victims from being unfairly grilled about their past sexual activity. Michigan's comprehensive 1974 rape reform law has been the model. At a preliminary hearing for the man who offered Alice a ride, the defendant's lawyer started asking her questions about her penchant for hitchhiking with men. Citing Michigan's shield law, the prosecutor successfully objected to that line of questioning. Unable to discredit Alice's testimony, the defense lawyer quickly made a deal: his client would plead guilty to criminal sexual conduct in the first degree if the prosecutor agreed to drop charges of possessing a firearm and robbery. Still to be sentenced, the man will probably get 15 to 20 years.

Without the reform rule, the crime against Alice might never have been prosecuted. And if it had come to trial, says Susan Rohr, an adviser at the three-year-old Detroit Rape Counseling Center, "the defense attorney would have done everything to keep the jury from thinking about the facts of the crime. Instead, he would have tried to make it seem that the victim was in the habit of making quick acquaintances with strange men in a bar late at night."

Changes in rape laws have been pressed by women's rights groups, who argue that rape victims have too often been "raped a second time" by the criminal justice system, and by law reformers, who want rape treated rationally, like any other violent crime. One step has been to drop the word rape. Many of the new statutes speak in terms of sexual assault, sexual battery or criminal sexual conduct and carefully define the act.

A bill now before the Texas legislature would go even further and eliminate any mention of sex; instead, it lists in clinically bland terms the various forms that forced intercourse can take and calls them all assault. Aggravated rape becomes aggravated assault, a first-degree felony punishable by five years to life. The Texas bill would also follow those in other states by being "sex neutral," or containing no assumption that rape is only something done by men to women.

Almost all states no longer require the victim to prove that she resisted the rape to the utmost because lawmakers now recognize that resistance can risk further harm. Another feature of the old rape statutes that is disappearing is draconian penalties, which have been counterproductive: too often, juries would acquit rather than send a rapist to jail for a term of 20 years or more. Under the new laws, sentences are more flexible; basically, the greater the violence, the stiffer the penalty. In Michigan, a man who already had a rape on his record was convicted of another, this one at gunpoint, and sentenced to eight to 15 years. But in another case, a man who slapped and raped an acquaintance he occasionally met in a bar, but who used no other force and had no criminal record, got off with probation plus payment of court costs. Under the old law the prosecutor might not have bothered to take the case to trial, since the jury would probably not have convicted the man.

Along with changing social attitudes that have made women more willing to report rapes, as well as more careful and sensitive police work, the Michigan law has helped dramatically increase the number of rape convictions. In that state, there were 90% more successful prosecutions in 1977 than in 1972, while rapes that have been reported climbed by 30% and arrests by 62%. But defendants still get a fair trial. In Michigan, the law specifically admits proof of prior sex with the defendant. In some other states, the shield laws call for a balancing test; the judge considers whether the evidence of a woman's past history might prove that she really did consent to intercourse or if it would simply prejudice the jury against the victim. Usually he hears the evidence privately in his chambers before deciding whether the jury should hear it.

One change in the rape statutes that is likely to come more slowly is the abolition of the old common law rule that a husband cannot be convicted for raping his wife. A few states—Oregon, New Jersey, Delaware and Nebraska—have done so, and others are still considering whether to take that leap into the marital bedroom. But the difficulty was illustrated [in 1978] by the celebrated Rideout case in Oregon. Mrs. Rideout accused Mr. Rideout of rape and left him, but the jury acquitted, and two weeks later the Rideouts were reconciled, lovingly gazing at each other at a cocktail lounge for the benefit of a photographer. When last heard from they were separated again.[4]

The Rape Victim's Point of View

Rape victims typically go through what many psychologists have labeled the rape trauma syndrome. There appear to be three phases of victim reaction:

Phase 1 During phase 1, victims frequently experience a state of emotional shock. They cannot believe that the rape has occurred, and they may be unable to comprehend what has happened or what they should do. Victims are likely to experience a wide range of emotions at this time, including anger, shame, frustration, and anxiety. It is common for victims to exhibit all these emotions in the form of severe and abrupt mood changes.

Notification of the victim's parents or spouse is one of the early issues to arise during the first phase, and it is very common for women to state that their parents or spouse must not know what has happened. This is unfortunate, because in most instances a marked decrease in anxiety and other symptoms occurs after the victim has discussed the attack with her family. A decrease in severe anxiety marks the end of phase 1 of post-rape trauma.

Phase 2 In phase 2, the adjustment phase, victims often give every appearance that they have learned to cope with the impact of the rape assault. This phase is often mistakenly thought to represent a successful resolution; however, it is usually only a temporary period of outward adjustment, for at this time many victims have not fully come to terms with their experience.

---

[4] *Time*, April 2, 1979. Copyright 1979 Time Inc. All rights reserved. Reprinted by permission from TIME.

Phase 3   Phase 3 begins when the victim develops an inner sense of depression. Victims may perceive themselves as being changed by the rape, either because they feel different about themselves or because they believe that others view them as changed and stigmatized. Many victims find it difficult to return to normal responsibilities, such as work or school. When they do return, they are often unable to concentrate or perform their normal tasks. For some victims, this may lead to further depression. Family support is often crucial during this phase because of the victim's desperate need to communicate. In phase 3 the victim typically feels guilty—even though she has not done anything at all to deserve that feeling.

In an article in the February, 1985, issue of *Psychology Today*, Elizabeth Stark reports on some of the effects of sex crimes on women:

Is sexual attack the most psychologically devastating crime? Do attempted crimes affect victims as much as those that succeed? These are questions that clinical psychologist Dean Kilpatrick and his colleagues at the Medical University of South Carolina in Charleston addressed in a telephone survey conducted in the Charleston area.

They asked more than 2,000 women between the ages of 18 and 80 if they had ever been the victim of either completed or attempted rape, sexual molestation, robbery or assault. The women were also asked if they had ever suffered a nervous breakdown, thought of suicide or attempted suicide.

As expected, victims of crime suffered more psychological problems than nonvictims. Only 2.2 percent of the nonvictims had attempted suicide, as compared to 13.2 percent of victims of completed rape and attempted rape, molestations and robbery. Sex crimes, especially rape, caused the most severe mental consequences; 1 in 5 of the rape victims had attempted suicide, and more than twice that many said at one time thay had considered it seriously.

One surprising result was that while completed rape was psychologically worse for victims than was attempted rape, attempted sexual molestations and attempted robbery produced more serious mental problems than their completed counterparts. Kilpatrick speculates that imagination is the reason. When a threatening situation is left unresolved, victims are never sure what their assailants intended to do to them or how much danger they were actually in.

"For rape victims, their worst fears have been realized," he explains. "But victims of other attacks that were not completed do not know what they escaped." Kilpatrick believes that how a victim evaluates the danger that she was in will strongly affect whether emotional and psychological problems develop.[5]

---

[5] Elizabeth Stark, "The Psychological Aftermath," *Psychology Today* (February 1985).

The Rapist

Dr. Walter Bromberg, a psychoanalytically oriented psychiatrist who studied many rapists, perceived some as men who are afraid of women and who have no meaningful relationship with women.[6] A study by the staff of the Institute for Sex Research at Indiana University revealed that there is a good deal of similarity in the conduct of rapists despite the fact that the acts of one rapist are carried out quite independently of the acts of another rapist. The great majority of rapists try to avoid detection, do not join together to commit their crimes, and do not act compulsively. They can plan their crimes, and they give similar rationales for their behavior. The rapists' vocabularies of motives, according to the Indiana researchers, include "seemingly plausible accounts of their actions to prove their innocence." It was reported, for instance, that some rapists really believed that their victims willingly cooperated; "she didn't struggle," "she voluntarily removed her clothes," "she enjoyed it," "she encouraged me" are some of their descriptions of the woman's response.[7]

In a more recent study, Dr. A. Nicholas Groth, on the basis of his research with 500 convicted rapists, developed a classification system consisting of the following types of rape:

1. *Power Rape.* In this pattern, according to Groth, the rape becomes a form of domination and conquest. In many respects this fits the model Susan Brownmiller writes about, where the offender is acquisitory and sees the rape as a situation where he possesses the woman by physical force and dominance. This kind of rape usually involves a man who feels insecure about his masculinity, and the rape is his attempt to demonstrate that he has mastery over his victim. The rapist in this category often says, "Do what I say and you won't get hurt." He often holds his victim captive over a period of time, controlling her and raping her repeatedly.

2. *Anger Rape.* This is a form of rape in which the offender expresses his hostility towards women in general by selecting one woman and raping her. According to Groth, the sexual assault becomes a vehicle for discharging pent-up feelings of rage that have built up in the offender over a long period of time. The rape is an assault involving extreme physical brutality that goes far beyond the violence necessary simply to subdue the victim. Often, according to Groth, this type of rapist is not even sexually excited, and he may even be impotent during the attack. The

---

[6] Adapted from Walter Bromberg, *Crime and the Mind* (New York: Macmillan, 1965), pp. 88–91.

[7] Paul H. Gebhard, John H. Gagnon, Wardell B. Pomeroy, and Cornelia V. Christenson, *Sex Offenders, An Analysis of Types* (New York: Harper & Row, 1965), pp. 197–206.

offender in this type of rape often attempts to humiliate and degrade his victim by forcing her into acts of sodomy and fellatio.

3. *Sadistic Rape.* According to Groth, in this pattern of rape anger and power over the victim become eroticized. The offender finds mistreating his victim and performing sadistic acts on her erotically satisfying. This type of rapist often achieves orgasm by flagellating, burning, or cutting the victim. He often performs ritualistic acts on her. The Hillside Stranglers often tied their victims down and then shocked them with electric current. It is apparent that sadistic rapists suffer from a severe form of mental illness. The victim often represents someone the rapist believes has hurt him; he wants to harm his victim severely, and in many cases to murder her.[8]

On the basis of his research sample, Groth concluded that approximately 55 percent of his sample was comprised of power rapists, 40 percent were anger rapists, and about 5 percent were sadistic rapists.

The Dynamics of Sexual Assault

A pilot study was conducted by the Queen's Bench Foundation, an organization of female attorneys and judges, to explore the dynamics and interactions in sexual assault from the perspective of the sex offender. The research was directed toward understanding what precipitates a man to rape a particular woman, and what stops him. The 72 interviewed men were taken from a pool of 83 excessively violent rapists confined at Atascadero State Hospital, California, for treatment as mentally disordered sex offenders.

Over three-fourths of the offenders were strangers to the victims. In one-fifth of the cases, victim and offender were friends of some sort. Reasons for rapists choosing a victim are summarized in Figure 10.1.

According to most of the respondents in the study, power and dominance were the primary goals of the rapist. He wanted to overpower and control. Although no strategy of resistance was found to be 100 percent effective, perhaps the most important result of this study was the realization that women can, and do, deter sexual assault. Women can successfully resist violent rapists even in circumstances where resistance might appear to be futile. The study showed that victim resistance is highly correlated with deterrence of sexual assault. However, resistance incurred greater risks of injury.[9]

---

[8] Adapted from A. Nicholas Groth with Jean Birnbaum, *Men Who Rape* (New York: Plenum, 1979), Chapter 2.

[9] *Rape: Prevention and Resistance* (San Francisco: Queen's Bench Foundation, 1976), pp. 5–28.

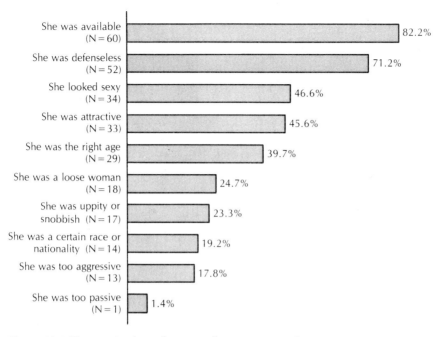

Figure 10.1 Factors in the selection of rape victims. [*Source: Rape: Prevention and Resistance* (San Francisco: Queen's Bench Foundation, 1976), p. 70.]

Most rapists attack total strangers. The women they attack are not necessarily young, beautiful, or seductive. In Los Angeles, for example, several women in their seventies and eighties were raped and killed. The man charged by the police with these brutal offenses was in his early thirties. More frequently, rapes are committed on young children. Rapists tend to attack in their own neighborhoods, principally in the late evening or early morning, and indoors. More than half the rapes are committed in the home of the victim, where she is likely to feel more secure and be less cautious.[10]

The Queen's Bench Foundation also conducted research into the circumstances of rape, the modes of rapists, and the strategies used by rape victims and attempted rape victims to resist sexual assault. In the four months between March and July, 1976, 68 victims of rape and 40 victims of attempted rape were interviewed. Most demographic differences between rape victims and attempted rape victims were not statistically significant. Most of the women were between 17 and 29, the majority were single, and most were living in metropolitan areas in neighborhoods they considered "safe" or "very safe." The attacker's age

[10] "Rape Alert," *Newsweek*, November 10, 1975, pp. 70–79.

and physique were not significantly associated with completion of the assault. Some of the findings were:

1. In 65 percent of the incidents the attacker's initial interaction with his victim was casual or even friendly.
2. Most of the women (61 percent) responded in a friendly or polite manner.
3. A period of interaction between the woman and her future assailant often preceded the attack.
4. The assault usually began with physical force or restraint.
5. Approximately half the attacks occurred indoors.

Some of the differences noted between the actions of rape victims and those of attempted rape victims were:

1. Attempted rape victims were more likely than rape victims to be suspicious of their future assailants.
2. Rape victims were more panicked and fearful than attempted rape victims.
3. Rape victims thought primarily of survival and death. Attempted rape victims considered methods of resistance.
4. Victims of attempted rape employed stronger forms of verbal resistance.
5. Attempted rape victims were more assertive physically.
6. More attempted rape victims screamed than did rape victims.[11]

In a study of 13 women, Pauline Bart concluded that

Women were more likely to avoid rape under the following circumstances: 1) when they were attacked by strangers, 2) when they used multiple strategies, screamed and physically struggled, 3) when the assault took place outside, and 4) when their primary concern was with not being raped. Women were more likely to be raped under the following circumstances: 1) when they were attacked by men they knew, particularly if they had had a prior sexual relationship with them, 2) when the only strategy they used was talking or pleading, 3) when the assault took place in their homes, 4) when their primary concern was with not being killed or mutilated, and 5) when there was a threat of force. . . .

Although we did not find prior experience to be an important variable differentiating outcome, we found that struggling and screaming were associated with avoiding rape, and talking (including pleading) as the sole strategy was the modal strategy when rape was not prevented. Moreover, the use of more than one strategy was associated with rape avoidance. In addition, we found that women were primarily concerned with avoiding murder and/or mutilation in the episodes ending in rape, an understandable fear given the newspaper coverage of sexual assault . . . while when these women avoided being raped, their primary concern was with not being raped. It was also found that women were more likely to avoid rape in the

---

[11] *Rape: Prevention and Resistance*, pp. 5–28.

episode in which they were attacked by a stranger, while they were more likely to be raped in the episode when they were attacked by a man they knew.[12]

Some experts on rape advocate "fight back," and others recommended "play for time." The controversy was interestingly depicted in the following article in *Time:*

When Frederic Storaska—beefy, confident, macho—arrives on a college campus for one of his celebrated lectures, he knows that two things are likely to happen: 1) many women in the audience will be enthusiastic, even adoring; and 2) feminists outside will picket and denounce him as a leering chauvinist showman and just plain wrong on how to avoid rape.

Storaska vs. the feminists is the longest-running mongoose-and-cobra act in the field of rape prevention. Storaska, 39, holder of a black belt in karate, is the star of a 1975 film called *How to Say No to a Rapist and Survive,* still one of the most widely shown educational movies ever. . . .

Storaska's style can be abrasive. Feminists condemn as inappropriate his constant attempts at humor, which he says help women relax. (Sample: in ridiculing women who rely on Mace or any other spray to protect them, "What are you going to do if the wind is blowing in your face? Say to him, 'Excuse me, but would you mind raping me from the other direction?' ") He acts bewildered by the personal attacks. In interviews, Storaska out-feminizes the militant feminists, proclaiming that the rape impulse is deeply embedded in a male-dominated society. What, then, do the militants really have against him? "Testosterone," he quips.

He might have put it more delicately; many feminists are no longer interested in listening to lectures by men on rape, and some rape crisis centers do not welcome men on the premises. Still, the real issue is neither the Storaska style nor hormones, but his basic advice: Play for time, use your wits, and go along with the rapist until you have a chance to react safely. Feminists and many rape-resistance experts think it is far better to scream, run or struggle immediately. In one of Storaska's favorite examples, a female student is accosted by a male who says sharply: "I want you to get in that car." Thinking quickly, the woman says "Great!", tells the man she followed him out from the dance, then gives him a peck on the cheek. She says she has to go back inside to tell her friend not to wait for her. Once safely inside, she screams rape.

Some feminists hate the idea of using such seductive techniques even in self-defense. Says an anti-Storaska brochure from the Syracuse Rape Crisis Center: "We are concerned about the self-image of a woman who responds with feigned affection to a rapist, and is still unsuccessful in avoiding rape. Then what about her guilt, her anger, her feeling of being used?" Feminists also complain that if women use Storaska's system and fail, the rapist can rarely be convicted.[13]

---

[12] Pauline B. Bart, "A Study of Women Who Both Were Raped and Avoided Rape," *Journal of Social Issues* 37, no. 4 (1981).

[13] "Deadly Dilemma for Women," *Time,* September 21, 1981. Copyright 1981 Time Inc. All rights reserved. Reprinted by permission from TIME.

The research evidence is contradictory on whether a woman should fight back or not. In her study, Bart concluded that fighting back usually works. Another study concluded that while resistance or immediate flight notably increases a victim's chances of escape, it also increases the odds of sustaining heavy injuries. Another unknown factor is related to the victim's later feelings, after the crime. Perhaps if she attempts to fight back, she will feel less like a victim who has capitulated to her atrocious assailant.

The Child Molester

The molester of children usually has a long history of personal inadequacy and psychosexual immaturity. He is usually unable to relate intimately to adult women, whom he fears. Child molesters are not very active sexually, except for some very perverse psychopaths. They are generally sexually retarded; consequently, they resort to children as easy victims for their sexual advances. Some older men whose sexual activity is considerably limited may also turn to children.

One man who was an admitted pedophile gave an interview to a reporter; the resulting article, published anonymously in *Los Angeles* magazine, provides some insights into this type of offender:

> Nick looks like the Marlboro man, gracefully slipping into middle age. He's 49, six-foot-three and wears a blue quilted jacket, Levi's and boots, a black Stetson on his head. His furrowed face looks as if it were carved out of marble. Sipping coffee at Arthur J's, said by police to be a frequent Hollywood gathering place for teenage runaways, Nick talks frankly about his particular predilection—for young boys.
>
> A self-professed pedophile—with otherwise "normal" bisexual tendencies—Nick served three and a half years at Patton State Hospital for sexually molesting young boys. Two of his victims were 11-year-old twin brothers. He has three teenagers of his own, all in foster homes, and says he turned to sex with minors when his wife walked out on him. Now, thanks to therapy at Patton, he's managed to curb his appetite for underage boys, who, as he tells it, are not difficult to find.
>
> "I used to get young boys aged 14 to 16 to baby-sit my three children. I'd tell their parents I was going out to play poker and would probably not be home until 4 or 5 in the morning, and the boy could sleep overnight. I never went anywhere—I stayed home. People were fooled by my outward appearance. No one had the slightest idea that I was molesting their child. The parents knew me and my family, and trusted me completely."
>
> Nick says the average child molester is light-years from the stereotypic image of the lurker in a raincoat hanging around alleys and restrooms. "He's more likely to be that nice man who lives down the street who lets your kids play in his yard and fix their bikes in his garage. Or maybe he's working as a youth counselor or scoutmaster. The molesters I met at Patton said they found jobs that put them close to youngsters. Like me, many were married with kids of their own. This gives opportunities for them to molest children with the least risk of discovery."

In what is perhaps a self-serving statement, Nick claims that he seldom met a boy or girl over the age of 12 who had not already had some sexual experience with a peer or adult. And, in what is a sad commentary on the state of the American family, he felt that in many cases he gave the kids the kind of love, attention and affection they lacked in their own homes. "We looked for kids who were unhappy at home."[14]

In an attempt to sustain a definition of himself as a "normal" person, the pedophile may deny performing the act or claim that, at the time of the act, he was powerless to control his behavior. This process has been referred to as deviance disavowal. Disavowal by the child molester may take the form of claiming he was under the influence of alcohol at the time.

In a study designed to find out whether deviance disavowal is indeed employed, researchers interviewed 158 male child molesters. Each was asked to give an explanation of why he committed the offense for which he was convicted. He also was asked to explain why he thought others committed similar offenses. The explanations were divided as follows: (1) those admitting sexual contact with no mention of drinking, (2) those admitting sexual contact with mention of drinking, and (3) those denying any sexual contact. There was no mention of how much alcohol was consumed.

Of the 158 subjects, 109 suggested what should be done with other molesters. These divided into "punitive" and "nonpunitive" dispositions. Those who wanted a punitive disposition expressed some violent action, such as "break his neck"; those who preferred a nonpunitive disposition urged more understanding, such as "give him another chance" or "give him psychiatric help."

The difference between those who admitted to their offenses but claimed to be drinking at the time and those who denied their offenses was not significant. But the difference between *both these groups* and those admitting their offenses without reference to alcohol was significant. Reference to alcohol apparently enables many molesters to admit their offenses and yet avoid identity with other molesters.[15]

J. H. Fitch studied and classified 147 men convicted of sex offenses against children and received in Bristol prison in 1956. In 1960, a follow-up study indicated that 139 of those convicted had been out of prison for over a year and 8 had not yet been released. The 139 men who

---

[14] *Los Angeles* magazine, May 1981. Reprinted by permission of *Los Angeles* magazine. Copyright May 1981.

[15] Charles H. McCaghy, "Drinking and Deviance Disavowal: The Case of Child Molesters," *Social Problems* 16 (Summer 1968):43–49. See also Charles H. McCaghy, "Child Molesters: A Study of Their Careers as Deviants," in *Criminal Behavior Systems*, ed. Marshall B. Clinard and Richard Quinney (New York: Holt, Rinehart and Winston, 1967), pp. 76–88.

had been released were the subjects of the study. The 77 men who had been convicted of heterosexual offenses were compared with the 62 who had been convicted of homosexual offenses. No age differences were found between the two groups, the median age for each being about 36. This is above the median age of the general prison population, but it is usual for child molesters. The offenses that had resulted in conviction were gross indecency, buggery (sodomy), rape, carnal knowledge of a minor, and indecent assault. Indecent assault is a less serious offense than the others, although there is not much difference in actual behavior. A plea of guilty to indecent assault is often accepted to avoid trial for one of the more serious assaults. The study showed no significant difference between the homosexual and the heterosexual offenders in type of offense. Nor was there any difference in intelligence. The only significant difference between the two categories was in length of time served. The homosexual offender served a much longer sentence in prison for the same type of offense. More homosexuals had good employment records, principally as professionals, office workers, and entertainers. More heterosexuals were either unemployed or were manual or semi-skilled workers. More homosexuals were single men, and more of them were subsequently convicted of sex offenses. Twenty-six of the heterosexuals had committed incest, molesting children in their own families. Only two homosexuals had committed such acts.

The subjects were classified into five categories on the basis of Fitch's psychological evaluation:

1. *Immature* Those whose offenses appeared to be caused by their inability to identify themselves with an adult sexual role. Acting out infantile fantasies—emotionally immature.
2. *Frustrated* Those whose offenses seemed to be a reaction against sexual emotional frustration at an adult level. Reverted to primitive modes of behavior when made to feel insecure or rejected. Turned to their children (incest) when made to feel inadequate by their wives. [Of course, the wife is not at fault. Only emotionally disturbed men turn to their children to act out their frustrations.]
3. *Sociopathic* Generally those who committed the act with complete strangers. Impulsively acting out temporary aggressive moods.
4. *Pathological* Those who were unable to control sexual impulse as a result of psychosis, mental defect, organic impairment, or premature senile deterioration.
5. *Miscellaneous* Not included in any of the above. Those whose isolated and impulsive acts did not appear to relate to any obvious pattern of emotional or sexual difficulty.

The sociopathic group had the highest percentage of reconvictions for both sexual and nonsexual offenses. It should be noted, however, that the total number of sociopaths in the study was 19, or 14 percent of the total number of child molesters.[16]

My own research with child molesters I have treated in therapy groups in the late 1980s supports Fitch's earlier observations on pedophiles.

Child molesters are difficult to treat because many of them are compulsive repeat offenders. One view of what might be done with child molesters was revealed by psychiatrist Dr. Roland Summit in an article titled "Society Vs. the Child Molester":

> Every so often a sexually assaulted child is murdered. We understand murder. We *believe* murder. So we clamor for action and appeasement.
>
> We are appalled when we learn, as is so often the case, that the suspected killer is a known sexual offender—previously apprehended, convicted, treated and released. We are aghast to learn that the man driving the ice-cream truck, reading the meter or leading the choir could be a registered child molester. When a child is murdered, we worry about these things. In between killings, we tend to forget.
>
> For each tortured body there are thousands of tortured minds: children who are befriended, molested and betrayed, usually by someone whom they and their parents know and trust. The murdered child speaks louder than these silent prey; less than 5% of the surviving victims complain to the authorities, very few of these complaints are prosecuted, and still fewer lead to any meaningful control of the offender.
>
> The sadistic killer draws our righteous indignation against child predators as a whole. The vast majority of child molesters will never maim or kill a child. Most are convinced that they are doing a service, bringing love and joy to sexually neglected children. Pedophiles gain our trust and entrap our children with impunity. Children may protect their secret rather than risk rejection and punishment by telling. We believe that a stranger could kill a child for lust. We can't imagine that our neighbor could captivate our child for love. We believe in a lifeless victim; it's hard to trust a living one.
>
> While it is true that most child molesters are not homicidal, it also is true that those who eventually turn to murder started out with less violent patterns of sexual assault. Another truth crying for prevention is that career pedophiles begin early, even in childhood, molesting younger children as they themselves have been molested.
>
> The challenge for protecting children is not to single out the end-stage homicidal monsters, nor even to keep all known child molesters in jail. There is no jail large enough, no juries sure enough, no children strong enough to withstand the courtroom trauma, and no sentences long enough to keep most offenders behind bars. Our burden is to recognize the offenders in our midst, to challenge their access to children and to block their

---

[16] J. H. Fitch, "Men Convicted of Sex Offenses Against Children: A Follow-up Study," *British Journal of Sociology* 13 (July 1962):18–37. Copyright 1962 by Routledge & Kegan Paul Ltd. Reprinted by permission.

escalating addiction, even as we hold them responsible to lawful, productive citizenship.[17]

Incest

Child molestation, whether committed by a stranger or an acquaintance, has a devastating impact on the victim. When the perpetrator is a family member, the emotional consequences are even more devastating. Sexual abuse by close relatives produces severe long-term negative emotional effects on the child.

A case described by Rebecca Trounson, who interviewed one incest victim, reveals some of these effects:

THE RAPES ARE HISTORY BUT THE BITTERNESS NEVER ENDS

Each June, Susan, a 32-year-old mother of two, forces herself to buy a Father's Day card, scanning the displays for one with an innocuous, unsentimental message.

"I search and search for one that's plain, almost boring in fact," she said. "I just can't send him one that says, 'Thank you for the terrific childhood.' "

Susan was forced to submit to sexual intercourse with her father almost daily from the time she was 12 to the day she moved out of the house at 18, she said in a recent interview. She felt she could not tell her mother, who remained unaware of the abuse even though she was frequently in the house at the time it occurred, Susan said.

She had always been the favorite of her father's two daughters, said Susan, a Los Angeles County resident who asked that her real name not be used.

"He told me I was the brightest, the prettiest, the best at everything I did," she said. "We were inseparable. But the love turned into possessiveness and eventually into a distortion of itself.

"He kept telling me that it was okay—that it was normal. I was afraid . . . to say no, afraid that he would get mad at me."

When she grew older and began to resist him, he beat her with a belt.

Throughout the period of the abuse, she tried to maintain an outwardly normal appearance, Susan said. She did well in high school, was a cheerleader and dated a football player. She attended church regularly and sang in the choir.

"But when I got home, I was a prisoner," she said. "Once I got in the door, I could never leave. I had headaches and crying spells and nightmares. I was kept from going out and he stole my car out of the school parking lot once to punish me.

"I hated him with everything in me. I couldn't stand to be near him. I wished that he would die and then it would solve it. Once a friend of ours

---

[17] Roland Summit, "Society Vs. the Child Molester," *Los Angeles Times*, February 20, 1987.

was killed and I went to the funeral. I saw his children crying and I felt so guilty that I had wished my father would die."

According to child-abuse specialists, guilt is the single most common and potentially most serious effect of sexual child abuse. Like Susan, the victims almost always blame themselves—not only for hating the abuser, but for somehow causing the incident to occur. . . .

"Even a child of five or six can believe that it was her fault, that if she hadn't been so seductive he wouldn't have molested her," said Dr. Michael Durfee, who is in charge of the child-abuse unit of the Los Angeles County Department of Health Services. "How can a child that age be seductive?

"But they take responsibility anyway. That's one of the great truths—children take responsibility," he said. "Responsibility for what they think of as their role as temptress and also for not telling someone and stopping the abuse. And then if they do tell someone, they may take responsibility for breaking up their families or sending someone to jail."

Susan said she never told anyone because she was afraid that if her parents were to divorce, she might have to live with her father. "I just hoped that someone would notice there was something different about me. I wanted someone to know and come and take care of it."

Her attempts to maintain a normal appearance and family life have continued into her adulthood. Her parents visit her once a year, usually staying in her home for several weeks. And she continues to buy the Father's Day cards.

"I still love him because he's my father. But I hate him for what he did to me," she said.

Susan told her mother only last August. She learned then that her father had destroyed her credibility with her mother when Susan was a teenager by telling her that the girl was unruly and untrustworthy and that he would keep an eye on her.

"Now I have to talk to him, to get rid of the responsibility for this," she said. "I have to ask him why, if he's sorry, what he was thinking and what was going on with his life. I have to know, to get rid of the guilt."

Durfee and others said the guilt often leads to diminished self-esteem that can culminate in self-hate. Its short-term effects may include behavior problems, promiscuity, trouble in school, and depression.

Older victims of sexual abuse often become "psychological time bombs," according to Kee MacFarlane, program specialist of the National Center on Child Abuse and Neglect in Washington, D.C.

"For many of these people, it takes years before they can break out and tell someone," MacFarlane said. "By that time, they've tried to bury the memories, divorcing their minds from their bodies. They become so numb to pain and turmoil in their lives that they decide they'll never feel anything again, never be hurt again."[18]

The incest offender violates not only law, but universal taboo. Incest as a detected offense is relatively rare. Aggressive incest is primarily a

---

[18] Rebecca Trounson, "The Rapes Are History but the Bitterness Never Ends," *Los Angeles Times*, October 22, 1981. Copyright, 1981, *Los Angeles Times*. Reprinted by permission.

male activity, though the extent to which the female partner encourages or cooperates in the activity may indicate her deviation. Among detected incest offenders, fathers who commit incest with their daughters are most frequent. Young men may be more likely to commit incest with their sisters than fathers with their daughters, but their behavior is not so likely to be detected. Mothers rarely commit incest with their sons.

It is likely that a great deal of incest goes unreported. For incest to come to the attention of the police, one of the participants would have to inform on a member of his or her immediate family. All members of the family would then suffer from the resulting stigmatization. Where a young girl is partner to an incestuous relationship with her father, the most frequent type of incest, the publicity and the court experience would perhaps be far more damaging to her than the sex act itself.

In my psychotherapy work with over 600 female adolescents in a psychiatric hospital in recent years (1984–1989), I have noted that a considerable number of these delinquent girls had family problems and acted out as incorrigible runaways, substance abusers, or prostitutes. During this six-year period, I found that of this sample at least 40 percent, or 240 girls, revealed in therapy that they had been sexually abused by one or more members of their families. (I would estimate that at least another 10 percent were abused but would not reveal their secret.) The abuser was usually the father or stepfather, but the violators included older brothers and uncles. In the hundreds of group therapy sessions I directed with these girls, I determined that the emotional pain and sense of injustice about being a victim of sexual abuse was a primary factor in propelling them into delinquent behavior and, in many cases, a later life of crime. (This issue will be discussed more fully in Chapter 14.)

SEX OFFENSES NOT HARMFUL TO OTHERS

Prostitution and Crime

Prostitution stirs more mixed emotions than most other sexual offenses. It is a pattern of male-female sexual activity that is mentioned in all the annals of humanity. The Bible has many references to it. Through the ages it has at times been required of some women, at other times tolerated, and at still other times forbidden. In the Judaic tradition, the prostitution of Jewish women was forbidden and prostitution was confined to foreign women. Early Christianity was essentially antisex. However, in the Middle Ages prostitution was tolerated as a necessary evil. Saint Augustine held this view. "Suppress prostitution," he said, "and capricious lusts will overthrow society." In the thirteenth century, Saint Thomas Aquinas took a similar position, arguing in his *Summa*

Theologica that prostitution is a necessary evil, preventing seduction and rapes.

A study of 200 street prostitutes in San Francisco was directed by Dr. Mimi Silbert and funded by the National Institute of Mental Health; it revealed a great deal about how women become prostitutes. One interesting finding was that about two-thirds of the 200 prostitutes ran away from home to escape sexual or other brutality in their homes. Dr. Silbert is executive director of the Delancey Street Foundation, a residential program for various people, including former drug addicts and former prostitutes. Silbert noticed that most of the women who sought help at Delancey Street had early sexual abuse in common.

The women of Delancey Street made the study unique in that the research was carried out by former prostitutes. The study was reported in an article by Janice Mall in the *Los Angeles Times*. Her article was based on an interview with Ayola Pines, who had assisted Silbert with the study. Pines noted that:

> The prostitutes used as researchers "got the kind of information social scientists can't get. They knew the games, if someone was not being honest, and said so. They did interviews lasting two to four hours on the background, home, history of sexual abuse and life on the street." The study was not a representative study of prostitutes in general, Pines said, but a study of the bottom, street prostitutes. "There are," she said, "no happy hookers."
>
> "We found two major profiles or trends," said Pines. "The most prevalent was a surprise to us." That was the finding that two thirds of the girls had landed in the streets because of sexual abuse at home. "People say these are life choices," said Pines, "that prostitution is a career like any other. They should look at girls 10 or 11 or 12 who are prostitutes because they have no other way to live. They are afraid of the police because the police would take them home. In abusive homes children are reluctant to accuse, to testify. This was the most prevalent, most tragic background among prostitutes."
>
> The other third of the street girls were very poor minority young people who started [in] prostitution because nothing else was available to them, Pines said. One girl told the interviewer, "My mother was a whore, my grandmother was a whore, my sister is a whore. My sister took me out on the street and showed me what to do." These children's lives are not as pathological as those of the young runaways, Pines said, because they have support. "They're trapped, but it's not as terrible as for these young women who have no one in the world."
>
> Pines described an 11-year-old who was asked by the interviewer, whom she had just met, if she had anyone to whom she could talk about her life. "Not before, but now I have you," the girl replied. "Many of the girls said thank you to the interviewers," Pines said. "It was the first time they had ever had someone to talk to about themselves."
>
> Among the 200 girls interviewed only about 10 were addicted to drugs and started prostitution to support the habit. Many runaway children thought they could support themselves by working at jobs such as baby-

sitting. "But of course they can't," said Pines. "And they're really not thinking when they run away. They're just running from abuse. They come to the bus depot and there's no social worker waiting. There's a pimp or some woman who works for a pimp."[19]

Patterns of Prostitution

The Legalized Brothel　In some countries prostitution is a legal commercial venture. Brothels are licensed and regulated by the government in an effort to minimize the negative impacts of venereal disease and organized crime. These two side effects of prostitution are generally present in situations where prostitution is illegal.

In his classic book on prostitution, Charles Winick described Nevada prostitution. The practice is accepted in most counties of the state. Mustang Ranch, one of many licensed brothels, is the largest, doing an annual business in the millions. The house rules are not too strict, but drugs and sloppy clothes are not allowed. There are 50 women working for the establishment at any given time. They are regularly inspected by physicians and are required to hang their health certificates on the wall, a practice of some significance in the era of AIDS. The women are free to accept or reject customers for any reason. They may, for example, discriminate against clients from different ethnic backgrounds.[20] Whether or not the legal brothel has resulted in an increase or decrease in venereal disease cannot be established. It has, however, decreased the activity of police and courts in dealing with prostitution. The Mustang Ranch is so legitimate that in 1989 public stocks were sold on Wall Street and elsewhere by the owner, Joseph Conforte.

The Illegal Brothel　In the United States most brothels operate illegally. One such brothel was described as a luxurious East Side apartment house catering to New York businessmen. The apartment has two bedrooms, and after hours it is the residence of the madam in charge. The proprietor of the brothel receives a minimum of several thousand dollars every few days, tax free. A trick (a sexual act) costs anywhere from $100 to $500, and the money is divided with the hooker. The madam is always looking for new girls to satisfy her customers. She usually hears of girls from other hookers.

The owner considers her apartment a clean, respectable place that gentlemen can frequent. She avoids troublesome and aging hookers. Troublesome hookers are those who give out their home telephone

---

[19] Janice Mall, "A Study of S.F.'s Unhappy Hookers," *Los Angeles Times*, February 19, 1982. Copyright, 1982, *Los Angeles Times*. Reprinted by permission.

[20] Charles Winick and Paul M. Kinsie, *The Lively Commerce: Prostitution in the United States* (Chicago: Quadrangle, 1971), p. 221.

numbers and those who don't share the money they have made from a client. The police are often bribed to ignore the illegal brothel.

The Streetwalker In many respects the streetwalker is at the bottom of the prostitution hierarchy. According to various research, the typical "hustler" drifts to an urban area in her late teens or early twenties after experiencing unsatisfactory working conditions and social maladjustment at home. She obtains work as a waitress or counter help, and for a time she lives a rootless, disorganized life without friends and without ties to stabilizing social institutions. During this crucial period she is tense, dissatisfied, bitter, and bewildered. Her alienated way of life brings her into contact with established prostitutes, whose superficial finery and seeming security are appealing. Her morale is at a low ebb, and, hungry for some kind of friendship and affection, she accepts dates arranged for her by a prostitute friend (or by the prostitute's pimp).

She becomes aware that she is moving outside the pale of lawful society when she is arrested. After a time the arrest experience comes to be viewed as an occupational risk. Eventually she becomes stabilized in her calling, finds her friends almost exclusively in the underworld, and acquires recognized status as a prostitute. Many street hustlers are teenage runaways.

The Call Girl In the higher echelons of prostitution is the call girl, who usually maintains her own apartment and keeps a "book" in which she lists the names and phone numbers of her clients. Generally she responds to calls; however, she may also use her book of names to solicit. Harold Greenwald, who made an intensive psychiatric study of call girls in New York, maintained that they show a deep hatred of men, demonstrate a pattern of homosexuality, and have strong suicidal tendencies. He claimed that call girls are characterized in particular by biparental rejection of the most severe kind and that in many cases this factor is the most important explanation of their behavior.

Greenwald saw prostitution as an attempt to replace affection that was missed in childhood. The curious relationships between many prostitutes and pimps, to whom they turn over a large part of their earnings, he saw as an attempt by the call girls to overcome loneliness and form a relationship with someone who seems to be lower than themselves as a human being.[21]

Massage Parlors The massage parlor has, to an extent, come to be regarded as a type of illegal brothel. Police are raiding them frequently and harassing owners, in efforts either to enforce the law or to obtain payoffs. The numbers of massage parlors around the United States

---

[21] Harold Greenwald, *The Call Girl* (New York: Ballantine, 1958).

increased in the 1980s. They rank from hole-in-the wall dens to luxurious establishments. Some parlors cater to a hundred customers a day, seven days a week.

The Drug Addict–Prostitute A relatively recent addition to the world of prostitution, particularly in the United States, is the drug addict–prostitute. Like the male drug addict, the female addict finds after a time that she must turn to an illegal activity to support her expensive drug habit. Prostitution is the illegal activity most readily available to her.

A large percentage of streetwalkers are addicts. Call girls are not generally found on the drug scene. It is estimated that 90 percent of the female addicts engage in prostitution at one time or another because prostitution is a quick source of funds necessary to support their drug habits and the habits of the men with whom they live. In recent years, with the spread of heroin use to high schools and junior high schools, teenage streetwalkers have made their appearance.

Kingsley Davis made the point that prostitution is essentially caused by social and economic conditions. He also indicated that it is a most functional pattern in the web of our society and will not easily be eliminated. His commentary is interesting, although it is a more controversial position now than it was in 1961, when he made the following statement:

> The most persistent form of prostitution is the pure commercial form. Whether in brothels or in the streets, under bridges or in automobiles, this form is practiced everywhere and remains at the bottom of the social scale. Although its scope may be contracted by sex freedom and "amateur competition," the practice itself is not likely to be displaced. Not only will there always be a system of social dominance which gives a motive for selling sexual favors, and a scale of attractiveness which creates the need for buying them, but this form of prostitution is, in the last analysis, economical, enabling a small number of women to take care of the needs of a large number of men. It is the most convenient sexual outlet for armies and for the legions of strangers, perverts, and physically repulsive in our midst. It performs a role which apparently no other institution fully performs.[22]

In an effort to combat the problems of young prostitutes in major urban areas, especially New York and Los Angeles, halfway houses or havens for "hookers" have emerged. These organizations provide shelter, protection from the woman's pimp, and counseling. An organization of this type, Children of the Night, was established in Los Angeles. In an article in the *Los Angeles Times*, Michael Capaldi delineated the approach of these haven organizations:

---

[22] Kingsley Davis, "Prostitution," in *Contemporary Social Problems*, eds. Robert K. Merton and Robert A. Nisbet (New York: Harcourt Brace Jovanovich, 1961), p. 288.

PIONEER PROGRAM FOR YOUNG PROSTITUTES

Leann's blond hair frames eyes made larger from the makeup. She puts on an indigo chiffon blouse with flecks of silver, designer jeans, and sharp-heeled pumps under upturned cuffs.

As she dresses, it is 10:30 on a Saturday night. Soon she will meet the army of prostitutes in Hollywood. Tonight Leann will be back on Sunset Boulevard.

On the boulevard, as she watches the hookers stroll, she talks about the fear in the street life.

"You never know who you are in the car with. It could be anyone. A cop, some guy who is going to stab you or beat you up. Some girls get killed. But you never want to refuse money because your pimp sets a quota. Never, unless you're really scared."

Leann was a prostitute for nine years. In those years—from age 15 to 24—she was arrested several times, strung out on heroin (for seven years) and labeled incorrigible by police and social workers. She worked Sunset Boulevard most of the time.

But tonight she is here for a different reason. She is approaching young prostitutes and telling them that there is a way out of the life.

That way out is Children of the Night, a pioneer program to aid child prostitutes. The program began virtually by accident in 1979 when Lois Lee, then a UCLA graduate student in sociology, was studying the bond between prostitutes and their pimps.

"I wondered," Lee recalled, "why a girl would stand on a street corner and do something deplorable, then give all her money to a pimp."

In the course of the interviews, Lee's heart went out to the young hookers, some in their early teens, and she began offering her small apartment as a temporary shelter for boys and girls seeking to escape the pimps and street life.

Leann was among the first of Lee's street contacts, and eventually asked to be taken in.

Since then Leann has become one of the most effective of the 20 full- and part-time counselors who have had marked success in convincing young prostitutes to stay off the streets. Children of the Night offers workable alternatives to the life. When Leann goes back to the prostitution hot spots of Hollywood, her objective is simply to meet the kids and give them Children of the Night's hot line phone number.

Like Lee and the rest of Children of the Night's staff, Leann's style is bold. Typically, she walks up to a young hooker, engages her in conversation and offers help if she wants it. The help offered is usually advice, food, legal assistance or refuge from an abusive pimp.

Many of the teenagers are skeptical. They may suspect that Children of the Night is a cult group, a religious outreach program or a con outfit. Leann remembers when Lee first approached her about five years ago.

"I told her, 'Go away, I don't have time for you. My pimp won't let me talk to anybody unless they're a customer.'"

Her reaction was not rare. But like most of the kids, Leann took a business card. Later she called.

Lee has spent the last four years refining this approach, but still seems an unlikely sort for this kind of work when she is on the street. She is blonde, sweet-faced, smiling and seemingly too young to be a mother figure to these runaway prostitutes. Lee is only 10 years older than many of the girls and boys she has taken in.

Leann remembers the late nights, years ago, when she called Lois Lee in tears.

"I never had a key to my house because I lived with my pimp. I used to call Lois when I first met her and say, 'Lois, I can't go home, I didn't make $500, I only have $375 and Rob won't let me come home.'"

Lee took her in. Since those days Lee and her staff have housed more than 250 reforming prostitutes and have placed hundreds more in foster homes.

What began as an informal and temporary attempt to help a few kids soon ballooned. Crowding into her two bedroom south Beverly Hills home was a constant flock of kids, as many as eight at a time. They stuck with Lee wherever she went.

"I used to pack them all up into my old car," Lee smiled, "and drive all the way to San Diego where I had classes to take. We were a strange group, like a mother hen and her line of kids piling into the classroom."

Sometimes a pimp has sought retribution for his loss.

Lee tells of a time when one of her girls testified against her former pimp and the pimp threatened to have the girl killed. Lee informed the detectives working on the case who responded with their own threat to the pimp.

"They told him," Lee said, "that if that girl so much as skins her knee, they'd come down on him like a ton of bricks." . . .

Lee's new facility is aimed at one thing: To build a family for the children who do not know one.

People familiar with street life agree that the sometimes incredible bond between a young hooker and her pimp is predicated on her desire for a strong father figure. A pimp will abuse his girls, beat them mercilessly and feed them drugs. But it is treatment not overwhelmingly different than what they knew at home. Even in the face of such brutality, a pimp's girls generally compete for his attention.

"A lot of these girls are addicted to the life. Their pimps are the substitute fathers that they are usually lacking at home. Believe it or not, a lot of girls even call their pimps 'daddy,'" said Clapp, a 17-year police veteran.

Lee sums up the approach: "We take care of everything. Essentially, we assume the role of the pimp."[23]

OTHER SEX-RELATED OFFENSES

The Decriminalization of Abortion

On January 22, 1973, the U.S. Supreme Court, in a landmark decision, ruled that women have the constitutional right to abortion in the first six

---

[23] Michael Capaldi, "Pioneer Program for Young Prostitutes," *Los Angeles Times*, August 9, 1981. Copyright, 1981, Michael Capaldi. Reprinted by permission of the author.

months of pregnancy, and that in the first three months of pregnancy the decision of whether or not an abortion is to be performed is to be left solely to the woman and her doctor. The effect of this decision is to prohibit regulation of abortion by the states in the first three months of pregnancy.[24] In July, 1976, the Supreme Court handed down two important decisions reinforcing the 1973 ruling. In a five-to-four decision the Court ruled that states may not impose blanket restrictions requiring women under 18 to obtain parental permission for an abortion. In a six-to-three ruling in the same case, the Court held that a woman's husband need not consent to her abortion.

Prior to this decision, most states in the United States had laws providing for punishment of anyone committing an abortion. Penalties ranged from 1 year in prison in Kansas to 20 years in Mississippi. In 15 states, the woman upon whom the abortion was performed was guilty of a felony. The pressure of church organizations, most particularly the Roman Catholic church, kept strict abortion laws in force. The destruction of a fetus was viewed as equivalent to the murder of a human being.

The liberalization of the abortion laws has greatly reduced criminality by providing people who had a need for a service with a lawful way of satisfying that need. However, the controversy over abortion continues. So-called "Right to Life" groups see abortion as being the murder of a human being; more liberal feminist organizations see antiabortion legislation as an invasion of a woman's right to control her own body. I favor the latter group's position for two reasons: First, women do have the right to decide whether or not they wish to have a child; and second, if this right is denied it will not prevent abortions—it will only create a dangerous situation through the revival of totally unnecessary criminal abortions. I see no good reason for enlarging the crime problem and, at the same time, creating a dangerous situation for women who choose to abort a fetus. However, the controversy about legal abortion and the issues involved rages on in the United States. "Right to Life" advocacy groups picket abortion clinics, and at this writing the Supreme Court is considering a number of cases that could overturn its 1973 decision.

Pornography and the Sex Offender

Many federal, state, and local statutes make pornography illegal. New York and San Francisco permit almost every type of pornography with the exception of actual sex acts. Even state laws that are very restrictive and punitive differ greatly, however. Many people are in prison for violating laws against pornography, and a great many more people are prosecuted each year for such acts as selling or showing "obscene" films, books, pictures, and so on. Despite these facts, pornography is big

---

[24] Betty Liddick, "Effects of Supreme Court Abortion Ruling," *Los Angeles Times,* February 11, 1973.

business in the United States, a business which, according to some estimates, amounts to billions of dollars each year.

The press releases of law enforcement people give the impression that pornography causes sex crimes. Former FBI director J. Edgar Hoover, for example, was quoted as saying, "We know that in an overwhelming number of cases, sex crime is associated with pornography. We know that sex criminals read it, and are clearly influenced by it. I believe that if we can eliminate the distribution of such items among impressionable children, we shall greatly reduce our frightening crime rates." Mr. Hoover offered no statistics to support this extreme claim. In fact, none exist. Most studies indicate that pornography does not in any way influence the commission of sex crimes and may, in fact, through a sort of catharsis, tend to reduce them.

Despite considerable evidence to the contrary, a government study by then–attorney general Meese's Commission on Pornography in 1986 released a report that alleged a connection between pornography and sex offenses such as rape.

The basic research question—does pornography cause people (mostly men) to abuse, rape, and exploit others (mostly women)?—was never satisfactorily answered by the commission's report. The commission members, like many of their predecessors, did not even agree on what pornography is.

Among the members of the commission who dissented from the main report were Judith Becker, a behavioral scientist at Columbia University whose career has been devoted to evaluating and treating the victims and perpetrators of sex crimes, and Ellen Levine, the editor of *Woman's Day* magazine. They argued that the short time and the limited funds that had been granted to the commission meant that a "full airing of the differences" between its members, much less the issuing of a comprehensive report, was impossible, and that "no self-respecting investigator would accept conclusions based on such a study." Among their objections were the following:

- No effort was made to procure an accurate balanced sample of the varieties and distribution of pornography. Visual materials "were skewed to the very violent and extremely degrading." Portrayals of the violent degradation of women were limited to hard-core pornographic films. Many horror movies and popular films were ignored.
- Little effort was made to acquire testimony from people who enjoy pornography and do not believe they are harmed by it. The commission members were understandably sympathetic toward the victims of sex crimes who tearfully testified that their abusers loved pornography. However, the commission did not have any witnesses from the sample of millions of consumers of X-rated films, soft-core magazines, and erotica who freely admit that they enjoy this material—and are not sex offenders.

- Social science studies used in the report were conducted mostly on male college students who were volunteers; their results cannot be extrapolated to sex offenders or any other group.

The dissenters on the Commission on Pornography concluded: "To say that exposure to pornography in and of itself causes an individual to commit a sexual crime is simplistic, not supported by the social-science data, and overlooks many of the other variables that may be contributing causes."

Legal View of Pornography

The most recent ruling on pornography by the U.S. Supreme Court, in May, 1987, states that in deciding whether sexually explicit material is legally obscene, judges and juries must assess the social value of the material from the standpoint of a "reasonable person" rather than applying community standards. The five-to-four decision largely reaffirmed the Court's previous rulings on the restraints placed by the First Amendment on the government's power to make the sale of obscene materials a crime. The majority reversed a decision by an Illinois appellate court, which had upheld a trial judge's instruction that a jury should apply community standards in deciding the social value of sexually explicit works.

The Court said community standards should be considered only in deciding whether the prosecution has established the other two components of the three-part definition formulated in 1973 in *Miller* v. *California*. In that decision, the Court held that descriptions or depictions of sexual conduct may be banned as obscene in "works which, taken as a whole, appeal to the prurient interest in sex, which portray sexual conduct in a patently offensive way, and which, taken as a whole, do not have serious literary, artistic, political or scientific value."

In his opinion for the Supreme Court, Justice Byron R. White said, "The proper inquiry is not whether an ordinary member of any given community would find serious literary, artistic, political or scientific value in allegedly obscene material, but whether a reasonable person would find such value in the material, taken as a whole."

Homosexuality and Crime

Homosexuality is a form of sexual behavior that became more widely accepted in the late 1980s. Despite this, there are still laws on the books in many states that proscribe this form of sexual preference.

It is obviously not unlawful to be a homosexual. The basic illegality of homosexual behavior is the behavior proscribed in many states by sodomy laws. These laws, apart from their penalties, have two characteristics. First, while the laws have been applied almost exclusively to homosexual behavior, they make no distinction between heterosexual and homosexual acts. Second, the sodomy laws are variously expressed; the laws are not uniform as to the particular acts that are punishable.

Homosexuals in California may be prosecuted for violating Section 647 of the penal code, which provides that "every person who commits any of the following acts shall be guilty of disorderly conduct, a misdemeanor: *(a)* Who solicits anyone to engage in or who in any public place or in any place open to the public or exposed to public view engages in lewd or dissolute conduct . . . *(b)* Who loiters in or about any toilet open to the public for the purpose of engaging in or soliciting any lewd or lascivious or any unlawful act." There have been efforts to pass legislation in many states revolving around a concept of "consenting adults." In brief, this means that any sexual relationship between "consenting adults" in private is legal. Although Section 647 of the California penal code was still in force in the 1980s, "consenting adult" legislation was passed in that state in 1976.

Homosexuals are frequently harassed by the police, and police brutality toward them has frequently been alleged. The general public reveals a degree of hostility and prejudice toward homosexuals. The result is discrimination in employment and in many professions, including the armed forces. Men applying for employment with the government or with companies that require security clearance suffer severe discrimination if they have ever been arrested and charged with homosexual behavior. A California attorney has informed me that several of his clients who had been found guilty of homosexual activity on the basis of very limited evidence were subsequently unable to secure employment in the large California factories working on government contracts. Job applicants are required to report any arrest and the reason for it. An arrest for homosexual solicitation usually results in the denial of security clearance. Even when security clearance is granted, the mere statement that a person had been arrested for homosexual behavior would cause many employers to refuse to hire him or her. The military forces have not responded in a uniform manner to personnel who admit to being homosexual.

Despite the continued existence of many outmoded and absurd laws on homosexuality, the major crime problem related to homosexuality in today's society is not the behavior of homosexuals. Rather, the problem is the behavior of many violent homophobic men's reactions to gay people. These individuals participate in what has become known as gay-bashing. An editorial by Damien Martin in the September 1, 1988, issue of the *New York Times* analyzed this insidious form of violence:

> The anti-gay attack on the Upper West Side of New York City—in which a group of teenagers surrounded two young men, taunted them with epithets, then beat and stabbed them—is neither surprising nor unusual. What is surprising is the amount of attention the event has received. But attention should also be focused on the factors that contribute to such violence, especially the hostile anti-gay statements of religious and political leaders.
>
> The institute of which I am executive director serves lesbian and gay

youth and their families. Every year, about 1,000 young people seek our help. By the time they call us, more than 40 percent have suffered from violence related to their sexual orientation, more than half of it at the hands of peers. All the others live in fear of discovery and thus of violence.

Harvey Milk High School in New York City was created by gay youths, partly because violence inflicted on young homosexuals made it impossible for some to stay in other schools. The homosexually oriented are constantly slandered by people at all levels of society. Indeed, some of those who should be in the forefront of the fight against bias-related violence—religious and political leaders—often encourage or condone physical attacks against gay men and lesbians.

In 1982, the Rev. Jimmy Swaggart published a pamphlet about the Bible in which he said that "God is saying here that not only is the homosexual worthy of death, but perhaps also those who approve of homosexuality."

In a book widely distributed to state and Federal legislators by right wing groups, the Rev. Ernst Rueda, a Roman Catholic priest, defended those who physically attack gay people "as social agents of the majority of the population."

Noach Dear, a New York City Councilman and an Orthodox Jew, has claimed on television that homosexuals would not be beaten up if they did not let people know they were gay—blaming the victims, not the perpetrators of violence.

In 1986, the Vatican issued a pastoral letter that stated that violence against homosexuals is "understandable." . . .

The message that they and our other so-called leaders send is quite clear: Beating up gay people is okay.

I could give page after page of instances of how violence against gay and lesbian adolescents by peers and others is fostered by those who should be their protectors. In front of an entire class, a New York City gym teacher told a gay male adolescent that since he wanted to "act like a girl" he could stay in the girls' section. Afterward, his classmates verbally and physically harassed him until he dropped out of school.

In Bangor, Maine, the school district cancelled a proposed Tolerance Day—organized after three students killed a gay man—because one of the scheduled speakers was a lesbian.

Concern about the corruption of children is often a rallying cry for anti-gay forces. The real corruption occurs when the majority of young people are given the idea that violence against someone who is different can be justified.

The danger in this is not just to gay and lesbian people. History should have taught us that once violence against any group is acceptable, other stigmatized groups are in danger.[25]

THE LAW AND THE SEX OFFENDER

As we have noted, our laws define certain types of sexual behavior as crimes and provide punishment for violators of these laws. Forcible

---

[25] Damien Martin, *New York Times*, September 1, 1988.

rape, for example, is defined as a crime in every state in the United States and is categorized in FBI statistics as a serious crime, second only to murder and nonnegligent homicide. Prostitution and commercialized vice are also specifically defined and penalized in all 50 states. The statutes are neither as clear nor as uniform with respect to voyeurism, exhibitionism, and other deviant sexual behavior.

Some forms of sexual deviance are specifically prohibited; others are included in the broad categories of assault, disorderly conduct, and vagrancy. There are major differences in the ways these offenses are defined and offenders are dealt with. Treatment of offenders depends greatly on local community attitudes and enforcement policies. In some communities, the minor sex offender is regarded merely as a nuisance, and police interfere only with public activities. In others, police agents and informers often stop just short of entrapment to develop evidence on which to base prosecutions for offenses amounting to relatively minor sexual deviance.

Many states have enacted sexual-psychopath laws providing for special treatment of repeat sex offenders, often without the protection of trial procedures. Two assumptions underlie these laws: (1) that the sex offender is dangerous, and (2) that the offender is a psychopath with a compulsion to commit sex offenses. We find, however, that "sexual psychopath" is a legal rather than clinical category. A court may determine that a person is a sexual psychopath without defining the term *psychopath* in the way it is understood by psychiatrists or psychologists. One analysis of the sexual-psychopath statutes in effect in 26 states that had enacted such laws led to the following conclusions:

1. All of them provide for the commitment of "psychopathic" sex offenders.
2. They are not in agreement on the definition of "psychopathic" sex offenders.
3. The most commonly used definition identifies him as "a person lacking the power to control his sexual impulses or having criminal propensities toward the commission of sex offenses."
4. Sixteen of the statutes provide that the offender must have been *convicted* of some *crime* or of a *specific sex crime* before the court can commit him for treatment.
5. Seven of the statutes *do not require a conviction.* All that is necessary is that the offender be *charged* with some crime.
6. Five statutes require only that cause be shown that the accused is probably a sexual psychopath.
7. Every sexual-psychopath statute provides for either compulsory or voluntary examination of the accused. In many states the qualifications of the examiner are not specified.
8. A hearing of some kind is usually provided for the purpose of determining whether one is a sexual psychopath. In some states the judge may hear or read any evidence . . . and make a determination without a hearing.

9. In most states, if the judge or jury decides that the accused is a sexual psychopath, he is sent to a state mental hospital or to the psychiatric division of the state penitentiary to receive special treatment for an *indeterminate period.*
10. Release is usually on parole and only after a determination that the individual is cured.[26]

Sexual-psychopath laws permit the state to deprive persons of liberty for indeterminate periods without the usual safeguards provided by criminal courts. Such persons are neither insane nor feebleminded, and they have not been successfully defined as a distinct class of abnormal persons. Most of the individuals committed pursuant to this leglislation are sex deviates in minor ways: Peeping Toms, exhibitionists, and the like. The more serious sex criminals are rarely touched in the operation of these laws.

THE COMMUNITY'S REACTION TO SEX OFFENDERS

When the public becomes disturbed by newspaper accounts of horrible sex crimes, it tends to lose sight of the fact that these accounts are published because the events they describe are *infrequent.* Those who would repeal sexual-psychopath statutes are not suggesting that the behavior of the sex criminal should be condoned. What they are suggesting is that laws against murder, rape, and aggravated assault can, if properly enforced, adequately protect society. The rate of serious sex crime is far below that of minor sex offenses.

When minor sex deviates become public nuisances, they can be charged with violations of statutes prohibiting disorderly conduct. A voluntary relationship between two adults need not be a matter of public interest unless it is carried on in a public place.

To formulate meaningful proposals for the treatment of the sex offender we must first rid ourselves of the misleading concept *sexual psychopath* and define the term *sex offender.* We have defined crime as an act in violation of the criminal law and made punishable by law as a felony or misdemeanor. What distinguishes the sex offender from any other offender is that the law violated prohibits a particular form of sexual activity. Persons convicted of forcible rape, who are usually aggressive heterosexuals, and persons found guilty of illegal homosexual behavior, whether passive or aggressive—all are classified as sex offenders. So are the shy withdrawn peeper and the extroverted exhibitionist. The term *sex offender,* therefore, does not indicate homogeneity of behavior or personality. All that sex offenders have in common is their

---

[26] Alan H. Swanson, "Sexual Psychopath Statutes: Summary and Analysis," *Journal of Criminal Law, Criminology and Police Science* 51 (July–August 1970):215–218.

conviction by the courts for the violation of statutes prohibiting certain forms of sexual activity.

A person convicted of a crime is generally given a psychological or psychiatric examination. In most states this is part of the presentence investigation. If such examination should reveal sexual or psychological deviation or a combination of the two, the individual could be sent to an instititution, one with a treatment program, if such an institution exists. A sexual or psychological deviate who is not dangerous can be placed on probation and treated in the community.

Many "sex offenders," like the witches of old, are branded for life. A penetrating statement by Duncan Donovan, a vice president of the American Civil Liberties Union, analyzes this issue:

> The law requiring former "sex offenders" in California to register with their local police departments is one of the dehumanizing practices reminiscent of the Puritans' branding adulterers with a scarlet "A." It contributes almost nothing to the well-being of the community while inflicting a crippling stigma on an otherwise law-abiding person.
>
> What constitutes a "sex offender" varies from place to place and from time to time. It seldom refers to an ax-murderer. In California, it is anyone convicted of rape, child molestation or lewd conduct—or seduction by the promise of marriage. The bulk of registrations are for so-called "victimless crimes" involving lewd conduct. Most of these are for sexual activity, or solicitation of sexual activity, in more-or-less public places—streets, parks, bars, theaters.
>
> A sampling of Southern California police departments indicates that registration has little or no value in criminal investigations. Yet registration endures, with devastating effect on individuals and, ultimately, on all society.
>
> The kind of personal damage that registration as a former "sex offender" can do was recently brought to the attention of the Lesbian and Gay Rights Chapter of the American Civil Liberties Union of Southern California. It was the case of an upper-middle-class man, happily married, the father of three children. I repeat, he was happily married. He had been convicted of an act of lewd conduct with another man. Now, totally beyond the price that he had to pay for that offense, he is registered, stigmatized with a criminal status and open to the whims of any police investigation. Long after the sentence against him has been passed and executed, the trauma to him and to his family remains, a continuing presence not unlike the scarlet letter of Hester Prynne. She lived in 17th Century Salem when that Puritan town was really a theocracy. But he lives in a democracy in which the church is separated from the state. . . .
>
> If this man had been a mass murderer, his "debt to society"— whatever that means—would be considered paid. But society is still pursuing him in the form of a police procedure that at any time can rip away his privacy and the privacy of his family. At any moment his past could be exposed to his neighbors, his employer, his co-workers. Can you imagine him moving into a small town? Not a small town in the Deep South with a caricature sheriff, but a small town right here in the metropolitan area—a town like Signal Hill.

His past would be an open book. As a former newspaper reporter who covered the police beat both here and in San Francisco, I can assure you that any interesting story is grist for gossip in a police department. And "The Scarlet Letter" has long been interesting.[27]

I believe that some balance must be struck on the issue of the sex offender in the community. The public has a clear right to be protected from dangerous sex offenders; at the same moment, in a civilized society, we should not brand for life a person who has violated a minor sex law. Incapacitation of some kind might be required for clearly dangerous sex offenders, but we should proceed with greater leniency concerning individuals who commit victimless crimes such as prostitution. We could then redirect the enormous energy and power of the police and courts from these issues to the clearly destructive criminal acts that are perpetrated on a daily basis in our society.

---

[27] E. H. Duncan Donovan, "Scarlet Letter Still Brands Sex Offenders," *Los Angeles Times*, March 11, 1982. Reprinted by permission of the author.

POWER-STATUS CRIME

White Collar Crime

Before exploring the pattern of white collar crime, it is appropriate to place it in the context of power-status crime. There are three forms of power-status crime: white collar crime, political crime, and organized crime.

THE CONCEPT OF POWER-STATUS CRIME

White Collar Crime

The form of power-status crime first identified in the sociological literature was white collar crime. Although this form of crime has been part of the American crime problem since our country's inception, this criminal pattern was most cogently discussed and identified at a speech delivered in 1939 to the American Sociological Association by the then president of the association, Edwin M. Sutherland. Sutherland stated that criminological sociologists should shift their research and theoretical focus from offenders in the lower socioeconomic groups to people of higher status in American society who commit crimes in the course of their occupations. It was Sutherland's position that white collar crime was more costly, created more social disorganization, and had more of a deleterious impact on American society than all other types of crime combined. A considerable amount of sociological research over the past 50 years, including Sutherland's book *White Collar Crime*, has validated Sutherland's viewpoint.

The only problem with Sutherland's assertion about white collar crime is that his conceptualization did not, in my view, encompass all patterns of upper status crimes. Two other virulent forms of crime round out what I term power-status crime: in addition to white collar crime there are political crime and organized crime.

Political Crime

Although a variety of political crimes have been committed in different presidential administrations, in recent history President Richard M. Nixon's offenses brought the concept of political crime into sharper focus. In 1971, when then-president Nixon wanted more data about the Democratic party's strategy in the forthcoming 1972 election, through a chain of command he authorized a burglary break-in at the Democratic party's offices in the Watergate apartment and office complex. Then, in order to cover up what has since been characterized as a second-rate burglary, through his presidential aides, he authorized a series of further crimes. Thousands of dollars from the Republican party's coffers were spent in an attempt to ensure a cover-up of the crime. Ultimately the conspiracy unraveled and Nixon was forced to resign under the clear threat of being convicted by Congress of an impeachable offense and being removed from office. Most of his staff—including his two closest presidential aides, John Ehrlichman and H. Robert Haldeman, and then–attorney general John Mitchell—were convicted and went to prison.

In a somewhat similar fashion in the Reagan administration, various crimes were alleged to have been committed in order to further the president's foreign policy and political goals in Central America. The basic similarity between the Nixon and Reagan administrations' complex offenses is that in the main, these political crimes were committed not for profit but for greater power to achieve political objectives and goals. In my view, this basic emphasis on goals and political issues rather than profit separates the political criminal from the white collar criminal, although political crime does encompass the use of political office or power for financial gain.

Organized Crime

Another form of power-status crime that pervades our social system is organized crime. Originally imported from Italy, but not restricted to Italian-Americans, the so-called Mafia or Cosa Nostra consists of a powerful, affluent underground criminal system. Individuals involved in organized crime necessarily utilize corrupt political and corporate connections in carrying out their nefarious activities. Many people involved in organized crime have succeeded in infiltrating and controlling quasi-legal business organizations and labor unions for their own illegal profit.

A case that illustrates the quasi-legal characteristics of organized crime was a business enterprise that was known to me when I was an adolescent growing up in Newark, New Jersey, in the early 1940s. Abner "Longy" Zwillman was a "heroic" and notorious mob figure in Newark. Longy lived in a suburban mansion and was a friend of the mayor, a philanthropist who contributed to his Newark synagogue, and a close friend of Mafia bosses Lucky Luciano and Frank Costello. Longy owned the Public Service Tobacco Company, which controlled *all* the cigarette machines in the state of New Jersey. In my naïveté, I once asked of a man who was important in New Jersey crime and political circles, "How come Longy owns every cigarette dispensing machine in the state?" His response was succinct: "If anybody selects any competitor of the Public Service Tobacco Company, the machine and the business that takes in the machine will be blown up." The power of organized crime is vested in implied and activated threats of violence, even including homicide, used to enforce this covert criminal empire's objectives and position.

Notable in organized crime's homicides was the apparent murder and disappearance of former Teamsters union president James Hoffa. Hoffa was convicted for tampering with a jury and was in prison for ten years. When he was released, he went up against organized crime's wishes and attempted to regain the union presidency. The Mafia responded in prototypical fashion: they removed him permanently from aspiring to the position by having him—in the parlance—"hit." Hoffa simply disappeared, and his body was never found.

The Three Types of Power-Status Crime

The major subforms of power-status crimes are defined as follows:

1. *White Collar Crime*   Criminal acts are sometimes committed by people of high status in the course of their occupations. The objective in committing such crimes is primarily financial gain. For example, some corporate executives bribe government officials in the United States and other countries in order to secure business contracts, and some people participate in "insider trading" by illegally acquiring secret corporate information and then using it for their own profit.

2. *Political Crime*   Some officials use their political power in illegal ways for the purpose of affecting political decisions or for personal financial gain. For example, some people in Congress and in other government positions allow bribes to influence legislative decisions; former president Nixon conspired in illegal activities to attempt to ensure his reelection; and some government officials attempt to circumvent the law in the pursuit of foreign policy objectives.

3. *Organized Crime*   A loose federation of crime "families" or criminal organizations is involved in narcotics trafficking, gambling, quasi-legal business organizations, and the illegal control

of unions. For example, various drug cartels import large quantities of illegal drugs into the United States; crime families exercise hidden control over some labor unions, over some hotels and gambling enterprises in Nevada, and over some contracting firms, garbage collection businesses, and hotel laundry firms.

Power-status crimes have several factors in common: (1) Power-status criminals have political and/or financial power in the social system. (2) Criminals in this category spend less time in courts, jails, and prisons than traditional criminals. (3) Perpetrators are often sociopaths who tend to have a noncriminal self-concept. (4) The public usually perceives power-status crime as inevitable corruption and often rationalizes such criminal activity as justifiable behavior. Because the victims—the general public—cannot clearly see the harm such crimes do to them, there is no vociferous or coherent effort to control these forms of crime.

We will analyze these varied aspects of power-status crimes in detail: this chapter discusses white collar crime; Chapter 12, political crime; and Chapter 13, organized crime. The balance of this chapter will focus on white collar crime.

DEFINING WHITE COLLAR CRIME

Edwin Sutherland, originator of the concept, defined white collar crime as a crime committed by a person of respectability and high social status in the course of an occupation. Sutherland included the following as white collar crimes: violations of antitrust laws; misrepresentation in advertising; infringements of patents, trademarks, and copyrights; violations of labor laws; and breaches of trust of various types.[1] A business person who committed a murder or rape, whether in a business office or out of it, would not have committed a white collar crime, nor would a lawyer who committed an aggravated assault upon another person, even though the act occurred in the lawyer's office or in the courtroom.

When he introduced the concept, Sutherland was primarily interested in formulating an overall theory of criminal behavior. He rejected the conventional explanations of criminality because he believed that the statistics that supported them erroneously indicated a concentration of crime in the lower socioeconomic class of society. He believed the statistics were distorted by two factors: (1) upper-class persons who commit crimes are frequently able to escape arrest and conviction because their money and social position make them more powerful politically, and (2) laws that apply exclusively to business and the

---

[1] Edwin H. Sutherland, *White Collar Crime* (New York: Holt, Rinehart and Winston, 1961), pp. 9–10.

professions, and which therefore involve only upper-class people, are seldom dealt with by criminal courts.

Herbert Edelhertz, former chief of the Fraud Section of the Criminal Division of the U.S. Department of Justice, found Sutherland's definition too restrictive in that it limited the concept to crimes committed in the course of one's occupation. Edelhertz included as white collar crime filing false income tax returns, making fraudulent claims for social security benefits, concealing assets in a personal bankruptcy, and buying on credit with no intention or capability of paying. He also included the criminal manipulation of a business, such as planned bankruptcy or old-fashioned confidence games operated in a business milieu. His definition of white collar crime included any illegal act or series of illegal acts committed by nonphysical means and by concealment or guile in order to obtain money or property, to avoid the payment or loss of money or property, or to obtain a business or personal advantage.[2]

THE NATURE AND EXTENT OF WHITE COLLAR CRIME

A study conducted in 1985 by sociologist Amitai Etzioni of George Washington University found that two-thirds of the nation's 500 largest industrial corporations had been convicted of such serious crimes as bribery (overseas bribery cases were excluded), falsification of records, tax law violations, and gross violations of workplace safety rules.

The findings did not surprise many Americans. A poll conducted in 1987 by the Roper Organization concluded that 62 percent of American adults thought that white collar crime was a "serious and growing problem that shows a real decline in business ethical behavior."

This problem of a decline in business ethics and white collar crime as a growing phenomenon was detailed in an article titled "Fraud, Fraud, Fraud" in the August 15, 1988, issue of *Newsweek:*

> The current dragnet for white-collar criminals culminates a roaring, greedy decade that created not only legitimate prosperity but also boundless motivation for stealing. Fraud was never so tempting or remorseless, thanks to the proliferation of electronic money and fast, faceless financial transactions. In the past the primary safeguard against such theft had been trust, but in the go-go '80s that ethical obstacle blew away like an old cobweb . . . [The article went on to describe a number of different white collar crimes which appeared in the headlines during the week of August 15, 1988.]
>
> • Hertz, the largest U.S. auto-rental agency, pleaded guilty in federal court to overcharging customers and their insurance companies for repairs to cars that the motorists had damaged in collisions. The company agreed to

---

[2] Herbert Edelhertz, *Nature, Impact, and Prosecution of White-Collar Crime* (Washington, D.C.: Government Printing Office, 1970), p. 12.

pay a fine of $6.9 million and to make full restitution to some 100,000 victims, who overpaid at least $13.7 million from 1978 through mid-1985. According to the Government's probe, which was first disclosed in January, Hertz paid wholesale prices for auto repairs but charged customers full retail price without advising them of the markup. In other cases, Hertz prepared phony repair appraisals and charged customers for work that was never done. . . .

- Investigators in New York City uncovered a "blood-trafficking" ring in which suspects bought samples from drug addicts and other poor people and then sold the blood to medical labs that bilked the state's Medicaid program of at least $15 million for useless tests. At 14 of the 41 labs examined, investigators found sufficient improprieties to bar the operations immediately from the Medicaid program. A grand jury handed up the first criminal indictments from the probe, charging ten people with cheating Medicaid out of $3.6 million since 1986. . . .

- In one of the first uses of racketeering laws against securities traders, a federal grand jury indicted six men on criminal charges that they evaded taxes through dozens of fraudulent Wall Street stock deals. The accused companies' top officers could face prison terms of up to 20 years each and fines totaling $19 million.

- The probe of insider trading based on purloined early copies of *Business Week* magazine expanded to include at least 16 suspects on both coasts. In the most fully investigated case so far, a former Merrill Lynch Broker is believed to have paid employees at a magazine printing plant in Connecticut to give him copies of *Business Week* a full day before the issue was available to the general public so he could buy stocks recommended in the "Inside Wall Street" column before the price went up. The broker typically paid $30 an issue, but allegedly reaped profits of $2,000 or more a week.

- Mario Biaggi, a Bronx Democrat who had served for 20 years in Congress, was convicted of 15 felony counts for his part in the Wedtech scandal. The federal jury found Biaggi guilty of extorting $1.8 million in Wedtech stock and $50,000 in cash in return for his influence in getting federal military contracts for the Bronx-based manufacturing company. The day after the conviction Biaggi tearfully resigned his seat in Congress. . . .[3]

As these cases indicate, hardly a week goes by without a newspaper account of charges filed by the government alleging that some large corporation has engaged in price-fixing, rigging of bids, forming illegal combinations in restraint of trade, making false claims in advertising, or some other business activity in violation of the law. Business executives and corporations are occasionally convicted of such violations. The punishment imposed is usually in the form of a fine. When executives are sentenced to jail, the terms are short, seldom in excess of 30 days.

In the over 100-year history of the Sherman Antitrust Act, business people have been sent to jail on very few occasions. A typical question raised is, "How can jurors send that well-dressed, white, wealthy father

---

[3] "Fraud, Fraud, Fraud," *Newsweek*, August 15, 1988.

of three to jail with unkempt, nonwhite, poor, uneducated criminals?" In one case, Judge John Ford was quoted as saying, "All are God-fearing men, highly civic-minded, who have spent lifetimes of sincere and honest dedication and service to their families, their churches, their country, and their communities. . . . I could never send Mr. ———— to jail." So, while the executives of seven electrical manufacturing corporations convicted of a price conspiracy involving over $1 billion were sentenced to 30 days in jail each, poor people convicted of crimes often involving thefts of less than $100, are given harsh sentences.

When business people are the victims of crimes committed by poor people, punishment is particularly severe. For example, persons convicted of bank robbery are sentenced to an average of 11 years of imprisonment and actually serve an average of 5 years. The amounts of money they steal from banks vary from a few hundred to a few thousand dollars. The sums realized by the crimes of corporate executives run into billions of dollars.

This condition of unequal sentencing was revealed in a 1987 United States Justice Department research report. The research revealed that the number of federal convictions for white collar crime rose 18 percent in the first five years of the Reagan administration and convictions for other types of crime went up more than twice as fast. The department reported that 10,733 defendants were convicted of federal white collar crimes in 1985, up about 1,600 from 1980. The average length of a prison sentence for a white collar criminal rose 20 percent to 29 months in 1985, compared with 2 years in 1980. The report stated that the average length of a prison sentence for other types of federal criminals was 50 months in 1985, about the same as it had been five years earlier.

Tax fraud convictions of organized crime figures and drug dealers contributed to the trend of somewhat longer sentences for white collar criminals. The Justice Department study cited an 86 percent increase in the average length of prison sentences handed out to those convicted of tax fraud from 1980 to 1985, from 11 months to 21 months. The department found that 40 percent of convicted white collar criminals were sentenced to prison in 1985, compared with 54 percent of non–white collar criminals. The study noted that financial losses caused by white collar crime dwarf the amounts lost through other types of crime.

Prototypical Cases of White Collar Crime

There are many forms of white collar crime. Following are a number of prototypical cases that reveal the dynamics and complexity of white collar crime.

Corporate Tax Fraud According to one recent commissioner of the Internal Revenue Service, corporate tax avoidance schemes have reached shocking proportions. Known losses from corporate tax avoidance have increased enormously. He states, "It is unbelievable that large, publicly held corporations engage in such schemes. Yet, they do. This is flouting the law—deliberate, willful attempts to avoid and evade taxes." Among the examples cited were the following:

- Corporation A understated its income by claiming depreciation on a patent that did not exist.
- Corporation B had a president who was losing $250,000 to $750,000 a year at the crap tables. To pay his debts he set up an artificial firm to which he wrote corporate checks for supplies that were never actually bought or delivered. He cashed the checks, and the gambling losses became expenses of the corporation, reducing its tax bill.
- Corporation C instructed its 1,000 salespeople to pad their expense accounts by $50 to $100 a week. The funds were then deposited in a special account used to pay off favored customers and public officials.

Unless the IRS is able to prove criminal intent, such cases usually go to civil courts. There the corporations may be required to pay 6 percent interest and possibly a 50 percent fraud penalty.

Defense Contracts Using the "buy-in" technique, a defense contractor bids low to obtain a contract. The cost of production is actually much higher than the estimate, and the contractor is paid additional money because of this "cost overrun." When a defense contract permits this practice, the contractor is guaranteed large profits at no risk whatsoever.

Since in many contracts the percentage of profit is regulated, hiding excess profit is a fraudulent practice. In a closed hearing before the House Banking and Currency Committee, then–vice admiral Hyman G. Rickover, deputy commander for nuclear propulsion of the Naval Ship Systems Command, charged that many corporations with defense contracts were making excessive profits and that the Department of Defense was both unwilling and unable to stop it. He also charged that excessive profits were hidden by bookkeeping procedures. Inordinate profits can easily be hidden just by the way overhead is charged, by the way component parts are priced, or by the way intracompany profits are handled: the company reports as cost what actually is profit. Rickover cited one contractor who submitted cost breakdowns on several multi-million-dollar contracts indicating a profit of 10 percent. The auditors from the General Accounting Office found profits of 45 and 65 percent.

These illegal profits on defense contracts in the past may be perceived as minor offenses compared to the revelations made in 1988 on what has become known as the Pentagon procurement scandal. Defense contractors used lobbyists and others to acquire illegally data from the Pentagon that would give these companies an edge in the competition for billions of dollars' worth of defense contracts. The first wave of the scandal was discussed in an article titled "Payoffs at the Pentagon" in the June 2, 1988, issue of *Newsweek:*

Forget the $400 hammers and the $7,000 coffee pots; forget the dreary litanies of waste, fraud and abuse. The latest by-product of the Reagan defense buildup seems to be a new form of corruption within the military-industrial complex—a conspiracy of greed that resembles nothing so much as insider trading come to the nation's defense establishment. That, at least, is the import of the sensational story that galvanized Washington last week—a fragmentary and still evolving tale of bribery within the Pentagon itself, and one that may ultimately involve billions of dollars in top-secret government contracts and perhaps a dozen major aerospace manufacturers.

The scandal became public after a sweeping, tightly coordinated raid by the FBI and the Naval Investigative Service on 38 separate locations in Maryland, Virginia, the District of Columbia and 10 other states. The targets of the raid included five highly placed civilian employees of the Department of Defense and the offices of 14 leading defense contractors, including the McDonnell Douglas Corp., United Technologies Corp., Litton Data Systems, Unisys Corp. and Northrop Corp. The raid was the culmination of a two-year-long investigation into the alleged theft of technical or contractual information that had enormous competitive value to companies bidding on Defense Department contracts.[4]

The breadth and depth of the scandal set off shock waves all across Washington, and the reverberations quickly spread to Capitol Hill. Approximately 250 individuals have already been supboenaed in the scandal, and the cases may take five to ten years to go through the courts. In 1989 over 14 people either were convicted or pleaded guilty to fraud in Pentagon procurement.

Stock Market White Collar Crime   Previous white collar crimes involving stock manipulations have been dwarfed by recent criminal capers. American white collar crimes appear to increase with time. The ingenious white collar crimes of Ivan Boesky, Michael Milken, and many other tycoons who operated like them in the late 1980s shook the foundation of Wall Street and the world financial market.

Boesky's criminal activities in the stock market were revealed in 1986. Essentially, those activities involved trading on insider information not known to the general public. His illicit profits came from taking unfair advantage of price movements in a broad range of stocks.

On November 14, 1986, the Securities and Exchange Commission announced that Boesky, 49, one of America's most eminent and successful stock market speculators, had been caught in an ongoing probe of insider trading. Boesky agreed to pay $100 million in penalties, to return profits, and to cease to trade stock professionally for the rest of his life. In December, 1986, Boesky was sentenced to a three-year term. He began serving his sentence at the minimum security federal prison in Lompoc, California, on March 24, 1988. Boesky's conviction has led to a number of important indictments of other individuals and financial corporations.

Shortly after the Boesky incident, the public learned of even more astounding crimes in the Wall Street investment firm of Drexel Burnham Lambert and the alleged illegal activity of its California branch's high-yield bond investment chief executive, Michael Milken. On April 14, 1988, after months of negotiations, Drexel Burnham Lambert Inc. and the Securities and Exchange Commission reached a settlement of civil charges involving securities law violations, with the influential Wall Street firm agreeing to sweeping changes in how it does business and how it will be regulated in the future by the government.

The settlement ended a two-and-a-half-year investigation into Drexel's trading practices at its junk bond unit in Beverly Hills, California. "Junk bonds," risky high-yield bond issues, were developed by Milken and used as part of the financial packages in flamboyant corporate takeovers during recent years. Drexel agreed to plead guilty to criminal charges and to pay $650 million in fines and other penalties. Also, as part of its settlement with government prosecutors, Drexel was required to dismiss Milken.

Milken was indicted on March 29, 1989, on criminal charges including racketeering, securities fraud, and mail fraud. At his arraignment on April 14, 1989, Milken agreed to put up assets totaling $700 million as security for the $1.85 billion the government is seeking to seize from him on federal racketeering charges. Milken's brother, Lowell, who also was named in the indictment, agreed to pledge $50 million in assets as security for the amount that the government wants to seize on the racketeering charges against him. Lowell was allowed to remain free on bail by posting a $1 million bond plus his home and two California vacation houses he owns.

The Milken brothers pleaded not guilty to racketeering, mail fraud, securities fraud, and insider trading charges. They denied violating any laws, and the trial, due to begin in 1989, will no doubt be the white collar criminal trial of the century.

The March 29 indictment of the Milkens stunned Wall Street because it disclosed for the first time the staggering amounts paid to Michael Milken in recent years. Over a four-year period beginning in 1984 and ending in 1987, he was paid $1.1 billion. In 1987 alone Drexel paid him $550 million for his legally questionable services.

Prosecutors in the court case will attempt to get $1.85 billion from Michael Milken under the terms of the Racketeer Influenced and Corrupt Organizations Act, known as RICO. This law, originally developed to prosecute organized crime, allows the government to seize an amount equal to all of the proceeds of a continuing criminal enterprise. The government claims that Milken's junk bond operation in Beverly Hills amounted to such an enterprise because it allegedly involved defrauding customers, insider trading, and securities fraud.

If the Milkens hadn't reached agreement on putting up the total of over $750 million, the U.S. Attorney's Office in Manhattan could have asked the judge to freeze their assets or require them to post bond for the full $1.85 billion. Under the arrangement they agreed to, the Milkens will still receive the interest earned on the amount they pledged as security.

The connections between Boesky and Milken will be revealed in the trial since Boesky, as part of his sentence, has agreed to testify against Milken.

The billions of dollars involved in these recent crimes, even taking into account an inflated dollar, makes the amounts of money involved in past United States white collar crimes look small. It is apparent that financial investment fraud has escalated dramatically in the past decade.

Fraud in Banks and Savings and Loan Companies Two hundred ten savings and loan companies failed in the United States between 1984 and 1988. Regulators have found serious abuse, fraud, and misconduct in half, according to the Federal Savings and Loan Insurance Corporation (FSLIC), which regulates the industry. In California, the rate is as high as 77 percent.

The 31 savings and loans in California that were seized or closed by regulators between 1984 and 1988 cost the FSLIC an estimated $5.6 billion. That is more than half the $10.8 billion that Congress appropriated in 1988 to rescue the insolvent deposit insurance fund.

It takes much more time and experience for law enforcement officials to unravel the sophisticated plots of savings and loan insiders than, say, the plots of ordinary bank robbers. And sentences for white collar criminals, when they are caught and convicted, can be light in comparison to sentences for robbers who make off with a fraction of the cash.

One chairman of a savings and loan saw his bank as a cash machine. At his disposal was a luxurious corporate jet, complete with a $4,000 burgundy leather toilet seat. He gave $250,000 to his church and a Ferrari to his secretary. All of this was derived illegally from savings and loan funds. The bank examiners responsible for uncovering the diversion of funds were making salaries far below those of the white collar criminals they were attempting to convict.

The mismatch of resources between white collar criminals and the agents trying to apprehend them illustrates one problem in trying to crack down on fraud. Salaries are, however, just part of the difficulty. Regulating the savings and loan industry has been in recent years an uneven proposition at best. This situation is the result of rapid deregulation, a lack of cooperation between federal regulators, flimsy sentences for offenders, and understaffing of watchdog agencies.

Police Corruption On December 28, 1972, a 283-page report based on one and a half years of investigations was submitted by the Knapp commission. The five-member commission was appointed in May, 1970, by New York's Mayor John Lindsay to investigate allegations of corruption in the New York City Police Department. According to this report, which was praised by the then police commissioner of New York City, more than *half* the 29,600 officers on the city police force took part in corrupt practices in 1971. The most common violations were accepting payoffs from builders, tow truck operators, bar owners, and gamblers. Also reported were such crimes as robbing bodies and participating in auto theft rings.[5] These crimes were committed as *police officers* and not as individuals who happened to be police.

Knapp commission investigators found a report from the federal Bureau of Narcotics and Dangerous Drugs requesting help in investigating New York police officers believed to be involved in drug traffic. On the request, which was never acted upon, they found the notation that Walsh, the deputy police commissioner, "doesn't want to help the feds lock up local police. Let them arrest federal people."

The commission found that the acceptance by police officers of gifts, cash, and merchandise was the most widespread form of misconduct. According to the report, *almost all police officers* either sought or accepted favors of one kind or another, and the practice was widely accepted by both police and citizenry. Many did not consider it corruption at all, "but a natural perquisite of the job."

The most serious corruption involved the enforcement of narcotics laws. Crimes attributed to police included keeping money or drugs confiscated in raids, selling drugs, storing narcotics paraphernalia in police lockers, illegally tapping suspects' phones for purposes of blackmail, and introducing potential customers to pushers. Some police reportedly had provided armed protection for narcotics dealers and had offered to obtain "hit men" to kill witnesses in drug cases.

In 1988 another major police bribery case involving narcotics was revealed in New York. A number of police officers, known as the Buddy Boys, were involved in confiscating drugs and then selling them. In several instances they literally took over crack cocaine houses in New York, taking possession of drugs and cash for their own use. *In several situations they stayed in the crack houses, in uniform, using holes in the doors for selling the cocaine they had confiscated.* These police officers were convicted and sentenced to long terms in prison.

Medicaid Fraud The Medicaid program was established pursuant to congressional action in 1965. It was intended to help finance health services for an estimated 20 million poor persons in need of such services. The complex program was funded by federal, state, and local governments. After a great many reports of abuses in the administration

---

[5] John J. Goldman, "Over Half of New York Police Force Took Graft in '71, Inquiry Finds," *Los Angeles Times*, December 26, 1972.

of the Medicaid program, a Senate committee sent out six staff investigators to pose as Medicaid beneficiaries. These investigators made 200 visits to 100 clinics in New York, New Jersey, Michigan, and California.

In a 287-page report of one committee in 1976, the following charges were made regarding offenses that continued to be a problem in the 1980s:

1. Medicaid money is being lost to "Medicaid mills," small neighborhood health clinics set up in rundown store fronts.
2. Business people, doctors, dentists, optometrists, and chiropractors were making large sums of money by taking advantage of the program. Three hundred sixty-five physicians received $100,000 or more from the program.
3. Such clinics take in more than $2.2 billion a year with 70 percent of that going to business people who, for the most part, own the clinics.
4. Often the medical services rendered were substandard and unnecessary, with facilities ill-equipped, unlicensed, and unregulated. A few examples of the frauds uncovered are:
   A. One investigator with perfect vision received three prescriptions for eyeglasses.
   B. An investigator was x-rayed on a machine that had no film.
   C. At a Los Angeles clinic, an investigator submitted a soap and cleanser concoction as a urine sample, which was tested as "normal."
   D. Although in good health, investigators were diagnosed to be afflicted with everything from bronchitis to a severe infection of the urinary tract.
5. Doctors spent little time with patients, some doctors seeing no patients at all.

Abuses that were found included the following:

1. "Ping-ponging," or referring patients from one doctor to another throughout a clinic, often regardless of need. A patient who complained of a simple stomach ache might see an internist, a dentist, a podiatrist, a chiropractor, and even a psychiatrist during a single visit.
2. "Ganging," the practice of requiring all members of a patient's family to be examined by doctors in the clinic, even though they do not have a medical complaint.
3. "Upgrading," or billing for a more expensive service than is actually provided. A physician may treat a suspected cold and bill for treating acute bronchitis.
4. "Steering"—the directing of a patient to a particular pharmacy by a physician or other practitioner. This often involves kickbacks. It is a violation of the patient's freedom of choice as well as of Medicaid regulations.

5. "Billing for services not rendered," either adding services not performed to legitimate bills or turning in totally fraudulent bills for a patient the doctor has never seen or an ailment that has not been treated.[6]

Computer Crimes   Computers are increasingly becoming an integral part of the American way of life. As such, they are prone to utilization by skillful manipulators who in effect are white collar criminals. The potential problems of computer fraud have not gone unnoticed by computer manufacturers. The following article delineates some of them:

BIG THREAT TO COMPUTER SECURITY FOUND

Computer experts are scurrying to plug what may be the most serious threat to computer security to crop up since the machines were invented.

A group of students at the University of California at Berkeley figured out an extremely simple and undetectable way to crack a large number of computer systems and remove, change or destroy the information they contain.

News of the existence of this method has leaked out into the computer community before manufacturers have been able to devise a way to neutralize the threat.

"We've been sitting around for years thinking about what if some day something like this happened," said Donn Parker of SRI International in Menlo Park, one of the world's leading experts on computer crime. "All of a sudden it has, and we're now trying to deal with it."

There is no evidence that anyone has actually used this method to commit a crime, but, then again, it would not be noticed immediately if anyone had.

Although SRI is distributing detailed instructions on the method to computer operators with a need to know, it is reluctant to discuss the specifics with the public at large.

However, Parker said that the method works by allowing a person at a computer terminal to impersonate another user at another terminal and have access to all of the data that the other user has.

Computers have long been known to be notoriously insecure, a major concern to society as increasing amounts of financial and personal information are stored and transmitted electronically.[7]

In the late 1980s there were a number of major entries into computer systems, mainly by individuals who wanted to demonstrate their ingenuity. Many judges and prosecutors have called for stiffer sentences for those convicted of computer crimes.

---

[6] *U.S. News & World Report,* September 13, 1976, p. 55. See also *Newsweek,* September 6, 1976, p. 18.

[7] Lee Dembart, "Big Threat to Computer Security Found," *Los Angeles Times,* March 3, 1982. Copyright, 1982, *Los Angeles Times.* Reprinted by permission.

One major computer crime can result in the white collar criminal theft of millions. A case in point is the $21 million caper committed against the Wells Fargo Bank of California. This one modern computer bank robbery dwarfs the combined efforts of such notorious bank robbers as Willie Sutton and John Dillinger, along with all the rest of the bank robbers of the 1930s. The case was cogently analyzed in *Time:*

It was a bank heist bigger than the Brink's job, but the bandits used no guns or getaway cars. Rather than being fast on the draw, they had fast fingers on computer keyboards. The Wells Fargo Bank of San Francisco last week filed suit charging that a group of boxing promoters and a key accomplice inside the bank had pulled off a colossal $21 million embezzlement. The alleged sting was by far the largest computer bank fraud in history and raised some troubling questions: How could such an unlikely ring of conspicuous sports personalities so easily rob a multibillion-dollar bank? How vulnerable is the banking industry to a wave of similar computer capers now that punch cards and print-outs have replaced ledger books?

The central figure in the affair is Harold Smith, 37, who has already been dubbed "the black Jesse James" by Don King, a rival boxing impresario. . . . Smith suddenly burst onto the boxing scene in 1979 flashing mysteriously huge sums of cash. As chairman of Muhammad Ali Professional Sports (MAPS), he became almost overnight the leading big-time fight promoter. One of the members of the MAPS board of directors is Benjamin Lewis, 47, who until three weeks ago was an operations officer at a Beverly Hills branch of Wells Fargo and had authority to use the bank's computers.

Wells Fargo contends that the two men and associates illegally withdrew a total of $21 million from that Beverly Hills branch and one in Santa Monica, where MAPS had deposits. Wells Fargo officials refuse to reveal how the scheme was accomplished, except to say that it involved elaborate computer transfers of money over at least the past year into 13 accounts controlled by MAPS. . . .

Smith and Lewis allegedly first made a series of legitimate deposits in the bank, some in excess of $500,000. That was done so that bank officials would not become suspicious later when MAPS began transferring large sums of money. Then someone working for Wells Fargo, purportedly Lewis, began to type bogus instructions into a computer terminal, perhaps transferring money from other deposits into the MAPS accounts. When Smith later started making large withdrawals, he attracted no notice. After all, he was a lord of the boxing ring and regularly paid fighters six-figure purses. Three weeks ago, however, the ruse unraveled. During some routine accounting work, a bank employee spotted serious irregularities in the records and sounded the alarm. Before the investigation picked up steam, both Smith and Lewis were gone. Smith's whereabouts were unknown at week's end . . . [but Lewis turned himself in].

Law enforcement officers and computer experts say that the MAPS caper was typical of the kind of embezzlement that computers make possible. Transactions that once required several signatures on a piece of paper are now carried out instantly by the use of silicon microchips. With modern communications networks, money can be sent in a moment to a bank branch in the next county or in the next country. For example, the transfer of

$7.9 billion . . . from American banks to the Bank of England as part of the deal to free the American hostages in Iran took less than ten minutes.

The sophisticated technology multiplies the opportunities for theft. Warns Philip Wynn, deputy district attorney for Los Angeles County: "Computer crime is an extremely serious problem. I see it as a monster." No one knows exactly how much computer con men are raking in, but the numbers are big. Federal officials say that the average loss in a bank robbery is $3,200. A typical nonelectronic embezzlement comes to $23,000. But the average computer fraud is $430,000.

Moreover, computer criminals are rarely caught. Jay Becker, director of the National Center for Computer Crime Data, estimates that 99 out of 100 electronic swindles go totally undetected. In most cases security procedures are lax, or clever crooks have learned how to beat the system without leaving a trail. Says FBI Agent Paul Nolan: "In many instances, the criminal can punch just one button, which tells the computer to forget everything. Once that's done, the evidence is destroyed."

Recognizing the threat from computer cons, many banks have installed complex safeguards. Complicated codes are used to thwart unauthorized computer use, and some systems use special programs called audit trails that record every transaction and the user. Computer-security experts, however, admit that many criminals are easily staying one step ahead of the precautions. Says Robert Campbell, president of Advanced Information Management Inc.: "I guess we're at the same stage as when we first started putting locks on the doors of our houses. They kept schoolchildren and stray animals out, but for the person who is really determined, there's still little or no challenge." . . .

Banks are not the only targets. Computer criminals are pilfering money from all kinds of companies. Employees at large corporations, for example, have used computers to print out paychecks to fictitious persons. Department-store workers have credited their charge accounts with a thousand dollars or so and have then gone on shopping sprees.

The Federal Government is now beginning to face the problem. The FBI has given 500 of its 7,800 agents a course in computer-crime detection. A bill before Congress would provide new and tougher penalties for computer tampering: up to 15 years in prison and fines as high as $50,000. When he introduced the legislation last year, Republican Senator Charles Percy of Illinois warned that computer theft could be as high as $3 billion per year. Even with stepped-up law enforcement, companies themselves will have to be much more vigilant. The MAPS scandal showed how simple it is to bilk a bank electronically. Though the scheme was discovered, the alleged leader had plenty of time to drop out of sight and reportedly to stash much of the missing $21 million in numbered Swiss bank accounts.[8]

CONTROLLING COMPUTER CRIME

In recent years major blockades have been instituted against computer crimes, and many corporations are becoming more open about their

---

[8] "The Wells Fargo Stickup," *Time*, February 16, 1981. Copyright 1981 Time Inc. Reprinted by permission from TIME.

problems. Many corporate executives are stepping up efforts to stop computer hackers and disgruntled employees from manipulating data-processing systems in order to embezzle funds, uncover secrets, and destroy data. Among other things, security-conscious businesses are installing sophisticated "access control" gadgetry, bringing in special consultants, and working more closely with other companies and law enforcement authorities.

Just as the outlaws of the Old West spurred security companies to design better vaults, modern-day electronic bandits are inspiring the development of advanced computer security gadgetry. The most sophisticated new equipment includes biometric machinery—products that verify the identity of a would-be computer user by analyzing the person's unique physical characteristics. For example, an eye-scanning device detects the unique blood vessel patterns in the retina, a sort of "eye signature." Made by EyeDentity, an Oregon firm, it is designed to restrict access to computer data bases. To use a computer equipped with the scanner, an individual first has to look through a scope. The scanner then takes a reading of the person's retina. Computer access is granted only to authorized users whose blood vessel patterns have been recorded and stored in the scanner's electronic memory.

Other biometric devices work on the same principle. For example, one company produces devices that use fingerprints to control access to computers. Fingerprints are read by a rectangular sensor about the size of a large index card. Another company has developed voice-based identity verification equipment. Other companies are experimenting with lasers to scan body cells for characteristics that determine a person's identity.

Some access-control equipment relies more on the way people do things than on their biological characteristics. For example, there are devices that analyze signatures on the basis of writing patterns, speed, and pen-to-pad pressure. Similarly, there is an identity verification gadget designed to distinguish a "keyboard signature"—an individual's typing speed, acceleration patterns, and finger-to-key pressure.

Although these new devices are being employed, the use of passwords is still the most common means of controlling computer access. Many companies assign a password—typically a one-word code—to their computer-using employees. To gain access to computer data, employees type these passwords on the computer keyboard. The password system also has been improved. There are circuit-bearing "smart cards" for traveling employees who use personal computers to communicate with the company's main computer. These cards flash the password needed to gain access to the main computer. They flash new passwords continuously, a feature designed to thwart intruders who try to gain computer access by guessing or stealing the code. Typically, the passwords change one to four times a minute.

Such access controls are sufficient for many companies, but some corporations—firms involved in top-secret U.S. Defense Department contracting, for example—provide an extra layer of protection. They install cryptographic ciphers, equipment that turns English into a gibberish-like code. The devices, used when sensitive data are transmitted from one computer to another, are intended to thwart industrial spies who try to intercept messages. Another device translates the code back to readable form. New efforts are constantly in process to develop even more sophisticated computer security devices to thwart white collar criminals in an increasingly computerized society.

SOME VIOLENT CONSEQUENCES OF WHITE COLLAR CRIME

Most white collar crime simply involves the theft of considerable money from citizen victims who are usually unaware they are being robbed. The money finds its way into corporate coffers, and the top executives in these companies personally benefit through lucrative stock splits, high salaries, and bonuses. In some cases, however, white collar crime can result in bodily harm and death. The violence may be indirect and hard to trace, but the results are, nevertheless, assaults on people.

As we have noted, criminal behavior involves either the commission of an act or an omission—in which someone neglects to do something prescribed by law. Notable in this latter context are neglect to clean up pollution-producing industrial wastes, to institute proper health and safety measures for employees, and to observe building and safety codes. Such white collar crimes and others that lead to bodily harm—to violence—are committed in the name of maximization of profits by corporations that place the value of the dollar above human values.

In one important case, for example, the Ford Motor Company was indicted, tried, and convicted of homicide in Indiana. The case stemmed from an accident in which three girls died when their Ford Pinto car burst into flames after being hit in the rear by another car. It was alleged that a defect in some Pintos was responsible for such catastrophic results, that Ford knew about the defect and the possible results, and that Ford did not take sufficient action, soon enough, to remedy the defect.

This was the first time that an American auto manufacturer was charged with a criminal offense. The conviction indicates that Ford was guilty of a white collar crime of omission. A significant issue is that of *mens rea*, literally meaning "guilty mind." Were Ford executives aware of the lethal possibilities of the omission to correct the Pinto defect? In his article "Pinto Madness," Mark Dowie alleged that they were.

According to Dowie, the Ford executives responsible for the Pinto were interested in profit maximization and carried out a cost-benefit analysis of the car. They pressured the National Highway Traffic Safety Administration to make an estimate of the dollar value of a human life.

When the Administration provided a figure of $200,725, Ford executives argued that they should not be required to fix the Pinto because the expected benefits (avoiding an estimated 180 burn deaths per year at $200,725 per person) were considerably less than the cost of fixing some 12.5 million Pintos at $11 per car.[9]

The Pinto case is thus a clear example of the deadly game of profit maximization within the auto industry. The General Motors (Chevrolet) Corvair provides another example. The car had a tendency to go out of control and flip over.[10] According to a former GM executive, the engineering staff took a very strong stand against the Corvair as an unsafe car long before it went on sale. Although he was a member of the engineering staff, he was told, in effect, "You're not a member of the team. Shut up or go looking for another job." The dissident executive asked for authorization to install a stability bar in the rear of the Corvair to offset its tendency to flip over. He was told the $15 per car cost was too high.[11]

The aircraft manufacturing industry provides still another example of corporate violence. In the early 1970s the engineering director at General Dynamics sent a memo to his superiors advising them that the cargo doors on the DC-10 were insecure. He suggested that fixing them might well be less expensive than damages from the loss of a planeload of people. His superiors disagreed. Two years later a DC-10 crashed in France after its cargo doors opened; all 346 passengers were killed.[12]

Regarding another kind of corporate violence, Lawrence Backow estimated that in the United States there are "at least 390,000 new cases of occupational disease each year" and "as many as 100,000 deaths per year from occupationally caused diseases." Job-related injuries disable approximately 2.2 million workers each year and kill at least 14,000.[13]

On the basis of his research, Backow further estimated that the percentage of industrial accidents that involve unsafe conditions ranges from 12 to 98 percent. Serious accidents very often involve unsafe conditions which violate safety codes. In his book Backow cited a New York study in which 57 percent of the serious accidents investigated involved code violations, and a Wisconsin study in which 35 out of 90 fatal accidents were found to involve violations of safety regulations. In many plants, falls are a frequent cause of injury. Most such falls could

---

[9] Mark Dowie, "Pinto Madness," in *Crises in American Institutions*, eds. Jerome Skolnik and Elliot Currie (Boston: Little, Brown, 1979), pp. 23–40.

[10] Ralph Nader, *Unsafe At Any Speed* (New York: Grossman, 1972).

[11] J. Patrick Wright, *On a Clear Day You Can See G.M.* (Detroit: Wright Enterprises, 1979).

[12] Ralph Nader, Mark Green, and Joel Seligman, *Taming the Giant Corporation* (New York: Norton, 1976).

[13] Lawrence Backow, *Bargaining for Job Safety and Health* (Cambridge: M.I.T. Press, 1980), p. 23.

easily be avoided by providing guardrails and warning markers. Machines that create flying particles or dust can be properly shielded or ventilated but often are not. Electrical hazards can often be inexpensively eliminated by proper grounding or shielding. Industrial processes are usually designed to accomplish a task as rapidly as possible, and the health and safety of the worker who must operate the machine is seldom considered.

Evidence indicates that a large percentage of cancers result from exposure at the workplace, yet new chemicals are being introduced into industry at an enormous rate, much faster than they can be tested to see if they contain carcinogens. Where carcinogenic properties have been proved, as with asbestos, the companies involved fight to keep health standards as slack as possible so as to minimize the cost of meeting them.[14]

Among the employer costs related to industrial accidents and disease are workers' compensation premiums, sick pay, medical and life insurance, the costs of a medical staff and plant dispensary, recruiting and training costs for replacements, down time and resulting production losses, and lower employee morale. However, corporation executives have usually calculated these costs as less than the costs of providing a healthier, safer workplace, and they have usually made improvements only when forced to do so by the government or unions.

In a study of the drug industry, Clinard and Yeager determined that all 17 U.S. drug corporations had been charged with at least one federal violation.[15] The drug industry is somewhat unusual in that the person who makes the purchase decision, the prescribing physician, is not the person who pays for the drug. This has led to a colossal advertising campaign directed at the physician, which, in turn, has led to overprescription and sometimes addiction and death. A *Washington Post* article estimated that overprescription promoted by drug companies leads to 60,000 to 140,000 deaths each year in the United States.[16]

The testing of drugs is also suspect—although it should be realized that some chemicals are introduced into the workplace with no testing whatsoever, and food additives are presumed safe unless clear evidence exists to the contrary. A Food and Drug Administration and General Accounting Office study of 238 clinical investigations found that three out of four of those investigations failed to comply with one or more legal requirements. In 1979 Biometric Testing Inc. was brought before a federal grand jury for falsifying reports on drugs. Two former executives pleaded guilty.[17]

---

[14] Larry Agran, "Getting Cancer on the Job," in Skolnik and Currie, *Crises in American Institutions*, pp. 432–442.

[15] Marshall Clinard and Peter Yeager, *Corporate Crime* (New York: Free Press, 1980).

[16] *Washington Post*, May 1, 1974.

[17] Clinard and Yeager, *Corporate Crime*, p. 112.

The marketing and/or use of substances whose toxic effects are not known—and in some cases cannot be known—until people become ill or die has led to a variety of lawsuites, or "toxic torts." Asbestos fibers, the synthetic hormone diethylstilbestrol (DES), and the defoliant Agent Orange are among the substances that have led to such litigation, which is usually in the form of a class-action suit against the manufacturer. In 1988 a number of Lockhead Aircraft employees who were working on the "stealth" bomber in a hangar full of chemicals instituted a lawsuit because they had a variety of illnesses. The paradox in their case was that because of security issues, they could not reveal the type of work they performed in the hangar. Among the problems in such cases are (1) the fact that the victim may not discover the injury or harm until years after exposure to the substance and (2) the difficulty of showing a direct link between the substance and the injury. These tend to work to the benefit of the corporate profit maximizer and to point out the degree to which current laws pertaining to violent corporate white collar crime are outmoded.

ATTITUDES TOWARD WHITE COLLAR CRIME

As we have seen, the profit system and the principle of caveat emptor have widespread support. Leisure class psychology, with its emphasis on material wealth and spending, exerts a great influence on all strata of our society. Getting something for nothing or for as little effort as possible is acceptable behavior for businesses and workers alike. Business people may pad expense accounts, inflate deductions on income tax returns, exaggerate insurance claims, and overcharge when they can. Workers may goldbrick on the job, take as many breaks as possible, feign illness, and use other methods to cheat employers. Both can engage in such forms of cheating with peer-group support or, at the very least, indifference. Hard work is deemed undesirable, and the hard worker is often considered a fool.

Individualism and competitive achievement are values in our culture that are overemphasized by business people engaged in sharp practices, by criminals, and by white collar criminals. These values are considered so important that violations of law are condoned and even undertaken when considered essential to "victory" or "success." Equal importance is attached to individualism and competitiveness by the professional criminal, the burglar, and the thief. Business people and others in our society who do not attach the same significance to these values have difficulty succeeding in our "free enterprise" competitive society.

The goals set for themselves by the leaders of finance and industry become the goals of others in business and politics. Most people on the lower rungs of the corporate ladder have fewer opportunities than their superiors to attain these goals by completely legitimate means. Since the goals are all-important to many of these people, they may employ means that others consider unprincipled, immoral, and unethical, yet they stay within the law.

When this sort of behavior becomes obnoxious to too many people, we pass laws regulating it, and so we have laws for pure food and drugs, laws for truth in packaging, and laws regulating advertising claims. Some business people who have difficulty making as much money as they would like within the limits set by government regulations simply ignore the regulations. They usually get away with it. The few who are caught and brought to trial arouse a considerable amount of sympathy. They are regarded as unfortunate rather than criminal, not only by their peers but by the public in general, and often even by the agencies charged with their prosecution.

The success of white collar criminals tends to make them models for some people in lower social strata, many of whom decide that these deviant values are worth imitating. The behavior patterns of the con artist, the professional thief with the highest status, closely resemble those of the business person engaged in white collar crime, particularly the one who uses misleading advertising. Both are intent on enriching themselves by misrepresenting the products or services they are selling. Despite the sharp increase in unethical practices and criminal activities, it should be emphasized that the great majority of people working in corporate America are ethical, law-abiding citizens.

CONTROLLING WHITE COLLAR CRIME

Why is white collar crime so extensive? White collar crime, by definition, involves acts and violations of the criminal law by corporate executives, business people, and professionals. These persons are members of the upper strata of society and would not be expected to participate deliberately in behavior that would tend to weaken and undermine that society. They are likely to be conservative and opposed to changes in the status quo, a social system in which they have thrived. Perhaps it is for that reason that they violate laws regulating business practices, particularly those laws designed to bring about social change. To a considerable extent, white collar crime represents resistance to such laws. Laws enacted to effect social change tend to give rise to two major groupings in our society—one potentially benefiting from the change and the other fearful of it. The business people whose practices such laws are intended to deter see them as unfair, biased, and serving the interests of a special interest group.

As Sutherland noted, practically all large corporations engage in illegal restraint of trade.[18] Official determinations of misrepresentation

---

[18] Sutherland, *White Collar Crime*, p. 61.

in advertising have been made against 28 of the 70 large corporations studied by Sutherland. Should the executives of all these corporations be given the status of criminal? If so, this same question may be raised with respect to violators of patent laws, labor laws, and other laws regulating business activities.

It is apparent that as a nation we are reluctant to confer the status of criminal upon our business leaders, persons close to the top of the power structure of our society. There is no recognized need for the "rehabilitation" of these people, nor have we created prison facilities for them. Those who drafted laws regulating business practices obviously intended to encourage the business person or professional to refrain from certain activities. There was no intent to change the *way of life* of those affected by these statutes. The fact that it is these very people who would be stigmatized as criminals if laws regulating business activities were strictly enforced is indicative of the need for a reconsideration of these laws. Social scientists and lawyers could share the responsibility for preparing appropriate statutes.

I suggest that statutes for the regulation of business practices be drafted according to the following principles:

1. Unless there is a general consensus that the status of criminal should be conferred on a violator of a statute, that statute should not be included in the criminal law. Only statutes designed to deter violations of the mores, behavior that is seriously detrimental to members of the society and which constitutes a threat to the society as a whole, should be included in the criminal law.

2. The criminal law of a state should be contained in *one* document, a criminal code. If we limit the criminal law to the functions outlined above, it would be possible to publish all of it in one document.

3. Statutes designed to establish norms of acceptable behavior in a business or profession should be incorporated in an administrative code for that business or profession. The administrative code may be used effectively as an instrument of social change and as a means of regulating behavior intended to deter social change.

4. Administrative codes may be enforced without conferring the status of criminal on anyone. The agency or board in charge of administering a code may proceed in the following manner:
   A. By licensing persons or corporations engaged in any of certain specified activities. In the United States most professional people are licensed. Lawyers, doctors, dentists, optometrists, teachers, psychologists, and other professionals are certified, accredited, or otherwise licensed by state agencies. Many business activities are also licensed. Liquor store owners, barbers, restaurant owners, trucking companies, and transportation companies are among those licensed by state agencies.
   B. By drafting and publicizing a code of conduct for licensees.

C. By providing administrative procedures for ascertaining violations.
D. By taking administrative action against violators in accordance with powers granted to it by statute. Some of the possible sanctions an agency or board may impose are:
   1. Withdrawal of products from the market.
   2. Suspension of license.
   3. Revocation of license.

The sanctions listed above are to be used only when the business person or professional refuses to comply with directives of the code. Violators are not stigmatized in any way. They lose none of their rights as citizens, nor do they lose their freedom. Anyone who wishes to engage in a professional or business enterprise must accept the rules set forth by the society for engaging in that activity or lose the right to engage in the activity.

The federal government has the power to enforce such regulations with respect to businesses engaged in interstate commerce. It may bar violators from use of the mass media for advertising purposes and from engaging in interstate commerce. The powers of state governments to regulate corporate entities are unlimited. The corporation is a creature of the state and exists only at the discretion of the state. The police powers of the state also permit the regulation of business and professional activities.

The decision as to whether a statute should be included in the criminal code or in an administrative code is not as difficult to reach as it may appear to be. Some norms are clearly established, and consensus makes the criminal code appropriate. What is required is greater specificity. Statutes forbidding the sale of adulterated food or poisoned food clearly belong in the criminal code. Those regulating the packaging of food can be handled by an administrative code. Misrepresenting in advertising the quality of a product that is physically harmful clearly belongs in the criminal code; misrepresenting the value of a product may not.

Many corporations are notoriously devious in their advertising. Traditional criminals do not have the ingenuity or the resources to glamorize their deviant acts. If they did, the general public might view them in a more favorable light. Large corporations, however, can advertise their products and their motivations in a glamorous fashion. For example, many oil companies spend millions of dollars falsely advertising their "service to the community" in so-called house advertising. A properly organized public could run ads countering the oil companies' extravagant claims and fallacious ads with true statements. These community ads would reveal how oil companies commit acts of white collar crime through selling products that pollute the environment. They would discuss automobile emissions and how the sea is polluted by offshore oil drilling and spills into the ocean, killing sea life and ruining beach areas. The monstrous 1989 Exxon oil spill in Valdez, Alaska, and the feeble efforts of Exxon and the Bush administration to control the damage is a case in point.

A representative case of fallacious advertising was carried out by the Occidental Petroleum Company in California before the 1988 elections. One ballot issue was whether the oil company should be allowed to drill right off the highway near a beautiful beach in the Pacific Palisades. The issue had been in the courts for at least a decade. Occidental ran television advertisements that claimed that millions of dollars would be generated for crime prevention and education if the public allowed the company to drill in the Pacific Palisades. The potential victims, private citizens, organized and ran ads showing how the drilling would be a violent criminal assault on the people who lived in this region of the United States. The oil company's ballot issue in this case was defeated. The public's rejection of Occidental's fallacious safety claims echoes Exxon's inability to control the devastation of their Alaska oil spill.

Many who favor more severe penalties for perpetrators of white collar crimes are committed to this position because they believe that persons convicted of traditional crimes are by comparison punished excessively. They seek to correct the injustice to the poor by increasing the punishment of the rich, thus making justice more equitable. Perhaps equity may be better achieved by reducing or eliminating the punitive aspects and concentrating our efforts on the effective deterrence of practices considered undesirable. White collar crime can be controlled, and there appear to be methods of control more effective than mere punishment.

There remains the problem of enforcement of regulations applied to big business. We know that criminal codes do not deter because our law enforcement personnel and courts are reluctant to stigmatize business people. After all, business people, even those who violate the law, are closely related to the power segment of our society. Those regulatory agencies that exist tend to be dominated by the business enterprise they are supposed to regulate. How, then, can we expect regulatory agencies effectively to eliminate, reduce, or otherwise deal with those who violate regulations? It is obvious that the consuming public must somehow be heavily represented on the regulatory boards. Perhaps a nonpartisan organization such as Common Cause or a consumer advocate like Ralph Nader could supply the leadership that would dictate the membership of the regulatory agencies. In any event, the battle for control of regulatory agencies is worthwhile. Attempts to stigmatize individual business people who violate regulations do not appear to be productive.

Segments of big business may even be willing to accept more impartial and effective regulatory agencies. As Page Smith has noted:

Any substantial loss of faith in the integrity of the business community, it can be argued, would strike at the very foundations of our economic system, and the consequences would be beyond calculating.

The success of American capitalism—indeed its very existence—has been dependent on the Protestant ethic. That moral code has always, if sometimes fitfully, imposed restraints, essentially moral in character, which have prevented captialism from devouring us all in its lust for power and profits.[19]

Part of the reason for the seeming acceptance of white collar crimes by the general population is that, in many cases, private citizens are the only ones in a position to expose certain forms of white collar crime, and they are reluctant to do so. In an article in *The Nation*, James Lieber pointed out that there are risks involved in "blowing the whistle" on another person within the community. These risks often include ostracism, isolation, and ruin. They, in turn, lead to marital breakups, firings, and nagging personal doubts.

Lieber pointed out what has happened to people who have thrust themselves into the public eye by exposing those involved in white collar crimes. Lois Gibbs is a prime example. When she "became alarmed by the carcinogens that seeped into her basement from the Love Canal, she led a militant movement to force the government to relocate endangered citizens." This action prompted a former Hooker Chemical Company engineer to go public with information that plant workers had been exposed too. In retaliation, the Love Canal community "poisoned" Gibbs's marriage and then made it impossible for the former engineer to find a job in the chemical industry.

In his article Lieber further stated that a person's beliefs can be radically changed by the effects of "snitching." William Kuykendall, who worked at a Virginia nuclear power plant, was a fundamentalist Christian and active in his church's functions. After he discovered that he and his fellow employees were being exposed to radiation and waste that contaminated the James River, he voiced his grievances. However, little or nothing was done. Kuykendall's frustration at his employer's indifference, his union's lack of attention to safety, and the ineffectiveness of the Nuclear Regulatory Commission then affected him to the point that he took matters into his own hands and sabotaged the plant's control rods.[20]

It appears that looking the other way is often the common denominator among individuals where white collar criminal behavior is concerned. So the problem weighs heavily on the potential informer who must rely on his or her own conscience in deciding whether or not to do

---

[19] Page Smith, "Equity Funding Scandal: It Strikes at the Heart of the American Business Ethic," *Los Angeles Times*, July 11, 1973.

[20] James Lieber, "Acts of Conscience," *The Nation*, January 2–9, 1982.

anything. None of these people have profited materially from "blowing the whistle"; they did so—and took the attendant risk—because of their own conscience, character, and sense of community. This may be the best or only way to control white collar crime, since the perpetrators often commit their crimes in secret collusion with other white collar criminals. Unlike traditional crime, where the victim will report the crime to the police, in white collar crime the victims (the public) are often unaware of the crimes perpetrated on them. Society therefore has to rely on regulatory agencies and honest whistle-blowers to respond to these crimes on behalf of the victims—who are you and me.

Chapter
12

Political Crime

An editorial titled "The President's Men, Under Law" in the June 30, 1988, issue of the *New York Times* summarized various issues related to a landmark Supreme Court decision that is highly relevant to the prosecution of political criminals now and in the future:

> For the Reagan Administration, it was humiliating. For almost everyone else, yesterday's Supreme Court decision on special prosecutors deserves celebration, starting with the main point: When the President's men come under suspicion, the nation need not helplessly leave the investigation and prosecution to the President's men. Congress has the power to create a court-appointed counsel to conduct an independent investigation when the need arises.
>
> The 7-to-1 margin makes the decision more convincing, as do Chief Justice Rehnquist's prose and background. The lean language, devoid of political rhetoric, vindicates Congress's careful Ethics in Government Act of 1978 and its high purpose, the safeguarding of nonpolitical justice.
>
> That the judgment comes from Mr. Rehnquist adds to its authority. He was, it will be recalled, appointed to the Court by Richard Nixon and promoted by Ronald Reagan, two Presidents who have been investigated or embarrassed by special prosecutors. . . .
>
> The Justice Department [under the supervision of then Attorney General Edwin Meese III], having argued so imperiously for an opposite result, must find the decision a humiliation. The only constitutional prosecutor, it maintained, is one who can be fired at the President's whim. . . .
>
> Appropriately, Chief Justice Rehnquist offered no opinion about the wisdom or need for the law authorizing independent prosecutors. . . . The Chief Justice focused entirely on the main issue, legislative power.
>
> Could Congress require the Attorney General to apply for an indepen-

dent counsel to pursue substantial suspicions about the Attorney General's colleagues in the executive branch? Yes, without undue invasion of executive authority.

Could Congress create a special court in Washington to appoint the prosecutor? Yes. In the clear language of the Constitution's appointments clause, Congress may vest the appointment of certain officers, even some who do executive jobs, in the courts of law. What more logical place, the Chief Justice asked, for a Congress concerned about the conflicts of interest that could arise in situations when the executive branch is called upon to investigate its own high-ranking officers?[1]

There are three basic types of political crime:

1. *Crimes Committed to Effect Political Change*   One form involves acts or omissions in violation of the criminal law for the purpose of making changes in the political or social system. The particular acts may be traditional crimes such as murder, assault, or theft; however, what makes these political crimes is that the goal is not personal profit. Rather, it is to influence the political or social situation. The actions of revolutionary and terrorist groups, for example, clearly fit this pattern.

2. *Crimes Committed to Maintain Political Power*   Another form of political crime involves acts committed for the purpose of maintaining political power. This type of political crime can involve the use of government power to spy on one's political opponents, the illegal arrest of individuals who challenge the incumbent's political power, the dissemination of confidential or false data about individuals who challenge the incumbent's social policies, or the illegal use of campaign funds. The Nixon administration's abuse of its power in the Watergate affair and the use of "dirty tricks" in an election are cases of this form of political crime. The Reagan years, 1980 through 1988, were marked by a variety of political crimes, especially the illegal use of political position and power by government officials for the maintenance or furtherance of their positions or goals. In the Iran-Contra scandal, for example, government money was illegally used to fund rebel troups in Nicaragua, in violation of the Boland amendment. (This issue is more fully discussed later in this chapter.)

3. *Crimes Involving the Use of Political Position or Power for Personal Monetary Gain*   The third form of political crime involves the use of an elected or appointed office for personal profit. The case of Spiro T. Agnew is an example. While governor of Maryland, he received bribery money from building contractors, and he continued to receive such illegal funds while he was vice

---

[1] "The President's Men, Under Law," *New York Times*, June 30, 1988. Copyright © 1988 by The New York Times Company. Reprinted by permission.

president of the United States. A number of Reagan's appointees, including Attorney General Edwin Meese, engaged in quasi-illegal and unethical activities, using their political power for personal gain.

To trace political crime to its origin, we would probably have to go back to the first organized groups in human history in which one or more members found themselves dissatisfied with the way the group was being led and were unable, for whatever reason, to effect changes. Political assassination, for example, probably goes back to prehistory, when one member of a group killed the leader to take over control. In the United States there have been many political assassinations. The killings of presidents Abraham Lincoln, William McKinley, and John F. Kennedy and the assassinations of Martin Luther King, Jr., and Robert F. Kennedy all can clearly be described as political crimes.

It has often been said that such assassinations have no real influence on the course of events in a democratic nation. Yet several presidential elections in the United States were decisively influenced by such acts of terror. Few would deny that the assassination of John F. Kennedy in 1963, which put Lyndon B. Johnson in the White House, greatly influenced the presidential election of 1964. In fact, many contend that this change in leadership was directly responsible for the escalation and continuation of the Vietnam war.

The assassination of Senator Robert F. Kennedy in 1968 greatly influenced the presidential election of that year. Had he not been assassinated, the popular senator would most certainly have gained his party's nomination and would very likely have been elected president. This assassination, followed by the election of Richard Nixon, is considered by many to have been responsible for the continuation and expansion of United States involvement in the Vietnam war for at least four years. Moreover, it is apparent that had the attempted assassination of Ronald Reagan in 1981 been successful, it would have changed American history.

IN-POWER AND OUT-OF-POWER POLITICAL CRIMINALS

A major delineator of political crime is the dichotomy between those who are *in power* and those who are *out of power*. Those who are out of power and who commit criminal acts confront enormous obstacles to their efforts to change the system. They usually have limited resources, and they usually do battle to change the political system through borderline criminal activities involving marches, sit-ins, and the commission of acts for which they expect to be arrested. Political crimes are by no means restricted to people who are politically to the left. In the late 1980s many politically conservative people, members of so-called right to life groups that oppose current abortion laws, were arrested; and members of militant right-wing groups such as the Ku Klux Klan, the White Aryans, and the American Nazi Party have committed political crimes.

In the most significant case in point in the century, the then criminal acts of Martin Luther King, Jr., and his followers achieved high levels of success in changing our sociopolitical system. King's leadership and behavior, now viewed as glorious acts of martyrdom, were, in the early days of the civil rights movement, clearly political crimes. His "criminal" behavior, however, contributed to changes in our political system and laws that have benefited all citizens, whatever their color. Many of his former followers, who contributed to the civil rights victories, have become significant political leaders in America. Two notable examples are Andrew Young, who was an ambassador to the United Nations and was later elected mayor of Atlanta, and the Reverend Jesse Jackson, who was a candidate for the Democratic presidential nomination in 1988.

Beyond the civil rights movement in America, there are and have been out-of-power individuals whose criminal acts have been terroristic. In the 1960s and 1970s, such quasi-military groups as the Weathermen and the Symbionese Liberation Army carried out bombings and assassinations, with limited effects on the political and social systems of the United States.

Radical political dissenters are distinguished from terrorists, who reject the legitimacy of the existing political system and reject compromise. The hope of terrorist groups is to overthrow the existing order and substitute one of their own. To them, the ends justify the means they employ. The "counterrevolutionaries" who functioned in the executive branch of government during the politically criminal Nixon regime also rejected compromise and sought to maintain themselves in power at any cost. To them, also, the ends justified the means they employed. As we know, many of them (but not their leader) were indicted, convicted, and served jail sentences for their political crimes. The biggest difference between these two factions—a vital one—is that one group was in control and had access to almost all the devastating power accumulated by this government since the birth of the nation. The misuse of this power *exclusively* for political ends is, in my view, a more heinous crime than most of the political crimes committed by citizens not in power.

It is useful to review the causes and nature of political crime in the context of significant cases in American history. We shall examine first the political crimes of people out of power, then those of people in power.

OUT-OF-POWER POLITICAL CRIMES

Ideally, in a democratic country people are expected to express their political differences in the course of political campaigns and to accept the decision of the electorate. Perhaps it is for this reason that political leaders seldom resort to political deviance or political crime. However, when it appears to minority groups, either on the political right or the political left, that their views are ignored and that government is not responsive to their needs or desires, they may resort to unlawful means to influence change. Such acts constitute political crimes. The various riots in the ghettos during the 1960s, draft evasion, and the extreme acts of resistance to the Vietnam war qualify as political crimes by people without political power.

Attempts to influence change may take the form of active dissent at either the individual or mass level. Protest rallies on college campuses in favor of or against abortion and demonstrations against South African apartheid are examples of the latter type of activity. Jean-Paul Sartre, the great French writer and philosopher, expressed his lack of faith in our democracy when he refused to participate in a "teach-in" in the United States for fear he would reinforce the myth that America was a democratic society. In fact, people who do participate in such actions are demonstrating considerable faith in the democratic process, even though in some cases, as in the Nixon era, the dissenters are viewed and treated as criminals.

When active dissent is ignored or meets with repression, some of those seeking to influence change in this way resort to other means. Some of these means may be grouped under the heading of nonviolent disruption. This category includes such activities as blocking the road to the nuclear weapons test site in Nevada. Should these efforts also prove futile, some persons may attempt to attract attention and influence change by acts of terror. Certain banks, the Pentagon, defense plants, nuclear plants, police stations, telephone exchanges, and other government facilities have been the targets of terrorists. Finally, if all efforts to influence change prove unsuccessful and the minority group dissatisfied with the response of government leaders is large enough, it might resort to guerrilla warfare.

Violent social conflict in the United States has generally occurred when the established order resisted efforts of new or excluded groups to gain access to rights and opportunities supposed to be available to them. The deprived may feel justified in taking whatever action is necessary to gain those rights that the egalitarian values of the society promise them. The fact that some see themselves denied access to the benefits of the society while others appear to have them in abundance creates a feeling of relative deprivation in the have-nots.

In a society founded on egalitarian principles and the tolerance of dissent, protest movements tend to be a corrective mechanism; they signal the need for change before the frustrations of the deprived precipitate violent rebellion. In order of severity, civil disobedience, rioting, and insurrection are the principal forms of civil protest—short of revolution—through which people express objection to injustices.

In the United States, people seeking to influence change have largely depended on the electoral process. At times, however, there has been a resort to nonviolent disruption. In the 1890s, workers dissatisfied with working conditions and the laws favoring employers engaged in active dissent in the form of marches, demonstrations, and strikes. The federal government and most state governments used laws and police repression to break the strikes and demonstrations. By 1935, dissatisfaction took the form of nonviolent obstruction such as sit-down strikes. For example, strikers took over the General Motors plants and barricaded themselves inside. Steelworkers followed the same course of action in some of the mills of U.S. Steel and other companies. These sit-down strikes led to concessions and, ultimately, more favorable labor laws. Unions became stronger, working conditions better, and wages higher. Had these efforts failed, there might well have been terroristic acts against the plants.

In the United States, however, the tendency in the past has been for the government to respond to a mass movement by making significant concessions when nonviolent obstruction was moderately effective. The government responded to the civil rights marches, demonstrations, and freedom rides of the 1950s by enacting civil rights legislation. During the 1960s, a great many people dissatisfied with the treatment of minority groups, the draft, and the war in Vietnam engaged in active dissent. While some concessions were made in the area of civil rights, for the most part the government remained indifferent to the antiwar movement and to minority problems attributed to war spending. Minority groups continued to suffer economic and social discrimination; the draft and the war in Southeast Asia went on. In the 1970s there was an increase in nonviolent obstruction by some, while others resorted to terrorism and a few undertook small guerilla-type actions. It was not until 1977 that President Carter pardoned those who had violated our draft laws. In the 1980s, political dissent was rather conservative and was generally restricted to actions against the use of nuclear power and against U.S. policy related to wars in Central America.

Dissent on Campus

A historical review of dissent on campus related to the Vietnam war reveals some of the political crimes of the past. On many campuses in the United States during the 1960s and 1970s, students participated in demonstrations, marches, sit-ins, and other forms of mass action in opposition to the war in Southeast Asia and to the draft. While these actions attracted the most attention, minority group students, particularly black students, were demonstrating for changes they considered necessary. While black militants were included in the leadership of these demonstrations, there was no evidence whatsoever that any national or even statewide conspiracy was involved. Nor did the students use weapons in any of these mass actions. Nevertheless, in many instances the reaction of state officials was repressive and severe.

The incident that came to be known as the Orangeburg Massacre occurred on February 8, 1968, at South Carolina State College at Orangeburg. The students, who had been conducting a sit-in, were ordered by state police to evacuate the building they occupied. They refused. State police fired into the building and around the outside, killing 3 students and wounding 27, some seriously. There was no evidence that the students fired at the police. All but 2 of the 30 who had been hit by police bullets were shot in the back or side while running or crawling or lying on the ground. Nine state highway patrolmen were tried on federal charges related to these shootings and killings. The state of South Carolina took no action against any of the state police. The only person convicted by a South Carolina court as a result of this incident was not a police officer but a black student. Cleveland Sellers, a former official of the Student Nonviolent Coordinating Committee, was found guilty of participating in a riot and sentenced to a year in jail. None of the 10 prosecution witnesses testified to a specific violation of the law on Sellers's part, and he was the only person charged out of more than 600 people on the scene at the time of the riot.[2]

In 1970, two years after the Orangeburg Massacre, two black students were killed by Mississippi police controlling a mass action at Jackson State College. The President's Commission on Campus Unrest accused the Mississippi police of needlessly causing two deaths by gunshot and lying to their superiors and to the FBI. The state department took no action against the police involved, and a Mississippi grand jury refused to indict any of them.[3]

In 1962, at Oxford, Mississippi, a riot occurred when the federal government attempted to integrate the University of Mississippi. United States marshals were fired upon by white snipers, and 29 marshals were wounded. More than 100 marshals were injured by acid, bricks, and rocks. The marshals twice requested permission to fire on the mob, but their commanders, determined to avoid bloodshed, refused to allow them to do so. The commanders of the marshals must be commended for their forbearance and their desire to avoid bloodshed. They were not criticized for refusing to authorize firing into a hostile white mob. Unfortunately, the police chiefs of Orangeburg and Jackson did not exercise equal forbearance when the demonstrators were black students. Despite the fact that no weapons were used by the black demonstrators, law enforcement authorities sanctioned police violence against nonviolent mass action.

At Kent State University in Ohio, in response to a student demonstration protesting the invasion of Cambodia by U.S. troops, Governor James A. Rhodes called out the National Guard to "control" the students, after

---

[2] Jack Nelson and Jack Bass, *The Orangeburg Massacre* (New York: Ballantine Books, 1972).

[3] Tom Wicker, "Jackson State and Orangeburg," *Los Angeles Times*, October 8, 1970.

they had set the Reserve Officers' Training Corps (ROTC) headquarters on fire. On campus, National Guardsmen held back the student demonstrators at bayonet point. There was considerable resentment, and some demonstrators threw rocks to harass the guardsmen. No shots were fired by any student, nor were any guardsmen injured by the rocks. Nevertheless, guardsmen fired a fusillade into a crowd of students, killing four of them.

Two of the students, Jeff Miller and Allison Krause, were actually participating in the demonstration. Jeff's mother expressed the view that he was protesting against what was going on in Cambodia because he was "nonviolent." She said: "President Nixon wants people to believe Jeff turned to violence. That is not true. When four kids are dead he gave no comfort. Nixon acts as if these kids had it coming. But shooting into a crowd of kids—*that* is violence. . . . They consider stones threat enough to kill children. I think the violence comes from the government."[4]

The father of Allison Krause, commenting on her opposition to the war, said: "She spoke her mind because we taught her to. She resented being called a 'bum' because she disagreed with someone else's opinion. She felt the war in Cambodia was wrong. Is this dissent a crime? Is this a reason for killing her?"[5]

The other two, Sandra Lee Scheuer and Bill Schroeder, were merely observers and were not even active in the demonstration. Bill Schroeder was a basketball star and an ROTC student, second in his class. A friend said of his killing: "Make sure you say one thing if nothing else. Say that Bill was not throwing rocks or shouting at the Guardsmen. It would have never crossed his mind to do that. He was there watching it and making up his own mind about it and they shot him."[6]

There was no evidence that any of the students was armed, yet the guardsmen fired into a body of student demonstrators, killing four.

A county grand jury exonerated all National Guardsmen; 25 students were indicted for rioting. The Justice Department's investigation into the killings was dropped in August, 1971, with an announcement by Attorney General John Mitchell (who was later convicted as a Watergate criminal) that "there is no credible evidence of a conspiracy between National Guardsmen to shoot students on the campus and that there is no likelihood of successful prosecution of individual guardsmen."[7]

It may be argued that mass action in dissent is not illegal; indeed the

---

[4] "Kent State: Four Deaths at Noon," *Life*, May 15, 1970, p. 32.

[5] Ibid., p. 33.

[6] John Pekkanen, "A Boy Who Was There Watching and Making Up His Mind," *Life*, May 15, 1970, pp. 36–37.

[7] Nathan Lewin, "Another Skeleton in the Closet? Kent State Revisited," *New Republic*, August 18 and 25, 1973, p. 17.

right to such dissent is guaranteed by the U.S. Constitution. Nevertheless, thousands of people in the United States have been beaten, clubbed, arrested, and convicted of offenses arising out of their participation in marches and demonstrations organized to express dissent.

The instances of mass action that we have discussed to this point relate to people engaged in active dissent. Those participating did not believe they were doing anything unlawful, and when charged by the police or prosecuting agencies they all protested their innocence, even when they acknowledged their participation in the events alleged. The protesting students in Orangeburg and Kent State felt they were participating in lawful demonstrations to protest the war in Vietnam, the draft, or the injustices done to them as members of a minority group. The riots, they contended, were started by the police in an effort to continue repression. They considered themselves to be the victims of deliberate efforts by government leaders to suppress and destroy their organized efforts to influence changes in the society, changes that they considered necessary.

Nonviolent Dissent Against Political Policies

By the mid-1960s, it had become apparent to some that the right to dissent against the Vietnam war and the draft was under attack. A battle of conscience had begun between people who considered the Vietnam war illegal and immoral and those who used their political power to launch the war and carry it on.

Many influential religious leaders and others whose consciences were aroused by what they considered to be an unjust and immoral war began to engage in activities calculated to obstruct the draft and force an end to the war. Their efforts were not without considerable success. In 1968 a *Harvard Crimson* questionnaire, to which 529 seniors responded, indicated that 94 percent disapproved of U.S. policy in the Vietnam war, 60 percent would make a determined effort to avoid the draft, and 22 percent of those would refuse to be inducted if their appeals were turned down. College students all over the country were expressing similar attitudes in mass meetings, teach-ins, and demonstrations. The trial of Dr. Benjamin Spock, Rev. William Sloane Coffin, Jr., and others represented government reaction to those who were perceived as "obstructing" the draft. The trials of Father Daniel Berrigan, Father Philip Berrigan, and other members of the Catholic left for obstructionist action of a more serious nature represented an even more drastic reaction. So, too, did the trials of Daniel Ellsberg and Anthony Russo.

The Trial of Dr. Spock On January 5, 1968, five men were indicted, charged with a conspiracy "with each other, and with diverse other persons, some known and others unknown to the Grand Jury" to counsel, aid, and abet violations of the Selective Service Act and to hinder administration of the draft. In addition, four of the men were charged with conspiring to "sponsor and support a nationwide program of resistance" to the draft. Indicted were Dr. Benjamin Spock, a pediatrician and author of the best-selling *Baby and Child Care;* the Rev. William Sloane Coffin, Jr., a Yale University chaplain; Mitchell Goodman, a writer; Michael Ferber, a Harvard graduate student; and Marcus Raskin, a former White House aide. Although all were indicted for conspiring together, they hardly knew each other. Each had met the others at different times, and they were acquainted largely because of their involvement in the peace movement.[8]

The Rev. Coffin explained his action as follows:

> I think we had our first resort, writing letters and petitions, seeing congressmen—our second, third, fourth, and fifth resorts, and then the question was, having done all that, did you put your conscience to bed with the thought that you've done everything you could while the war continues to escalate and the President remains indifferent to the cries of protest? Or do you choose to follow the route of protest to the end even if it means going to jail?[9]

For Dr. Spock, the idea of breaking the law and exposing himself to arrest was something new. He explained:

> We wanted to force a confrontation, but I don't want to be a martyr. I don't consider myself guilty. It is a challenge—to say I'm going to prove to you that the war is illegal, and that draft resistance will be effective in proportion to the number of men involved. If 100,000 or 200,000 or 500,000 young men refuse to be drafted, they will make it difficult, if not impossible, for the government to continue the war.[10]

These men were trying actively to express their dissent from our government's policies in Vietnam and voice opposition to the draft. At their trial, the judge refused to permit consideration of the legality of the Vietnam war. All except Raskin were found guilty and sentenced to two years in prison and fined. Their convictions were later reversed by the U.S. Supreme Court. However, they were punished for expressing their dissent through a long, expensive trial and much harrassment.

U.S. v. *Daniel Ellsberg and Anthony Russo*   On June 13, 1971, the *New York Times* began publishing a series of documents and analyses purportedly derived from a *History of United States Decision-Making Process on Vietnam Policy.* This compilation of documents was ordered by Secretary of Defense Robert S. McNamara in 1967 in an effort to determine objectively how we became involved in the Vietnam war. The total

---

[8] Jessica Mitford, *The Trial of Dr. Spock* (New York: Knopf, 1969).

[9] Donald Jackson, "The U.S. Versus Coffin and Spock," *Life*, May 17, 1968, p. 68B.

[10] Ibid.

compilation consisted of 47 volumes of narratives and documents, containing approximately $2\frac{1}{2}$ million words. It was prepared by 36 political scientists, economists, systems analysts, and other experts.[11] The portion published first by the *New York Times* and later by the *Washington Post* became known as the Pentagon Papers. The government did not deny the authenticity of the documents; rather, it took court action to enjoin the newspapers from publishing them on the ground that the documents were classified. Senator Mike Gravel of Alaska then proceeded to read an even larger portion of the *History* on the Senate floor. This larger version was later published by Beacon Press in four volumes.[12]

Those who dissented from government policy during the 1960s were generally within their rights as citizens, as we can see from our later perspective. Daniel Ellsberg was a respected economist who served as an advisor to high government officials. Dr. Spock was a famous pediatrician with an interest in peace. Others—the Berrigans, who were Catholic priests; the Chicago Seven; the Black Panthers; the student demonstrators—added a wide range of diversity to the dissenters. But they seemed to have the following characteristics in common:

1. They aspired to influence change in actions or policies of the government.
2. They considered government leaders insensitive to demands for change.
3. They felt powerless to produce change through the electoral process, petitions, letters, or individual protests.
4. They considered government leaders to be engaging in unlawful or morally wrongful behavior.
5. They claimed moral superiority.
6. They were recognized by their supporters as morally superior to the government leaders.
7. They did not consider themselves criminals, nor were they considered criminals by their followers. They had no criminal self-concept.
8. Their violations of law were not for personal gain.
9. They were perceived as dangerous to established order by the authorities.
10. They were often victims of unusually severe repressive measures by the government.

---

[11] Irving Louis Horowitz, "The Pentagon Papers and Social Science," *Transaction* 8 (September 1971):37–46.

[12] *Senator Gravel Edition: The Pentagon Papers*, 4 vols., ed. Mike Gravel (Boston: Beacon Press, 1971).

IN-POWER POLITICAL CRIMES

To highlight the nature of the political crimes of people in power, we shall focus on three general types. The first involves overreaction to dissenters by the state, often through law enforcement agencies. The FBI response to the war dissenters provides an interesting case in point. The second involves actions of the government—the people with the ultimate political power. In this regard I shall discuss the crimes of the Nixon administration, especially the Watergate affair. The third involves people using their political power for personal gain. The Abscam offenses highlight this type of political crime and raise the fundamental criminological issue of the distinction between entrapment and the ferreting out of crime. The various political crimes committed by members of the Reagan administration are also related to this pattern.

Government Overreaction as Political Crime

The government's response to the dissenters of the 1960s was in the nature of overkill and, from the perspective of the present time, bordered on, involved, or actually was political crime. In fact, a number of legal decisions have supported the allegation that the people in power committed political crimes to suppress the dissenters. Court decisions in the late 1970s revealed that the dissenters' marches and moratoriums were legal, that the dissenters were illegally subjected to wiretapping and spied upon, and in one case that the FBI acted illegally.

The government of the United States, at various times in its history, has enacted laws intended to repress groups considered to be a threat to the power structure of the society. Examples are the Sedition Act of 1798, criminal anarchy laws and criminal syndicalism laws enacted in the early twentieth century, the Smith Act of 1940, the McCarran Act of 1950, and the Rap Brown portion of the 1968 Omnibus Crime Bill. We may include with these the antiriot provisions of the Civil Rights Act of 1968.

The courts have also been used to suppress dissent. Eight anarchists were tried in Chicago for conspiracy to commit murder after participating in a riot on May 4, 1886, during which a bomb killed seven people. They were sentenced to hang; one killed himself, and four were executed. The governor of Illinois pardoned the three survivors in 1893 because he thought that the trial had been a judicial disgrace. The judge had instructed the jury that it was sufficient for a finding of guilt "to believe that there was a conspiracy to overthrow the existing order of society and that the defendants were party to such a conspiracy and that the policeman was killed by a bomb thrown by a party to the conspiracy." Governor Altgeld said of this, "Until the state proves from whose hands the bomb came, it is impossible to show any connection between the man who threw it and the defendants."

In Massachusetts, Nicola Sacco and Bartolomeo Vanzetti, two anarchists, were convicted and executed for a robbery and murder which they denied committing. Protests came from all parts of the world, maintaining that the case represented judicial murder. In 1977 the governor of Massachusetts announced that the conviction of Sacco and Vanzetti was not supported by the evidence and ordered that their memory be honored on Memorial Day.

Tom Mooney, a pacifist and anarchist, participated in a demonstration against World War I during which a bomb exploded and killed someone. He was convicted of the crime by a California court. After years of imprisonment and international protest, Mooney was pardoned.

Many other examples of judicial repression of radicals can be cited. Committees in both houses of Congress used hearings to destroy the careers of political dissenters in the 1940s and 1950s. Senator Joseph McCarthy headed a Senate committee which participated in an anticommunist crusade to destroy dissenters. Very few, if any, of the people who were "investigated" by Senator McCarthy were actually members of the Communist party, and no illegal activity was established on the part of anyone. Yet a great many people lost their jobs, their careers, and their reputations in the course of this quasijudicial repression.[13]

Prosecutions Alleging Violent Action The reaction of Attorney General Mitchell and the Nixon administration to those who expressed their opposition to the draft and to the Vietnam war through nonviolent obstruction was to prosecute the dissenters for their "illegal" acts. In essence, the Justice Department won a major victory and suffered two defeats in court. Nevertheless, Mitchell and the administration succeeded in attaining their objectives. Through these expensive and lengthy trials, costing millions of dollars and taking years, the government had effectively silenced many leaders of the peace movement and the draft resistance movement. They had gained additional time to carry on the war in Vietnam and even to expand it. The rank and file of the peace movement were diverted from protesting to defending court actions against their leaders and arousing support for defendants.

While high-status dissenters were being tried for conspiracies to obstruct the draft and oppose the war, the less popular radical leaders and black militants were subjected to much harsher treatment. Mitchell and the Department of Justice alleged conspiracies to engage in violent actions. The Chicago Seven were charged with conspiracies to riot, and Black Panther leaders were charged with murders. Efforts were made by innuendo to associate the people involved in these cases with efforts to

[13] Jason Epstein, *The Great Conspiracy Trial* (New York: Random House, 1970), pp. 4–6.

overthrow the government by force and violence. Ties to "communist" revolution, while not alleged, were subtly and not so subtly implied.

The major riots in the black urban ghettos were cited as examples of guerilla warfare in the cities. Extensive property damage was done in the course of the black uprisings and their repression. Considerable losses were suffered by the rioters, in numbers killed or injured and in the number of persons arrested. If we consider those arrested as the equivalent of prisoners of war, the number killed and injured as war casualties, and the property damage done as war damages, we can better evaluate the outcome. The insurrections were effectively suppressed. The ruthlessness of the suppression made it unlikely that such mass actions would be attempted again. Nevertheless, a series of conspiracy trials was initiated to harass dissenters who were not directly connected with any of these riots but were active in the anti–Vietnam war movement and the black liberation movement.

Trial of the Chicago Seven   In August, 1969, the federal government began the prosecution of eight men charged with conspiracy to start riots in Chicago before and during the national convention of the Democratic party in August 1968. The eight men charged were Rennie Davis, Dave Dellinger, John Froines, Tom Hayden, Abbie Hoffman, Jerry Rubin, Bobby Seale, and Lee Weiner. Jerry Rubin and Abbie Hoffman had formed an organization called the Youth International Party (Yippies). It represented an attempt to gather into one political movement people identified with the "new left" and "hippies." Bobby Seale was chairman of the Black Panther party. The other five persons charged were in one way or another publicly opposing the war in Vietnam and the draft. There was evidence that all these men were urging people to go to Chicago to protest the war in Vietnam and what they considered a "controlled" Democratic convention. There was no direct evidence that they had planned jointly to organize riots in Chicago.

The prosecution insisted that the trial was not political, but simply the prosecution of a criminal indictment: "conspiracy to cross state lines with the intention of organizing, promoting, or encouraging a riot." Yet the evidence was presented largely through the testimony of Chicago police officers, undercover and FBI agents, and army and navy personnel (some of whom claimed to have infiltrated the organizations of the defendants), testifying principally about events in Chicago. There were only two witnesses for the prosecution without police connections. The prosecutor acknowledged that he had no evidence of any conspiratorial meetings or of any other meeting including all seven defendants. Bobby Seale had never met any of the others before coming to Chicago for the Democratic convention and had met only Jerry Rubin after arriving in Chicago. No evidence was presented of any lawbreaking by David Dellinger, Rennie Davis, or Abbie Hoffman. The only unlawful activity of Jerry Rubin, according to witnesses, was to throw a sweater at a policeman and a bottle of paint at a police car (and miss). Tom Hayden (who later was elected to the California State Assembly) was arrested for letting air out of a tire of a police car, spitting at an arresting officer, and disguising himself. These were the unlawful acts testified to at the trial.[14]

The planned demonstrations, the defense contended, would have been peaceful antiwar demonstrations had not the demonstrators been attacked by the police. Indeed, an investigation of the riots that coincided with the Democratic convention indicated that police overreactions to taunts and verbal abuse were the principal causes of the riots.[15]

The treatment of Bobby Seale at this trial attracted both national and international attention. He was first arrested on August 19, 1969. At the time his attorney, Charles Gary of San Francisco, was hospitalized subsequent to an operation. Seale requested a three-week postponement of the trial so that his attorney could be present to represent him. This request was arbitrarily denied. Bobby Seale refused to accept any other counsel and insisted on his right to represent himself. The reaction of Judge Julius Hoffman to his protests was extreme, culminating with the judge's having Bobby Seale bound and gagged in the courtroom while the trial was proceeding. Finally, the judge declared a mistrial for Bobby Seale and cited Seale for contempt of court on 16 separate counts. The government ultimately dropped the case against Seale for lack of sufficient evidence. However, he spent two years in confinement as a result of the contempt citation.

The trial of the remaining seven continued for five months. All were acquitted on the conspiracy charges. Five of the accused —Rennie Davis, David Dellinger, Tom Hayden, Abbie Hoffman, and Jerry Rubin—were convicted of having crossed state lines individually to incite a riot at the 1968 Democratic national convention. Each was sentenced to five years in prison and fined $5,000. Judge Hoffman also held all seven defendants in contempt of court for making a mockery of justice in his courtroom. A federal appeals court unanimously reversed the convictions because of the antagonistic behavior of the prosecutor and the judge. The prosecutor had referred to the defendants as "violent anarchists," "liars and obscene haters," and had urged the jury to consider their appearance, hairstyles, and conduct in court, none of which had any bearing on their guilt or innocence.

---

[14] Jason Epstein, *The Great Conspiracy Trial* (New York: Random House, 1970). This book contains a great deal of information regarding the activities of the defendants prior to the indictments as well as a detailed account of the trial. For an excellent discussion of the improprieties of Judge Julius Hoffman during the trial, see Arthur Niederhoffer and Alexander B. Smith, "Power and Personality in the Courtroom: The Trial of the Chicago 7," *Connecticut Law Review* 3 (Winter 1970–71):233–243.

[15] Daniel Walker, *Rights in Conflict: Convention Week in Chicago, August 25–29, 1968* (New York: Dutton, 1968).

That this trial was essentially a political trial is evidenced by the unusual measures the prosecution took to attempt to establish a "conspiracy," although it had no evidence at all that a conspiracy existed.

Activities of Law Enforcement Agencies For some years there have been claims of illegal actions by the police and FBI against individuals and organizations whose activities were disapproved of by the directors of the FBI and/or police. Break-ins and burglaries by the FBI, for example, admittedly illegal, were supposedly sanctioned by former FBI director J. Edgar Hoover.

In September, 1975, the FBI told the Senate Intelligence Committee that 238 burglaries had been carried out against 14 domestic organizations during a 26-year period ending in April, 1968. Documents indicated complicity of the New York City police department in arranging for and carrying out the burglaries that took place in New York City. According to FBI documents, agents broke into the offices of the Socialist Workers Party and its youth affiliate as often as twice a month for a total of 92 past-midnight raids in the 1960s. The documents showed that FBI agents photographed at least 8,700 pages of party files, including financial records and personal letters, during the break-ins. One agent testified that he committed at least 50 burglaries with the approval of his superiors and that he received an incentive award for the burglaries from the head of the New York City field office.

The use of agents provocateurs by the FBI and other law enforcement agencies was particularly effective in smashing organizations in opposition to the established order. An agent provocateur is an undercover agent who infiltrates an organization and then tries to subvert it. Such covert agents are the link between the system and its opponents. According to Andrew Karmen, "Provocation by undercover agents is one phase of political suppression which includes electronic and photographic surveillance, dossiers, data banks, harassment, intimidation, frame-ups, and mass arrests."

Executive-Branch Crime: Watergate and the Iran-Contra Affair

Watergate The political crime that eventually toppled the Nixon administration was, in Nixon's own words, "a third-rate bungled burglary." At 2:30 A.M. on June 17, 1972, five men were arrested inside the seventh-floor suite of the Democratic National Headquarters at the Watergate, a lavish office-apartment complex in Washington, D.C. They were wearing rubber gloves to avoid leaving fingerprints and carried electronic listening devices, cameras, two-way radios, and burglar tools. On the persons of the men and in their hotel rooms were found $6,000 in consecutively numbered $100 bills. Bernard L. Barker, the man in charge, had, in one personal bank account, $89,000 that had been donated to the Committee to Re-Elect the President. In addition, he had a check in the amount of $25,000 made out to Maurice Stans, a former secretary of commerce in the Nixon administration who was, at the time of the arrest of the five, finance chair of the Republican campaign. Barker, a former employee of the CIA (Central Intelligence Agency), had been active in working with anti-Castro Cuban refugees in Miami. Arrested with Barker was James W. McCord, Jr., a security director for the Committee to Re-Elect the President. For 19 years McCord had been an employee of the CIA and a special agent of the FBI. The other three arrested, Frank A. Sturgis, Eugenio R. Martinez, and Virgilio R. Gonzales, had, like Barker, been employed by the CIA in connection with anti-Castro work in Miami.[16]

Charged with the five men who were arrested at the scene of the crime were two other persons closely associated with the Nixon administration: E. Howard Hunt, Jr., former CIA agent, sometime author, and a White House consultant, and G. Gordon Liddy, ex-FBI agent and counsel to the finance committee of the Committee to Re-Elect the President. Hunt had been employed by the CIA for 20 years and was one of the people actively engaged in the Bay of Pigs invasion of Cuba. He was in the Watergate Hotel at the time of the break-in, talking to the break-in team by walkie-talkie when police arrived. He succeeded in making his escape. Liddy was with Hunt at the time. All seven men were charged with conspiracy to use illegal means, including wiretapping, to monitor conversations, steal documents, and intercept telephone conversations, and with illegal entry to steal. The penalties provided by law for these offenses included 34 years in prison and $80,000 in fines.[17]

Despite the seriousness of the charges and the implicit involvement of people very close to the leadership of the Nixon campaign (including a former attorney general, John N. Mitchell, and a former cabinet member, Maurice Stans), the press repeatedly referred to the crime as a "caper."

The case against the Watergate Seven did not come to trial until January, 1973, some two months after the presidential election. The four Miami men who were arrested at the scene of the crime pleaded guilty, as did Hunt. According to *Newsweek*, Hunt held out the promise of financial support and a "presidential pardon" to get the others to plead guilty. "Reliable sources said that the four Miami men had no doubt been working for Mitchell and Stans—and that they were persuaded by Hunt that they could expect pardons after the publicity died down."[18]

---

[16] "What the Watergate Case Is All About," *U.S. News & World Report*, September 25, 1972, p. 27.

[17] "Seven Down on Watergate," *Time*, September 25, 1972, p. 21. For brief descriptions of the men involved, see TRB, "Moral Novocain," *New Republic*, August 19, 1972, p. 4.

[18] "The Watergate Case: Rush to Judgment," *Newsweek*, February 5, 1973, p. 29.

The jury took 90 minutes to convict on all counts G. Gordon Liddy and James W. McCord, Jr., the two defendants who pleaded not guilty.

Despite the convictions, the trial left a number of questions unanswered. For instance: How high did knowledge of the Watergate operation go? Were operatives of the Committee to Re-Elect the President involved in other shady activities? The government charged that Liddy had obtained $235,000. The Watergate break-in accounted for $50,000. What was the rest of it used for? Total cash allotments for other "operations" were estimated to reach $900,000.

In April, 1973, some ten months after the original arrests at the Watergate, President Nixon appeared on television and cast aside a year of official denials that anyone important had been involved in the bugging and burglarizing of the Democratic National Committee headquarters. He conceded the possibility of indictments at the very top level of his administration. Before it was over, many of President Nixon's closest associates resigned under a cloud, and several faced indictments. By this time Watergate had come to mean more than the break-in at the Democratic headquarters in June 1972. It included all the "dirty tricks" alleged to have been undertaken by the Committee to Re-Elect the President, among them the following:

- Illegal and unethical activities to hamper the presidential candidacy of Senator Edmund Muskie. For example, telephone calls were made at 2:00 A.M. to large numbers of Democratic voters in New Hampshire on the eve of the state primary. The caller, who was or claimed to be black, identified himself as representing the Harlem Committee to Elect Muskie President and urged the listener to vote for Muskie. This was an obvious effort to both exploit racial prejudice and annoy voters by awakening them.
- Illegal and unethical activities to hamper the presidential candidacy of Senator Henry Jackson by publishing and distributing letters, purporting to come from Senator Muskie, claiming that Senator Jackson was a homosexual. This fraudulent activity was intended to hurt the candidacies of both Jackson and Muskie. Donald H. Segretti, a California lawyer who reportedly carried on espionage and sabotage activities against Democratic presidential candidates on the West Coast, was indicted for this offense and others by a Florida court. He was alleged to be acting under the supervision of a White House appointments secretary and a White House assistant to H. R. Haldeman, President Nixon's chief of staff.
- Illegal and unethical activities to hamper the presidential candidacy of Senator Hubert Humphrey by publishing and distributing letters allegedly from Senator Muskie attributing immoral sexual activities to Senator Humphrey. This was another activity charged against Mr. Segretti in Florida.
- Illegal and unethical activities to hamper the presidential candi-

dacy of Senator Edward M. Kennedy by preparing a fraudulent file attempting to link President John F. Kennedy with the assassination of President Diem of South Vietnam.

- Illegal and unethical activities to conceal campaign contributions. These included a $200,000 "donation" from Robert Vesco in $100 bills, which was returned two months after the election. A large amount of cash, some $350,000 or more, was collected in Texas and not reported. Other large sums, kept in safes in the White House, were alleged to have been used for illegal purposes.

- Efforts by close associates of the president to discourage investigation of illegal activities of the Committee to Re-Elect the President. The extent to which the president personally involved himself in these activities is not clear and may never be. However, the president's two closest associates, H. R. Haldeman, his chief of staff, and John D. Ehrlichman, his chief assistant for domestic affairs, knew about these activities and were alleged to have either approved them or approved of covering them up. That the president knew for many months that people close to him were involved was made clear by the testimony of L. Patrick Gray, former acting head of the FBI; he testified to Senate investigators that less than three weeks after the Watergate burglary he personally told the president that White House topsiders were using both the FBI and the CIA to cover up the scandal. Gray admitted handing over FBI files on Watergate bugging and burglary to White House counsel John Dean and confessed to destroying papers from E. Howard Hunt's safe given to him by Dean.[19]

Many other activities were engaged in by the "secret police operating out of the White House:

> Senate probers, *Newsweek*'s Washington bureau learned, have been told by high Administration officials that illicit methods—including burglary and unauthorized wiretaps—were widely used to try to stop sensitive leaks, to monitor the domestic left and gather information for the prosecution of cases against radicals. The investigators have been told specifically that burglaries were committed in connection with the Seattle Seven, Chicago Weather people, Detroit Thirteen and Berrigan cases. They are also looking into allegations that Administration operatives broke into the Brookings Institution, a respected Washington think tank, looking for information on former National Security Council staffer Morton Halperin.[20]

In 1976 a federal judge ordered Nixon, Mitchell, and Haldeman to pay damages to Halperin for illegal wiretaps in his home for two years.

---

[19] "How Gray Tried to Warn Nixon," *Newsweek*, May 21, 1973, p. 18. © 1973 Newsweek, Inc. All rights reserved. Reprinted with permission.

[20] "What the Secret Police Did," *Newsweek*, June 11, 1973, p. 20. © 1973 Newsweek, Inc. All rights reserved. Reprinted by permission.

In May, 1973, a Senate Select Committee on Presidential Campaign Activities was established to investigate the Watergate affair in all its ramifications. Chaired by Senator Sam Ervin of North Carolina, a country lawyer who graduated from Harvard Law School with honors, the committee began open hearings that were broadcast over national television. The testimony before the committee clearly illustrated the counterrevolutionary character of the activities of Mr. Nixon's supporters. Witness after witness involved in the cover-up of criminal activities testified that they participated because they believed it was necessary to protect the country from "radicals" and to reelect the president. Statements by the president, which admitted in effect that he discouraged full exposure of the criminal activities, claimed that this was necessary for "national security reasons." These men were not simply trying to steal an election. They had high-minded purpose—national security—and for this the end justified the means.

The attorney general of the United States and the assistant attorney general were present at a meeting in the Department of Justice where serious crimes were being planned. While there is a dispute as to whether the attorney general did or did not approve of the plan to carry out the criminal activities, he did not deny being present on at least two occasions when they were discussed, and he admitted on national television that he took no action. Why? Because he felt that the reelection of President Nixon was more important than preventing serious crimes from taking place.

As the top law enforcement official in the United States, he was tough. He advocated such dubious techniques as wiretaps, preventive detention, no-knock laws, and stop-and-frisk laws. He also rode roughshod over the rights of people he considered to be in the radical left. He was largely responsible for the criminal indictments against Daniel Ellsberg, the Chicago Seven, the Harrisburg Seven (the Berrigans and the Catholic left), and several other leftist groups. While the government won few convictions, the enormous cost of the defense in these trials destroyed the dissenters' effectiveness in stopping the war in Vietnam.[21]

The activities of the Committee to Re-Elect the President were different from the usual "white collar crimes" of politicians. In the past, white collar crimes by politicians involved personal enrichment, graft, and excessive feeding at the government trough by greedy people occupying public office. Their crimes were committed for personal gain. In Watergate, in the broad sense, we had political associates of the president subverting the electoral process in the United States because they believed that the election of President Nixon was more important than obeying laws. To them, again, the end justified the means. They were engaged in political crime. According to Stewart Alsop, a journalist who strongly supported the candidacy of Mr. Nixon,

---

[21] "The Rise and Fall of Mr. Law and Order," *Newsweek*, April 30, 1973, p. 18.

The people who were running the President's election campaign were not really running the kind of campaign this country has known since the party system was founded. They were not practicing politics. They were making war, a special kind of war. The kind of war they were making has been made between nations for a long time now, and it is still being made. But this special kind of war has not before been made within a nation, certainly not within this nation.[22]

Prosecution of the Watergate cases was entrusted to Archibald Cox (until his discharge by President Nixon in October of 1973) and then to Leon Jaworski. Both Cox and Jaworski tried unsuccessfully for nearly a year to obtain 64 tapes involving conversations about Watergate between President Nixon and one or more of the defendants.

In November, 1973, the Judiciary Committee of the House of Representatives began hearings relative to the possible impeachment of President Nixon. After gathering evidence for six months, the Judiciary Committee held five days of open hearings, broadcast over national television, in which the impeachment of the president was debated. All 21 Democrats and 6 of the 17 Republican members approved three articles of impeachment. Pursuant to a unanimous decision of the U.S. Supreme Court, President Nixon began turning over taped conversations to the district court. Three tapes released on August 5, 1974, clearly indicated Mr. Nixon's participation in the cover-up of Watergate. Immediately following these disclosures, congressional support for the president disintegrated. To forestall impeachment, President Nixon resigned his office on August 8, 1974, in the "interest of the nation."

Less than a month after taking office, President Gerald Ford pardoned Richard Nixon for all crimes he may have committed during his term of office. Many people suspect collusion in Nixon's appointment of Ford as vice president to succeed Spiro Agnew. They allege that Ford was appointed in exchange for an agreement to pardon Nixon later. By mid-January, 1975, some 40 members of the Nixon administration, including H. R. Haldeman, John Ehrlichman, and John Mitchell, had been convicted of serious crimes or of covering up serious crimes. On June 22, 1977, H. R. Haldeman and John Mitchell began serving sentences of from two and a half to eight years in federal prisons. Ehrlichman was already in prison serving the same sentence.

At the time of the Nixon pardon, Senator Floyd Haskell of Colorado was quoted as saying, "This is the final chapter of the Watergate cover-up . . . it could only confirm what too many Americans already believe: that there is one set of laws for the rich and powerful, another for everyone else."[23] The repressive actions of the Nixon administration

---

[22] Stewart Alsop, "War, Not Politics," *Newsweek*, May 14, 1973, p. 132. © 1973 Newsweek, Inc. All rights reserved. Reprinted by permission.

[23] *Newsweek*, September 17, 1974, p. 20.

and law enforcement agencies were cogently described by Kirkpatrick Sale in an article in the *Los Angeles Times:*

THE RADICALS WERE RIGHT ALL ALONG: THE GOVERNMENT WAS OUT TO DO THEM IN

Watergate has lifted the lid on a box of political "horrors" that have come as a searing shock to most of the American public. But some were not shocked, and they were the ones who had been telling us all along that the box was there and it was real: the young radicals against whom many of those political "horrors" were used.

From 1968 on, radical groups were claiming that the government was out to do them in—by foul means more often than fair—but no one seemed to have been listening back then.

More than four years ago a president of the Students for a Democratic Society charged on national television that President Nixon, Atty. Gen. John N. Mitchell, et al., were mapping a campaign of repression against SDS and other radical groups, but he was ridiculed by his questioners and no follow-up story ever appeared in the overground press. Even after FBI informers, *agents provocateurs* and wiretappers became publicly acknowledged in succeeding years, few people seemed to give credence to the radicals' charges.

Hence, this spring, the papers and the public treated it as big news when some of the radicals' most paranoid warnings were confirmed—the President himself admitted having approved the illegal operation of repression against campus and other radical groups.

But it wasn't news to the leaders of SDS: FBI spokesmen had acknowledged back in 1969 that the bureau was infiltrating and spying on every chapter, and that spring no fewer than six regional offices of SDS were broken into and records and membership lists stolen.

It wasn't news to the Weathermen, two of whose members were fingered by an FBI infiltrator in the spring of 1970 and most of whose leaders now face heavy conspiracy charges in Detroit on the basis of evidence from wiretaps and informers.

It wasn't news to the Seattle Eight, whose trial in December, 1970, featured an acknowledged FBI informer and provocateur and whose lawyers were the victims of five mysterious break-ins during which only legal papers relating to the trial were taken.

It wasn't news to the Harrisburg Conspiracy, the Camden 28, the New York "Crazies," the Brown Berets or the Gainesville Veterans Against the War—all of whom faced court proceedings as the result of federal agents and informers in their midst—or to the lawyers for the Chicago Eight, for the Black Panthers, for assorted Weathermen members and for Daniel Ellsberg —all of whom were the acknowledged victims of wiretaps and bugs.

The amazing thing, really, is that it *was* news to so many people so long after it all began. For the evidence was there—in public comments from FBI agents and defectors, in obscure congressional testimony, in stories in the underground and campus press, in documents liberated from FBI offices, in out-of-the-way newspaper articles and elsewhere.

For example, in early 1969 an FBI spokesman admitted that "we keep watching" SDS and "nothing the SDS does surprises us." Not much later, a former FBI agent acknowledged that the bureau was sending out forged letters trying to create factionalism in SDS and antiwar organizations.

In 1970 it was public knowledge that the FBI had added 1,200 agents for its campus work, that federal funds for local police surveillance were increased by 300%, and that the Justice Department was turning its Internal Security Division into a national Red Squad devoted to massive surveillance and harassment.

By 1971, wiretaps, infiltrators, break-ins and even mail-openings had been exposed at fully 50 campuses and in a dozen radical organizations—and still no public outcry.

Perhaps the public's failure to protest is the most frightening thing of all—even more chilling than the fact that a federal administration could set up formally a massive campaign of repression.

Only a nation that could willfully avert its gaze from the unpleasantness all around, that could choose to ignore the evidence of a growing police state, that could even acquiesce in the belief that anything was justified in getting rid of the "longhairs" and "subversives"—only such a nation would have allowed itself to be pulled so far along the road toward totalitarianism.

Unless we realize just how close we came to losing our basic freedoms—and how close we might yet come—the box of political "horrors" may have been opened in vain.[24]

In a television interview with David Frost in May, 1977, former president Nixon acknowledged that many of these actions took place with his consent and insisted that if the president ordered them, they were legal. In pronouncements made by Nixon in various speeches and interviews there is no evidence whatever that he has any definition of himself as a criminal. From his "I am not a crook" speeches that preceded his resignation to his more recent comments, he remains self-righteous and, like his counterparts in organized crime, sees nothing wrong with his criminal years in the White House. In his resignation speech he said he was resigning because he had lost his support in Congress. He did not say why he had lost that support. He reminded the world again that he was no "quitter," said he would have preferred to fight on but, instead, felt obliged to "put the interest of America first." He injected into his departure a note of martyrdom. He talked about the accomplishments of his administration. He compared himself to Theodore Roosevelt's "man in the arena whose face is marred by dust and sweat and blood . . . who knows in the end of the triumphs of high achievement and . . . if he fails, at least fails while daring greatly."

In the Nixon administration, freedoms were expendable; safeguards in the Constitution were ignored. In the minds of the president's underlings any means were acceptable. Nixon was reelected, but even

---

[24] Kirkpatrick Sale, "The Radicals Were Right All Along: The Government Was Out to Do Them In," *Los Angeles Times*, July 30, 1973. Reprinted by permission of the author.

with all the power of the government at his disposal, he could not keep the presidency. Despite his attempts to destroy it, democracy worked.

Was Nixon a sociopath? We can only quote one of his most egocentric comments at the height of the unraveling of Watergate. He was consumed with saving himself, and his lack of compassion was revealed in a comment to Henry Kissinger, who would often call him about the progress of the war in Vietnam. In this particular call, Kissinger reported to Nixon the large number of Americans killed in a major Vietnam battle. According to Kissinger, Nixon's response was, "Oh screw 'em." He then went on to discuss some issues related to his impending Watergate impeachment.

There are some parallels between the paranoia that evolved in the Nixon White House years and in the Nazi regime of Adolf Hitler. Close associates of Adolf Hitler burned down the Reichstag, the building that housed the German parliament, and blamed Communists for this terroristic act. Ten Communists were actually convicted of the crime at a large public trial. Adolf Hitler was swept into office after this Reichstag fire on a "law and order" platform to protect the national security of Germany from radicals. One wonders if the whole Nazi era and World War II might not have been averted if some alert guards had caught the Nazi perpetrators of the Reichstag fire, the German "Watergate." The Watergate political crimes of people in power, as it turned out, were not as disastrous to the people of the United States as the Reichstag fire was to the people of Germany and the world. We recovered from the Nixon crimes largely as a consequence of the self-correcting nature of our political system, but the parallel between Hitler's Nazis and Nixon's staff is clear. Both regimes were controlled by politically criminal zealots who committed political crimes that subverted the electoral process because they equated loss of power by their leader with national disaster.

The Iran-Contra Case   Nixon's regime and his overkill use of executive privilege were mainly related to his personality. In contrast, during the Reagan years a series of crimes unfolded related to foreign policy issues. A preliminary conclusion on these executive crimes and the president's role is that Nixon was clearly personally involved in his regime's offenses. In contrast, Reagan was characterized as a hands-off president, or, by some of his political enemies, as a fool who did not even know what went on in his presidency. The evidence to date is that he did not know about the Iran-Contra crimes. Nixon may have committed crimes of commission, whereas Reagan committed crimes of omission. Reagan himself characterized the crimes as his responsibility, saying they took place "on my watch."

Reagan was not charged with any offense in the alleged Iran-Contra crimes, since he and Vice President George Bush claimed they never knew what was going on in the White House. The targets were Ronald

Reagan's National Security Adviser, John Poindexter; National Security Council (NSC) aide and Marine Colonel Oliver North; and two arms dealers, former Air Force Major General Richard Secord and Iranian-born businessman Albert Hakim. They were charged with conspiring to defraud the United States by establishing and concealing a plan for illegally supporting the Nicaraguan rebels known as the Contras. A federal grand jury also charged all four defendants with theft of government property for siphoning off more than $17 million in proceeds from U.S. arms sales to Iran and with wire fraud resulting from the movement of the money through Swiss bank accounts. The three counts together could carry maximum penalties of 20 years in prison and fines totaling as much as $750,000.

In addition, Poindexter and North were accused of trying to cover up their illicit actions by destroying and removing documents related to the alleged crimes and with making false statements. North was charged with lying to Attorney General Edwin Meese about NSC involvement in the diversion of funds to the Contras and with writing misleading letters to Congress denying that the NSC was supporting the Contras. Former national security adviser Robert McFarlane had pleaded guilty to misdemeanor charges for signing the letters. Poindexter was accused of a peculiarly high-tech cover-up: he purged his NSC computer files of all messages relating to the Contra supply operation.

North, who told Congress that he and Poindexter were the designated "fall guys" for the Iran-Contra affair, bore the brunt of the indictment. Piled onto the conspiracy and obstruction charges were accusations that the Marine lieutenant colonel had embezzled $4,300 worth of traveler's checks and received an illegal gratuity by accepting a $13,800 home security system from Secord.

North was also accused of conspiring to defraud the Internal Revenue Service by using the tax-exempt National Endowment for the Preservation of Liberty (NEPL) to solicit $3.2 million in contributions, which he used to buy lethal Contra aid. NEPL president Carl "Spitz" Channell and public relations consultant Richard Miller pleaded guilty to the same charges in 1987.

North refused to take the bad news quietly. "I did not commit any crime," North declared in a press conference at his lawyer's office, his voice trembling with emotion. "I have been caught up in a bitter dispute between Congress and the president over the control of foreign policy, the power of the president to deter communism in Central America, and his duty to protect our citizens from terrorist acts abroad. . . . I intend to fight allegations of wrongdoing for as long as necessary. (In this context, North obviously has no criminal self-concept.)

North held another emotional news conference to announce his resignation from the Marine Corps. True to his sense of theater, expressed at the congressional hearing in 1987, he had traded in his olive-green uniform and chestful of ribbons for a business suit. Continued service in the Marines, said North, would be incompatible with defending himself against the charges, particularly since his lawyer may subpoena the "highest-ranking officials of our government." The implication seemed clear: if North was to play the fall guy, he intended to drag his superiors down with him. At his trial in March and April of 1989, North's primary defense was the Adolph Eichmann defense, "I was only following orders."

Richard Secord responded to his indictment with contempt, appearing on TV news shows to denounce the investigation as a "witchhunt." He declared, "The charges are absolutely ludicrous, and I intend to grind them to dust." Poindexter and Hakim, the more self-effacing participants in what Secord called the "enterprise," commented only through their lawyers. While he was president, Ronald Reagan refused to concede that some of his former aides may have violated the law. Reagan commented, "I have no knowledge of any law that was broken."

The 101-page indictment on the conspiracy sheds some light on the tangled Iran-Contra affair, placing events in a criminal framework. The grand jury treated the initiative to sell arms to Iran in exchange for U.S. hostages as a legitimate covert operation, not a crime. It was the abuse of that operation, the diversion of funds and other related activities, that led to the possible breaking of laws. The grand jury reached the same conclusion as the Tower Commission Report in 1987 and the congressional committees about Reagan's involvement in the Contra scheme: the president was practically an innocent bystander in his own administration, oblivious to the machinations of his overzealous aides. The North trial produced evidence that seriously challenged Reagan's "innocent bystander" defense.

According to the grand jury, North was cagey and aggressive in securing profits for the enterprise managed by Secord and Hakim. In January, 1986, for instance, North arranged to sell 4,000 TOW missiles to Iran for $10,000 each. The Iranians paid $10 million for the first shipment of 1,000 TOWs. But North told the CIA he had sold the weapons for only $3,469 apiece. The U.S. government, through the CIA, received just $3.7 million on the deal. Some of the remaining $6.3 million was used to aid the Contras, but the bulk of it was retained by Secord and Hakim, and possibly North. Special Prosecutor Walsh charged that the money was the rightful property of the United States, but the arms merchants have repeatedly said the money belongs only to their enterprise.

The grand jury alleged that Secord and Hakim encouraged North to remain on the NSC staff so they could continue to realize "opportunities for substantial revenue and profits." To persuade North to stay in his White House post, Secord gave North an expensive security system and Hakim established the "B. Button" investment account, a $200,000 fund to be used for the education of North's children. During his congressional testimony and subsequent trial, North passionately denied any knowledge of the Button account and any use of funds for his private use, and said he needed the security system to protect his family.

North's protracted criminal trial in March and April of 1989 revealed, among other things, that former president Reagan and then–vice president Bush were much more involved in the Iran-Contra scandal than either the Congressional investigation or the Tower report revealed.

On May 4, 1989, Oliver North was convicted on three felony charges: altering, concealing, and destroying National Security Council top secret documents; helping to mislead Congress; and illegally accepting a gift of $13,800 for a home security system.

Political Crimes for Personal Gain

People in power are often in a position to sell their offices for personal gain. Their election or appointment provides them with a special position in the system, which depends to a great extent on the trust of the populace. The violation of this trust for personal gain is a crime of the highest order that tends to corrode and subvert our social system and government.

Despite this, the use of political power for personal gain has almost become a part of the American way of life. From the founding of our country, people at all levels, from local government to the White House, have violated their positions of trust to commit political crimes. The political crimes of former vice president Spiro T. Agnew and those convicted in the FBI Abscam cases reveal the nature, extent, and implications of political crimes for personal gain in recent times.

Spiro T. Agnew   Mr. Agnew's problem began in 1972, when a director for the Bureau of Internal Revenue's intelligence unit, Robert Brown, told U.S. Attorney George Beal that he had recently checked into the tax returns of some Maryland officials and they "didn't jibe." The attorney countered by commenting that he had heard rumors of officials receiving cash kickbacks from local contractors. This conversation eventually led to an investigation.

Department of Justice investigators uncovered evidence of widespread corruption in the allocation of state and local government contracts in Maryland. Included were claims that then–vice president Spiro T. Agnew, while he was Baltimore County Executive, received payoffs of $1,000 a week from contractors. It was further alleged that payments continued while Mr. Agnew was governor of Maryland, and that he had been given a lump-sum payment of $50,000 after he moved to Washington as vice president.

Agnew, in a press conference, denied the charges. After weeks of allegations and denials, Agnew appeared in U.S. District Court on October 10, 1973, and pleaded *nolo contendere* to charges of having evaded taxes on funds contributed to him in 1967. The judge informed him that his plea was equivalent to a guilty plea. He then imposed a fine of $10,000 and three years' unsupervised probation.

The plea of guilty and the sentence resulted from weeks of plea bargaining during which the Justice Department insisted on prosecuting Agnew for bribery, extortion, and tax evasion unless he agreed to resign, plead guilty to some charges, and serve nine months in prison. Agnew, according to news reports, was willing to resign but refused to accept imprisonment. The final bargain included Agnew's resignation and government prosecution of the case against Agnew in the federal investigation of tax evasion, alleged bribery, and extortion. This then–attorney general Elliot Richardson accomplished in a 40-page document setting forth the prosecution's evidence.

From the outset of the case against him through his televised explanations, Agnew insisted that he was innocent of any wrongdoing, that he had never violated a public trust in return for political contributions. Given his criminal personality, he might truly have believed he was innocent. For Agnew, it was all essential to survival; it was a platform from which he could continue to pursue higher office. Having entered big-time politics without benefit of wealth, he felt constant pressure to live up to the standards of his wealthier peers.

He accepted groceries from a supermarket executive. His restaurant tabs were usually picked up by someone courting his favor. He used funds given to him when he was governor to stock a wine cellar. When, as vice president, he traveled to Palm Springs, California, his expenses were paid by Frank Sinatra or Bob Hope. Attorney General Richardson saw Agnew's acceptance of gifts and kickbacks as criminal. Agnew perceived his behavior as noncriminal.

Agnew held several press conferences during which he denounced his accuser, and the ironic aspect of his self-righteous "defense" is that he might really have believed what he said. With the aid of lawyers, he prepared a brief statement acknowledging that he was being investigated and proclaiming complete innocence. He conducted a news conference at which he called the charges against him "damned lies," pledged cooperation with the prosecutors, and said he had "absolutely nothing to hide."

The political crimes of Agnew in taking bribes were expounded by the prosecution in great detail, and he had no alternative but to resign. Agnew made only one slight admission of guilt in an interesting comment after his resignation: "I suppose by the standards of post-Watergate morality I did something wrong." This cynical remark parallels the statements of some of his criminal colleagues. They fit in well with Al Capone's comment on his way to Alcatraz ("I'm no criminal, I was just providing a service") and Richard Nixon's remark at the height of his infamy ("I am not a crook"). In 1989 Agnew had the audacity to claim that he was entitled to a $29,197 tax refund for the $142,500 he paid Maryland as restitution for the bribes he criminally collected while he was governor of Maryland. The deduction was denied.

The Abscam Political Crimes   The FBI has for many years utilized undercover operations in its pursuit of federal criminals. Its nets have captured many power-class criminals engaged in illegal activities. The arrests in the Abscam undercover law enforcement effort, however, produced an enormous controversy because the FBI net ensnared a number of high officials, over 100 political figures were named in undercover tapes, and eight congressmen, including one senator, were convicted.[25]

The Abscam undercover operation began with a relatively routine investigation and "sting" attempt. In 1977, after a 35-year career as a skilled and slippery confidence man, Melvin Weinberg was arrested for the first time. After his conviction and in exchange for a suspended sentence, Weinberg agreed to work undercover for the FBI in a sting operation which required the talents, respect, and plausibility that a known criminal could bring to such a project. In the summer of 1978 the FBI set up an operation to lure organized crime figures into selling stolen art works and securities to its own agents in what was essentially a fencing operation. At that time there was no thought that the operation would reach into the upper levels of American government.

Things had gone so well in the first few months that the bureau decided to expand the operation and adopt a new cover. Weinberg and a small number of agents were established as Abdul Enterprises Ltd. in a building in Long Island, New York. Passing themselves off as business representatives of wealthy Arab sheiks, the group put out the word that their establishment would purchase stolen or forged U.S. Treasury certificates of deposit which, under a complicated system, would be sold to the governments of the sheiks in exchange for cash that could then be invested in the United States by the sheiks. Weinberg was able to convince prospective "marks" with the plausible story that because of Islamic religious laws against usury, the sheiks could not invest profitably in their own countries; thus, they were willing to give securities to their governments in exchange for cash to be invested elsewhere. Since the securities would never be redeemed, the agents explained, it was not necessary that they be authentic. The hook was thus baited for the criminal—Abdul Enterprises (the FBI) would pay a straight commission of 7 percent of the face value for such securities, regardless of origin. Of course this was all a hoax, but the many petty criminals looking for action failed to notice that. In fact, no funds were ever paid for these bogus or stolen securities. Weinberg, the career con artist, was able to keep an army of hopeful yet insistent claimants at bay for over a year with a myriad of stalling techniques, including references to the Iranian hostage crisis.

By creating the illusion of tremendous wealth and investment capital, Abdul Enterprises was able to enlarge the web and ensnare even

---

[25] I wish to acknowledge the participation and help of my student, Paul Kelleher, who collated data on Abscam from a variety of sources.

more criminals. By putting out the word among the various crooks and mobsters already participating that Emir Kambir Abdul Rahman desired to build a gambling casino in Atlantic City, the FBI was able to attract a number of interested "investors." It was at this point that a small-time operator, Bill Rosenberg, brought Angelo J. Errichetti, the mayor of Camden, New Jersey, and a state senator, into the trap. Errichetti promised Weinberg and the other FBI agents that financing for the casino would be available and that he could ensure the issuance of all necessary licenses for a "fee" of $400,000. He was given $25,000 and promised more as his role developed. As the scam progressed, Errichetti, with an eye on kickbacks and personal power, kept proposing management teams for the casino and suggested numerous locations. This brought a number of Errichetti's corrupt associates into the deal, each with his own proposed investment projects for Abdul Enterprises. Peripheral dealings such as these were numerous and frightening in the degree of corruption they exposed.

It was one of these secondary deals that led Abscam into its second and most notorious phase—high-level political corruption. According to FBI tapes, New Jersey lawyer Alexander Feinberg and a group of his friends—among them Senator Harrison Williams—wanted investment money from Abdul Enterprises to complete the purchase and clear the title of a titanium mine and processing plant in Georgia in which the group already had a partial interest. With Harrison's contacts and an expected shortage of titanium for government defense projects, the group expected to reap millions. To obtain proof of the criminal intent of Williams, the Abscam team set up a meeting with Williams and promised to obtain capital of $100 million, of which he would get 17 percent ($17 million) in exchange for his promise to use all his contacts for the good of the enterprise. He did so, and he received $17 million in bogus stock certificates in an exchange that was carefully recorded on videotape. Alexander Feinberg was to hold the stocks so that Williams could seek contracts from the government without any apparent conflict of interest.

As the investigation moved into the area of political corruption, FBI and Justice Department officials were notified and informed. On the strength of the evidence, they authorized new "fronts" for Abscam to test leads which were being uncovered by low-level intermediaries. A second sheik, Yassir Habib, was created and given the problem of needing extralegal immigration assistance. The plausible cover story was that both Yassir Habib and Abdul Rahman were raping their countries and wanted a safe haven so they would not end up like the Shah of Iran. Word went out through political channels, and soon representatives, most with the prodding of lawyer and former district attorney Howard L. Criden, were lining up to collect fees for influence or private legislation. Numerous other officials and criminals were eventually charged.

The Abscam videotapes are fascinating in their revelation of how many corrupt officials are streetwise, cagey, and very suspicious—traits presumably acquired through experience in political crime that is never detected. For example, one political criminal in Abscam, Representative Michael Myers of Philadelphia, in demanding his illegal money, remarked: "Money talks and bullshit walks." He pocketed $25,000 in cash at that time.

It is of value to examine more closely some of the power-class criminals convicted as a result of Abscam.

Representative John W. Jenrette, Jr. Jenrette, a Democratic candidate from South Carolina's Sixth District, won elections to the House of Representatives in 1974, 1976, and 1978 by large and increasing margins. His popularity with his constituents was not matched by popularity with his political rivals or business associates. In 1975 the Justice Department investigated charges that Jenrette had accepted large contributions from a federal contractor who had already been hired to build a federal facility in Jenrette's district. A kickback scheme was suspected, but the Justice Department took no action after Jenrette returned the contributions. In 1976 a business partner charged Jenrette with converting company funds to personal use. The matter was eventually settled out of court without formal charges being brought. Also in 1976, Heritage Shores, a land development company in which Jenrette had a substantial interest, came under federal scrutiny. It was alleged that underwater land was being sold to unsuspecting investors. These charges were still under investigation during the Abscam sting; the tapes themselves contain allusions to Jenrette's efforts to get the investigation killed.

Representative Richard Kelly Kelly, a Republican, was first elected from his Florida district in 1974 and would serve three terms of office before being repudiated by his constituents in the wake of his involvement in the Abscam affair. Prior to his election, Kelly had served 11 years as a judge in Florida's Sixth Judicial Circuit and had served as an assistant U.S. district attorney. Ironically, he had also served as a lawyer for the FBI. In 1968, Kelly was officially reprimanded by the Florida Supreme Court for "conduct unbecoming a member of the judiciary." This was his first official censure—Kelly had nearly been impeached from the Florida state bar in 1963 for misconduct in office. It was Kelly who, when the Abscam revelations began, offered the absurd defense that he was "conducting an investigation of shady characters on his own." He kept $25,000 in cash that he had stuffed in his pockets on leaving one Abscam meeting in the glove compartment of his car. He used the money for personal expenses.

Representative Raymond F. Lederer According to Abscam videotapes, Lederer accepted a $50,000 bribe in return for his influence in the

House and a promise to introduce a private immigration bill for the mythical Arab sheik Emir Kambir Abdul Rahman. Of all the implicated congressmen, Lederer was the only one to be reelected in 1980. However, the Pennsylvania Democrat, when faced with a 10 to 2 vote for expulsion by the House Ethics Committee, resigned his seat. Prior to the Abscam affair, Lederer, who served on the Ways and Means Committee, had an untainted record and was not known to have any criminal propensities.

Representative John M. Murphy   New York's contribution to the Abscam operation was first elected to the House in 1962. Ranked first in his West Point class of 1950, Murphy was also a highly decorated veteran of the Korean war. His first decade in public service was uneventful and unmarred. By 1973, Murphy was under federal scrutiny after arranging a meeting between Thomas Gambino (the gangster's son and a college friend of Murphy) and the secretary of the Interstate Commerce Commission. No charges were filed. During the oil embargo of 1973 and 1974, Murphy was involved in negotiations to build an oil refinery in Nicaragua in partnership with college chum Anastasio Somoza, then president and dictator of Nicaragua. Murphy was to assure a flow of oil from Iran in return for a share of the profits, critics alleged. Murphy also came under official investigation by the House Standards Committee in the "Koreagate" scandal of 1977 and 1978. No evidence of wrongdoing could be produced. This was also the outcome of investigations into an alleged kickback scheme with the Pahlavi Foundation, an agency entrusted with the management of the assets of the deposed Shah of Iran. In December, 1980, as a consequence of Abscam, Murphy was charged with and convicted of receiving an unlawful gratuity, conflict of interest, and conspiracy. He was fined $20,000 and given prison terms which he served concurrently. He was freed in 1983.

Representative John P. Murtha   This Democrat from Pennsylvania's Twelfth District held seats on two powerful House committees: Appropriations and, ironically, Standards of Official Conduct. Murtha was the first Vietnam veteran to serve in the House and was elected in 1974, 1976, and 1978. He was enormously popular in his district and would probably have continued to be elected in the absence of Abscam. It should be noted that although Murtha agreed to use influence with regard to the immigration of Yassir Habib, the phony sheik, he persistently refused a payoff.

Representative Michael O. Myers   The most candid and self-incriminating of all participants and the first to accept a bribe, Myers was elected from the Democratic First District of Philadelphia, serving from 1976 to 1980. A former longshoreman and state representative, Myers had strong support from his blue collar constituents. Of blue collar origins himself, Myers showed real savvy in political affairs.

He was fined $20,000 and given three 1-year sentences to run concurrently.

Representative Frank Thompson Jr. Despite a shining reputation for integrity, Thompson, chair of the Administration Committee, is on videotape accepting a bribe for his influence through his middleman lawyer and coconspirator Howard L. Criden. Both were convicted of bribery and conspiracy in December, 1980.

Senator Harrison A. Williams, Jr. Probably by any measure the most culpable of all the Abscam defendants, Williams exceeded all the rest in the degree of his corruption. The senator promised to delay deportation proceedings against Yassir Habib, the mythical sheik. While refusing a $50,000 cash bribe directly, Williams did divide the money with his intermediary and lawyer Alexander Feinberg. Williams promised to use his close contacts with the Pentagon, President Carter, and other Democratic party leaders to obtain government contracts for a business venture in which he would be given a secret interest. The Democratic senator from New Jersey had served since 1958 and was considered to be the fourth-ranked Democrat in the Senate.

Williams was the most self-righteous of the prominent Abscam political criminals. He was convicted on nine counts of bribery and conspiracy by a federal court and sentenced to three years in prison. The Senate Ethics Committee unanimously condemned his behavior, and in March, 1982, the Senate held a trial to determine whether to expel him. As did many of the others, Williams claimed that he was entrapped. He assailed the FBI Abscam undercover activity as a "vile and heinous" operation. Under the threat of a certain vote by the Senate for his expulsion, he resigned his Senate seat on March 11, 1982. He vowed to continue to fight "the wretchedness and rottenness of the FBI operation whenever I could." In response to his charge of FBI entrapment, the chairman of the Senate Ethics Committee that condemned Williams's behavior commented: "Senator Williams attended meeting after meeting [with the Abscam group] and promised to fully cooperate in an illegal bribery scheme for which he was convicted in federal court."

The Question of Entrapment An obviously highly significant issue is related to the ethics of the FBI operation and the issue of entrapment. This issue was assessed in a penetrating article in *Newsweek*:

> *Did the FBI illegally entrap any politicians?* The biggest danger in any "sting" operation is that overeager investigators can become *agents provocateurs*—inciting crimes that otherwise would not have been committed. Some critics have said that entrapment may have taken place in operation ABSCAM. . . .

Still, it would be difficult for any politician charged with a crime as a result of the ABSCAM investigation to base his defense on a claim of entrapment. For one thing, he might first have to admit that he did indeed accept a bribe—and while such a defense might make legal sense, it would amount to political suicide. For another, a suspect claiming entrapment opens himself up to a wide-ranging look at his past. Finally, the U.S. Supreme Court has narrowed the definition of entrapment over the years to the point where the government can provide the idea, the opportunity and the means for a crime—and still win a conviction. As long as the government can prove that the victim of a sting operation was *"predisposed to commit the crime,"* [italics added], the court has ruled, it doesn't matter if the undercover men encourage the crime. Because presumably sophisticated politicians were willing to meet with shadowy figures under dubious pretenses, the government is given a good chance of demolishing any entrapment claims that might arise. To be on the safe side, Justice Department attorneys tried to make sure that the FBI stayed within the court's expansive guidelines by listening in on every meeting the ABSCAM agents had with a potential bribe-taker.

But the larger ethical question is whether the government has [the] right, as Washington attorney David Povich puts it, "to run around and test innocent people to see if it can corrupt them."

FBI director William Webster says his bureau has "an obligation, when information about criminality comes to us, to run down leads and pursue them." Former U.S. Attorney General Nicholas de B. Katzenbach believes that the FBI did something more. Entrapment or not, he says, "I don't think it's the government's business to go out and create a crime."[26]

Several Supreme Court decisions are worthy of review in assessing the entrapment question. In 1932 the Court granted a positive decision in a state appeals case, *Sorrells* v. *United States;* the case firmly established a defense for entrapment in the federal courts. The principle that emerged from this case was that the function of law enforcement was to be the prevention of crime and the apprehension of criminals. The government could not " . . . implant in the mind of an innocent the *disposition* to commit the alleged offense and induce its commission in order that they may prosecute."

In the years since *Sorrells* there have been three major Supreme Court entrapment cases: *Sherman* v. *United States* (1958), *United States* v. *Russell* (1973), and *Hampton* v. *United States* (1976).

In *Sherman* the court reversed the conviction unanimously but was divided on the appropriate standard. The numerical majority adopted what would come to be called the "subjective" test, which emphasized the culpability of the defendant. Yet, because it was not the intent of Congress to "tempt the innocent," this faction of the court would look at two things in evaluating a case. First, the origin of the crime was to be

---

[26] "Some Questions of Ethics," *Newsweek*, February 18, 1980. Copyright 1980, by Newsweek, Inc. All rights reserved. Reprinted by permission.

considered; the crime must originate with the defendant to the extent that while the government may provide an opportunity for the commission of a crime, they cannot actively create crime by inducing the person to so act. Second, this wing of the court focuses on the intent of the defendant—summed up in the question of a "predisposition" to commit the crime. Basically this means that *if the defendant can be shown to have an element of intent to commit the crime, then there is no issue of entrapment. Entrapment would occur only if a person was demonstrated to have no original intent to commit a crime but was nonetheless persistently pressured by government agents to the point of its commission.*

The minority wing of the court advocated an "objective" standard which rejects the intent of Congress and focuses instead on police activity. In all three cases they argued that the origin of "intent" was irrelevant since it was impossible to ascertain the "predisposition" of the defendant to commit the crime. Instead they asserted that entrapment should be based solely on whether or not the conduct of government agents was likely to induce a normally law-abiding person to commit the offense. Because the court would still be forced to infer the threshold of blandishments that the common citizen could withstand, the test would not be perfect, just better. This is primarily a judicial argument; the court, if it ever adopts this test (and all cases have thus far been decided on "subjective" grounds), would have to declare entrapment any time the conduct or role of government agents exceeded some statutory level.

Assessing the conduct of the government in Abscam and the action of the various congressmen, I maintain that, regardless of which legal test is used, the defendants cannot be said to have been entrapped. Clearly the government agents created an opportunity for the commission of crimes by offering bribes. However, the level of involvement of government agents was far less than in either *Hampton* or *Russell*, and in these cases the original convictions were sustained. Nor did government agents pressure or persistently solicit their targets in the face of reluctance. Furthermore, the origin of the criminal act rested solidly with the congressmen and those who operated as their fronts. All approached the sting operation with the intent of making a mutually beneficial exchange of influence for money or for promised investments in their districts. As New York Federal District Court Judge George Pratt said when sentencing a group of Abscam defendants:

> The court is convinced that the defendant Congressmen appeared through a self selecting procedure that involved other defendants as well. The agents did not set out to offer bribes to any particular Congressmen. They set no standards, established no criteria. Instead, the middlemen . . . carried the word that money was there for the taking by any Congressmen who would promise legislative aid to the sheik's need for asylum in the United States. . . . In short each was a willing volunteer.

On a subjective test the origin of the crime rests with the defendants and the issue of intent or predisposition is demonstrated and therefore settled. If an "objective" standard were to be used, the defendants would fare no better. They could each have simply refused the proffered deal. Fifty thousand dollars may be tempting, but it is hardly an overwhelming inducement. Three legislators—Senator Pressler, Congressman Patten, and Congressman Murtha—were able to withstand the temptation.

When these cases appear before the Federal Supreme Court, the law of entrapment which has been operating for 50 years may be re-evaluated. Since its subject will be congressmen and not drug addicts or pushers, it is likely that the court may moderate and refine the rules and tests of entrapment in a desirable manner. The Senate's assessment will also add some insights and conclusions about the political crimes of Abscam.

I do not take the extreme position of Mark Twain, who said about the U.S. Congress that it was "the only distinctively native criminal class." I do believe, however, that Abscam can be viewed in one context as an interesting criminological situation test. The research results revealed a high level of potential congressional political criminals who are amenable to the commission of power-status crimes for profit. Many of these offenses are socially perceived as "crimes." A case in point involves then—Democratic Speaker of the House Jim Wright, who in April, 1989, was cited unanimously by the House Ethics Committee for 69 violations of House rules.

Lyn Nofziger and Michael Deaver: Political Power for Rent   The intent of the 1978 Ethics in Government Act is clear. It was written to prohibit former federal officials from selling their influence with friends in government. The law is not unduly restrictive. A would-be lobbyist must wait only one year after leaving the government before contacting former associates. One of Reagan's chief assistants, Lyn Nofziger, was convicted in 1988 for violating the Ethics in Government Act. He violated the law by using his position to acquire special favors from lobbying clients, criminally profiting from this practice.

The case of Lyn Nofziger, 63, a onetime California newsman who served as Ronald Reagan's political director until January, 1982, reveals how certain political criminals violate the law for profit and see nothing wrong with their behavior. After a 16-day trial, a federal jury in Washington found Nofziger guilty of illegally contacting the White House for three clients of his "communications" firm: New York City's scandal-plagued Wedtech Corp., which paid Nofziger's agency $1 million to help secure a small-engine contract with the Army; Fairchild Republic Co., which paid his firm $25,000 to promote continued federal funding of the A-10 antitank aircraft; and the National Marine Engineers'

Beneficial Association, a maritime union that retained him at $90,000 a year to advocate the use of more civilian sailors on U.S. fleet support ships.

Nofziger's lawyers did not deny that on April 8, 1982, he wrote to Edwin Meese, then counselor to the president, urging that Wedtech get the $32 million Army contract. They conceded that Nofziger talked to National Security Council aides on September 24, 1982, about the Fairchild planes and wrote to a Meese deputy on August 20 of that year about the sailors' jobs. But these overtures did not violate the Ethics in Government Act, they argued, because the law prohibits lobbying only on matters of "direct and substantial interest" to the contacted agencies. Nofziger dismissed his crime as being "kind of like running a stop sign." He received a 90-day prison sentence.

Another former Reagan aide, and a close personal friend of President Reagan, Michael Deaver was convicted of lying about lobbying and using his former White House connections. He was accorded a $100,000 fine, placed on probation for three years, and ordered to perform 1,500 hours of community service. Deaver, like Nofziger, had no criminal self-concept. On the courthouse steps after sentencing, he commented, "It was a very fair sentence, if I had been guilty."

Deaver claimed he had been an alcoholic and that his alcohol problem should have exonerated him from his crime. If alcoholism or substance abuse were a valid defense, at least half of America's criminal population should be released from prison.

Representative John Dingall, a Democrat from Michigan and chairman of the House Energy and Commerce Commission, before which Deaver was convicted of lying, criticized the sentence as being too lenient: "It sends the wrong message. The message is that the powerful can get away with things most people can't. That's the standard to which this administration has lowered the country." President Reagan commented on the Deaver sentence: "I never thought he did anything wrong. I believe he's innocent."

It is apparent that neither Nofziger, Deaver, nor Reagan perceived the behavior involved as criminal. This, as has been indicated, is a common characteristic of white collar criminals. They do not have a criminal self-concept. In addition, even when they are convicted, their sentences are moderate when compared to the severe sentences meted out to traditional criminals.

Attorney General Edwin Meese: Criminal or Political Victim? At the center of any federal administration's handling of judicial matters is the Department of Justice and its attorney general. No attorney general in history (with the possible exception of John Mitchell in the Nixon administration) has been as severely confronted with attacks on his ethical perceptions and behavior as has Edwin Meese III. He was maintained in office by President Reagan (February, 1985, to August, 1988) despite a series of unethical situations and criminal allegations.

In all the following allegations, no criminal act was conclusively proved; however, one can speculate that some of Meese's dealings, like Agnew's, might emerge after he retired from the attorney general position and was no longer in the spotlight.

July 25, 1983 White House counsel Fred F. Fielding begins reviewing allegations that Meese, then White House counselor, and Michael K. Deaver, at the time White House deputy chief of staff, received $118,000 in loans arranged by their California tax accountant, John R. McKean, at a time they were getting McKean a $10,000-a-year presidential appointment to the U.S. Postal Service's Board of Governors.

September 27, 1983 The Army's inspector general finds irregularities in Meese's promotion to colonel in the Army Reserve but says that there is no evidence of undue influence. The investigator recommends against revoking Meese's promotion, which had been approved by Major General William R. Berkman, an old friend of Meese.

March 27, 1984 Attorney General William French Smith asks a three-judge federal panel to name an independent counsel to investigate broad allegations against Meese, who recently had been nominated to be Smith's successor. The inquiry is prompted by reports that Meese failed to list on his financial disclosure form an interest-free $15,000 loan his wife received from Edwin Thomas. Thomas, his wife, and their son had been appointed to federal jobs.

January 28, 1985 Two staff lawyers in the Office of Government Ethics conclude that Meese, then attorney general–designate, twice violated federal conflict of interest rules, but the staff report is overruled by the agency director. The report alleges that Meese should have disqualified himself when two men who had helped him financially were considered for federal jobs.

December 17, 1986 The Justice Department's Office of Professional Responsibility investigates Meese's decision to delay for ten days an FBI investigation of an airline involved in Iranian arms deals and weapons shipments to the Nicaragua Contras. The Justice Department says that the central figure in the Iran arms sale operation, then National Security Council aide Oliver North, had asked Meese in October to delay the inquiry into Southern Air Transport, formerly owned by the CIA.

January 7, 1987 The Justice Department requests an independent counsel to investigate allegations that former White House aide

Lyn Nofziger may have violated federal ethics laws by lobbying Meese and other former colleagues on behalf of the Wedtech Corp. shortly after leaving office in 1983.

April 6, 1987   Meese acknowledges that he intervened on behalf of Wedtech to ensure that it got a fair hearing from the Army in its effort to win the $32-million engine contract. Meese also says that his close friend and former lawyer, E. Robert Wallach, sent him a series of memorandums in 1981 and 1982 promoting Wedtech.

May 11, 1987   Meese announces that he has terminated his financial partnership with W. Franklyn Chinn, a financial advisor. In February, Chinn had been forced to resign from the Wedtech board because of allegedly questionable financial transactions. (Chinn was later indicted for his alleged illegal involvement with Wedtech.)

June 30, 1987   The Office of Government Ethics says that Meese violated financial disclosure requirements after investing $60,000 with Chinn. (Meese earned a sizable increase in his investment over a two-day period.) The agency's director says that Meese voluntarily invested the money in 1985 under an arrangement that failed to qualify as a blind trust under the 1978 Ethics in Government Act.

January 7, 1988   Independent counsel James C. McKay's investigation of Meese is extended to include charges that he may have had a conflict of interest when he met with the heads of regional telephone companies to discuss legal restrictions on their firms at a time when he and his wife still owned telephone stock.

January 29, 1988   Sources say that the independent counsel is focusing on a 1985 memo from Wallach to Meese that allegedly cited a plan to pay off a high-ranking official in Jerusalem to help head off Israeli interference in a $1-billion Iraqi pipeline project. Meese later says that he did not recall noticing the mention of the payoff plan in the memo. Wallach received $150,000 in fees from a financier for exploring the deal, and it was alleged that Meese might receive a share of this $150,000 for helping create the project.

March 23, 1988   McKay widens the investigation of Meese, looking into the Justice Department's renewal of a ten-year, $50 million office lease that was signed after the building's owner had provided a $40,000 annual salary for Meese's wife for her work at a public service organization.

March 29, 1988   Deputy Attorney General Arnold Burns, the second-ranking official in the department, and Assistant Attorney

General William Weld, who oversaw all federal criminal investigations, resigned along with four of their aides, telling associates that Meese's legal problems hampered the operation of the department.

When Meese finally announced that he was resigning as attorney general in August, 1988, the *Los Angeles Times* printed an editorial titled "Good Riddance," which reflected the sentiments of many public officials and citizens:

Attorney General Edwin Meese III purports to find vindication in the findings of independent counsel James C. McKay, but we can't imagine where. What we find, as we study the 814-page report released Monday, is a dossier of chiseling, cronyism and conflict of interest whose disclosure would embarrass almost anyone who cared one whit about professional ethics or the standing of the Justice Department. Anyone except Ed Meese.

Most Americans, for example, would have trouble sleeping if they had failed to report $20,000 in income to the Internal Revenue Service. But, as McKay's report reveals, Meese couldn't put his hands on the right documents when his 1985 tax return was due, so he neglected to report $20,706 in capital gains from the sale of stocks. Only when his accountants were summoned before a grand jury in February of this year did Meese file an amended return and pay the government what was due two years earlier. McKay decided that a jury would probably convict Meese for filing a "materially false tax return," but he declined to prosecute partly because the attorney general had paid up.

On paper, it would also appear that Meese violated a federal conflict-of-interest law by participating in the breakup of AT&T while owning $14,000 in regional telephone company stock. The independent counsel, showing Meese every benefit of the doubt, decided not to prosecute because Meese, while working at the White House in the early 1980s, got special permission to work on AT&T matters despite his stockholdings and again in 1987 sought another waiver. The intervening years were not covered by waivers, but McKay chose to ignore what would have been a very technical infraction.

McKay's investigation of Meese's involvement in the proposed construction of a $1-billion Iraqi oil pipeline, the central issue in the case, was hampered by uncooperative witnesses, especially E. Robert Wallach. As McKay reported, Meese "undertook unusual activities" for Wallach, his longtime friend and lawyer. Meese asked then–National Security Advisor Robert C. McFarlane to meet with Wallach, who had been retained by a Swiss-based businessman to help with the project. At the very same time, Wallach was performing all sorts of favors for Meese—helping him refinance his house and finding his wife a job. McKay noted "the coincidence . . . between Mr. Meese's acceptance of things of value from Mr. Wallach and Mr. Meese's official acts that benefited Mr. Wallach." But after Wallach invoked his Fifth Amendment privilege against self-incrimination and declined to testify, McKay concluded that there was not enough evidence to prove that Meese *knew* that Wallach expected favors in return. In essence, McKay couldn't prove Meese's criminal intent.

No matter how loudly Meese protests his innocence or denounces McKay's probe as a waste of money, the facts that the prosecutor has laid out belie his claims. On this record the Justice Department's Office of Professional Responsibility would be justified in recommending Meese's censure; we can't think of a better send-off as the attorney general returns to private life next month. Meese escaped prosecution only because the prosecutor was not certain that he could prove him guilty on the major counts and considered it unwise to pursue the minor ones alone. Good prosecutors make just these kinds of decisions all the time. The ultimate irony in this case is that Meese, a bad prosecutor who disgraced the Justice Department, should be spared by a good prosecutor.[27]

As we have seen, people commit political crimes in order to maintain political power, acquire political power, or use political power for personal gain. Two categories of people commit these crimes: disenfranchised people *out of power* amd a group of higher-status people *in power*.

The motivations for the maintenance or the acquisition of political power are more apt to be ideological, whereas the acquisition of power for financial gain involves the base human trait of greed. In many respects the form of political crime motivated by greed is more reprehensible than the ideological; it involves a clear abuse of public trust. People who have been given political power in the social system, either through the vote or through appointment by an elected public official, owe honest service to their fellow citizens.

Voting ethically lax or sociopathic leaders into power ensures the appointment of their own kind into high political offices. This creates a government environment that spawns political crimes. People who commit them usually do not have a criminal self-concept; they have the sociopath's limited concern about the ethics of their behavior. In many respects, political crime is more insidious and costly, and has a more deleterious impact on society through corroding the public trust, than all other forms of crime combined.

---

[27] "Good Riddance," *Los Angeles Times*, July 19, 1988. Reprinted by permission.

Chapter
13

Organized Crime

Members of organized crime are full-time career criminals, and many of them are homicidal sociopaths. In the hierarchy, as in most corporations, potential executives usually start at the bottom and attempt to rise in the structure; they engage in various criminal activities, especially violent street crime, and use "family" or friends to help them move up the ladder.

The sociological and popular literature abounds with descriptions of organized crime—varyingly called the syndicate, the Mafia, or the Cosa Nostra (Italian for "our thing")—as being a cohesive and coherent group organization. My speculation is that organized crime does exist but it may be more a "near-group" than a cohesive group. There appear to be many criminal organizations that make up "organized crime," and they are not all interconnected into one criminal empire.

Another significant factor about organized crime is that its criminal activities do not flourish in a social vacuum. As will be further delineated, various research reveals that organized crime would not exist without interconnections to corrupt people and organizations in politics and business. These three corrupt factions—political, white collar, and organized crime systems—use and feed on each other.

THE HISTORY, NATURE, AND EXTENT OF ORGANIZED CRIME IN AMERICA

There is much folklore about organized crime in America. Much of the myth has been fostered by various books and films. It was not until 1951, however, that a United States Senate committee named after its chairman, Senator Estes Kefauver, produced relevant data about the nature and extent of organized crime in America.

After completing an investigation of organized crime—which lasted over a year, involved traveling over 52,000 miles, and included 92 days of hearings—the Kefauver committee reached several conclusions:

1. Organized criminal gangs operating in interstate commerce were firmly entrenched in the operation of many gambling enterprises, such as bookmaking, policy rackets, and slot machines, and in the sale and distribution of narcotics and commercialized prostitution.
2. Criminal syndicates in this country made tremendous profits, owing primarily to their ability to secure monopolies in the illegal operations in which they engage.
3. The two major crime syndicates in the country at that time were the Accardo-Guzik-Fischetti syndicate, with headquarters in Chicago, and the Costello-Adonis-Lansky syndicate, in New York.
4. There was a sinister criminal organization known as the Mafia operating throughout the country, with ties in other nations, in the opinion of the committee.
5. Despite arrest records and well-documented criminal reputations, the leading criminals in the country remained largely immune to prosecution and punishment, although their underlings were on occasion prosecuted, convicted, and punished.
6. Gambling profits at that time were the principal support of big-time racketeering and gangsterism.[1]

CHARACTERISTICS OF ORGANIZED CRIME

Organized crime has the following characteristics:

1. *Hierarchic Structure*　There is a chain of command in many respects resembling that of an army or a large corporation. The people at the top give orders to junior executives, who transmit the orders to persons further down in the hierarchy for ultimate communication to the individuals designed to carry them out. Members of ordinary criminal gangs are usually partners who know each other well, so the apprehension of one often leads to the apprehension of others and to the termination of their criminal activity. Because of its hierarchic structure, this is not necessarily true of organized crime.

---

[1] *Third Interim Report of the Special Committee to Investigate Organized Crime in Interstate Commerce* [Kefauver Committee], Senate Report no. 307 (Washington, D.C.: Government Printing Office, 1952), pp. 1–2 (hereafter cited as Kefauver Committee Third Interim Report).

2. *Threatening or Using Force*   Violence is used to enforce the will of the overlords of organized crime. A criminal syndicate will often recruit career criminals as enforcers of its will.

3. *Extensive Planning*   Planning deals with the operation of enterprise, management of personnel, relationships with political figures and police, and distribution of profits.

4. *Relative Immunity to Prosecution at the Higher Echelons*   Organized crime syndicates seek protection against arrest and prosecution for all personnel employed by them. According to the Kefauver committee, there was evidence of corruption of public officials in several forms: (*a*) direct bribe or protection payments made to law enforcement officials so that they would not interfere with specific criminal activities, (*b*) political pressure to protect criminal activities or further the interests of criminal gangs, and (*c*) direct participation by law enforcement officials in the business of organized crime.[2]

5. *Interlocking Leadership*   The Kefauver committee established that there were relationships between leaders of gambling enterprises and between these gambling bosses and the leaders of groups engaged in the distribution of narcotics, commercialized vice, and other illegal enterprises. The committee also reported evidence of infiltration into many legitimate business activities.

The President's Commission on Law Enforcement at that time described organized crime as consisting of 24 groups allied with other racket enterprises to form a loose confederation operating in large and small cities. Each of the 24 groups is known as a "family," with membership varying from as many as 700 men to as few as 20. In 1971 the Department of Justice reported the existence of 26 families operating in 21 metropolitan areas. The structure and activities of a typical family are shown in Figure 13.1.

Maintaining a Low Profile

Many films about organized crime, seen by millions of Americans, have served to glamorize the Mafia but have done little to familiarize the public with its criminal operations.

Despite some modest knowledge about the "family," organized crime is an enigma to those outside its ranks. It takes an enormous toll of life and property, yet the overlords of organized crime are relatively immune to prosecution and seldom inhabit our prisons or burden our parole systems. Their victims include compulsive gamblers, drug addicts, workers swindled by racketeer unions, and business people exploited by protective associations. In the course of their activities these criminals succeed in influencing or controlling many public

---

[2] Kefauver Committee Third Interim Report, p. 184.

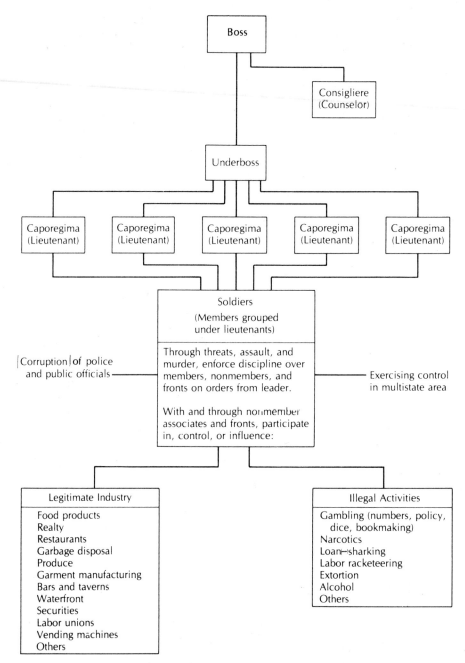

Figure 13.1 An organized crime family. [*Source:* President's Commission on Law Enforcement and Administration of Justice, *The Challenge of Crime in a Free Society* (Washington, D.C.: U.S. Government Printing Office, 1967), p. 194.]

officials and business people through either intimidation or corruption.

The success of organized crime in influencing public officials gives its leaders relative immunity from arrest, prosecution, and conviction. Because the Mafia has succeeded in penetrating many echelons of the political and business spheres, many informed authorities consider it a serious threat to the democratic form of government.

When Robert F. Kennedy was attorney general, he testified before a Senate subcommittee that the physical protection of witnesses who cooperated with the federal government in organized crime cases presented serious problems. Witnesses had to change their appearances and their names, and some of them even had to leave the country. The government was apparently unable to protect its friends from its enemies without obliterating their identities.[3] The situation had changed very little by 1972, and has persisted to the present. Charles H. Haight, a longtime informer for the FBI and other federal agencies, who provided evidence against an opium smuggler in 1972, maintained that his life was in danger and the government was not adequately protecting him. With respect to this he said:

> I've got a $35,000 contract out on my life. . . . I've been threatened . . . I've been shot at . . . I've had my car "tampered" with and the government won't protect me. I've got to have an operation to save my life and the Veterans Administration won't let me into their hospitals because they say I'm a danger to other patients. I was shot at the last time I checked into a VA hospital.[4]

Many witnesses hesitate to give evidence against members of organized crime because they are afraid to face the consequences experienced by Mr. Haight. In recent years, the government's Witness Protection Program approach has helped to improve this situation. This program is discussed more fully in a later section of this chapter.

Organized Crime and Deviant Business

The illegal enterprises of organized crime thrive because of the following conditions:

1. A desire or demand for a particular service, product, or activity on the part of a substantial portion of the population. This desire or demand produces the potential consumer.
2. The failure of society to provide lawful means of satisfying the desire or demand.

---

[3] President's Commission on Law Enforcement, *The Challenge of Crime in a Free Society*, p. 187.

[4] Mary Neiswender, "Informer Says Life Periled, U.S. No Help," *Long Beach* (Calif.) *Press Telegram*, December 11, 1972.

3. The existence of an organized group ready and willing to supply the desired service, product, or activity.

In this section we shall analyze some of the illegal business enterprises of organized crime. Historically, the Mafia's deviant businesses originated with bootlegging.

Smuggling whiskey from abroad and distributing it in the United States required national and in many cases international syndication. The nationwide crime syndicate of which Kefauver spoke was probably formed to deal with hijacking and internecine rivalries within the loosely federated bootlegging industry. Relationships with law enforcement officials and politicians were also cemented during the Prohibition era. The unlimited consumer market for liquor accounted in large part for the growth of organized crime in America.

After Prohibition was repealed, organized crime concentrated its efforts on gambling, the distribution and sale of narcotic drugs, strikebreaking, labor racketeering, and other forms of racketeering. The group that had been organized to provide liquor when it could not be sold lawfully was now ready and willing to provide offtrack betting on horses, lotteries, other forms of gambling, drugs, and "muscle." Gambling was by far the most lucrative of these enterprises.

Beginning in the middle of the nineteenth century, most states in the United States outlawed various types of gambling. These laws represented attempts by the dominant groups to protect poor people from their own "folly." It was believed that workingmen who gambled and lost their money would be more likely to turn to stealing and other forms of crime and would be less likely to meet their obligations to their families. Gambling, however, like drinking, was traditional in almost every ethnic group that makes up the population of the United States. In Great Britain during the seventeenth and eighteenth centuries, gambling was highly respectable. Horse racing was considered the "sport of kings," and nobility was present at all racetrack openings. Betting parlors were prevalent, and even betting on credit was permitted. So were lotteries. In the United States, margin speculations in stocks, futures speculation in commodities, trading in commodity options, stock options, and many high-risk business ventures are lawful forms of gambling. So is wagering at a racetrack. Why, then, pass laws making gambling a crime outside these limited areas? Poor people see this as an attempt by the rich to harrass them, to keep them in constant unfavorable contact with the police, and to interfere with a traditional or customary activity that provides hope and sometimes joy. By making some forms of gambling illegal, we have given to organized crime a virtual monopoly over many activities.

For many years the man reputed to be the head of the organized crime syndicate's gambling activities was the late Meyer Lansky. During Prohibition, Lansky had been a partner of two organized crime leaders,

Joe Adonis and Frank Costello, in three distilleries. Later his interests included casinos, narcotics, and a bookie network. In the 1930s Lansky became a member of the Mafia "commission" to establish a supreme council. After the liquidation of former partner Bugsy Siegel in 1947, Lansky took over the syndicate's gambling interests in Las Vegas and the rest of the United States. Syndicate-owned hotels made substantial contributions to the campaigns of Governor Grant Sawyer, Paul Laxalt, Senator Alan Bible, and other Nevada politicians. All of them protested the FBI's bugging of Lansky's telephone conversations. His personal assets were estimated to be about $300 million by the Internal Revenue Service. In 1970 Lansky went to Israel to avoid indictment. He was referred to there as a "philanthropist" and a "Miami Beach socialite." He and a group of associates built the multimillion-dollar Dan Hotel in Tel Aviv, the largest hotel in Israel, with 1,000 air-conditioned rooms, and large chain hotels in three other cities. In 1973 Lansky was extradited to the United States to stand trial for some of his activities. Although active in organized crime for over half a century, Meyer Lansky served only one jail sentence—three months for an illegal gambling operation in Saratoga, New York.[5]

In the 1980s, the strong link established by Lansky between the Las Vegas hotel gambling empire, state and local politicians, and organized crime continued. According to FBI reports, the illegal skimming of billions of dollars from hotel receipts continues, and most of this money ends up in the hands of organized crime leaders. One earlier report on gambling for the Organized Crime Task Force of the President's Crime Commission stated that the turnover of illegal gambling in the United States was not less than $30 billion per year, with annual profits of about $7 billion.[6] An FBI agent estimated that in the 1980s organized crime netted around $50 billion a year from illegal gambling, including skimming in Atlantic City and Las Vegas.

At present, legal state-run gambling operations net billions of dollars. Instant lotteries, in which winners are announced immediately, have been particularly successful. Despite this, the evidence remains that organized crime, through skimming and various other illegal gambling activities, nets billions of tax-free dollars.

Organized Crime and Legitimate Business

We have no way of knowing how far organized crime has penetrated legitimate business. On this matter in 1960 Robert Kennedy concluded:

---

[5] William Schulz, "The Shocking Success Story of 'P.E. No. 1,'" *Reader's Digest* 96 (May 1970):54–59. See also Hank Messick, *Lansky* (New York: Putnam, 1971).

[6] Rufus King, *Gambling and Organized Crime* (Washington, D.C.: Public Affairs Press, 1969). See also Donald R. Cressey, *Theft of the Nation* (New York: Harper & Row, 1969).

The results of the underworld infiltration into labor-management affairs forms a shocking pattern across the country. We found and duly proved that the gangsters of today work in a highly organized fashion and are far more powerful now than at any time in the history of the country. They control political figures and threaten whole communities. They have stretched their tentacles of corruption and fear into industries both large and small. They grow stronger every day.[7]

In a later book, *Crime in American Society*, sociologist Charles H. McCaghy cogently pointed out how and why organized crime participates in legitimate businesses:

Not all businesses operated by organized criminals are strictly illegal. Criminals own hotels, construction and trucking companies, catering services, bars, and a variety of sales and service establishments; gangsters are involved in some labor unions; and they control other businesses which are legal, though of marginal respectability, such as casinos and pornography-distributing companies.[8]

There are several possible reasons why organized criminals participate in legitimate organizations.

1. *Emergence into Legitimacy* Ownership of legal businesses may openly signal the beginning of withdrawal from illegal businesses. Younger generations of established crime families may be unwilling to continue the activities of their parents; these new generations have the financial resources to obtain good educations and to establish themselves in respectable enterprises. The criminal enterprises are relinquished to those more willing to take the risks.

2. *Laundering Money* The immense profits from illegal businesses can present a problem for organized criminals. Law enforcement officials tend to become curious about where the money came from and whether all appropriate taxes have been paid. This kind of attention can be minimized by channeling the funds through a legitimate business, which effectively "launders" them because their source is disguised as legal profit from the business. [Laundering is a major aspect of the illicit drug business today.]

3. *Scams* Scams involve using a legitimate company to acquire funds illegally by employing the company's established credit. For example, suppose the owner of a small store finds himself hopelessly in debt to a loan shark. The shark and his buddies may become "partners" and begin a scam: they order merchandise on the store's credit, the merchandise is sold to a fence or anyone

---

[7] Robert F. Kennedy, *The Enemy Within* (New York: Harper & Row, 1960), p. 240.

[8] Reprinted with permission of Macmillan Publishing Co., Inc., from *Crime in American Society* by Charles H. McCaghy. Copyright 1980 by Macmillan Publishing Co., Inc.

who does not ask questions, the funds are pocketed by the gangsters, and the store eventually goes into bankruptcy. In 1988 a scam of this type was operated at the 222 Carpet Company, when the young owner invited organized crime figures to share in his "business."

4. *Labor Racketeering* Offhand, it might seem that when organized criminals participate in labor unions they are identifying with the common worker's cause. Unfortunately, gangster infiltration of unions is not unselfishly motivated. To be a union official is to control the union's members, its pension funds, and its contract negotiations with employers. Controlling members in some instances means determining who works and who does not; this encourages shakedowns of members for employment privileges and provides plush jobs for loyal gang members. Controlling members also opens opportunities for organized on-the-job pilferage, especially from construction sites and waterfront loading docks. Union pension funds provide vast pools of money to enrich union officials and to finance friends' pet projects.

The classic example of the connection between organized crime and labor unions is found in the case of the International Brotherhood of Teamsters, which has had a history of such activity throughout most of the twentieth century.

Organized Crime and Labor Unions

In his cogent book *Organized Crime,* August Bequai delineated the connections between organized crime, labor unions, and racketeering. This interrelationship is a unique characteristic of American society. As Bequai wrote:

> In late March 1978 Salvatore Briguglio, a syndicate-connected union leader, was shot to death by two hired assassins in New York. During this time an official high in the Labor Department was reassuring on audience of concerned citizens that the federal government's crackdown on labor racketeering had proved a success. In Las Vegas federal sources were expressing concern that a key Mafia leader had made an attempt to gain control of some local unions. Other government sources were expressing concern that one of the nation's largest labor unions might soon elect an ex-felon as its president. The individual involved is alleged to have strong links with organized crime, has been under investigations by federal authorities for more than a dozen years, was once convicted for obstruction of justice, and served a brief prison term. His second-in-command also has a history of criminal involvement and has been indicted three times by federal prosecutors.[9]

---

[9] August Bequai, *Organized Crime* (Boston: Lexington Books, Heath, 1979).

Frauds involving pension and welfare funds have become a serious problem, another example of the relationship of labor unions to organized crime. Many of these funds have been depleted by loans to anyone willing to give a kickback to corrupt union officials; organized crime–owned businesses have received loans under these terms. Funds have also been invested in elaborate securities schemes. Union funds have been used to hire racketeers as consultants at exorbitant salaries, as well as to buy boats, airplanes, and even homes for corrupt labor officials.

The Teamsters Union The Teamsters union's history as a labor union and its connection with organized crime are a sordid issue in the labor union movement. In the early years, organized criminals were hired by employers as strikebreakers. In recent years, organized crime infiltrated many labor unions. The most serious and pervasive infiltration is found in the Teamsters union.

An article in the July 11, 1988, issue of *Time* delineated some of the issues involved and described a hotly debated government approach to the problem:

> "He was ridiculed. He was vilified. He was hated irrationally—but he was right." With that paean to Robert Kennedy and his long battle against the crime-ridden leadership of the International Brotherhood of Teamsters, U.S. Attorney Rudolph Giuliani took on the task that has stymied Kennedy and other prosecutors for the past thirty years. Giuliani, however, comes to the fight armed with a powerful weapon.
>
> Last week in New York City, he unveiled a far-reaching civil lawsuit, charging 26 reputed mobsters and the Teamsters' 18 top executives with making a "devil's pact" to subvert the nation's largest union. Filed under the Racketeer-Influenced and Corrupt Organization Act, the suit aims to oust the union's entire leadership, replacing it with a court-appointed trustee who will supervise the "free and fair" election of a new executive board.
>
> Earlier prosecutors were forced to fight the union's corruption by charging individual leaders with specific crimes: Teamsters President Jackie Presser, for example, is under indictment for racketeering and embezzlement, and past Presidents Dave Beck, Jimmy Hoffa and Roy Williams all went to jail. RICO frees the Justice Department to take action against an entire institution. Building on more than 300 convictions of Teamsters and union-related Mob figures since 1970, the lawsuit portrays the leadership of the 1.6 million-member union as a front for the Mafia. Organized crime, charged Giuliani, "has deprived union members of their rights through a pattern of racketeering that includes 20 murders, a number of shootings, bombings, beatings, a campaign of fear, bribery, extortion, theft and misuse of union funds."[10]

Although the Reagan administration professed enthusiasm for the Teamsters suit and for a government takeover of the Teamsters union,

---

[10] "Breaking a Devil's Pact," *Time*, July 11, 1988. © 1988 Time Inc. Reprinted by permission.

the announcement caused some embarrassment. The Teamsters endorsed the Reagan-Bush ticket in 1980 and 1984 and the Bush-Quayle ticket in 1988. Presser was named advisor to the 1980 Reagan transition team, headed by none other than Edwin Meese III. "Had this information been available at the time," Attorney General Meese said last week, "President Reagan . . . would obviously not have accepted that kind of support." But evidence of the Teamsters' pact with organized crime was known well before 1980. As the 1985 report of the President's Commission on Organized Crime pointed out, "Jackie Presser had . . . an extensive record of organized-crime associations through organizations that were infested with La Cosa Nostra associates and convicted felons." It was revealed after Presser's death on July 9, 1988, that he had been a government informer for the FBI for a period of over nine years. Although he worked closely with the Mafia, Presser provided valuable information which was later useful in prosecuting many Mafia leaders.

Organized Crime and the Drug Business

During the nineteenth century and the early part of the twentieth century, most doctors carried morphine, codeine, and other opium derivatives in their medical kits and dispensed them to patients to relieve suffering. These drugs were inexpensive and in most cases quite effective. In addition to being directly administered to patients by physicians, these drugs were sold to the public in pharmacies, grocery stores, and general stores in the form of patent medicines. Although there is evidence that medical doctors were aware of the dependence created by the use of these drugs, they continued to administer them because the dependence was deemed less harmful to the patient than the suffering the drug alleviated.

After 1915, as a result of the passage of the Harrison Anti-Narcotic Act and an interpretive regulation of the Treasury Department, there was no longer any lawful way for a person addicted to any of the opium derivatives to acquire these drugs. It is estimated that by that time there were over 100,000 addicts and an additional 250,000 users of narcotic drugs in the United States. The nation thus found itself with a large number of people who had a need for a product with no means of lawfully satisfying it. The evidence obtained by various Senate Crime Investigating Committees clearly indicated that organized crime began to supply the narcotics necessary to satisfy that need.

In the 1980s, cocaine smuggling became an even bigger business than heroin smuggling for organized crime in the United States. Heroin use is, for the most part, restricted to the lower socioeconomic class, but cocaine use pervades all strata of society and constitutes an enormous business that has been infiltrated by organized crime. This illicit business was described in a *Time* cover story:

> Of all drugs in the U.S., cocaine is now the biggest producer of illicit income. Some 40 metric tons of it will be shipped into the country this year. As coke

experts like to point out, if all the international dealers who supply the drug to the U.S. market—not even including the retailers—were to form a single corporation, it would probably rank seventh on the FORTUNE 500 list, between Ford Motor Co. ($37 billion in revenue) and Gulf Oil Corp. ($26.5 billion). Last year street sales of cocaine, by far the most expensive drug on the market, reached an estimated $30 billion in the U.S. (Sales of marijuana, the runner-up and still the most widely used illicit drug, amounted to some $24 billion.) . . .

The cocaine trade may be the most lucrative form of commerce in the world. Periodic glimpses of its staggering scale are afforded by headlines such as those in Wilmington, N.C., early this month. DEA and U.S. Customs officials swooped in on a twin-engine Cessna that made an unscheduled nighttime landing, arresting the pilot and a passenger and seizing their cargo of 440 lbs. of cocaine. The estimated wholesale value of the shipment: $16 million.

The drug's main port of entry is Miami. By no coincidence, the Miami branch of the Federal Reserve Bank of Atlanta is the only branch bank in the U.S. Reserve system to show a cash surplus—$4.75 billion worth in 1980. A likely explanation: laundered cash from drugs.

Allan Pringle, deputy regional director for the DEA, says of Miami: "The brokers are here, the financiers are here, the heads of the organizations are here." More than 80% of all cocaine seized worldwide is confiscated in Florida—yet by the most optimistic estimate, seizures of smuggled dope account for no more than 10% of the total traffic entering southern Florida. Arrests of cocaine smugglers and dealers pose a huge logistical problem. . . . Pringle: "In some cases we've had so much cash on our hands that we've had difficulty transporting it for storage. We're talking literally about billions in small bills."[11]

Cocaine smuggling, because of its lucrative possibilities, is a prime enterprise for organized crime. Its members have the ready cash, the connections, and the criminal organization to smuggle cocaine into the country and sell it to the variety of users at all levels of our society.

The retail value of the heroin and cocaine required to support the habits of U.S. drug addicts is estimated to be in the billions of dollars each year. In an effort to determine the structure of criminal organizations engaged in the importation, distribution, and sale of heroin, I interviewed drug addicts, pushers, peddlers, and police officers specializing in the apprehension of narcotics offenders. Practically all people involved in the drug trade are men. While there may be several echelons in each of the categories, the following specializations and methods of operation emerged:

The Importer-Smuggler   The importer is a representative of the upper echelon of a crime organization. He may never actually touch narcotic

---

[11] "Cocaine: Middle Class High," *Time*, July 6, 1981. Copyright 1981 Time Inc. Reprinted by permission from TIME.

drugs. He may order a shipment directly or through a representative from Hong Kong, Peru, Colombia, Mexico City, Ankara, Paris, Rome, or some other city in which suppliers are represented. Payment is generally made at the time of the order, and a delivery date and time are set. Various devices may be employed to camouflage the shipment. It might, for example, be concealed in automobile tires. The purchaser would then be advised to order 40 tires for delivery to an auto parts supply company in New York City. The importer need never claim the tires or handle the drugs. All he does is transfer the bill of lading to the purchaser, who then claims the shipment. It is virtually impossible to catch the importer unless someone else in the business informs on him. Since he is usually a high-ranking member of his criminal organization, this would be a very unhealthy thing to do. In any case, very few people know much about his business.

The Wholesale Distributor   The wholesaler is also a member of the organized crime syndicate. He very seldom receives a direct delivery of narcotics from the importer. In the instance cited above, a bill of lading changes hands. The bill of lading is assigned to an auto parts dealer, who acts for the distributor by picking up the tires. If apprehended, the auto parts dealer claims that he is participating in a legitimate transaction and denies all knowledge of the drugs. His bill of lading covers 40 tires at the regular price for those tires, and there is no indication that the tires contain narcotics. Even if the police and agents of the Bureau of Narcotics know the distributor by reputation, search the tires, and confiscate the narcotics, they may still have difficulty obtaining a conviction because of lack of evidence of guilty knowledge on the part of the purchaser. The parts dealer is most unlikely to supply evidence against the wholesale distributor.

The Supplier-Distributor   The supplier-distributor generally deals directly with the wholesale distributor in his area of operation. He pays the wholesale distributor for the drugs, which are subsequently delivered to a designated point by an agent of the wholesaler. If either the wholesaler or the supplier is followed and any part of the transaction witnessed by an enforcement officer, there is insufficient evidence to result in a conviction. The delivery agent is occasionally picked up by the police and convicted of possession of drugs. He seldom testifies against his employer. The supplier sells to peddlers in his area, and these transactions are handled in much the same manner as the transaction between the supplier and the wholesale distributor. Money changes hands and the drugs are later "dropped." In a large city the supplier may give the peddler a key to a locker at a bus terminal or railroad station. The two know each other and, to an extent, trust each other.

The Peddler   The peddler is a member of the lowest echelon of organized crime. He is usually not an addict himself. He purchases from distributors in his area and sells to pushers, most of whom are addicts. He is in a highly exposed position and knows it. Occasionally he is picked up after identification by pushers. The addict-pusher may tell the police the name of the peddler who supplies him and how best to make a purchase. Delivery by the peddler to the pusher is generally direct. However, when the peddler is selling to someone not known to him, he takes great precautions. He may use a drop delivery or have an addict-pusher he does know make the delivery for him. He does not solicit business directly but encourages his pushers to expand their own activities.

The Dealer-Addict   The pusher is not a member of the criminal organization; he is not acceptable to the syndicate. He is generally an addict who has been encouraged by his pusher to start selling as an agent of the pusher. When an addict begins to require more drugs than he can pay for, he generally asks for credit. At this point he is urged to sell to his friends and thereby make enough to pay for his own supply. Of the 70 drug users I interviewed in a study at Riker's Island Penitentiary in New York City, all but two acknowledged that at one time or another they had pushed drugs, and that their first sales had been to their friends.

The pusher or "connection" deals directly with customers and is extremely vulnerable to arrest. An addict picked up by the police for a burglary or larceny will frequently give the police the name of his or her connection. Arrests and convictions are frequent. However, the street dealer can seldom lead the police higher than the peddler, who seldom if ever will provide evidence against those in the higher echelons. The result is that the enterprise thrives, despite the best efforts of the Bureau of Narcotics and local law enforcement agencies.

The Addict   At the end of this line of criminals is the user-addict. If the addict is wealthy, he or she can support a habit through personal resources. If not—and most addicts are "street junkies"—then built into the addiction syndrome is the practice of traditional crime. The male street addict usually mugs, robs, or burglarizes to support his habit. Most female addicts turn to prostitution for this purpose.

ORGANIZED CRIME: ITALIAN, BLACK, AND HISPANIC

The organized crime concept has spread to various racial and ethnic groups in high-crime urban areas. According to Francis Ianni, who carried out direct research into the subject, organized crime is more than just a criminal way of life; it is an American way of life. It is a viable and persistent institution within American society with its own symbols, its own beliefs, its own logic, and its own means of transmitting these systematically from one generation to the next. As an integral part of economic life in the United States it can be viewed as falling at one end of a continuum which has the legitimate business world at the other end.

Viewed in this way, organized crime is a functional part of the American social system and, while successive waves of immigrants and migrants have found it an available means of economic and social mobility, it persists and transcends the involvement of any particular group and even the changing definitions of legality and illegality in social behavior.

Ianni noted that, at present, organized crime is in a period of transition. Italian domination has begun to give way to that of a new group: the blacks and Hispanics. This black and Hispanic involvement can be examined as part of the process of ethnic succession. They, like other minorities before them, are inheriting a major instrument of social and economic mobility. Although Ianni focused on the patterns of black and Hispanic crime activists, previous research on Italian-American patterns was utilized for comparison.

Ianni, in the course of his field study of the Lupollos, a pseudonym for an Italian-American family in organized crime, discovered that each succeeding generation of the Lupollo family had been moving quietly but certainly out of crime. Tracing the family through 70 years, he found that only 4 of the 27 males of the most recent generation were involved in organized crime.

The Lupollos had lost all their gambling activities in Harlem to blacks. In Brooklyn the family held some control through franchise arrangements with blacks and Puerto Ricans. The Lupollos supplied working capital and the necessary police and political protection in return for a share of the profits. Ianni later learned that this same change was occurring in other Italian-American crime families. In introducing his book, *Black Mafia*, he stated in part:

> By the time I completed my research in 1970 the pattern was so clear that I was able to report in A *Family Business* that as the Italians move or are forced out of organized crime, they are replaced or displaced by blacks and in some cases by Puerto Ricans. Following my study of the Lupollos, I spent eighteen months studying the emerging but as yet not clearly identifiable process of succession of blacks and Puerto Ricans in organized crime in the United States. What I put forward here as the major conclusion of this new study is the thesis that if this pattern continues, we shall witness over the next decade the systematic development of what is now a scattered and loosely organized pattern of emerging black control in organized crime into a black Mafia.[12]

Ianni described the relationships between ethnicity, politics, and organized crime in American cities as follows:

> The Irish came first, and early in this century they dominated crime as well as big-city political machinations. As they came to control the political machinery of large cities they won wealth, power and respectability through

---

[12] Francis A. J. Ianni, *Black Mafia* (New York: Simon & Schuster, 1974), p. xii. Copyright © 1974 by Francis A. J. Ianni. Reprinted by permission of Simon & Schuster, a Division of Gulf + Western Corporation.

subsequent control of construction, trucking, public utilities and waterfront. By the 1920's and the period of prohibition and speculation in the money markets and real estate, the Irish were succeeded in organized crime by the Jews, and Arnold Rothstein, Lepke Buchalter and Gurrah Shapiro dominated gambling and labor racketeering for over a decade. The Jews quickly moved into the world of business and the professions as more legitimate avenues to economic and social mobility. The Italians came next, and what Phil had been telling me—and what is now becoming increasingly obvious—was that as the Italians are leaving or are being pushed out of organized crime they are being replaced by the next wave of migrants to the city: blacks and Puerto Ricans.

Ethnic groups move in and out of organized crime and their time in control comes and goes. Even the specific crimes may change, as bootlegging is replaced by drug pushing and prostitution gives way to pornography. But organized crime as an American way of life persists and transcends the involvement of any particular group and the changing social definitions of what is illegal and what is not.[13]

He found the relationship between corrupt political structures and organized crime to be symbiotic, with success in one dependent on the right connections in the other. The aspiring member of a minority group, blocked from access to wealth and power, is permitted to produce and provide illicit goods and services that society publicly condemns but privately demands—gambling, stolen goods, sex, and drugs—always paying tribute to the political establishment. In return for payments, immunity from prosecution is provided by political machines. Crime is not viewed as an American problem and syndicates are safe in the ghetto as long as the slum dwellers "do it to each other."

Ianni attributed the recruitment of black and Puerto Rican youth into organized crime to the absence of deterrents. The formation of organized crime networks he blamed on the complicity of the police, the failure of the schools to reach these youngsters, and the broken structure of most of their families. He noted that

not a single force in the neighborhood where these boys grew up presented a vigorous deterrent—a serious threat, a danger, a fright or a compelling alternative set of values—to those of the street [gang] society, which justified most of their activities.[14]

The latest development in black and ethnic gangs are the black drug gangs of Los Angeles and the Jamaican gangs based mainly in New York. In 1988 there were over 400 gang-related murders in Los Angeles. Many of these can be directly attributed to the crack cocaine wars. The business aspect of crack is so lucrative that gang members literally kill over territorial rights. In some respects these murders have more logic

---

[13] Ianni, *Black Mafia*, pp. xiv–xv.

[14] Ibid., p. 141.

than the "turf murders" of the past. Many former gang members pursuing large profits have become involved in the drug trade of large cities around the United States.

THE FUTURE OF ORGANIZED CRIME IN AMERICA

The 1980s were characterized by efforts to prosecute various Mafia families. This happened in part because various former members of organized crime became government witnesses. One major penetration into the operations and activities of organized crime was the testimony of Jimmy "The Weasel" Fratianno, as detailed in the book *The Last Mafioso,* which Fratianno coauthored with Ovid Demaris. Fratianno's qualifications as an informant are impeccable. Born in 1913, he was a mob member for most of the 60 years he spent in criminal activities. He was a "capo," a "made man" who had been ritually accepted into the Mafia, a "hit man" who admittedly had killed at least nine men to fulfill his role in organized crime, and he had spent over a third of his life in prison.

According to the book, after Frantianno was inducted into the Cosa Nostra, he worked his way up the organized crime ladder until he reached the point where he was an associate of the top bosses and ultimately became a boss himself. He had access to many secrets and knew of the various links between the Mafia and legitimate business. During his Mafia years, from 1946 to 1975, Fratianno made both friends and enemies; around 1975, he became aware that a contract was out on his life.

At that point, Fratianno did not have enough money to leave the country. He decided, instead, to try to kill the leaders of the Mafia family that had put out the contract. He enlisted a prison friend, associated with the Mexican Mafia, to do these "hits," but his plan did not work out. Jimmy then realized that his association with organized crime was ended and that by working with the FBI he could get exactly what he wanted: safety and revenge. According to Jimmy, the Mafia had reached a point where respect was on the decline. He felt he had played according to Mafia rules for 30 years, only to be turned on in his later years (he was then in his sixties) by treacherous associates.

Fratianno began to talk in private to the police and was finally induced to testify in open court against his former "friends and family." His testimony before various grand juries and at many criminal trials produced a potent blow against organized crime. Following are some of the results of Fratianno's acceptance of the U.S. government's Witness Protection Program, as detailed in *The Last Mafioso:*

- The FBI was able to plug a leak in its Cleveland office when Geraldine Rabinowitz, an FBI file clerk, and her husband Jeffrey, an automobile salesman, pleaded guilty to two counts each of accepting bribes totalling $15,900 from Kenneth Ciarica. They were sentenced to five years in prison. Jimmy had turned the two in.

- Jimmy's testimony before a Fort Lauderdale federal grand jury led to the indictment of Aniello Dellacroce and Tony Plate on charges of violating the Racketeer-Influenced and Corrupt Organizations Act (RICO) and for the 1974 murder of Charles Calise.

- While in Florida, Fratianno testified in the West Palm Beach federal court. Marshall Caifano, who earlier had been convicted of possessing and transporting stolen securities valued at $4 million, was awaiting sentencing under the Special Offenders Act; this act empowered the judge to add 10 years to the maximum sentence of 15 years for the fraud conviction if it could be shown that Caifano was a "special dangerous offender." As a result of Fratianno's testimony, the judge sentenced Caifano to a 20-year prison term.

- On the basis of information from Fratianno, the Las Vegas casino empire of Allen Glick came tumbling down when agents from the Nevada Gaming Control Board's audit division discovered that $7,200 in quarters had been placed in the auxiliary vault at the Stardust casino without being recorded for tax purposes. A search of another section of the vault produced $3,500, also unrecorded. Searches at the Fremont revealed similar unrecorded caches. The agents estimated that the skimming of slot machines at both casinos amounted to nearly $12 million.

- In a trial in San Francisco, a jury found Rudy Tham guilty on 15 felony counts and 4 misdemeanor counts involving the misuse of Teamsters union funds. Twelve of the felony counts were for picking up Jimmy's hotel and restaurant tabs.

- Acting on Jimmy's information, FBI agent James Ahearn, who had induced Fratianno to cooperate with the government, made arrests that involved the recovery of 15 pounds of cocaine that was 92 percent pure. The wholesale value of the cocaine was estimated at well over $2 million.

- In February, 1978, following Fratianno's appearance and testimony before a federal grand jury, a six-count indictment was handed down against six leaders of a major Mafia family. They were charged with racketeering, extortion, obstruction of justice, conspiracy, and murder.

- Fratianno's testimony in June, 1980, before a New York federal grand jury led to a four-count indictment of Frank "Funzi" Tieri, who became the first boss ever accused by a federal grand jury of running a Mafia crime family. He was engaged in "various criminal activities," including murder, loan-sharking, extortion, interstate transportation of stolen property, and bankruptcy fraud.

- In 1987 Fratianno was unceremoniously dropped from the federal government's Witness Protection Program. A spokesperson from the Justice Department said that they had spent $1 million on Fratianno's protection and that witnesses are terminated sooner or later. Fratianno indicated enormous displeasure with this severance and claimed the payments were more like $500,000. He believed that he was now a man marked for death by the Mafia— and that he would be murdered in the future.

Fratianno's confessions and courtroom testimony were valuable in revealing the manner in which the Mafia had infiltrated our society at all levels. The Mafia was clearly intertwined with union activity, big business, gambling, the entertainment world, and corrupt government officials. Because of the criminal web, organized crime poses a far more serious threat to society as a whole than does traditional crime. Its hierarchic structure leaves its top echelons virtually immune to prosecution. Its use of force and the threat of force, combined with an interlocking leadership and extensive planning, make its operations highly profitable. The large profits and ready cash obtained from drug trade and other illegal operations provide funds for corrupting public officials, buying into legitimate business, and expanding criminal activities. Organized crime is a destructive force whose greedy tentacles are twisted about many segments of our social and political system. The government's inability to convict the Mafia in court was revealed in several judicial setbacks in the late 1980s.

ORGANIZED CRIME ON TRIAL

From 1981 through 1989, federal prosecutors brought over 1,000 indictments against over 2,500 mafiosi and convicted over 800 Mafia members or their uninitiated "associates." Many of the remaining cases are still pending. Regarding all criminal organizations, including such non-Mafia types as motorcycle gangs and Chinese and Latin American drug traffickers, the FBI compiled evidence that in 1987 alone led to over 3,800 indictments and almost 3,000 convictions.

In Chicago, where organized crime has always been strong, the conviction in January, 1985, of four top local mobsters for directing the tax-free skimming of cash from two Las Vegas casinos forced the ailing Anthony Accardo, 80, to return from a comfortable retirement in Palm Springs, California, to keep an eye on an inexperienced group trying to run the rackets. The same skimming case crippled organized crime leadership in Kansas City, Milwaukee, and Cleveland. The New England Mafia was jolted by the convictions in April, 1985, of underboss Gennaro Anguilo, 67, and three of his brothers, who operated out of Boston. Their organization was described by the FBI as being in a "state of chaos."

In 1983, Joseph Bonanno, former organized crime leader in New

York, published *A Man of Honor,* an autobiography about his Mafia years. Rudolph Giuliani, a federal prosecutor in New York, read the book and concluded that the 1970 RICO act could be used to prosecute the Mafia. From 1986 to 1988 the Mafia was placed on trial in a number of jurisdictions, including Manhattan and Brooklyn, New York.

The New York Mafia Trials

In a cover story titled "Hitting the Mafia," *Time* magazine provided some insight into the New York Mafia trials. (Assistant United States Attorney Michael Chertoff, who prosecuted one of the cases, affirmed to me that the data in the *Time* article were accurate.)

> The aging bosses seated at the defense table in the packed federal courtroom in lower Manhattan look harmless enough to be spectators at a Sunday-afternoon boccie game. Anthony (Fat Tony) Salerno, 75, the reputed head of the Genovese crime family, sits aloof and alone, his left eye red and swollen from surgery. White-haired Anthony (Tony Ducks) Corallo, 73, the alleged Lucchese family chief, is casual in a cardigan and sport shirt. Carmine (Junior) Persico, 53, is the balding, baggy-eyed showman of the trio. Elegant in a black pinstripe suit, a crisp white shirt and red tie, the accused Colombo crime boss is acting as his own attorney. "By now I guess you all know my name is Carmine Persico and I'm not a lawyer, I'm a defendant," he humbly told the jury in a thick Brooklyn accent. "Bear with me, please," he said, shuffling through his notes. "I'm a little nervous."
>
> As Persico spoke, three young prosecutors watched, armed with the evidence they hope will show that Junior and his geriatric cohorts are leaders of a murderous, brutal criminal conspiracy that reaches across the nation. In a dangerous four-year investigation, police and FBI agents had planted bugs around Mafia hangouts and listened to endless hours of tiresome chatter about horses, cars and point spreads while waiting patiently for incriminating comments. They pressured mobsters into becoming informants. They carefully charted the secret family ties, linking odd bits of evidence to reveal criminal patterns. They helped put numerous mafiosi, one by one and in groups, behind bars. But last week (September 22, 1986), after a half-century in business, the American Mafia itself finally went on trial.
>
> . . . Assistant U.S. Attorney Michael Chertoff, whose busy mustache could not hide his tender age of 32, addressed the anonymous jurors in calm, methodical tones. Chertoff charged flatly that the Mafia is run by a coordinating commission and that the eight defendants, representing four of New York City's five nationally powerful Mob families, were either on this crime board or had carried out its racketeering dictates. "What you will see is these men," he said, "these crime leaders, fighting with each other, backstabbing each other, each one trying to get a larger share of the illegal proceeds. You are going to learn that this Commission is dominated by a single principle—greed. They want more money, and they will do what they have to do to get it."
>
> Across the East River in another federal courthouse in Brooklyn, a jury was being selected for the racketeering trial of the most powerful of all U.S. Mafia families: The Gambinos. Here a younger, more flamboyant crime

boss strutted through the courtroom, snapping out orders to subservient henchmen, reveling in his new and lethally acquired notoriety. John Gotti, 45, romanticized in New York City's tabloids as the "Dapper Don" for his tailored $1,800 suits and carefully coiffed hair, has been locked in prison without bail since May, only a few months after he allegedly took control of the Gambino gang following the murder of the previous boss, Paul Castellano.

Gotti, who seemed to personify a vigorous new generation of mobster, may never have a chance to inherit his criminal kingdom. Prosecutor Diane Giacalone, 36, says tapes of conversations between Gotti and his lieutenants, recorded by a trusted Gambino "soldier" turned informant, will provide "direct evidence of John Gotti's role as manager of a gambling enterprise." If convicted, the new crime chief and six lieutenants could be imprisoned for up to 40 years.[15]

The Aftermath   The Manhattan and Brooklyn trials were concluded in 1987. The Manhattan trial ended with a smashing success for the government. All defendants were convicted on all counts. Seven organized crime leaders received sentences of 100 years in prison, and one received a 40-year sentence.

In the John Gotti–Gambino family trial in Brooklyn all the defendants were acquitted. In true Mafia style, the government's informer, Wilfred "Willy Boy" Johnson, a former associate of John Gotti, was shot to death two years later. On August 29, 1988, at 6:20 A.M., as he was leaving his home for work on a construction job, Johnson was apparently killed by the first bullet fired from a .38-caliber automatic handgun. After this lethal shot, at least six more bullets were put into Johnson's head. The Mafia was apparently sending a message to other possible informers.

A later, 21-month-long trial in federal court in Newark, New Jersey, involved 20 alleged organized crime figures. This trial ended August 25, 1988, with all 20 defendants of the Lucchese crime family acquitted of 77 criminal counts. The federal prosecutors had presented 89 witnesses and hundreds of hours of tape recordings in an effort to prove that the defendants had operated a "criminal enterprise" in New Jersey and Florida between 1976 and 1985, but all the defendants were found not guilty on all charges. According to several, they thought that the evidence was not strong enough to back up the allegations.

ORGANIZED CRIME INTO THE 1990s

Despite the fact that two of the three major Mafia trials resulted in acquittals, a side effect of the trials was the development of techniques and the surfacing of new data about organized crime in America.

---

[15] "Hitting the Mafia," *Time*, September 29, 1986. © 1986 Time Inc. Reprinted by permission.

For example, the Mafia no longer seems to dispute its existence when on trial. In the preliminary hearing related to the New York trials, a defense attorney for several of the organized crime figures stated: "This case is not about whether there is a Mafia. Assume it. Accept it. There is. Nevertheless, just because a person is a member of the Mafia doesn't mean he has committed the charged crime or even agreed to commit the charged crime." The lawyer depicted the Mafia "commission" as a sort of underworld executive roundtable that approves new Mafia members and arbitrates disputes. Its purpose, he insisted, is "to avoid conflict."

Many conspiracies were revealed and described by government witnesses in the Brooklyn trial of John Gotti and the Gambinos. The prosecutors contended that the commission directed loan-sharking and an extensive extortion scheme against the New York City construction industry and approved the 1979 murders of Bonanno boss Carmine Galante and two associates. Bonanno soldier Anthony Indelicato, 30, and alleged current Bonanno boss Philip (Rusty) Rastelli, 68, were accused of plotting the hit, with the commission's blessing, to prevent Galante from seizing control of the Gambino family. The jurors saw a videotape of Indelicato being congratulated shortly after the killings by high-ranking Gambino family members.

The crux of the government's case in the previously cited Manhattan trial involved detailing a commission-endorsed scheme to rig bids and allocate contracts to mob-influenced concrete companies in New York City's booming construction industry. Any concrete-pouring contract worth more than $2 million was controlled by the Mafia, according to the indictment, and the gangsters decided who should submit the lowest bids. Any company that disobeyed the bidding rules might find itself with unexpected labor problems, and its sources of cement might dry up. Mafia "dues," actually a form of extortion, amounted to $1.8 million between 1981 and 1984. The Mafia also demanded a 2 percent cut of the value of the contracts it controlled.

The key defendant on this charge was Ralph Scopo, 57, a soldier in the Colombo family—and, just as important, the president of the Cement and Concrete Workers District Council before he was indicted. Scopo was accused of accepting many of the payoffs from the participating concrete firms. Scopo's lawyer admitted the union leader took payoffs, but he and the other attorneys denied it was part of a broader extortion scheme.

Although the New York trials involved four of New York's five Mafia families, a murder plot prevented the Gambino family from being represented. Former Gambino boss Paul Castellano and underboss Aniello Dellacroce had been indicted. But Dellacroce, 71, died December 2, 1985, of cancer. Fourteen days later Castellano, 72, and Thomas Bilotti, 45, his trusted bodyguard and the apparent choice to succeed

Dellacroce, were the victims of yet another sensational Mafia hit as they walked, unarmed, from their car toward a mid-Manhattan steak house.

The major evidence in the Gotti case was provided through a complex bugging scheme. In 1984 Gambino soldier Dominick Lofaro, 56, was arrested in upstate New York on heroin charges. Facing a 20-year sentence, he agreed to become a government informant. Investigators wired him with a tiny microphone taped to his chest and a miniature cassette recorder, no bigger than two packs of gum, that fit into the small of his back without producing a bulge. Equipped with a magnetic switch on a cigarette lighter to activate the recorder, Lofaro coolly discussed Gambino family affairs with the unsuspecting Gotti brothers. Afterward he placed the tapes inside folded copies of the *New York Times* business section and dropped them in a preselected trash bin. Lofaro provided the government with more than 50 tapes over the two years prior to the trial.

Both New York Mafia trials depended heavily on tapes as evidence, as have numerous RICO cases around the country. The FBI's bugging approach increased sharply, from just 90 court-approved requests in 1982 to more than 150 in 1986 and 1987. The trials revealed that various investigating agencies, including state and local police, found novel places to hide their bugs, including a Perrier bottle, a stuffed toy, a pair of binoculars, shoes, an electric blanket, and a horse's saddle. Agents even admitted to dropping snooping devices into a confessional at a Roman Catholic church frequented by mobsters, as well as a church candlestick holder and a church men's room. All of this, the agents insist, was done with court permission.

In the process of their bugging, the agents learned fascinating data about mob mores. One Mafia leader was heard explaining how dangerous it is to kill just one member of a gang: "If you're clipping [killing] people always make sure you clip the people around him first. Get them together, 'cause everybody's got a friend. He could be the dirtiest [expletive] in the world, but someone that likes this guy, that's the guy that sneaks [kills] you." They also heard two Mafia leaders complaining about a competing gang of Irish hoods: "They don't have the scruples that we have. . . . You know how I knew they weren't Italiano? When they bombed the [expletive] house. We don't do that."

The New York trials involved a number of former gangsters who have proved willing to violate the Mafia's centuries-old tradition of *omertà* (silence), and, like Valachi and Fratianno, they provided evidence against their former partners.

John Gotti, in the Brooklyn trial, was very disturbed by the deception of Wilfred "Willie Boy" Johnson. Caught carrying $50,000 in a paper bag in 1981, Johnson had invited New York City detectives to help themselves to the cash. They charged him with bribery. After that, Johnson, who frequented Gotti's Bergen Hunt and Fish Club, kept the police posted on how Gotti was progressing in the hierarchy. He also suggested where bugs might be placed.

The willingness of some hoodlums and victims to defy the Mafia and talk is partly due to the existence of the federal Witness Protection Program, which since it started in 1970 has helped over 5,000 people move to different locations and acquire new identities and jobs. At a cost to the government of about $100,000 for each protected person, the program has produced convictions in around 80 percent of the cases in which such witnesses were used.

A more significant reason for the breakdown in Mafia discipline in recent years was revealed by the trials: the new generation of crime family members is not as dedicated to the old Sicilian-bred mores. Many new members believe that a long prison sentence is too stiff a price to pay for crime family loyalty. The younger mafiosi are much more Americanized than the "old boys." They often enjoy the good life and are not as committed to the old rules.

Prosecutor Rudolph Giuliani contended in a TV interview that as the Italian-American community has grown away from its immigrant beginnings, the Mafia has been losing its original base of operations and recruits. Pointing to the relatively small number of "made" Mafia members, Giuliani said: "We are fighting an enemy that has definable limits in terms of manpower. They cannot replenish themselves the way they used to in the twenties, thirties, and forties."

Despite Giuliani's predictions about organized crime's demise, the Mafia remains a wealthy organization that reputedly earned at least $26 billion in 1988 from its various illicit sources. The Mafia has deep roots in unions and labor-intensive industries such as building construction, transportation, restaurants, and clothing. In many industries, says Ray Maria, the Labor Department's deputy inspector general, "the Mob controls your labor costs and determines whether you are reputable and profitable."

Repeated prosecution alone will not put the organization out of its costly and deadly business. Veteran observers of organized crime recall the prediction of the imminent demise of the Chicago Outfit in 1943 when its seven highest-ranking bosses were convicted of shaking down Hollywood movie producers. The bell of doom seemed to be tolling nationwide in 1963 when Joseph Valachi's disclosures set off an FBI bugging war against the families. In 1975 the most successful labor racketeering prosecution in United States history was supposed to have cleaned up the terror-ridden East Coast waterfront from Miami to New York. None of those highly publicized events have had lasting impact.

Despite these failures, today's zealous prosecutors have a new tool that gives them a fighting chance to take the organization out of organized crime. The same RICO law that allows prosecution against criminal organizations also provides for civil action to seize their assets, from cash and cars to real estate. This aspect of RICO may become a more effective weapon against organized crime in the 1990s.

Organized crime in too many branches and forms continues to plague and loot American society. Despite RICO, the Witness Protection Program, and aggressive prosecutors, organized crime remains a significant and integral part of our society. It is important to note that this criminal pattern of power-status crime could not persist without a continuing connection between organized crime and various political and corporate institutions in American society.

THE CAUSAL
CONTEXT OF CRIME

Chapter
14

Causation: Individual Theories

A fundamental pursuit of criminology and the study of delinquency is the search for causes. The endeavor to understand the causal
context or background of crime and delinquency has historically challenged the best minds of all civilized societies. In examining the variety
of causal explanations of crime and delinquency, we must keep in mind
several concepts and issues as guides to their scientific validity:

1. A relationship of factors is not necessarily a causal nexus. The fact
   that a preponderance of criminals and delinquents come from
   broken homes does not necessarily mean a broken home must
   cause delinquency and crime.
2. No single theory explains all crime and delinquency. Different
   patterns of crime and delinquency require different causal explanations. The sex offender, the burglar, and the violent gang youth
   do not tend to emerge from the same causal context.
3. Primary and secondary causes should not be confused. The lack
   of social workers and poor school facilities are not primary causes
   of delinquency; however, a broken home *may* be a primary causal
   factor.
4. One cannot logically isolate one single cause of crime or delinquency. Causation is a multifactored condition. The relative
   weight of each factor is difficult to determine.
5. In examining causal explanations based on research with offenders, we have the problem of separating the causal force from
   the impacts of the administration of justice (arrest, jail, courts,
   prison).

These factors and others make the issue of causation a complex matter for analysis. The following analysis makes it clear that a search for a theory inclusive enough to explain all criminality would be unproductive:

> A skid-row drunk lying in a gutter is a crime. So is the killing of an unfaithful wife. A Cosa Nostra conspiracy to bribe public officials is crime. So is a strong-arm robbery by a 15-year-old boy. The embezzlement of a corporation's funds by an executive is crime. So is the possession of marijuana cigarettes by a student. These crimes can no more be lumped together for purposes of analysis than can measles and schizophrenia, or lung cancer and a broken ankle. As with disease, so with crime; if causes are to be understood, if risks are to be evaluated, and if preventive or remedial actions are to be taken, each kind must be looked at separately.[1]

Although traditional crime and delinquency, organized crime, white collar crime, and political crime may have some elements in common, the differences are so great that some theories explaining criminal behavior are likely to be more relevant to one than to another.

I have divided what I consider to be significant causal theories into two broad categories:

1. Some theories attempt to explain the criminal or delinquent behavior of people who are given the status of criminal or delinquent. An assumption basic to all these theories is that the cause or causes of criminality can be attributed to some characteristic or characteristics of the offender or the subculture with which the person is identified. Constitutional, psychological, and subcultural deviance theories, grouped into this broad category, will be delineated in this chapter.
2. Some theories seek to explain criminality or delinquency as a response to some societal attribute or policies. Some of the questions these theories deal with are: Why does a society have a high incidence of crime and delinquency? Why is there a high incidence of a particular type of crime? Why do some subgroups in the society have higher crime or delinquency rates than others? These theories, most of which may be regarded as macrosociological, will be delineated in Chapter 15.

The inclusion of a causal theory or concept in this section does not necessarily mean that I agree with that viewpoint. It does mean that the concept cited has had a significant influence on thinking about delinquency in some historical period and that the viewpoint currently has an influence on society's perception of delinquents, the administration of justice, and treatment strategies.

---

[1] *The Challenge of Crime in a Free Society: A Report by the President's Commission on Law Enforcement and Administration of Justice* (Washington, D.C.: Government Printing Office, 1967), p. 3.

DEMONOLOGY

The demon theory, or some modification of it, has been presented as an explanation of crime and juvenile delinquency for a long period of recorded history. This fundamentalist religious viewpoint posits that people who fail to follow the basic norms of the group are possessed by demons. From this viewpoint, there is little or no distinction between crime and sin, and the offender is regarded as an antagonist to both the group and the gods. The offender's criminal action is thought to be caused by evil spirits, who take possession of the person's soul and force him or her to perform their evil will. During the Middle Ages, when Christianity dominated Western life, the theory of possession by the devil tended to merge with the Christian concept of original sin.

The influence of theories of demonology and "natural depravity" upon the legal codes and the practices of the courts is evidenced by the fact that as late as the nineteenth century a formal indictment in England accused the criminal of "being prompted and instigated by the devil." In the United States, as late as 1862 a state supreme court declared that "to know the right, and still the wrong pursue, proceeds from a perverse will brought about by the seduction of the evil one."[2] Even in contemporary society, people will say that a delinquent is "full of the devil," or threaten, "I'm going to shake the devil out of you."

In an address to 6,000 people at his weekly public audience in Rome on November 29, 1972, Pope Paul VI said that the devil is dominating "communities and entire societies" through sex, narcotics, and doctrinal errors. His address included the following references to the devil: "We are all under obscure domination. It is by Satan, the prince of this world, the number one enemy." He criticized those who question the existence of the devil, saying: "This obscure and disturbing being does exist."

The Reverend John Narvone, an American professor at the Gregorian University in Rome, has studied Satan and narcotics. He has a theory that drug addicts risk becoming outright "apprentices" of the devil. The concept of demonology is generally believed to be of no value by most criminologists. However, the pronouncements of many members of the clergy and some judges, along with the continuing belief in a devil by a large part of the society, make demonology a consideration in treating criminals in many communities even today.

THE CLASSICAL SCHOOL OF CRIMINOLOGY

A significant effort to explain crime in a philosophical manner was made in the eighteenth century by Cesare Beccaria, the founder of what is now

---

[2] John M. Gillette and James M. Reinhardt, *Current Social Problems* (New York: American Book Company, 1933), pp. 652–653.

known as the classical school of criminology. Beccaria's theory postulated that only conduct dangerous to the state or to other people should be prohibited and that punishment should be no more severe than deemed necessary to deter persons from committing such crimes. The importance of knowing in advance the amount of punishment to be administered led to the adoption of the fixed or "determinate" sentence.

Accepting the Christian doctrine of free will, the classical school postulated that people could choose between good and evil alternatives. The explanation of crime included the notion that human beings were essentially hedonistic, desiring a maximum of pleasure and the avoidance of pain. A person committed a crime because the pleasure anticipated from the criminal act was greater than the subsequent pain that might be expected.

A major proponent of the classical explanation was Jeremy Bentham. In 1825 he published a book called *An Introduction to the Principles of Morals and Legislation,* in which he proposed a "penal pharmacy" where definitely prescribed punishments were to be applied for specific crimes. The assumption was that people had free will and could decide whether or not it was personally profitable to commit a crime. It was assumed that if the punishment or pain was always more than the pleasure or benefit from a crime, the potential offender would be rational and be deterred from committing the offense.

The classical philosophical and judicial view of crime is still held by many contemporary courts. The counterpoint position to the classical view is determinism. This position asserts almost no free will. It postulates that the socialization process and all the social factors that impinge on an individual determine personality. In this framework an individual has no free will or individual choice. People are propelled by social forces and other conditions beyond their control. The controversy over the contradictory positions of free will and social determinism is still discussed in contemporary society.[3]

PHYSIOLOGICAL EXPLANATIONS OF CRIMINALITY

The Italian Positivist School

Cesare Lombroso, an Italian medical doctor, on the basis of research with military personnel and inmates of Italian military prisons, developed a theory that challenged Beccaria and the classical school. His chief investigative work was done between 1864 and 1878. Lombroso and his followers became known as the positive school of criminology, essentially because they attempted to base their conclusions on objective firsthand empirical data.

---

[3] The argument was revived in a probing analysis by David Matza. See *Delinquency and Drift* (New York: Wiley, 1966).

Lombroso's major early conclusions were that criminal tendencies were hereditary and that "born criminals" were characterized by physical stigmata. To Lombroso the born criminal was an *atavism*, a throwback to an earlier, more primitive species of human. Lombroso concluded that

1. Criminals are at birth a distinct type.
2. They can be recognized by certain stigmata (e.g., "long lower jaw, scanty beard, low sensitivity to pain").
3. These stigmata or physical characteristics do not cause crime but do enable identification of criminal types.
4. Only through vigorous social intervention can born criminals be restrained from criminal behavior.

After his initial studies, Lombroso greatly modified his theories. A central error in his early studies was that he neglected to note that most of the criminals in the Italian army were Sicilians and thus were a distinct physical type. They did not, however, commit more crimes than the general population because of their *physical typology*, as Lombroso alleged, but because they came from a culture that was more criminally oriented. Lombroso and his followers in the Italian school—Ferri, Garofalo, and others—later included more social factors in their analyses of criminality.

Although Lombroso was obviously wrong about his born-criminal thesis, he did make significant contributions to the field of criminology. His research (1) caused a focus on the firsthand study of criminals and moved the field from a philosophical posture of analysis to empirical research; (2) broadened the discussion of crime causation; (3) produced a school of criminology that attracted many distinguished students to the field; and (4) produced a reform of the Beccaria-Bentham classical school.

Enrico Ferri described the impact of the new "positivist school" on the classical school:

> The general opinion of classic criminalists and of the people at large is that crime involves a moral guilt, because it is due to the free will of the individual who leaves the path of virtue and chooses the path of crime, and therefore it must be suppressed by meeting it with a proportionate quantity of punishment. This is to this day the current conception of crime. And the illusion of a free human will (the only miraculous factor in the eternal ocean of cause and effect) leads to the assumption that one can choose freely between virtue and vice. How can you still believe in the existence of a free will when modern psychology, armed with all the instruments of positive modern research, denies that there is any free will and demonstrates that every act of a human being is the result of an interaction between the personality and the environment of man?
>
> It has continued in the nineteenth century to look upon crime in the same way that the Middle Ages did: "Whoever commits murder or theft is alone the absolute arbiter to decide whether he wants to commit the crime or

not." This remains the foundation of the classic school of criminology. This explains why it could travel on its way more rapidly than the positive school of criminology. And yet, it took half a century from the time of Beccaria before the penal codes showed signs of the reformatory influence of the classic school of criminology. So that it has also taken quite a long time to establish it so well that it became accepted by general consent, as it is today. The positive school of criminology was born in 1878, and although it does not stand for a mere reform of the methods of criminal justice itself, it has already gone quite a distance and made considerable conquests which begin to show in our country. It is a fact that the penal code now in force in this country represents a compromise, so far as the theory of personal responsibility is concerned, between the old theory of free will and the conclusions of the positive school which denies this free will.[4]

Later Studies of Genetics, Physical Types, and Crime

In 1901 Dr. Charles B. Goring, an English prison official, tested Lombroso's theory by measuring 3,000 criminals and comparing these measurements with those of 1,000 students at Cambridge University. He found no significant differences in physical types between criminals and noncriminals.[5] Later studies by Hooton and Kretschmer on physical types and crime postulated a degree of support for Lombroso's original thesis.[6] A close appraisal of their research methods, however, tends to make their conclusions suspect.

In the 1940s William Sheldon also concluded that there was a relationship between certain physical characteristics and temperamental characteristics. Sheldon divided human beings into four physical types on the basis of body measurements: *endomorphs,* who tend to be fat; *mesomorphs,* who tend to be muscular with large bones and athletic build; *ectomorphs,* who are inclined to be thin and fragile; and *balanced types,* a "combination category" composed of people who show no marked dominance of any single type.

Each body type, according to Sheldon, was characterized by a distinctive temperament. Endomorphs were described as viscerotonic, submissive, and little interested in physical activity or adventure. Mesomorphs were described as somatotonic, physically active, self-assertive, and daring. Ectomorphs were categorized as cerebrotonic, inhibited, and introverted.

Sheldon attributed the various body types and their characteristics to heredity, maintaining that they were genetically determined. In a study

---

[4] Enrico Ferri, *Criminal Sociology* (Boston: Little, Brown, 1901).

[5] Charles Goring, *The English Convict* (London: His Majesty's Stationery Office, 1913).

[6] Earnest A. Hooton, *Crime and the Man* (Cambridge, Mass.: Harvard University Press, 1939); Ernest Kretschmer, *Physique and Character* (London: Kegan Paul, Trench, Trubner, 1936).

of 200 juvenile delinquents, he found that about 60 percent were mesomorphs. Since most police officers, army officers, football players, and other energetic leaders of our society are also likely to be mesomorphic, this correlation between mesomorphy and delinquency was not considered to be a causal explanation of delinquency.[7]

In an analysis of Sheldon's work in the *American Sociological Review*, Sutherland virtually demolished his conclusions. Here are some of Sutherland's criticisms:

1. Sheldon defines delinquency in terms of "disappointingness" and not in terms of violation of the law.
2. His method of scoring delinquents is subjective and unreliable. For example, he defines "first-order psychopathy" in terms of subjectively determined interference with adjustment, apparently the same as "disappointingness."
3. The varieties of delinquent youth he presents are overlapping and inconsistent. They do not differ significantly from each other in their somatotypes or psychiatric indices.
4. The relationship of the psychiatric indices to social fitness is not made clear.[8]

Sheldon and Eleanor Glueck revived interest in William Sheldon's somatotypes in the 1950s. They found that 60.1 percent of the delinquents they studied were mesomorphs, as against 30.7 percent of the nondelinquents. They were cautious in their interpretation of these findings, concluding that "there is no 'delinquent personality' in the sense of a constant and stable combination of physique, character, and temperament which determines that a certain individual would become delinquent."[9]

Although no causal relationship has been established between any physical characteristic and criminal behavior, there is some evidence that the muscular mesomorphic child is more likely to become delinquent than children with other body types, *all other things being equal.* The mesomorph, who is by definition muscular, active, and relatively uninhibited, may be more likely than others to take action defined as delinquent by society when confronted with a favorable social environment. Research exploring the possibility of using body types as a predictive device has been going on for many years. The conclusions so far have been inconclusive, if not outright specious.

A study by James Q. Wilson and Richard J. Hernstein revived the

---

[7] William H. Sheldon, *The Varieties of Delinquent Youth* (New York: Harper & Row, 1949).

[8] Edwin H. Sutherland, "Critique of Sheldon's *Varieties of Delinquent Youth*," *American Sociological Review* 16 (February 1951):10–13.

[9] Sheldon Glueck and Eleanor Glueck, *Unraveling Juvenile Delinquency* (New York: Commonwealth Fund, 1950), p. 221.

assessment of biological and genetic factors in looking at crime and delinquency. In their book *Crime and Human Nature*, they assert that to understand street crime we must redirect attention away from an excessive concern with social and economic factors and focus instead on differences among individual people. These often reflect biological and genetic differences. Wilson and Hernstein state that different types of family upbringing also play a role: "One way or another bad families produce bad children. The interplay of genes and environment creates, in some people but not in others, the kind of personality likely to commit crime."[10]

In another assessment of the biological connection to crime, Sarnoff A. Mednick and William F. Gabriella reported in an article in *Science:* "We conclude that some factor transmitted by criminal parents increases the likelihood that their [biological] children will engage in criminal behavior. This claim holds especially for chronic criminality. The findings imply that biological predispositions are involved in the etiology of at least some criminal behavior."[11]

Chromosomes and Criminality   Studies of chromosomal abnormalities have attempted to show a correlation between criminal behavior and males possessing an extra Y (male) chromosome; that is, they are XYY rather than the normal XY. In spite of varied and conflicting results in different studies, some suggestive consistencies of behavior and traits do emerge. The chance of possessing an extra Y chromosome is up to 60 times greater among criminals than it is among the general population; also, a higher frequency of aggressive and disturbed behavior and higher rates of violent crime are found among those having an extra Y chromosome.

One theory holds that the criminal act itself is biologically and hereditarily determined; that is, there is a direct relationship between the biological structure and the behavior that is supposedly determined by it. A second theory is that what is genetically transmitted is a general tendency to maladjustment and that, given certain environmental pressures, this disposition leads to criminal behavior. Inherent in this theory is the supposition that crime is just one of many possible outcomes of a defective physiological structure.

If criminality is inherited, then noncriminality or conforming behavior must also be inherited. If we accept the premise that the factors determining criminal behavior already exist at birth, then it follows that the influence of environment is not very important. If, however, criminal

---

[10] James Q. Wilson and Richard J. Hernstein, *Crime and Human Nature* (New York: Simon & Schuster, 1984).

[11] Sarnoff A. Medwick and William F. Gabriella, "Genetic Influence in Criminal Convictions," *Science* 224 (May 1984).

behavior is frequently found among persons lacking genetic defects, or if biological defects are found among a great many noncriminals, then the genetic theory of crime becomes questionable. Before we can reach any conclusions on the relationship between chromosomes and criminality, we need to know what proportion of criminals do not have genetic or biological defects. If the number is large, the theory is defective.[12]

In the journal *Science*, in 1976, Herman Witkin (a research phychologist with the Educational Testing Service) and his colleagues commented on earlier studies. First, the search for XYY men has often been conducted in selected groups presumed to be likely to contain them, such as institutionalized men and tall men. Second, a number of reports now in the literature are based on observations of a single case or just a few cases. Third, many studies of XYYs have not included control XYs; in those that did, comparisons were often made without knowledge of the genotype of the individuals being evaluated. The control groups used have varied in nature, and comparison of results from different studies has therefore been difficult. Rarely were psychological, somatic, and social data obtained for the same individual XYY men. Finally, there do not yet exist adequate prevalence data for the XYY genotype in the general adult population with which the XYY yield of any particular study may be compared.

To avoid these problems, Witkin and his colleagues chose to gather data in Denmark by using social records that were available for a sample of the general population. They then compared normal males with males having different patterns of chromosomal abnormalities and attempted to identify the factors that might account for any predominance of abnormalities among inmates or among men with criminal records. Out of a sample of 4,139 men, they found 12 XYY cases, 16 XXY cases, and 13 XY cases that had other chromosomal anomalies. Of the 12 XYY cases, 5 (or 42 percent) were found to have been convicted of one or more offenses, as compared to 3 of the 16 XXY cases (19 percent) and 9 of the 13 abnormal XY cases. There did appear to be an inordinately high probability that XYY men would have criminal records. However, there were 389 men with records, and only 5 of them were XYY cases. The abnormality is so rare that it cannot account for very much criminal activity.

Further analysis by Witkin and his colleagues yielded no evidence that XYY males are more prone to violent crimes than XY males. The elevated crime rate reflected property crimes, not aggressive acts against persons. The XYY males were found to have lower scores on intelligence tests and to be taller than XY males. However, even with these

---

[12] Menachim Amir and Yitzcham Berman, "Chromosomal Deviation and Crime," *Federal Probation* 34 (June 1970):55–62. See also Robert W. Stock, "The XXY and the Criminal," *New York Times Magazine*, October 20, 1968, p. 30.

differences in intelligence and height taken into account, there was still a difference between XYY and XY cases. The researchers suggested that chromosomal anomalies may have pervasive developmental consequences, but there is no evidence that aggression against persons is one of them.[13]

MODERN POSITIVISM: FREE WILL AND DETERMINISM

The classical and the positivistic conceptions of crime and delinquency continue as central subjects for discussion. Each view projects its own image of people and their motivations. The classical school of criminology (Bentham, Beccaria) sketched people as essentially having free will, implying that a person who chooses to violate the law can be restrained from this impulse by a proper measure of punishment. In counterpoint, the positivists believed in what is today more often called determinism. They viewed the criminal as something of a billiard ball, propelled by conditions outside any individual's control.

As early as 1906 Ferri stated these opposing views most succinctly:

> "Whoever commits murder or theft is alone the absolute arbiter to decide whether he wants to commit the crime or not." This remains the foundation of the classic school of criminology. . . . The positive school of criminology maintains, on the contrary, that it is not the criminal who wills; in order to be a criminal it is rather necessary that the individual should find himself permanently or transitorily in such personal, physical, and moral conditions, and live in such an environment, which become for him a chain of cause and effect, externally and internally, that disposes him toward crime. This is our conclusion, which I anticipate, and it constitutes the vastly different and opposite method, which the positive school of criminology employs as compared to the leading principle of the classic school of criminal science.[14]

Matza, after closely reviewing each of these conceptions in depth, presented a more middle-of-the-road viewpoint. He first pointed to the danger of being overdeterministic. Using the juvenile court concept as an example of overdeterminism, he commented:

> To philosophically attribute fault to underlying conditions, but to actually hold the immediate agent responsible is an invitation to distrust. And to refer to penal sanction as protective care is to compound the distrust. Thus, by its insistence on a philosophy of child welfare and its addiction to word magic, the juvenile court systematically interferes with its alleged program. By its own hypocrisy perceived and real, it prepares the way for the

---

[13] Herman Witkin, "Criminality in XYY and XXY Men," *Science* 193 (August 1976): 547–555.

[14] Enrico Ferri, *The Positive School of Criminology* (Chicago: Kerr, 1906), p. 23.

delinquent's withdrawal of legitimacy. Without the grant of legitimacy, the court's lofty aspirations cannot be effectively pursued.

Thus, the ideology of child welfare supports the delinquent's viewpoint in two ways. It confirms his conception of irresponsibility, and it feeds his sence of injustice. Both support the processes by which the moral bind of law is neutralized. Both facilitate the drift into delinquency.[15]

Matza believed that contemporary theorists in the field of criminology went too far in the direction of positivism. Although he did not attempt fully to revive the classical viewpoint, he did attempt to incorporate "some modified versions of the classical viewpoint into the current framework of positive criminology." Matza posited what he referred to as "soft determinism" in discussing his basic concept of delinquency and drift. He contended that human beings are neither wholly free nor wholly constrained, but somewhere midway between the two. The delinquent is never totally a lawbreaker but *drifts* into delinquency.

> The image of the delinquent I wish to convey is one of drift; an actor neither compelled nor committed to deeds nor freely choosing them; neither different in any simple or fundamental sense from the law abiding, nor the same; conforming to certain traditions in American life while partially unreceptive to other more conventional traditions; and finally, an actor whose motivational system may be explored along lines explicitly commended by classical criminology—his peculiar relation to legal institutions. . . . The delinquent transiently exists in a limbo between convention and crime, responding in turn to the demands of each, flirting now with one, now the other, but postponing commitment, evading decision. Thus, he drifts between criminal and conventional action.[16]

One argument against this theory of drift preceded Matza. Ferri stated back in 1906:

> It is evident that the idea of accident, applied to physical nature, is unscientific. Every physical phenomenon is the necessary effect of the causes that determined it beforehand. If those causes are known to us, we have the conviction that the phenomenon is necessary, is fate, and, if we do not know them, we think it is accidental. The same is true of human phenomena. But since we do not know the internal and external causes in the majority of cases, we pretend that they are free phenomena, that is to say, that they are not determined necessarily by their causes.[17]

Matza's belief that most delinquents are drifters is stated as follows: "The delinquent as drifter more approximates the substantial majority of juvenile delinquents who do not become adult criminals than the

---

[15] Matza, *Delinquency and Drift*, pp. 97–98.

[16] Ibid., p. 28.

[17] Ferri, *Positive School of Criminology*, pp. 35–36.

minority who do." To Matza, delinquency is seldom a youth's total career. Most delinquents, he believes, participate in juvenile delinquency as a part-time enterprise.

Gresham Sykes and David Matza described five ways in which delinquents deny that their behavior is bad. These techniques tend to neutralize their responsibility for delinquent activity.

1. *The denial of personal responsibility.* Here the delinquent uses a kind of social word play. "Of course I'm delinquent. Who wouldn't be, coming from my background?" He then can neutralize personal responsibility by detailing the background of a broken home, lack of love, and a host of other factors.

2. *The denial of harm to anyone.* In this pattern of neutralization, stealing a car is only borrowing it; truancy harms no one; and drug use "doesn't hurt anyone but me."

3. *The delinquent denies that the person injured or wronged is really a victim.* "The (assaulted) teacher was unfair"; the victim of a mugging "was only a queer"; and the gang youth assaulted was "out to get me."

4. *The delinquent condemns the condemners.* "Society is much more corrupt than I am."

5. *Delinquent group or gang loyalties supersede loyalty to the norms of an impersonal society.* "When I stabbed him I was only defending my turf." The youth places his gang or delinquent group and its values (even if delinquent) above the law, the school, and society.[18]

All these factors tend to neutralize the delinquent youth's belief that he is delinquent or has done anything wrong. These rationalizations enable him to deny any real personal responsibility for delinquent behavior.

In any case, according to Matza, most delinquents are really not delinquent but are acting out the "subterranean values" of the society. Who can deny that the mass public admires and respects a smart operator, even if such actions are illegal? The delinquent may in his own self-concept merely be acting out the norms he sees beneath the surface of the law. In some respects, the delinquent may see himself as a lower-class white collar criminal. He thinks there is really nothing wrong with his behavior. In fact, he believes he is being unfairly treated by being punished for what society does not really condemn.

By adapting concepts found in the large society, the delinquent rationally negates his own offense. Since the law supports self-defense as a justification for violent action, it is easy for the delinquent to justify in his own mind the use of violence to defend his gang turf. The delinquent also uses the concept of insanity ("I went crazy") to negate his offense, and he widens the extenuating circumstance of "accident" to include recklessness. The sense of injustice found in the delinquent

---

[18] Gresham Sykes and David Matza, "Techinques of Neutralization: A Theory of Delinquency," *American Sociological Review* 22 (December 1957):665–666.

subculture is thus reinforced by the vagaries of many societal laws and norms. Many of society's irrational prescriptions weaken prohibitions of certain actions by the juvenile and facilitate the drift to juvenile delinquency, and in time into a criminal career.

THE PSYCHOANALYTIC VIEW OF CRIME AND DELINQUENCY

Psychoanalytic theory, as originally formulated by Sigmund Freud, has been offered as an explanation of delinquent and criminal behavior. According to psychoanalytic theory, the individual begins life with two basic instincts or urges: Eros, the life or love instinct, and Thanatos, the death or hate instinct. The personality of the normal adult is composed of the id, the ego, and the superego. At birth there is only the *id*, the reservoir of both the life and the death instincts. The id seeks immediate gratification and is concerned with striving after pleasure. It is governed by the *pleasure principle*, seeking the maximization of pleasure and the avoidance of pain. It has no idea of time or reality.

In the first few years of life the individual develops an ego and a superego. The *ego* is the part of the self in closest contact with the social reality. It directs behavior toward the satisfaction of urges consistent with a knowledge of social and physical reality. In living out the *reality principle* through the ego, the individual may postpone immediate gratification but does not abandon it.

Morality, remorse, and feelings of guilt arise with the development of the *superego*, the chief force in the socialization of the individual. The superego is sociologically or culturally conditioned. It includes the development of a *conscience* and an *ego ideal*. The ego ideal represents what we *should* do and the conscience gives us guilt feelings when we do "wrong."

The following oversimplified model serves to illustrate operation of the Freudian id, ego, and superego: A child sees cookies on the table. His id demands immediate gratification, and he is governed by the pleasure principle. He grabs a cookie. His parents take the cookie away from him. When he has developed an ego, he waits for his parents to leave before taking a cookie, or he asks for one and coaxes if it is denied him. In either case he has applied the reality principle and postponed gratification. When he has developed a superego, he will not take the cookie if it is defined as wrong for him to do so. If he does take the cookie without being observed, he feels guilty.

Psychoanalytic theory tends to attribute delinquency or criminality to any of the following causes:

1. Inability to control criminal drives (id) because of a deficiency in ego or superego development. Because of faulty development,

the delinquent or criminal is believed to possess little capacity for repressing instinctual (criminal) impulses. The individual who is dominated by the id is consequently criminal.

2. Antisocial character formation resulting from a disturbed ego development. This occurs during the first three years of life.

3. An overdeveloped superego, which makes no provision for the satisfaction of the demands of the id. Offenders of this type are considered neurotic.

Freudians, neo-Freudians, and other psychoanalytic schools attribute criminality to inner conflicts, emotional problems, or unconscious feelings of insecurity, inadequacy, and inferiority. They regard criminal behavior and delinquencies as symptoms of underlying emotional problems. Psychoanalytic theory does not explain the criminal acts of the "normal" criminal, who simply learns to be criminal from differential association with criminal teachers. Psychoanalysis offers an explanation for the impulsive behavior of the psychotic, the neurotic, and the sociopath. This behavior, in psychoanalytic terms, would generally be id-dominated behavior evidencing ego deficiency, the inability to control criminal impulses.[19]

For criminologists the most important assertion of psychoanalytic theory is that to understand criminality we must understand unconscious motivation. In this context everyone is basically, in terms of the id, a criminal. Freud further asserts that if this is true, we must condemn in others the criminal thrust that lurks in all of us. This accounts for the psychoanalytic assumption that *the public demands severe punishment for certain crimes because the offender has acted as the rest of us would like to act ourselves.* Another philosopher put it this way: "We stamp out in others the evil we dimly perceive in ourselves."

The classical Freudian view of the interplay of crime and punishment has been most comprehensively and cogently presented by Franz Alexander and Hugo Staub in *The Criminal, the Judge, and the Public.* Several of its central themes are worth pondering for the light they cast on past and present attitudes toward offenders:

1. *Psychodynamically, all people are born criminals.* The human being enters the world as a criminal, that is, socially not adjusted. During the first years of life the child preserves this criminality to the fullest degree, concerned only with achieving pleasure and avoiding pain. Between the ages of 4 and 6 the development of the criminal begins to differentiate itself from that of the normal person. During this period (the latency period), which ends at

---

[19] For a detailed presentation of the psychoanalytic explanation of criminality and delinquency, see Kate Friedlander, *The Psychoanalytic Approach to Juvenile Delinquency* (New York: International Universities Press, 1947), and Walter Bromberg, *Crime and the Mind* (Philadelphia: Lippincott, 1948).

puberty, the future normal individual partially succeeds in re-pressing genuine criminal instinctive drives and stops their actual expression. He or she converts or transforms these criminal libidinal drives into socially acceptable forms. The future criminal fails to accomplish this adjustment.

The criminal carrries into action the natural, unbridled instinctual drive, acting as the child would act if it only could. The repressed and therefore unconscious criminality of the normal person finds a few socially harmless outlets, such as dream and fantasy life, neurotic symptoms, and also some transitional forms of behavior that are less harmless, such as dueling, boxing, bullfights, and occasionally the free expression of criminality in war. According to Alexander and Staub, "The universal criminality of the man of today demands violent, purely physical outlets."[20]

2. *The Oedipus complex is a fundamental psychodynamic fact that produces criminality unless it is successfully resolved.* The Freudian doctrine of the Oedipus complex asserts that all boys have a natural hostility toward their fathers and a love for their mothers that encompasses sexual desire. The guilt and anxiety aroused by these feelings must be resolved, according to Freud, if the youth is to grow up to become a psychologically healthy man. Alexander and Staub are extreme and dogmatic about the "fact" of the Oedipal condition:

> It took two decades of psychoanalytical research to prove conclusively that the Oedipus complex presented the chief unconscious psychological content of neurotic symptoms. It was found that all those psychological undercurrents which the adult person usually represses are affectively connected with the Oedipus situation of early childhood; these psychic currents, after they are repressed, continue in the unconscious, tied as with a navel cord to the infantile Oedipus complex.[21]

A major concomitant of the Oedipus complex is the assumption that a youth who represses his hostility toward his father will displace his aggression elsewhere. For the Freudian psychoanalyst, this accounts for much of the violent behavior (including homicide) of delinquent youths. The Freudian asserts that when the Oedipal situation is resolved through psychoanalysis, the analysand, now aware of the real object of his aggression, can curb his hostility.

---

[20] Franz Alexander and Hugo Staub, *The Criminal, the Judge, and the Public* (Glencoe, Ill.: Free Presss, 1956), p. 52.

[21] Ibid., p. 73.

3. *Uncovering unconscious motives is the fundamental task of criminology.* Alexander and Staub state:

> Theoretically speaking, every human being's responsibility is limited, because no human act is performed under the full control of the conscious ego. We must, therefore, always evaluate the quantitative distribution of conscious and unconscious motivations of every given act. Only such evaluation will provide us with definite criteria for purposes of diagnosis, or of sentencing or of any other measure which we might consider necessary to take in regard to a given act. The task of the judge of the future will be the establishment of such a psychological diagnosis; the measures resulting from such a diagnosis will, therefore, be founded on the psychological understanding of the criminal.[22]

Among those who take the extreme psychoanalytic view, certain criminal patterns are symbolic reflections of unconscious motivation. For example, the use of a gun by an armed robber is considered a reaction formation to a sense of male impotence. The gun is considered a symbol of male potency, and without attempting to be facetious, some extremists of the psychoanalytic school contend that when the armed robber says, "Stick 'em up," he is symbolically trying to adjust his unconscious sense of impotence. Similarly, the crime of breaking-entering and theft is considered to be displaced unconscious rape. These are the things the courts must understand, according to Alexander and Staub, before taking any "measures" against offenders.

4. *The first rebellious act or crime is committed in early childhood and is an important determinant of one's sense of justice.* "The first crime which all humans, without exception, sooner or later commit is the violation of the prescription for cleanliness. Under the rule of this penal code of the nursery, man for the first time becomes acquainted with the punishment which the world metes out to the individual transgressors."[23]

Therefore, according to Alexander and Staub, Ferenczi was right when he spoke of "sphincter morality" as the beginning and the foundation of adult human morality.[24] A refractory criminal who persists in spiteful rejection of social demands is like "a baby sitting on its little chamber pot persistently rejecting any demands coming from the outside; it sits in this sovereign position and feels superior to the grown-ups."[25]

---

[22] Alexander and Staub, *The Criminal, the Judge, and the Public*, p. 85.

[23] Ibid., p. 55.

[24] Sandor Ferenczi, "Psychoanalysis of Sexual Habits," in *Sex in Psychoanalysis*, trans. Ernest Jones (New York: Basic Books, 1950).

[25] Alexander and Staub, *The Criminal, the Judge, and the Public*, p. 55.

Alexander and Staub allege that the moment when a child begins to impose inhibitions on elimination is the first decisive step toward adjustment to the outside world, because at that moment the child creates an inhibitory agency within his or her own personality. In brief, the child begins to develop internal reference points for conduct and a sense of justice or injustice from the process of toilet training. The justice (or lack of it) of this training becomes a prototype of future restrictions on the child's instinctual life, and a disturbance during this phase of development may naturally serve as a cause of future disturbance in one's social adjustment.

Freudian psychoanalytic theory remains a prevalent construct among social workers and psychiatrists treating offenders, but criminologists today tend to a greater inclusion of social factors and the societal framework in their search for an understanding of the causes of crime and delinquency.

REINFORCEMENT THEORY AND CRIME

A widely accepted psychological theory that explains the learning process is called *reinforcement theory*. Fundamental to this theoretical approach is the idea that learning does not take place unless there is some sort of reinforcement, some equivalent of reward or punishment. Trasler applied this theory in an effort to determine *how a person learns not to be a criminal or delinquent*. The basic assumption of the theory is that *the individual learns not to become a criminal by a training procedure*, learning to inhibit certain kinds of behavior, some of which are defined as criminal. Trasler tested his assumption in an experiment with rats, using *passive avoidance conditioning*.

In this experiment, the rat first learned how to obtain food by depressing a lever. An electric shock was then substituted for the food. The rat learned to avoid depressing the lever, even though the original drive, hunger, remained. Even when the unpleasant stimulus was removed, the rat would not touch the lever. The researchers concluded that it was in this way that the rat acquired "anxiety." An individual's aversion to criminality is believed to develop in the same way. The individual is conditioned to feel anxiety in anticipation of punishment, even though the punishment originally used in conditioning is no longer present.

According to this theory, the degree of anxiety is in direct proportion to the amount of punishment meted out during one's early conditioning or socialization process. The intensity of the anxiety is a function of the severity of fear stimulated at the time of conditioning. The theory alleges that persons predisposed to criminal behavior have not been adequately punished for criminal acts during childhood. No anxiety is aroused by contemplating a criminal act because there was little or no fear-producing punishment.

Trasler lists the following as points of importance in adequate social conditioning:

1. The effectiveness of social conditioning will depend upon the strength of the unconditioned reaction (anxiety) with which it is associated.
2. Where there is a strong dependent relationship between a child and his parents, the sanction of withdrawal of approval will evoke intense anxiety.
3. The relationship between a child and his parents is likely to be one of dependence if it is (*a*) exclusive, (*b*) affectionate, and (*c*) reliable.[26]

Differences in conditioning methods, differences in sensitivity and family attitudes toward crime, and differences in class attitudes toward crime determine whether or not an individual will be predisposed to criminal behavior.

DIFFERENTIAL ASSOCIATION AND CRIME

A noted French scholar, Gabriel Tarde, was among the first to contend that patterns of delinquency and crime are learned in much the same manner as any other occupation. Learning, according to Tarde, occurs by imitation and in association with others. Imitation, as Tarde conceived it, involves more than simply emulating the behavior of another. The process is similar to that of *identification,* as the term is used in modern psychology. The individual is assumed to have selected a role model and fashioned his or her behavior after that model. To Tarde, crime is not a characteristic or a disease that the individual inherits or contracts; it is an occupation that the person learns from others. The only difference between crime and any lawful occupation is in the content of what is learned.[27]

A more systematic explanation of the way criminal behavior patterns are acquired was developed by Edwin Sutherland and later elaborated upon by Donald Cressey, his student and collaborator. The central thesis of the theory, known as differential association, is that "criminal behavior is learned through interaction with others in intimate personal groups. The learning includes techniques of committing criminal acts, plus the motives, drives, rationalizations, and attitudes favorable to the commission of crime."[28] The basic principles of differential association are stated as follows:

---

[26] Gordon Trasler, *The Explanation of Criminality* (London: Routledge & Kegan Paul, 1962).

[27] Gabriel Tarde, *Penal Philosophy* (Boston: Little, Brown, 1912).

[28] Edwin H. Sutherland and Donald R. Cressey, *Criminology,* 8th ed., 1970, p. 75. By permission of the Estate of Donald B. Cressey.

1. *Criminal behavior is learned.* Negatively, this means that criminal behavior is not inherited, as such; also, the person who is not already trained in crime does not invent criminal behavior, just as a person does not make mechanical inventions unless he has had training in mechanics.

2. *Criminal behavior is learned in interaction with other persons in a process of communication.* This communication is verbal in many respects but includes "the communication of gestures."

3. The principal part of the learning of criminal behavior occurs within *intimate personal groups.* Negatively, this means that the impersonal agencies of communication, such as movies and newspapers, play a relatively unimportant part in the genesis of criminal behavior.

4. When criminal behavior is learned, the learning includes (*a*) *techniques of committing the crime*, which are sometimes very complicated, sometimes very simple; (*b*) *the specific direction of motives, drives, rationalizations, and attitudes.*

5. The specific direction of motives and drives is *learned from definitions of the legal codes as favorable or unfavorable.* In some societies an individual is surrounded by persons who invariably define the legal codes as rules to be observed, while in others he is surrounded by persons whose definitions are favorable to the violation of the legal codes. In our American society these definitions are almost always mixed, with the consequence that we have culture conflict in relation to the legal codes.

6. *A person becomes delinquent because of an excess of definitions favorable to violation of law over definitions unfavorable to violation of law.* This is the principle of differential association. It refers to both criminal and anti-criminal associations and has to do with counteracting forces. When persons become criminal, *they do so because of contacts with criminal patterns* and also because of isolation from anti-criminal patterns. Any person inevitably assimilates the surrounding culture unless other patterns are in conflict; a Southerner does not pronounce "r" because other Southerners do not pronounce "r." Negatively, this proposition of differential association means that associations which are neutral so far as crime is concerned have little or no effect on the genesis of criminal behavior. Much of the experience of a person is neutral in this sense, e.g., learning to brush one's teeth. This behavior has no negative or positive effect on criminal behavior except as it may be related to associations which are concerned with the legal codes. This neutral behavior is important especially as an occupier of the time of a child so that he is not in contact with criminal behavior during the time he is so engaged in the neutral behavior.

7. *Differential associations may vary in frequency, duration, priority, and intensity.* This means that associations with criminal behavior and also associations with anti-criminal behavior vary in those respects. "Frequency" and "duration" as modalities of associations are obvious and need no explanation. "Priority" is assumed to be important in the sense that lawful behavior in early childhood may persist throughout life, and also that delinquent behavior developed in early childhood may persist throughout life. This tendency, however, has not been adequately demonstrated, and priority seems to be important principally through its selective influence. "Intensity" is not precisely defined but it has to do

with such things as the prestige of the source of the criminal or anti-criminal pattern and with emotional reactions related to the associations. In a precise description of the criminal behavior of a person these modalities would be stated in quantitative form and a mathematical ratio be reached. A formula in this sense has not been developed, and the development of such a formula would be extremely difficult.

8. The process of learning criminal behavior by association with criminal and anti-criminal patterns involves all of the mechanisms that are involved in any other learning. Negatively, this means that the learning of criminal behavior is not restricted to the process of imitation. A person who is seduced, for instance, *learns criminal behavior by association*, but this process would not ordinarily be described as imitation.

9. While criminal behavior is an expression of general needs and values, it is not explained by those general needs and values since non-criminal behavior is an expression of the same needs and values. Thieves generally steal in order to secure money, but likewise honest laborers work in order to secure money. The attempts by many scholars to explain criminal behavior by general devices and values, such as the happiness principle, striving for social status, the money motive, or frustration, have been and must continue to be futile since they explain lawful behavior as completely as they explain criminal behavior. They are similar to respiration, which is necessary for any behavior but which does not differentiate criminal from noncriminal behavior.[29]

This theory does not explain why some people associate with those who approve of violation of the law while others do not, nor does it explain why some individuals become intensely committed to definitions *favorable* to the law while others with similar associations do not. It remains significant, however, because most current theorists have adopted the emphasis that differential association places on social learning through interaction in intimate groups as the principal method of the transmission of criminal values.

The impact of Sutherland's theory on criminology was detailed by Cressey in an article in *Social Problems*. Sutherland's theory has had such a profound impact on the field of criminology in the United States that it is pertinent to present most of Cressey's remarks on the origin and development of the theory of differential association.

> The first formal statement of Edwin H. Sutherland's theory of differential association appeared in the third edition of his *Principles of Criminology*, in 1939. Sutherland later pointed out that the idea of differential association was stated in an earlier edition of the text, and he confessed that he was unaware that this statement was a general theory of criminal behavior. At the insistence of his colleagues, he drew up a formal set of propositions based on this earlier notion and appended it to the 1939 edition of the textbook.
>
>   In one sense, this first formal statement of the theory of differential association was short lived. For reasons which never have been clear, the

---

[29] Sutherland and Cressey, *Criminology*, pp. 77–79.

statement of the theory was qualified so that it pertained only to "systematic criminal behavior," rather than to the more general category, "criminal behavior." Further, the statement was redundant, for it proposed generally that individual criminality is learned in a process of differential association with criminal and anti-criminal behavior patterns, but then went on to use "consistency" of association with the two kinds of patterns as one of the conditions affecting the impact of differential association on individuals. Thus, "consistency" of behavior patterns presented was used as a general explanation of criminality, but "consistency" also was used to describe the process by which differential association takes place. . . .

He also deleted the word "systematic," principally because it led to errors of interpretation. He believed that "systematic criminal behavior" included almost all criminal behavior, while his readers, colleagues, and students considered only a very small proportion of criminal behavior to be "systematic." The theory now refers to all criminal behavior.

The current statement of the theory of differential association holds, in essence, that "criminal behavior is learned in interaction with persons in a pattern of communication," and that the specific direction of motives, drives, rationalizations, and attitudes—whether in the direction of anti-criminality or criminality—is learned from persons who define the codes as rules to be observed and from persons whose attitudes are favorable to violation of legal codes. "A person becomes delinquent because of an excess of definitions favorable to violation of law over definitions unfavorable to violations of law." In any society, the two kinds of definitions of what is desirable in reference to legal codes exist side by side, and a person might present contradictory definitions to another person at different times and in different situations. Sutherland called the process of receiving these definitions "differential association," because the content of what is learned in association with criminal behavior patterns differs from the content of what is learned in association with anticriminal behavior patterns. "When persons become criminals, they do so because of contacts with criminal behavior patterns and also because of isolation from anti-criminal patterns." These contacts, however, "may vary in frequency, duration, priority, and intensity."

When this idea is applied to a nation, a city, or a group, it becomes a sociological theory, rather than a social psychological theory, for it deals with differential rates of crime and delinquency. For example, a high crime rate in urban areas, as compared to rural areas, can be considered an end product of a situation in which a relatively large proportion of persons are presented with an excess of criminal behavior patterns. Similarly, the fact that the rate for all crimes is not higher in some urban areas than it is in some rural areas can be attributed to differences in probabilities of exposure to criminal behavior patterns. The important general point is that in a multi-group type of social organization, alternative and inconsistent standards of conduct are possessed by various groups, so that individuals who are members of one group have a higher probability of learning to use legal means for achieving success, or of learning to deny the importance of success, while individuals in other groups learn to accept the importance of success and to achieve it by illegal means. Stated in another way, there are alternative educational processes in operation, varying with groups, so that a person may be educated in either conventional or criminal means of achieving success. Sutherland called this situation "differential social organization" or "differential group organization," and he proposed that "differential group organization should explain the crime rate, while differential association should explain the criminal behavior of a person. The two explanations must be consistent with each other."

Sutherland's theory has had an important effect on sociological thought about criminality and crime, if only because it has become the center of controversy. Strangely, it seems to have received more discussion, comment, and research attention in the last five years than in the first fifteen years of its existence. Also, there rapidly is developing a situation in which probation, parole, and prison workers have at least heard of the theory, even if they are barely beginning to try using it for prevention of crime and rehabilitation of criminals. A social worker has recently written, "The hallmark of this new departure (in delinquency prevention) is the recognition that delinquency is not primarily a psychological problem of neuroses but a social problem of differential values. Essentially most delinquent behavior arises from the fact that core concepts of what is right and wrong, what is worth striving for and what is attainable, are not transmitted with equal force and clarity throughout the community."[30]

SOCIAL ALIENATION AND CRIMINALITY

Clarence R. Jeffery proposed a theory of social alienation to explain criminality. He pointed out that the concept of crime must exist before the concept of the criminal is possible. Antisocial behavior is not criminal behavior until a system of criminal law emerges. He stated that all the theories of crime put forth in criminology are theories of criminal behavior, attempting to explain the behavior of the criminal. Regardless of the adequacy of the theories of behavior, they do not explain why the behavior is regarded as criminal. This is why Jeffery believed that criminologists need a theory of crime that explains the origin and development of criminal laws in terms of the institutional structure of society.

Jeffery's Theory of the Development of Law

Law came into existence at a time when the tribal system was disintegrating and social cohesion was no longer available as a means of social control. Primitive law is custom enforced by the kinship group and

---

[30] Donald R. Cressey, "The Theory of Differential Association: An Introduction," *Social Problems* 8 (Summer 1960):2–6. Reprinted by permission of the Society for the Study of Social Problems.

based on the cohesiveness of the group. It is private and personal in nature and in operation.

Law is a product of impersonalization and the decline in social cohesion. It is a product of urbanization. Law emerges in a society whenever intimate, personal relationships are no longer efficient as agents of social control.[31]

Jeffery grouped explanations of criminal behavior into two schools: the psychological and the sociological.

The *psychological* school is based on the proposition that criminals differ from noncriminals in terms of personality traits that are expressed in some form of antisocial behavior. Criminal behavior is caused by emotional or mental conflict. The most damaging criticism raised against the psychological school is the observation that few neurotics are criminals and that most criminals are neither neurotic nor psychotic.

Jeffery chose Sutherland, with his theory of differential association, to represent the *sociological* school. Jeffery described it as basically a theory of learning and stated that criminal behavior is learned from contact with those who maintain criminal attitudes and practices. Criminal behavior is learned by association with criminal and antisocial patterns. He pointed out the following criticisms of the theory of differential association:

1. The theory does not explain the origin of criminality.
2. It does not explain crimes of passion or accident.
3. The theory does not explain crimes by those with no prior contact with criminal attitudes.
4. It does not explain the noncriminal living in a criminal environment.
5. The theory does not differentiate between criminal and noncriminal behavior.
6. It does not take into account motivation or "differential response patterns." People respond differently to similar situations.
7. The theory does not account for the differential rate of crime associated with age, sex, urban areas, and minority groups.[32]

Jeffery advanced a *theory of social alienation* in an attempt to integrate the psychological and sociological concepts of criminality. His theory states that crime rates are highest in groups where social interaction is characterized by isolation, anonymity, impersonalization, and anomie.

According to this theory, the criminal is one who lacks interpersonal relationships and suffers from interpersonal failure. The typical criminal

---

[31] Clarence R. Jeffery, "An Integrated Theory of Crime and Criminal Behavior," *Journal of Criminal Law, Criminology and Police Scinece* 50 (March 1959):533–552. Summary on p. 536.

[32] Ibid., p. 537.

has failed to achieve satisfactory interpersonal relations with others; is lonely and emotionally isolated; lacks membership in lawful primary groups; is insecure, hostile, and aggressive; feels unloved and unwanted; and has an inadequate sense of belonging. The criminal is the product of social impersonalization.

The theory of social alienation is in essential agreement with the psychological thinking that places emphasis on such concepts as feelings of rejection, emotional starvation, psychological isolation from others, and so forth.

Jeffery's theory is in agreement with Sutherland's theory in that both emphasize the importance of social interaction that occurs in the primary group. It differs from differential association in the following respects: (1) It explains sudden crimes of passion. (2) It explains why an individual can live in a delinquent subculture and yet remain isolated from delinquent patterns. (3) It explains why a person with no history of association with criminals can commit criminal acts. (4) It explains the origin of criminal behavior in the first place by suggesting that high crime rates exist in areas characterized by anonymous, impersonal relationships. The theory of social alienation represents an attempt to integrate the sociological and psychological schools. It retains emphasis on social interaction with emphasizing the emotional content of human interaction.

In support of his theory, Jeffery pointed to the fact that crime rates are high for young adult males who live in urban slum areas, who are from lower socioeconomic groups, and who are members of minority groups. In these areas one also finds social isolation, a preponderance of impersonal relationships, and anonymity.

Types of Alienation

Jeffery divided social alienation into three types. First there is *individual alienation*. The individual is alienated and isolated from interpersonal relations. This person is often characterized as a sociopath, who does not accept the values of society.

The second type is *group alienation*. The group to which the person belongs is alienated and isolated from the larger community. The individual who identifies with such a group is often characterized as a cultural deviate or a dyssocial person. A lack of integration of the various segments of society produces alienation of those segments.

The third type is *legal alienation*. The differential treatment of blacks and whites, and of lower-class and upper-class individuals, in courts of law illustrates the fact that different social groups have differential access to justice. In a large, complex society, government by representation replaces government by direct citizen participation. The function and processes of government are removed from the people and placed in the hands of a corps of professional politicians and lobbyists. A type of alienation exists between legal values and those expressed in other institutions of our society.[33]

CONTAINMENT THEORY

To explain the way in which criminal behavior is influenced by a variety of factors, Walter Reckless offered the containment theory:

1. At the top of a vertical arrangement impinging on an individual is a layer of *social pressures*. Pressure factors include adverse living conditions and economic conditions, minority group status, lack of opportunities, and family conflicts.

2. The pressures include what Reckless refers to as *pull factors*. These draw the individual away from the accepted norms. They include bad companions, delinquent or criminal subculture, and deviant groups.

3. In the situation immediately surrounding the individual is the structure of effective or ineffective *external containment*. This structure consists of effective family living and supportive groups.

4. The next layer is the *inner containment* within the individual. It is a product of good or poor internalization. When external containment is weak, inner containment must be additionally strong to withstand the pushes from within and the pulls and pressures from without.

5. The bottom layer consists of the *pushes*. These include inner tensions, hostility, aggressiveness, strong feelings of inadequacy and inferiority, and organic impairments.[34]

Reckless used outer containment and inner containment as intervening variables. The individual may be pressured into criminality by unfavorable economic conditions or pulled into it by association with a delinquent subculture if the outer containment is deficient. The lack of outer containment is evidenced by the lack of well-defined limits to behavior, the breakdown of rules, the absence of definite roles for adolescents to play, and failure of family life to present adequate limits and roles to the youth.

Reckless contended that a child in a high-delinquency area where outer containment is weak remain nondelinquent if inner containment is good. Inner containment consists of good ego strength, self-control, good self-conceptualization, and strong resistance against diversions.

Containment theory does have the advantage of merging the psychological and the sociological viewpoints of crime causation. It facilitates

---

[33] Jeffery, "Integrated Theory of Crime and Criminal Behavior," pp. 550–551.

[34] Walter C. Reckless, *The Crime Problem* (New York: Prentice-Hall, 1961), pp. 355–356.

an analysis of the inner personal forces that propel a person to commit a crime, and at the same time permits an examination of the sociocultural forces that shape an individual's motivation and personality.

SELF-CONCEPT: CRIME AND DELINQUENCY

On the basis of my four decades of research and observation, I have developed the theory that a significant causal factor in delinquency and crime relates to the offender's self-concept. This factor has several roots and several implications. Children who are physically, sexually, or emotionally abused, usually by their parents, develop low self-esteem and are more apt to be prone to commit delinquent acts as adolescents and to grow up to become criminals. They also denigrate themselves, feel worthless, and are less likely to care about what happens to them. These social-psychological forces push these juveniles toward self-destructive behavior such as drug abuse and violent crime. Their suicidal tendencies make them more likely to commit senseless, destructive delinquent acts which are as harmful to themselves as the behavior is to their victims.

In my work with delinquents, especially in psychiatric facilities, I have observed the impact of self-concept on delinquent behavior in thousands of youths who are the end result of their negative socialization process. One prototypical example is 14-year-old Andy. He was emotionally and physically abused from the age of 4, three to five times a week, by his alcoholic father. The physical beatings and verbal abuse administered by his father often had little relationship to Andy's behavior. He would be beaten or verbally abused for such offenses as poor school grades, not keeping his room clean, or being suspected of smoking marijuana; and he would also be beaten whenever his alcoholic father had a need to act out his personal frustrations on his son. According to Andy, "He would hit me or scream at me at times when I deserved it. Like I knew I did something wrong. He would also beat the shit out of me for no reason—just because he was loaded [drunk] and mad at the world. I've always felt like a punching bag, or maybe more like a piece of shit."

The irrational behavior of Andy's father led to several consequences. The indiscriminate beatings and verbal abuse had the effect of producing low self-esteem in the youth. He tended to feel humiliated and worthless. As a result of these feelings he thought he was a "loser" and did not deserve to feel he was a worthwhile person.

In the family's dynamics, Andy's mother was almost totally dominated (and sometimes battered) by his father into a subservient role. Consequently, the father's perception of Andy was a significant factor in the development of Andy's low self-esteem in particular and of his personality in general. As Andy stated in a moment of self-revelation, "If my own father thinks I'm a punk and a loser, maybe that's what I am."

Feelings of *low self-esteem* are acted out in self-destructive delinquent behavior that often involves violence. Some researchers and reporters have misperceived gang members as "fighting for their turf" and committing Rambo-like acts of violence in a coherent defense of their comrades in arms. A more accurate perspective on their violent behavior is that these youths are, because of their low self-esteem, acting out self-destructive behavior; they have limited concern about whether they live or die.

Low self-concept is one consequence of abuse; another is extreme rage. The *rage* created in the child by the physical and emotional abuse of the parents is a significant facet of the causal theory of delinquency and self-concept. In this context, I recall a 15-year-old gang member with whom I worked in New York City, who accounted for his being wild in the streets in this way:

> My father always beat me up since I was a little kid. When I hit 14 we would wrestle and fight even. Sometimes I would beat him up—but mostly he won. Our fights would totally piss me off, and when I hit the streets I was looking for trouble. I had fights every day, and when our gang would go bopping I was always up in the front line. I never cared what happened to me or anyone else.

A considerable amount of senseless violence is cooked up in a cauldron of family violence that involves the physical abuse of a child.

Substance abuse is another facet of a delinquent's abuse-generated low self-concept. Substance abuse and alcoholism are ways of ameliorating the painful feelings of having low self-esteem. Substance abuse is also a form of self-destructive behavior.

A case in point is Jane, a drug abuser with whom I worked in a therapy group in a psychiatric hospital. She had been sexually abused by her stepfather for three years. In addition to her drug problem, one of the fallouts from her sexual traumas was the practice of self-mutilation. She slashed herself with razor blades and almost died on several occasions. She very obviously had a low self-concept and considerable rage; Jane did not care what happened to her.

In one encounter group–therapy session I directed, I delivered a diatribe about the deadly, destructive effects of drug abuse and remarked, "Drug addiction is a form of slow suicide." As I said this, I noticed Jane's eyes light up. I asked her about her response and she commented, "You're absolutely right. Now I know why I do drugs. I feel like a worthless piece of shit and if I had enough courage I would kill myself. I often feel, especially when I smoke crack, maybe I'll die painlessly and suddenly from the coke like those two football players."

Child abuse, low self-esteem, a delinquent self-concept, and suicidal tendencies are intertwined factors in the cases of most juvenile delinquents. In some respects, teenage suicide is a type of homicide. I worked with one delinquent youth, 16-year-old Pete, who was in the hospital for stabbing himself in the chest with a hunting knife. He almost died from this self-inflicted wound. Although he was in the hospital for attempted suicide, he had a long delinquent career that included drug addiction and robbery. In a psychodrama session I had him act out the specific dramatic episode that involved his suicide attempt. A number of dimensions of his feelings about his father, his delinquent behavior, and his self-concept as a delinquent emerged in the session.

In Pete's psychodrama, a key dramatic episode involved a screaming battle with his "father." In the core dialogue, Pete screamed at his "father" as he brandished a rolled-up magazine that represented the knife he had actually held in his hand during the real fight.

> PETE: You drunken bastard, you've been beating on me since I was a little kid. I'll never forget that day you threw me up against the wall when I was ten. And I really didn't do anything.
>
> "FATHER": You deserved every beating I gave you.
>
> PETE: Bullshit. No kid deserves the things you did to me. I'm going to end this pain now. I'm going to kill you!

I intervened in the psychodrama at this point and used a psychodramatic technique known as a soliloquy.

> L.Y.: Pete, I want you to hold off your next move. Here you are in this terrible situation. Like Hamlet, just say your inner thoughts out loud.
>
> PETE: I hate this man. He's never been a father to me. He doesn't deserve to live. With one move of this knife [the rolled-up magazine in his hand] I can wipe him out of my life and get rid of all my pain. . . . It's either him or me. [Begins to cry.] But there were times when he was good to me. We went to ball games and fishing. I guess I love him, and maybe he's right about me. I'm no fucking good. I'm everything he's accused me of. I'm just worthless. It's never going to work out, and I can't stand it any more.

Sobbing, Pete stabbed himself in the chest with the symbolic knife in the psychodrama. This was the act he had committed *in reality*—which had resulted in his placement in the psychiatric hospital.

The session was a classic representation of the feelings of many delinquent youths who have these conflicting emotional vectors at work in their lives. They have low self-esteem because they have been physically and emotionally abused. They are full of rage toward the perpetrator of the abuse, in Pete's case his father. They *displace* a lot of their aggression onto people other than the primary object of their hostility, and this accounts for their violent delinquent behavior. Yet on some level their low self-esteem persists and is reflected in self-destructive behavior. In Pete's case, it resulted in his horrendous self-inflicted wound. It was almost a toss-up between killing his father or himself. Pete believed that either act, killing his father or himself, would end his emotional pain.

Another factor that produces a delinquent self-concept and that perpetuates delinquent behavior is a *criminogenic* family background that fosters the adoption of deviant values. As a case in point, a young man, Bill, with whom I worked in juvenile detention, had a father who was a "biker." All his life Bill was surrounded by a biker culture which included drugs, violence, and sexual acting out. These behavioral patterns constituted a normal part of his family's day-to-day life situation. When he went to school he began to notice that he came from what he later termed "a criminal family." Others in the community, including his teachers and neighbors, perceived Bill as being delinquent, and in time Bill's family background tended to reinforce his self-image as a delinquent. His deviant behavior, which involved drug abuse and violence, was reinforced by his self-concept and the deviant values he learned from his family.

Society finally places the stamp of delinquency on a youth in the juvenile court. Being labeled a delinquent by the juvenile court validates a delinquent's self-concept and the delinquent behavior that emanates from this self-description. Following is an example of this dynamic factor in defining delinquency. I recall escorting a youth, George, who was 14 at the time, into juvenile court when I worked in a juvenile detention institution in Newark, New Jersey. Prior to this court appearance George had been involved in various thefts, gang fighting, and the abuse of drugs. Despite several court appearances for these varied offenses, he had managed to avoid being sent away to the state reformatory. In our conversation prior to George's court appearance, he was concerned, and he revealed a great deal of anxiety about his behavior, his parents' reactions, and what was going to happen to him in court. The judge determined that probation was no longer feasible and that George should be sent to the state reformatory for 18 months.

When George and I left the court to return to the detention facility to prepare him for his transfer to the state reformatory, his earlier attitude of concern and anxiety was radically changed. He seemed angry, he swaggered, and he had a determined look on his face. On the way to the detention facility, I vividly recall, he looked up at me with a snickering smile and flatly stated, "I guess I am now a juvenile delinquent."

George now had the self-concept of "delinquent" officially conferred upon him by the courts. When I probed further about his feelings and attitudes, he revealed that this meant he had more status in his gang, and that from that time on "nobody cares and I may as well do anything I want."

This youth's attitude was prototypical of many: when they are defined as delinquent by the courts, they define themselves in this way more definitively and take on the attitudes and behavior of delinquents.

The label becomes more of a fact. In brief, the definitiveness of a delinquent self-concept tends to reinforce further delinquent behavior as a prelude to later adult criminal behavior.

On this issue, Walter Reckless, Simon Dinitz, and Ellwyn Murray stated:

> The concept of self as a delinquent may work negatively. To attribute certain abstract characteristics and predictions of delinquency to certain individuals or groups could possibly influence persons to accept the ascribed roles, a self-fulfilling prophecy. Applying labels and epithets such as "juvenile delinquent" and "young criminal" does not help anyone to think well of himself. Active, aggressive, impetuous, sometimes violent and irrational behavior does not automatically mean that a child is a junior public enemy. Equating healthy defiance with delinquency may encourage a child to think of himself as a delinquent.[35]

In summary, child abuse, neglect, and their impact on a juvenile's self-concept all affect delinquent behavior. I posit the following sequence leading to a low self-concept, which helps explain a considerable amount of crime and delinquency. (1) The child is abused (sexually or physically) or neglected by the primary socializing agents—the parents. (2) Because the child is treated in negative ways and with limited respect, the child feels humiliated, demeaned, and unworthy. As a consequence of this pattern of socialization, the child develops a low self-concept and feels self-hatred. The child thinks, on some deeper emotional level, "If these important, powerful people in my life think that I am stupid, inadequate, and unworthy of love and respect, I must be a terrible person." (3) Mixed in with the child's low self-esteem is a rage against the parents who have abused or neglected their child, and this rage is often displaced onto people in the general society. (4) The juvenile court reflects society's viewpoint and puts the final stamp of "delinquent" on the juvenile.

Children with a low self-concept tend to care little about what happens to them. They not only do not value themselves; this attitude carries over in regard to other people in their world. This "I don't give a damn about anything" attitude, combined with the rage that derives from being abused, creates a youth who is apt to be violent and has a disrespect for the rights or property of others. This type of juvenile, who has little regard for anyone, is most likely to be delinquency-prone. The delinquent's emotional pain, which results from abuse and a low self-concept, facilitates law-violating behavior. A significant facet of this low self-esteem is a suicidal tendency that is characteristically acted out in the later criminal behavior of violence and substance abuse.

---

[35] Walter C. Reckless, Simon Dinitz, and Ellwyn Murray, "Self-Concept as an Insulator Against Delinquency," *American Sociological Review* 21 (December 1956):744–746.

Chapter
15

Causation: Group and Society Theories

*T*he noted French sociologist Emile Durkheim considered crime an integral part of all societies. Having defined crime as an act that is punished, he expressed the view that a society exempt from crime was utterly impossible. The dominant group in the society invariably defines certain behavior as undesirable and punishable. It is this social definition that confers criminal character upon the act, and not the intrinsic quality of the act. According to Durkheim:

> Crime is present . . . in all societies of all types. Its form changes; the acts thus characterized are not the same everywhere; but, everywhere and always, there have been men who have behaved in such a way as to draw upon themselves penal repression. If, in proportion as societies pass from the lower to the higher types, the rate of criminality . . . tended to decline, it might be believed that crime, while still normal, is tending to lose this character of normality. [Actually] it has everywhere increased. . . . There is, then, no phenomenon that presents more indisputably all the symptoms of normality, since it appears closely connected with the conditions of all collective life.[1]

Durkheim did recognize that some criminal behavior was pathological and was made punishable with the complete consensus of the society—murder, for example. With respect to other behavior classified as criminal there is less general agreement.

In a society that permits individuals to differ more or less from the

---

[1] Emile Durkheim, *The Rules of Sociological Method*, 8th ed., trans. Sarah A. Solvag and John H. Mueller (Glencoe, Ill.: Free Press, 1950), pp. 65–66.

collective type, it is inevitable that some acts are criminal. However, since nothing is "good" indefinitely and to an unlimited extent, people must be free to deviate; otherwise, social change would be impossible.

As Durkheim saw it, if progress is to be made, individual originality must be able to express itself. For the originality of the idealist to find expression it is necessary that the originality of the criminal also be expressible. It should be remembered that the founders of the United States were at first considered legally criminals in the context of the British Empire. Crime is thus a valuable force for social change.

ANOMIE AND CRIME

Anomie, as first presented by Emile Durkheim in his search for the cause of suicide and later elaborated upon by Robert K. Merton and others, is characterized as a condition in which an individual feels a loss of orientation; the person is without outside controls he or she can trust or believe in. For such an individual, little is real or meaningful; this person cannot relate to society wholly and finds its norms and values without meaning. This individual is free of the restrictions imposed on those belonging to society and, free, is lost.[2] In his treatise on anomic suicide, Durkheim pointed out the dangers of such freedom from acceptable restraint: "Those who have only empty space above them are almost inevitably lost in it, if no force restrain them." Durkheim pointed out that "no living being can be happy or even exist unless his needs are sufficiently proportioned to his means." Society limits the means available to the individual. Society also sets goals appropriate to each category of people in it. There may be some flexibility, but there are also limits. "To pursue a goal which is by definition unattainable is to condemn oneself to a state of perpetual unhappiness," Durkheim continued. Yet, in our society, as in the France of Durkheim's time, *all classes contend among themselves because no established classification any longer exists.* Society, according to Durkheim, is the only agency that is acceptable to people as a regulator of human desires; it is the only agency recognized as superior to the individual, with the acknowledged right to make demands and impose restrictions. Yet " . . . discipline can be useful only if considered just by the peoples subject to it. When it is maintained only by custom and force, peace and harmony are illusory; the spirit of unrest and discontent are latent; appetites superficially restrained are ready for revolt."

Merton related crime to anomie through the four following concepts:

1. Society, in the United States, places an emphasis on success as

---

[2] Emile Durkheim, *Suicide*, trans. John A. Spaulding and George Simpson (Glencoe, Ill.: Free Press, 1951).

represented by possessions and their consumption, and at the same time, for some people, blocks legitimate paths to the achievement of that goal. Success is assumed to be achievable by all.

2. The access to legitimate means of achievement are effectively denied to many members of the lower classes and to members of minority groups.

3. The conflict thus established is often resolved by resorting to illegal means of achievement of acceptable goals.

4. On the other hand, an individual may deny the value of the goal and act out that denial in the destruction of property.

Resorting to either illegitimate means or destruction of the goal is anomie. It is an inability to correlate the ends of action and the action to the values of society. Since legitimate means and shared goals become contradictory, the individual must relieve anxiety and frustration by denying the one or the the other as meaningful. As distance grows between institutional means and cultural goals, anomie grows more prevalent.[3]

CRIME AND DISLOCATIONS IN THE SOCIAL SYSTEM

In the larger context of society, Robert K. Merton examined the way in which the social structure exerts definite pressure upon some persons to engage in nonconformist behavior. He asserted that deviant behavior results from discrepancies between culturally defined goals and the socially structured means of achieving them.

According to Merton, American society defines success as a goal for everyone. Some of the socially approved means of achieving success are hard work, education, and thrift. The emphasis in our society, he pointed out, is on the *goals*—winning the game—not on the *means*—how you do it. Since some people do not have equal access to approved means, they have a more limited chance to achieve the goals of the society unless they deviate.

Merton described five basic modes of adaptation to the goals and means of the society:

- *Adaptation I*   Conformity to both culture goals and means. This is the most commonly used adaptation in every society.
- *Adaptation II*   Innovation, the acceptance of the cultural emphasis on success goals without equally internalizing the morally prescribed norms governing the means for their attainment. The individual accepts the goals of wealth and power, but does not

---

[3] Robert K. Merton, *Social Theory and Social Structure* (Glencoe, Ill.: Free Press, 1957), pp. 131–160.

accept work as means. The innovator may choose illegal means and become a criminal. This choice is particularly attractive to the person who concludes that he does not have access to approved means of achieving his goals.

- *Adaptation III* Ritualism, the rejection of culturally defined goals with conformity to the mores defining the means. The ritualistic individual does not try to get ahead; he is overly involved with the ritualistic means of success.
- *Adaptation IV* Retreatism, the rejection of both the culturally defined goals and the institutionalized means. The individual escapes by becoming a drug addict, an alcoholic, a psychotic, or by some other method.
- *Adaptation V* Rebellion, the rejection of both the goals and the means of attaining them. The rebel attempts to introduce a "new social order."[4]

In general, Merton's fundamental explanation of the tendency to criminality is that the emphasis on goals rather than on the means of attaining them causes many people who cannot achieve material success goals through legitimate means to resort to any means, including crime. Merton's point of reference for accounting for criminality is found in the analysis of social dislocations. This is the fundamental direction taken by many recent sociological students of crime causation.

ECONOMIC DETERMINISM

The Dutch criminologist William A. Bonger, a Marxist, was the principal proponent of a theory of economic causation of crime. Bonger attributed criminal acts, particularly crimes against property, directly to the poverty of the proletariat in a competitive capitalistic system. Poverty, which resulted from unsuccessful economic competition, led to personal disorganization and was an inherent part of a capitalist society. The solution to crime, according to this theory, could be achieved only through the reorganization of the means of production and the development of a classless society. Bonger described this viewpoint this way:

> The egoistic tendency does not by itself make a man criminal. For this something else is necessary. . . . For example, a man who is enriched by the exploitation of children may nevertheless remain all his life an honest man from the legal point of view. He does not think of stealing, because he has a surer and more lucrative means of getting wealth, although he lacks the moral sense which would prevent him from committing a crime if the thought of it occurred to him. . . . As a consequence of the present

---

[4] Adapted from Merton, *Social Theory and Social Structure*, pp. 141–156.

environment, man has become very egoistic and hence more capable of crime, than if the environment had developed the germs of altruism.

The present economic system is based upon exchange. . . . Such a mode of production cannot fail to have an egoistic character. A society based upon exchange isolates the individuals by weakening the bond that unites them. When it is a question of exchange the two parties interested think only of their own advantage even to the detriment of the other party. . . .

No commerce without trickery is a proverbial expression (among consumers), and with the ancients Mercury, the god of commerce, was also the god of thieves. This is true, that the merchant and the thief are alike in taking account exclusively of their own interest to the detriment of those with whom they have to do.[5]

There has been sufficient evidence since Bonger wrote to indicate that poverty alone does not cause crime and that most poor people are not criminals. Most Western societies, however, have assumed greater responsibility for care of the unemployed and the poor than they did in Bonger's time. A commentary of Bonger's that still appears to hold true is his observation that conspicuous consumption tends indirectly to set goals impossible of legitimate achievement by people in the lower strata of society. Bonger's postulate of the discrepancy between culturally approved goals and institutionalized means of achieving them as a cause of crime has been incorporated into the theoretical positions of many recent sociologists.

Economic determinism as part of a contemporary radical criminology has been supported by the work of Gordon and others.[6] According to this view, capitalist societies depend on basically competitive forms of social and economic interaction and upon substantial inequalities in the allocation of social resources. Without competition and a competitive ideology, workers might not be expected to struggle to improve their relative income and status in society by working harder. Although property rights are protected, capitalist societies do not guarantee economic security to most individual members. *Driven by fear of economic insecurity and by a competitive desire to gain some of the goods unequally distributed throughout the society, many individuals will eventually become "criminals."*

The following three different kinds of crime in the United States provide examples of functionally similar rationality:

1. *Ghetto Crime*   The legitimate jobs open to many young ghetto residents typically pay low wages, offer relatively demeaning

---

[5] William A. Bonger, *Criminality and Economic Conditions* (Boston: Little, Brown, 1916), pp. 401–402.

[6] David M. Gordon, "Capitalism, Class and Crime in America," *Crime and Delinquency* (April 1973):163–186.

assignments, and carry constant risk of layoff. Many types of "crimes" available in the ghetto offer higher monetary return, higher status, and often low risk of arrest and punishment.

2. *Organized Crime* Activities such as gambling, prostitution, and drug distribution are illegal for various reasons, but there is a demand for these activities. Opportunities for monetary rewards are great, and the risks of arrest and punishment low.

3. *Corporate Crime* Corporations exist to protect and augment the capital of their owners. If it becomes difficult to do this lawfully, corporate officials will try to do it another way.

Gordon also pointed out that current patterns of crime and punishment in the United States support the capitalist system in three ways:

1. The pervasive patterns of selective law enforcement reinforce a prevalent ideology in the society that *individuals rather than institutions are to blame for social problems.*

2. The patterns of crime and punishment manage "legitimately" to neutralize the potential opposition to the system of many oppressed citizens. The cycle of crime, imprisonment, parole, and recidivism denies to the poor, particularly the black poor, meaningful participation in a society, denies them decent employment opportunities, and keeps them on the run.

3. By treating criminals as animals and misfits, as enemies of the state, we are permitted to continue to avoid some basic questions about the dehumanizing effects of our social institutions.

A critical theory of criminal law that generally supports Gordon's position is stated by Quinney in the following terms:

1. American society is based on an advanced capatilist economy.

2. The state is organized to serve the interests of the dominant economic class, the capitalist ruling class.

3. Criminal law is an instrument of the state and ruling class to maintain and perpetuate the existing social and economic order.

4. Crime control in capitalist society is accomplished through a variety of institutions and agencies established and administered by a governmental elite, representing ruling class interests, for the purpose of establishing domestic order.

5. The contradictions of advanced capitalism—the disjunction between existence and essence—require that the subordinate classes remain oppressed by whatever means necessary, especially through the coercion and violence of the legal system.

6. Only with the collapse of capitalist society and the creation of a new society, based on socialist principles, will there be a solution to the crime problem.

As capitalist society is further threatened by its own contradictions, criminal law is increasingly used in the attempt to maintain domestic order. The underclass, the class that must remain oppressed for the triumph of the dominant economic class, will continue to be the object of criminal law as long as the dominant class seeks to perpetuate itself.[7]

Radical theorists like Quinney draw heavily on economic and Marxist theory. They argue that delinquency is the product of the perpetual class struggle in capitalist societies. The ruling class creates the conditions out of which delinquency arises, and nothing short of revolution will alter the situation. Such theorists tend to see delinquency as a result of the *marginalization of youth*. Capitalism is viewed as a "criminogenic" system that perpetuates inequities based on age, sex, race, and occupation. Thus, merely "tinkering" with the system by investing time and resources into rehabilitation, diversion, or prevention will not rectify the delinquency problem. They assert that when children are freed from the evils of class struggles and reintegrated into the mainstream of life, the cooperative instincts of the young will become dominant, and a society free of crime and delinquency will emerge. The prescriptions for this revolution are stated by Quinney as follows:

> Our task as students is to consider the alternatives to the capitalist legal order. Further study of crime and justice in America must be devoted to the contradictions of the existing system. At this advanced stage of capitalist development, law is little more than a repressive instrument of manipulation and control. We must make others aware of the current meaning of crime and justice in America. The objective is to move beyond the existing order. And this means ultimately that we engage in socialist revolution.[8]

Most of the theories expressed by Gordon and Quinney focus on male delinquency. A body of Marxist theory and research being developed by feminists asserts that "the special oppression of women by . . . [the criminal justice] system is not isolated or arbitrary, but rather is rooted in systematic sexist practices and ideologies which can only be fully understood by analyzing the position of women in capitalist society."[9]

The relationship among capitalism, sexism, and crime is interestingly stated by Rafter and Natalizia. On various aspects of this issue, they write:

> Capitalism and sexism are intimately related, and it is this relationship that accounts for the inferior status traditionally given to women by the American criminal justice system. Sexism is not merely the prejudice of individuals; it is embedded in the very economic, legal, and social framework of life in the United States. The criminal justice system, as one part of that institutional

---

[7] Richard Quinney, *Criminal Justice in America* (Boston: Little, Brown, 1974), p. 24.

[8] Ibid., p. 25.

[9] Dorie Klein and June Kress, "Any Woman's Blues: A Critical Overview of Women, Crime and the Criminal Justice System," *Crime and Social Justice* (Spring/Summer 1976):45.

framework, reflects the same sexist underpinning tht is evidenced throughout capitalist society.

Capitalism relies upon the traditional structure of monogamy and the nuclear family to fulfill its economic potential. The division of labor essential to the capitalist system is one that cuts off those who produce from control over the means of production. And it dictates that men shall be the chief producers of goods, while women shall function primarily as nurturers of the next generation of producers.

Legal policy and structures evolve in response to the particular system of morals prevalent in a given society. This means that, in a capitalist system, law reflects a bourgeois moral code which restricts women to specific roles within the economic scheme. Women are properly chattel of the dominant men in their lives (husbands, fathers, lovers, pimps), and women's work is defined as unworthy of significant remuneration. Violations of the moral code defining women's proper role are labeled deviant and punished by stringent sanctions. Law becomes an instrument of social control over women and a means of preserving the economic status quo.

Historically, the entire justice system in America has been dominated by men. Our legal framework has been codified by male legislators, enforced by male police officers, and interpreted by male judges. Rehabilitation programs have been administered by males. The prison system has been managed by men, primarily for men.

Chivalrous motives are the ostensible grounds for a particularly discriminatory instrument for the oppression of female juveniles—status offense statutes. These statutes specify that juveniles can be prosecuted for behaviors or conditions that would not be illegal if committed or manifested by an adult, such as running away, incorrigibility, and being in danger of falling into vice. Although theoretically applying to juveniles of both sexes and all economic levels, these laws reflect efforts to uphold bourgeois standards of femininity—standards glorifying submissiveness, docility, and sexual purity. That these statutes function with sexual bias is borne out by studies revealing that the prosecution rate for status offenses is much higher among girls than among boys, and that female status offenders are punished more severely than are boys who commit more serious property or violent offenses. And, as in the case of their adult counterparts, low-income and minority girls bear most of the burden of such sanctions. At an early age therefore, these girls learn that deviance from economically based sex role patterns will result in legal sanctions, despite the chivalrous intent of our justice system.

The second way in which the legal system oppresses women is through its almost total failure to respond to issues of concern to women. Wife abuse, sexual harassment, incest, rape, production of unsafe methods of birth control, forced sterilization for eugenic purposes—these are critically important problems to women, whose needs the legal system has either failed to consider or has glossed over with token, ad hoc efforts. Such problems, moreover, have the greatest significance for poor and working-class women, indicating that class is at least as critical as sex in the struggle to obtain legal equality for women.[10]

---

[10] Nicole Rafter and Elena Natalizia, "Marxist Feminism: Implications for Criminal Justice," *Crime and Delinquency* (January 1981):81–87. Used by permission.

There is considerable awareness of the conditions Rafter and Natalizia focus on, and efforts are being made to remedy the problems cited.

SOCIAL DISORGANIZATION AND CRIME

Social ecologists are largely involved in establishing relationships between residential areas and the natural groups that inhabit them. Among others, sociologist Clifford Shaw, in an early study of social ecology, found that the greatest concentration of delinquents occurred in urban areas of marked social disorganization and described the process as follows:

> In the process of city growth, the neighborhood organizations, cultural institutions and social standards in practically all of the areas adjacent to the central business district and the major industrial centers are subject to rapid change and disorganization. The gradual invasion of these areas by industry and commerce, the continuous movement of the older residents out of the area and the influx of newer groups, the confusion of many divergent cultural standards, the economic insecurity of the families, all combine to render difficult the development of a stable and efficient neighborhood organization for the education and control of the child and the suppression of lawlessness.[11]

In the slum area, delinquent traditions were transmitted to the new arrivals. There were adult criminal gangs engaged in theft and the sale of stolen goods. Children were exposed to a variety of contradictory standards and forms of behavior. They were often found guilty in the courts for behavior that was approved by the neighborhood in which they lived. High-delinquency areas developed social values and patterns of behavior that conflicted with the values of the larger society. Thus behavior that was considered "correct" by the norms of the slum neighborhood was considered delinquent and criminal by the norms and laws of the larger society. This condition of social disorganization is often referred to as culture conflict. These social dynamics observed by Shaw in the 1930s still have relevance to the contemporary urban scene.

LABELING THEORY

A person convicted of a crime is given the status of criminal. The term *criminal* may therefore be viewed as a stigmatizing label. Once given the stigmatizing label the individual may be subjected to isolation, segregation, degradation, incarceration, and chemical or psychological

---

[11] National Commission on Law Observance and Enforcement, *Report on the Causes of Crime* 2, no. 13 (Washington, D.C.: Government Printing Office, 1931), p. 387.

treatment. These things can happen to anyone found guilty of a crime and labeled criminal *whether or not that person actually committed the crime.* In a sense, we may view all this punishment as the result of the labeling rather than of the behavior.

Becker, a leading exponent of labeling theory, put it this way:

> *Social groups create deviance by making the rules whose infraction constitutes deviance,* and by applying those rules to particular people and labeling them as outsiders. From this point of view, deviance is *not* a quality of the act the person commits, but rather a consequence of the application by others of rules and sanctions to an "offender." The deviant is one to whom that label has successfully been applied; deviant behavior is behavior that people so label.[12]

It is clear from the above that the labeling theorist does not consider criminality a property inherent in certain types of behavior, but rather a status conferred upon a person who is found to have engaged in the behavior.

Another implication of this theory is that the process of labeling is itself a critical determinant of the subsequent deviant or conforming career of the individual. For example, Tannenbaum says:

> The young delinquent becomes bad because he is defined as bad and because he is not believed if he is good. . . .
>
> The person becomes the thing he is described as being. Nor does it seem to matter whether the valuation is made by those who would punish or those who would reform. . . . Their [police, courts, parents, etc.] very enthusiasm defeats their aim. The harder they work to reform the evil, the greater the evil grows under their hands.[13]

One of the institutions most often guilty of labeling juveniles is the school. The school is in a position to be the greatest influence upon the lives of juveniles—particularly toward career orientation. Students who are labeled negatively in the school will likely come to regard themselves as inferior and are unlikely to succeed at school or elsewhere. Students who are given failing grades seldom make a comeback. They tend to view themselves as failures and drop out of school.

A third implication of this theoretical position is that one of the factors determining whether deviancy will be reduced, repeated, or even broadened to include a wider range of acts is the nature of the reactions of the group to the initial act. The reactions may have several possible effects. On the one hand, if the reprimanding institution wisely and discreetly imposes firm sanctions on the individual and attempts to involve the individual in acceptable activities, the chances are good that the individual will conform to the acceptable ways of the society and

---

[12] Howard S. Becker, *Outsiders* (New York: Free Press, 1963), p. 9.

[13] Frank Tannenbaum, *Crime and the Community* (New York: McGraw-Hill, 1951), p. 18.

will develop a good self-image. On the other hand, if the sanctions are harsh, degrading, public—particularly if the actor is forced to leave the acceptable mainsteam of society—chances of future deviancy may be heightened. It is possible that institutions contribute highly to delinquency by reacting to misbehaving juveniles in such a way that they are pushed away, excluded, further alienated from more responsible persons and standards, rather than pulled back in and rescued. In other words, there seems to be a tendency to shut out rather than open up opportunities for a juvenile to become involved in a legitimate, acceptable, conforming-to-the-norm situation. The person labeled criminal is excluded even more.[14]

Labeling theory raises serious questions about the advisability of recklessly stigmatizing people with labels such as *criminal* and *delinquent* when the objective is principally to deter the behavior. When we attach the stigmatizing label we may actually contribute to an increase in the undesirable behavior by seriously handicapping the individual's efforts to secure employment, training, licenses, and so on. Labeling theory does little to explain delinquent or criminal behavior. It does a great deal, however, to emphasize the damage that can be done by attaching stigmatizing labels.

CONFLICT THEORY OF CRIMINAL BEHAVIOR

The explanation of criminality as a form of deviant behavior must deal with at least two problems:

1. The process by which individuals come to commit acts that are defined by society as crimes
2. The kinds of groups and areas that produce certain kinds of criminality

Those criminologists who seek to explain why certain behavior is defined as criminal tend toward a conflict theory explanation. What becomes defined as a crime is related to the power of some groups in the society to include in the criminal law their values and interests. The same power structure, or one closely related to it, by its enforcement of the law imposes a variation of the same values and interests.

This point of view leads to the conclusion that the passage of virtually all criminal laws, the policies of nearly all law enforcement agencies, and the operation of the criminal justice system are in some way influenced by political pressures of competing interest groups.

---

[14] Albert K. Cohen, "The Sociology of the Deviant Act: Anomie Theory and Beyond," *American Sociological Review* 30 (February 1965):5–14. For the effect of sanctions, see John Delamater, "On the Nature of Deviance," *Social Forces* 4 (June 1968):445–455.

Economic interest groups exercise a predominant influence on the governmental system, including the legislative, enforcement, and criminal justice systems.

Culture Conflict and Crime

The criminal law is a body of rules or norms of conduct that prohibit specific forms of conduct and provide for punishment for them. The type of conduct prohibited often depends upon the character and interests of the groups that influence legislation. Everyone is required to obey the rules set forth by the state, as described in the penal code. Some people, however, belong to groups that have sets of rules or norms of conduct different from those required by the overall society's criminal law. Culture conflict arises when an individual is committed to rules that are contrary to those of the overall society. Whether behavior is criminal or noncriminal depends upon which conduct norms are applied.[15]

Culture conflict is a common experience among immigrants to the United States. They come with many customs and traditions that are not acceptable in this country. Prior to World War II, when American influence was less pervasive than it is now, the problem was even more acute. Consider the Oriental tradition of "family honor." Under this system, if a woman committed adultery, it was the duty of either her elder brother or her father to kill her. This was not something that he *might* do; he was *obligated* to do it. If a man were to kill his daughter for that or for any other reason in this country, he would be convicted of murder.

There are still many conduct norms of foreign countries that clash with those found in the United States and lead immigrants into trouble with the law. When culture conflict arises in this way, it is referred to as *primary* culture conflict.

Another type of culture conflict arises when people are committed to a subculture within the country that differs in some respects from the norms of the overall society. This sort of conflict is experienced by a person migrating from a rural area to an urban center—the Puerto Rican migrating from the island to New York City or a black family moving from the rural south to the urban north. When culture conflict arises as a result of conflicting conduct norms within the society, it is referred to as *secondary* culture conflict.

The overall society has defined the "right ways" of doing things. "The hallmark of the delinquent subculture is the explicit and wholesale repudiation of middle class standards and the adoption of their very antithesis."[16]

---

[15] Thorsten Sellin, *Culture Conflict and Crime* (New York: Social Science Research Council, 1938).

[16] Albert K. Cohen, *Delinquent Boys* (New York: Free Press, 1955), p. 3.

Whether we regard the delinquent subculture as a repudiation of middle-class standards or simply as a way of conforming to lower-class standards, it contains rules of behavior at variance from those of the overall culture of our society and often leads to behavior that is legally viewed as delinquent.

Group Conflict Theory as Explanation of Crime

In developing a group conflict theory, George Vold began with assumptions long established in sociology: first, that human beings are always involved in groups, and second, that action within groups and between groups is influenced by opposing individual and group interests. Society is a collection of such groups in equilibrium; that is, opposing group interests are in some way balanced or reconciled. There is a continuous struggle within and between groups to improve relative status. Groups come into conflict when the interests and purposes they serve tend to overlap and become competitive. As conflict between groups intensifies, loyalties to groups intensify. The outcome of group conflict is either victory for one side and defeat for the other or some form of compromise. Politics is primarily a way of finding practical compromises between antagonistic groups. In a democracy, a struggle between conflicting groups often culminates in legislation translating compromise into law. Those who produce legislative majorities dominate policies that decide who is likely to be involved in violation of the law. Crime, then, may be seen as minority group behavior. Some of those whose actions have become illegal as a result of legislation violate the law as individuals. Many of those who belong to groups that oppose the law react as a group—a conflict group. The juvenile gang, in this sense, would be an example of a "minority group" in opposition to the rules of the dominant "majority."

In a group-centered conflict, "criminal" behavior occurs when action is based on the principle that *the end justifies the means* and *the end object is the maintenance of the group position.* This principle is the rationalization offered to justify the actions of a juvenile gang, of organized crime running gambling operations, of the white collar criminals who fix prices, and of the people involved in Watergate. Whenever there is genuine conflict between groups and interpretations, correctness is decided by the exercise of power and/or persuasion.[17]

Richard Quinney has developed a comprehensive group conflict theory which he calls the *social reality of crime.* As he sees it, the legal order gives reality to the crime problem in the United States.

The theory of the social reality of crime, as formulated, contains six

---

[17] George B. Vold, "Group Conflict Theory as Explanation of Crime," in *Deviance, Conflict and Criminality*, eds. R. Serge Denisoff and Charles H. McCaghy (Chicago: Rand McNally, 1973), pp. 77–88.

propositions and a number of statements within each. These may be summarized as follows:

1. The official definition of crime. *Crime as a legal definition of human conduct is created by agents of the dominant class in a politically organized society.* Crime, as *officially* determined, is a *definition* of behavior that is conferred on some people by those in power. Legislators, police, prosecutors, judges, and other agents of the law are responsible for formulating and administering criminal law. Upon formulation and application of these definitions of crime, persons and behaviors become criminal. The greater the number of definitions of crime that are formulated and applied, the greater the amount of crime.

2. Formulating definitions of crime. *Definitions of crime are composed of behaviors that conflict with the interests of the dominant class.* Definitions of crime are formulated, and ultimately incorporated into the criminal law, according to the interests of those who have the power to translate their interests into public policy. The definitions of crime change as the interests of the dominant class change. From the initial definitions of crime to the subsequent procedures, correctional and penal programs, and policies for controlling and preventing crime, those who have the power regulate the behavior of those without power.

3. Applying definitions of crime. *Definitions of crime are applied by the class that has the power to shape the enforcement and administration of criminal law.* The dominant interests intervene in all the stages at which definitions of crime are created and operate where the definitions of crime reach the application stage. Those whose interests conflict with the ones represented in the law must either change their behavior or possibly find it defined as criminal. Law enforcement efforts and judicial activity are likely to increase when the interests of the dominant class are threatened. The criminal law is not applied directly by those in power; its enforcement and administration are delegated to authorized legal agents. As legal agents evaluate more behaviors and persons as worthy of being defined as criminal, the probability that definitions of crime will be applied grows.

4. How behavior patterns develop in relation to definitions of crime. *Behavior patterns are structured in relation to definitions of crime, and within this context people engage in actions that have relative probabilities of being defined as criminal.* The probability that persons will develop action patterns with a high potental for being defined as criminal depends on structured opportunities, learning experiences, interpersonal associations and identifications, and self-conceptions. Personal action patterns develop

among those defined as criminal because they are so defined. Those who have been defined as criminal begin to conceive of themselves as criminal, adjust to the definitions imposed upon them, and learn to play the criminal role.

5. Constructing an ideology of crime. *An ideology of crime is constructed and diffused by the dominant class to secure its hegemony.* An ideology which includes ideas about the nature of crime, the relevance of crime, offenders' characteristics, appropriate reactions to crime, and the relation of crime to the social order is diffused throughout the society in personal and mass communications. The President's Commission on Law Enforcement and Administration of Justice is the best contemporary example of the state's role in shaping an ideology of crime. Official policy on crime was established in a crime bill, the Omnibus Crime Control and Safe Streets Act of 1968. This bill, a reaction to the growing fears of class conflict in American society, created an image of a severe crime problem and, in so doing, threatened to negate some of our basic constitutional guarantees in the name of controlling crime. The conceptions that are most critical in actually formulating and applying the definitions of crime are those held by the dominant class. These conceptions are certain to be incorporated into the social reality of crime.

6. Constructing the social reality of crime. *The social reality of crime is constructed by the formulation and application of definitions of crime, the development of behavior patterns in relation to these definitions, and the construction of an ideology of crime.*[18]

CULTURAL DIMENSIONS OF CRIMINALITY

Social Theory of Crime

Donald R. Taft and Ralph W. England, Jr., formulated a social theory that attempts to explain the high rate of crime in the United States and other Western societies. They see criminality resulting from a combination of the following aspects of the culture:

1. *American culture is dynamic.* Our standards are constantly changing. "The wrong of yesterday is the right of today."

2. *American culture is complex.* According to Taft, crime is the product of culture conflict, and culture conflict is widespread as a result of immigration and internal migration.

---

[18] This revised version of the theory is contained in Richard Quinney, *Criminology* (Boston: Little, Brown, 1975), pp. 37–41.

3. *American culture is materialistic.* "Speaking generally, the underprivileged and unsuccessful accept the same values as the successful and aspire to imitate their success." It is apparent that the underprivileged have a more difficult time achieving success goals than the privileged.
4. *American social relations are increasingly impersonal.* Primary relationships in the family and neighborhood have declined. Anonymity breeds alienation and a greater impetus to crime and delinquency.
5. *American culture fosters restricted group loyalties.* "Preference for men, not wholly because of their personal qualitites, but because they are natives, neighbors, Masons, or of our race, class, or creed, is widespread and not essentially different in quality from gang loyalty." This leaves people out, produces conflict, hostility, and crime.
6. *Survival of frontier values.* Among frontier values that have survived into the present are the tradition of extreme individualism and the tendency of some groups within our society to take the law into their own hands.[19]

All these factors in American culture, according to Taft and England, "normally" produce a high incidence of crime.

The Criminogenic Society

Barron presented an analysis of the criminogenic aspects of the American society and culture. He discussed several official and unofficial American values likely to encourage norm-violating and illegal behavior:

1. *Success*   There is an emphasis in our culture on the importance of succeeding and asserting one's self. The well-known quotation of football coach Vince Lombardi is cited: "Winning isn't everything, it is the only thing." Americans hate to admit failure. They feel frustrated if they do not achieve success. There is also a very high value placed on moving up, going higher on the scale toward ultimate success. When people realize that they are not going to succeed and are not moving up through hard work, thrift, study, and so on, many turn to crime and delinquency as ways of achieving success.
2. *Status and Power Ascendance*   The answer to the question "How far can I get?" is found in terms of social status. Evidence of higher status is provided by high grades, expensive cars, expensive clothes, jewelry, and so forth. Dollars provide the power. Money and material goods have become values in themselves. People who cannot obtain them lawfully may violate laws to get them.
3. *Resistance to Authority*   Independence, individuality, and nonconformity are encouraged. All these involve resistance to au-

---

[19] Reprinted with permission of Macmillan Publishing Company from *Criminology* by Donald R. Taft and Ralph W. England, Jr. Copyright © 1964 by Macmillan Publishing Company.

thority. Americans tend to ridicule literal observance and strict conformity. This tendency applies to observance of laws. The Caspar Milquetoast is an object of ridicule.

4. *Toughness*   There are class differences in the emphasis on toughness. However, in every subculture people are encouraged to fight back. Violence is celebrated in crime and gangster programs, on TV, in films, in magazines, and so on.

5. *Dupery*   People are rewarded for getting the better of others. The observation attributed to P. T. Barnum that "there's a sucker born every minute" meets with general agreement if not approval. Official norms and laws are violated with the tacit acceptance of the society or group as long as violations are concealed. People are proud of getting the better of others.

6. *Dynamic Culture*   Changes in norms are so rapid in the United States that differences between right and wrong are weakened.

7. *Conflicting Values and Norms*   Behavior that is defined as illegal in American society may not necessarily be "wrong" in the subcultures of some groups.

8. *Impersonal Social Relations*   Urban living, in which one hardly knows one's neighbor, does not provide the informal controls of rural society.

9. *Loyalty Versus Ethics*   Many people apply one code of ethics in their relations with members of their own group and a different code with nonmembers.[20]

Barron tempered the impact of criminogenic theory by acknowledging that widespread crime and corruption existed at other times in history and occur in places other than the United States. Nevertheless, although they are not peculiar to American society, they appear to be part of it.

CRIMINAL AND DELINQUENT GANG THEORY

The phenomenon of gangs has been a significant dimension of crime and delinquency in the United States. This includes both juvenile gangs and adult gangs—especially organized crime structures. In this regard, many juvenile gangs in high-crime neighborhoods serve as the training system for a later life in the big league of crime. A number of theorists in social psychology have attempted to research and analyze the structure and relationship of gangs to crime and delinquency in the United States. Notable among these gang theorists are Albert Cohen, Richard Cloward

---

[20] Derived from Milton L. Barron, "The Criminogenic Society: Social Values and Deviance," in *Current Perspectives on Criminal Behavior*, ed. Abraham S. Blumberg (New York: Knopf, 1974), pp. 68–86.

and Lloyd Ohlin, Walter Miller, and Herbert Block and Arthur Nieder-hoffer. Their viewpoints are presented along with my theory of gangs in the following analysis of adult and juvenile gangs and their relationship to criminal and delinquent causal theory.

The Gang as a Subculture of Delinquency

Albert Cohen viewed delinquent youths as a subculture with a value system different from the dominant one found in the inclusive American culture. Lower-class children, according to Cohen, use the delinquent subculture as a mode of reaction and adjustment to a dominant middle-class society that indirectly discriminates against them because of their lower-class position. Lower-class youths, trained in a different value system, are not adequately socialized to fulfill the status requirements of middle-class society. Despite this differential socialization, they are unfairly exposed to middle-class aspirations and judgments they cannot fulfill. This conflict produces in the lower-class youths what Cohen has termed status frustration. In reaction, they manifest a delinquent adjustment, acting out their status frustrations in "nonutilitarian, malicious, negativistic" forms of delinquency.

In such settings as the school and community center, the lower-class youth is exposed to generally middle-class agents of the society (teachers and social workers). Their efforts to impose their middle-class values of orderliness, cleanliness, responsibility, and ambition are met with sharp negativism.

Cohen listed nine middle-class values that are specifically rejected by the lower-class child: (1) ambition; (2) responsibility; (3) the cultivation of skills and tangible achievement; (4) postponement of immediate satisfactions and self-indulgence in the interest of long-term goals; (5) rationality, in the sense of forethought, planning, and budgeting of time; (6) the rational cultivation of manners, courtesy, and personality; (7) the need to control physical aggression and violence; (8) the need for wholesome recreation; and (9) respect for property and its proper care.

The lower-class child, in reaction against these unfair impositions, substitutes norms that reverse those of the larger society: "The delinquent subculture takes its norms from the larger subculture, but turns them upside down. The delinquent's conduct is right by the standards of his subculture precisely because it is wrong by the norms of the larger culture."[21] The dominant theme of the delinquent subculture is the explicit and wholesale repudiation of middle-class standards and the adoption of their very antitheses. In this negative polarity of "just for the hell of it" vandalism and violence, lower-class youths attempt to adjust their status frustration and hostility toward the larger society's

---

[21] Cohen, *Delinquent Boys*, p. 19.

unfair imposition of middle-class values upon them; and the gang is the vehicle for their delinquencies. The individual delinquent is "the exception rather than the rule."

Cohen's position on the gang's relation to the community and the family paralleled the conceptions of the early Chicago school:

> Relations with gang members tend to be intensely solidary and imperious. Relations with other groups tend to be indifferent, hostile or rebellious. Gang members are unusually resistant to the efforts of home, school and other agencies to regulate, not only their delinquent activities, but any activities carried on within the group, and to efforts to compete with the gang for the time and other resources of its members. It may be argued that the resistance of gang members to the authority of the home may not be a result of their membership in gangs but that membership in gangs, on the contrary, is a result of ineffective family supervision, the breakdown of parental authority and the hostility of the child toward the parents; in short, that the delinquent gang recruits members who have already achieved autonomy. Certainly a previous breakdown in family controls facilitates recruitment into delinquent gangs. But we are not speaking of the autonomy, the emancipation of *individuals*. It is not the individual delinquent but the gang that is autonomous. For many of our subcultural delinquents the claims of the home are very real and very compelling. The point is that the gang is a separate, distinct and often irresistible focus of attraction, loyalty, and solidarity.[22]

The delinquent subculture described by Cohen represents a collective effort on the part of the youths to resolve adjustment problems produced by dislocations in the larger society. In the gang the norms of the larger society are reversed so that nonutilitarian deviant behavior (especially violence) becomes a legitimized activity. The gang thus serves lower-class children as a legitimate opportunity structure for striking back at a larger society that produces their status-frustration problems.

Delinquent Opportunity System

In their analysis of delinquency causation, Cloward and Ohlin "attempt to explore two questions: (1) Why do delinquent 'norms,' or rules of conduct, develop? (2) What are the conditions which account for the distinctive content of various systems of delinquent norms—such as those prescribing violence or theft or drug-use?"[23]

Cloward and Ohlin rely heavily on the concept of the delinquent subculture. In their view, "A delinquent subculture is one in which

---

[22] Cohen, *Delinquent Boys,* p. 46.

[23] Reprinted with permission of The Macmillan Company from *Delinquency and Opportunity* by Richard A. Cloward and Lloyd E. Ohlin. © The Free Press, a Corporation, 1960.

certain forms of delinquent activity are essential requirements for the performance of the dominant roles supported by the subculture. It is the central position accorded to specifically delinquent activity that distinguishes the delinquent subculture from other deviant subcultures."[24]

They define three dominant kinds of delinquent subculture—the "criminal," the "conflict," and the "retreatist." Cloward and Ohlin recognize that the extent to which the norms of the delinquent subculture control behavior will vary from one member to another. Their description of each subculture is therefore stated in terms of the fully doctrinated member rather than the average member: The criminal subculture is devoted to theft, extortion, and other illegal means of securing an income; some of its members may graduate into the ranks of organized or professional crime. The conflict group commits acts of violence as an important means of securing status. The retreatist group stresses drug use, and addiction is prevalent.

Their central explanation for the emergence of delinquent subcultures is derived from the theories of Durkheim and Merton. Their basic view is "that pressures toward the formation of delinquent subcultures originate in marked discrepancies between culturally induced aspirations among lower class youth and the possibilities of achieving them by legitimate means."[25]

Cultural goals become an important aspect of Cloward and Ohlin's thesis. In describing two categories of need, physical and social, Durkheim makes the point that physical needs are satiable, whereas social gratification is "an insatiable and bottomless abyss." Given this condition, Cloward and Ohlin state that when people's goals become unlimited, their actions can no longer be controlled by norms, and a state of normlessness or anomie exists.

Cloward and Ohlin turn to Merton's elaboration of Durkheim's basic postulate to account for the various patterns of deviant behavior. In Merton's view, anomie (normlessness) and the breakdown of social control emerge not because of insatiable goals alone but because of a lack of fit between the goals and the legitimate means for attaining them. As Merton specifies, "Aberrant behavior may be regarded sociologically as a symptom of dissociation between culturally prescribed aspirations and socially structured avenues of realizing these aspirations."[26]

Merton's formulation, according to Cloward and Ohlin, helps to explain the existence of a large proportion of law violators among lower-class youths. Because they are denied equal access to normative social opportunity, they experience a greater pull toward deviance.

---

[24] Cloward and Ohlin, *Delinquency and Opportunity*, p. 7.

[25] Ibid., p. 36.

[26] Merton, *Social Theory and Social Structure*, p. 134.

The ideology of common success-goals and equal opportunity may become an empty myth for those who find themselves cut off from legitimate pathways upward. We may predict, then, that the pressure to engage in deviant behavior will be greatest in the lower levels of the society.

Our hypothesis can be summarized as follows: The disparity between what lower class youth are led to want and what is actually available to them is the source of a major problem of adjustment. Adolescents who form delinquent subcultures, we suggest, have internalized an emphasis upon conventional goals. Faced with limitations on legitimate avenues of access to these goals, and unable to revise their aspirations downward, they experience intense frustrations; the exploration of nonconformist alternatives may be the result.[27]

Cloward and Ohlin view the gang as one of the "nonconformist alternatives" these children may explore. Alienated youths band together in the collectivity of the gang in an effort to resolve their mutual problems. The same theme is used to explain the normative patterning of gangs: the conflict, criminal, and retreatist. A youth's selection of one type of subcultural adjustment over another is related to the degree of availability of these illegitimate "opportunity structures" in various sociocultural settings.

We believe that the way in which these problems are resolved may depend upon the kind of support for one or another type of illegitimate activity that is given at different points in the social structure. If, in a given social location, illegal or criminal means are not readily available, then we should not expect a criminal subculture to develop among adolescents. By the same logic, we should expect the manipulation of violence to become a primary avenue to higher status only in areas where the means of violence are not denied to the young. To give a third example, drug addiction and participation in subcultures organized around the consumption of drugs presuppose that persons can secure access to drugs and knowledge about how to use them. In some parts of the social structure, this would be very difficult; in others, very easy. In short, there are marked differences from one part of the social structure to another in the types of illegitimate adaptation that are available to persons in search of solutions to problems of adjustment arising from the restricted availability of legitimate means. In this sense, then, we can think of individuals as being located in two opportunity structures one legitimate, the other illegitimate. Given limited access to success-goals by legitimate means, the nature of the delinquent response that may result will vary according to the availability of various illegitimate means.[28]

Cloward and Ohlin tend to minimize the importance of individual personality factors and characteristics. "The social milieu affects the

---

[27] Reprinted with permission of The Macmillan Company from *Delinquency and Opportunity* by Richard A. Cloward and Lloyd E. Ohlin. © The Free Press, a Corporation, 1960.

[28] Cloward and Ohlin, *Delinquency and Crime*, pp. 151–152.

nature of the deviant response whatever the motivation and social position (i.e., age, sex, socioeconomic level) of the participants in the delinquent subculture."[29]

Criminal subcultures, according to Cloward and Ohlin, are most likely to occur in the somewhat stable slum neighborhoods that provide a hierarchy of criminal opportunity. In some conflict with Cohen's description of delinquency as "malicious, negativistic, and nonutilitarian," Cloward and Ohlin argue that for many youths in this type of neighborhood, the desire to move up in the neighborhood criminal hierarchy may cause them to overconform to delinquent values and behavior to show off their criminal ability. Such criminal overconformity, Cloward and Ohlin maintain, accounts for rash, nonutilitarian delinquent acts:

> The criminal subculture is likely to arise in a neighborhood milieu characterized by close bonds between different age-levels of offender, and between criminal and conventional elements. As a consequence of these integrative relationships, a new opportunity structure emerges which provides alternative avenues to success-goals. Hence the pressures generated by restrictions on legitimate access to success-goals are drained off. Social controls over the conduct of the young are effectively exercised, limiting expressive behavior and constraining the discontented to adopt instrumental, if criminalistic, styles of life.[30]

Conflict subcultures, according to Cloward and Ohlin, tend to arise in disorganized slums that provide no organized hierarchy for criminal development. These slums, with their high degree of disorganization and their orientation toward the present, offer limited legitimate and illegitimate opportunity structures. The social disorganization of such slums contributes to the breakdown of social control:

> The young in such areas are also exposed to acute frustrations, arising from conditions in which access to success-goals is blocked by the absence of any institutionalized channels, legitimate or illegitimate. They are deprived not only of conventional opportunity but also of criminal routes to the "big money." In other words, precisely when frustrations are maximized, social controls are weakened. Social controls and channels to success-goals are generally related: where opportunities exist, patterns of control will be found; where opportunities are absent, patterns of social control are likely to be absent too. The association of these two features of social organization is a logical implication of our theory.[31]

The lack of opportunity in these areas causes such youths to seek it in other ways. "Adolescents turn to violence in search of status. Violence

---

[29] Cloward and Ohlin, *Delinquency and Crime,* p. 160.

[30] Ibid., p. 171.

[31] Ibid., pp. 174–175.

comes to be ascendant, in short, under conditions of relative detachment from all institutionalized systems of opportunity and social control."[32]

The *retreatist subculture* emerges, according to Cloward and Ohlin, as an adjustment pattern for those lower-class youths who have failed to find a position in the criminal or conflict subculture and have also failed to use either legitimate or illegitimate opportunity structures. "Persons who experience this 'double failure' are likely to move into a retreatist pattern of behavior."[33]

Some youths who either drop out of other types of subcultures or find the conflict or criminal subculture no longer functional may also resort to the retreatist pattern. Cloward and Ohlin conclude that limitations on both legitimate and illegitimate opportunity structures produce intense pressures toward retreatist behavior. All three types of delinquent behavior are viewed by Cloward and Ohlin as adjustment patterns that utilize the most available opportunity structure provided by the anomic social system.

Lower-Class Culture and "Normal" Delinquency

Using cultural concepts in a somewhat different fashion, Walter Miller projects a lower-class adolescent theory of gangs. He maintains (in a fashion somewhat similar to Cohen's position) that the values of lower-class culture produce deviance because they are "naturally" in discord with middle-class values. The youth who heavily conforms to lower-class values is thus automatically delinquent. Miller lists a set of characteristics of lower-class culture that tend to foster delinquent behavior. These include such focal concerns as trouble, toughness, "smartness" (ability to con), excitement (kicks).

According to Miller, gang activity is, in part, a striving to prove masculinity. Females are exploited by tough gang hoods in the "normal" process of relating. Girls are "conquest objects" utilized to prove and boost the masculinity of the street-corner male.

Miller further theorizes that the gap between levels of aspiration of lower-class youths and their general ability to achieve produces distinct types of lower-class categories, which reveal the degree of delinquency proneness of a youth.

1. *"Stable" lower class.* This group consists of youngsters who, for all practical purposes, do not aspire to higher status or who have no realistic possibility of achieving such aspiration.
2. *Aspiring but conflicted lower class.* This group represents those for whom family or other community influences have produced a desire to elevate their status, but who lack the necessary personal attributes or

---

[32] Cloward and Ohlin, *Delinquency and Crime*, p. 178.

[33] Ibid., p. 181.

cultural "equipment" to make the grade, or for whom cultural pressures effectively inhibit aspirations.

3. *Successfully aspiring lower class.* This group, popularly assumed to be the most prevalent, includes those who have both the will and the capability to elevate their status.[34]

Miller emphasizes the fact that lower-class youths who are confronted with the largest gap between aspirations and possibilities for achievement are most delinquency-prone. Such youths are apt to utilize heavily the normal range of lower-class delinquent patterns in an effort to achieve prestige and status:

> . . . toughness, physical prowess, skill, fearlessness, bravery, ability to con people, gaining money by wits, shrewdness, adroitness, smart repartee, seeking and finding thrills, risk, danger, freedom from external constraint, and freedom from superordinate authority. These are the explicit values of the most important and essential reference group of many delinquent youngsters. These are the things he respects and strives to attain. The lower class youngster who engages in a long and recurrent series of delinquent behaviors that are sanctioned by his peer group is acting so as to achieve prestige within his reference system.[35]

The Adolescent Striving for Adulthood

Herbert Bloch and Arthur Niederhoffer, in a somewhat different interpretation, view delinquent behavior as a universal and normal adolescent striving for adult status. Their hypothesis is reached by the utilization of considerable cross-cultural material that attempts to reveal the differences and similarities of the adolescent condition in a variety of societies. Their basic position is presented in the following concise statement:

> The adolescent period in all cultures, visualized as a phase of striving for the attainment of adult status, produces experiences which are much the same for all youths, and certain common dynamisms for expressing reaction to such subjectively held experience. The intensity of the adolescent experience and the vehemence of external expression depend on a variety of factors, including the general societal attitudes toward adolescence, the duration of the adolescent period itself, and the degree to which the society tends to facilitate entrance into adulthood by virtue of institutionalized patterns, ceremonials, rites and rituals, and socially supported emotional and intellectual preparation. When a society does not make adequate preparation, formal or otherwise, for the induction of its adolescents to the adult status, equivalent forms of behavior arise spontaneously among

---

[34] William C. Kvaraceus and Walter B. Miller, *Delinquent Behavior* (Washington, D.C.: National Education Association, 1959), vol. 1, *Culture and the Individual*, p. 72. Copyright 1959 by the National Education Association of the United States. Reprinted with permission.

[35] Kvaraceus and Miller, *Delinquent Behavior*, p. 69. Copyright 1959 by the National Education Association of the United States. Reprinted with permission.

adolescents themselves, reinforced by their own group structure, which seemingly provide the same psychological content and function as the more formalized rituals found in other societies. This the gang structure appears to do in American society, apparently satisfying deep-seated needs experienced by adolescents in all cultures. Such, very briefly, is our hypothesis.[36]

In their analysis they attempt to assess the effects of such cultural patterns as puberty rites, self-decoration, and circumcision on adolescent behavior. Gang behavior, with its symbolic evidence of the "urge for manhood," is seen as an American equivalent of the puberty rites of other cultures. The gang is thus viewed as a vehicle for accomplishing the assumed highly desired status of adulthood.

Using data about adolescents from such diverse groups as the Mundugumor of New Guinea, the Manus of the Admiralty Islands, the Kaffirs of South Africa, the Comanche and Plains Indians, and a tightly knit delinquent New York gang, Bloch and Niederhoffer attempt to draw the inference that the ganging process provides symbolic evidence of the urge to adulthood. They conclude:

1. Adolescent gangs may be profitably studied by using as a frame of reference the theory of power.
2. The gang's attempt to gain status and power through the domination and manipulation of persons and events is a collective representation of the individual gang member's guiding fiction, which is "to prove he is man." In passing it is worthy of note that Alfred Adler's system of psychology is "tailor made" for the analysis of the gang since it is principally concerned with the struggle for power and the "masculine protest."
3. The presence of the gang, real, constructive or symbolic, gives the individual member ego support and courage. He gains a psychological sense of power and manhood which he does not possess at all when he is on his own.
4. If single gangs can pose a threat to the peace and safety of community— and they certainly do so—then the well-meaning efforts to organize several gangs into a confederation may be a very grave error. Without significant changes in behavior and values on the part of such gangs, this maneuver may only multiply to extremely dangerous proportions the looming menace which even now we find difficult to control.[37]

THE VIOLENT GANG AND NEAR-GROUP THEORY[38]

Sociologist Emile Durkheim exhorted the sociologist to "emancipate himself from the mind of the layman; we must throw off, once and for all,

---

[36] Herbert A. Bloch and Arthur Niederhoffer, *The Gang* (New York: Philosophical Library, 1958), p. 17. Reprinted by permission.

[37] Ibid., p. 217.

[38] This section is derived from Lewis Yablonsky, *The Violent Gang* (New York: Macmillan, 1962; reprint, New York: Irvington Press, 1988).

the yoke of these empirical categories which from long continued habit have become tyrannical."[39]

Not only is a freedom from preconception urged; Durkheim's second canon is the necessity of being explicit:

> Every scientific investigation is directed toward a limited class of phenomena, included in the same definition. The first step of the sociologist, then, ought to be to define the things he treats, in order that his subject matter may be known. This is the first and most indispensable condition of all proofs and verifications. A theory, indeed, can be checked only if we know how to recognize the facts of which it is intended to give an account.[40]

A Classification of Gangs

Three types of gangs appear most persistently in gang neighborhoods: (1) social gangs, (2) delinquent gangs, and (3) violent gangs. Although these prototypes seldom appear in pure form, the structure and behavior of the ideal type may be described. The *social gang* is a social group composed of tough youths who band together because they find their individual goals of a socially constructive nature can most adequately be achieved through a gang pattern. The *delinquent gang* is characterized by delinquent patterns of activity, such as stealing, assault, or dealing drugs, with material profit as the essential objective. The *violent gang* is characterized by sociopathic themes of spontaneous prestige-seeking violence, with psychic gratification (kicks) as the goal. There are, of course, youths who belong to more than one type of gang during their gang careers, and some youths belong to several simultaneously. These types of gangs are depicted in Figure 15.1.

Social Gangs   The social gang is a relatively permanent organization that centers around a specific neighborhood location. All members are intimately known to one another and there is a strong sense of comradeship. Members are the in-group; all others are outsiders. Members may wear club jackets or sweaters with insignia that identify them to the external community.

Activities are socially dominated and require a degree of responsible social interaction in the group: organized athletics, personal discussions, dances, and other socially acceptable activities characteristic of most youths. Membership is not based on self-protection (as in the violent gang) or on athletic prowess (as on an athletic team) but upon feelings of mutual attraction. Cohesiveness is based on the feeling that through the group the individual can lead a fuller life. Members are willing to

---

[39] Emile Durkheim, *The Rules of Sociological Method*, 8th ed. (Glencoe, Ill.: Free Press, 1950), p. 32.

[40] Ibid., pp. 34–35.

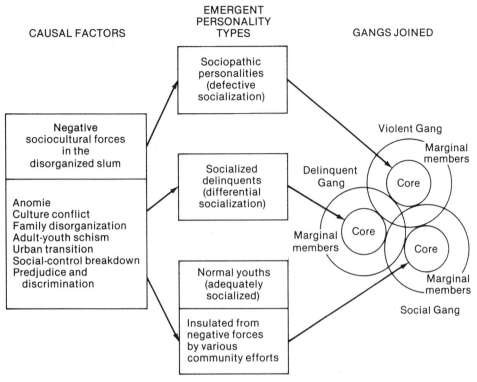

Figure 15.1 Gang patterns of slum youths.

submerge individualistic interests to group activities. Leadership is based upon popularity and constructive leadership qualities and generally operates informally. The leader is apt to be the idealized group member.

This type of gang seldom participates in delinquent behavior, gang warfare, or petty thievery except under unusual circumstances. Members may become involved in minor gang clashes, but only under pressure. The social gang has considerable permanence. Its members often grow up together and develop permanent lifelong friendships that continue when they leave the "corner" and move into adult life patterns.

The social gang is closely associated with and acts in accordance with the values of the larger society. It draws its memberships from the most emotionally stable and socially effective youths in the neighborhood—those most closely influenced by and involved with the norms and values of the more inclusive society. Thus, of all gang types, the social gang is the one least dissociated from the overall society.

Delinquent Gangs The delinquent gang is primarily organized to carry out various illegal acts. The social interaction of the members is a secondary factor. Prominent among the delinquent gang's activities are drug dealing, burglary, petty thievery, mugging, assault for profit (not simply kicks), and other illegal acts directed at "raising bread." It is generally a tight clique, a small, mobile gang that can steal and escape with minimum risk. It would lose its cohesive quality and the intimate cooperation required for success in illegal ventures if it became too large. Membership is not easily achieved and must generally be approved by all gang members.

The delinquent gang has a tight primary-group structure. The members know each other and rely heavily upon each other for cooperation in their illegal enterprises. The group has some duration and lasting structure. It usually continues in action until interrupted by arrest or imprisonment. Members lost in this way are usually replaced. The leader is usually the most effective thief, the best organizer and planner of delinquent activities.

Often members of these cliques also participate in the activities of violent or social gangs, but such participation is only a sideline; their basic allegiance is to the delinquent gang.

With some exceptions, delinquent gang members are emotionally stable youths. Their delinquency is more likely to result from being socialized into delinquent behavior patterns than from emotional disturbance. The emotionally disturbed delinquent is more likely to steal or commit assault alone in a bizarre way. Such a youth does not usually have the social ability required to belong to the organized delinquent gang.

In summary, the delinquent gang is composed of a cohesive group of emotionally stable youths trained into illegal patterns of behavior. Violence may be employed as a means toward the end of acquiring material and financial rewards, but it is rarely an end in itself since the activities of the gang are profit-oriented. The delinquent gang accepts the materialistic success goals of the society but rejects the normative ways of achievement. Many delinquent gang members in the late 1980s became dealers in the developing criminal drug empire that grips all major cities in the United States. In connection with their drug-dealing activities, many of these gang members, after proper socialization as delinquents, move up the criminal opportunity ladder and become part of organized crime.

Violent Gangs In contrast with the other gang types, the violent gang is primarily organized for emotional gratification, and violence is the theme around which all activities center. Sports, social activities, even delinquent activities are side issues to its primary assaultive pattern. The violent gang's organization and membership are constantly shifting in accord with the emotional needs of its members. Membership size is exaggerated as a psychological weapon for influencing other gangs and for self-aggrandizement. Small arsenals of weapons are discussed and, whenever possible, accumulated. This arsenal in the 1980s included Uzis, various machine guns, shotguns, and high-powered handguns. The violent gang is thus essentially organized around gang-war activities, although occasionally certain youths will form delinquent cliques or subgroups within the overall violent gang.

Membership characteristics are unclear in the violent gang's structure. Leaders are characterized by megalomania, a strong need to control, and an emotionally distorted picture of the gang's organization. The image of the leader is often exaggerated and glorified by gang members to enhance their own self-concepts. Strong power drives in the violent gang are demonstrated by attempts to control territory. Territorial disputes are constant sources of conflict between gangs.

Because of the unclarified nature of its structure, the violent gang has a chameleonlike quality. Its organization shifts with the needs of its members and is always in a state of flux. Conflicts with other groups go on constantly, either in discussion or in actuality. Other gangs are allies one day and enemies the next, according to the whims of the sociopathic gang members and leaders.

The expression of violence by the group appears to be more acceptable than individual violent behavior. The consensus factor of the group seems to permit a wider range of "legitimate" abnormal behavior. A disturbed youth may therefore cloak his pathology in the group image, which simultaneously aggrandizes him and lends him anonymity.

Many gang leaders appear to be involved in an attempt to redefine earlier years when they were disturbed, insecure, and unhappy. At this later period in their lives (approximately between the ages of 18 and 25), they act out the powerful role they could not achieve when they were younger.

Gang warfare in gang neighborhoods usually has no clear purpose or consensus of definition for all participants. For many gang members, it is an opportunity to channel personal aggressions and hostilities. Many gang wars originate over trivia. Territory, a "bad look," an exaggerated argument over a girl, or a nasty remark may stir up a large collection of youths into gang warfare. Such surface provocations give disturbed youths a cause célèbre and a banner under which they can vent hostilities related to other issues in their lives, such as a sense of hopelessness about their futures. The gang members' emotions are fanned through interaction and produce a group contagion. What starts out as a "bad look" from one youth toward another can thus develop into major violence. Each youth who becomes involved can project into the battle whatever angers or hostilities he has toward school, his family, the neighborhood, the police, or any other problems he may be living through at the time.

At actual gang-war events, most youths on hand have little or no idea why they are there or what they are expected to do. Leaders, gang members, citizens, and sometimes the police and the press are caught up in the fallout of gang-war hysteria. Although violent gang members may not be clear about their motives or their gang's organization, the gang war can result in homicide—a very clear situation indeed. In fact, the confused nature of the gang and its fantasies help to make it a highly destructive instrument of violence. The revved-up violent feelings in gang members account for the large number of so-called drive-by shootings in many large cities. These homicides are senseless; partial proof of this is that most victims of these murders have no gang affiliations.

Thus, gang violence results from the following set of interrelated circumstances:

1. Varied negative sociocultural dislocations exist in the disorganized, rapidly changing urban slum area.
2. These dislocations produce dysfunctional gaps in the socialization process that would ordinarily train youths for normative social roles.
3. Adolescents not adequately socialized may develop asocial or sociopathic personalities.
4. The resulting sociopathic personalities are essentially characterized by (*a*) a lack of social conscience; (*b*) a limited ability to relate to, identify with, or empathize with others except for egocentric objectives; and (*c*) impulsive, aggressive, and socially destructive behavior when impulsive, immediate needs are not satisfied.
5. Because of these personality deficiencies, the sociopathic individual cannot relate adequately to more socially demanding groups (including delinquent and social gangs).
6. Individualized emotional outbursts are more stigmatized, are considered more bizarre, and to some extent are more unrewarding than group pathological expressions. In the context of the violent gang, such individualistic expression becomes socially "legitimate."
7. The malleable nature of the violent gang makes it a compatible and legitimate vehicle for adjusting the emotional needs of the sociopathic youth, who cannot relate adequately in more demanding social groups.

The violent gang, and its homicidal behavior, lends itself to social-psychological analysis. Why do sociopathic youths form violent gang structures?

Normal groups are constellations of roles defining prescribed ways in which members may interact effectively and harmoniously. The normal group may be viewed partially as a projected model for behavior toward the accomplishment of the mutually agreed-upon goals of its members. A dominant characteristic of such a group is the fact that most members are in consensual agreement about the important norms and reciprocal expectations that regulate and determine each group member's behavior. Thus, essential elements in a normal group are its members' agreement upon and ability to fulfill certain prescribed norms or standards of behavior. This is not the case with violent gangs.

The Violent Gang as a Near-Group   The organization of human collectives may be viewed as a continuum of factors. At one extreme, an organized cohesive collection of persons interacting around shared functions and goals for some period of time forms a normal group. At the other extreme of human organization, a loose collection of individuals, generally characterized by anonymity and spontaneous leadership, motivated and ruled by momentary emotions, forms a mob or crowd. Although the term *mob* fits a youth riot and *group* fits a cohesive delinquent gang, neither term seems especially appropriate to describe the structure of violent gangs.

Groups that emerge midway on a continuum of organization are distorted in one direction or the other by most perceivers. It appears as though there is a psychological (autistic) need to consolidate one's view of the world. Violent gangs, therefore, despite considerable evidence to the contrary, are often mistakenly perceived by observers as cohesive groups, and in some youth riots observers see no organization despite the fact that in most cases a degree of organization exists.

Because no existing group conceptions seem suitable for describing the violent gang, it may be referred to as a near-group. The group stands midway on the continuum from mob to group (see Figure 15.2). It is differentiated from other collectivities that are temporarily midway because it has some degree of permanence or homeostasis. A cohesive group may be partially disorganized for a period of time, but it is in a state of becoming either organized or disorganized.

The violent gang as an ideal type of near-group structure includes most of the following characteristics:

1. Participants in the violent gang near-group are generally sociopathic personalities. The most sociopathic are core participants or leaders.
2. To these individuals the near-group is a compensatory paranoid

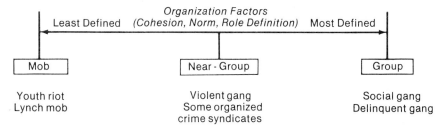

Figure 15.2 Collective structures.

pseudocommunity, which serves as a more socially desirable adjustment pattern than other pathological syndromes available in the community.

3. Individualized roles are defined to fit the emotional needs of the participants.
4. The definition of membership is diffuse and varies for each participant.
5. Behavior is essentially emotion-motivated within loosely defined boundaries.
6. Group cohesiveness decreases as one moves from the center of the collectivity to the periphery.
7. Membership requires only limited responsibility and social ability.
8. Leadership is self-appointed and sociopathic.
9. There is a limited consensus among participants in the collectivity as to its functions or goals.
10. There is a shifting and personalized stratification system.
11. Membership is in flux.
12. Fantasy membership is included in the size of the collective.
13. There is a limited consensus of normative expectations for behavior.
14. Norms and behavior patterns are often in conflict with the inclusive social system's prescriptions.
15. Interaction within the collectivity and toward the outer community is hostile and aggressive, with spontaneous outbursts of violence used to achieve impulsively felt goals.

It should be noted that the concept of the near-group has application beyond juvenile violent gangs. I speculate that many organized crime "families" or syndicates are not as cohesive or coherent as many law enforcement agencies perceive them. It is my view that many "Mafia-type" and organized crime organizations have near-group characteristics.

Speculations on the Future of Violent Gangs   For a time during the 1960s and early 1970s, there was a diminution of violent gang activities. This decrease in violence may have resulted from a sense of hope that positive social change might take place, and perhaps because potential members of violent gangs were involved in the then vibrant civil rights movement. But as apathy and despair reappeared in the urban ghetto, violent gangs reemerged as vehicles for venting anger and frustration.

Gang forms were modified in the 1960s. Violence was used as a vehicle for social change. For example, during the riots in the Watts area of Los Angeles, black gangs that had previously fought each other joined forces against their common enemy—"Whitey." Many ghetto youngsters who in the 1950s would almost automatically have joined a violent gang became members of quasi-political militant groups such as the Black Panthers or the Brown Berets. Their violence was no longer senseless: it appeared to have purpose.

The extravagant faith in these minority group militant organizations has clearly diminished. Intensive leadership battles, "ego trips," and selling out to impotent bureaucratic programs seem to have taken their toll, and many of these organizations became unattractive or defunct. As these vehicles for social change diminish, the despair, alienation, and hopelessness of many young people are now being rechanneled into structures that parallel earlier violent gangs.

A sense of despair and alienation produces this type of violent gang. For an individual who sees little hope or opportunity for achievement in the overall society, the violent gang becomes an acceptable substitute. In it, the youth has identity and an extravagant hope for "stardom" in a success- and power-oriented society. With a stroke of a knife or a bullet from a gun, the individual can achieve status among his peers and, in a perverted way, in the larger society.

The youth most susceptible to violent-gang membership emerges from a social milieu that trains him inadequately for assuming constructive social roles. In fact, the defective socialization process to which he is subjected fosters a lack of humanistic feelings. At hardly any point is he trained to have feelings of compassion or responsibility for other people.

The selection of violence by gang youths is not difficult to understand. Violent behavior requires little in the way of training, personal ability, or even physical strength. (As one gang member stated, "A knife or a gun makes you ten feet tall.") Because violence is a demonstration of easily achieved power, it becomes the paramount value of the gang. Violence requires characteristics that gang members have in quantity: limited social ability and training, considerable resentment and aggression, and a motivation to retaliate against others and the system. Violence serves as a quick and sure means for upward social mobility within the violent gang and, to some extent, in the overall society.

The very fact that it is "senseless" rather than "rational" violence that appeals to the gang member tells us a great deal about the meaning of violence to him. It is an easy, quick, almost magical way of achieving power and prestige. In a single act of unpremeditated intensity, he establishes a sense of his own identity and impresses this existence on others. No special ability is required to commit this brand of violence—not even a plan—and the guilt connected with it is minimized by the gang code of approval, especially if the violence fulfills the gang's idealized standards of a swift, sudden, and senseless outbreak.

One aspect of senseless violence is related to a concept I term *existential validation*, the validation of one's existence. This basically involves the individual's sense of alienation from human feeling or meaning. People have an increasingly limited awareness of their personal human value in a vast, technological, dehumanized society. Many people feel a social death. Extremist violence is one way of establishing identity and experiencing some feeling of existence.

Most people have a sense of identity and existence in their everyday activities. They do not require intense emotional excitement to know they are alive, that they exist. In contrast, some people, including the sociopath, do need such arousal; indeed, their sense of being a human and having feelings requires increasingly heavier dosages of bizarre and extreme behavior to validate the fact that they really exist. Extreme violent behavior is one pattern that gives the sociopath a glimmer of feeling. Existential validation through violence (or other extremist bizarre behavior involving, say, sex or drugs) gives the socially dead person some feeling. As one gang killer reported, "When I stabbed him once, it felt good. I did it again and again because it made me feel alive for the first time in my life."

Violence is not exclusively the prestige symbol of the gang. The larger society covertly approves of, or is at least intrigued by, the outrageous as depicted in literature and in television, movies, and other mass media. On the surface most members of society condemn violence; however, on a covert level there is a tendency to aggrandize and give recognition to violent people. The sociopathic personality who commits intense acts of violence is the "hero" of many plays and stories protrayed in the contemporary mass media.

The continuance into the 1990s of "senseless" violent gangs, in conjunction with the increased use of enormously destructive drugs, is an indicator of the deep despair and alienation experienced by many minority and ghetto youths. The phenomenon of the violent gang is closely correlated to many significant social dislocations that persist in American society. New social policies and treatment approaches are required to solve this deadly crime and delinquency problem.

CAUSAL THEORY AND TREATMENT OF THE CRIME PROBLEM

Theories about the causal context of crime and delinquency tend to point to strategies for treating the problem. For example, economic theories point up the necessity of modifying the social system to provide more occupational hope for depressed socioeconomic groups; theories related to anomie indicate a greater emphasis is needed on providing more equal opportunity for all; and near-group theory emphasizes that youths who have low self-esteem require therapy that gives them a greater sense of social competence so they can participate more effectively in the larger society. In Chapters 16 through 18, I present and analyze a variety of correctional control and treatment programs and strategies designed to ameliorate the crime and delinquency problem in American society.

PART Six

THE TREATMENT AND CONTROL OF CRIME

Chapter
16

Corrections: Prevention and Treatment Approaches

*T*he prison as a social system is at best a difficult environment within which to resocialize criminals. This, coupled with the fact that most criminals were juvenile delinquents, leads us logically to believe that an effective way to combat our crime problem is to reach the offender at an early age in the community, before he or she is caught in the net of the law and sent to an adult institution. Effective social-psychological treatment programs include community-based programs, such as probation and parole. This chapter encompasses (1) recommended prevention programs, (2) community approaches, and (3) various treatment methods and strategies that should be incorporated into existing correctional institutions and community programs that attempt to control crime.

The general advantages of community-based programs are that they have a better chance for success than institutional programs because the environment is more natural than the onerous and artificial milieu of the prison. The prime disadvantage of treating the offender in the community is the fact that the individual is apt to be living within the same environment, with the same set of causal forces, that originally produced the crime or delinquency. These negative forces must be vitiated or overcome if the individual is to function as a law-abiding citizen, whether or not he or she later spends time in a correctional institution.

Neighborhood community programs have been designed to reduce the incidence of criminality and delinquency in problem areas. These programs are based on the assumptions that certain urban areas with high delinquency rates tend to foster crime and delinquency, and that the development of indigenous anticriminal leadership and services in these areas would reduce the incidence of criminal and delinquent behavior by minimizing or blocking out these negative elements in the community. Programs of this type are attempts to change the social environment in which the offender grows up. Such programs coordinate the activities of existing facilities and agencies and establish additional facilities if this seems advisable. Community organization experts attempt to activate or organize councils representing as many social welfare agencies as will cooperate and sometimes seek to organize the people from the problem area into neighborhood committees for action.

COMMUNITY PROGRAMS

The Chicago Area Project

A pioneer community program was developed by Clifford Shaw and others in the 1930s in Chicago. It has served as a model for crime prevention community programs that were developed in the late 1980s. The program was initiated after the research of Shaw and his colleagues had clearly indicated that the slum areas of large cities were characterized by a disproportionately large number of delinquent children and criminals. The program was based on several assumptions that have become standard for such programs in recent years:

1. In high-delinquency areas, delinquency is symptomatic of deeper social ills. It is a product of the social milieu. The same blighted areas that have high delinquency rates also have high rates of economic dependency, illness, infant mortality, substandard housing, and poverty. (This is as true today as it was in the 1930s.)

2. Delinquency cannot be attributed to factors inherent in race or nationality groups.

3. Delinquency in deteriorated areas may frequently be regarded as conformity to the expectations, behavior patterns, and values of the groups of children in the neighborhood.

4. Most delinquents in deteriorated areas are not inferior to children in the more privileged communities in any fundamental way. Delinquency is a part of the social tradition of the neighborhood; a large segment of the population tolerates, reinforces, and even encourages delinquent behavior.

5. It is not possible to save a child apart from the family or community. A community with a new morale and new leadership directed in socially constructive channels is essential.

6. *The local neighborhood can be organized to deal effectively with its own problems. There exists in the neighborhood sufficient indigenous leadership to bring about changes in attitudes, sentiments, ideals, and loyalties for the construction of a more acceptable community lifestyle.*

The Chicago Area Project became a model for today's neighborhood crime prevention programs. The project organized community committees in six areas of Chicago. Twenty-two neighborhood centers involving over 7,500 children were developed in these areas. The community committees were organized with the aid of a staff member of the project. The staff member did not exercise control but was available to mobilize needed resources or act as an adviser only if called upon by the committee. The neighborhood committee selected a qualified local resident as director, and that person was then employed as a staff member of the area project. Policy decisions were left to the neighborhood committee, whether the "experts" on the staff of the area project agreed or not. The residents of the neighborhood were in control.[1] Ten years after its inception, the Russell Square Community Committee, for example, had 125 active members and 700 contributing members. These included local business people and political leaders, bartenders, plumbers, carpenters, workers, and some former delinquents and criminals.

The projects encouraged the expansion of existing facilities for recreation and the construction of new ones. Efforts were made to improve school-community relations and particularly to encourage teachers to remain in the schools. Club work, discussion groups, and hobby groups were used as tools for developing community spirit.

One of the most important aspects of the area-project program was the preparation of offenders for return to the community. Offenders soon to be released were visited in their institutions, encouraged to participate in committee activities upon their return, and helped to establish contacts with employers and other local groups. These legitimate activities furnish the framework within which the offender returning from an institution can become accepted and can come to feel like a full member of the community.

The social climate of a community can be expected to improve as the people in it assume greater responsibility for its direction. A community administered by outsiders is less likely to develop an esprit de corps. The Chicago Area Project demonstrated that people in the deteriorated areas of our cities are capable of supplying the leadership necessary to increase constructive action. While the effect of the Chicago Area Project on delinquency was not precisely measured, in all probability delinquency was substantially reduced as a consequence of the effort.

The Detached-Worker Program for Gangs

In the late 1980s, especially in Los Angeles, the violent gang problem reached horrendous proportions. In 1988 there were over 400 gang-

---

[1] Solomon Kobrin, "The Chicago Area Project: A 25-Year Assessment," *Annals of the American Academy of Political and Social Science* 322 (March 1959):19–29.

related murders in Los Angeles County. Many of these were associated with drug-dealing enterprises. How can we control violent gangs and their murderous behavior?

In the 1950s I developed a community-based program modeled after the Chicago Area Project in New York City. It was primarily directed at youth gangs; however, the approach proved of value in preventing other patterns of crime and delinquency. In this approach, a professional, usually a social worker, is assigned to a particular gang. The essential avowed goal of the youth worker is to redirect the gang from destructive behavior patterns into "constructive" activities.

Contrary to popular belief, getting in touch with the gang is not difficult for a detached worker. However, the meaning given to the relationship by gang members varies and is of major significance. If the gang worker appears as a "mark" to most members, a "do-gooder" who doesn't know the score, they will simply use the worker for money, cigarettes, or whatever favors they can obtain. The negative nature of this situation is not simply the gang worker's being duped, but an incorrect assumption of success. Many gang workers, rather than resocializing gang members, are themselves negatively affected by the gang. They may rationalize their personal motives toward "adventuresome" gang behavior as necessary to maintain their relationship. In fact, this behavior is not necessary. Becoming themselves "gang members" neutralizes their impact as adequate adult role models.

The detached gang worker who is duped by the gang or misinterprets the meaning of a situation is reinforcing rather than modifying illegal behavior. The gang worker is, in effect, a carrier of the values and norms of the larger society. Initially gang members resist the intrusion into the subculture they have created (to act out their problems). The gang will attempt to get what it can without changing and then seduce the detached worker into becoming part of the gang. The gang worker should be aware of the negative implication of compromising the relevant norms of the larger society to gain false acceptance and superficial approval. The worker who does this is fairly quickly eliminated as a force for changing the gang, since they begin to view the worker as a mark or sucker susceptible to manipulation. This defeats the objectives the worker is attempting to achieve.

The gang worker must have a realistic image of gang structure or is likely to be duped by the illusory conceptions of the gang as described by its members. The worker's acceptance of the fantastic stories created by core gang participants produces a reinforcement of undesirable gang mythology.

The validity of such antisocial patterns as gang warfare, territory, and peace meetings should be challenged and discouraged rather than accepted and, in some cases, aggrandized and given legitimacy. The enlightened detached gang worker can sometimes operate effectively through the use of ridicule, disbelief, and criticism.

The worker is often presented with wild stories of gang activity, some believed and some not believed by the gang participants themselves. By "buying" their story, the worker becomes a dupe who loses the potential for positive influence. On the other hand, by pushing the "gang stories" to their illogical conclusion by sensitive caricaturing, the worker makes treatment progress. First, the worker achieves stature with the gang as an adult person who can't be "conned" or manipulated. This the gang members respect. Second, the worker turns the gang and its members back upon self-evaluation and assessment. This process causes them to begin to look at themselves and their gang as it exists in reality.

A Case in Point Following is a transcript of a taped session in which I handled a potential gang fight using the foregoing principles.

Four gang youths entered my office. They were obviously nervous but were attempting to give a "cool" appearance:

FIRST GANG BOY: Well, that's it—we'll whip it on tonight at seven and then the whole city will rumble. I mean we're not going to sit still for that bullshit. The Dragons are through once and for all.

L.Y.: Now, really, what is all this bullshit anyway? Wait a minute, I have to make a call. [Makes an inconsequential phone call, emphasizing disinterest in the mass rumble that is supposed to engulf the city, then turns to the boys with a look of disgust.] Now, what's all this rumble stuff about?

GANG BOY: Well, they're suppose to whip it on tonight. Duke says . . .

L.Y.: Wait a minute now. Duke told you this? [In disbelief] He told you this and you believe him?

GANG BOY: Well, yeah—he and Pete met with Loco from the uptown Dragons, and he says that . . .

L.Y.: [Interrupting] Just a minute. You mean to tell me those nuts Duke, Loco, and Pete cook up some nonsense about a rumble and you guys jump right into the fire. [In disbelief] How stupid can you get?

SECOND GANG BOY: I told them it was a lot of crap and . . .

L.Y.: Don't tell them. Why didn't you tell Duke—right there? Besides, you guys don't really have anyone to fight for you anyway. [Refers at length to a previous meeting with twelve of the "gang" where they finally agreed they were the only twelve they could count on in a fight.]

THIRD GANG BOY: Well, Duke and Jerry say our ten divisions can. . .

FOURTH GANG BOY: [Interrupts] Oh, man, you guys still dig all that bullshit. [Turns] I didn't believe none of it—but they all got excited.

L.Y.: Maybe one of these days you guys will wise up. Let's talk about something important. Are you all set up for the game at the Columbia gym Sunday?[2]

At that time I maneuvered past the gang-war subject, but I picked it up later with the police and another social agency to check it out further. If I had become involved and called a "peace meeting" with relevant gang leaders, I might have poured gasoline on the fire by reinforcing, joining, and helping develop a possible gang fight. What occurred as a result of my not being drawn in was to destroy the potential support of many gang members for an attack, discredit the gang leader's fantasy, cause the youths to examine some of the mythology of their near-group structure, and change over to a positive subject. Another main goal in this type of ridiculing approach is to encourage the marginal members to confront the fantasy of the gang and the gang-war plans on their own at the source—the leader. In some cases they effectively mimic the worker's sarcastic and caustic comments with the provocative gang leader, vitiating the leader's negative impact toward violence. Castrating his fantasy through sarcasm and ridicule helps to minimize his negative effect, rather than support and reinforce the gang leader's potential impact.

The "conned" detached worker tends unwittingly to reward what is in fact sociopathic behavior. The misguided worker not only legitimizes the gang and its core but also provides them with a type of "social director." In this role the worker aids the violent gang leader's nefarious activities by providing attractive activities, dances, athletic events, and so on for marginal members.

The worker may be incorporated into and become part of the gang's structure. Having a gang worker attached to one's gang then becomes a status symbol of being a real "down," "bad," or tough gang. As one violent gang leader expressed it: "We're a real down club. We got a president, a war counselor, and a Youth Board man."

The incorrectly oriented detached worker may indirectly help to produce and articulate violent gang culture.

Some Guidelines for Effective Use of the Detached-Worker Approach Reaching the gang in its own milieu through the detached gang worker is a significant approach to the problem of violent gangs. However, several issues require revision and redefinition if this approach is to modify

---

[2] Reprinted with permission of Macmillan Publishing Co., Inc. from *The Violent Gang* by Lewis Yablonsky, pp. 242–243. © Lewis Yablonsky 1962.

rather than solidify or reinforce the structure and behavior of violent gangs. On the basis of the near-group conception of gang organization and other factors that have emerged in the analysis, the following guidelines are suggested for a more effective approach to this problem:

1. It is necessary for the detached gang worker to be trained to diagnose accurately several types of gang structure. Different approaches are required for the social, delinquent, and violent gangs.

2. The accurate diagnosis of the violent gang reveals different degrees of participation and involvement. One may work with marginal members through more conventional treatment approaches; core participants and leaders of violent gangs require a different and more intense form of treatment.

3. A violent gang can be further integrated by working through the leaders. The detached gang worker should avoid giving the leader credence, since this may reinforce gang structure. Providing the sociopathic leader with "official" status and activity opportunities for the gang tends to defeat rather than achieve sound corrective goals.

4. The detached gang worker, as an official representative of the more inclusive society, must avoid sanctioning or participating in deviance to gain what will turn out to be a false acceptance and rapport. The worker should serve as an adequate law-abiding adult role model and in this way may become a bridge or vehicle for bringing the larger society's constructive values and norms to the gang.

Violent gangs should not be treated by any official community program as a "legitimate" social structure. Giving credence to the violent gang by providing it with an official representative of society is giving tacit authorization to pathology and violence. For example, peace meetings that involve gang leaders and paid representatives of city government implicitly provide an illegal, pathological enterprise with official support.

These conclusions are not based upon moral or legal considerations but upon the nature of gang organization. An entity such as the violent gang cannot be treated as a unit. The type of detached-worker policies and the programs that have been employed in the past appear to solidify and legitimize the violent gang, reinforcing its pathological behavior rather than modifying its antisocial activity.

Rather than "redirecting" and implicitly reinforcing the violent gang as an institutionalized and legitimized pattern of illegal behavior, the focus should be upon eliminating it as an entity. This goal may be worked toward by a combination of modified detached gang work, police action, incarceration, group therapy, and a new "milieu therapy" approach to sociopathic behavior. If these approaches are utilized, the violent gang may be dismembered and many of its participants may be resocialized and legally reconnected into the inclusive society. Core violent gang members require institutionalization because they cannot usually be helped in the community.

HALFWAY HOUSES AND COMMUNITY TREATMENT PROGRAMS

Most inmates of prisons and training schools were, prior to their incarceration, members of delinquent groups with subcultures deviating materially from that of the dominant culture in our society. While in these institutions, inmates are subjected to a continuous acculturation and assimilation of the delinquent value system. They tend to develop a vocabulary that reflects attitudes, beliefs, opinions, and orientations different from and often opposing those of the conventional person, if they did not have such attitudes when they arrived at the institution. The roles played by the inmates and the roles they are required to play upon release are vastly different in most important aspects. This is obviously true of the important family roles. The inmate is living apart from parents, brothers and sisters, and any other relatives with whom he or she normally resides. We often forget that the inmate is also away from community roles and normal occupational roles.

In spite of the fact that most inmates do some work while at an institution, the attitudes attached to this role of worker differ materially from the attitudes required for satisfactory achievement in a work situation on the outside. Workers in the correctional labor system are encouraged to be nonproductive, dilatory, and contentious. Institutionally developed attitudes affect the individual's concept of the role of the job seeker. In reform school or prison, the inmate does not have to seek a job. It is considered to be the duty of the officials to provide inmates with work, and they come to feel that they have a right to a job. Supervisors in prison are content with a limited amount of productivity, the standards being far lower than those set by employers outside the institution. Far more cooperation than the inmate is accustomed to give is expected by fellow workers, supervisors, and employers when the person works on the outside.[3]

As a result of the stay at a correctional institution, the person is disconnected from ordinary occupational, family, and community roles. While inside, the individual adjusts to prison life, and upon his release may be expected to have difficulty reestablishing occupational and family roles in the community. This person needs time to adjust and to

---

[3] Martin R. Haskell, "An Alternative to More and Larger Prisons: A Role Training Program for Social Reconnection," *Group Psychotherapy* 14 (March–June 1961):30–38.

reconnect to society. Institutions organized to facilitate the necessary transition are called *halfway houses,* to symbolize their status as an establishment between a prison and the residence of a free citizen. The halfway house as now constituted is a temporary residence for released offenders, usually located in the community in which the inmates resided before they were incarcerated, or as near to that community as possible. At the halfway house, a building housing 20 to 50 people under the supervision of a correctional authority, the released prisoner can look for a job, work on a job, meet with family and friends, and begin to assume the roles normally acceptable in the community.

Highfields

A prototype for a new type of treatment-oriented halfway house is the residential group center of the Highfields program, originated in 1950 in New Jersey. This institution has served as a model for programs in a number of other states. The program was not designed for deeply disturbed or mentally deficient offenders. Each Highfields unit is limited in population to 20 offenders assigned directly by the court— offenders who have not previously been committed to a correctional institution. Although the original Highfields concept as described here was developed for younger offenders of ages 16 and 17, I perceive the program as potentially adaptable to older offenders.

The youths who lived in the first experimental Highfields center stayed there for an average of four months. During the day they worked at a nearby institution or in the community, performing menial labor. There were few security measures and there was little or no authoritarian leadership. Every evening the boys were divided into two groups of ten each for a meeting built around the technique of guided interaction.

The guided group interaction sessions are at the heart of the Highfields approach. The method is explained as follows by Dr. Lloyd McCorkle, one of the creators of the Highfields approach:

> Rehabilitation begins with changes in attitudes. But how can these be brought about? The boys entering Highfields have for years identified themselves as delinquents. Their close friends are delinquent. Group pressure has generally pushed and pulled them into delinquency and prevented their rehabilitation. Most delinquents feel rejected and discriminated against by their parents. They generally manifest strong emotional reactions, particularly against their fathers, but often against their mothers, brothers, and sisters. By the time they are confronted with law-enforcing agencies they have developed strong ego defenses. They do not take the responsibility for their delinquency. Instead, they tend to blame others— their parents, their associates, and society.
>
> The whole Highfields experience is directed toward piercing through these strong defenses against rehabilitation, toward undermining delin-

quent attitudes, and toward developing a self-conception favorable to reformation. The sessions on guided group interaction are especially directed to achieve this objective.

Guided group interaction has the merit of combining the psychological and the sociological approaches to the control of human behavior. The psychological approach aims to change the self-conception of the boy from a delinquent to a nondelinquent. But this process involves changing the mood of the boy from impulses to law breaking to impulses to be law abiding.[4]

At Highfields, emphasis was placed on normal social activities and values. This was accomplished by four devices intended "to help the boys be like everybody else." (1) Family members and friends of boys were encouraged to visit them at Highfields and see how they were getting along. (2) An effort was made to educate the surrounding community to accept the boys rather than to show suspicion or reject them entirely. (3) Perhaps most important, the boys did useful work and were paid for it. (4) The stay at Highfields was limited to a maximum of four months. This time factor was considered an important device that contributed to successful rehabilitation.

Institutions modeled after the original Highfields have been developed around the country. Some are now located in central city areas. Much like the original, they house about 20 persons each, and custodial personnel are held to a minimum. Residents are permitted to receive visitors frequently and to leave the premises with visitors. They usually work outside the institution, and they participate in group therapy sessions on a regular basis.

The philosophy, operation, effect, and potential of the Highfields program have been summarized as follows:

1. Its thoroughgoing use of the group as an instrument of rehabilitation is social-psychologically sound and has been verified by experience.
2. The method of guided interaction directs group influences toward rehabilitation rather than, as in the large reformatory, to the reinforcement of attitudes of delinquency and hostility to authority.
3. In the guided group interaction sessions the youth achieves an understanding of himself and his motivations which enables him to make constructive plans for his future.
4. Highfields greatly reduces the time of treatment from the usual one to five years in training schools or reformatories to three or four months.
5. It requires a minimum of staff as compared with other methods of treatment.
6. Highfields has far lower per capita costs than other institutions for the treatment of delinquents.
7. There is every reason to believe that Highfields can be successfully

---

[4] Lloyd W. McCorkle, *The Highfields Story* (New York: Holt, 1958), p. v.

established elsewhere provided the new projects incorporate its philosophy, its design of operation, and a specially trained staff.[5]

The Highfields experiment has been considered generally successful by several research evaluations. With some variations, it was successfully replicated in Provo, Utah.[6] While Highfields was originally designed for adolescents, similar types of institutional approaches are now used for adult probationers and parolees. I would recommend the expansion of the Highfields approach to include offenders up to age 30. Additional programs of the Highfields type can diminish the populations of our adult prisons, can resocialize many young offenders, and can help to ameliorate our general crime problem in a more humane way.

THE BASIC APPROACHES OF PROBATION AND PAROLE

Prisons and therapeutic communities are dependent on probation and parole for their success. This is because most offenders can benefit from supervision in the community. The two actions of a correctional system that leave the greatest autonomy to the person serving a sentence of a court are probation and parole. The first, probation, represents the sentence imposed by a court in lieu of confinement. The person sentenced spends no time at all in a correctional institution, with the exception of time spent in detention prior to trial. Once sentenced to probation by a judge, the offender is relatively free as long as he or she conforms to the conditions imposed by the judge or the judge's agent. The individual is placed under the supervision of a probation officer, who is a peace officer charged with seeing that these conditions are met. (The probation officer has many other duties and problems, some of which will be discussed in this chapter.)

Parole is similar to probation in that the parolee is also relatively free in the community. The parolee, too, is supervised by a peace officer, usually called a parole agent. The major difference between probation and parole is that the parolee has served at least part of a sentence in a correctional institution. The parolee is released from the correctional institution prior to the expiration of the sentence and allowed to serve the remainder of the sentence in the community, provided he or she lives up to the conditions imposed by the releasing authority.

---

[5] H. Ashley Weeks, *Youthful Offenders at Highfields* (Ann Arbor: University of Michigan Press, 1958), pp. xvii–xviii. See also McCorkle, *Highfields Story.*

[6] LaMar T. Empey and Jerome Rabow, "The Provo Experiment in Delinquency Rehabilitation," *American Sociological Review* 26 (October 1961):679–696.

Probation

Probation is a treatment program in which the final action in an adjudicated offender's case is suspended, so that the person remains at liberty, subject to conditions imposed by or for a court under the supervision and guidance of a probation officer. The correctional system provides for the treatment and supervision of offenders in the community by placing them on probation in lieu of confinement in a custodial institution. In most states, probationers serve the sentence of a court under the supervision of a probation officer assigned by the court. The judge has broad powers in this situation and sets the conditions of probation and the length of the supervision period. He or she retains the power to order revocation of probation, usually for a violation of one of the conditions of parole or for the commission of another offense. The effect of revocation is to send a probationer to a custodial institution.

A few states have centralized probation systems, but most of the counties in the United States exercise autonomy within limits set by state statutes. For example, the probation system in California is a centralized system that authorizes each county to provide facilities, services, and regulations. In many states, probation is an activity of the court—criminal, juvenile, or other—with the probation officer serving as an appointee of the judge. There is therefore considerable variation in the use of probation and the manner in which it is administered.

In general, adult probation services are state functions, and juvenile probation services tend to be local functions. In 32 states, juvenile courts administer probation services. In 30 states, adult probation is combined with parole services. In terms of the number of persons served and of total operating costs, the juvenile probation system has approximately twice as many resources per capita as the adult system.

More than half the offenders sentenced to correctional treatment are first placed on probation. The average caseload assigned to a probation officer is usually around 75. The typical probation caseload is usually a random mixture of cases. Some probation departments manage short-term institutional facilities for certain probationees.

The probation officer sees that the probationer lives up to the conditions of the probation. The officer assists the probationer with problems at work or school, or with family members, and provides guidance. David Dressler notes four central techniques used by the probation officer.

1. *Manipulative techniques.* The environment may be manipulated in the interests of the person seeking help. The end product is usually something material and tangible received by the individual under care, for example, financial aid rendered by the agency or an employer persuaded to rehire a discharged worker.
2. *Executive techniques.* The probation officer may refer the individual to other resources in the community for help that the correctional agency

cannot render. For example, the probation officer may refer the individual to a legal aid society or secure public assistance for him.

3. *Guidance techniques.* The probation officer may give personal advice and guidance on problems not requiring complex psychological techniques. The advice is likely to be fairly direct and the guidance comparatively superficial. The end product is intangible, although it may facilitate the achievement of tangible goals. For example, the individual is advised how to budget his income or helped to explore the possibilities of training for a trade.

4. *Counseling techniques.* These are based largely upon psychological orientations and require considerable skill. The services are intangible, concerned with deep-seated problems in the emotional area—for example, aid in adjusting a marital situation or help in overcoming specific emotional conflicts.[7]

In addition to these probation approaches, in recent years many new techniques have been developed for treating offenders in the community in lieu of warehousing them in custodial settings or releasing them prematurely into the community without any controls.

In an incisive article, "Practical Alternatives to Jail's Fast Shuffle," in the *Los Angeles Times,* March 20, 1989, Barry J. Nidorf, chief probation officer of Los Angeles County, one of the largest and most effective probation departments in the United States, analyzes the problem of increasing overcrowding in our nation's jails and mentions some of the innovative new probation techniques that can be utilized in the community to effectively control and rehabilitate criminals:

The local manifestation of the nationwide epidemic of overcrowded jails, prisons and juvenile facilities became evident recently when Los Angeles County Sheriff Sherman Block was forced, under federal court order [because of overcrowding], to increase the number of early releases of county prisoners.

News of the announcement was accompanied by a disturbing photograph. It showed a just-released inmate, a smile on his face, who had served his 14-day county jail sentence in 14 hours—or at the rate of $2\frac{1}{2}$ minutes on the hour. . . .

With no end in sight to the serious jail overcrowding problem, it is time that the community look to new criminal sanctions that can protect its citizens and satisfy the demands of justice without depending on scarce jail beds. Jail may be where most citizens want criminals to be, but that is not a reality today. There is just not enough space to hold any but the most dangerous and violent criminals. New sanctions, strong enough to deter, are needed for criminals who are released early—or do not go to jail at all—because of overcrowding. [In addition to Los Angeles, and other cities around the country, one of the most publicized manifestations of the problem Nidorf delineates is found in our nation's capital, Washington,

---

[7] David Dressler, *Practice and Theory of Probation and Parole* (New York: Columbia University Press, 1969), pp. 151–152. Used by permission.

D.C., notoriously described in the press as "the murder capital of the United States."]

If new sanctions are not found and used, a never-ending cycle of greater overcrowding and earlier release will embolden confirmed criminals to continue committing crimes, while failing to discourage would-be criminals.

Which new sanctions are needed? Examples include "house arrest," electronic monitoring of criminals confined to their homes on probation; "work sentencing," using supervised crews of probationers sentenced to work improving community buildings, parks, roads and other public areas; [and] "work furlough," a program in which employed probationers work their regular jobs by day and are sentenced to stay in a contracted residential center by night.

Sanctions like these are obviously not appropriate for every criminal. Violent offenders and habitual criminals belong in jail or prison. But for petty criminals and even many nonviolent felons, such sanctions are not only appropriate but needed. They help to mitigate the jail overcrowding crisis by imposing penalties right in the community. They attach a cost to crime that is more demanding than just sitting in jail for a few hours. Coupled with a beefed-up, quick-to-respond surveillance capability, these community-based sanctions are effective, tough and affordable.[8]

Parole

Parole is a treatment program in which the offender, after serving part of a term in a correctional institution, is conditionally released under the supervision and treatment of a parole officer. There are basically three types of agencies that are empowered to grant parole: a board set up for the correctional institution; a central parole board for a state; and a group of officials, usually called a parole commission, whose principal functions are other than granting parole. The institutional board is composed mainly of personnel from the specific prison in which the candidate for parole is confined. It usually includes the warden. This means that conformity to the rules of the prison may be the principal criterion applied. However, even where representatives of a central parole board come to the prison to conduct parole hearings, they are greatly influenced by the recommendations of the warden and other custodial people. The prisoner who does not conform to prison rules is not likely to be released on parole. The advantage of the central parole board is that it provides uniform standards throughout the state.

Parole is not a right of every individual in prison. It is viewed as a privilege granted to a prisoner for good behavior and progress while in prison and is considered useful in rehabilitation outside the prison. In practice it is a system of conditional release that permits a prisoner to leave the prison before the completion of the maximum sentence and to live in the community under supervision of a parole officer.

---

[8] Barry J. Nidorf, "Practical Alternatives to Jails Fast Shuffle," *Los Angeles Times*, March 20, 1989.

Parole is beneficial to society in that, to some extent, it protects society from the individual during that time. It is also beneficial to the parolee, who may serve part of the sentence in relative freedom, outside the prison; the individual may assume most community roles and possibly get some assistance in obtaining employment. If a parolee violates the conditions of parole, the parole may be revoked and he or she may be taken back to prison. The parolee may have an extremely hard time obtaining employment and otherwise adapting in the community. A parole officer may help with personal problems so the parolee will be able to reassume normal community roles.

Before being placed on parole, a prisoner must receive a determination of readiness by the parole authority. After receiving this determination, the prisoner has a parole hearing. This is an interview with a representative of the parole authority to determine the prisoner's willingness and ability to obey the law and the conditions of the parole agreement. Once all the necessary hearings have been held, the final decision rests with the parole board. The board reviews all the pertinent reports and records on the individual, such as a complete social history revealing the nature of the offense, a family history, and statements of teachers, clergy, employers, or others who may furnish information relative to the prisoner's readiness for parole. Also considered is a complete record of past and present offenses. The reports of prison officials regarding the prisoner's behavior in prison and efforts at rehabilitation are given great weight. The individual is given medical and psychological tests to help determine his or her ability to function once again in society. The parole officer must draw up a plan for the parolee to follow outside the prison. This must include plans for employment, housing, and the resolution of other anticipated problems.[9]

It is expected that the prison will provide job training or some vocational skills that will better prepare the individual for life in the community. Recreational, educational, and vocational training facilities in prison are intended to help in rehabilitation. Medical, psychological, and counseling programs, group therapy sessions, and other therapeutic processes are supposed to prepare the individual to reenter society.

A counseling program is one important aspect of a prerelease preparation program. The prisoner may be deemed ready for release when he appears before a parole hearing officer. However, the individual may suffer anxieties and fears about the outside world. Whether or not the parolee leaves the prison with hostile attitudes will depend in part on the way the parole hearings are held and the way the person has been treated in prison.

Parole is in every sense a continuation of the correctional process.

---

[9] See Dressler, *Practice and Theory of Probation and Parole*, Chapter 7, for a detailed discussion of the process of selection for parole. See also Reed K. Clegg, *Probation and Parole* (Springfield, Ill.: Thomas, 1964).

The goal is to help reestablish the parolee in the community as a law-abiding citizen. Parole supervision includes efforts to discover the strengths in the parolee's personality and ways of dealing with emotional problems. The parolee cannot become dependent on the parole officer for all decisions and solutions to personal problems. The individual on parole must learn to handle successfully difficult situations that may arise. However, the parole officer should be able to obtain help for the parolee when required.

The parole officer has three main functions in the relationship with the parolee. The first is to use knowledge of community resources to help the parolee and the parolee's family adjust to society. The second is to provide or obtain treatment for the parolee when required. This includes dealing with psychological problems. The third function is supervision. The parole officer is supposed to try to keep the parolee from violating the conditions of parole. The officer may visit the parolee's home or work location to determine progress and may also interview family members and other important persons who can help in determining the parolee's progress. The necessity of field visits depends on each individual case. Visits may occur as often as once a week or as seldom as once a month, depending on the parolee's adjustment.

The parolee is required to accept and sign the parole agreement and is told that breaking any conditions will be cause for revocation of parole and a return to prison.

The period of parole varies from state to state and between individuals as well. It depends largely on the progress made by the parolee in the community. In most cases, parole lasts from two to five yers.

There has been a tendency in recent years to combine probation and parole operations under one organization, and this is always done for those convicted in federal courts. Both probation and parole deal with adjudged criminals and delinquents outside institutions, and since the services they render are similar, it is logical that they should be placed under one administrative agency. If that agency also controls the confinement facilities, coordination and integration of the various correctional services and institutions are facilitated.

PSYCHOTHERAPY WITH CRIMINALS: SPECIAL PROBLEMS

For many years, qualified psychotherapists have worked in prison and community institutions with offenders of all kinds. The treatment has included various modalities from psychoanalysis to group therapy. My general conclusions, based on a review of the research on therapy with offenders, are that (1) therapy for people in prison or people with the threat of imprisonment hanging over their heads poses special problems, and (2) most therapeutic programs for offenders, in prisons or in the community, are "window dressing" and have reached only a small percentage of offenders.

Despite a very limited effort at therapy for offenders during this past century, it has become fashionable among many criminologists, law enforcement experts, and politicians to conclude erroneously that therapy with criminals does not work, and punishment is the only solution.

I take the position that we really do not know whether the infusion of therapy into correctional programs works because it has never been extensively and effectively tried. In places such as Highfields and other institutions, in certain probation and parole projects, and in therapeutic communities, when real group or individual therapy was used it was effective in redirecting certain offenders from a life of crime to a law-abiding way of life.

Having a few psychologists, sociologists, or psychiatrists assigned to an institution with hundreds of inmates is an obviously ineffectual attempt at therapy. Developing specialized treatment teams, however, offers some possibility for reaching offenders and, in fact, resocializing them into law-abiding citizens.

I have worked directly as a therapist with criminals and delinquents of every type, in and out of prisons, over the past 40 years. The following discussion encompasses various problems and issues related to therapy with offenders and the types of treatment strategies I have found to be effective in my practice and in the therapeutic work of others.

Individual Counseling and Therapy in Prison

In individual or therapy counseling, there are two persons present—the therapist or counselor and the patient or counselee. What occurs in the course of the counseling depends largely on the philosophy, training, and ability of the therapist. There are some special problems that occur in working with criminals, especially in prisons.

Drs. Richard Korn and Lloyd McCorkle reveal some of the problems involved in counseling offenders in prison in the following "tough love" dialogue between a counselor and an inmate client. The counselor opens the session by asking why the inmate had come to see him:

> *Inmate:* Well, I've been talking to a few of the guys. . . . They said it might be a good idea.
> *Counselor:* Why?
> *Inmate* (in a fairly convincing attempt to appear reticent): Well—they said it did them good. . . . They said a guy needs somebody he can talk to around here . . . somebody he can trust. A . . . a friend.
> *Counselor:* And the reason you asked to see me was that you felt that I might be a friend? Why did you feel this?
> *Inmate* (a little defensively): Because they told me, I guess. Aren't you supposed to be a friend to the guys?
> *Counselor:* Well, let's see now. What is a friend supposed to do? (Inmate looks puzzled.) Let's take your best buddy, for example. Why do you consider him a friend?

Inmate (puzzled and a little more aggressive): I dunno . . . we help each other, I guess. We do things for each other.
Counselor: And friends are people who do things for each other?
Inmate: Yes.
Counselor: Fine. Now, as my friend, what is it you feel you'd like to do for me?
Inmate (visibly upset): I don't get it. Aren't you supposed to help? Isn't that your job?
Counselor: Wait a minute—I'm getting lost. A little while ago you were talking about friends and you said that friends help each other. Now you're talking about my job.
Inmate (increasingly annoyed): Maybe I'm crazy, but I thought you people are supposed to help us.
Counselor: I think I get it now. When you said "friends" you weren't talking about the kind of friendship that works both ways. The kind you meant was where I help you, not where you do anything for me.
Inmate: Well . . . I guess so. If you put it that way.
Counselor: Okay. (Relaxing noticeably from his previous tone of persistence.) Now, how do you feel I can help you?
Inmate: Well, you're supposed to help people get rehabilitated, aren't you?
Counselor: Wait. I'm lost again. You say I'm supposed to do something for people. I thought you wanted me to do something for you. Do you want me to help you get rehabilitated?
Inmate: Sure.
Counselor: Fine. Rehabilitated from what?
Inmate: Well, so I won't get in trouble anymore.
Counselor: What trouble?

At this point the inmate launched into a vehement recital of the abuses to which he had been subjected from his first contact with the juvenile authorities to his most recent difficulties with his probation officer immediately prior to the offense (stealing a car) leading to his present sentence. During the entire recital he never referred to any offense he had committed but, instead, laid exclusive emphasis on his mistreatment.

The counselor heard this account out with an expression of growing puzzlement which was not lost on the inmate, who continued with increasing vehemence as his listener appeared increasingly puzzled. At length the counselor, with a final gesture of bewilderment, broke in:

Counselor: Wait. . . . I don't understand. When you said you wanted me to help you stop getting into trouble I thought you meant the kind of trouble that got you in here. Your difficulties with the law, for example. You've talked about your troubles with different people and how they get you angry but you haven't talked about what got you into jail.
Inmate (visibly trying to control himself): But I am talking about that! I'm talking about those bastards responsible for me being here.
Counselor: How do you mean?

The inmate again repeated his tirade, interspersing it with frequent remarks addressed to the counselor. ("What about this? Do you think that was right? Is that the way to treat a young guy?" etc.) The counselor once more looked puzzled, and broke in again.

> *Counselor:* I still don't see it. We'd better get more specific. Now take your last trouble—the one that got you into the reformatory. This car you stole . . .
> *Inmate* (excitedly): It was that————P.O. [probation officer]. I asked him if I could get a job in New York. He said no.
> *Counselor:* What job?

(The inmate admitted that it wasn't a specific job, just "any job in New York.")

> *Counselor:* But I still don't follow. The probation officer wouldn't let you work in New York. By the way—don't the regulations forbid probationers from leaving the state?
> *Inmate:* Well, he could've given me a break.
> *Counselor:* That may be—but I still don't follow you. He wouldn't let you work in New York, so you and a few other guys stole a car. How does that figure?

(Here the inmate "blew up" and started to denounce "bug doctors who don't help a guy but only cross-examine him.")

> *Counselor:* Wait a bit, now. You said before that you wanted me to help you. We've been trying to find out how. But so far you haven't been talking about anything the matter with you at all. All you've talked about are these other people and things wrong with them. Now are we supposed to rehabilitate them?
> *Inmate:* I don't give a————who you rehabilitate. I've had about enough of this. If you don't mind, let's call the whole thing off.
> *Counselor:* But I do mind. Here you've been telling me that my job is to rehabilitate you and we haven't talked five minutes and now you want to call the whole thing off. Don't you want to be rehabilitated?

(Inmate is silent.)

> *Counselor:* Let's see if we can review this thing and put it in the right perspective. You said you wanted to be rehabilitated. I asked you from what and you said from getting into trouble. Then I asked you to talk about your troubles and you told me about this probation officer. He didn't give you what you wanted so you stole a car. Now as near as I can understand it, the way to keep you out of trouble is to get people to give you what you want.
> *Inmate:* That's not true, dammit!
> *Counselor:* Well, let's see now. Have I given you what you wanted?
> *Inmate:* Hell, no!
> *Counselor:* You're pretty mad at me right now, aren't you?

(Smiles. Inmate is silent, looks away.)

> *Counselor* (in a half-chiding, half-kidding tone): Here, not ten minutes ago you were talking about what good friends we could be and now you're acting like I'm your worst enemy.

Inmate (very halfheartedly, trying not to look at the counselor's face): It's true, isn't it?
Counselor: C'mon now. Now you're just trying to get mad. You won't even look at me because you're afraid you'll smile.

(Inmate cannot repress a smile. Counselor drops his kidding tone and gets businesslike again.)

Counselor: Okay. Now that we've agreed to stop kidding, let's get down to cases. Why did you come to see me today?

(Inmate halfheartedly starts to talk about rehabilitation again, but the counselor cuts in.)

Counselor: Come on, now. I thought we agreed to stop conning. Why did you come?
Inmate: Well . . . I heard you sometimes see guys . . . and . . .
Counselor: And what?
Inmate: Help them.
Counselor: How?
Inmate: Well, I tell you my story . . . and . . .
Counselor: And then? What happens then?

(Inmate is silent.)

Inmate (finally): You tell them about it.
Counselor: Who do I tell?
Inmate: You know—people who read them.
Counselor: Should I write a report on this session?
Inmate: Hell, no!
Counselor: What do you think we should do?
Inmate (looking away): Maybe I could . . . (Falls silent.)
Counselor (quietly): Maybe you could come and talk to me when we really have something to talk about?
Inmate: Yeah. . . . Aw, hell. . . . (Laughs.)[10]

This interview illustrates the problems and possibilities inherent in the crucial first counseling session with an adaptive offender of average intelligence who attempted to conceal his true feelings and his motive to manipulate under the disguise of a request for friendly help.

The special character of the adaptive criminal's motivations concerning treatment requires a special counseling technique. The usual methods of permissiveness, nondirection, and acceptance require modification. To have permitted the offender to "define the relationship" would have been an error, because the counselor would have fallen into the offender's manipulative and self-defeating trap. In counseling criminals the therapist has to be direct, tough, and honest in order to break through most offenders' manipulative techniques.

---

[10] Richard Korn and Lloyd McCorkle, *Criminology and Penology* (New York: Holt, Rinehart and Winston, 1959). Reprinted by permission of the authors.

Reality Therapy

Dr. William Glasser, a psychiatrist who has worked with many delinquent groups, has developed a treatment strategy that he calls *reality therapy*. It has some parallels with the Korn and McCorkle approach to psychotherapy with prisoners. Dr. Glasser maintains that from a treatment standpoint both the theory and practice of reality therapy are incompatible with the prevalent concept of mental illness. He describes the task of the therapist as one of becoming *involved* with the patient and then inducing the patient to face reality and take the *responsible* path. Dr. Glasser believes that reality therapy with offenders differs from conventional therapy on six points related to involvement:

1. Because we do not accept the concept of mental illness, the patient cannot become involved with us as a mentally ill person who has no responsibility for his behavior.
2. Working in the present and toward the future, we do not get involved with the patient's history because we can neither change what happened to him nor accept that he is limited by his past.
3. We relate to patients as ourselves, not as transference figures.
4. We do not look for unconscious conflicts or the reasons for them. A patient cannot become involved with us by excusing his behavior on the basis of unconscious motivations.
5. We emphasize the morality of behavior. We face the issue of right and wrong which we believe solidifies the involvement, in contrast to conventional psychiatrists who do not make the distinction between right and wrong, feeling it would be detrimental to attaining the transference relationship they seek.
6. We teach patients better ways to fulfill their needs. The proper involvement will not be maintained unless the patient is helped to find more satisfactory patterns of behavior. Conventional therapists do not feel that teaching better behavior is a part of therapy.[11]

The case of Maria illustrates Dr. Glasser's method:

Apathetic and despondent, Maria, a seventeen-and-a-half-year-old girl, was a far different problem from Jeri. Jeri was at least capable of taking care of herself fairly well, albeit illegally. She had good intelligence and some sort of warped self-reliance. Maria, on the other hand, had almost nothing. In institutions since she was about twelve, before then in foster homes, with no family, few friends, not too much intelligence (although test results are misleadingly low on these deprived girls), she came to my attention after she was involved in a serious fight in her cottage. I was asked to see her in the discipline cottage because she seemed so hopeless. She had been sitting in her room, eating little, and making no effort to contact any of the cottage staff. There seemed to be little we could do for her because she had given up herself. The fight that brought her into discipline was the result of a building frustration caused by an older, smarter girl, Sonia, who, recognizing Maria's

---

[11] Excerpts from *Reality Therapy: A New Approach to Psychiatry* by William Glasser, M.D. Copyright © 1965 by William Glasser, Inc. Reprinted by permission of Harper & Row, Publishers, Inc.

desperate need for affection, pretended to like her in order to get Maria to be a virtual slave. Maria had attacked another girl whom Sonia had openly preferred to her and joined with Sonia in making fun of Maria.

When I sat with her in the day room of the discipline unit, she refused to speak, just sitting apathetically and staring at the floor. I asked her my routine getting-acquainted questions, such as, How long have you been at the school? What are you here for? What are your plans? Do you want to return to your cottage? Marie just sat and stared. Finally she asked me to leave her alone. She had seen plenty of psyches (as our girls call psychiatrists) before, but she never talked to them. It was a discouraging interview, if it could be called an interview at all. We were worlds apart. After about twenty very long minutes I said, "I will see you next week." Saying nothing, she walked quietly back to her room. I felt that I had made no impression whatsoever. None!

Each week for seven weeks the same scene was repeated, except for different questions, and few enough of them because I could not think of what to ask. My most frequent question was, "Don't you want to get out of here?" Her reply, on occasions when she did reply, was, "What for?" My attempts to answer were met with silence. I did not have a good answer because she was obviously involved with no one and had no way to fulfill her needs—her isolated room was probably the most comfortable place for her. At least in a room by herself she did not have to see others doing and feeling what was not possible for her.

At the eighth visit I detected the first glimmer of hope. She said "Hi" in answer to my "Hi" and looked at me occasionally during the interview. I decided on a whim to ask her about her tattoos. Tattoos are the rule with our girls, nine girls out of ten have some. On her legs and arms Maria had twenty or thirty self-inflicted tattoos—dots, crosses, words, initials, and various marks, all common with our girls. I asked her if she would like a large, particularly ugly tattoo removed. Unexpectedly, she said she would; she would like them all out. Her request surprised me because girls like Maria are more apt to add tattoos rather than want them out. Lonely, isolated girls, particularly in juvenile halls, derive some sense of existence through the pain of pushing ink or dirt into their skin and by the mark produced by the act. It is a way they have, they tell me, of making sure they are still there. On the next visit we talked further about her tattoos and her feelings of hopelessness. In addition, she brought up her fear that her housemother, toward whom she had some warm feeling, would not take her back into the cottage because of what she had done. Although a housemother can refuse to take a girl back into the cottage when there are serious fights between girls, she rarely does so. I said I did not know whether or not her housemother would take her back, but that I would have her housemother stop by and see her if Maria wished it. She said she would appreciate seeing her housemother very much.

Maria now started to make progress. Her housemother, who liked her and recongized the loneliness in her quiet, uncomplaining ways, visited her and told her she was welcome back in the cottage. Her housemother also said how much she missed Maria's help with the cottage housework. Maria had been a tireless worker in the cottage. I told Maria that I had discussed her problems with the girls in my therapy group and that they wanted her to join the group. My few interviews, together with the powerful effect of the housemother's visit, had already caused some change in Maria when she left discipline. The girls in my therapy group took a special interest in her, something which might have been resented by a more sophisticated girl, but was deeply appreciated by Maria. The technique of getting girls who are more responsible to become particularly interested in someone like Maria is strongly therapeutic for them because it directly leads to fulfilling their needs and helps them to identify with the staff, thereby helping to sever ties with their own delinquent group.

Taking more interest in school, Maria began to learn to read for the first time. In the group we talked at length about what she might do, and it was decided that a work home with small children, whom she could love and who might love her in return, would be best. Older girls who have no families do well in carefully selected homes where they are paid to do housework and childcare. Although by then she was no problem, we kept her a few extra months so that some of her worst tattoos could be removed and to allow her to become more accustomed to relating to people.

The case of Maria illustrates that the key to involvement is neither to give up nor to push too hard. No matter how lonely and isolated a girl may be, if the therapist adheres to the present and points to a hopeful future and, in cases like Maria's, expands her initial involvement into a series of involvements as soon as possible, great changes can take place. Here the need for group therapy was critical for there she could gain strength from relating to more responsible girls and could see how she might emulate their more responsible behavior. Through our persistence Maria, perhaps for the first time in her life, was able to fulfill her needs.

From her good relationship with her housemother, Maria was able to go to a work home where her hard work and love for children were deeply appreciated. Later she married and our assistant superintendent has several pictures of Maria's growing and successful family in her "grandchildren" picture gallery.[12]

Group Therapy with Offenders

Virtually every correctional institution for criminals and delinquents now has some form of group therapy included in its program. Some programs are therapist-centered; that is, the therapist attempts to treat each member of the group individually or together but does not intentionally use the members of the group to help one another. Other programs are group-centered. In such groups, the therapist considers every member of the group to be a therapeutic agent for every other member. Guided group interaction, the method used at Highfield, is a group-centered method. Here the group is treated as an interactional unit. Some groups are psychoanalytically oriented, with the therapist seeking to give individual members of the group insight into their problems from a psychoanalytic point of view. Others are spontaneous and free and encourage members of the group to develop spontaneity.

---

[12] Glasser, *Reality Therapy*, pp. 80–82.

Psychodrama and role training are action methods designed to develop spontaneity and to modify illegal behavior.

In individual therapy sessions, an offender can rationalize, distort, or simply lie about what is taking place. However, in group therapy all members must necessarily be aware that their description of the group process is subject to a wider commentary and audience. Group methods, therefore, usually have broader impact than individual methods. An interesting anecdote that partially illustrates this point, with special reference to social control, was described by Richard Korn in an article on a group therapy program that he directed in Vermont. Two youths, both members of the same therapy group, found some money on the grounds of the institution. Both knew that if they kept the money, one or the other, or both, might discuss the find in the group session. If they accepted the need to tell the truth in their therapy, they were confronted with a role conflict, and one or both might "cop out," tell the truth on the other. This group process produces an open situation that tends to merge the prison underworld with its more formal structure.

In addition to blending the subculture of the institution with its upper world, group therapy also opens up the therapist's activity to wider inspection and more critical analysis, not only by peers, but by clients. What the therapist does in group sessions is much more open to discussion than what a therapist does in an individual therapy situation. The process of group therapy, therefore, presents the possibility for much greater impact than individual therapy, not only upon offenders, but also upon staff and the total social system of the institution.

In dyadic therapeutic interaction (single therapist–single patient), two personalities who may be far apart in intellectual abilities attempt to communicate about one of the individual's problems (usually the offender's). Generally speaking, therapists tend to come from a different sociocultural milieu than criminals. Therapeutic communication may therefore be significantly impaired. This is not necessarily the case in group therapy. Those in group therapy are (by definition) in interaction with others who have comparable levels of understanding and usually a similar set of difficulties.

In group therapy, criminals become co-therapists with each other, and this seems to increase the potentiality of group understanding. Often in group psychotherapy, offenders who have difficulty interpreting and diagnosing their own problems are experts vis-à-vis their fellows. In fact, many sociopaths, generally considered the most difficult type of criminal to treat, are excellent diagnosticians and interpreters of the problems of other criminals. Sociopaths can thus be enlisted as effective co-therapists, and this sometimes has a positive effect on their own behavior.

In comparing group therapy with individual therapy (formal psychoanalysis in particular), one finds that the average offender's educational background and intellectual abilities are more adaptively geared to the group process. In psychoanalysis with offenders, for example, the therapist may develop excellent and appropriate formulations about the offender's problem. However, the analyst may have considerable difficulty inducing the offender to understand himself or herself in the same way that the psychoanalyst thinks he or she understands the criminal. In group psychotherapy, which tends to operate on a less sophisticated intellectual level, the offender, with other offenders as co-therapists, is more likely to develop insights and understanding of his or her behavior beneficial to treatment. The offender can thus relearn behavior patterns on an emotional and action level in the group process, rather than being required to attempt an intellectual analysis that may be foreign to accustomed thought processes.

PSYCHODRAMA AS A GROUP THERAPY METHOD

Psychodrama was first created by Dr. J. L. Moreno in Vienna in 1910. He introduced the technique into the field of corrections in the United States in 1931. It has been used continuously since that time in various psychiatric and correctional institutions for offenders.

Psychodrama

Psychodrama is an exploration by dramatic methods of the relationships a person has to others and the problems he encounters in his relationships. It may be viewed as an experimental procedure in which the individual may observe his relationship with others and manipulate them for any socio-analytic purpose. He may in the course of a psychodrama recognize the existence of problems; he may also become aware of alternative solutions to problems and experiment with possible choices between alternatives. In the course of these experiments he may examine several possible responses of others to each course of action upon which he embarks.

The director begins the session by a "warming up" process in which he helps the group to select a protagonist, the person around whose problems the session will revolve. The protagonist is asked to be himself on the stage and to enact situations in which he was involved in the past, is involved in at present, or anticipates for the future. He is urged to choose scenes involving his relationships to others. The choice of enactment is left to him. Some forms of enactment commonly selected are:

1. The reenactment of a past scene or situation.
2. The enactment of a problem that presently involves the individual with someone else in the group or with the director.
3. The enactment of a situation which one anticipates for the future. This is called a future projection.

The objective of psychodrama, and the techniques employed, is not to train the individual for theatrical excellence but to provide him with an opportunity to play himself in all sorts of relationships, particularly those in which he has experienced difficulties, and to experiment with different forms of behavior. Unsatisfying relationships may be explored in the laboratory situation provided by the psychodramatic stage, a director, his assistants (called auxiliary egos), and a psychodramatic group. The individual examines his social relationships in the *here and now*. He presents his view of them on the stage in the presence of and with the help of other members of his psychodrama group led by the director. Members of the group are encouraged to refer to their experiences in dealing with similar problems and the difficulties they encountered.

Role perception and skill in role enactment develop hand in hand. Because our culture does not define roles with sufficient precision to provide all the answers for satisfactory performance in them, some degree of spontaneity or creativity is necessary to meet situations which had not been anticipated in the culture. As the individual becomes more secure in action he becomes more spontaneous. Thus, participation in psychodrama should result in an increase in spontaneity.[13]

Reducing Aggressive Behavior with Psychodrama

John G. Hill, a correctional counselor in a Los Angeles County probation camp, describes the rationale for and the methodology of using psychodrama to reduce aggressive behavior in an institution. Hill's approach has value for correcting the prison gang problem and thereby reducing violence in prisons:

> One of the major problems faced by correctional counselors in the care and treatment of . . . offenders in the institutional setting is that of the aggressive, assaultive ward. He presents unique difficulties in terms of control and adaptability especially in the group living situation, and as his behavior directly affects the behavior of his peers, his negative acting out exerts undue pressures upon the group as a whole. . . .
>
> With these thoughts in mind the possibility of utilizing psychodrama as a treatment tool in dealing with the aggressive ward became readily apparent based on four major assumptions.
>
> 1. Aggressive and assaultive impulses could be channeled in a controlled monitored setting allowing full expression without the danger of physical injury.
> 2. Motives behind these impulses could be explored in a manner readily visible to the wards involved.
> 3. Immediate catharsis could be achieved, reducing the probability of uncontrolled aggression and pressure in the group living situation.
> 4. Precipitating problems could be alleviated, examined, and explored as they occurred by a restaging of the problem in a psychodramatic setting.

---

[13] Martin R. Haskell, *An Introduction to Socioanalysis* (Long Beach, Calif.: California Institute of Socioanalysis, 1967), pp. 11–12. For a further discussion of psychodrama, see Lewis Yablonsky, *Psychodrama* (New York: Gardner Press, 1989).

An examination of the case of David M. will serve as an example of the process in action. David M. is a Mexican-American youth of seventeen years, committed to Camp Fenner for murder. He is a large, heavyset boy, intensively gang oriented. His case file reveals a record of seventeen arrests ranging from assaults and robberies to the committing offense.

David entered "A" dormitory reluctantly. His initial reaction to camp was negative in the extreme. Within three hours of entering the program he had managed to alienate virtually everyone in the dormitory, staff and peers alike. His answer to every reasonable request was a resounding obscenity. The consensus of opinion by staff was that David should be removed to a security or "lock up" facility as soon as possible. This would probably have been initiated in short order had he not become involved in an incident with the reigning Chicano in the dorm, Leon, a member of a rival gang. Staff intervened before blows were struck and David and six other wards were taken to the office for counseling. . . .

It was felt that the psychodramatic approach might prove effective in this case, and the transition from encounter group to psychodrama was made by setting the stage for a reenactment of the confrontation between David and Leon. Initially an *auxiliary ego* staff member played the part of Leon to alleviate the bad emotional climate.

David was seated in a chair facing Staff, who assumed the *role* of the *other*, Leon.

> *David:* You bastards (indicating the group as a whole) are always messin' with me.
> *Staff:* Man, you come walking in here like *vato loco* [a crazy person] trying to prove how tough you are, what do you expect?

David does a double take and demands to know who Staff is. Is he to be a staff or is he supposed to be Leon? The ground rules are repeated, indicating that what we are trying to accomplish is to relive the incident so that we can see what the problem is.

> *David:* How come that punk [indicating Leon] don't do it himself?

Leon becomes visibly agitated and starts to get out of his chair. He is waved back. Staff explains that because of the charged atmosphere and raw feelings a substitute for Leon is being used. David is to regard Staff as Leon for purposes of the psychodrama and respond to him accordingly. The initial confrontation is reviewed with the wards explaining that David had challenged Leon and that Leon had reacted by questioning David's right to enter the dormitory as a new boy and throw his weight around. Staff, assuming the *role* of Leon, picked it up from there.

> *Staff:* How come you think you're such a badass? You can't come walking in here talking all that crap and shoving people around. You better get your act together.
> *David:* Screw you, man! You don't tell Mad Dog what to do or not to do!
> *Staff:* Mad dog? Mad dog? They usually put mad dogs to sleep. What does that mean, Mad Dog? Everyone here knows where dogs come from.

Leon laughs from the sidelines as David balls up his fists and glares about him.

> *David:* I'm going to waste you. . . . [This is directed toward the vacant space halfway between Staff and Leon.]

The interchange continues for some minutes and is evidently a source of some satisfaction to David who begins to relax as he realizes that he can express himself verbally without fear of physical retaliation. Another ward, James, a black who has been in obvious delight over the exchange, is moved into position next to David to act as his *double*.

> *Staff:* [Continuing] I don't know how a punk like you stayed alive on the outs. . . .
> *David:* [Reddening at this reflection on his manhood, struggles with himself for a moment before answering]. . . . You ain't nothing at all unless you got your homeboys around.

At this point James, who has obviously been anxious to participate, interjects as David's *double*—helping David to present himself more effectively.

> *James* [As David]: Yeah, you think you runnin' this dorm, tellin' everybody what to do all the time. You think you cool but you ain't crap!

David is somewhat taken aback at the unexpected support he has found and warms to his role. He begins to reflect on his statements, picking up cues from James.

> *David:* Yeah, how come when I come in here you all of a sudden start giving orders? You ain't no better than me even if you been here longer. . . .

Leon now enters the session to play himself. The interchange between the two boys was now taking place in fairly normal tones as Leon, having vented his personal feelings from the group, begins dealing with David on the level of a person of authority trying to reason with a recalcitrant underling. David was resisting this process by pointedly ignoring Leon's arguments and discussing his own feelings of right and justice. While he played the *role* of wronged party with obvious relish it was apparent that he had little or no insight at this point into his role in the problem.

Staff suggested that the wards physically exchange places and Leon play the *role* of David while David assume the *part* of Leon. Both boys initially balked at the idea of role reversal but at the urging of others in the group reluctantly exchanged seats. Leon was the first to begin the dialogue. He assumed an exaggerated stance of braggadocio, fists clenched and lips drawn back. He stared defiantly at David.

> *Leon:* [As David] You ain't gonna tell me what to do!

David was obviously struggling at this point, not sure of how he should react. Then, apparently remembering Leon's tirade against him, launched into a vituperative monologue which continued for some minutes despite Leon's attempts to interrupt. The other members of the group seemed to be enjoying the performance immensely.

When David finally ran out of words Staff asked him what he was feeling at that moment.

> *David:* I don't know man, but I really got pissed off. . . It made me feel like just kicking him and going off on him.
> *Staff:* Do you want to go off on him now?
> *David:* Yeh, yeh I do!
> *Staff:* [Handing David a towel] Okay, hit the desk with this. Hit the desk like it was Leon.

David takes the towel and tentatively hits the desk; once, twice, three times. Then he knots the end and brings it crashing down a half a dozen times.

> *Staff:* Who are you hitting, David?
> *David:* Him, Leon, the Flores.
> *Staff:* [Turning to the *audience*] What's happening here?
> *Jerry:* It seem to me that he's getting pissed off at Leon for doing the same thing to him that he did to Leon.
> *Mike:* I think he's pissed off at himself.
> *Staff:* [To David] What do you think about that?
> *David:* I don't know what you're talking about.
> *Leon:* Look man, I was doing the same thing you were doing from the first minute you walked in here. So maybe you can see how you was coming off.

David struggles with this concept for a moment, then crashes the towel violently against the desk.

> *David:* You guys don't know crap!

David does not say this too convincingly, however. The rest of the group have had a glimpse of the truth and immediately begin to belabor the point.

> *Steve:* Hey man, maybe you got angry because you know the way it really is. Maybe you better face it instead of copping out.
> *Jerry:* [Changing allegiance] Yeah, don't seem like you can take what you was giving out.
> *Leon:* I don't know, sometimes it's hard to be real. I mean to really see yourself. (He reflects for a moment.) When I was on the outs . . . when I was a kid, I got into fights all the time . . . everybody thought I was crazy, even my parents. I was in the hospital maybe five or six times. When I was fifteen I got shot and everybody thought I was going to die. When I got back on the streets I was a big man. I was tough. Then I started thinking how weird it was that it took almost getting killed and having a hole in my side to make me a person of respect. Anyway, now I had my rep and didn't have to go around personally going off on people. Sure, I done some gang banging but most of the time since then I kept laid back out of sight. I got things I want to do. I got a *vieja* and a kid. I

guess I know what David feels like. I guess he still got to make his rep.
He's just not going about it the right way. Going off on *vatos* in camp
ain't gonna make it. That way somebody going to do him when he gets
back on the street. We all got to get along here and do our time the best
way we can. We got to stick together. When I was sitting here doing his
trip I was getting next to how he was feeling. I guess because I been
there myself.

Leon has appeared to have lost all his animosity, and during the course
of his soliloquy David listened intently. David seemed surprised that Leon
expressed empathy with his feeling, especially in view of the towel incident.
He was having difficulty in controlling his tears.

Staff: [To David] Okay, how are you feeling now?
David: I don't know man. I don't know how I'm feeling. I feel all
washed out. I feel like I don't give a damn about anything. I'm tired.
Leon: You got to get with it. You were talking that everyone was down
on you without giving you a chance. Well it seems to me that you were
down on everybody without giving us a chance.
David: I don't know. With the *putos* on the street you got to get them
before they get you, you know that, otherwise they walk all over you. I
know you got homeboys here but no one is going to walk over me.
Leon: Okay, no one is going to walk over you here as long as you take
care of business. There's too many dudes out there that want to see us
firing on each other. You're just going to make it harder on yourself and
the rest of us unless you're cool.
David: [Shaking his head to indicate doubt, reflects for a moment
then tentatively holds out his hand. He finds it hard to meet Leon's
eye.] Okay, okay. I'm sorry about the towel, huh? I guess I was pretty
pissed off.

Leon takes David's hand and shakes it firmly, making the comment that
he can clearly see why they call him Mad Dog. At this point David has some
recognition of responsibility to the group.

For David the psychodrama was both a catharsis and an initiation into the
group living setting of "A" dormitory. While the session could not be
considered a panacea for David's problems it did provide the initial step
which allowed him to remain in the program instead of being transferred to
maximum security prison. Perhaps most important, for the first time, it
allowed him to see himself as others saw him; the beginnings of insight.[14]

The foregoing examples were cases handled in an institutional
setting. In my work with violent gangs, I often used role playing on a
continuing basis and in crisis situations. Gang life moves so fast that it is
not possible to wait until gang members are apprehended and placed in
an institution. To prevent crime, one must respond to emergencies. In

---

[14] John G. Hill, "Reducing Aggressive Behavior in the Institutional Setting through
Psychodrama," *Group Psychotherapy, Psychodrama, and Sociometry,* ed. Zerka T.
Moreno, vol. 48 (June 1977):83. Reprinted by permission.

the following account, the underlying theory and elements of a psychodrama session (warm-up, action, and postdiscussion) are applied to (1) an immediate "live" problem (2) of an "emergency" nature, (3) in the "open community," that (4) emerged unexpectedly:

A disturbed gang leader, accompanied by two friends, accosted me as I was walking down the street, pulled out a switchblade knive, and announced that he was on his way to kill a youth who lived in a nearby neighborhood on the upper west side of Manhattan. I moved into action armed with a psychodramatic approach.

First, I was prepared for this emergency-possibility, since on a continuing basis I had made sociometric tests which revealed the relationships of various gangs and gang networks in the area. I knew the gangs that were feuding and the leadership patterns of each group. More than that, the youth facing me already had had previous exposure to psychodrama; this was helpful, as we could move right into action. In short, the groundwork was set for this emergency use of psychodrama.

I asked myself: why did the youth stop me before he want to stab the other youth? I suspected the chances were good that he really did not want to commit this violence and wanted me to help him find a way out.

The "Ape," as this boy was called by the gang, was openly defiant and upset. His opening remark was:

"Man, I'm packin'; I got my blade (switch-blade knife) right here. I'm going to cut the s_____ out of those m_____ f_____ Dragons. I'm going up and get them now . . . once and for all."

In short, he had a knife and was going to stab any Dragon gang boys he met that day. It was also reasonable to assume that he would stab any youth who, in his hysterical judgment, was a Dragon.

The boys followed me to my nearby office and the session began with the use of another gang boy as an auxiliary ego in the role of the potential victim. A paper ruler replaced the knife (for obvious reasons), and the "killing" was acted out in my office under controlled psychodramatic conditions.

The psychodrama, in brief, had all of the elements of a real gang killing. The Ape (the subject) cursed, fumed, threatened, and shouted at the victim, who hurled threats and insults in return. Ape worked himself into a frenzy and then stabbed the auxiliary ego (the gang boy playing the part) with the paper knife. The psychodramatic victim fell dead on the floor.

The Ape was then confronted with the consequences of his act in all of its dimensions, including the effect on his family. He began to regret what he had done and was particularly remorseful when (psychodramatically) an auxiliary ego playing the role of a court judge sentenced him "to death in the electric chair."

The psychodrama accomplished at least two things for this very potential killer: (1) He no longer was motivated to kill, since he had already accomplished this psychodramatically. (2) He was confronted with the consequences of this rash act; this was an added dimension of consideration. Many gang boys are unable to think ahead in a situation to the outcome. These factors possibly served as a deterrent to the actual commission of a murder. Of course, this boy required and received further therapy, which sought to deal with his more basic personality problems. Moreover, considerably more work was attempted on the gang networks, so as to minimize their potential for violence. However, the emergency psychodrama, *in situ*, the immediate situation, did deter the possibility of Ape's committing a homicide, at least on that particular day.[15]

Group psychotherapy and psychodrama provide the opportunity for actual direct role training. Here offenders can view themselves and others by presenting their problems for group discussion and analysis. More than that, they are in a position to correct (or edit) their illegal actions in the presented situations. The offender can try out or practice legally conforming roles in the presence of criminal "experts," who quickly detect whether a member is conning the group or playing it straight. In a role-playing session in which offenders were being trained for future employment, for example, one offender (who was soon to be released from prison) went through the motions of getting a job with apparent disinterest. This fact was quickly and forcefully brought out in the open by other members of the group, producing a valuable discussion on the basic need of employment for going straight. In another session I observed a violent offender learn to control his assaultive impulse by talking about, rather than acting out, his wish to assault a member of the group. He learned to talk about violent impulses rather than assault first and discuss later.

A characteristic of group treatment, therefore, is that it provides an opportunity for violent offenders to talk or act out their illegal motivations in a controlled setting. After acting out their destructive impulses in the session, they may no longer have the need to carry them out in reality. The group also gives offenders and their peer co-therapists an opportunity to assess the meaning of violence through discussion. An empathic group can help the violent offender understand compulsive emotions. Among other things, these people learn they are not alone in their feelings.

Many offenders have difficulty controlling immediate compulsions for future goals. They tend to live in the moment and often lack the ability to relate the past to the present, the present to the future. The thought of future punishment or past experience doesn't usually enter their conscious deliberations to serve as a deterrent to illegal action. Training in understanding time dimensions is therefore often useful in crime prevention.

Psychodrama as a group process provides such time flexibility. The offender can act out the past, immediate, or expected problem situations

---

[15] Lewis Yablonsky, "Sociopathology of the Violent Gang and Its Treatment," in *Progress in Psychotherapy*, eds. Jules H. Masserman and J. L. Moreno (New York: Grune & Stratton, 1956–1960), vol. 5, *Reviews and Integrations* (1960), pp. 167–168. Reprinted by permission.

that are disturbing him. The process is useful in working with criminals who manifest impulsive behavior. Psychodrama, in particular the "future-projection technique," by means of which a person propels himself or herself into a future situation, provides an opportunity for the offender to plan for a legally conforming future. This technique has been used with offenders about to be released into the open community, to project them into relevant future social situations in which they will find themselves. These role-test situations include potential problems in the community, on the job, with the family, with supervising probation officers, and others.

The role-training process tends to build up the offender's resistance to efforts on the part of delinquent friends to seduce the person back into criminal activity. Psychodrama provides an opportunity for the "immediate-situation-oriented" offender to review past and future behavior with its many implications for resisting criminal activity. To the offender with con-artist or sociopathic characteristics, words are cheap. Considerable research indicates that it is very difficult to lie in action during psychodrama. Because group pressures make distortion so difficult, the offender is forced to assess personal behavior and its rationale closely. This, combined with opportunities to try out legally conforming behavior patterns before such severe judges as one's peers, helps the offender to reexamine and reject past illegal behavior patterns and learn socially conforming practices.

The total array of treatment processes described in this chapter—including community programs, probation, and parole, individual therapy, group therapy, and psychodrama—constitutes a significant body of treatment methodologies for effectively treating criminal offenders.

Chapter 17

The Correctional System: Prisons

*A*ll societies have institutionalized systems for responding to and attempting to control crime and delinquency. In Western societies, traditional systems are the police, courts, and various methods of supervising and treating offenders in the community, including the use of probation and parole. The avowed basic objective of most of these community responses to crime and delinquency is the prevention of crime and delinquency and the ultimate resocialization of offenders. When a convicted criminal is considered to be incapable of functioning in the larger society, or it is believed that the offender requires punitive and rehabilitative efforts to control and modify behavior, he or she is placed in a correctional custodial institution, which in reality is a prison.

BASIC FUNCTIONS OF THE CORRECTIONAL SYSTEM

When a person has been found guilty of violating a law and is turned over to a correctional system, the criminal justice system has, through its authorized agents, decided that

1. The individual's behavior will be more or less closely supervised for a period of time.
2. The individual is to be deprived of some or all of his or her liberty for a period of time.
3. Some change in the person's values, attitudes, and behavior is desirable.
4. This experience with the correctional system will make the person less likely to violate laws in the future.

The correctional system may thus be seen as having three basic functions: (1) protective, (2) punitive, and (3) rehabilitative.

The Protective Function: Incapacitating the Offender

The correctional system is assigned the function of protecting society from the actions of those people whose behavior or potential behavior is believed to be dangerous to the person or property of others. We do not screen our population to isolate such people for this treatment. When the court convicts an individual of a serious offense, a presentencing investigation often reveals personality characteristics that make the offender a threat to others. Many criminals are confined in prison for long periods on the assumption that they are a menace to society when at liberty. The custodial institution, at least temporarily, serves the function of incapacitating the offender.

What is not generally recognized is that any form of supervision in the community also can perform a protective function. Probation or parole supervision helps to protect society by setting limits on the activity of an individual and discouraging behavior that might be dangerous to the person or property of others. To be sure, an individual cannot be supervised as strictly in the community as in prison. The question that must be raised with respect to each person sentenced is: How much supervision is necessary if society is to be adequately protected? A corollary question is: How dangerous is this person? Obviously, we need greater protection from the potential attacks of an aggressive sociopath than we do from a "normal" individual who has committed burglaries, larcenies, or other property offenses to take care of immediate needs or even as a career. While probation or parole may not be as effective in performing the protective function with career criminals, we must consider that it may be far more effective than the prison in performing a rehabilitative function (by getting the probationer or parolee a job, additional training, etc.).

The Punitive Function

In primitive societies, when it was believed that the criminal was possessed by the devil, punishment was administered to exorcise the devil or to exile or execute the wrongdoer. This was done in part to protect the society from further outrages by the dangerous offender, but it was done also to *placate the gods*. In the Hebrew tribes, beginning with the Law of Moses, punishment was a means of substituting collective vengeance for individual or family vengeance. This use of criminal law, which in a theocracy was also religious law, combined the concepts of sin and crime and established punishment as social vengeance. The medieval Christian church continued this practice in a modified form by emphasizing the doctrine of free will. Since individuals were free to act as they pleased, their behavior and destinies were in their own hands. The church popularized the notion that sin and crime were dangerous to the group and hateful to God. By this theory, the individual could choose to be an exemplary citizen and escape punishment here or hereafter, or the person could be immoral or criminal and *deserve* to be punished. The wrongdoer must suffer punishment to *atone* for sins and crimes and thus gain salvation. In the middle of the eighteenth century, Cesare Beccaria made recommendations that provided the basis of the classical system of criminology. Essential to that system was the idea that punishment could be justified only as a deterrent to the commission of crime and not as a means of providing social revenge. Enrico Ferri, a leading exponent of this school, proposed in 1921 that all concepts of punishment and notions of retribution for moral culpability be eliminated. Punishment should be used only to deter. From this point of view, the more severe the punishment, the greater the deterrent power. Thus, probation would provide some deterrent; imprisonment a greater deterrent, with increasing deterrent power as length of sentence increased; and finally, capital punishment would provide the maximum deterrent power.[1]

Punishment is not currently considered a central technique for controlling crime. Yet a spirit of retaliation exists in most societies, and it is difficult to erase. The basic goals of punishment as specifically employed in the correctional field are twofold. One alleged function of punishment is to deter future crime on the part of the individual punished. A second is, as Emile Durkheim has indicated, to reinforce the existing norms by demonstrating to the larger society that there is a response to deviance. It is assumed that punishment gives the law-abiding members of society a greater sense of solidarity and cohesion.

In summary, therefore, punishment has some deterrent impact on offenders, validates the norms, and gives the larger society a sense of solidarity.

The concept of punishment as a deterrent poses a debatable question. The degree to which the threat or imposition of punishment on an individual actually affects future behavior differs from person to person. Several speculations, unsupported by hard research evidence, are in order:

1. Crimes of passion are less apt to be controlled by punishment than crimes involving clear monetary gain. Thus, for example, an individual assaulting someone in a fit of rage is less likely to consider the consequence of the act than a burglar, who may take into account the penalty for the crime before committing it.

---

[1] Harry Elmer Barnes and Negley K. Teeters, *New Horizons in Criminology* (New York: Prentice-Hall, 1945), pp. 391–404, contains an excellent discussion of the history of punishment for crime.

2. The individual's status or position in the community may affect the deterrent power of punishment. It is logical to assume that someone who is wealthy and living the "good life" has more to lose by punishment (especially deprivation of freedom) than someone who is poor and living a marginal existence. The threat of punishment is more likely to control the person with high status than to control the person in a lower socioeconomic position.

3. The possibility of swift and certain punishment is more likely to control criminal behavior than a fuzzy and delayed reaction to crime. When there is a long period between the crime and the punishment, the offender is less likely to link the two factors together.

4. The amount and degree of punishment should be administered to offenders as equitably as possible. Otherwise the individuals who are "unjustly" punished may well become embittered recidivists.

Punishment to Deter   The principal justification for punishment at the present time is to deter the person punished from engaging in criminal activity again and, by making an example of the person punished, to deter others from committing the act. Yet even Beccaria had reservations. He pointed out, for example, that the deterrence was not guaranteed by the severity of punishment but rather by the certainty and speed with which it was administered. Most people who commit crimes do not expect to get caught. The data gathered by the FBI and published in the 1987 *Uniform Crime Reports* confirm this judgment. Only about 20 percent of the serious crimes known to the police are cleared by arrest. Furthermore, fewer than half of those cleared by arrest are prosecuted, and only about half the prosecutions result in someone being imprisoned. The odds are about 20 to 1 against a crime known to the police resulting in a prison sentence. If we consider that the experts estimate that two or three times as many crimes are committed as are known to the police, then the odds are still higher. The people betting on horse races or at the gambling tables in Las Vegas would love to have such odds in their favor. How can the prospect of punishment deter when it is so uncertain? Yet some of our public officials, faced with high crime rates, continue to advocate increased severity of punishment. For example, in 1989, the Bush administration's director of drug policy, William Bennett, advocated the suspension of certain citizens' civil rights in the war on drugs. The ACLU and other civil rights organizations vigorously dissented with Bennett's extreme position. There is evidence that punishment does deter certain individuals from perpetrating certain crimes; however, punishment alone is insufficient to control crime effectively.

The Rehabilitative Function

When the penitentiary system in the United States was first advocated in Pennsylvania in 1829, it was considered fundamental that education and religious instruction should go hand in hand if a prisoner was to be reformed. Aside from religious instruction through "moral instruction," there was no formal educational instruction in the Pennsylvania penitentiary until 1845. Even then education was introduced because it was considered an important force in reformation, and recreation was considered important as an essential part of education. It soon became apparent, however, that if the inmates were to succeed in the community they had to be rehabilitated. That is, they had to acquire skills that would help them to find employment in the community.

Prison work programs did not help much in that direction. Most work programs were introduced into the prisons as a form of punishment. Even the sentences reflected this purpose. A criminal was sentenced to "confinement at hard labor." The work, whatever was assigned, was intended as punishment. Later on, when introduced by the Quakers, hard labor was viewed as useful in reform. The prisoner was developing good work habits.

When prisons began to assume a rehabilitative function, they improved their educational programs and their vocational training programs. In the twentieth century, education came to be seen as both reformative and rehabilitative. The clearly reformative aim was to induce the inmate to adopt goals and attitudes in accord with those of society. The clearly rehabilitative aim was to develop skills, understanding, and knowledge that would enable the individual to perform the ordinary duties of every efficient citizen. This led to the emphasis on vocational education. A typical prison, for example, offered instruction in barbering, carpentry, masonry, tailoring, machine shop, printing, arithmetic, and grammar. Virtually all prisons have some rehabilitation programs offering some training. Yet very little is accomplished. A convict in the midst of a psychodrama session involving convicts, judges, and correctional staff put it rather succinctly when he said, "Let's get one thing straight, baby, I've heard a lot of talk about rehabilitation from you people here, but I've never seen any in jail. I was a laborer when I came in and the only thing I learned is how to make license plate tags. I'll go out for six months, but I'll be back."

Most prisons do provide instruction in occupations related to work in the community. However, this is inadequate or incomplete as rehabilitation unless parole supervision in the community is effective. Even a prisoner who taught a trade needs help in getting employment and in handling relationships with employers. Prisoners may also need help in developing meaningful relationships with their families and with others in the community. Some of this is provided by psychologists and social workers in prison, and some by parole agents in the community.

Some research evidence reveals that in terms of financial costs it is less expensive to keep criminals in prison than to attempt to rehabilitate them in the community. A 1988 United States Department of Justice study stated that it is cheaper to build new prisons and jails than to relieve overcrowding in penal facilities by releasing repeat offenders. The cost of building a new cell and maintaining a prisoner in it is $25,000 a year, according to the study by the department's National Institute of Justice, but new crimes committed by each released prisoner cost society an estimated $430,000 a year in victims' losses, police and court work, and private security expenses. The study of 2,190 inmates in California, Michigan, and Texas stated that each repeat offender given early release committed an average of 187 crimes a year. The institute treated each drug deal as a separate crime. Sentencing 1,000 additional offenders to prison each year would have required about $25 million a year but would have averted 187,000 felonies that cost society a total of $430 million, according to the study.

THE PRISON POPULATION

The percentage of Americans in prison has more than doubled since 1970. According to the Justice Department, there were over 600,000 inmates in state and federal prisons as of June, 1989.

This imprisonment surge has been assailed as neither effective nor affordable. Such doubts have helped bring on experiments with such alternatives as confining a convict at home with electronic monitoring and a reconsideration of some of the harsher sentencing approaches developed over the last 15 years.

But despite yearly prison construction costs of more than $1 billion and desperate overcrowding throughout the nation's prisons, the widespread fear of crime makes a dramatic shift downward in the prison population unlikely. In fact, new federal sentencing guidelines are expected to add to the prisoner population. A study released by the National Conference on Crime and Delinquency projected a 21 percent increase in the prison population by 1992.

If only because of cost constraints, many states across the nation are grappling with alternatives to prison. Some states have decided that the harshest mandatory sentencing plans developed over the last decade are too inflexible to be effective. There is particular interest in state sentencing commissions such as one used in Minnesota, which adjusts prison terms to reflect available prison space.

The battle in the justice system over imprisonment has crystallized. On one side are calls for "lock 'em up" justice and contentions that any reported moderation in crime rates partly reflects the numbers of criminals behind bars. On the other side there is a growing concern about the devastating costs and questionable long-term results of the historic increase in imprisonment.

The movement toward increasing prison sentences and putting more criminals behind bars toward the end of the twentieth century is related to a more callous attitude toward criminals and an increased fear of them by the general law-abiding public. This attitude by the general public is, in part, fueled by the recent increases in violent behavior by young adult offenders. There is a trend toward incarceration of these young offenders, most of whom go on later in life to do time in adult prisons.

The Institutionalization of Violent Youths

Research reveals that increasing numbers of violent youths (including many members of violent gangs) are being placed in correctional institutions. A 1987 Justice Department study of violent young offenders determined that nearly 39 percent of the 18,226 juveniles in long-term youth correctional institutions were jailed for violent crimes, and that nearly three out of five used drugs regularly.

The study was based on interviews with a nationally representative sample of 2,621 residents in long-term, state-operated juvenile institutions. The interviews were conducted in 50 facilities in 26 states. In the sample, 52.5 percent of the individuals were white, 41.4 percent black, and about 14.5 percent Hispanic. The rest were American Indians, Asians, Alaskan natives, or Pacific Islanders.

The study revealed that more than half of those who used drugs said that they began by the age of 14. Nearly a quarter of the group reported using drugs such as heroin, cocaine, PCP, or LSD. The study also found that a large percentage of these youths had long delinquent histories. Almost 43 percent of the juveniles had been arrested more than five times. Almost 60 percent had been committed to a correctional institution at least once before their current confinement.

The study also found that nearly 41 percent of those convicted of a violent offense had used a weapon while committing their crimes. Nearly one in five of those held for violent offenses used a gun. The majority of the violent offenses committed were robbery and assault.

The research also found that many of the young adult offenders had criminal histories that were just as extensive as those of adults in state prisons. For example, more than half of the young adults surveyed—as well as a comparable sample of state prisoners—were found to be incarcerated for violent offenses. Among the juveniles, 57.5 percent said that they had a current violent offense, had been on probation previously, or had been incarcerated at least once for a violent crime.

The Justice Department report also indicated a high incidence of broken homes and poor education: nearly 72 percent of the juveniles interviewed said that they had not grown up with both parents. (In contrast, a 1986 study found that nearly 74 percent of the nation's estimated 62.8 million children were reported to be living with both parents.) Only 41.7 percent of the juveniles and young adults between the ages of 15 and 17 in correctional facilities had finished more than eight years of school. More than 76 percent of this age group in the general population had completed more than eight years of school.

The research further noted that more than half the juveniles and young adults in correctional institutions reported that a family member had served time in jail or prison. Almost 25 percent said their fathers had been incarcerated in the past year.

In the study, the young offenders claimed to be influenced by their friends. Many reported that their friends had committed crimes such as smuggling, selling drugs, burglary, stealing cars, shoplifting, and selling stolen property. An estimated 62 percent of the offenders were with others when they committed the offense for which they were currently incarcerated.

The Prison Community Structure

Prisons remain dominantly organized as custodial systems for people, despite the fact that most institutions attempt to institute some occupational or treatment programs. A castelike system exists, with inmates frozen in position. Prisoners can obviously never aspire to rise above the status of inmate as long as they remain in the institution. This fact tends to inhibit motivation toward personal growth and development. The emphasis is clearly custodial. The prison system that Donald Clemmer described over 30 years ago has not changed a great deal. He wrote:

> With only slight changes the same body of rules has been in use for over fifteen years. Excepting those ordinances which deal with the cleanliness of institutions, the basic thought in every rule is to prevent riots and escapes. The attitude of the officials that the essential purpose of the prison is incapacitation is traditional. When new officials take office they are in communication for weeks or months with the employees they are to replace. There is sufficient time to indoctrinate the neophyte employee. Even if the tradition was not transferred from officer to officer, newly appointed workers would hold to the orientation that the purpose of prison is incapacitation and retribution, having assimilated these ideations from a society in which they are prevalent.[2]

In the large correctional institution, most inmates have meaningful communication and relationships (if any) only with other inmates. The castelike system inhibits really meaningful communication between inmates and custodial personnel. When significant relationships begin to develop between inmates and professional persons, custodial staff members tend to fear that their authority will be undermined. The dilemma created by these two antithetical sets of relationships has been cogently described by Richard Korn and Lloyd McCorkle:

---

[2] Donald Clemmer, *The Prison Community* (New York: Holt, Rinehart and Winston, 1958), p. 183.

The total result of the interacting trends and processes . . . has been to isolate the confined offender from socially beneficial contact with individuals outside the inmate social world and to prevent the formation of relationship bonds which might redefine him as an acceptable member of the noncriminal community. This is the major dilemma of penology.

The writers see little possibility of a resolution of this dilemma within the universally prevailing context of a large institutional approach. Large institutions (walled and unwalled) are dependent on the development of a bureaucratic apparatus based on formal structuring of human relationships. This formal structuring, which is required for the efficient and secure operation of the large institution, is in turn dependent on the maintenance of a social distance which sets crippling limits on contact with members of the official community—the only available representatives of the larger society. Where these limits have been redefined—as in the case of the professional worker—the results, to date, have largely been supportive to the inmate social system and have contributed to the weakening of measures of control.[3]

There are more treatment programs in our correctional institutions than ever before. The number of teachers, psychologists, social workers, and other professionals has, therefore, gone up to some extent. Nevertheless, the control of virtually every one of our prisons is in the hands of people who emphasize custody. This is true not only because the philosophy of prison administrators is punitive but also because the public has been educated to demand custody. I was present in a prison from 1:00 to 2:30 P.M. while a head count of some 3,000 inmates was conducted again and again in an effort to locate an inmate who was missing at the 1:00 P.M. roll call. The prison—the Riker's Island Penitentiary, New York—was on an island completely surrounded by very deep, navigable waters. When the warden was asked why there was so much emphasis on custody and security, he replied: "If 500 inmates are rehabilitated at this penitentiary no one will ever know about it. If one man escapes it will make headlines." Unfortunately, the warden was right. An escaped convict loose in New York City might very well be the subject of headlines. Over half the 3,000 prisoners would be released on parole at some time during the year. Yet if even one inmate escaped, the warden might be considered to be at fault.

The relationship between treatment personnel and custodial personnel is lukewarm at best. Cooperation on paper is considerable; in reality it is minimal. The warden and his staff see their task as one primarily of custody. Rehabilitation and treatment are acceptable but must not interfere in any way with custody and security. The inmates try to play one against the other. Some prisoners cater to the guards and custodial people to obtain special privileges. They are rejected by the inmate

---

[3] Richard R. Korn and Lloyd W. McCorkle, "Resocialization Within Walls," *Annals of the American Academy of Political and Social Science* 293 (May 1954):97–98.

value system, particularly if they inform on other inmates. Informers are referred to as "stool pigeons" and "rats." However, those inmates who get good jobs in the prison by conning the treatment staff are looked up to. Those who get assigned to the classification section, records section, library, school, hospital, or other sections of the prison that offer work assignments considered "easy" are not rejected. Both staff members and other prisoners expect them to do favors for their fellow inmates. They all do favors for other prisoners, some at a price and some as a sign of identification and sympathy.

Prison Organization and the "Doing-Time" Problem

Meaningful rehabilitation in prison is often sabotaged by two dominant dimensions of the prison's social structure: first, the fact of the inmate underworld system, with its heavy emphasis on maintaining criminal values and behavior; and second, the overwhelming administrative theme of security and custody that dominates the prison's social structure and atmosphere.

Because of the complex and onerous conditions in prison, most inmates simply "do time." This central problem of the prison may be more clearly revealed by an analysis of the differential views of prisons. There are three main protagonists concerned with prisons: the inmate, the staff, and the public. The following soliloquies reflect a consensus of attitudes on the part of these three protagonists as they enter a contemporary correctional institution:

JOHN Q. PRISONER: Here I go again—back in stir. I thought I could make it this time, I wanted to stay clean, but I can't seem to help it. It was an easy mark and I should have made it without getting busted—but that's the breaks. . . . Well, five-to-ten won't be too rough this trip. I wonder who's still in. Things were working pretty smoothly with my old bunch when I left last time. I hope they're still here. Let's see—Jim is still in, and Joe. . . . I hear they're still trying that new program. That rehabilitation stuff is still B.S. for my money. What can they do for me? I began talking to the headshrinker last time, and each trip made me feel worse. Who needs it? . . . I'll do my time, no sweat, get out in two years, and go back into action. I can do two years standing on one foot.

JOHN Q. STAFF: Here I go again. I remember the first time I walked into this place ten years ago. I really had my mind made up—I was going to save the world. I thought everybody had some good in him, if you just knew how to bring it out, and I thought I had what it takes. But I soon wised up. . . . At first, when the older staff smiled at my ambitious ideas for helping the inmates square up, I could shrug it off. And when they called me aside and told me I was rocking the boat and "you can't help these punks anyway," I didn't pay much attention. . . . But then I began to feel as they did. These guys are impossible and you can't really change them. There are a few good ones—at least they behave themselves while they're here—but they always come back. Most of them are impossible hoods. The only place they'll straighten out is in a coffin. . . . Just the other day I had to take that new guard aside and wise him up on that score. What a dreamer! It's funny to have a new character like that around. He really acts like he can change some of these hoods. He'll learn! . . . We have to do our time, just like the prisoners. Of course, we get out evenings and weekends. But next morning we're right back in. We're doing time, just like them.

JOHN Q. PUBLIC: I've never visited one of these places before. Frankly, I really didn't want to come. I'm too busy these days at the office to take time off for this nonsense. But with all the other lodge members coming, I just couldn't refuse. Anyway, I always wanted to see whether these places really look like they do in the movies. . . . I must admit that I'm actually a little frightened. That prison riot they had last year was no picnic. You can't really change a criminal, so the least they can do is keep them under control. They should be locked in their cells and kept there. These places are turning into country clubs, from what I hear. I sometimes wonder where our tax money goes in these places. The least they can do is have these criminals do their time quietly.

The real problem in correctional institutions today is not only outmoded physical plants, undercut budgets, overcrowding, prison sociopaths, violence, understaffing, riots, and other such difficult conditions. An essential problem is the absence of active rehabilitative attitudes and objectives, and an attitude of simply doing time. This attitude is not restricted to inmates; it is too prevalently shared by prison administrators, custodial officers, and the public, despite occasional utterances to the contrary. Although most prisons throughout the country today have both individual and group therapy programs and all sorts of occupational training programs, by and large the inmates are expected to serve out their sentences quietly, and the prison administration is on hand to see that they do. As one offender stated, "Rehabilitation is still a dirty word." It is taken lightly, not only by most offenders, but unfortunately, and more significantly, by many prison administrators and custodial officers as well. Although some lip service is paid to rehabilitative efforts, in general the prevalent doing-time philosophy continues to militate against correction.

The central problem of the so-called correctional institution is found in a closer analysis of the prison community. A central theme in the literature in this field is that the prison social structure not only militates against correction inherently but, in fact, reinforces negative and illegal behavior patterns that are in conflict with the overall social system.

The social structure in a men's prison is divisible into two categories of participants: the inmate population and the institution's personnel. Each stratum is clearly and easily identifiable. Each tends to view the other with mingled distrust and suspicion. There is a reinforcement of mutually hostile attitudes between prison personnel and inmates through stereotyping. There is a tendency toward praise of one's own group and deflation of the other. To the prisoner, the prison doctor is a sawbones or croaker, the warden is a political hack, and the psychiatrist is a headshrinker. Institutional personnel, in turn, tend to stereotype prisoners as stupid, shiftless, immoral, and recalcitrant hoods. Some inmates and staff attempt to walk the line between these two divisions, but this is usually a precarious position. They find at one point or another that it is necessary to take sides, and it is too difficult and even dangerous to leave one's defined membership group.

When the offender is sentenced, he is, in effect, being rejected by society. His status as prisoner forces him to make some adjustments in his self-concept. He can accept his sentence as being "just what I deserve" (few do), or he can rationalize and project the blame for his incarceration on an unfair society. The nearest objective representation of the outside world is the institutional staff. Most prisoners therefore respond to the guards and prison administration as negative symbols of the society that has "wronged" them.

Advantages accrue to the prisoner who becomes an "organization man," stays with his group, and conforms to inmate values. The prisoner who continues to accept the outside society and its values by not being continually hostile toward the prison administration (the inside-the-walls symbol of the outside society) may find himself in the difficult situation of being rejected by both worlds. Few inmates have the resources or courage to stand up against the expectations of the prison world, which are imposed by fellow inmates with persistent force and clarity. In many instances their norms are more precise than the regulations prescribed by the administration.

The enculturated or conforming inmate does better in prison. He becomes, as Clemmer has termed it, "prisonized." If he accepts "stir" rules, he is accepted not only by his fellow inmates, but also by custodial officers, who learn to have this kind of negative expectation of inmate behavior. The maintenance of this equilibrium is reinforced by all factions in the doing-time society.

There is a similar pressure on guards toward conformity to certain generally accepted negative attitudes (negative in the sense that they militate against correction). The new guard is quickly instructed by the old-timer about the "correct" attitudes to have toward "shiftless, recalcitrant, no-good hoods" who will never change. The correctional officer (at whatever level up to warden) who enters the prison social structure with a degree of correctional idealism will soon be cajoled or forced into submitting to the shared doing-time norms of both personnel and inmates. He is quickly admonished by both fellow officers and even some old-line inmates with such expressions as: "You'll learn"; "You'll see what I mean about these characters"; "No con ever really changes."

To resist these pressures to conform to the "we're all doing time" philosophy takes more courage and strength than most new correctional officers can muster and still do their difficult, demanding, and at times dangerous job. Moreover, to do their work they require the cooperation of their fellow officers (particularly in dangerous situations), and this may not be forthcoming for "eager beavers," "rate-busters," or "inmate fraternizers."

The understaffed and underfinanced prison administration often falls into the trap of cooperation with the inmate social system to maintain at least an overt image of order and discipline in the institution. It may use "squealers," allow prison sociopaths to dole out favors, look the other way when misconduct takes place, and so forth, all to maintain a degree of order. This practice of "playing ball" with the inmate system may produce short-range benefits, but at some point the administration gets the uneasy feeling that the reins of control have slipped quietly into the too willing hands of the inmate population. In particular, the "prison politician," usually a long-termer and sociopath, maneuvers himself into a position of central power. When the administration moves toward tightening and enforcing administrative rules, resistance sets in.

The sociopathic leader, who has the most to lose from a return to institutional administrative order (since he has developed a system of contraband favors and power beneficial to himself), may threaten a shake-up of the quiet doing-time situation. His extreme reaction often explodes into a prison riot.

Riots are only one minor price paid for the maintenance of the doing-time society. The main cost is in salvageable inmates, who do their time and come out with the same criminal behavior patterns with which they went in, if they have not become more recalcitrant.

If either the administrators or the inmates shift their responses or attitudes about the prison as a doing-time society, the other faction may feel threatened. An inmate who sincerely defines the prison as a therapeutic community and attempts to change his behavior can make the administrators feel very uncomfortable. They may have to reshuffle their attitudes and discard their stereotyped views of the the prisoner as someone who will never change; they may even have to attempt to provide therapeutic services. This is a real threat. It may add burdens to an already demanding job and impose on the administration demands that are impossible to fulfill in terms of budget, staff, and therapeutic resources.

On the other hand, if the prison administrators take the view that the prisoner's behavior pattern can be modified, that he is reachable and can "straighten out," this may produce great anxiety in the offender, who will have to modify his rationalized view of society as unfair, disinterested, and unable to help him. In addition, if he accepts help he is forced to admit there is something wrong with himself, something that should be changed. This is hard for anyone to do, and especially hard for an inmate with a calcified set of rationalizations about himself and society. The status quo, although painful and self-defeating in many respects, is less anxiety-producing for him than the drastic changes required if he accepts efforts to modify his pattern of behavior.

Given these complex conditions, there is a silent agreement on the part of both staff and inmates to maintain the equilibrium of the existing social system.

Unfortunately, the doing-time problem is not restricted to the prison community. A certain apathy and maintenance of a negative status quo between correctional officers and their clients can be similarly identified in other correctional efforts, such as probation, parole, and detention, and to some extent in court practices. The doing-time philosophy generally pervades the field of correction and is the most significant problem to be overcome if rehabilitation is to be more than just a word.

Dr. Richard Korn, a prominent criminologist who has studied a number of prison systems, perceives the "time" factor in prison as follows:

> Over the centuries the strange structures and their strange or commonplace names arise, disappear on the human landscape: Maison de Force, Bastille, Devil's Island, Sing Sing, Attica. But on the Yard the topic is interminably the same: "Where have you done time?" "How much time?" No other subject so deeply engages men in confinement, not even the trauma of physical confinement itself. Prisoners have survived or transcended every other pain of imprisonment. No man can overcome his time.[4]

---

[4] Richard R. Korn, "Action Is the Only Way You Can Keep Sane," *New York Times*, September 19, 1971. Copyright © 1988 by the New York Times Company. Reprinted by permission.

SOME GENERAL EFFECTS OF IMPRISONMENT

Even under ideal conditions, which seldom exist in prison, social-psychological forces inherent in the system produce a dehumanizing effect. A landmark psychological study conducted at Stanford University is revealing in this regard. Stanford psychologists, in a study of the behavior of "guards" and "prisoners" under simulated prison conditions, concluded that common notions about prison behavior were largely myths. The prevailing belief is that prison guards are particular kinds of people with inherent sadistic traits and that prisoners are weak, emotionally unstable persons prone to crime. The researchers found that these behavior patterns were developed in a matter of days by "normal" young American males.

The subjects were 22 young men who responded to advertisements seeking men to participate in an experiment at $15 a day. The experiment, all were told, would last two weeks. Most of the subjects were middle-class college students who were determined by means of personality tests to be emotionally stable. A replica of a prison was constructed in the basement of a laboratory at Stanford, including barred cells and a solitary confinement room. Some of the subjects were chosen to be guards, others to be prisoners. Selection was made at random. The guards were given no instructions except that they were to gain the respect of the prisoners and to maintain law and order.

It became apparent very soon that the guards liked their authority roles and began to abuse them. The prisoners tried to please the guards. The researchers concluded that the subjects were behaving in much the same way that real guards and prisoners who cooperated with the guards would behave. At first the psychologists thought the subjects were merely taking their assignments seriously and were role-playing to please the experimenters. They soon concluded, however, that the subjects had slipped completely into prison-life behavior. They commented, with respect to the prisoners, "We used scales to measure their moods daily and they steadily became depressed and negative. They'd say, 'I only care about myself—I don't give a damn about the others.'"[5]

The guards became aggressive and sadistic. They forced prisoners to clean out toilets with their bare hands. They walked them into door jambs, denied them smoking and reading privileges, and forced them to move boxes from one closet to another for hours without giving a reason.[6]

Professor Philip G. Zimbardo, who directed the research, said about this: "We had to call it off after six days because of the amount of suffering we'd seen and the amount of brutality. We had to release one

---

[5] Philip G. Zimbardo, "Pathology of Imprisonment," *Trans-Action* 9 (April 1972):4–8.

[6] Philip G. Zimbardo, "Brutality in a Mock Prison," *Los Angeles Times*, April 8, 1973.

on the first day, and then another on each successive day. We even saw signs of sexual abuse begin to emerge."[7]

All but two prisoners were willing to waive the $15 a day if they would be given parole. All prisoners were happy to have the experiment terminated after the sixth day.

The guards all came to work on time and even worked extra hours without extra pay. Most of the guards seemed to enjoy the power their roles gave them and did not want the experiment to end.

One prisoner said, "I began to feel I was losing my identity, that the person I call _____ was distant from me, was remote until finally I wasn't that person, I was 416. I was really my number and 416 was really going to have to decide what to do." Another prisoner said, "I learned that people can easily forget that others are human."

The Stanford study had a real-life counterpart that, if anything, revealed a more horrendous situation. A former prison official, testifying at a Senate hearing, spoke of murders, beatings, torture, stomping and kicking, and sexual perversions as punishments. Black prisoners, he said, ate only table scraps left by white inmates. Brass knuckles, ax handles, blackjacks, and devices that gave electric shocks to prisoners— to the point that they lost consciousness—were used routinely.

Persons released from prisons have reported such dehumanizing experiences for years. Somehow these reports were generally regarded as exaggerations or were attributed to the emotional problems of the individual prisoner. The Stanford experiment and actual reports of prison life suggest, however, that the role of guard, with all the power attached to it, tends to brutalize normal people. Clearly, faced with such brutality and sadism, an individual who is powerless to effectively protect himself or herself from it is, to an extent, dehumanized. In the process, a hatred for the system may develop that can be extremely difficult to overcome.

RACIAL GANG PROBLEMS AND PRISON VIOLENCE

John Irwin, in his classic book *Prisons In Turmoil*, describes a fundamental problem in contemporary prisons around the country. Irwin maintains that gang-type structures have developed along racial lines in prisons, and the level of violence and potential violence has grown. According to Irwin:

> The hate and distrust between white and black prisoners constitute the most powerful source of divisions. After being forestalled by the moves toward unity during the prison movement [previous] conditions and trends . . . were reestablished. Black prisoners continued to increase in numbers and

---

[7] William Chapman, "Mock Prison Guards Turn into Sadists," *Los Angeles Times,* December 10, 1972.

assertiveness. Whites, led by the more prejudiced and violent, increasingly reacted. Hate, tension, and hostilities between the two races escalated. An Illinois black prisoner describes the posture of black prisoners toward whites:

> In the prison, the black dudes have a little masculinity game they play. It has no name, really, but I call it whup or fuck a white boy —especially the white gangsters or syndicate men, the bad juice boys, the hit men, etc. The black dudes go out of their way to make faggots out of them. And to lose a fight to a white dude is one of the worst things that can happen to a black dude. And I know that . . . the white cats are faggots. They will drop their pants and bend over and touch their toes and get had before they will fight.[8]

White prisoners, whether or not they were racially hostile before prison, tend to become so after experiencing prison racial frictions. Edward Bunker, who served several terms in California prisons and has written cogently about contemporary prison processes and relationships, described a middle-class white prisoner's entrance into racial hatred:

> After 10:30, the noise dropped a decibel or two, and from the morass of sound Ron began to recognize certain voices by timbre and catch snatches of conversation. Above him, perhaps on the second tier, he picked up a gumboed black voice saying he'd like to kill all white babies, while his listener agreed it was the best way to handle the beasts—before they grew up. A year earlier, Ron would have felt compassion for anyone so consumed by hate, and whenever whites casually used "nigger" he was irked. Now he felt tentacles of hate spreading through himself—and half an hour later, he smiled when a batch of voices began chanting: "Sieg Heil! Sieg Heil! Sieg Heil!"[9]

The racial conflicts among blacks, whites, and Hispanics in American prisons have produced a situation in which groups of prisoners regularly rob and attack other prisoners and retaliate when members of their clique or gang have been threatened or attacked. This has intensified the fear and widened the gap between prisoners, particularly between prisoners of different races. The problem of racial conflict has substantially increased the level of prison violence and made many prisons almost impossible to manage.

In recent years the problem of racial violence has been accentuated by the evolution of more clearly defined prison gangs. Most of these groups have some connection to the neighborhood gangs the inmates formerly belonged to in their communities of orientation. In a *Newsweek* article, the prototypical gang problem that has developed in prison was delineated in detail as it relates to the so-called Mexican Mafia:

---

[8] From John Irwin, *Prisons in Turmoil.* Copyright © 1980 by John Irwin. Reprinted by permission of the publisher, Little, Brown and Company.

[9] Edward Bunker, *Animal Factory* (New York: Viking, 1977), p. 92.

In the prisons of California, push has too often come to kill. From its early days as a self-defense unit, the prison gang called La Nuestra Familia (Our Family) has grown into a regiment of disciplined predators, unencumbered by any rules except its own rough code. Recruits train openly in prison yards. They stab their foes in full sight of prison guards. And when they are paroled, they carry their murderous skills back to the streets. Last week, after a five-year Federal investigation, a grand jury indicted 25 leaders and members of Nuestra Familia, hoping to cripple a gang that seems equally at home on either side of prison walls. . . .

Like many gangs, Nuestra Familia owes its start to ethnic rivalry. When chicanos from central California were sentenced to prison in the late 1960s, they were often greeted by groups of Los Angeles toughs known as the Mexican Mafia. The older inmates sneered at the new cons and regularly preyed on them for money and sex. The victims responded in kind; they, too, formed a gang. Pitched battles for turf became common in prison and out. "We did the same things that the Mexican Mafia did," says Art Beltran, a former gang leader who is now cooperating with the government. . . .

The gangs once operated openly under an informal system of peaceful coexistence with state prison officials. The leaders were sometimes permitted to roam the halls at will, to enter the normally secure solitary areas for private meetings and even to use the staff conference room. Prison officials admit to having cooperated. "We were trying to use them as a way to control the violence inside," a Corrections Department spokesman said. "It didn't work." At times the cooperation seemed like collusion. . . .

The gang demands unquestioning loyalty from its members. They memorize names of enemies who are to be killed on sight—no matter where they may be spotted. Sammy Venegas, a Nuestra Familia lieutenant, allegedly ordered his own brother Lupe killed because he suspected that the youth was keeping drug profits. When Beltran told this story to a grand jury last March, the jurors were stunned. "It disturbed them," he says. "It still chills my spine." Beltran, the gang's former third-ranking officer, admits to killing three people himself. He turned state's evidence as part of a plea bargain.

Disturbing as the prison violence was, law-enforcement officials targeted the gang only after paroled members caused trouble in the barrios. The Fresno group proved especially difficult. In an effort to muscle in on the prostitution trade, Neustra Familia members killed several reluctant women and their pimps, and rival drug dealers met similar fates. In all, cops blame the gang for 136 murders since 1975.[10]

The Escalation of Violence and Homosexuality

Violence has always been a popular solution for inmates in prison conflicts. Short of a prison riot, violence is a constant element in contemporary prison life. According to Irwin, the meaning of violence has become related to an exaggerated form of masculinity:

---

[10] *Newsweek*, February 1, 1982. Copyright 1982, by Newsweek, Inc. All Rights Reserved. Reprinted by Permission.

Violent groups who, in the pursuit of loot, sex, respect, or revenge, will attack any outsider have completely unraveled any remnants of the old codes of honor and tip networks that formerly helped to maintain order. In a limited, closed space, such as a prison, threats of attacks like those posed by these groups cannot be ignored. Prisoners must be ready to protect themselves or get out of the way. Those who have chosen to continue to circulate in public, with few exceptions, have formed or joined a clique or gang for their own protection. Consequently, violence-oriented groups dominate many, if not most, large men's prisons. . . .

Toughness in the new hero in the violent men's prisons means, first, being able to take care of oneself in the prison world, where people will attack others with little or no provocation. Second, it means having the guts to take from the weak. . . .

In addition to threats of robbery, assaults, and murder, the threat of being raped and physically forced into the role of the insertee (punk or kid) has increased in the violent prison: "Fuck it. It's none of my business. If a sucker is weak, he's got to fall around here." . . .

Prison homosexuality has always created identity problems for prisoners. Long before today's gang era, many prisoners, particularly those with youth prison experiences, regularly or occasionally engaged in homosexual acts as insertors with queens, kids, or punks, though not without some cost to their own masculine definitions. There has been a cynical accusation repeated frequently in prison informal banter that prisoners who engaged in homosexual life too long finally learn to prefer it and, in fact, become full, practicing homosexuals, both insertees and insertors: "It was a jocular credo that after one year behind walls, it was permissible to kiss a kid or a queen. After five years, it was okay to jerk them off to 'get 'em hot.' After ten years, 'making tortillas' or 'flip-flopping' was acceptable and after twenty years anything was fine." The constant game of prison dozens among friends and acquaintances, in which imputation of homosexuality is the dominant theme, reflects and promotes self-doubt about masculinity. Presently, the threat of force has been added to the slower process of drifting into homosexuality, and fear about manhood and compensatory aggressive displays of manhood have increased drastically.

Today the respected public prison figure—the convict or hog—stands ready to kill to protect himself, maintains strong loyalties to some small group of other convicts (invariably of his own race), and will rob and attack, at least tolerate his friends' robbing and attacking, other weak independents or their foes. He openly and stubbornly opposes the administration, even if this results in harsh punishment. Finally, he is extremely assertive of his masculine sexuality, even though he may occasionally make use of the prison homosexuals or, less often, enter into more permanent sexual alliance with a kid.[11]

AIDS in Prison

Homosexuality has produced another significant problem that has emerged in men's prisons in recent years in the specter of AIDS.

---

[11] Irwin, *Prisons in Turmoil*, pp. 192–195.

Homosexual behavior in prison is a well-known fact of life, and this pattern of sexuality has had a significant effect.

The United States Bureau of Prisons began segregating federal inmates displaying "predatory or promiscuous behavior" who tested positive for the virus that causes AIDS. In 1987 statistics showed that nearly 500 prison inmates, about 3 percent of those tested under a pilot program in the federal prison system, have tested positive for the AIDS virus.

As of October, 1987, 16,372 federal prisoners had been tested for the virus under a program that began in June. Of that number, 494, or 3 percent, tested positive, the government reported. There currently are 31 cases of AIDS in the federal prison system out of a population of more than 44,000. No doubt these figures have increased each year since 1987.

The Justice Department issued a statement saying that the government will launch a new five-part, mandatory AIDS testing program effective immediately. Among those to be tested under the program are those "who have exhibited predatory or promiscuous behavior," said the statement, which did not elaborate on what would constitute such behavior. Inmates in that category who test positive for the AIDS virus are increasingly separated from the general inmate population in prisons around the United States.

Prison Riots: The Case of Attica

This mix of emotionally destructive factors, pseudopolitics, violence, and homosexuality contributes to a racial revolutionary fervor in American prisons. In the past two decades these forces have produced prison riots in Michigan, New Mexico, Texas, and Arizona. One of the most destructive prison riots in American history was the conflagration at Attica Prison in New York. It resulted in the slaughter of 26 inmates and the wounding of dozens of others. A close analysis of this situation reveals many factors that lead to prison riots.

Attica Correctional Facility is one of the 170 major correctional institutions in the United States. It occupies 55 acres in upstate New York and is rated a maximum security installation. This means that it is surrounded by a wall guarded by armed officers and that one cannot move in or out of a cellblock without passing through two locked doors. In such institutions inmates are not permitted to move from their cells to a place of work, to the dining area, to a treatment facility, or anywhere else unless accompanied by a guard.

The prison had an educational program, a recreation program, a religious program, and a vocational training program; it also had a machine shop, a metal shop, a carpentry shop, and other work programs. According to inmates involved in the riot, none of these programs was effective. The entire setting was repressive and oppressive.

Former inmates of Attica contended that solitary confinement was frequently imposed for minor infractions and that beatings on the elevator en route to the "box" (solitary confinement cell) were frequent. The box was conveniently located over the prison hospital. Inmates were allowed only one shower a week, even though many worked (for as little as 25 cents a day) in the metal shop, known as "the black hole of Calcutta," where temperatures exceeded 100 degrees. Former inmates claimed that one bar of soap and one roll of toilet paper was the monthly allotment. They also maintained that there was little useful vocational training.[12]

At Attica inmates protested against what they considered to be intolerable conditions. Among their demands were religious freedom to worship as Black Muslims, permission for political meetings without intimidation, the end of mail censorship, the right to communicate with anyone they wished, law libraries, vocational programs, better food, and regular grievance procedures.

Such protests against conditions and against the racism of the guards were strongly articulated in July. Many of the inmates were self-styled revolutionaries who had been transferred to Attica from other prisons because of their militancy. They smuggled banned books by Malcolm X and Bobby Seale into their cells and held secret political meetings at the chapel or when engaged in athletics. They passed around writings of their own.

In July demands were sent to Governor Nelson Rockefeller and State Corrections Commissioner Russell Oswald by a group calling itself "the Attica Liberation Faction." It labeled Attica a "classic institution of authoritative inhumanity upon men," but noted: "We are trying to do this in a democratic fashion. We feel there is no need to dramatize our demands."

A rumor of brutality swept the prison on September 8. The riot started on September 9, at 8:30 A.M., when a group of inmates refused to line up at the rap of guards' clubs for a work detail. The guards were outnumbered and overpowered. The inmates rushed through three cellblocks and set fire to six buildings. The chapel, prison school, and machine shop were gutted. Using knives, pipes, baseball bats, and spears made out of broom handles and scissor blades, the rebellious inmates captured guards and civilian employees as hostages. The prison staff regained control of two cellblocks by using tear gas, and they confined about half the inmates in their cells. About 1,200 prisoners continued to hold one cellblock and several dozen hostages. From all indications the hostages were not mistreated.

In the course of three days of negotiations, Commissioner Oswald agreed to 28 of the inmates' 30 demands. The principal stumbling block

---

[12] "War at Attica: Was There No Other Way?" *Time*, September 27, 1971, pp. 18–26. See also Bruce Jackson, "Comment: Beyond Attica," *Trans-Action* 9 (November/December 1971):4–10.

was the demand for complete amnesty. The hostages and inmates requested Governor Rockefeller to come to the negotiations. Four important observers pleaded with Rockefeller to come. He refused. At 7:00 A.M. on the fifth day, an army of 500 troopers was assigned to specific funtions: sharpshooting, rescue, barricade removal, backup security. The instructions were to "use force to meet force." After some further unsatisfactory negotiations, the troopers attacked at 9:32, after first dropping tear gas from two helicopters. According to a police sergeant, "The ones that resisted—throwing spears and Molotov cocktails—were cut down. We caught some men with arms extended to throw weapons. Anybody that resisted was killed."

Doctors who treated prisoners reported indiscriminate firing by officers and the calculated slaying of unresisting convicts. According to Dr. Lionel Sifontes of Buffalo, "Many of the ringleaders were approached by guards and shot systematically. Some had their hands in the air surrendering. Some were lying on the ground." Twenty-six inmates were killed and 83 seriously wounded in the attack. That there must have been some indiscriminate firing by the troopers is evidenced by the fact that they killed nine hostages dressed in convicts' clothes. The troopers claimed that the hostages all died by having their throats slit. The commissioner made a public announcement to that effect. Autopsies proved, however, that they were killed by the troopers. There was no evidence of slashed throats.

The ferocity of the police attack did not end with the shooting. Guardsman James P. Watson, a law student, testified in a federal court that unresisting naked convicts, standing with hands on heads, were poked in the groin, rectum, and legs with clubs to make them run through a guantlet of guards, who kicked and beat them. Some inmates fell, he said, and guards chased others into a building. Standing nearby, Watson heard "screams and moans and the sounds of clubs hitting flesh and bone." Days later, four outside physicians confirmed reports of brutality. The bodies of fallen guards were tagged with their names, and families notified. As late as four days after the riot, relatives of some convicts were still refused information about whether their sons or husbands were alive or dead.

The New York State Special Commission on Attica, after interviewing 2,500 persons including 1,600 inmates, 400 correctional officers, 270 state police, 200 National Guardsmen, and 100 sheriffs and deputies, concluded:

1. The Attica Correctional Facility in September 1971 was not perceptibly better or worse than the other maximum-security prisons which at that time housed nine out of every ten adult male offenders incarcerated in the State's system. Attica is every prison and every prison is Attica. [Not much has changed at Attica or other American prisons since 1971.]
2. The promise of rehabilitation has become a cruel joke. If anyone was

rehabilitated, it was in spite of Attica, not because of it. . . . If Attica was a true model, then prisons served no one.

3. The commission found no evidence that the Attica uprising was planned, either by avowed revolutionaries or anyone else. The evidence points in the other direction.

4. The assault of September 13, 1971 and its aftermath were marred with excesses. Thirty-nine persons were killed by gunfire and eighty others suffered gunshot wounds during the assault. One out of every ten persons in D yard that morning was struck by gunfire and more than a quarter of the hostages died of bullet wounds (all firing was by police and guards).

5. In the aftermath of the assault, hundreds of inmates, stripped of their clothing, were brutalized by correction officers, troopers, and sheriff's deputies. . . . Forty-five percent of the inmates who had been in D yard suffered bruises, lacerations, abrasions, and broken bones.

6. No effective steps were taken on September 13 to see that reprisals did not occur and no satisfactory explanation has been given for that failure. *"An uprising in which inmates had demanded above all that they be treated as human beings thus ended with their being treated inhumanly."*[13]

PRISON DEATH ROWS AND CAPITAL PUNISHMENT

A powder keg that exists today in most major state prisons is the "death row" for capital offenders awaiting execution. The very existence of a death row has a deleterious impact on the entire prison population.

At the end of 1988 there were more persons awaiting execution than at any other time since a national count has been kept. Thirty-six states have a death penalty statue in force, 30 states were holding prisoners on death rows, and 25 states had imposed the death penalty during the year. Over 2,100 prisoners were under sentence of death in the United States at the end of 1989.

During the 1930s, persons who received the death penalty did not spend many years on death row. In the mid-1930s, close to 200 executions occurred annually. Consequently, the death row population was relatively stable from year to year. By the 1950s, the number executed annually had declined to fewer than 100, and it declined to fewer than 50 in the early 1960s.

In the face of mounting challenges to the legality of capital punishment, an unofficial moratorium on executions was in effect for some ten years, starting in June, 1967. Recent trends in executions and in the size of the death row population generally appear to coincide with a shift in public opinion about punishment by death. In the mid-1960s, only two of every five participants in U.S. public opinion polls favored capital punishment for persons convicted of murder. However, this changed

---

[13] William L. Wilbanks, "The Report of the Commission on Attica," *Federal Probation* 37 (March 1973):3–13. Reprinted by permission.

during the 1970s. And in 1988, most polls showed that about two of every three persons favored the death penalty.

Most current capital punishment laws date from 1976 Supreme Court decisions upholding laws that carefully define the types of cases in which the death penalty may be applied. The new laws provided for guided discretion on the part of the judge or jury by specifying capital crimes in detail and spelling out aggravating and mitigating circumstances that must be considered in deciding on the sentence.

Since 1976, further refinements have taken place as standards gradually evolved from cases before the U.S. Supreme Court. In 1977, for example, the Court held in *Coker* v. *Georgia* that the rape of an adult female is not a capital offense, thereby eliminating a sanction that had been applied almost exclusively to black men. (Over 90 percent of all persons executed for rape since 1930 were black.)

During the 1980s, the Court generally considered litigation concerning penalty by death on a case-by-case basis, handing down decisions that did not, as a rule, have a broad impact on previous convictions. However, the Court made it clear that it would continue to monitor the ways in which the states apply their capital punishment laws.

In 1988, U.S. Supreme Court Justice Sandra Day O'Connor expressed her opinion on capital punishment. Citing delays that can last for decades, she noted that it is hoped that proposed changes, including a time limit for seeking federal court reviews, will streamline the appeals process. She commented:

> There is no doubt that the capital cases across the country are posing a significant strain on the system. We see it very acutely at the Supreme Court. In the last year the California Supreme Court has affirmed a large number of capital convictions on direct review. That's because there are no time limits on appeals against capital punishment. Some Death Row inmates are seeking federal court reviews of their cases as long as ten years after their convictions.

The following editorial by Tom Wicker provides a relevant viewpoint on the death penalty. Mr. Wicker is a journalist expert on prisons. His firsthand reports from the Attica prison riots resulted in a book on prison problems, which was a significant contribution to the analysis of the prison community:

> Lewis F. Powell Jr., the former Supreme Court Justice, put a pertinent question to the recent meeting [August, 1988] of the American Bar Association: If the death penalty in the United States isn't swift and certain, should it be retained?
>
> The tenor of Mr. Powell's speech suggested that he might be willing to limit post-conviction appeals in capital cases, so that executions could be carried out more certainly and speedily. But since in any humane country, the death penalty *cannot be swift and certain*, the better response would be to do away with it altogether.
>
> When a civilized state decides to take the life of a citizen, it's obligated to grant every opportunity for appeal, for new evidence to be presented, for

mistakes in police or court procedure to be rectified. Some of these appeals may lack validity; but they can't be eliminated or restricted without similarly affecting appeals that might be serious and warranted. The A.B.A. itself opposes limiting death penalty appeals.

It seems equally clear that the death penalty cannot be administered so that all those to whom it might apply are treated equitably. Mr. Powell has been appointed by Chief Justice Rehnquist to lead a committee of judges studying the present capital punishment system, which Mr. Rehnquist termed "disjointed and chaotic." What's the substantive difference between that and the death penalty being "capricious" or "freakish," the descriptions used in Justice Potter Stewart's opinion in 1971, when the Supreme Court held that death sentences "are cruel and unusual in the same way that being struck by lightning is cruel and unusual"?

In 1976, however, the Court held a Georgia capital statute constitutional on the grounds that its system of determining guilt separately from the sentence supposedly would eliminate caprice in its application. Other states then adopted Georgia's law. Mr. Rehnquist's complaint, a dozen years later, suggests that the Georgia model still has not made death sentencing equitable—or any more constitutional than it was in 1971.

Mr. Powell's concern about delay is well justified, but for the wrong reasons. He pointed out that, on the average, eight years pass between commission of a capital crime and the execution of a person convicted for it—which means that the delay is often considerably longer. Many convicted people remain on death row more than eight years before the execution or some other resolution—sometimes a finding that they are innocent after all. Since 1976, only about 100 executions have resulted from the Supreme Court's ruling in the Georgia case, though thousands have been sentenced to death.

"If capital punishment cannot be enforced even where innocence is not an issue and the fairness of the trial is not seriously questioned," Mr. Powell asked the A.B.A., "is retention of a punishment that is not being enforced . . . in the public interest?" The delay between the crime and punishment, he said, "hardly inspires confidence in or respect by the public for our criminal justice system."

These remarks might be taken to mean that only questions concerning guilt or innocence or the fairness of the trial should be heard on appeal. That would be a narrow view of a complicated matter; still not finally decided by the Supreme Court, for example, is whether someone can be executed for a crime committed while a minor—surely a proper subject for appeal.

Even after hearing Mr. Powell, the A.B.A., for another example, voted to support legislation "which alleviates any racial discrimination in capital sentencing which may exist." Plenty does, though Mr. Powell in his last term on the Court was the author of its opinion rejecting statistical evidence that blacks who murdered whites were sentenced to death more often than whites who killed blacks. And what about those instances in which one person is sentenced to death, but another is not, for essentially the same crimes—even in the same state?

Nor is loss of public confidence the main issue raised by delays in executions. Every authority on crime holds that swift and certain punishment is the only real deterrent. But nothing in the criminal justice system is less swift or certain than an execution—which is one good reason the death penalty is not and can't be the deterrent many people think it is.

It scarcely commends the humanity of a society or a system, moreover, if they keep even the perpetrators of heinous crimes—much less people convicted wrongly, as they often are—suspended 8, 10 or more years in the expectation of being electrocuted, gassed or poisoned by the state.[14]

A PLAN FOR A FEDERAL VIOLENCE RESEARCH CENTER TO REPLACE DEATH ROWS

If the current trends in death sentences, the law, and stays of execution continue, by the year 2000 there will be at least 2,500 people living on death rows in prisons around the country. I here propose a viable plan for dealing with people convicted of committing homicide.

Several factors related to the social dynamics of homicide place this plan in context. First, a variety of research carried out over the past century on whether capital punishment deters murder has produced mixed conclusions. Some data reveal that states with the death penalty have a higher per capita murder rate than states without the death penalty, and other data indicate the opposite. There are cases of states whose murder rates increased after they enacted the death penalty, and there are states where the per capita murder rate decreased after the death penalty was eliminated from the law. Many countries that do not have the death penalty have lower per capita murder rates than the United States.

In brief, we must conclude that there is no clear correlation, one way or another, between the existence of capital punishment and the murder rate. In other words, capital punishment does not necessarily deter murder. But if it doesn't prevent murder, then what function does capital punishment perform? There is evidence that the sentencing of a murderer and the execution of a murderer provide many people in society with satisfying feelings of both revenge and catharsis. Moreover, many people have a sense of equanimity when they feel "justice has been done" through the execution of an offender.

On an emotional level I share the convicted murderer's rationale that when society performs an execution it makes us all murderers. In effect, when the convicted killer is executed, we all have shared in some way in pulling the switch. We have in fact committed premeditated murder.

Another significant factor related to capital punishment and death rows is that when a killer is executed we have clearly kept that person

---

[14] Tom Wicker, "The Death Penalty Can't Be Saved from Itself," *New York Times*, August 12, 1988. Copyright © 1988 by the New York Times Company. Reprinted by permission.

from killing again. If a murderer lingers on death row, with shifting laws and appeals the killer may return to society and kill again.

Given all these vectors related to the issue, I would like to propose a bold new federal plan for dealing with convicted murderers. First, we need to propose clear federal legislation that would eliminate the death penalty in the United States. I then recommend the building of a federal maximum security prison research center that could comfortably house 3,000 prisoners. The complex would be escapeproof; yet within its walls the inmates would be treated humanely. All those convicted of first-degree murder from around the country would be sentenced to this federal prison for life, with *no* possibility of parole. They would have their own individual rooms and do some kind of meaningful work, but basically all of these convicted murderers would become subjects of research.

Qualified social and medical scientists (sociologists, psychologists, psychiatrists, and medical doctors) would be invited to carry out research with these subjects. A scientific research committee would screen all research applications and applicants. The research would generally be into the causes of violent behavior. In this context, qualified research people might in time discover much concerning the case histories, the physiology, and the psychodynamics of people who commit murder. Simply stated, we would learn more about the causes of violence, especially murder.

The situation would provide an opportunity for murderers to atone in some way for their destructive behavior, by giving something back to society in the way of valid information. As we learned more about the social, psychological, and physiological makeup of murderers, we might be in a better position to develop prevention programs.

No doubt, some of the inmates would choose not to cooperate as research subjects. These could be separated from the main body of cooperative subjects and provided with fewer privileges than the subjects. In time, some might decide to cooperate, as they saw the advantages of participating in the research.

The goal of the program would be solely research, not therapy or rehabilitation. Any therapy carried out with the inmates would be only to help them adjust to their immediate life situation, since they would never be released. If they developed any occupational skills (such as writing), they would be free to communicate with people outside the walls in their respective fields. Visiting could become liberalized. At all times, however, it would be clear that under no circumstances would any of these prisoners be allowed in a situation where he or she might kill or commit violence against another person. In a sense, the one act of murder would have disqualified each of them from free interaction with others in situations where they might pose a danger.

Obviously, many details must be worked out for such a plan to succeed. I can say, however, that a program of this type would solve several problems: (1) It would provide qualified researchers with an opportunity to research murderers, violence, and murder in a compatible, unique setting. (2) It would no doubt produce valuable insights into the subject of violence in general and therefore might equip society to prevent future violence. (3) It would eliminate the horrendous death row situation, including its negative emotional impact on the populations of prisons in which death rows exist. (4) It would incapacitate dangerous people. (5) It would eliminate the necessity for future executions. And, generally, it would provide a more humane system for dealing with murderers in a democratic society.

SOME CONCLUSIONS ABOUT PRISONS

Dr. John Irwin is a criminologist who has had the unique experience of studying prisons both as a prisoner and later as a social scientist. He is now a professor of sociology at San Francisco State University and has for the past decade been a leader in the Prisoner's Union movement in the United States. Irwin has a very unique and insightful understanding of corrections and prisons. On the basis of his extensive research, he has developed a number of perceptive conclusions concerning this subject. I fully share his viewpoint and therefore present his perspective in detail.

> We must assume that to some extent the threat of imprisonment does deter, and a legitimate purpose of prisons is deterrence.
>
> The main purpose of imprisonment, however, should be punishment. We are dishonest and foolish if we do not admit that punishment is basic in our response to crime. This is not a brutish retributive atavism in human beings; it is an essential part of the bargain that we make to live by rules. When they are breached, particularly in a manner producing extreme harm to others, we want something done. When nothing is done, the rules lose their meaning and persons lose their social commitment.
>
> Historically, societies have used a variety of forms of punishment, many of which (such as whipping, mutilation, and perhaps execution) are presently unacceptable to us and others (such as banishment) are impossible. In the last hundred years, many new and apparently more humane forms (such as probation, fines, and mandatory work in public institutions) increasingly have been used. Each has some minor problems, such as the tendency of organizations to misuse free labor and the differential capacity to pay fines. All share one inherent flaw: they are not sufficiently punitive for serious crimes. We must keep in mind that the public will continue to want persons guilty of crimes like murder, violent rape, and mayhem to receive more than probation, fines, or work in public service.
>
> The only humane option that is seen as sufficiently punitive is imprisonment, a modern form of banishment. If our intention is to find the least inhumane form of punishment that society will accept for serious crime, we shall do better by drawing the line at imprisonment. Then we can insist that imprisonment is sufficient, and we can work to remove all punishment

beyond that which is necessary to maintain a system of incarceration. If we want to reduce the number of people who receive imprisonment, our most extreme form of punishment, then we must alter the social arrangements that promote serious crime and remove some crimes from the category of serious offenses. It is neither fair nor effective to reduce the number of persons who receive imprisonment by selecting a few out of the pool of persons convicted of serious crime. If we want to reduce prison populations, short sentences can be added to the two changes just recommended. But we are stuck with prisons, so let us be fair in sending people to them and remove from them any unnecessary, added punishment.

I defend prisons because they are the only feasible punishment for serious crime. Perhaps the purpose of general deterrence is served, but the main purpose is punishment. Rehabilitation and incapacitation are impossible, unjust, and inhumane. Therefore, I accept prisons *because* they are punitive. However, once this hurdle is crossed, the path is open to consider other positive functions of imprisonment. One potential positive function, atonement, was envisioned by the Quakers when they planned prisons, but they considered it only as part of a total religious conversion. Many persons who complete their prison terms, although they experience no contrition for their preprison activities and are not "born again," do feel atoned. They express this in frequently repeated statements, such as "I did my time!" They are out of debt, stronger in knowing that they took their punishment, and securer in knowing that they have a response to any blame aimed at them after imprisonment.

Another potential benefit is imprisonment as a "respite." This runs against the dominant, humanitarian opinion on incarceration: imprisonment is necessarily damaging to the prisoners and their social lives because it extricates and segregates them from their outside communities, families, and work. I would argue that many, if not most, convicted felons were not nestled in the types of communities, families, or work situations that persons who believed the above had in mind or even in which, given a real choice, felons would like to remain. More likely, they were caught in somewhat destructive social webs or were being swept along out of control, careening and ricocheting through the days. Imprisonment affords these persons a respite from their involvements, during which they can extricate themselves from destructive dynamics, sort through their values and beliefs, pull themselves together, and make new plans and preparations for a new effort at life. The longer the respite lasts, the more likely it becomes that prisoners drift into special prison-nurtured belief systems and lose subtle skills required to function in the outside world. Short periods of confinement, perhaps one year or less, particularly if they are accompanied with resources that prisoners may use at their own discretion to equip themselves, can allow many benefits of a respite and avoid the deterioration of long imprisonment.

By and large, these benefits are realized only when convicts serve their time in a setting that is safe and not excessively mean, deprived, and arbitrary and has resources, meaningful options, and freedom to choose and plan so that they may pull themselves together and improve themselves. Privacy, some educational and vocational training resources, and voluntary systems of change (for example, individual therapy, group therapy, TM, yoga, or whatever prisoners believe to be effective) should be available. The benefits are reduced or disappear if convicts are constantly confronted with murderous violence and whimsical, arbitrary, and malicious control practices.

A first order of business is reducing the violence in the violent prisons. This is no easy task. But methods being pursued by administrators, classification and segregation, are ineffective and escalate the other negative conditions, the whimsical, arbitrary, and malicious control practices. The new hope is small prisons, but fiscal conservatism may thwart this solution. It would not necessarily work, anyway. If small prisons are filled, administered, and controlled in an arbitrary manner, then they will be as punitive and unconducive to the benefits mentioned above as the old fortresses.

We need a new system of control over prisoners that is not based on arbitrary decision making or on the old informal convict social system and its single prisoner code. There is only one possibility, a formal system of decision making in which all diverse parties (prisoners and guards included) have some input and in which the conditions of work and confinement, the rules of the institution, and the special problems and grievances of different parties (individuals and groups) are negotiated. Since a prison will always have special problems of social control, the administration will need the preponderance of power. But there could be systematic and open negotiation of policy and rules, a swift procedure for the inferiors (prisoners, guards, and other employees) to bring grievances to the administration, and an appeal mechanism involving outside authorities, preferably an independent body with a mixture of private and governmental representatives. The administration would not lose control of the prison under these arrangements, but would only be pressured to act openly, reasonably, and fairly. This is the direction taken when differences and hostilities divide people, groups, states, colonies, and nations. But in the prison realm, where authoritarianism has prevailed and prospered in the past and where one of the most significant groups is prisoners, who have been considered less than human or not entitled to any rights, the idea is repulsive. The big barrier is allowing prisoners to have organizations that formally represent prisoners in decision making. It was considered seriously in California, and the plan and its history are instructive. We described both in a issue of the *Outlaw* [The Prisoner's Union publication]:

> For over eight months, the Prisoner's Union has been meeting with top administrators of the California Department of Corrections. The meetings have proceeded on two tracks. One has dealt with general problems of access to prisons—media, visitation, correspondence, etc. The other has been an effort to see if we could arrive at a plan for allowing prisoners to participate in organizations. . . .
>
> Most everyone who knows about prisons regards them as a terrible failure; full of misery, despair, and violence. We believe a root cause of these problems is the isolation and powerlessness of people who are locked up. Our goals of abolishing the Intermediate Sentence, ending economic exploitation and restoring civil and human rights (including the right to organize) all seek in one way or another to empower prisoners. The empowerment of prisoners is important for everyone. No

one point of view can encompass all the complexities of a vast system of prisons. Participation by everyone concerned is necessary for any part of our political system to work and this includes prisoners. At present, there is no way for the prisoners' point of view to be effectively presented, either on behalf of an individual or for the class. This results in many stupid, uninformed, or accidental decisions that have very destructive effects on people inside and ultimately on us all.

What we need is a new theory of crime and penology, one that is quite simple. It is based on the assumption that prisoners are human beings and not a different species from free citizens. Prisoners are special only because they have been convicted of a serious crime. But they did so in a society that produces a lot of crime, a society, in fact, in which a high percentage of the population commits serious crime. Those convicted of serious crimes must be punished and imprisoned, because it is the only option that satisifes the retributive need and is sufficiently humane. Knowing that imprisonment itself is very punitive, we need not punish above and beyond imprisonment. This means that we need not and must not degrade, provoke, nor excessively deprive the human beings whom we have placed in prison. It also means that we must not operate discriminatory systems that select which individuals should be sent to prison and, once incarcerated, who should be given different levels of punishment.

Since we assume that convicts are humans like us and are capable of myriad courses of action, honorable and dishonorable, we also assume that they will act honorably, given a real choice. This means that we provide them with the resources to achieve self-determination, dignity, and self-respect.[15]

HUMANIZING PRISONS: THE SYNANON EXPERIMENT

The Synanon therapeutic community movement for criminal-addicts, founded by Charles E. Dederich in 1958, spawned a major breakthrough for the treatment of offenders in prison. The name Synanon was coined by Dederich when he heard a recovering alcoholic slur two words, *symposium* and *seminar*, into one word, "synanon." There are now hundreds of Synanon-like therapeutic communities around the country, and many of them have their residents set up programs for people doing time in prison.

The therapeutic community concept for treating offenders in the community is more fully developed in Chapter 18, "The Therapeutic Community: An Alternative to Prison." In this chapter I will delineate an experimental Synanon program that operated for four years in the Nevada State Prison.[16] It was a valiant effort to institute a program that

---

[15] Irwin, *Prisons in Turmoil*, pp. 238–242, 247–248.

[16] This section is, in part, derived from Lewis Yablonsky, *The Tunnel Back: Synanon* (New York: Macmillan, 1965; Baltimore: Penguin Books, 1968).

could fulfill the lofty goal of providing a valuable program in a prison in which prisoners could, as John Irwin states, "be provided with the resources to achieve self-determination, dignity, and self-respect."

Although the program at the Nevada State Prison was ended after four years by a new prison administration, it was a valuable experimental effort worthy of consideration as a methodology that could be, and in several states has been, instituted in contemporary prison systems.

BREAKTHROUGH IN CORRECTIONS: THE NEVADA STATE PRISON EXPERIMENT

There has been little significant progress in the management of prisons since communities began to incarcerate offenders. "Progress" has essentially been measured not from the inmates' point of view, but from the position of prison administrators, the press, and the public. To the large majority of prisoners, being physically unchained and receiving humane treatment are only minor mitigations of the problem of being *deprived of liberty and placed in a homosexual environment.*

Historically, a few landmarks have been cited as "breakthroughs" in penology. Southern chain gangs have been, to the best of our knowledge, abolished (although chaining men to walls and manacling them has not disappeared). In 1913, Thomas Mott Osborne, then chairman of a New York State prison reform committee, spent a week (incognito) in the Auburn, New York, prison. He later published a book (*Within Prison Walls,* 1914) based on his prison experience. The book was important, setting off a chain reaction of public sentiment to make prisons more humane. To a great extent, this has been accomplished. The brutalities of whipping and torturing inmates have virtually disappeared from the contemporary prison. The modern prison is reasonably humane, in the sense that sanitary food and living conditions usually prevail.

A trend has developed, since World War II, involving efforts at therapy behind walls. Various treatment approaches, with group counseling and psychotherapy in the foreground, have been implemented. There are some indications that these new approaches have had some impact. However, most of the evaluations of "success," "landmark," or "breakthrough" in the treatment of prisoners are those of the "enlightened outsider."

The first real breakthrough in the history of prisons, from the viewpoint of the prisoner, has come from Synanon. The first report on the project appeared in *Time* magazine:

MUTUAL AID IN PRISON

Since Synanon House set itself up in Santa Monica four and a half years ago as a mutual self-help cure station for drug addicts, it has seen its fame spread across the country. And for good reason. Addicts given intensive treatment at special federal hospitals have a relapse rate as high as 90 percent; Synanon, which models itself on Alcholics Anonymous and uses ex-addicts to give junkies the support and understanding they need to kick the habit and stay clean, has cut the relapse rate to as low as 20 percent.

Most striking outpost for the addicts' mutual-aid method is Nevada State Prison. Authorities invited Founder Charles "Chuck" E. Dederich, 49 (never a drug addict himself, but a graduate of Alcoholics Anonymous), to set up Synanon's system in the cell blocks and maximum freedom honor camp at Peavine, northwest of Reno. The result has been an unexpected bonus. Not only is Synanon taking hold with 18 addicts, but because the same personality weaknesses that drive some people to narcotics are also present in many non-addict prisoners, the Synanon program at Nevada now covers twice as many convicts with no addiction history.

The Unconnables At the prison, Warden Jack Fogliani has set aside a whole tier of cells for Synanon. Occupying it are men who normally would be under maximum security. Yet this tier is the only one in which the cells are left unlocked at night. Each 4-ft. by 8-ft. cubicle is spick-and-span. On the walls, instead of calendar nudes, are reproductions of Van Gogh and art work done by the inmates. Neither Fogliani nor the prison guard captain visits the Synanon tier unless invited.

"Punishment is not the answer, nor keeping a man locked up," says Warden Fogliani. "These Synanon people can approach the convicts in a way that we can't. They've been at the bottom of the barrel, too, so other convicts listen to them. It's the voice of experience." Bill Crawford, one of the Synanon leaders who moved to Reno, and an ex-addict himself, goes further: "The prisoners suddenly found they were with guys who, like themselves, have conned people—and therefore can't be conned by the prisoners."

Socrates in the Cells Synanon depends heavily on group therapy, and it insists on a tough regime. Since both addict and non-addict cons have made lying a way of life, absolute truthfulness is demanded. Any hedging, any attempt to shift the blame for their plight to others, is ruthlessly torn apart within the group. Even foul language is banned, because it might snowball into a rumble. And the ultimate punishment is expulsion from the program. But in return, Synanon gives the addict, often for the first time, a sense of belonging to a group. Instead of a "fix," it offers by the example of the ex-addict leaders, hope that a cure is possible. And because the group governs and disciplines itself, it gives the addicts and other convicts a jolt of self-respect.

Often the starting point for hope is a timeworn epigram that is chalked on a slate, such as Socrates' "All I know is that I know nothing," or Emerson's "Discontent is the want of self-reliance." From there the prisoners take it on their own, analyzing themselves and one another. But the strongest prompting toward cure is the living example of the ex-junkies themselves.

Such a one is Candy Latson, 26, a Houston-born Negro who started using dope when he was 15. He has twice done time in Los Angeles County jail. "I got to the honor camp once there. I went in clean, but I came out hooked again," he says. Through Synanon, Candy learned insight: "I kept telling myself I had four strikes against me: I had only a seventh-grade education, I was black, I was a dope addict, and I had a record. I was using my misfortunes for an excuse to keep using dope." Last week Candy Latson was in Nevada State Prison—not as a prisoner but as an honored guest and Synanon counselor. He has been clean now for three years, and is working full time for nothing more than his keep and $2 a week spending money, to help others kick the habit and stay clean.[17]

Phases Involved in Introducing Synanon into a Prison

On the basis of my direct research at the Nevada State Prison, I have concluded that there are several marked phases in introducing Synanon into a prison structure:

> *Phase 1: The Party*   At first, there is a large attendance of inmates at the Synanon sessions. In part, there is a curiosity to see so-called live ex-addict criminals. (Some addict inmates later said they didn't really believe that the Synanon people were "clean" and came to see whether they could "score"!) Most prisoners look for some activity to relieve the monotony and boredom of prison life.
>
> The party phase is the initial situation. It rapidly becomes apparent to many of the "partygoers" that the Synanists "mean business" and will not be deterred from their goals. Resistance is thrown up by the Synanists, and many members of the original "party group" disappear; they were not serious in the first place. Some of these men withdraw, take a "wait-and-see" attitude, and then attempt to get back into Synanon at a later time.
>
> *Phase 2: Early Attempt at Inmate Takeover*   The "prison politicians" and upholders of the most negative inmate creeds attempt to take over the Synanon intrusion, since it may interfere with their prison "games." This phase of possible "takeover" is permitted by Synanists to operate for a short period of time. After Synanon gets its foot firmly in the door, the takeover contingent is openly challenged by Synanists. They get this faction to reveal its real motivations. This quickly builds up into a "join-us-or-get-out" attitude on the part of the Synanists. In the Nevada State Prison project, several takeover individuals were tolerated for several months and then the vise was tightened. Some stayed in the program, and several left.
>
> *Phase 3: The Battle*   In the next phase, a pitched battle develops between Synanon values and the "doing-time" elements in the overall prison. The fact that the Synanist is free, leading a "clean," constructive life is the most powerful demonstration of the Synanon argument.

---

[17] *Time*, March 1, 1963.

It requires considerable strength and belief in the Synanon position for an inmate Synanist to stand up against the criminal code. Synanists are normally accused by many inmates of being snitches, of selling out, and being tools of the administration. As described by Candy, in the early days of Synanon at Nevada State Prison, Synanists were "booed" by inmates as they walked through the prison yard. One Synanist, a relative newcomer, eight months in Synanon, revealed how, when he first "went to work" as a Synanist in the Terminal Island project, he had considerable guilt about pushing the Synanon idea. He revealed how, at first, he gave in to a type of apology. In effect, he was at the outset saying to some of the inmates, "Forgive me for being free and happy."

Phase 4: The Showdown   The inmate resisters are culled out of the program when they do not cooperate properly in this phase. The Synanist shakes the group down to those truly involved in the program. After the showdown, it might be expected that a select group of inmates would remain. The evidence is to the contrary. At Nevada State Prison, the Synanon group of about 100 contained a random sample of the prison population.

Phase 5: Opening Up   After the Synanon group has solidified, many inmates begin to feel free and "open up" and reveal their inner conflicts and feelings. A real step forward then takes place. Unlike the professional institutional group therapy situation, where, for the most part, "opening up" is geared toward impressing the administration, in Synanon the inmate is doing it for himself. (No prison staff members are allowed in the synanon sessions.) The Synanon groups become almost a family association. At Nevada State Prison, the Synanon-tier members refer to one another as "brothers." Practically all secrets, problems, and feelings are revealed to one another in this phase of growth.

The Impact on Administration-Inmate Relations

In my research, I found that the warden, other prison administrators, and many inmates were in general agreement that Synanon produced some remarkable changes at Nevada State Prison. Many dramatic developments occurred in the prison after Synanon moved in.

There was a decrease of tension in the prison yard and in the general prison environment. This produced a higher degree of communication and interaction between inmates and guards and resulted in a considerable breakdown in the "we-they" situation.

There were fewer prison offenses in general and a reduction of severe disciplinary problems. In particular, prison officials observed fewer battle scars on inmates, a "quieter prison yard," and the virtual elimination of knife fights. This general reduction of hostility in the prison was attributed to Synanon by Warden Fogliani, who observed, "The fact that the men could fight their battles verbally in the synanon sessions helped to prevent their carrying out the actual physical fights."

Synanon produced a greater emphasis on inmate self-discipline. According to the warden, this was "particularly true of the honor camp situation." The state official who administered the forestry camp part of the honor camp operation commented favorably on the spirit, behavior, and self-discipline of the honor camp men: "When there was any infraction of rules, the Synanon men took care of their own problems in their groups." This seemed to foster the development of the inmates' "inner controls."

Participation in Synanon became a factor in parole consideration. Inmates came to recognize that there was something to be gained from Synanon participation. (There was a paradox in this situation. When the men sincerely involved themselves in Synanon, they were, in fact, increasingly better parole risks.) Progress in Synanon was determined by the judgments of prison officials, by Synanist analyses, and by the opinions of inmate peers in the Synanon program. This appeared to be a most useful collection of opinions and analyses for determining who was "ready" for parole. (In some respects, it was a new kind of parole prediction method.)

The sharing of opinions among these different, yet cooperating, factions seemed to have a side effect of bringing staff and inmates into greater harmony.

Synanon's apparent success had a degree of positive fallout that affected the therapeutic action of many guards and other prison personnel. Synanon somewhat smashed the "doing-time" myth of the "tough con who cannot change." Startling changes in behavior occurred in many former "hard-core, difficult inmates." This resulted in a greater staff belief in the possibilities of rehabilitation in general.

Back to Reality

The new "prison-to-freedom" tunnel carved out by Synanon in the Nevada State Prison program may very well represent the opening of a new trail in American correction. Taking the Synanon path, a prisoner can move from complete custody to freedom. At each turning point, the inmate must positively affect the critical judgments of inmate peers, Synanists, and the prison administration.

The paths of transition available through Synanon provided several more "gateways to freedom" for the offender—not only a personal freedom but the freedom to learn how to live effectively with others. The inmate had an available set of achievable goals that could transport him from the "hole" to life in a Synanon in the community. He could progress through these levels as he outgrew his apparent need to live in the womblike atmosphere of the cell and demonstrated an apparent ability to assume greater responsibility at a higher level of life.

The movement is analogous to movement from the womb (solitary confinement) into various stages of life. In the "hole," the inmate vegetates and is almost totally inactive. The "hole" is dark, and there is no interaction or communication with other people. In maximum security, the inmate functions like a child. He makes sounds and mutterings in groups that are usually concerned with his physical comfort. At another Synanon level, he is beginning to interact with others in the yard (adolescence). On the Synanon tier, a still higher level of expectations and demands requires a more adult role. In the Synanon Honor Camp, he more clearly demonstrates his ability to function as an adult. He is given and assumes responsibility. He does significant work and begins to interact with people in the society at large. In the next step, living in a Synanon community outside the walls, he is to a great extent on his own and has earned the right to function on the outside as an adult. There he can round himself out and grow up, along with his hundreds of newfound "brothers" and "sisters."

Starting from inside the walls, Synanon has carved a path back into a world of new reality. The only price the formerly encapsulated inmate has to pay is clearly stated in a brochure written and printed by Nevada State Prison Synanon members: "The only requirement for new members is honesty, for this is a basic necessity in making the concepts of Synanon practical."

Since its founding in 1958, the original Synanon organization has remained in existence. It has sparked a worldwide movement now known as the therapeutic community. Chapter 18 presents an appraisal of therapeutic communities and the ways in which they are, and can be, used as an "outside the walls" residential alternative to prisons for some criminals.

Chapter
18

The Therapeutic Community: An Alternative to Prison

EX-CRIMINALS HELP TO REFORM FELONS
"Criminal therapy," the use of ex-criminals to treat criminals, is a major breakthrough in criminology, according to Dr. Lewis Yablonsky, University of California at Los Angeles criminologist. In an article in the September issue of Federal Probation, *a leading criminology publication of the Federal Government, Dr. Yablonsky described the important new treatment for criminals.*

The technique originated, he pointed out, at Synanon House in Santa Monica, California, a unique self-help community for rehabilitation of drug addicts. Over the past year several "graduates" of Synanon have effectively introduced "criminal therapy" at the Federal Terminal Island Prison near Long Beach, California.

Dr. Yablonsky, who is also Synanon research director, said, "We have found that former addicts with long criminal backgrounds and prison experience often make the most effective therapists for younger addicts and delinquents who have embarked on similar criminal careers.

The ex-criminal therapist has 'made the scene' himself. He cannot be 'conned' or outmaneuvered by his 'patient.' He quickly gains the grudging respect of his 'patient' and there is rapport. The result is a communication that penologists and others in authority find difficult to establish with others who by their criminal background, are defiant of authority."

In this new approach "being clean" (of crime, drugs, and violence) becomes the status symbol. A reverse of the criminal code occurs and any slip back into criminality means great loss of face in the group.
[New York Times, *September 30, 1962. Copyright © 1962 by The New York Times Company. Reprinted by permission.]*

*T*he therapeutic community methodology briefly described in the *New York Times* article highlights the Synanon approach in its early years. The original method has been developed, modified, and replicated all over the United States and worldwide. An organization in the United States is known as Therapeutic Communities of America, and a worldwide association is the World Federation of Therapeutic Communities.

Although it is not applicable to all types of criminals, the therapeutic community has had a profound and positive rehabilitative result for tens of thousands of former criminal-addicts in the thousands of therapeutic communities that are currently in existence. Although Synanon in prison is a valuable treatment, the therapeutic community (TC) is a viable alternative to placement in prison for many and is also effective for working with criminals in residential community treatment centers. Many TCs focus on offenders' substance abuse problems; however, given the significant linkage between substance abuse and criminality (over 70 percent of criminals abuse some substance), the TC system has a role in helping to solve the crime problem.

In this chapter I will delineate and analyze the therapeutic community as a community treatment methodology that has the potential for rehabilitating criminals and also for converting many people in the criminal population into paraprofessionals who can significantly contribute to controlling crime. The chapter is derived, in part, from my book *The Therapeutic Community.*[1]

ORIGINS OF THE TC CONCEPT

The concept of utilizing former offenders or former patients for the purpose of treating people with a problem has a long history that precedes the creation of Synanon. In this century several contributions to the TC model are notable. Psychiatrist J. L. Moreno, who invented the psychodrama and many dimensions of group therapy around 1910, early on perceived the value of people acting as cotherapists in a small group therapy process. He wrote extensively about the concept of the professional group therapist's and psychodramatist's major role of getting people in group therapy to help each other to resolve their problems. The effective professional's role was, according to Moreno's basic viewpoint, mainly as a catalyst and coordinator of the group's therapeutic energy.

Maxwell Jones, in the 1940s, utilized "patient power" principles in setting up a form of therapeutic community in mental hospitals in England. He attempted to have the mental patients in his group work

---

[1] Lewis Yablonsky, *The Therapeutic Community* (New York: Gardner Press, 1989).

with each other toward strengthening their ability to function in the outside social system.

A major breakthrough in paraprofessional therapy, related to the TC movement, was the creation and development of Alcoholics Anonymous (AA). AA began in 1935 when a stockbroker and a medical doctor, both alcoholics, pooled their knowledge about the ravages of alcoholism. They spent over three years in developing, on a trial-and-error basis, the basic tenets of AA that were utilized in their own recoveries. The AA program—reports of success stories, support group meetings, the utilization of recovering alcoholics as sponsors, and a 12-step method that an alcoholic can work through—has had a profound impact on reducing the problem of alcoholism on a worldwide basis. AA has also become a significant methodology used in prison work for criminals.

In my own work with violent gangs in New York City, I formulated a TC method when I hired former gang members to work with gangs.[2] These "paraprofessionals" knew the turf—and intuitively understood the problems that violent gang youths were struggling with, since they had "been there" themselves. This enabled them to help many youths extricate themselves from the gang warfare, drug abuse, and crime that were rampant in their neighborhoods. I also utilized the treatment energy of parolees who were leading successful lives to help resocialize neighborhood violent gangs and delinquents in small group therapy sessions. These were former criminals effective in communicating the benefits of a crime-free lifestyle to delinquents in small group situations that I constructed as part of my overall crime prevention program. Consequently, when I first hear about Synanon, I was enormously interested in researching the organization.

I first learned about Synanon at a United Nations conference on crime and delinquency in London in the summer of 1960. One evening, at an informal gathering, this new experiment for treating criminal addicts was described to me by noted criminologist Dr. Donald Cressey. According to Dr. Cressey, Synanon involved a small group of criminal-addicts living together in an old beach house then located in Santa Monica, California. Synanon was a residential counterpart of the community-based AA. Since the inception of the TC approach in Synanon, the method has been developed and utilized to control crime and addiction problems on a worldwide basis. Bona fide TCs have definitive structural and functional characteristics that have evolved over the years.

Defining the Therapeutic Community

In my view, a true therapeutic community incorporates the basic AA approach of using recovering offenders as cotherapists in a supportive

---

[2] See Lewis Yablonsky, *The Violent Gang* (New York: Macmillan, 1962; reprint, New York: Irvington Press, 1988).

group environment. In this anticrime setting, former offenders can be motivated to explore their social-psychological problems and become resocialized into a law-abiding approach to life.

On the basis of my extensive research into TCs around the world since 1961, I have concluded that there are several basic factors that must exist in order for an organization to be defined as a true TC: (1) voluntary entrance; (2) the use of various methods, especially the encounter group process; (3) the proper use of former offenders in combination with college-trained psychotherapists as cotherapists in the program; and (4) an open-ended social structure that allows the resident to move up the status ladder of the organization into an increasingly responsible therapeutic position in the TC.

Voluntary Entrance   By "voluntary entrance" I mean there is some level of motivation on the part of criminals to participate in the TC program and that they are not being "sentenced" to the treatment program against their will. There has to be some commitment on the part of the offender to change past criminal behavior, even though such motivation may be fueled by other considerations. There are many factors that influence a criminal's "commitment" to a TC program on entrance. For example, the person may have a sense of hopelessness about life as a criminal. Many criminals are on the verge of becoming totally alienated from family and real friends. A criminal may choose a "commitment" to a TC instead of being involuntarily confined to prison as the result of a court decision.

Thus, voluntary entrance means that there is some level of participatory motivation on the part of people who enter the program. Even though the motivation may be low in the beginning, the criminal has made a decision to change his or her behavior; and unlike the situation in a prison or closed hospital ward, the individual can leave at will. From this weak beginning, the embers of commitment must be fanned by TC compatriots, in a community setting that is radically different from a prison, into a glowing fire of motivation to become and remain free from a future life of crime.

Group Processes   The encounter group in a TC is a basic vehicle through which the recovering criminal explores personal problems and the commitment to become drug-free. In addition, various supportive, educational, and psychodramatic groups are of great value in the recovery process. All bona fide TCs utilize some form of encounter group at the core of their treatment program. One reason for doing so is that *all* criminals practice some pattern of self-deception about their lives. To combat the self-delusions that keep these people on their self-destructive paths, a small group situation is required in which they can be confronted by group members who will help them better understand the realities of their life situations and positively change their values from criminally oriented perceptions to law-abiding viewpoints.

The encounter group enables a recovering criminal to become a cotherapist to his or her peers. When this type of "doctor" is giving treatment to another criminal in an encounter group, the recipient of the verbal attack may hear and accept this truth—but of equal importance is the fact that the statement may apply as well to the person who made it.

The group process in a TC, especially the encounter group, not only deals with the self-delusion of the recovering criminal; it is also a situation in which each resident's progress is evaluated, work and organizational problems in the TC are resolved, each person's responsibility for recovery is discussed, and family problems are analyzed and treated. The group process in a TC, therefore, does not always involve harsh verbal battles—participants are often supportive of each other and rationally analyze the variety of problems that they mutually share in their movement toward personal growth and changing their values.

Most TCs use varied forms of groups. Some involve long-term group sessions, which last two or three days and are often called "trips" or "marathons." "Group probes" on significant problems are a form of intellectual investigation into relevant issues. Many TCs in their group process utilize a form of psychodrama, both on a regular basis and when the need arises. The essence of these varied groups is that the residents become cotherapists to each other in a drive for personal and social growth. Their relationship has many parallels to the processes that occur in AA support groups.

Former Criminals as Cotherapists An important element in a TC is the fact that shortly after entrance the residents assume considerable responsibility for their own treatment. They are forced to confront the realities of their life situations by others who have made the trip from feeling abject helplessness to a point where they have taken considerable control over their own lives.

Former criminals are equipped to be effective peer therapists for at least three important reasons. First, they have been through the throes and conflicts of their original problems. They know many of the rationalizations and self-deceptions that keep a person on the criminal merry-go-round: from the streets, to jail, to prison, and back. They comprehend on a deep emotional level from their own experience what a criminal life is like; they have "been there" themselves.

Second, they have gone through the complex resocialization process of personal change in a TC program. They know, on a firsthand basis, the painful emotional crises and traumas of confronting their own lives more directly. They have experienced the various phases of reorganizing their relationships with their families and friends. They have developed coping mechanisms for dealing with the temptations of sliding back into their former states of existence, and for breaking off relationships with former partners in crime.

Third, because of these two sets of experiences—life as a criminal and firsthand knowledge about the recovery process—former offenders have usually developed some special insights and skills. They are not easily outmaneuvered or conned. They quickly acquire the respect of the "copatients," because they can see through the rationalizations and ploys that they once used themselves. The result is a communication that has more therapeutic power than that usually achieved in more traditional professional therapy. These paraprofessionals also know from their day-to-day experiences the self-discipline required to continue to lead a crime-free life.

The significant value of these former criminals as cotherapists in a TC does not exclude the university-trained psychiatrist, psychologist, social worker, or counselor. The management and leadership of most TCs are shared by former offenders who have become paraprofessionals and by trained professionals. The TC approach has, therefore, become a more cooperative venture, and this is revealed by an analysis of the social structure of contemporary TCs.

The Social Structure of TCs   One of the most important contributions of the TC to the treatment of criminals is found in the TC's social structure. It has a distinctly different organizational form than is found in other, more traditional therapeutic institutions.

Most traditional prisons or correctional institutions have a two-tier caste system of organization. There are the doctors and the patients, the correctional officers and the prisoners, the healers and the sick. This castelike division is based on the premise that if patients follow their doctor-therapists' instructions, they will get well. Most correctional organizations and prisons reflect this type of medical model.

A true TC does not have a "we-they" caste system. It provides an open-ended stratification situation. Upward mobility is distinctly possible in the organization, and, in fact, upward movement in the system is encouraged and is perceived as a positive factor in self-growth. As one TC leader, a former criminal, told a newcomer during an indoctrination session: "In a couple of years . . . you just might be a big shot around here and have my job." Not only is upward social mobility possible in a TC, but healthy status seeking is encouraged. This type of upward mobility is not possible in a traditional institution, since the professional therapist has a lock on the power-status position and "patients," or prisoners, remain in their clear-cut inferior role for the duration of their time in the institution.

A TC organization assumes, with some supportive evidence, that a person's position in its hierarchy is a correlate of social maturity, "mental health," increased work ability, and a clear understanding of the organization. Another assumption is that the social skills learned in a TC structure are useful within the larger society. The "we-they" problem does not exist in a true TC structure since the administration and the patients are one and the same, and upward mobility is encouraged in this open-ended stratification system.

In a TC, criminals find *a new society*. They receive support, understanding, and affection from people who have had life experiences similar to their own. They find a community in which they can identify with people, toward whom they can express their best human emotions rather than their worst. They find special friends (or in AA terms, sponsors) who will assist them when they begin to deviate or fall short of what they have set out to do—to develop personal growth and remain law-abiding. In the new society of the TC, they develop the ability to express their best human qualities and potentialities; this personal growth is transferable to living in a happier, more productive life in the larger society.

Group Therapy Methods and Processes

The overall environment of a TC is therapeutic. A positive ethos that is both supportive and caring is transmitted to the recovering resident informally on a daily basis in all individual and group interactions. Everyone experiencing emotional problems or pain has access to another person on a one-on-one basis in order to receive individual caring and counseling, on almost a 24-hour basis.

In addition to this overall healing environment, on a more specific level, in almost all TCs I have studied there are various groups that focus on such issues and topics as (1) indoctrinating the newcomer into the TC, (2) family treatment, (3) self-disclosure and nurturing, (4) educational therapy, (5) occupational issues, and (6) social-psychological analysis and treatment.

Indoctrination and Orientation   These groups are primarily for newcomers. They focus on various phases and ramifications of the TC program that will be encountered in the recovery process. These group sessions analyze the structure of the organization and the value and purpose of various methods, such as the encounter group and psychodrama. The goal of these sessions is to integrate the newcomer into the community and serve as a constant reminder to the more senior members who participate in these groups they are involved in the TC.

Most TCs have a waiting list. The Italian TC system (there are over 40 bona fide TCs in Italy) utilizes this waiting time by having applicants and their families attend indoctrination groups, where they learn about various aspects of the TC program. In this way they get a head start on joining the program. Typically, in these groups work is begun on the potential resident's problems. He or she may work out a family contract for improving behavior and for becoming drug- and crime-free as a prelude to entering the TC. These orientation and indoctrination groups facilitate a more effective learning experience when the newcomer finally becomes a full-time resident.

Family Groups Some discussion groups on family issues involve only residents. Other groups also include parents, spouses, siblings, and other relatives. The concept that hovers over every type of family-issue session is that the recovering resident is the nucleus of a familial social atom, and his or her problems are inextricably bound up with the family system. This concept encompasses J. L. Moreno's admonition that "treatment must always take into account the person's social atom, including family relationships."

These family-system treatment groups deal with specific proto-typical issues such as the following: (1) *Denial*—"My parents knew I was an addict but they chose to ignore my problem." (2) *Abuse*—"My mother beat me almost every day of my childhood for no good reason. I killed my rage and pain with drugs, and later when I was older I physically abused women to get back at my mother." (3) *Separation*—"I will not go back to the husband who abused me and my kids." (4) *Neglect*—"My parents were never there for me when I needed them. My father gave me material things, but he never showed any love." All these issues, and others, are focused on in family groups in order to help the recovering resident and his or her parents understand and resolve the family dynamics that produced their crime and drug abuse problems.

Self-Disclosure and Nurturing Groups Most criminals and delinquents, no matter how tough they appear to be on the outside, have a "hurt child" inside them and usually have never been able to disclose their painful feelings to another person. As one recovering woman resident told me:

> After I was in the TC for six months, I got in touch with my feelings, and I finally admitted that my father had sexually abused me for many years. When it was happening, my mother denied it was going on and I had no one to talk to about my rage and pain. I believe my secret caused me to use cocaine to kill the emotional pain of my problems. I also became a prostitute. This I stupidly believed gave me control over the sex act—and in some ways I felt that abusing masochistic men [tricks] was a real kick. I felt I was getting back at my father. After I discussed these painful things in a group, I cried for days. Other women, and some of the guys, helped me past my painful feelings.

After disclosure in a group, where this is encouraged, the group provides a nurturing environment in the TC for the resident. In this way emotional pain and rage that have been repressed for years surface, the resident tends to feel less alone and less guilty, and his or her self-esteem is often enhanced by the accepting, nurturing response of the group.

Educational Groups   Most delinquents and criminals in the process of their lives block out most of the real world. Many of them have learning disabilities. On their path to social reality in a TC, they often become enormously motivated to learn, read, and in general pursue the education they missed. This educational hunger is fed in educational groups in the TC that focus on all kinds of subjects, including philosophical discussions analyzing such philosophers as Emerson, Plato, Kant, and Spinoza; current events related to a range of contemporary social and political events; social and psychological theories about mental health, including those of Freud, Moreno, Fromm, and Erikson; the analyses of biological sciences; study groups and reading in literature, music, and art; and, in many TCs, spiritual and religious theories and practices. In brief, TC educational groups cover the range of human subjects. The process often motivates residents to complete their formal high school or college educations and to better determine the kind of life work they will pursue when they graduate from the TC.

Occupations and Work Groups   All TC residents work in and for their organization. As in most organizations, there are business office jobs, housekeeping and kitchen jobs, and manual labor, and these jobs are filled by residents. Many TCs have gas stations, light manufacturing plants, and advertising specialty businesses for the purpose of helping to finance the organization's work. Most of these jobs are staffed by residents. In "occupational groups" discussions, each resident's efficacy and proclivity for meaningful work are analyzed. The group's goal is to help residents, many of whom have had work problems in their pasts, to clarify the kind of work they would like to engage in when they graduate, and to perform more effectively in their occupations of choice. These groups foster on-the-job training and clarify occupational goals. The groups are beneficial for the residents in their future occupations in society.

Social-Psychological Treatment Groups   The overall goal of all the types of groups delineated here is to help the recovering residents deal more effectively with their emotional problems. In this regard, various TCs, depending on their social-psychological orientation, have different forms of group therapy. Some have professionally trained psychiatrists, psychologists, or social workers direct the group therapy sessions. Other TCs are more inclined to utilize leaderless rap groups in which people share and discuss their emotional problems and explore ways to resolve them. Some TC group therapy sessions are highly analytic and focus on problem-solving discussions. Also, in most TCs with which I have been involved or have studied, psychodrama and role training are significant therapeutic group methods. Most TCs utilize a range of group methods and techniques, including encounter groups, for resolving their residents' social and emotional problems.

The encounter group approach is at the core of most group methods in a TC. Consequently, the following discussion and analysis will focus exclusively on this important TC group method.

The Encounter Group

A method that is basic to the difficult process of dealing with a resident's problem, and which is utilized in all TCs, is what is variously called the encounter group, the game, or the dynamic group. Although most TCs effectively use the other group methods discussed, the encounter group is at the core of proper functioning of the overall organization of a TC, and it is a method that is vital for successfully treating the offender. The basic process involves a group attack on the self-deception that characterizes the resident. An important consequence of this verbal encounter is that it forces the recovering resident to examine his or her behavior and lifestyle introspectively. In my view, the encounter group is a necessary process in all TC work because the criminal personality does not respond to the other, more supportive approaches until basic self-deception devices are vehemently encountered by the group. (The encounter process for confronting an offender on an individual level in therapy was discussed in Chapter 16.)

A conscious dimension of the TC group encounter process is the use of a senior member as a role model, and this is often done in the group session. A role model is a person who has been in the situation of the new person and has made progress to a higher level of performance in the TC and in life. The role model is a dynamic example of what the newcomer can become after growing and developing in the TC.

The senior person in an encounter group will often make a comment to the effect that "I remember when I was like you, when I was here *x* amount of time." The role model then shares why he or she no longer feels, for example, in imminent danger of returning to drugs or a life of crime. This permits the newcomer to identify with someone who has experienced the same internal conflicts and has resolved these issues.

Open self-revelation by the senior patient-therapist in a TC is a factor not usually found in professional group therapy. Professionals seldom use their own problems as examples for the patient. In fact, this is counterindicated in most therapeutic methodologies. In a TC, however, it is standard technique for the acting "doctor" to identify with the "patient's" problem. In the group, therefore, a recovering resident points out an achievable positive goal. This is a person who can guide his or her growth from the successful position of personal experience. The role-model concept is openly discussed in TCs as a basic socialization process for positive behavioral change.

It is important to note that related to the senior role-model concept is the fact that both the senior patient and the junior patient are involved in a therapeutic interaction that is of value to both of them. As Donald Cressey stated, "When criminal A *helps* criminal B, criminal A is helped."[3] A role model who explains why a new resident should make positive changes in behavior is reinforcing his or her own resolution. Therefore, the person in a TC playing "therapist" is being helped personally by performing the therapeutic role. And since all residents of a TC at various times play therapist, they are helping resolve their own problems in the process.

The dynamic that should be emphasized in this interaction is that the junior patient can perceive in the role model what he can become, and the senior patient can see where she was in her earlier approach to life. This constant reminder of the way the senior resident was as a newcomer is important in reinforcing the resolve to lead a crime-free life.

The encounter group approach is especially therapeutic for formerly physically abusive or violent people. As a result of their training in encounter groups, they can learn how to channel their rage into verbal rather than physically violent behavior.

The power of an individual's confrontation abilities in a TC encounter group appears to be correlated with the emotional strength of the attacker and the attacker's position in the hierarchy. Old-timers in a TC have developed more powerful verbal weapons and speak from a more powerful position in the hierarchy. Their verbal sword has a sharper edge, but at the same time, they have learned to level their verbal encounter with more precision. They are more likely to direct their critique at the person's behavioral problems than the "self," and they seem to know when to give a person positive support. They are also less likely to be doing it out of their own emotional needs to attack another person.

It is important to emphasize the fact that the encounter group is always supplemented and enriched in a positive way by later informal discussions in a "caring circle" of friends in the TC. All residents in a TC are encouraged to develop and nurture a caring circle of people with whom they can discuss issues brought up forcefully in the group in a more casual interpretive, analytic, and supportive way. These nurturing, supportive discussions with a caring circle of friends are most significant in the overall group process in TCs.

THE THERAPEUTIC COMMUNITY FROM THE VIEWPOINT OF TWO FORMER RESIDENTS

Zev

Some of the processes, characteristics, and phases of entering and growing up in Synanon were articulated by Zev Putterman, who had

---

[3] Donald Cressey, "Changing Criminals: The Application of the Theory of Differential Association," *American Journal of Sociology* 61, no. 2 (September 1961):116–120.

then been a member of Synanon for a year, in a lecture to one of my graduate seminars. For the lecture, Zev was asked to compare his past role as an inmate in a variety of treatment settings with his Synanon experience.

Zev was 33 when he arrived at Synanon in 1962. He had been a criminal drug addict for around 14 years. Partially because of his upper-middle-class background, he had managed to complete a college education. After college, Zev had some success as a theatrical producer and director. Zev described the experiences felt by many TC members. The unique quality that differentiated Zev from others was that because of his educational background he had a more exceptional ability to articulate his growth process:

> I will try to give you the benefit of my contact with various institutional approaches to my disorder, which has been labeled by psychoanalysts as "constitutional psychopathy, complicated by drug addiction." I guess, in your frame of reference, "sociopath" would be more applicable. At any rate, this diagnosis was made fourteen years ago by Dr. Abram Kardiner, a pretty reputable Freudian psychiatrist, after I spent eight months with the man.
>
> Over a period of thirteen years, I wound in and out of private, public, state, county, and federal institutions for drug addicts; also private hospitals for people with the whole spectrum of emotional and psychological disorders. What I think is relevant to examine here today in the light of my experience is what happened to me in the thirteen months that I've been at Synanon that has made it possible for me not to behave as I did previously.
>
> There is no evidence, as yet, as to whether I have been changed on a deep and meaningful level. But there is plenty of face evidence that my behavior has manifested a change so drastic from what it was thirteen months ago that to me, and people who knew me before coming to Synanon, it's almost unbelievable.
>
> What I wanted to point out to you, in brief, is that what happened at Synanon did not happen at the Menninger Clinic in Topeka; the Institute of Living in Hartford; three times at Lexington, Kentucky; New York Metropolitan Hospital; Manhattan General; the Holbrook Sanatorium; or the Westport Sanatorium. . . .
>
> When you think of an addiction history of fourteen years, people have the image of fourteen years of constant drug use. The thing that makes a person a drug addict, to me, is the equation that they learn after their first detoxification. A drug addict becomes a drug addict not when he just becomes addicted to drugs, but when he learns this equation. They kick their habit physiologically; they have decided consciously to change their behavior; they are going to manipulate themselves in every way that they know in order not to repeat what they've been doing, and—bingo—they repeat exactly those processes which got them to the point that they didn't want to get to. This, to me, is when a drug addict becomes a drug addict. The drug addict, to me, is the person who has taken his first cure and then gone back to dope. The institution he goes to is part of his addiction process.
>
> Now, let's discuss institutional settings and their differences. I think the very first difference between Synanon and other setups is that the addict on

the outside has heard something about this thing called Synanon. He knows that it has something to do with drug addicts and that there are no psychiatrists there. He hears that they're all drug addicts and that they're not using drugs. Of course, the drug addicts don't believe this—not for a second. This is absurd! "Of course they're using drugs. If they are a group of drug addicts, they're using drugs; and if they are not using drugs, they're not the kind of drug addict that I am. Because if they were the kind of drug addict that I am, why, they would use drugs." So this is the first impact that Synanon has. In other words, you're convinced that this sounds very nice but that it's not true.

Certain circumstances force people to come to Synanon. The AA always uses the phrase "You reach your own bottom." So, let's assume that I had reached a "bottom": I had tried everything else in the Western world, I think, just about everything else; you know, chemical cures as well, which I didn't bother to mention.

Anyway, I came to Synanon. At first, something very strange happened to me. I came into this place early in the morning. I had just gotten off the plane; I'd flown three thousand miles. The usual reception at a place where a person has volunteered for a cure is "Welcome aboard!" This was not the case. I was told to sit down and shut up, in just about those words; you know, literally, "Sit down. Shut up."

I figured I was talking to a disturbed person who didn't understand who he was talking to. In the first moment of contact, instead of being told, "Welcome aboard," you're told to shut up and sit down. Whereupon, being loaded on a variety of opiates, I explained that I had just arrived in California; that I flew in from New York; and that I had talked to a board member; whereupon the magic words "Shut up and sit down" were readministered. I began to realize that reason has nothing to do with the behavior of these people; these are not reasonable people, obviously; because I was being perfectly reasonable. So I shut up and sat down, because I had no alternative. If I'd had an alternative, I would have said, "I'll come back another time." But I was three thousand miles away from my connection. I didn't have that resource.

I sat down for a number of hours, and then I was called by some people into a room. Oh, first of all, my luggage was taken away from my possession. And one of my pieces of luggage contained a variety of drugs, nonnarcotic in nature, that were prescribed for me by my psychiatrist. When I left New York I said, "I'll be gone for six months," and he wrote five prescriptions for six months' worth of five different kinds of medication—you know, to ease withdrawal . . . nonnarcotic psychic energizers, tranquilizers, sleeping medication—a whole satchelful of it.

The intake interview . . . I've been subjected to many intake interviews, by social workers, psychiatrists, psychologists, and charge nurses, you know. And I was usually asked a variety of questions, and I had my pat answers; you know, am I white or black—"I'm white." In this instance, I wasn't asked anything. They didn't even want to know my name. I mean, literally, they did not say to me, "Who are you?" They proceeded to tell me who I was. Their only contact with me had been a phone call from Westport, which lasted maybe a minute, and then my contact with the guy at the desk, who didn't listen to what I was saying. So they were telling me who I was.

They told me things like I would never make it, I was a mama's boy, I was spoiled, I was a compulsive talker, I was unable to learn anything, I was probably incurable; that if I didn't shut up they would throw me out; that they were not interested in learning anything from me, because I had nothing to teach them—which, of course, to me was absolutely absurd, because, you know, I had come there to enlighten the West Coast. This is a shocking experience. I'm making it humorous, but it shook me up; it shook me down to my feet.

After being screamed at by Reid Kimball, who has tapped sources of rage better than anyone I've ever met, and being thoroughly humiliated by six dope fiends staring at me . . . He would use devices like this: he said, "There's an accumulative thirty-seven years of sobriety in this room and eighty-two years of dope addiction in this room; so therefore, your fourteen years of addiction and three seconds of sobriety don't count." Now, that was reasonable to me. So you see, I was being hit on a reasonable and nonreasonable level as I saw it.

So, they were talking about me as if I wasn't there, after this thing happened. You know, "Let's take him downstairs, let's do this to him . . ." I wasn't being consulted, and the first thing I thought, when I heard about Synanon, was: There won't be any "we" and "they" alienations, because these are folks like me and they know how sick I am.

I was then taken outside by a man by the name of James Middleton. A gargantuan character that I would never have an opportunity to communicate with—even shooting dope. It would just be a matter of conning him, or him hitting me over the head. And he proceeded to take my little satchel with medicine in it—you know, he looked to me like Alley Oop—and he took this satchel of medicine and led me downstairs to the basement, which is pretty grim, and looked like the Twenty-third Precinct in New York. He took the satchel and opened the bottles and proceeded to pour them into the toilet. I said, "Now wait. You see, you don't understand. These are nonaddicting drugs—none of these drugs are addicting drugs, and they're legitimate. See, my name is on them." And while I'm saying this, he is like grunting and pouring my medicine out.

This is another important aspect of Synanon as different from another institution. The first thing I picked up in this indoctrination, being a manipulative type of guy, was this: When people didn't want me or didn't seem to want me, I, of course, wanted them. The appeal to me was somewhat like a fraternity appeal in a college. The fraternity which is most difficult to get into is naturally the most desirable.

Well, what had been communicated to me immediately by "Sit down and shut up," you know, as if I were rushing the house, was: This club is rather exclusive. They're not particularly impressed with me, so naturally they must be pretty good—because my self-esteem was pretty shitty, although it didn't look that way.

Then, my personal property . . . I think a person's property represents who you are—you know, your résumés. For people in my business, your eight-by-ten glossies [pictures] and your theater programs—you know, this is who you are. I had a few pieces of clothing and an electric shaver—things you picked up that are pawnable. These things were taken away from me—brusquely. And I was given—*schmatas* [rags] is the only word I can think of—I was given unseemly clothing.

There was nothing institutional about the clothing. There was a plaid shirt which didn't fit. And I was very specific in asking for cotton, because my skin gets sensitive during withdrawal. I was given a wool plaid shirt, because I asked for cotton, and a pair of khaki pants that didn't fit, and rubber go-aheads, or flip-flops, or suicide-scuffs, which were very uncomfortable. And then I was taken upstairs.

There I was. My luggage was gone, my résumés, my identity, my drugs . . . my pride. I also got a haircut, just because I protested too much. I had my hair cut off rather short, and by a guy who didn't particularly care for the cosmetic value of a haircut. I didn't need a haircut. The day before, I had been to Vincent of the Plaza and had a haircut.

I went into the living room and was introduced to a few people. I recognized a couple. I recognized a couple as drug addicts. Like I saw scar tissue on their arms. I saw that they were—like maybe they really were drug addicts.

Kicking my habit at Synanon had a big effect on me. It was a process which, again, was very different from the institutions. The institutions I had been to all had detoxification procedures of one kind or another. All the detoxification procedures that I've ever been involved in, although they may be medically necessary for people with a heart condition or people who are over ninety-three, really were not necessary, I discovered at Synanon. In all of the settings I had been in, the bit was to exaggerate your symptoms so that you could get medication. Because if you get medication, you feel better. Which is very simple: if you get medication, you feel better; if you don't, you feel bad. I don't think there is anything pathological in this kind of behavior. So the thing to do, of course, is to get medication.

Well, at Synanon, of course, I was told, with the flushing down the drain of the medications I had brought, that I was not getting any medication. And I said, you know, "I'm going to get quite sick—I'm not feeling very good." "You will not get any medication."

I said, "You don't understand. You see, I'm going to be really sick. You see, I'm from New York, and they've got good dope in New York, and I'm strung out—and I'm going to get really sick."

They again repeated, "You will not get medication. If you want medication, you can leave and get medication. But here you won't get medication."

This immediately stopped a whole process which would have gone on for two or three weeks if medication were given. This is another important thing: I had my biggest manipulative device taken away from me, because there was nothing to manipulate for, except maybe a glass of water. That's about it, you know. And how much of a con game would I have to run down to get a glass of water? . . .

I was up off the couch in four days. Now, I had been kicking habits. I was a specialist in observing myself kicking habits—you know, reading Cocteau as another frame of reference in kicking habits . . . how he kicked his habit—and all of my evidence crumbled. You see, all of my evidence was destroyed by the experience that I was sleeping by the seventh day—I hadn't slept without medication in or out of a place in seven years. I had not been able to sleep. I was now sleeping within seven days.

On the fifth day, I was rewarded for kicking my habit by receiving a mop! I thought the least I deserved—you know, the least—for what I'd been subjected to was a week at a country club. Instead, I was not rewarded at all. Because there really was not any reason for a reward. I heard things like "Not shooting dope is not worthy of a reward. People don't shoot dope! Therefore, not shooting dope doesn't earn any reward." It's like saying, "Congratulations for not beating your wife," or "Thank you for not murdering my sister." You know, one doesn't do this, so naturally you're not going to get a big hand.

No one at Synanon is going to applaud you because you're not shooting any dope and you're mopping the floors. Somebody's got to mop the floors, and you're constantly told you don't know how to do anything else. You begin to think that maybe they're right—because at this point, you're pretty broken, psychically and physically—so you find yourself mopping a floor.

And then the magic thing begins to go to work, this thing about the secret. I think this is what motivates you to mop the floor well. You begin to see that if you mop the floor well, you won't feel as guilty as if you mop the floor badly.

In most institutional settings, and in most psychoanalytical or socially oriented or tradition-directed treatment centers for dope fiends, your guilt is usually ameliorated: "You're a sick fellow; you can't help yourself; you have an acting-out disorder; together we'll work this thing out, resocialize you, and everything will be crazy. So of course what people like myself do is, they take all this ammunition, they fuel themselves with the fact that they are acting out a disorder. What can they do? They have all the data, so they go and act out.

You see, at Synanon, they lay guilt upon guilt. In other words, every time the energy flags a little bit—like mopping the floors and the corners aren't done—instead of being told, "Well, you know, he's still sick; he hasn't really kicked yet; he's new and he hasn't done much floor-mopping in his time," you are made to feel that the dirty corner represents a dirty corner in your psyche, your gut. You think that you really are ridiculously bad at mopping floors, and you get guilty, you see, and your guilt is fueled.

Now, whenever you are in an institutional setting, your guilt is explained away—it's lightened. The burden of guilt is lightened. In Synanon, whenever things begin to get buoyant and you permit your insanity to return as self-compensation for your low self-esteem, you're told you're not unique in nature and get smashed on the head with a velvet mallet. If it doesn't crush the tissue, you still feel the impact of it, which is an important thing.

Now, by this stage in Synanon, you are beginning to learn something. You are beginning to find out that everybody there, from the members of the Board of Directors down to yourself, has had a history akin to your own, somewhat akin. In other words, most of them came in and kicked their habit. Most of them came in and anticipated something completely else. You know, no drug addict anticipates being humiliated because he has decided to kick a habit. He does not conceive of this. I conceived maybe that because these were other drug addicts, maybe they'd be kind of tough. But I did not expect to be laughed at for doing the right thing, like kicking a habit.

Now, how much of what I'm saying is exaggerated because I'm that type of person? There are people who come to Synanon without the résumés and the eight-by-ten glossies . . . who are not smashed quite as hard as I was. They come in with a birdcage on one foot, a boxing glove on the other, and, like, they are in bad shape. You can see that they don't have any totems of success or any illusions, so there's no reason for them to be ridiculed the way I was ridiculed. But they still will not be able to get rewarded for bad behavior.

For instance, I think this is significant in looking at the total Synanon picture: A friend of mine arrived from New York about three months after I got here. My friend Herb was addicted to barbiturates as well as heroin, and he got pretty damn sick and began to act pretty crazy. This is interesting. Reid Kimball, who is one of the directors, came down and told Herb that if he acts like a nut, we'll have to throw him out, because we can't handle nuts. In other words, "Herb, you'll have to go to Camarillo or someplace where they handle crazy people. We don't handle crazy people, so you're not allowed to be crazy here." Now, I've been in three hospitals with Herb, and I know how crazy he is. Now, literally, this happened to work. "Don't be a nut." And, you know, he wasn't! He just couldn't act crazy if he wanted to stay at Synanon, so he didn't.

Herb was a pretty sick guy physically, but he was able to curb his emotional symptoms because of the Synanon approach to him. Candy would not go over to Herb and say things like "When are you going to get sick, little brother?" But, you know, he also didn't go over to him and say things like "Aw, poor boobie-baby-baby-boy," so that Herb would act crazy to get some more "poor boobie-baby-baby-boy," which is symptom reinforcement. Instead, he got what he could get. There were three or four other guys over there who had themselves convulsed when they came in, who said, "Well, man, you go into one of these wingdings every eight or ten hours; and you know, we're all here, and you'll be cool, and don't worry, and stay away from the furniture so you won't fall off."

Here is another significant thing in terms of an institution, and in terms of understanding the Synanon thing: About this time, about three or four weeks after my arrival, I began to notice that the place was full of me. The place was full of me. In other words, in every other institution I had ever been at, I had had a very schizzy feeling. There were the doctors, and I was kind of like them . . . but by some fluke, they became doctors and I was a dope fiend. And I'd look at them, you know, and I felt like I kind of had a foot in their camp. And then I was with the dope fiends, and there, you know, I'm a dope fiend. And there was kind of this "we-them" thing, and I kind of felt that I was straddling them both; and I really know that my soul was with the dope fiends, because the doctors did not know where it was at. They really didn't.

At Synanon, in contrast, I saw a million manifestations of me—in everyone—even the guy called Alley Oop, Jimmy Middleton, who's extremely different. Candy's different. He's colored. Yet Candy can spot things in me so quickly that are exactly me. He knows when I'm gaming; he knows when I'm conning, when I'm lying to myself. I can't do this when he's around, because he sees himself in me too.

The contract that had been set up all my life, the "we-they"—my father and me, my psychiatrist and me, the warden and me, the teacher and me—you know, this contract was smashed by Synanon. I became aware that the place was run by a hundred Zevs—different aspects of me. Different aspects of me were all there. So when I hated somebody's behavior, I hated me; when I approved of somebody's behavior, I approved of me. My sense of alienation with the "we-they" equation—the hip and the square, the culture and the subculture, the in-group and the out-group, the Jews and the Gentiles, the white and the black—all of the "we-they" equations that we had learned, primarily for me they had been a square . . . they had been destroyed.

I began to see that if I mopped a corner right, first of all I wouldn't be so guilty. Even if nobody saw the corner, you see, I felt funny. Secondly, I didn't have to be afraid of being busted by people like me if I did the corner right. And thirdly, I'd probably be able to stop mopping soon; I wouldn't have to mop for the rest of my life. Because it seems eternal—absolutely eternal. You know, they'll tell you, "You'll be mopping for the next three months, brother," and it seems like a long period of time. A long period of time. Since then, I have moved up into more important jobs in Synanon.

I begin to see what Lew Yablonsky articualtes as "social mobility" at Synanon. We don't have a caste system. We have a kind of class system, based on clean seniority, productivity, mental health, talent, and so on. I've just begun to climb this status ladder, and I'm beginning to understand now that I'm hooked into the organization and want to move up. The side effect may be getting well and growing up from being a baby to my thirty-four chronological years of age.

Zev graduated from Synanon and went on to a successful career in public television and film. He married, had children, and was a productive member of society.

Frankie: Delinquent to Artist

The transition of Frankie, a former member of a violent street gang in New York and a drug addict, from a different social background than Zev, revealed some other aspects of the therapeutic community process. The following story and analysis of Frankie's odyssey from criminal to artist is based on observing Frankie's progress over a three-year period in a TC and a number of interviews with him later when he was leading a productive life in society.

Frankie's "family" was a violent gang, until heroin took over his life. He had some talent in his early years in school and might have become an artist, but nothing in his environment permitted him to pursue his career. Violence and drugs pervaded his life when he was growing up on the Upper West Side of Manhattan.

After a youth in violent gangs, Frank turned to a criminal career of using and dealing drugs, especially herion. This life resulted in his doing time in a federal prison (Danbury), New York City's Riker's Island Penitentiary (five times), Bellevue Hospital in New York City, and the federal hospital for drug addicts in Lexington, Kentucky.

In addition to a pattern of drug addiction, pimping, and theft, Frank had a violent streak. "Frankie would never use a knife, unless he had to. Mostly with his fists he would beat a guy down and try to kill him right there. They pulled him off this big guy one time—he wouldn't stop punching him in the face." This was a casual observation by Frankie's former crime partner, a prostitute with whom he had lived for five years in New York City and who had also been rehabilitated in the same TC.

When Frankie was 26, a New York judge who was tired of seeing him go through the city's revolving-door prison system gave him a choice: a long prison sentence at Sing Sing or a last-chance effort in a TC. Frankie chose a TC alternative in California.

Frankie's first reaction to the TC was confusion: "The first thing they hit me with flipped me. This tough-looking cat says to me, 'There are two things you absolutely can't do here, shoot drugs or fight.'" Frankie said, scratching his head, "I was all mixed up—these were the only two things I knew how to do."

Despite his confusion he found the environment interesting and exciting and quite different from prison. There were, for him, "lots of hip people." Among this group was Jimmy, who at 48 had been an addict, a criminal, and a con man for more than 30 years, and had been clean for over 5 years in the TC. He was assigned as Frankie's sponsor. Jimmy ran the kitchen at that time. Frankie got his first job, scouring pots and pans and mopping floors. According to Frankie, Jimmy could not be conned or manipulated out of position like the guards and therapists that Frankie had encountered on Riker's Island and at various federal hospitals. Jimmy, of course, knew the score; to him, Frankie, with all his exploits, was a "young punk" who could give him no trouble. "I've met kids like this all my life—in and out of the joint," he said.

According to Frankie, "At first, I hated this bastard. I used to sometimes sit and plan ways to kill him." When Frankie wanted to fight Jimmy over a disagreement about work, Jimmy laughed and told him that if he wanted to fight, he would be thrown out of the place and get sent back to New York and a long prison term.

The usual prison situation was reversed, and this confused Frankie. In prison, if Frankie got into trouble, confinement became increasingly severe, with the "hole" (solitary confinement) an end point. In the Bellevue Hospital psychiatric ward, where Frankie had also spent time, it was a straitjacket. What made Frankie behave in order to stay in the TC? It was not only the potential threat of prison. In another setting his low impulse control would have propelled him out the door.

What was important for Frankie was that there were others who understood him, had made the same "scenes," and intuitively knew his problems and how to handle him. Although he would only grudgingly admit it, he respected people he could not con. He belonged and was now part of a "family" he could accept.

Frankie could also make a reputation in the TC without getting punished or locked up. In prison the highest he could achieve in terms of the values of other prisoners was to become king of the inmate world, acquire a "stash" of cigarettes, obtain some unsatisfactory homosexual favors, and land in the hole. In the TC he felt he could acquire any role he was "big enough or man enough to achieve," and "growing up" carried the highest approval of his fellows. He could actually move up the status ladder and become a director in this organization. For the first time in his life, Frankie was receiving status—in his gang terms, a "rep"—for being clean and nondelinquent.

Of course, when he first arrived, Frankie attempted to gain a rep by conniving and making deals, in accord with his old mode of relating. When he did, he was laughed at, ridiculed, and given severe "haircuts" by other old-time con men in group sessions. They were, he learned, ferociously loyal to the organization, which had literally saved their lives and given them a new life status. He too began to develop an esprit de corps in the TC. As he once put it, "I never would give three cheers for Riker's Island prison. But I'm part of this place. It's a home to me."

Frankie found that rep was acquired in this social system (unlike the ones he had known) by truth, honesty, and industry. The value of his other life required reversal if he were to gain a rep in the TC. These values were not goals per se that someone moralized about in a meaningless vacuum, but were means to the end of acquiring prestige in this tough social system with which he increasingly identified.

In the groups, three nights a week, Frankie participated in a new kind of group psychotherapy, unlike the kind he had "fooled around with" in prison. Here the truth was viciously demanded. Any rationalizations about past or current deviant behavior were brutally demolished by the group. There was an intensive search for self-identity. He found that in the process, which he began to trust, he learned something of what went on beneath the surface of his thoughts. Frankie admitted that for the first time in his life, he had found other people who had some idea of his underlying thoughts. He had had individual and group therapy in prison, but there he could con the therapist and, most important, "I said what I thought they wanted to hear so I could get out sooner."

Frankie, who at first had followed his usual pattern of self-centered manipulation of others, now began to care about what happened to others, who were real friends to him. He began to identify with the organization and learned on a gut level that if any other member failed, in some measure he, too, failed.

Frankie began to comprehend what others thought in a social situation. The concept of empathy, or identifying with the thoughts and feelings of others, became a significant reality.

In the status system, Frankie's rise in the hierarchy was neither quick nor easy. He first moved from the "dishpan" to serving food at the kitchen counter. After several months he began to work outside on a pickup truck that acquired food and other donations.

Here he had his first slip, no doubt, in part, to test the waters. With two other individuals who worked with him on the truck, a group decision was made one day that "smoking a joint might be fun." They acquired some grass from a dealer known to one of the group.

When they arrived back from work, their slightly "loaded" appearance immediately became apparent to the group. ("They spotted us right away.") They were hauled into the main office and viciously (verbally) attacked and ordered to cop out (tell) or "get lost." A general meeting was called, and they were forced to reveal all before the entire group, in a fireplace scene. That night Frankie was back washing dishes.

Frankie learned the hard way that the norms of the TC were the reverse of the criminal code he knew. In another slip situation, Frankie, with two other members, went for a walk into town. One of them suggested buying a bottle of wine. (Of course, no drinking was permitted in the TC.) Frankie and the other member rejected the proposal. However, no one revealed the incident until two days later, when it came up in group. The group jumped hardest on Frankie and the other individual who had vetoed the idea, rather than on the one who had suggested buying the wine. Frankie and the other "witnesses" were expected to report such slips immediately, since the group's life depended on keeping one another straight. For the first time in his life, Frankie was censured for *not* being a "snitch." The maxim that "thou shalt not squeal," basic to the existence of the usual underworld criminal culture, was reversed and ferociously upheld.

In another area for the criminal addict, the no-physical-violence rule was at first difficult for Frank to grasp and believe, since his usual response to a difficult situation was to leap, fists first, past verbal means of communication, into assault. As a result of the group's and other new patterns of interaction, Frankie's increasing ability to communicate began to minimize his assaultive impulses. Although at first he was kept from committing violence by the fear of ostracism, he later had no need to use violence, since he then had some ability to interact effectively. He learned to express himself, in what was for him a new form of communication, on a nonviolent, verbal level. On occasion Frankie would regress and have the motivation for assault, but the system had taken hold. In one session I heard him say, "I was so fucking mad yesterday, I wished I was back at Riker's [prison]. I really wanted to hit that bastard Jimmy in the mouth."

Unlike Zev, who had been somewhat successful in the theater, Frankie had a sketchy work record. Since most of his time was taken up with gang fighting, pimping, armed robbery, or pushing heroin, aside from some forced menial labor in prison, he was seldom engaged in anything resembling formal work. His theme had been "work was for squares." He learned how to work in the TC as a side effect of his desire to rise in the status system. He also learned, as a side effect of working, the startling new fact that "talking to someone in the right way made them do more things than threatening them."

As a consequence of living in this new social system, Frankie's social ability continued to increase. His destructive pattern of relating to others withered away. It was no longer functional for him in this new way of life. The TC developed his empathic ability. It produced an attachment to different, more socially acceptable values and reconnected him to the larger society in which the TC functioned as a valid organization.

The TC process unearthed a diamond in the rough. Frankie always had a proclivity for art. As he later described it to me, "When I was a kid, I always liked to draw—but no one paid any attention to my sketches. The only thing I got was that I was teased by other kids. I did some secret artwork in prison but tore it up. One day in group in a 'status probe,' they asked me what I really liked to do 'when I grew up.' I was scared to say it, but I said, 'I want to be an artist.' It was amazing that for the first time in my life no one laughed. They even encouraged me to go to art school."

The TC truly worked for Frankie and the society. It converted a potential gang killer into an artist. Frankie to date has been drug- and crime-free, works now as a lithographer, and has created many interesting works of art.

CROSS-COMPARING TCs WITH PRISONS

In a traditional institution, the assumption is that if the inmates or patients follow the rules of the institution and properly interact with their professional trained therapist, they will change and become better citizens who can function more effectively in the larger society. This model does not have as effective a success rate as the TC.

Most offenders have a close familiarity with traditional "correctional" systems. For example, Frankie and Zev learned how to do their time in reformatories, prisons, jail, mental hospitals, and addict hospitals which did not help them. They were programmed with a set of attitudes for handling encounters with society's traditional treatment facilities. They had learned the proper set of attitudes and responses and these were reinforced in the institution.

Most members of hospitals and prison officialdom are sterotyped by the inmate code as authority figures. For most inmates, the officials are perceived as objects to be manipulated for quick release, or they are tricks to beat for small scores to relieve the boredom and monotony of custody.

In contrast, offenders entering a TC are usually baffled by what they encounter in this very different treatment system. Frankie learned in the TC that everyone was a "right guy," including many of the administrators, most of whom had been in his position at one time.

TC members are not usually identified as inmates, wards, prisoners, or patients, and this also makes a big difference in their self-identities and outlooks. The person can identify with the constructive goals of the organization for which he or she works. He or she automatically becomes an employee in the TC organization, at first on a menial level, and later on is encouraged to take part in the TC's management and development.

In traditional institutions most inmates or patients tend to feel helpless, dependent, and hopeless about their destinies. They have limited power in the institution, since it is run by administrators who are usually indifferent to the inmates' or patients' opinions about its management. Moreover, as I have noted, the institution's administrators are seen as representatives of society's rejection of the inmates, and this sets up additional blockades to their progression in the institution. Inmates have a clear authority object for their frustrations and hatreds—the staff. In a TC there is no such split, since the administration consists of co-workers and colleagues. There is no "they" to rebel against within the organization.

Involvement in a TC helps to foster empathy in a person whose basic problem is alienation from society. Identification with the TC involves feelings of caring and concern for the other members and for the destiny of the totality of the organization. The development of these empathic qualities reverses the person's past, often sociopathic, lack of concern and has a real impact on positive personality change. Vital to this personality change are various group processes, such as the encounter group, the resident's sponsor, and a caring circle of friends.

Group sessions in the TC are more closely related to the real-life interpersonal and work problems that confront the members. Given the lack of caste division, lines of communication are open throughout the organization. This, plus a goldfish-bowl atmosphere, is conducive to a more extensive examination of a resident's deeper underlying problems. TC group sessions make intense efforts to surface all possible data about a member since this is vital to the protection and growth of both the person and the TC organization. Since all TC members work for the organization, many real on-the-job problems are funneled into the TC's group psychotherapy. All these factors give the TC group process a reality not found in the closed-off social systems of most traditional institutions and prisons.

There have been attempts at self-government in prisons and mental hospitals. In these settings, however, the inmates recognize that final decisions on important policy matters remain with the administration. In a TC, perhaps for the first time in an individual's life, the member assumes a significant role in controlling his or her future. These people have, often for the first time in their lives, a degree of power in their new "family" and community. Leadership in a constructive situation is a new experience, and it appears to develop personal responsibility and a sense of independence in the TC resident.

Because there is a generally held belief by the residents that "the TC saved our lives," the esprit de corps in the organization is quite powerful. Few inmates would proclaim the excellence of a hospital or a prison, but residents in a TC enjoy praising the organization that saved their lives. The Zevs and Frankies who are the residents of a TC, unlike patients and inmates, are involved with the growth and development of *their* organization.

In summary, the following elements reflect the significant difference between the social structure and organization of effective TCs and traditional correctional institutions:

1. There is a qualitative difference between indoctrination in the TC and in other settings. The contractual arrangements for therapy and the prospect's expectations of success are different. The indoctrination of the prospect by people who have themselves been in the newcomer's shoes and have succeeded appears to be a significant element, providing the newcomer with a role model. Also, the "indoctrinator" sees where he or she was on looking at the newcomer, and this is valuable for reinforcing personal growth.

2. TCs provide the possibility of upward mobility, whereas most institutions are caste systems. Becoming a TC member provides incentive for changing one's negative attitudes to antidrug, anticriminal motivation. The TC resident can, with the proper attitude and behavior, achieve any role in the organization. In contrast, in the custodial institution, inmates or patients are locked into their dependent positions.

3. There is a qualitative difference between the TC and the form of group therapy carried on in prisons and hospitals. This is partly a function of the described differences in the overall social system. The TC resident, as a voluntary participant, has little to gain by faking progress, whereas in other institutions, the appearance of being "rehabilitated" may be rewarded by an earlier release from custody. The TC member is encouraged to reveal and deal with problems honestly by others who have traveled the established TC route to recovery and independence.

4. The work assigned in a TC is real work, unlike the often contrived jobs in prison and mental hospitals. All work serves the real needs of the organization. These include the procuring of food and the work of the office staff, maintenance and service crews, automotive crews, and coordinating staff. Everyone in a TC is employed in meaningful work, which gives residents a greater sense of belonging to the TC and the feeling that they are, perhaps for the first time in their lives, self-supporting.

5. The TC subculture is integrated into the larger societal structure in a way that traditional institutions seldom are. The flow of members of the community through a TC and the participation of TC members in the larger society place it closer to the real-life situations of the outer world than do the artificial communities of

the traditional institutions that attempt personality and behavioral change in an unreal social system.

THE MAIN SOCIAL-PSYCHOLOGICAL FORCES AT WORK IN A TC

The elements listed in the foregoing section make up the essential social-psychological forces at work in an ideal TC. These elements affect the personality and behavior of the recovering offender in many ways:

Involvement   Initially the TC society is able to involve and control the newcomer by providing an interestng social setting made up of understanding associates who will not be outmaneuvered by manipulative behavior. The indoctrinators understand the newcomer because they were once in the same position.

Achievable Success Goals   Within the context of this system, the newcomer can (perhaps for the first time) see a realistic possibility for legitimate achievement, independence, and prestige. A TC provides a rational opportunity structure for the newcomer. Individuals are not restricted to inmate or patient status, since there is no inmate-staff division and all residents are immediately *staff members.*

New Social Role   Being a "TC professional" is a new social role. It can be temporarily or indefinitely occupied in the process of social growth and development of new projects. TC-trained staff people are increasingly in demand. (Therapeutic Communities of America now endorses TC professionals, who can qualify for an Addict Counselor Certificate.)

Social Growth   In the process of acquiring legitimate social status in a TC, the resident necessarily, as a side effect, develops the ability to relate, communicate, and work with others. The values of truth, honesty, and industry become necessary means to this goal of status achievement. With enough practice and time, the individual socialized in this way reacts according to these values— naturally. This is a most effective system for people who, upon entrance into a TC, had an egocentric-sociopathic posture toward life.

Empathy and Self-Identity   The constant self-assessment required in daily TC life and in the group sessions fostors the consolidation of self-identity and empathy. The individual's self-estimation is under constant assessment by relevant others, who become sensitive to and concerned about that individual. The process provides the opportunity for a person almost literally to see himself or herself as others do. The individual is also compelled, as part of this process, to develop the ability to identify with and understand others, if only to acquire higher status in the system. The side effects are personal growth, greater social awareness, an improved ability to communicate, and a greater facility for being empathic about the needs of others.

Social Control   Better control of the former criminal's deviance is a by-product of the individual's status seeking. Conformity to the norms is necessary for achievement in a TC. Anomie, the dislocation of social goals and the means for acquiring them, is minimalized. The norms are valid and adhered to within the social system, since the means are available for *legitimate goal* attainment in the TC.

Another form of control is embodied in the threat of ostracism. This, too, becomes a binding force. The relative newcomer in a TC usually does not feel adequate at first to participate in the larger society in a law-abiding way. However, after a sufficient period of TC social living, the resident no longer fears banishment and is adequately prepared for life outside (if this is his or her choice). However, residents may remain voluntarily because they believe a TC is a valid way of life. In a TC they have learned and acquired gratifying new social roles that enable them to help others who can benefit from the approach that saved their lives. They can become licensed and/or certified paraprofessionals.

Yet another form of social control is the group process. Here people are required to tell the truth, which helps to regulate their behavior. Transgressions are often prevented by the knowledge that any deviance will rapidly and necessarily be brought to the attention of their peers in a group session. Residents are living in a community where others know about and, perhaps more important, care about their behavior. This process enhances the resident's motivation to learn about and follow the rules of the community. This learning process enhances the possibility that the resident will have a greater respect for the rules and laws of the larger society.

TCs AND THE SOCIAL VACCINE CONCEPT OF CONTROLLING CRIME

The combined effects of the therapeutic community produce a person with a new identity who can become insulated from the need to return to a life of crime. The former offender develops an attitude and personal identity that enables the person to lead a happier, more productive, crime-free life.

In addition to their personal success, TC graduates can be valuable assets in society's overall war against crime and substance abuse. In a sense, they are antibodies in the overall social system. They have been "immunized," and they can be a vital force in preventing and helping others to resist the "disease."

The social vaccine concept may be summarized as follows: The individual who has been a criminal and who has gone through the process of recovery and is now functioning effectively in society provides a kind of antibody or social vaccine for the overall social system. A definition in *Webster's* states that "a vaccine is a living attenuated organism that is administered to produce or increase immunity to a particular disease." The immunization process was first introduced to the West by an English physician, Edward Jenner. Jenner demonstrated that inserting a low level of virus into a person's physiological system stimulated antibodies that would defend and prevent an immunized person from having a more virulent form of the disease.

Loosely transposing this concept from a physiological to a social system, I speculate that former criminal paraprofessionals properly employed in TCs create antibodies to the disease in the larger society. In this context, I suggest that once their problem has been overcome, paraprofessional former criminals can, in time, and in sufficient numbers, serve as antibodies to the "criminal disease" that exists in the overall society. To some degree the force of antialcoholic AA members has acted as a kind of social vaccine on an international level for helping to prevent and control alcoholism. The successful AA member is a zealot in the war on alcoholism. Similarly, the criminal resocialized in a TC can become an evangelical positive force in the war on crime. The explosive development and proliferation of therapeutic communities around the world has produced a social vaccine that can, if properly applied, significantly reduce the crime and substance abuse problem.

In brief, I perceive TC development as a vital therapeutic system for immunizing people who have passed through the fire—and have recovered from their disease. These people can provide valuable experimental data and can serve as law-abiding role models who help prevent others—especially young, vulnerable people—from falling into the morass of the crime problem. As the TC movement develops in quality and numbers, the TC system and its graduates, in the role of paraprofessional role models or as active concerned citizens, can significantly contribute to the prevention and control of the crime problem.

A platitude (which, like all platitudes, has a kernel of truth to it) is that most reformatories and prisons are breeding and training schools for crime. In reverse, the anticriminal, anti–substance abuse TC can, if properly developed and supported, become a "university" for resocializing some former offenders to become people with emotionally healthy values who can live positive and law-abiding lives in society. Moreover, these former offenders, if properly motivated, can act as positive role models in the context of serving as a social vaccine for preventing and controlling crime.

Name Index

Subject Index